Dewey Decimal Classification and Relative Index

Dewey Decimal Classification and Relative Index

Devised by Melvil Dewey

EDITION 23

Edited by

Joan S. Mitchell, Editor in Chief

Julianne Beall, Assistant Editor

Rebecca Green, Assistant Editor

Giles Martin, Assistant Editor

Michael Panzer, Assistant Editor

VOLUME 1

Manual ■ Tables

OCLC

OCLC Online Computer Library Center, Inc.

Dublin, Ohio

2011

Library of Congress Cataloging-in-Publication Data
Dewey, Melvil, 1851-1931.
  Dewey decimal classification and relative index / devised by Melvil Dewey. — Ed. 23 / edited by Joan S. Mitchell, Editor in Chief ; Julianne Beall, Assistant Editor ; Rebecca Green, Assistant Editor ; Giles Martin, Assistant Editor ; Michael Panzer, Assistant Editor.
    v. cm.
  Includes bibliographical references and index.
  Contents: v. 1. Manual. Tables — v. 2. Schedules 000-599 — v. 3. Schedules 600-999 — v. 4. Relative index.
    ISBN-13: 978-1-910608-81-4 (set : alk. paper)
    ISBN-10: 1-910608-81-5 (set : alk. paper)
    ISBN-13: 978-1-910608-80-7 (vol. 1 : alk. paper)
    ISBN-10: 1-910608-80-7 (vol. 1 : alk. paper)
    [etc.]
    1. Classification, Dewey decimal. I. Mitchell, Joan S. II. Beall, Julianne, 1946- III. Green, Rebecca, 1952- IV. Martin, Giles. V. Panzer, Michael. VI. Title.
    Z696.D52 2011
    025.4'31—dc22   2011001112

OCLC Online Computer Library Center, Inc.
6565 Kilgour Place
Dublin, OH 43017-3395 USA
www.oclc.org/dewey

ISBN-13: (set) 978-1-910608-81-4; v. 1 978-1-910608-80-7;
v. 2 978-1-910608-76-0; v. 3 978-1-910608-79-1; v. 4 978-1-910608-78-4

ISBN-10: (set) 1-910608-81-5; v. 1 1-910608-80-7; v. 2 1-910608-76-9;
v. 3 1-910608-79-3; v. 4 1-910608-78-5

 Recycled paper

Dedicated
to
the
worldwide Dewey community

Contents

Volume 1

Contents

Foreword by the Decimal Classification Editorial Policy Committee

The journey from Edition 22 to the published version of Edition 23 has seen significant developments within the world of Dewey Decimal Classification (DDC): developments within the schedule have been matched by those within the process for change, and by expansion in the technical framework that supports the use of DDC.

Work on Edition 23 began in March 2004 with a planning retreat to discuss the direction and aims of Edition 23; the retreat included members of the Decimal Classification Editorial Policy Committee (EPC), the Dewey editors, invited researchers in knowledge organisation from OCLC and elsewhere, and a representative from the DDC translation community. The areas of development in Edition 23 include those that were highlighted but could not be incorporated in Edition 22 and those that have emerged during the cycle of production for Edition 23.

Edition 23 includes extensive changes and updates in the terminology used throughout the schedules and tables to improve currency and accessibility for classifiers. There is significant development of schedule areas impacted by rapidly changing technology over the life cycle of Edition 23 such as computing, and extensive changes to aid interoperability between the different language translations that have been developed during the process of Edition 23.

Edition 23 has continued the best practice established during work for earlier editions by seeking expert advice from as wide a community as possible both within and beyond the DDC user base to ensure we continue to represent accurately complex knowledge areas and continue to improve the international applicability of the DDC schedules. This new edition is the work of a wide community including the editors, EPC, the European DDC Users' Group (EDUG), and colleagues from translation projects. Each has contributed to the proposed areas for review and discussions about new schedules to ensure accuracy and relevancy for as wide a community as possible.

The revision process aims to improve the currency of the schedules, whilst continuing to be sensitive to the use of DDC as a shelving tool. Any major changes inevitably bring challenges to libraries not least the costs of relocating and re-labelling stock. To help alleviate these problems expansion and revision have been preferred to relocation where possible. Significant changes have only been made after careful thought and debate of the relative merits of each action.

During preparations for Edition 23 the DDC has moved in new directions and is increasingly used beyond the traditional application as a classification at shelf. DDC is now widely used as a tool for organising materials in the Web, as a tool for gathering management information to support collection development, and as a tool for mapping thesauri or natural language subject schemes. DDC is moving into the digital environment with much to offer the arena of online knowledge management. The challenges are many, but the value of DDC in emerging areas of information management has begun to form a significant part of the discussions that shape the development of the classification.

Decimal Classification Editorial Policy Committee (EPC)

EPC was established in 1937 to serve as an advisory body to the DDC. In 1953, it was reconstituted into a joint committee of the Lake Placid Foundation and the American Library Association (ALA). In 1988, when OCLC acquired the DDC, Forest Press requested that the EPC continue its advisory role to the DDC.

The ten-member international board works closely with the DDC editors to suggest changes, facilitate innovations, and monitor the general development of the DDC. EPC acts as a channel for national committees and library communities beyond OCLC and the Library of Congress, gathering information from the user community to provide feedback and commentary to the editors. After the publication of Edition 22, EPC opened its private mailing list to include representatives of national libraries and translation teams; comments and suggestions received from this broader group have contributed to the development of Edition 23. In 2008, EPC members elected a chair from the United Kingdom; this marked the first time the post had been held by someone from outside North America. EPC also had another first during the period of development of Edition 23: a member from South Africa.

Since the publication of Edition 22, the following people (accompanied by the affiliation they had or now have as members) have served on EPC:

Migell Acosta (County of Los Angeles Public Library)
Richard Baumgarten (Johnson County [Kan.] Public Library)
Chew Chiat Naun (University of Minnesota)
Janice M. DeSirey (Hennepin County [Minn.] Library)
Lucy Evans (British Library), vice-chair, 2001–2004
David Farris (Library and Archives Canada)
Jonathan Furner (University of California, Los Angeles)
Andrea Kappler (Evansville Vanderburgh [Ind.] Public Library)
Caroline Kent (British Library), chair, 2008–
Jessica MacPhail (Racine [Wis.] Public Library)
Lyn McKinney (Billings [Mont.] Senior High School)
Anne Robertson (Australian Committee on Cataloguing), vice-chair, 2004–
Deborah Rose-Lefmann (Northwestern University)
Sandra Singh (Vancouver [B.C.] Public Library)
Andrea Stamm (Northwestern University), chair, 2000–2005
Arlene Taylor (University of Pittsburgh)
Welna van Eeden (University of South Africa)
Beacher Wiggins (Library of Congress)
Deane Zeeman (Library and Archives Canada), chair, 2006–2007

EPC would like to say an especially huge thank you to Joan S. Mitchell, editor in chief, and the current assistant editors of the Dewey Decimal Classification: Julianne Beall, Rebecca Green, Giles Martin, and Michael Panzer. We also thank former assistant editors Jonathan Furner and Winton E. Matthews, Jr., who contributed to Edition 23. EPC acknowledges with gratitude the energy, patience, diligence and passion that the Dewey editorial team brought to the production of every paper, and every meeting during the cycle for the new edition of DDC.

Caroline Kent
Chair, 2008–
Decimal Classification
Editorial Policy Committee

Acknowledgments

The publication of Edition 23 comes 135 years after the publication of the first edition of the Dewey Decimal Classification. The fact that the DDC continues to flourish as a relevant knowledge organization tool today is in no small part due to contributions of the worldwide community of Dewey users. The Dewey editorial team's ongoing interactions with the Dewey user community have helped to shape the content, representation, and use of the system.

We are extraordinarily grateful to the current and past members of the Decimal Classification Editorial Policy Committee (EPC). EPC members represent and bring the voice of the user to the table. EPC's guidance and critical review are essential in ensuring that the DDC continues to be a useful knowledge organization tool in a wide variety of environments and applications.

We acknowledge the contributions of the American Library Association (ALA), Chartered Institute of Library and Information Professionals (CILIP), and the European DDC Users' Group (EDUG) for their ongoing advice on the content and strategic direction of the DDC. Each of these organizations has committees that meet regularly to review proposals related to the DDC. We acknowledge the suggestions of Dewey Breakfast/Update attendees at ALA, American Association of School Librarians, and the Public Library Association conferences. We are also grateful for the advice of participants in International Dewey Users Meeting (formerly known as the Dewey Translators Meeting), held each year in conjunction with the World Library and Information Congress (IFLA General Conference and Assembly).

We thank national libraries throughout the world, our translation partners, and members of translation advisory teams who reviewed proposals and made suggestions throughout the tables and schedules. We are especially grateful for advice provided in history, geography, language, literature, and politics. We acknowledge the contributions in the aforementioned areas of the staff and/or translation teams associated with the following institutions (contributions to additional areas are noted below):

    ASTED
    Australian National Library
    Biblioteca nazionale centrale di Firenze
    Bibliotheca Alexandrina (also 281, 297)
    Bibliothèque nationale de France
    British Library
    Deutsche Nationalbibliothek (also 610, 636, 641, 663, 794)
    Israeli Center for Libraries
    Library and Archives Canada
    National Documentation Centre (Athens, Greece)
    National Library of Indonesia
    National Library of Norway
    National Library of South Africa (also 780)
    National Library of Sweden (also 610, 636, 796)
    National Library of Vietnam

Österreichische Nationalbibliothek
Rojas Eberhard Editores Ltda
Russian National Public Library for Science and Technology (also 281)
Swiss National Library

The following individuals from institutions other than those listed above offered advice on proposed updates:

004–006 Computer science
Ebe Kartus (Deakin University)

006.35 and 410.285 Computational linguistics
Nizar Habash (Columbia University)
Eduard Hovy (University of Southern California)
Jimmy Lin (University of Maryland)
Tom M. Mitchell (Carnegie Mellon University)
Philip Resnik (University of Maryland)

020 Library and information sciences (subject access; archives)
Susan E. Davis (Drexel University)
Daniel N. Joudrey (Simmons College)
Mary Lacy (Library of Congress)

160 and 511.3 Logic
Jeremy Avigad (Carnegie Mellon University)
Horacio Arló-Costa (Carnegie Mellon University)

200 Religion
Ia McIlwaine (University College London, and former editor in chief, Universal Decimal Classification)

281 Eastern churches
Paul Burns (University of British Columbia)
Hal Cain (Dalton McCaughey Library)
Monk Prodromos (Library of the Holy Monastery of Paraklitos [Malakasa, Greece])

297 Islam (historical periods; Hadith)
Kamal Lounaci (Bibliothèque et Archives nationales du Québec)
Charles Riley (Yale University)
Muhannad Salhi (Library of Congress)

305 Groups of peoples; 306 Culture and institutions; 362 Groups of people
Gillian Lord (Australian Institute of Family Studies)
Nancy Silverrod (San Francisco Public Library)

364.1 Criminal offenses
Pauline de Graaf (New South Wales Police College)

610 Medicine and health (adolescent medicine)
Joycelyn F. Brand (Dakota County Library)

646 Sewing, clothing
Rachel Clarke (Fashion Institute of Design and Merchandising)

741.5 Comic books, graphic novels, fotonovelas, cartoons, caricatures, comic strips
Leonie Bourke (Schools Catalogue Information Service [SCIS])
Robin Brenner (Cary Memorial Library)
Ann Case (H.W. Wilson Co.)
Olivier Charbonneau (Concordia University)
Neil Cohn (Tufts University)
Courtney Deines-Jones (The Grimalkin Group, LLC)
Ian Fairclough (Marion Public Library)
Joanna Fountain (Sam Houston State University)
Francisca Goldsmith (Berkeley Public Library)
Joel Hahn (Niles Public Library District)
Valerie Hodges (Kansas City, Kansas Public Library)
Rich Johnson (DC Comics)
Elmer Klebs (Library of Congress)
Esther Mandel (Sarasota County Public Libraries)
Scott C. Markham (Hennepin County Library)
Michael Martens (Dark Horse Comics)
Dale Martin (Lawrence Public Library)
Jean-Pierre Mercier (Centre national de la bande dessinée et de l'image)
Terry Moore (*Strangers in Paradise*)
Eric Norton (McMillan Memorial Library)
Michael G. Pawuk (Cuyahoga County Public Library)
Ruffin Powell (Culbreth Middle School, Chapel Hill, North Carolina)
Lisa Reynolds (Charlestown-Clark County Public Library)
Donna L. Schroeder (OHIONET)
Gail Mueller Schultz (Hennepin County Library)
David Serchay (Broward County Library System)
Brett Shanahan (DC Comics)
Karen Siracusa (Mercer County [NJ] Library System)
Jay Towne Smith (San Francisco Public Library)
Sheila Spence (Salt Spring Island Public Library)
Joseph Tennis (University of Washington)
Mike Tribby (Quality Books Inc.)
Alicia Wilson (DC Comics)
Patricia Wood (District of Columbia Public Library)

960 Africa
Joe Lauer (Michigan State University)
Peter Limb (Michigan State University)
Charles Riley (Yale University)

Table 2 (Asia Minor; Turkey)
Anthony Oddo (Yale University)

Table 5 (Hakka)
Ming Sun Poon (Library of Congress)

Table 6 (Indonesia)
Sulistyo-Basuki (Universitas Indonesia)

There were three formal review committees during the development period associated with the publication of Edition 23; all were established by EDUG. The following is a list of EDUG review committees and membership: ·

EDUG 340 Law Working Group: Yvonne Jahns (Deutsche Nationalbibliothek), chair; Federica Paradisi (Biblioteca nazionale centrale di Firenze).

EDUG 370 Education Working Group: Anne-Céline Lambotte (Université de la Méditerranée), chair; Kate Bunting (Leeds Metropolitan University); Bodil Gustavsson (Stockholms universitetsbibliotek); Caroline Kent (British Library); Karin Kleiber (Österreichische Nationalbibliothek); Patrice Landry (Swiss National Library); Ingebjørg Rype (National Library of Norway).

EDUG 930 Archaeology Working Group: Magdalena Svanberg (National Library of Sweden), chair; Bjørn Bandlien (University of Oslo Library); Patricia Bellec (Bibliothèque nationale de France); Brigitte Bernhard (Deutsche Nationalbibliothek); Ines Castellano-Colmenero (National Museums Scotland); Vera Uhlmann (Swiss National Library).

Many colleagues associated with the DDC at OCLC and the Library of Congress have made significant contributions to the development of Edition 23. First and foremost are the contributions of the current assistant editors of the Dewey Decimal Classification: Julianne Beall (Library of Congress), Rebecca Green (OCLC), Giles Martin (OCLC), and Michael Panzer (OCLC). Their scholarship, dedication, and commitment to our users are reflected throughout the Dewey Decimal Classification. We are also grateful to two former members of the Dewey editorial team for their continuing involvement and counsel. Jonathan Furner (UCLA) served as assistant editor 2005–2006 and was appointed a member of EPC in 2009. Winton E. Matthews, Jr., served as assistant editor 1985–2008 and returned to the Dewey editorial team in 2009 as a part-time consultant.

We are fortunate to have our editorial headquarters at the Library of Congress in the Dewey Section, where editorial work on the DDC is performed under an agreement between OCLC and the Library of Congress. The Dewey Section is currently headed by Eve M. Dickey. The section is part of the U.S. General Division, of which Karl E. Debus-López is chief. The Dewey Section was formerly the Decimal Classification Division, which Dennis M. McGovern headed 2002–2008, followed briefly by Jeffrey Heynen and Randall Barry as acting chiefs before the appointment of Mr. Debus-López. Dewey Section staff and other classifiers at the Library of Congress have continuously supported the editorial efforts by offering an expert view of new topics and areas requiring updating. In addition to assistant editor Julianne Beall and former assistant editor Winton Matthews, the following present and past Library of Congress staff members have also contributed to the development of Edition 23: Darlene Banks, Randall Barry, Mark Behrens, Anita R. Blaine, Michael B. Cantlon, Larry Ceasar, Karl E. Debus-López, Eve M. Dickey, Nate Evans, Ruth Freitag, Herbert Garrett, Donald Hardy, Jeffrey Heynen, Henry Lefkowitz,

Dennis M. McGovern, Nobuko Ohashi, Letitia J. Reigle, Robert Roth, Ida Shelton, Chay Tang, Cosmo Tassone, Carolyn Turner-Dixon, Dorothy A. Watson, and Ruby T. Woodard.

The staff and management of OCLC have provided the support and resources to enable the DDC to grow as a knowledge organization system. Thanks are due in particular to Jay Jordan, President and CEO; Robin Murray, Vice President, Global Product Management; and Karen Calhoun, Vice President, Metadata Applications. We also acknowledge our debt to the previous vice presidents to whom the Dewey editorial and business operations reported during the course of the development of this edition, Phyllis B. Spies and the late Gary Houk. We are immensely grateful to current and past OCLC staff members associated with business operations related to the Dewey Decimal Classification: Robin Cornette, Libbie Crawford, Steve Sattler, Eliza Sproat, Robert Van Volkenburg, and Christy Wallace. We also acknowledge the editorial assistance of Brad Gauder and Phil Schieber in final preparation of the front matter associated with this edition, and Rick Limes for the cover.

We thank Lorcan Dempsey, Vice President of OCLC Research & Chief Strategist, for his ongoing support of knowledge organization research. We especially note the numerous and ongoing contributions of Diane Vizine-Goetz and the Knowledge Organization Group in OCLC Research: Carol Hickey, Andrew Houghton, J.D. Shipengrover, Roger Thompson, and Harry Wagner. We also acknowledge the many contributions of other current and past OCLC Research staff, particularly Eric Childress, Jean Godby, Thom Hickey, Ed O'Neill, Stuart Weibel, and Jeff Young.

In addition to the contributions of editorial, business, and research team members, we are grateful to the following development team members who worked on ESS 4.0, the editorial support system from which Edition 23 was produced: Becky Babyak, Judy Barnes, Tom Baumgartner, Dena Bovee, Jui-wen Chang, Ho-chun Chin, Larry Evans, Amin Haghighi, Lenore Jones, Vicki Kushnir, Keith MacLaury, Barbara Norgard, Haiyan Qian, David Richards, Dave Ripp, Gary Shurgin, Mike Teets, Ed Tripp, Peter Werling (Pansoft), Dan Whitney, Marty Withrow, Jane Woodward, and Johan Zeeman. We are also grateful to Vicki Kushnir, Dan Whitney, and Marty Withrow for the support of ESS 3.0, the predecessor to the current system.

While work proceeded on Edition 23, OCLC introduced WebDewey 2.0, a new end-user web version of the DDC. In addition to the editorial, business, and research teams, the following staff worked on WebDewey 2.0: Helene Babich, Janet Bickle, Linda Bingham, Dena Bovee, Jui-wen Chang, Jim Clover, Erin Crego, Kristin Gain, Louann Gault, Amin Haghighi, Rob Hermance-Moore, Megan Hopkins, Maureen Huss, Jon Krause, Esther Lund, Joanne Murphy, Girija Parvate, Jeff Price, Renee Register, David Richards, Mike Robinson, Steve Smith, Dave Stallard, Megan Stypczynski, Linda Swope, Jeff Wallace, Peter Werling (Pansoft), Jane Woodward, and Johan Zeeman. Prior to the introduction of WebDewey 2.0, the following staff continued to support the delivery of updates to users in the original WebDewey: Greg Beaty, Jim Clover, and Amin Haghighi.

Underpinning the work on development and distribution of the DDC is a new representation based on the MARC 21 formats for Classification and Authority data. We collaborated on updates to the MARC 21 formats with colleagues at Deutsche Nationalbibliothek, the Library of Congress, and OCLC. The proposed changes were later approved by the ALA Machine-Readable Bibliographic Information Committee.

We have also begun to experiment with Dewey linked data and semantic web representations of the DDC; several members of the worldwide Dewey community have advised us on this endeavor. In addition to OCLC staff members, we are particularly grateful for the advice received from Marcia Lei Zeng (Kent State University), and the following members of the EDUG Technical Issues Working Group: Gordon Dunsire (University of Strathclyde), chair; Ulrike Reiner (Verbundzentrale des Gemeinsamen Bibliothekenverbundes [GBV]); and Lars Svensson (Deutsche Nationalbibliothek).

During the course of development of Edition 23, we lost six influential leaders and treasured colleagues:

David Balatti (Library and Archives Canada, and former EPC chair and member): among his contributions is the directive never to let an option be a substitute for a decision.

Dr. Luigi Crocetti (former president of Associazione italiana biblioteche): the leading Dewey expert in Italy, he oversaw the translation and publication of five editions of the DDC into Italian, starting with the Italian translation of Abridged Edition 11 in 1987.

David Farris (Library and Archives Canada, and EPC member from 2008 until his death in early 2011): the editor of Canadian Subject Headings (CSH), he worked on the prototype CSH–DDC mapping and advocated for the representation of Canadian topics in the DDC.

Magda Heiner-Freiling (Deutsche Nationalbibliothek): the force behind the first German translation of the DDC, the co-founder of EDUG, and the visionary who saw the power in making Dewey numbers "speak."

Gary Houk (OCLC): Electronic Dewey, Dewey for Windows, and WebDewey were launched under his executive leadership.

Peter J. Paulson (OCLC, and former executive director of Forest Press): he was a strong supporter of Dewey translations and a tireless promoter of the worldwide use of Dewey.

In closing, we thank the entire worldwide Dewey community, to whom this edition is dedicated.

Joan S. Mitchell
Editor in Chief
Dewey Decimal Classification
OCLC, Inc.

New Features in Edition 23

Overview

Edition 23 is the product of a new approach to development of print editions of the Dewey Decimal Classification. Like its predecessor Edition 22, it was prepared in the context of the web, but Edition 23 is the first to be produced as a by-product of the underlying database instead of as the sole focus of editorial development. Editorial development efforts since the publication of Edition 22 have focused on short-term and long-term updates. The long-term updates have been held for simultaneous introduction in the print and web versions of Edition 23, but most of the short-term updates have been continuously distributed to users. We have used WebDewey as our chief vehicle for delivering updates to our users. We have also featured selected new numbers and changes to the DDC on a monthly basis on our web site (www.oclc.org/dewey). All of these updates have been incorporated into Edition 23, plus additional updates.

In addition to the overall goal of keeping pace with knowledge, changes have been motivated by classifier efficiency and emerging requirements in machine representation and application. Our efforts have been informed by interaction with the worldwide community of Dewey users.

Major Changes in Edition 23

Edition 23 features a complete overhaul of the representation of groups of people, significant revisions to several standard subdivisions, numerous updates throughout the tables and schedules, and some structural changes. During the production cycle for Edition 23, we have migrated to a new editorial support system, adopted a different underlying data format, and introduced a new data distribution model. A brief discussion of the major changes follows.

GROUPS OF PEOPLE

We regularly reconsider the provisions for groups of people in the DDC. In the review concurrent with the development of Edition 23, we focused initially on the phrase "kinds of persons" in the caption at Table 1 —08 and elsewhere in the DDC. Users are sometimes confused about the difference between "kinds of persons" in Table 1 —08 versus "persons treatment" in Table 1 —092; more troubling is the unintended interpretation of "kinds of persons" as a definitive classification of people. We replaced "kinds of persons" with "groups of people" in Table 1 —08 and elsewhere in the DDC. At the same time, we deleted "History and description with respect to" entirely from the caption at Table 1 —08 and elsewhere in the DDC. We also substituted "Groups of people" for "Social groups" in the caption at 305 and elsewhere in the DDC.

We have long known that "persons treatment" itself is a confusing phrase, and questioned whether to continue using it in Table 1 —092. We changed the caption at Table 1 —092 to "Biography," and made a slight revision to the caption at Table 1 —09 at the same time (now "History, geographic treatment, biography" instead of "Historical, geographic, persons treatment"). There is a significant expansion for collected biography of groups of people by various attributes in Table 1 —092.

We have adopted consistent use of "people" versus "persons" when we are referring to a group of people by a specific attribute, e.g., homeless people. In a few cases, the term "persons" has been retained when it is part of the common name for a group of people, e.g., "stateless persons." Similar changes to terminology have been introduced in the Relative Index. In addition, we have replaced the current "Persons" index array with three new entries: Person (Legal concept), Persons (Individuals), and People. The index term for groups of people in general is "People"; the general index term for individuals is "Persons (Individuals)."

We have made small adjustments throughout Table 1 and 305–306 in the developments for groups of people by specific attributes. These changes are reflected elsewhere in the DDC, especially in 155 Differential and developmental psychology, 331 Labor economics, and 362 Social problems of and services to groups of people. In a related change, we have adjusted the preference order in 302–307 Specific topics in sociology and anthropology to topic first and the group of people second, e.g., friendship in women 302.34082, *not* 305.4 Women.

STANDARD SUBDIVISIONS

In addition to the changes in Table 1 with respect to groups of people and biography described in the previous section, there are other changes to standard subdivisions in Edition 23. Adjustments to specific standard subdivisions are highlighted under Table 1 in the selected list of changes in Edition 23 below. There are also several general improvements to the presentation of standard subdivisions in Edition 23. In records for standard subdivisions that introduce special expansions not found in Table 1, a new note is featured in the record: "Notation X from Table 1 as modified below." For example, the note "Notation 01 from Table 1 as modified below" is included in the record for 370.1 Philosophy and theory, education for specific objectives, educational psychology; there are several expansions under 370.1 that are not part of —01 Philosophy and theory in Table 1. In places where a standard subdivision concept has been displaced to a special provision, we have ensured that an add note appears under the special provision if addition in parallel to the standard Table 1 provision is desired. We have also looked carefully at provisions for standard subdivisions in add tables throughout the tables and schedules, and applied the same rules. In Table 1, we realized that the special provisions in the add tables under —08,—0901–0905, and —093–093 were incorrectly labeled as "standard subdivisions" in Edition 22. Subsequently, we have introduced a note under each noting that the provisions are "special notation," and have added the necessary preference instructions to each of the add tables in Table 1, plus the necessary notes to each entry.

In Table 3B, the notation labeled "Standard subdivisions" in the add table under —1–8 Specific forms lacked the usual initial 0 and thus did not look like regular standard subdivisions. We moved the contents of the add table from —1–8 to —1 Poetry as explicit subdivisions of the latter number, and revised the instructions under the rest of the forms in —1–8 to add using the notation following —100 in —1001–1009.

MAJOR UPDATES: TABLES

In addition to the aforementioned changes to groups of people and standard subdivisions, we have introduced several major updates in Edition 23 in Tables 2–6. In the heading for Table 2, "Persons" has been replaced by "Biography." There are significant expansions within the table for geographic areas in the ancient world, Italy, Switzerland, Sweden, Finland, Turkey, Indonesia, Vietnam, and Canada. In Table 3C, there is a significant expansion of —3 Arts and literature dealing with specific themes and subjects that draws the notation in closer alignment with parallel subjects in 001–999. In Table 4, there is a special expansion under —014 Communication; semantics, pragmatics, languages for special purposes. Tables 5 and 6 feature expansions for peoples and languages, respectively.

MAJOR UPDATES: SCHEDULES

We have updated 004–006 Computer science (and parallel provisions in 025.04 Information storage and retrieval systems and 621.39 Computer engineering) to reflect current technical trends. In 155 Differential and developmental psychology, we have provided for topics of environmental and applied psychology to be applied to groups of people. There is a revised and expanded development for logic in 160 Philosophical logic and 511.3 Mathematical logic (Symbolic logic).

In 200 Religion, we have initiated updates of provisions for the Orthodox Church and Islam; further work is planned on both of these areas after the publication of Edition 23.

In addition to the changes to groups of people, there are several major changes throughout 300 Social sciences. In 320 Political science (Politics and government), we have introduced revisions and expansions for ideologies and political parties. In 340 Law, we have updated and expanded provisions for the European Union and criminal courts. There is also a parallel expansion for criminal law to match the expansion for criminal offenses in 364 Criminology. The headings and developments at 366 Secret associations and societies and 369 Associations have been revised, and comprehensive works on associations have been relocated from 366 to 369. Several significant updates have been introduced in 370 Education to generalize provisions from an international viewpoint with respect to levels of education, kinds of schools, specific subjects in primary education, and policy issues in education. We have updated provisions for food and clothing in 390 Customs, etiquette, folklore (and related provisions in 640 Home and family management, 660 Chemical engineering and related technologies, and 680 Manufacture of products for specific uses).

The updates to languages in Table 6 are reflected in similar provisions in 400 Language. Throughout 400 Language, addition of Table 2 notation has been regularized for geographic variations of languages; special provision is no longer given for the country or countries where use of a language predominates.

There are numerous expansions featured throughout 610 Medicine and health, notably in nutrition, therapy, and diseases. We changed the heading at 690 from "Buildings" to "Construction of buildings," and expanded for special topics and parts of buildings. Similar changes to special topics and parts of buildings have been introduced in 720 Architecture and 721 Architectural materials and structural elements (the heading at 721 has been changed from "Architectural structure," which in turn has been discontinued from 721 to 720). Another change in a heading at the three-digit level occurs at 710, where "Civic and landscape art" has been replaced with "Area planning and landscape architecture."

The revised headings at 740 Graphic arts and decorative arts and 760 Printmaking and prints reflect the relocation of graphic arts from 760 to 740. There is a significant update at 741.5 Comic books, graphic novels, fotonovelas, cartoons, caricatures, comic strips. We have relocated cinematography and videography from 778.5 to 777 (a number that was last in use in Edition 14), and have introduced a major revision and expansion for the topics at the latter number.

In 780 Music, we have updated the distinction between 781.62 Folk music and 781.63–.66 Popular music for music that originates within and is associated with an ethnic or national group, and introduced a provision for hybrid styles in the add table under 781.63–.66. We have also eliminated distinctions among specific styles of rock music in 781.66 Rock (Rock 'n' roll); all are classed in 781.66. There are significant expansions throughout 796 Athletic and outdoor sports and games to address the variety of sports engaged in at the international level.

As in 400 Language, the updates to languages in Table 6 are reflected in similar provisions in 800 Literature (Belles-lettres) and rhetoric. We have made minor adjustments to literary period tables throughout 800, including recasting the notation in the special table for literary periods of Canada under 811–818 Subdivisions for specific forms of American literature in English from standard to optional notation.

The changes to geographic areas in Table 2 are reflected in 900 History, geography, and auxiliary disciplines; in addition, historical periods have been updated throughout 900.

STRUCTURAL CHANGES

We introduced two changes to modernize the structure of the classification for machine display and retrieval, and user convenience. The first is an elimination of dual headings. Dual headings are headings with two distinct terms separated by four hard spaces. In many cases, one of the topics of the dual heading has been moved to a class-here note. For example, the dual heading "Life sciences   Biology" at 570 is now simply "Biology" in Edition 23; the topic "life sciences" has been moved to the class-here note under 570.

The second structural change is the elimination of unbalanced spans in the schedules and tables. Records for spans in the tables and schedules are used to bring together information about a range of numbers or to provide add instructions. Generally, the numbers at both ends of the span have the same length, e.g. 810–890, 342–349, 616.1–.9, 943.01–.05, and 333.335–.339. This makes it easy to identify which numbers fall underneath the span in the hierarchy, and at what level the span is in the hierarchy. Sometimes, however, the numbers at each end of the span have a different length, e.g., 305.805–.89 Specific ethnic and national groups; this can cause confusion in the print and electronic editions with respect to the position of the span in the hierarchy. As part of the development of Edition 23, we have reviewed each unbalanced span. For example, 305.805–.89 has been replaced by two spans, 305.805–.809 and 305.81–.89.

DATA REPRESENTATION

The print version of Edition 23 has been produced using the fourth generation of the Editorial Support System (ESS), introduced in 2010. During the development of Edition 23, we have migrated the representation of DDC data from a proprietary format that has been in place since Edition 20 to a new data format based on the MARC 21 formats for Classification and Authority data. When we distribute the data for printing, for inclusion in WebDewey, and to translation teams and other users, we transform the representation from the internal MARC formats to a MARCXML representation. There are also other representations of the DDC data, e.g., SKOS.

Selected List of Changes in Edition 23

A complete list of relocations, discontinuations, and reused numbers, plus comparative and equivalence tables for the major revision of cinematography and videography, is available immediately following Tables 1–6. A selected list of new numbers, revisions, and expansions in Edition 23 follows.

Selected Changes in the Tables

TABLE 1. STANDARD SUBDIVISIONS

—0141   Discourse analysis
New number

—0286   Green technology (Environmental technology)
Revised

—0681   Organization and financial management
Fund raising for festivals relocated from —079*

—072   Research
Revised and expanded*

—074   Museums, collections, exhibits
Festivals relocated from —079*

—081   People by gender or sex
—0811   Men
Revised and expanded

—0865   People by marital status
Revised and expanded

—0867   Transgender and intersex people
New number; transsexuals relocated from —0866

—0925   Collected biography of people by specific gender or sex; age groups; relationships
—0926   Collected biography of people by miscellaneous social attributes
—0927   Collected biography of people with disabilities and illnesses, gifted people
—0928   Collected biography of members of specific religious groups
New numbers; relocated from —0922 and —0923

TABLE 2. GEOGRAPHIC AREAS, HISTORICAL PERIODS, BIOGRAPHY

—31   China to 420
—32   Egypt to 640
—33   Palestine to 70

*Introduced in an interim update prior to the publication of Edition 23

—34	South Asia to 647
—35	Mesopotamia to 637 and Iranian Plateau to 637
—363	Germanic regions to 481 and Pannonia
—364	Celtic regions to 486
—366	Iberian Peninsula to 415 and adjacent islands to 415
	Expanded
—368	Scandinavia to 481
	New number; relocated from —363
—369	Netherlands to 486, Belgium to 486, Luxembourg to 486, Switzerland to 486
	Relocated from —363 and —364
—37	Italian Peninsula to 476 and adjacent territories to 476
	Revised and expanded*
—393	Eastern Asia Minor to 640 and Cyprus to 640
—394	Middle East to 640
—395	Black Sea region to 640 and Caucasus to 640
—3971	Mauretania
—398	Southeastern Europe to ca. 640
	Expanded
—451–459	Italy, San Marino, Vatican City, Malta
—469	Portugal
	Revised and expanded*
—486–488	Sweden
	Revised and expanded*
—4897	Finland
	Revised and expanded*
—494	Switzerland
—4961	Turkey in Europe (Eastern Thrace)
—562–566	Turkey
	Expanded
—597	Vietnam
—5981–5986	Indonesia
	Expanded*
—71437	Urban agglomeration of Longueuil
	Expanded*
—951	Western New Guinea (Irian Barat)
	Expanded*

*Introduced in an interim update prior to the publication of Edition 23

TABLE 3B. SUBDIVISIONS FOR WORKS BY OR ABOUT MORE THAN ONE AUTHOR

—3082   Autobiographical and biographical fiction
New number*

—308768   Alternative histories
New number*

TABLE 3C. NOTATION TO BE ADDED WHERE INSTRUCTED IN TABLE 3B, 700.4, 791.4, 808–809

—3   Arts and literature dealing with specific themes and subjects
Revised and expanded*

TABLE 4. SUBDIVISIONS OF INDIVIDUAL LANGUAGES AND LANGUAGE FAMILIES

—014   Communication; semantics, pragmatics, languages for special purposes
Revised and expanded*

—0188   Corpus linguistics
New number*

—803   Translating materials on specific subjects
—804   Translating literature (belles-lettres) and rhetoric
New numbers; relocated from —802*

—823   Punctuation
New number*

TABLE 5. ETHNIC AND NATIONAL GROUPS

—59   Romanians; peoples who speak, or whose ancestors spoke, Rhaetian languages; Sardinians; Corsicans
Expanded*

—699   People who speak or whose ancestors spoke, Galician
New number

—914   South Asians
Revised and expanded*

—91829   Montenegrins
New number

—9183   Croats and Bosnians
New number and subdivision; Croats relocated from —9182*

—935   Cushitic and Omotic peoples
Expanded*

*Introduced in an interim update prior to the publication of Edition 23

—9423	People who speak, or whose ancestors spoke, Mongolian proper New number
—94823	Gond
—94824	Kandh (Kondh, Kui) New numbers
—948 9	Peoples who speak, or whose ancestors spoke, miscellaneous languages of south Asia New number and subdivision
—9517	Hakka New number
—954	Tibeto-Burman peoples Expanded*
—959	Miscellaneous southeast Asian peoples; Munda Revised and expanded*
—9838	Peoples who speak, or whose ancestors spoke, Tupí languages Revised and expanded*
—9922	Peoples who speak, or whose ancestors spoke, Malayo-Polynesian languages of Indonesia, Malaysia, Singapore, Brunei, East Timor; peoples who speak, or whose ancestors spoke, Chamic languages Expanded*
—9959	Fijians New number

TABLE 6. LANGUAGES

—599	Rhaetian languages; Sardinian, Corsican Expanded*
—699	Galician New number
—91489	Divehi (Maldivian) New number*
—91492	Languages of east central zone of Indo-Aryan languages (Eastern Hindi languages) New number
—91496	Pahari languages New number
—9183	Croatian and Bosnian New number and subdivision; Croatian relocated from —9182*

*Introduced in an interim update prior to the publication of Edition 23

—9457	Sámi (Saami) languages
	New number and subdivisions; relocated from —9455

—9489	Miscellaneous languages of south Asia
	New number and subdivisions

—95978	Yao
	New number*

—9838	Tupí languages
	Revised and expanded*

—9922	Malayo-Polynesian languages of Indonesia, Malaysia, Singapore, Brunei, East Timor; Chamic languages
	Expanded*

—99482	Tongan (Tonga)
—99484	Niue (Niuean)
	New numbers

—9959	Eastern Fijian languages
	New number

—9998	Sign languages
	New number and subdivisions

Selected Changes in the Schedules

003.72	Networks [as a kind of system]
	New number*

004.167	Handheld computing devices
	New number*

004.568	Semiconductor storage
	New number

004.65	Communications network architecture
	Revised and expanded*

004.6782	Cloud computing
	New number

004.695	Internet telephony
	New number*

005.717	Error-correcting codes
	New number; relocated from 005.72

005.74	Data files and databases
	Revised and expanded*

*Introduced in an interim update prior to the publication of Edition 23

006.2	Special-purpose systems New number and subdivisions
006.35	Natural language processing Computational linguistics relocated from 410.285*
006.75	Specific types of multimedia software New number and subdivisions*
017	General bibliographies and catalogs held in specific collections or offered for sale Revised; 018 Catalogs arranged by author, main entry, date, or register number and 019 Dictionary catalogs relocated here
025.042	World Wide Web New number and subdivisions*
025.4	Subject analysis and control Revised*
150.1985 150.1988	Personal construct psychology Positive psychology New numbers*
155	Differential and developmental psychology Revised and expanded
160.119	Specific systems of classical and nonclassical logic New number and subdivisions
176.2 176.22 176.3 176.4	[Ethics of] Reproductive technology [Ethics of] Human cloning [Ethics of] Birth control [Ethics of] Sexual relations New numbers
262.94	Codex iruis canonici (1983) Expanded*
281.5	Eastern churches Expanded
281.94–.99	Specific autocephalous, arbitrary autocephalous, autonomous, independent [Orthodox] churches Revised and expanded
296.76	[Religious experience, life, practice in Judaism for] Persons experiencing illness, trouble, bereavement New number

*Introduced in an interim update prior to the publication of Edition 23

297.0902	[Historical periods of Islam] 610–1499 Revised and expanded
297.125	Hadith (Traditions) [of Islam] New number and subdivisions relocated from 297.124
302.343	Bullying New number
320.54	Nationalism, regionalism, internationalism Revised*
320.56	Ideologies based on groups of people Revised and expanded; groups of people relocated from 320.508
324.2436 324.245 324.2494	Parties of Austria Parties of Italy Parties of Switzerland Revised and expanded*
331.114	Qualifications [of Labor force] Revised
331.5	Workers by personal attributes other than age Revised and expanded
332.04246	Emigrant remittances New number*
335.4346	Asian national variants [of Communism] New number*
340.114	Justice New number
341.2421	Council of Europe New number
341.2422	European Union Expanded
343.08114	[Law of] Retail channels by merchandising pattern New number and subdivisions
345.01	Criminal courts Expanded
346.02	Juristic acts, contracts, agency Revised and expanded
347.057	Legal costs and fees New number and subdivision

*Introduced in an interim update prior to the publication of Edition 23

361.43	Self-help groups New number*
361.772	International Committee of the Red Cross; International Federation of Red Cross and Red Crescent Societies New number*
362.19888	Abortion services Interdisciplinary works relocated from 363.46*
362.2993 362.2995	[Substance abuse of] Inhalants [Substance abuse of] Stimulants New numbers*
362.59	[Social problems of and services to] Homeless and unemployed people New number and subdivisions
362.682	Elder abuse [as a social problem] New number
362.77 362.78	[Social problems of and services to] Specific groups of young people [Social problems of and services to] Transgender and intersex young people, young people by sexual orientation, young people in intrafamily relationships New numbers and subdivisions relocated from 362.7086
362.8	[Social problems of and services to] Other groups of people Revised and expanded
363.32	Social conflict Revised and expanded*
363.3494	[Public safety aspects of] Tsunamis New number*
363.728493	[Environmental problems of] Sewage New number*
364.1	Criminal offenses Revised and expanded*
365.66	Services to prisoners Expanded*
366 369	Secret associations and societies Associations Both headings revised and comprehensive works on associations relocated from 366 to 369; standard subdivisions revised at 366 and 369*

*Introduced in an interim update prior to the publication of Edition 23

370.8	Groups of people Discrimination in education relocated from 379.26
371.05	Public schools distinguished by source of funding, locus of control, and mandate New number; relocated from 371.01
371.391	Waldorf method New number*
372.2	Specific levels of primary education Revised
372.37	Personal health and safety; social skills Expanded; comprehensive works on home and family management relocated from 372.82
372.65	[Primary education in] Foreign, official, second languages; bilingual instruction Expanded
372.7	[Primary education in] Mathematics Expanded
372.89	[Primary education in] History and geography Comprehensive works on social studies relocated from 372.82
373.23	Specific levels of secondary education
373.24	Academic, military, vocational [secondary] schools Revised
378.1035	Industry relations [in higher education] New number
379.1122	Support of public preschool education
379.12122	National support of preschool education
379.128	Support [of public education] by regional intergovernmental organizations
379.154	Control [of public education] by regional intergovernmental organizations
379.3222	Public support of private preschool education New numbers
391.4	Kinds of garments; accessories; buttons Revised and expanded
391.72	Finger rings New number
393.93	Funerals New number

*Introduced in an interim update prior to the publication of Edition 23

394.1	Eating, drinking; using drugs Revised and expanded
401.45	Pragmatics New number and subdivisions*
401.47	Languages for special purposes New number*
401.95	Speech perception New number*
410.188	Corpus linguistics New number*
413.15	Dictionaries of abbreviations, acronyms, symbols New number
413.17	Picture dictionaries New number*
418.07	Multilingual phrase books New number*
427.942	Geographic variations [of English] in England and Wales Revised and expanded; 427.9421–.9428 Geographic variations [of English] in parts of England relocated from 427.1–.8
437.943	Geographic variations [of German] in Germany and neighboring central European countries Revised
437.9431–.9435	Geographic variations [of German] in parts of Germany New numbers; relocated from 437.1–.5
437.9436	Geographic variations [of German] in Austria New number; relocated from 437.6
439.779485	Geographic variations [of Swedish] in Sweden New number
439.779486–.779488	
	Geographic variations [of Swedish] in parts of Sweden New numbers; relocated from 439.776–.778
439.8179489	Geographic variations [of Danish] in Denmark and Finland Revised and expanded; 439.81794891–.81794895 Geographic variations [of Danish] in parts of Denmark relocated from 439.8171–.8175
439.8279481	Geographic variations [of Norwegian] in Norway New number

*Introduced in an interim update prior to the publication of Edition 23

439.8279482–.8279484
 Geographic variations [of Norwegian] in parts of Norway
 New numbers; relocated from 439.8272–.8274

447.944
 Geographic variations [of French] in France and Monaco
 Revised and expanded; 447.9441–.9448 Geographic variations [of
 French] in parts of France relocated from 447.1–.8

457.9
 Geographic variations [of Italian]
 Revised and expanded; 457.9451–.9457 Geographic variations [of
 Italian] in parts of the Italian Peninsula relocated from 457.1–.7,
 457.9458 Geographic variations [of Italian] in Sicily relocated from
 457.8

459.9
 Rhaetian languages; Sardinian, Corsican
 Expanded*

467.946
 Geographic variations [of Spanish] in Spain, Andorra, Gibraltar,
 Portugal
 Revised and expanded; 467.9461–.9468 Geographic variations [of
 Spanish] in parts of Spain relocated from 467.1–.8

469.79
 Geographic variations [of Portuguese]
 Revised and expanded; 469.794691–.794696 Geographic variations
 [of Portuguese] in Portuguese parts of the Iberian Peninsula
 relocated from 469.71–.76

469.9
 Galician
 New number; relocated from 469.71–469.72 and 469.794

491.489
 Divehi (Maldivian)
 New number*

491.492
 Languages of east central zone of Indo-Aryan languages (Eastern
 Hindi languages)
 New number

491.496
 Pahari languages
 New number

491.83
 Croatian and Bosnian
 New number and subdivision; Croatian relocated from 491.82*

495.17951
 Geographic variations [of Chinese] in China and adjacent areas
 Revised and expanded; 495.179511–.179518 Geographic variations
 [of Chinese] in parts of China relocated from 495.171–.178

511.314   Modal logic
511.317   Conditional logic
511.318   Probabilistic logic
 New numbers

*Introduced in an interim update prior to the publication of Edition 23

514.746	Singularity theory New number
515.882	Convex functions New number
519.62	Stochastic optimization Expanded
523.49	Trans-Neptunian objects New number and subdivisions; relocated from 523.48*
551.417	Wetland geomorphology New number
581.39	Age characteristics [of plants] New number
590.723	[Zoological] Descriptive research Expanded
591.39	Age characteristics [of animals] Revised and expanded
612	Human physiology Revised and expanded; histology and cytology of specific systems, organs, and regions relocated from 611.018
613.2622 613.265	Vegan diet Raw food diet New numbers*
613.283 613.284 613.285	[Dietetics of] Carbohydrates [Dietetics of] Fats and oils [Dietetics of] Minerals Expanded*
613.71489	Qi gong New number*
613.719	Specific systems of exercises for health New number and subdivision*
615.79	Miscellaneous classes of drugs New number and subdivisions*
615.8514	Biofeedback therapy New number
615.85158	Therapeutic use of animals New number and subdivision*

*Introduced in an interim update prior to the publication of Edition 23

615.8548	Nutrition support [as a type of therapy] New number and subdivisions
616.00835	Young people twelve to twenty Clarification of scope of adolescent medicine (616.00835) and pediatrics (618.92)*
616.0475	Shock and multiple organ failure New number*
616.32	Diseases of pharynx and esophagus Expanded*
616.34473	Ulcerative colitis New number*
616.429	Sarcoidosis New number*
616.462	Diabetes mellitus Expanded*
616.57	Parasitic and fungal skin diseases Expanded*
616.85883	Other pervasive devclopment disorders New number and subdivision*
616.891425 616.89147	Cognitive therapy Brief psychotherapy New numbers*
616.91856	West Nile fever New number*
616.9693	Candidiasis New number*
617.1027	Athletic and dance injuries Revised and expanded*
618.18	[Gynecological aspects of] Birth control New number and subdivisions*
618.29	Nonsurgical methods of abortion New number*
621.384192	[Radio] Identification and locating New number; relocated from 621.384191
623.8282	Fishing boats New number

*Introduced in an interim update prior to the publication of Edition 23

623.893	Geonavigation aids
623.8942	Lighthouses
623.8944	Light beacons, buoys, daymarks
	Elimination of dual provision of same topics at 627.92 Navigation aids and its subdivisions
624.238	Cable-stayed bridges
	New number
629.272	Electronic systems [in motor land vehicles]
	New number
636.08321	Animal hospitals
	New number*
636.294	[Animal husbandry of] Cervidae (Deer)
	Revised and expanded*
641.22232	Rosé wine
641.2226	Fortified wine
	New numbers*
641.52	[Cooking] First meal of the day
641.53	[Cooking] Light meals
641.54	[Cooking] Main meal of the day
	Revised
641.8153	Crepes, pancakes, waffles
	New number
641.8157	Quick breads
	Revised
646.4	Clothing and accessories construction
	Revised and expanded
658.877	Auctions [as a type of marketing channels]
	New number and subdivision
659.1045	Use of images and themes in advertising
	New number*
663.2232	[Beverage technology of] Rosé wine
663.226	[Beverage technology of] Fortified wine
	New numbers*
663.29	[Beverage technology of] Nongrape wine
	New number
665.37	Biodiesel fuel
	New number

*Introduced in an interim update prior to the publication of Edition 23

667.75	Lacquers and lacquering Japans and japanning relocated from 667.8
668.4942	Glass-reinforced plastic New number
684.13	[Manufacture of] Chairs and tables Expanded
684.162	[Manufacture of] Shelving New number
690.3 690.4	Special topics of buildings Specific parts of buildings New number and subdivisions
709.04058	Minimalism New number*
709.04075	Conceptual art Expanded*
709.0408 709.0409	Specific composite media Outsider art (Art brut) New numbers and subdivisions*
709.05	21st century, 2000–2099 Expanded*
720.44	[Architecture of] Portable and temporary buildings New number and subdivisions
720.4724	Use of solar energy [in architecture] New number
725.37	[Architecture of] Agricultural buildings New number and subdivision; comprehensive works on agricultural structures relocated from 728.92
726.796	Cloisters New number; comprehensive works relocated from 726.69*
731.724 745.5946	Fountains Fountains [as handicrafts] New numbers*
740	Graphic arts and decorative arts Graphic arts relocated from 760
741.5	Comic books, graphic novels, fotonovelas, cartoons, caricatures, comic strips Revised and expanded*

*Introduced in an interim update prior to the publication of Edition 23

771	Techniques, procedures, apparatus, equipment, materials [of photography] Revised and expanded
777	Cinematography and videography New number and subdivisions relocated from 778.5
780.78	Performances (Concerts and recitals) Exhibitions and fairs relocated from 789.74; festivals relocated from 780.79*
781.648	Electronica New number
791.43	Motion pictures Made-for-television movies, video recordings of motion pictures relocated from 791.45*
791.66	Beauty contests
792.76	Stand-up comedy
795.36	Bingo New numbers*
796.16	Play with robots New number; relocated from 796.15
796.327	Team handball New number*
796.356	Hockey New number and subdivisions*
796.44	Gymnastics
796.47	Tumbling, trampolining, acrobatics, contortion Expanded*
796.524	[Walking and exploring by] Canyons and other depressions New number*
796.62	Bicycle racing Expanded
796.8157	Taekwondo New number
796.95	Sledding and coasting Expanded
796.963	Bandy
796.965	Broomball
796.966	Ringette New numbers*

*Introduced in an interim update prior to the publication of Edition 23

797.23	Underwater swimming Expanded*
797.252	Water polo New number*
798.242	Eventing New number
808.025	Plagiarism New number
808.03	Specific elements of rhetoric New number and subdivisions
808.512	Toasts and after-dinner speeches New number
808.81–.88	Collections in specific forms
809.1–.7	Literature in specific forms Revised to allow regular use of T3C—8–9 for literature for and by groups of people
809.98	[History, description, critical appraisal of] Miscellaneous writings New number and subdivisions
859.9	Literatures of Rhaetian, Sardinian, Corsican languages Expanded*
869.9	Galician literature New number and subdivisions
891.489	Divehi (Maldivian) literature New number*
891.492	Literatures of east central zone of Indo-Aryan languages (Eastern Hindi literatures) New number
891.496	Pahari literatures New number
891.83	Croatian and Bosnian literatures New number and subdivision; Croatian literature relocated from 891.82*
894.57	Sámi (Saami) literatures New number and subdivisions; relocated from 894.55
894.89	Literatures of miscellaneous languages of south Asia New number and subdivision

*Introduced in an interim update prior to the publication of Edition 23

907.2	Historical research Interdisciplinary works relocated from 001.432*
909.83	21st century, 2000–2099 Expanded*

910	Geography and travel
	    Travel by passenger automobile relocated from 796.78; travel by
	    motor homes, recreational vehicles, trailers relocated from 796.79*

930	History of ancient world to ca. 499 Revised and expanded

940–990	History of specific continents, countries, localities in modern
	world; extraterrestrial worlds
	    New historical periods introduced through 940–990, e.g., 973.932
	    Administration of Barack Obama, 2009–

945	Italy, San Marino, Vatican City, Malta Historical periods revised and expanded*
959.7	Vietnam Historical periods revised and expanded*

*Introduced in an interim update prior to the publication of Edition 23

Introduction to the Dewey Decimal Classification

About the Introduction

1.1   This Introduction explains the basic principles and structure of the Dewey Decimal Classification (DDC) system.

1.2   The Introduction is intended to be used in conjunction with the Glossary and the Manual. The Glossary defines terms used in the Introduction and elsewhere in the Classification. The Manual offers advice on classifying in difficult areas, and explains how to choose between related numbers.

Classification: What It Is and What It Does

2.1   *Classification* provides a system for organizing knowledge. Classification may be used to organize knowledge represented in any form, e.g., books, documents, electronic resources.

2.2   *Notation* is the system of symbols used to represent the classes in a classification system. In the Dewey Decimal Classification, the notation is expressed in Arabic numerals. The notation gives both the unique meaning of the class and its relation to other classes. The notation provides a universal language to identify the class and related classes, regardless of the fact that different words or languages may be used to describe the class.

History, Current Use, and Development of the Dewey Decimal Classification

3.1   The Dewey Decimal Classification—conceived by Melvil Dewey in 1873 and first published in 1876—is a general knowledge organization tool that is continuously revised to keep pace with knowledge. The system is further extended through number building, interoperable translations, association with categorized content, and mappings to other subject schemes.

3.2   The DDC is published in full and abridged editions by OCLC Online Computer Library Center, Inc. The abridged edition is a logical truncation of the notational and structural hierarchy of the corresponding full edition on which it is based, and is intended for general collections of 20,000 titles or less. Both editions are issued in print and electronic versions; the electronic versions are updated frequently and contain additional index entries and mapped vocabulary. OCLC owns all copyright rights in the Dewey Decimal Classification, and licenses the system for a variety of uses.

3.3   The DDC is the most widely used classification system in the world. Libraries in more than 138 countries use the DDC to organize and provide access to their collections, and DDC numbers are featured in the national bibliographies of more than sixty countries. Libraries of every type apply Dewey numbers on a daily basis and share these numbers through a variety of means (including WorldCat). Dewey is also used in a variety of applications on the web in support of categorization, browsing, and retrieval.

3.4   The DDC has been translated into over thirty languages. Since 1988, authorized translations of the full and abridged editions of the DDC have been published or are under way in Arabic, French, German, Greek, Hebrew, Icelandic, Indonesian, Italian, Norwegian, Russian, Spanish, Swedish, Turkish, and Vietnamese. The DDC Summaries, the top three levels of the Dewey Decimal Classification system, have been translated into Afrikaans, Arabic, Chinese, Czech, French, German, Hebrew, Italian, Norwegian, Portuguese, Russian, Spanish, Swedish, and Vietnamese.

3.5   One of Dewey's great strengths is that the system is developed and maintained in a national bibliographic agency, the Library of Congress. The Dewey editorial office is located in the Dewey Section of the Library of Congress, where classification specialists annually assign over 60,000 DDC numbers to records for works cataloged by the Library. Having the editorial office within the Dewey Section enables the editors to detect trends in the literature that must be incorporated into the Classification. The editors prepare proposed schedule revisions and expansions, and forward the proposals to the Decimal Classification Editorial Policy Committee (EPC) for review and recommended action.

3.6   EPC is a ten-member international board whose main function is to advise the editors and OCLC on matters relating to changes, innovations, and the general development of the Classification. EPC represents the interests of DDC users; its members come from national, public, special, and academic libraries, and from library schools.

Overview of the Dewey Decimal Classification

CONCEPTUAL FRAMEWORK

4.1   The DDC is built on sound principles that make it ideal as a general knowledge organization tool: meaningful notation in universally recognized Arabic numerals, well-defined categories, well-developed hierarchies, and a rich network of relationships among topics. In the DDC, basic classes are organized by disciplines or fields of study. At the broadest level, the DDC is divided into ten *main classes*, which together cover the entire world of knowledge. Each main class is further divided into ten *divisions*, and each division into ten *sections* (not all the numbers for the divisions and sections have been used).

4.2   The main structure of the DDC is presented in the *DDC Summaries* in the beginning of volume 2. The *first summary* contains the ten main classes. The *second summary* contains the hundred divisions. The *third summary* contains the thousand sections. The headings associated with the numbers in the summaries have been edited for browsing purposes, and do not necessarily match the complete headings found in the schedules.

4.3   The ten main classes are:

000	Computer science, information & general works
100	Philosophy & psychology
200	Religion
300	Social sciences
400	Language
500	Science
600	Technology
700	Arts & recreation
800	Literature
900	History & geography

4.4   Class 000 is the most general class, and is used for works not limited to any one specific discipline, e.g., encyclopedias, newspapers, general periodicals. This class is also used for certain specialized disciplines that deal with knowledge and information, e.g., computer science, library and information science, journalism. Each of the other main classes (100–900) comprises a major discipline or group of related disciplines.

4.5   Class 100 covers philosophy, parapsychology and occultism, and psychology.

4.6   Class 200 is devoted to religion.

4.7   Class 300 covers the social sciences. Class 300 includes sociology, anthropology, statistics, political science, economics, law, public administration, social problems and services, education, commerce, communications, transportation, and customs.

4.8   Class 400 comprises language, linguistics, and specific languages. Literature, which is arranged by language, is found in 800.

4.9   Class 500 is devoted to the natural sciences and mathematics.

4.10   Class 600 is technology.

4.11   Class 700 covers the arts: art in general, fine and decorative arts, music, and the performing arts. Recreation, including sports and games, is also classed in 700.

4.12   Class 800 covers literature, and includes rhetoric, prose, poetry, drama, etc. Folk literature is classed with customs in 300.

4.13   Class 900 is devoted primarily to history and geography. A history of a specific subject is classed with the subject.

4.14   Since the parts of the DDC are arranged by discipline, not subject, a subject may appear in more than one class. For example, "clothing" has aspects that fall under several disciplines. The psychological influence of clothing belongs in 155.95 as part of the discipline of psychology; customs associated with clothing belong in 391 as part of the discipline of customs; and clothing in the sense of fashion design belongs in 746.92 as part of the discipline of the arts.

NOTATION

4.15   Arabic numerals are used to represent each class in the DDC. The first digit in each three-digit number represents the main class. For example, 5̲00 represents science. The second digit in each three-digit number indicates the division. For example, 5̲00 is used for general works on the sciences, 51̲0 for mathematics, 52̲0 for astronomy, 53̲0 for physics. The third digit in each three-digit number indicates the section. Thus, 53̲0 is used for general works on physics, 53̲1 for classical mechanics, 53̲2 for fluid mechanics, 53̲3 for gas mechanics. The DDC uses the convention that no number should have fewer than three digits; zeros are used to fill out numbers.

4.16   A *decimal point*, or dot, follows the third digit in a class number, after which division by ten continues to the specific degree of classification needed. The dot is not a decimal point in the mathematical sense, but a psychological pause to break the monotony of numerical digits and to ease the transcription and copying of the class number. A number should never end in a 0 anywhere to the right of the decimal point.

PRINCIPLE OF HIERARCHY

4.17   *Hierarchy* in the DDC is expressed through structure and notation.

4.18   *Structural hierarchy* means that all topics (aside from the ten main classes) are part of all the broader topics above them. The corollary is also true: whatever is true of the whole is true of the parts. This important concept is called *hierarchical force*. Certain notes regarding the nature of a class hold true for all the subordinate classes, including logically subordinate topics classed at coordinate numbers. (For a discussion of notes with hierarchical force, see paragraphs 7.10–7.16 and 7.19–7.21.)

Because of the principle of hierarchical force, hierarchical notes are usually given only once—at the highest level of application. For example, the scope note at 700 applies to 730, to 736, and to 736.4. The words "Description, critical appraisal ..." found in the scope note at 700 also govern the critical appraisal of carving in 736 Carving and carvings, and of wood carving in 736.4 Wood. In order to understand the structural hierarchy, the classifier must read up and down the schedules (and remember to turn the page).

4.19   *Notational hierarchy* is expressed by length of notation. Numbers at any given level are usually *subordinate* to a class whose notation is one digit shorter; *coordinate* with a class whose notation has the same number of significant digits; and *superordinate* to a class with numbers one or more digits longer. The underlined digits in the following example demonstrate this notational hierarchy:

6̲00	Technology (Applied sciences)
63̲0	Agriculture and related technologies
636̲	Animal husbandry
636.7̲	Dogs
636.8̲	Cats

"Dogs" and "Cats" are more specific than (i.e., are subordinate to) "Animal husbandry"; they are equally specific as (i.e., are coordinate with) each other; and "Animal husbandry" is less specific than (i.e., is superordinate to) "Dogs" and "Cats."

4.20   Sometimes, other devices must be used to express hierarchy when it is not possible or desirable to do so through the notation. A see reference leads the classifier to subdivisions of a subject located outside the notational hierarchy. A centered entry (so called because its numbers, heading, and notes appear in the center of the page) constitutes a major departure from notational hierarchy. A centered entry is used to indicate and relate structurally a span of numbers that together form a single concept for which there is no specific hierarchical notation available. In the DDC, centered entries are always flagged typographically by the symbol > in the number column.

Classifying with the DDC

5.1   Classifying a work with the DDC requires determining the subject, the disciplinary focus, and, if applicable, the approach or form. (For a discussion of approach or form, see paragraph 8.3.)

DETERMINING THE SUBJECT OF A WORK

5.2   Classifying a work properly depends first upon determining the subject of the work in hand. A key element in determining the subject is the author's intent.

(A)   The title is often a clue to the subject, but should never be the sole source of analysis. For example, *Opera* could be the title of a work on the familiar dramatic musical art form or on the web browser Opera. Likewise, a title with specific terms that are subdivisions of a field may in fact use such terms symbolically to represent the broader topic. For example, titles containing terms like chromosomes, DNA, double helix, genes, and genomes may use these terms symbolically to represent the whole subject of biochemical genetics.

(B)   The table of contents may list the main topics discussed. Chapter headings may substitute for the absence of a table of contents. Chapter subheadings often prove useful.

(C)   The preface or introduction usually states the author's purpose. If a foreword is provided, it often indicates the subject of the work and suggests the place of the work in the development of thought on the subject. The book jacket or accompanying material may include a summary of the subject content.

(D)   A scan of the text itself may provide further guidance or confirm preliminary subject analysis.

(E)   Bibliographical references and index entries are sources of subject information.

(F) Cataloging copy from centralized cataloging services is often helpful by providing subject headings, classification numbers, and notes. Such copy appears in online services, and on the verso of the title page of many books as part of Cataloging-in-Publication (CIP) data. Data from these sources should be verified with the book in hand, since the cataloging record is based on prepublication information.

(G) Occasionally, consultation of outside sources such as reviews, reference works, and subject experts may be required to determine the subject of the work.

DETERMINING THE DISCIPLINE OF A WORK

5.3 After determining the subject, the classifier must then select the proper discipline, or field of study, of the work.

5.4 The guiding principle of the DDC is that a work is classed in the discipline for which it is intended, rather than the discipline from which the work derives. This enables works that are used together to be found together. For example, a general work by a zoologist on agricultural pest control should be classed in agriculture, not zoology, along with other works on agricultural pest control.

5.5 Once the subject has been determined, and information on the discipline has been found, the classifier will turn to the schedules. The summaries are a good means of mental navigation. The headings and notes in the schedules themselves and the Manual provide much guidance. The Relative Index may help by suggesting the disciplines in which a subject is normally treated. (For a discussion of the summaries, see paragraph 7.1; for a discussion of the Manual, see paragraphs 10.1–10.6; for a discussion of the Relative Index, see paragraphs 11.1–11.15.)

5.6 If the Relative Index is used, the classifier must still rely on the structure of the Classification and various aids throughout to arrive at the proper place to classify a work. Even the most promising Relative Index citations must be verified in the schedules; the schedules are the only place where all the information about coverage and use of the numbers may be found.

MORE THAN ONE SUBJECT IN THE SAME DISCIPLINE

5.7 A work may include multiple subjects treated separately or in relation to one another from the viewpoint of a single discipline. Use the following guidelines in determining the best placement for the work:

(A) Class a work dealing with interrelated subjects with the subject that is being acted upon. This is called the *rule of application*, and takes precedence over any other rule. For instance, class an analytical work dealing with Shakespeare's influence on Keats with Keats. Similarly, class a work on the influence of the Great Depression on 20th century American art with American art.

(B) Class a work on two subjects with the subject receiving fuller treatment.

(C)   If two subjects receive equal treatment, and are not used to introduce or explain one another, class the work with the subject whose number comes first in the DDC schedules. This is called the *first-of-two rule*. For example, a history dealing equally with the United States and Japan, in which the United States is discussed first and is given first in the title, is classed with the history of Japan because 952 Japan precedes 973 United States.

Sometimes, specific instructions are given to use numbers that do not come first in the schedules. For example, at 598, the note "class comprehensive works on warm-blooded vertebrates in 599" tells the classifier to ignore the first-of-two rule and class a work on birds (598) and mammals (599) in 599, which is the comprehensive number for warm-blooded vertebrates.

Also disregard the first-of-two rule when the two topics are the two major subdivisions of a subject. For example, collection systems (628.142) and distribution systems (628.144) taken together constitute 628.14 Collection and distribution systems. Works covering both of these topics are classed in 628.14 (not 628.142).

(For a discussion of the first-of-two rule versus preference order, see paragraph 9.6; for a discussion of comprehensive numbers, see paragraphs 7.16 and 7.19–7.20.)

(D)   Class a work on three or more subjects that are all subdivisions of a broader subject in the first higher number that includes them all (unless one subject is treated more fully than the others). This is called the *rule of three*. For example, a history of Portugal (946.9), Sweden (948.5), and Greece (949.5) is classed with the history of Europe (940).

(E)   Subdivisions beginning with zero should be avoided if there is a choice between 0 and 1–9 at the same point in the hierarchy of the notation. Similarly, subdivisions beginning with 00 should be avoided when there is a choice between 00 and 0. This is called the *rule of zero*. For example, a biography of an American Methodist missionary in China belongs in 266 Missions. The content of the work can be expressed in three different numbers:

266.0092	biography of a missionary
266.02373051	foreign missions of the United States in China
266.76092	biography of a United Methodist Church missionary

The last number is used since it has no zero at the fourth position.

MORE THAN ONE DISCIPLINE

5.8   Treating a subject from the point of view of more than one discipline is different from treating several subjects in one discipline. Use the following guidelines in determining the best placement for the work:

(A)   Use the *interdisciplinary number* provided in the schedules or Relative Index if one is given. An important consideration in using such an interdisciplinary number is that the work must contain significant material on the discipline in which the interdisciplinary number is found. For example, 305.231 (a sociology number) is provided for interdisciplinary works on child development. However, if a work that is interdisciplinary with respect to child development gives little emphasis to social development and a great deal of emphasis to the psychological and physical development of the child (155.4 and 612.65, respectively), class it in 155.4 (the first number in the schedules of the next two obvious choices). In short, interdisciplinary numbers are not absolute; they are to be used only when applicable. (For a discussion of interdisciplinary numbers, see paragraphs 7.16, 7.19–7.20, and 11.8–11.9.)

(B)   Class works not given an interdisciplinary number in the discipline given the fullest treatment in the work. For example, a work dealing with both the scientific and the engineering principles of electrodynamics is classed in 537.6 if the engineering aspects are introduced primarily for illustrative purposes, but in 621.31 if the basic scientific theories are only preliminary to the author's exposition of engineering principles and practices.

(C)   When classifying interdisciplinary works, do not overlook the possibilities of main class 000 Computer science, information & general works, e.g., 080 for a collection of interviews of famous people from various disciplines.

Any other situation is treated in the same fashion as those found in the instructions at More Than One Subject in the Same Discipline (paragraph 5.7).

TABLE OF LAST RESORT

5.9   When several numbers have been found for the work in hand, and each seems as good as the next, the following table of last resort (in order of preference) may be used as a guideline in the absence of any other rule:

Table of last resort

(1)   Kinds of things
(2)   Parts of things
(3)   Materials from which things, kinds, or parts are made
(4)   Properties of things, kinds, parts, or materials
(5)   Processes within things, kinds, parts, or materials
(6)   Operations upon things, kinds, parts, or materials
(7)   Instrumentalities for performing such operations

For example, surveillance by border patrols could be classed in either 363.285 Border patrols, or 363.232 Patrol and surveillance. Choose 363.285 since border patrols are a kind of police service, while patrol and surveillance are processes performed by police services.

5.10   Do not apply this table or any other guideline if it appears to disregard the author's intention and emphasis.

How DDC 23 Is Arranged

6.1   DDC 23 is composed of the following major parts in four volumes:

Volume 1

(A)   New Features in Edition 23: A brief explanation of the special features and changes in DDC 23

(B)   Introduction: A description of the DDC and how to use it

(C)   Glossary: Short definitions of terms used in the DDC

(D)   Index to the Introduction and Glossary

(E)   Manual: A guide to the use of the DDC that is made up primarily of extended discussions of problem areas in the application of the DDC. Information in the Manual is arranged by the numbers in the tables and schedules

(F)   Tables: Six numbered tables of notation that can be added to class numbers to provide greater specificity

(G)   Lists that compare Editions 22 and 23: Relocations and Discontinuations; Comparative and Equivalence Tables; Reused Numbers

Volume 2

(H)   DDC Summaries: The top three levels of the DDC

(I)   Schedules: The organization of knowledge from 000–599

Volume 3

(J)   Schedules: The organization of knowledge from 600–999

Volume 4

(K)   Relative Index: An alphabetical list of subjects with the disciplines in which they are treated subarranged alphabetically under each entry

Key Features of the Schedules and Tables

SUMMARIES

7.1   *Summaries* provide an overview of the structure of classes. Three types of summaries appear in the DDC:

(A)   DDC Summaries, the summaries of the top three levels of the DDC, are found in front of the schedules in volume 2. (For a discussion of DDC Summaries, see paragraphs 4.2–4.13.)

(B)   Two-level summaries are provided for each main class and division of the schedules and main numbers of Table 2 with subdivisions that extend beyond forty pages. See the summaries at the beginning of Table 2 —4 Europe and 370 Education for examples of two-level summaries.

(C)   Single-level summaries in the schedules and tables provide an overview of classes whose subdivisions cover between four and forty pages. For example, 382 International commerce (Foreign trade) has the following summary:

SUMMARY

382.01–.09	**Standard subdivisions**
.1	**General topics of international commerce**
.3	**Commercial policy**
.4	**Specific products and services**
.5	**Import trade**
.6	**Export trade**
.7	**Tariff policy**
.9	**Trade agreements**

ENTRIES

7.2   Entries in the schedules and tables are composed of a DDC number in the number column (the column at the left margin), a heading describing the class that the number represents, and often one or more notes. DDC numbers are listed in groups of three digits for ease of reading and copying. All entries (numbers, headings, and notes) should be read in the context of the hierarchy. (For a discussion of the principle of hierarchy, see paragraphs 4.17–4.20.)

7.3   The first three digits of schedule numbers (main classes, divisions, sections) appear only once in the number column, when first used. They are repeated at the top of each page where their subdivisions continue. Subordinate numbers appear in the number column, beginning with a decimal point, with the initial three digits understood.

7.4   Table numbers are given in full in the number column of the tables, and are never used alone. There are six numbered tables in DDC 23:

    T1   Standard Subdivisions
    T2   Geographic Areas, Historical Periods, Biography
    T3   Subdivisions for the Arts, for Individual Literatures, for Specific Literary Forms

        T3A   Subdivisions for Works by or about Individual Authors
        T3B   Subdivisions for Works by or about More than One Author
        T3C   Notation to Be Added Where Instructed in Table 3B, 700.4, 791.4, 808–809

    T4   Subdivisions of Individual Languages and Language Families
    T5   Ethnic and National Groups
    T6   Languages

Except for notation from Table 1 (which may be added to any number unless there is an instruction in the schedules or tables to the contrary), table notation may be added only as instructed in the schedules and tables. (For a detailed discussion of the use of the six tables, see paragraphs 8.3–8.20.)

7.5 Some numbers in the schedules and tables are enclosed in parentheses or square brackets. Numbers and notes in parentheses provide options to standard practice. Numbers in square brackets represent topics that have been relocated or discontinued, or are unassigned. Square brackets are also used for standard subdivision concepts that are represented in another location. Bracketed numbers should never be used. (For a discussion of options, see paragraphs 12.1–12.7; for a discussion of relocations and discontinuations, see paragraphs 7.23–7.24; for a discussion of bracketed standard subdivisions, see paragraph 7.25.)

7.6 Standard subdivisions are also bracketed under a *hook number*, that is, a number that has no meaning in itself, but is used to introduce specific examples of a topic. Hook numbers have headings that begin with "Miscellaneous," "Other," or "Specific"; and do not contain add notes, including notes, or class-here notes. For example:

> 652.302 Specific levels of skill
>
> [.302 01–.302 09] Standard subdivisions
>
> > Do not use; class in 652.3001–652.3009

NOTES

7.7 Notes are important because they supply information that is not obvious in the notational hierarchy or in the heading with regard to order, structure, subordination, and other matters. Notes may appear in the record for a number or a span of numbers. Notes may also appear at the beginning of a table. Footnotes are used for instructions that apply to multiple subdivisions of a class, or to a topic within a class. Individual entries in the Manual are also considered notes.

7.8 Notes in the schedules and tables generally appear in the following order: revision, former-heading, definition, number-built, standard-subdivisions-are added, variant-name, scope, including, class-here, arrange, add (including subdivisions-are-added), preference, class-elsewhere, see-reference, see-also reference, see-Manual, option, discontinued, and relocation notes.

7.9 The notes below do the following: (A) describe what is found in the class and its subdivisions; (B) identify topics in *standing room*, i.e., topics with insufficient literature to have their own number; (C) describe what is found in other classes; and (D) explain changes in the schedules and tables. Other notes are described in the sections on number building (paragraphs 8.1–8.22), citation and preference order (paragraphs 9.1–9.6), the Manual (paragraphs 10.1–10.6), and options (paragraphs 12.1–12.5).

Notes in categories (A) and (C) have hierarchical force (i.e., are applicable to all the subdivisions of a particular number). Those in category (B) do not have hierarchical force.

(A) Notes That Describe What Is Found in a Class

7.10   *Definition notes* indicate the meaning of a term in the heading. For example:

    364   Criminology

         Crime and its alleviation

7.11   *Scope notes* indicate whether the meaning of the number is narrower or broader than is apparent from the heading. For example:

    700   The arts

         Description, critical appraisal, techniques, procedures, apparatus, equipment, materials of the fine, decorative, literary, performing, recreational arts

7.12   *Number-built notes* identify and explain the source of built numbers included in the schedules and tables. Built numbers are occasionally included in the schedules or tables to provide additional information or to indicate exceptions to regular add instructions. For example:

    353.132 63   Foreign service

         Number built according to instructions under 352–354

         Class here consular and diplomatic services

7.13   *Former-heading notes* are given only when the heading associated with a class number in the previous edition has been altered to such a degree that the new heading bears little or no resemblance to the previous heading, even though the meaning of the number has remained substantially the same. For example:

    004.16   *Personal computers

         Former heading: Microcomputers

7.14   *Variant-name notes* are used for synonyms or near synonyms. For example:

    332.32   Savings and loan associations

         Variant names: building and loan associations, building societies, home loan associations, mortgage institutions

7.15   *Class-here notes* list major topics in a class. These topics may be broader or narrower than the heading, overlap it, or define another way of looking at essentially the same material. Topics in class-here notes are considered to *approximate the whole* of the class. For example:

    371.192   Parent-school relations

         Class here parent participation in schools; comprehensive works on teacher-parent relations

Standard subdivisions may be added for any topic in a class-here note. (For a detailed discussion of the use of standard subdivisions for concepts that approximate the whole of a class, see paragraphs 8.3–8.12 and the beginning of Table 1.)

7.16   Class-here notes are also used to indicate where interdisciplinary and comprehensive works are classed. *Interdisciplinary works* treat a subject from the perspective of more than one discipline. For example:

> 391   Costume and personal appearance
>
>> Class here interdisciplinary works on costume, clothing (apparel, garments), fashion; casual wear (sportswear)

Comprehensive works treat a subject from various points of view within a single discipline. Comprehensive works may be stated or implied in a class-here note. For example:

> 641.815   Breads and bread-like foods
>
>> Class here yeast breads, comprehensive works on baked goods   *(stated)*
>
> —411 5   Highland
>
>> Class here *Scottish Highlands   *(implied)*

(B) Including Notes (Notes That Identify Topics in Standing Room)

7.17   *Including notes* identify topics that have "standing room" in the number where the note is found. Standing room numbers provide a location for topics with relatively few works written about them, but whose literature may grow in the future, at which time they may be assigned their own number. For example:

> 362.16   Extended care medical facilities
>
>> Including convalescent homes, sanatoriums for persons suffering from chronic diseases

Standard subdivisions cannot be added for topics in standing room, nor are other number-building techniques allowed.

7.18   Entries in the taxonomic schedules in 579–590 may have two including notes. The first including note contains the scientific taxonomic names at or above the level of family. The second one contains common and genus names. For example:

> 593.55   Hydrozoa
>
>> Including Chondrophora, Hydroida, Milleporina, Pteromedusae, Siphonophora, Stylasterina, Trachylina
>
>> Including hydras, Portuguese man-of-war

(C) Notes That Describe What Is Found in Other Classes

7.19   *Class-elsewhere notes* lead the classifier to interrelated topics, or distinguish among numbers in the same notational hierarchy. They are used to show preference order, to lead to the comprehensive or interdisciplinary number, to override the first-of-two rule, or to lead to broader or narrower topics in the same hierarchical array that might otherwise be overlooked. They may point to a specific number, or to a concept scattered throughout the schedules. All notes that begin with the word "class" are class-elsewhere notes, except when they begin with "class here." For example:

641.7	Specific cooking processes and techniques

> Class specific processes applied to specific materials in 641.6; class specific processes applied to specific kinds of dishes, preparing beverages in 641.8

370.15	Educational psychology

> Class interdisciplinary works on psychology in 150. Class psychology of a specific topic in education with the topic, plus notation 019 from Table 1, e.g., psychology of special education 371.9019

155.4	Child psychology

> Class interdisciplinary works on child development in 305.231

7.20   *See references* lead from a stated or implied comprehensive number for a concept to the component (subordinate) parts of that concept in a different notational hierarchy. See references also lead from the interdisciplinary number for a concept to treatment of the concept in other disciplines. A see reference may point to a specific number, or to a concept scattered throughout the schedules. Each see reference begins with the word "For" and appears in italics. For example:

577.7	Marine ecology

> Class here saltwater ecology

> *For salt lake ecology, see 577.639; for saltwater wetland and seashore ecology, see 577.69*

305.4	Women

> Class here interdisciplinary works on women, on females

> *For a specific aspect of women not provided for here, see the aspect, e.g., women's suffrage 324.623, legal status of women 346.0134*

Throughout Table 2, see references (often in footnote form) lead from the implied comprehensive number for a jurisdiction, region, or feature to its subordinate parts in other classes. For example:

—411 5   Highland

Class here *Scottish Highlands

*For a specific part of this jurisdiction, region, or feature, see the part and follow instructions under —4–9

7.21   *See-also reference*s lead the classifier to related topics. They are reminders that minor differences in wording and context can imply differences in classification. Each see-also reference appears in italics. For example:

584.3   Liliidae

Class here Liliales, lilies

For Orchidales, see 584.4

See also 583.29 for water lilies

(D) Notes That Explain Changes or Irregularities in the Schedules and Tables

7.22   *Revision notes* warn users that there have been changes in the subdivisions of a class since the previous edition. A *new schedule, complete revision,* or *extensive revision* is always introduced by a revision note that appears first under the heading of the class affected. (For an example of a new schedule note, see 777 Cinematography and videography. There are no complete or extensive revision notes in DDC 23.)

7.23   *Discontinued notes* indicate that all or part of the contents of a number have been moved to a more general number in the same hierarchy, or have been dropped entirely. For example:

[025.393]   Recataloging

Number discontinued; class in 025.39

154.632   Panic disorder

Use of this number for other types of dreams discontinued; class in 154.63

7.24   *Relocation notes* state that all or part of the contents of a number have been moved to a different number. For example:

—[755 811]   Clifton Forge

Relocated to —755816

523.482   Optical, electromagnetic, radioactive, thermal phenomena

Pluto relocated to 523.4922

The former number is usually given at the new number, either in the heading or in the appropriate note. For example:

—755 816   Alleghany County

Including Clifton Forge [*formerly* —755811]

523.492 2   *Pluto [*formerly* 523.482]

7.25   *Do-not-use notes* instruct the classifier not to use all or part of the regular standard subdivision notation, but instead to use a special provision or standard subdivision notation at a broader number. When the whole standard subdivision is removed from use, the note appears under a bracketed standard subdivision; when only part of the standard subdivision is *displaced*, the part displaced is specified. For example:

[374.809]   History, geographic treatment, biography

Do not use; class in 374.9

320.409   History and biography

Do not use for geographic treatment; class in 320.41–320.49

Do-not-use notes are also used to instruct the classifier not to use all or part of an add table provision, but instead to use a special provision.

343.014   *Discipline and conduct

Including desertion

Subdivisions are added for either or both topics in heading

For discipline and conduct of a specific service other than the army in general, see the service in 343.015–343.019, e.g., discipline and conduct of mercenary troops 343.015354, naval discipline and conduct 343.01913

[343.014 026 9]   Courts and procedure

Do not use; class in 343.0143

*Add as instructed under 342–347

Number Building

8.1   The classifier will often find that to arrive at a precise number for a work it is necessary to build or synthesize a number that is not specifically listed in the schedules. Such *built numbers* allow for greater depth of content analysis. They are used only when instructions in the schedules make them possible (except for standard subdivisions, which are discussed in paragraphs 8.3–8.12). Number building begins with a base number (always stated in the instruction note) to which another number is added.

8.2   There are four sources of notation for building numbers: (A) Table 1 Standard Subdivisions; (B) Tables 2–6; (C) other parts of the schedules; and (D) add tables in the schedules.

(A) Adding Standard Subdivisions from Table 1

8.3   A *standard subdivision* represents a recurring physical form (such as a dictionary, periodical, or index) or approach (such as history or research) and thus is applicable to any subject or discipline that covers or approximates the whole of the meaning of the number. Here are a few examples with the standard subdivision concept underlined (in some cases an extra 0 precedes the standard subdivision according to instructions found in the schedules):

150.5	Philosophy and theory of psychology
230.003	Dictionary of Christianity
340.02573	Directory of lawyers in the U.S.
405	Periodical on language
507.8	Use of apparatus and equipment in the study and teaching of science, e.g., science fair projects
624.0285	Computer applications in civil engineering
796.912092	Biography of a figure skater
808.0071	Teaching of rhetoric

Further instructions on using Table 1 are found at the beginning of Table 1. See also Manual notes on selected standard subdivisions.

8.4   Standard subdivisions are not usually listed in the schedules except where needed to fill out three-digit numbers, e.g., 605 Serial publications, and in a few other instances. Standard subdivisions may be listed in the schedules when the subdivisions have extended or narrowed meanings. For example:

535.220 287 Testing and measurement   *(extended meaning)*

          Class here photometry

390.088   [Customs of] Religious groups   *(narrowed meaning)*

          Do not use for occupational groups; class in 390.4

Standard subdivisions may also be listed to introduce an expansion featuring special notation (the subdivisions in the expansion are not standard subdivisions). Such standard subdivisions are accompanied by a special note. For example:

370.1   Philosophy and theory, education for specific objectives, educational psychology

          Notation 01 from Table 1 as modified below

Sometimes, standard subdivisions are listed because references to other classes or the Manual are required. For example:

507.2   Research

Class research covering science in general in 001.4

See Manual at 500 vs. 001

507.21   Research methods

Class scientific method as a general research technique in 001.42

8.5   When standard subdivision notation from Table 1 is listed in Tables 2–6 and in the schedules, all of the notation's notes and subdivisions as given in Table 1 are applicable unless other instructions are given. Other Table 1 notation that is not listed in the schedules may also be used. For example, the fact that 610.7 is listed, but not 610.8 or the subdivisions of 610.7, does not exclude the use of 610.8 or 610.71.

8.6   Notation from Table 1 Standard Subdivisions may be added to any number in the schedules unless there is a specific instruction to the contrary. The classifier should never use more than one zero in applying a standard subdivision unless instructed to do so. If more than one zero is needed, the number of zeros is always indicated in the schedules. When using standard subdivisions with numbers built by adding from Tables 2–6 or other parts of the schedules, be sure to check the table or schedule used for the segment preceding the standard subdivision for special instructions on the number of zeros.

8.7   *The most important caveat with respect to standard subdivisions is that they are added only for works that cover or approximate the whole of the subject of the number.* For example, a work on mockingbirds of California should be classed in 598.844, the number for birds of the Mimidae family (not 598.84409794, the number for birds of the Mimidae family in California). The classifier should not attempt to specify California because mockingbirds are in the including note under 598.844 and therefore do not approximate the whole of 598.844 Mimidae in California. Likewise, class a work on the De Havilland 98 Mosquito (a specific British World War II fighter-bomber) in the number for fighter-bombers 623.7463 (not 623.7463094109044, the number for British fighter-bombers in World War II).

8.8   *Standard-subdivisions-are-added notes* indicate which topics in a multiterm heading may have standard subdivisions added for them because the designated topics are considered to *approximate the whole* of the subject. For example:

639.2   Commercial fishing, whaling, sealing

Standard subdivisions are added for commercial fishing, whaling, sealing together; for commercial fishing alone

Standard-subdivisions-are-added notes do not have hierarchical force beyond the standard subdivisions associated with the number itself. For example, the note under 639.2 governs the application of standard subdivisions to 639.2 itself, but not to 639.21–639.29.

8.9   Do not add multiple standard subdivisions to the same number except when specifically instructed to do so, and in the following instances. Standard subdivisions may be added to subdivisions of —04 Special topics that are specifically listed in the schedules. For example, standard subdivisions may be added to 155.9042 Stress, a subdivision of 155.904 Special topics in environmental psychology.

Standard subdivisions may also be added to special notation in the regular standard subdivision sequence. For example, under 370.1, there is an expansion for educational objectives at 370.11 Education for specific objectives. Standard subdivisions may be added to 370.11 and its subdivisions, since 370.11 and its subdivisions are special notation.

Standard subdivision concepts may be displaced to a special provision in the regular sequence of standard subdivisions or elsewhere; in either case, standard subdivisions may be added to the special provision. For example, 370.19 Psychological principles has been completely displaced to 370.15 Educational psychology, where the regular meaning of 370.15 (scientific principles) has been discontinued to 370.1. Notation 03 from Table 1, the standard subdivision for encyclopedias, may be added to 370.15 Educational psychology to represent an encyclopedia of educational psychology 370.1503.

The full range of standard subdivisions may also be added to standard subdivision concepts displaced to notation outside the regular sequence of standard subdivisions, e.g., the management of penal institutions in Great Britain 365.941068 (geographic treatment of penal institutions has been displaced from 365.09 to 365.9).

8.10   In many places in the schedules, there are numbers outside the regular sequence of standard subdivisions that look like standard subdivisions but are not standard subdivisions. If additional subdivisions are intended to be used at the special provision, an add note is provided. For example, at 027.009, a regular standard subdivision, geographic treatment is displaced to 027.01–027.09:

        027.009   History and biography

                       Do not use for geographic treatment; class in 027.01–027.09

        027.01–027.09   *Geographic treatment

                       Add to base number 027.0 notation 1–9 from Table 2, e.g., libraries in France 027.044

The special provision for geographic treatment at 027.01–027.09 is not a standard subdivision. If appropriate, standard subdivisions may be added to the resulting notation, e.g., libraries in France in the late 20th century 027.04409045.

8.11   Standard subdivisions should not be used where redundant, i.e., where the subdivision means the same as the base number, or where application of the standard subdivision would needlessly segregate material by aspects not emphasized by the author. For example, do not add notation 024694, which represents the subject for carpenters, to topics in 694, the number for carpentry, since works on a subject are written primarily for its practitioners. Likewise, do not add the subdivision of notation 0905 for the latest historical period to general works on a subject to represent the state-of-the-art because most users will expect to find such works in the main number. Special care should be taken in adding standard subdivisions to built numbers, since the standard subdivision applies to the whole number and not just to part of the number.

8.12   The table of preference at the beginning of Table 1 yields to two other rules, the rule of application and the rule of zero. By the rule of application, teaching financial management in hospital administration is classed in 362.110681, not 362.11071, even though notation 07 is above notation 068 in the table of preference. The rule of zero overrides the table of preference when standard subdivisions are displaced to notation outside the regular sequence of standard subdivisions (notation at nonzero positions or notation with fewer zeros), e.g., management of prisons in Great Britain 365.941068, not 365.068 as would be the case if prisons in Great Britain were classed in 365.0941. (For a discussion of the rule of application and rule of zero, see paragraph 5.7; for a discussion of displaced standard subdivisions, see paragraphs 7.25 and 8.9.)

(B) Adding from Tables 2–6

8.13   The classifier may be instructed to add notation from Tables 2–6 to a base number from the schedules or to a number from a table. A summary of the use of each table follows. Further instructions on using Tables 2–6 are found at the beginning of each table. See also the Manual notes for Tables 2–6.

8.14   *Table 2 Geographic Areas, Historical Periods, Biography.* The major use of Table 2 is with notation 09 from Table 1, where it can be added to every number in the schedule unless there are specific instructions to the contrary. For example, reading instruction in the primary schools of Australia is 372.40994 (372.4 reading instruction in primary schools + 09 History, geographic treatment, biography from Table 1 + 94 Australia from Table 2). Notation from Table 2 is also added through the use of other standard subdivisions from Table 1 (e.g., standard subdivisions 025, 074).

8.15   Area notation is sometimes added directly to schedule numbers, but only when specified in a note. For example:

      373.3–373.9   Secondary education in specific continents, countries, localities

                Add to base number 373 notation 3–9 from Table 2, e.g., secondary schools of Australia 373.94

8.16   *Table 3 Subdivisions for the Arts, for Individual Literatures, for Specific Literary Forms.* These subdivisions are used in class 800 as instructed, usually following numbers for specific languages in 810–890. Table 3C subdivisions are also added as instructed to numbers in Table 3B, 700.4, 791.4, and 808–809.

8.17   *Table 4 Subdivisions of Individual Languages and Language Families.* These subdivisions are used as instructed in class 400, following numbers for designated specific languages or language families in 420–490.

8.18   *Table 5 Ethnic and National Groups.* Notation from Table 5 is added through the use of standard subdivision 089 from Table 1, e.g., Ceramic arts of Chinese artists throughout the world is 738.089951 (738 Ceramic arts + 089 Ethnic and national groups from Table 1 + 951 Chinese from Table 5).

8.19   Table 5 notation may also be added directly to schedule numbers, but only when specified in a note. For example:

       781.621–.629   Folk music of specific ethnic and national groups

               Add to base number 781.62 notation 1–9 from Table 5, e.g., Spanish folk music 781.6261; then add further ...

8.20   *Table 6 Languages.* The major uses of Table 6 notation are to provide the basis for building a specific language number in 490 (to which notation from Table 4 is sometimes added) and to provide the basis for building a specific literature number in 890 (to which notation from Table 3 is sometimes added). Table 6 notation is also used in Table 2 under —175 Regions where specific languages predominate, and at various points in the schedules.

(C) Adding from Other Parts of the Schedules

8.19   There are many instructions to make a direct addition to a number from another part of the schedules. For example:

       809.935   Literature emphasizing subjects

               Add to base number 809.935 notation 001–999, e.g., religious works as literature 809.9352, biography and autobiography as literature 809.93592

In this example, the 2 in 809.9352 comes from 200 Religion, the 92 in 809.93592 from 920 Biography, genealogy, insignia.

8.20   In many cases, part of a number may be added to another number upon instruction. For example:

       372.011   Primary education for specific objectives

               Add to base number 372.011 the numbers following 370.11 in 370.111–370.119, e.g., character education 372.0114

In this example, 4 comes from 370.114 Moral, ethical, character education. Sometimes numbers are taken from more than one place in the schedules; in such cases the procedure for the second addition is the same as for the first.

(D) Adding from Tables Found in the Schedules

8.21   Add tables in the schedules provide numbers to be added to designated schedule numbers (identified by a symbol and accompanying footnoted instruction); these tables must be used only as instructed. For example:

616.973   *Contact allergies

Class here allergic contact dermatitis, allergies of skin

The asterisk in the entry above leads to the following footnote: "Add as instructed under 616.1–616.9." The add table at 616.1–616.9 is used only for diseases tagged with an asterisk or for diseases in class-here notes under headings tagged with an asterisk. Notation from the add table, such as 061 Drug therapy, may be used for 616.973 Contact allergies (tagged with an asterisk) and for allergic contact dermatitis and allergies of skin (in the class-here note).

8.22   *Subdivisions-are-added notes* indicate which terms in a multiterm heading may have subdivisions applied to them. For example:

616.51   *Dermatitis, photosensitivity disorders, urticaria

Subdivisions are added for dermatitis, photosensitivity disorders, urticaria together; for dermatitis alone

Citation and Preference Order

9.1   Citation and preference order must be considered when multiple aspects or characteristics of a subject (such as age, area, gender, historical periods, national origin) are provided for in the Classification, and a single work treats more than one of them.

CITATION ORDER

9.2   Citation order allows the classifier to build or synthesize a number using two or more characteristics (*facets*) as specified in instruction notes. Success in building a DDC number requires determining which characteristics apply to a specific work, and then determining from the instructions in the schedule the sequence in which the facets will be ordered.

9.3   Citation order is always carefully detailed in number-building instructions. For example:

909.04   [History with respect to] Specific ethnic and national groups

Add to base number 909.04 notation 1–9 from Table 5, e.g., world history of Jews 909.04924; then add 0* and to the result add the numbers following 909 in 909.1–909.8, e.g., world history of Jews in 18th century 909.0492407

For a work on the world history of the Jews in the 18th century, this note stipulates the following citation order for the individual facets of the full subject: world history + specific ethnic or national group + historical period. The historical period is introduced by the *facet indicator* 0.

PREFERENCE ORDER

9.4   If there is no provision to show more than one of the aspects or characteristics, it is a matter of preference (because a choice must be made among several characteristics). Preference notes supply either an instruction or table establishing the order in which to make the choice. An example of a preference instruction is found at 305.9:

> 305.9   People by occupation and miscellaneous social statuses; people with disabilities and illnesses, gifted people
>
> > Unless other instructions are given, class a subject with aspects in two or more subdivisions of 305.9 in the number coming last, e.g., unemployed librarians 305.9092 (*not* 305.90694)

In this case, the base subject is a group of persons; the two characteristics are employment status and occupational status. The occupation of librarian (305.9092) falls after unemployed status (305.90694) in the DDC hierarchy; following the instructions in the preference note, the characteristic that must be chosen is librarian (305.9092). (For an example of a preference instruction using a class-elsewhere note, see paragraph 7.20.)

9.5   An example of a table indicating preference order is found at 305:

> 305   Groups of people
>
> > Unless other instructions are given, observe the following table of preference, e.g., African American male youths 305.235108996073 (*not* 305.3889607300835 or 305.896073008351):

People with disabilities and illnesses, gifted people	305.908
Age groups	305.2
People by gender or sex	305.3–.4
People by social and economic levels	305.5
Religious groups	305.6
Ethnic and national groups	305.8
Language groups	305.7
People by occupation and miscellaneous social statuses	305.9
(*except* 305.908)	

9.6   Classifiers often must distinguish between preference order instructions and the first-of two rule in the same schedule. If the work treats two subjects, apply the first-of-two rule. If the work treats two aspects of the same subject, apply the preference order instructions. When the preference order instruction is to class with the last, the first-of-two rule and the preference order instructions may lead the classifier in opposite directions. For example, a bibliography of newspapers and pamphlets giving equal treatment to each would be classed according to the first-of-two rule in 011.33 (bibliography of pamphlets) rather than 011.35 (bibliographies of newspapers). A bibliography of microform newspapers (i.e., newspapers in microform form) would be classed according to the preference note at 011.1–011.8: "Unless other instructions are given, class a subject with aspects in two or more subdivisions of 011.1–011.8 in the number coming last …"; thus, the bibliography of microform newspapers would be classed in 011.36 (bibliographies of microforms) rather than 011.35 (bibliographies of newspapers). (For a discussion of the first-of-two rule, see paragraph 5.7.)

The Manual

10.1   The Manual gives advice on classifying in difficult areas, and provides guidance on choosing between related numbers.

10.2   *See-Manual references* in the schedules and tables refer the classifier to the Manual for additional information about a certain number, range of numbers, or choice among numbers. In some cases, the see-Manual reference refers only to a portion of a longer Manual note, or topic narrower than the numbers in the heading, e.g., "See Manual at 930–990: Historic preservation." The see-Manual reference is repeated in the entries for each of the numbers or number spans covered in the Manual note. For example, "See Manual at 004.21 vs. 004.22, 621.392" is listed in the entries for 004.21, 004.22, and 621.392.

10.3   Brief Manual-like notes are sometimes given directly in the schedule or table entry. For example:

631.583   Controlled-environment agriculture

Most works on use of artificial light in agriculture will be classed in 635.0483 and 635.9826

ARRANGEMENT AND FORMAT OF THE MANUAL

10.4   The Manual is arranged by table and schedule numbers, with the broadest span coming before entries for narrower spans or individual numbers. Manual notes are entered under the preferred or "if-in-doubt" number. If there is no if-in-doubt number, prefer the interdisciplinary number.

10.5   The Manual note heading summarizes the contents of the note. The terms in the Manual note headings need not match the terms associated with the same number(s) in the tables and schedules if the note is narrower than the number, or the note refers to more than one number. For example:

510

Mathematics

510, T1—0151 vs. 003, T1—011

Systems

10.6   If the Manual note is very long, or part of the note focuses on a topic narrower than the heading, subheadings may be provided. For example:

T1—068 vs. 353–354

Public administration and management in specific fields

Exceptions   *(subheading)*

The Relative Index

11.1   The Relative Index is so named because it relates subjects to disciplines. In the schedules, subjects are distributed among disciplines; in the Relative Index, subjects are arranged alphabetically, with terms identifying the disciplines in which they are treated subarranged alphabetically under them. For example:

Hospitals	362.11
accounting	657.832 2
American Revolution	973.376
animal husbandry	636.083 21
architecture	725.51
armed forces	355.72
Civil War (United States)	973.776
construction	690.551
energy economics	333.796 4
institutional housekeeping	647.965 1
landscape architecture	712.7
law	344.032 11
liability law	346.031
meal service	642.56
pastoral theology	206.1
Christianity	259.411
social theology	206.762 11
Christianity	261.832 11
social welfare	362.11
World War I	940.476
World War II	940.547 6
see also Health services	

In some cases the term implies rather than states the discipline. In the example above, the discipline of architecture is listed, but the discipline of military science is implied by "armed forces."

11.2   The Relative Index is primarily an index to the DDC as a system. It includes most terms found in the schedules and tables, and terms with literary warrant for concepts represented by the schedules and tables. The Relative Index is not exhaustive. If the term sought is not found, the classifier should try a broader term, or consult the schedules and tables directly. The schedules and tables should always be consulted before a number found in the Relative Index is applied.

ARRANGEMENT AND FORMAT OF THE RELATIVE INDEX

11.3   Index entries are arranged alphabetically word by word, e.g., Birth order precedes Birthday. Entries with the same word or phrase but with different marks of punctuation are arranged in the following order:

Term
Term. Subheading
Term (Parenthetical qualifier)
Term, inverted term qualifier
Term as part of phrase

Initialisms and acronyms are entered without punctuation and are filed as if spelled as one word. Hyphens are ignored and treated as a space. Terms indented below the main headings are alphabetized in one group even though they may be a mixture of disciplines, topical subheadings, and, to a limited extent, words that form phrases or inverted phrases when combined with the main heading.

11.4   Class numbers are listed in groups of three digits for ease of reading and copying. The spaces are not part of the numbers and do not represent convenient places to abridge the number.

11.5   See-also references are used for synonyms and for references to broader terms (but only when three or more new numbers will be found at the synonym or broader term), and for references to related terms (which may provide only one or two new numbers).

11.6   See-Manual references lead the classifier to relevant discussions in the Manual.

11.7   Numbers drawn from Tables 1–6 are prefixed by T1 through T6. (For a complete listing of table names and abbreviations, see paragraph 7.4.)

INTERDISCIPLINARY NUMBERS

11.8   The first class number displayed in an index entry (the unindented term) is the number for interdisciplinary works. If the term also appears in a table, the table number is listed next, followed by other aspects of the term. The discipline of the interdisciplinary number may be repeated as a subentry if the discipline is not clear. For example:

Adult education	374
	T1—071 5
federal aid	379.121 5
law	344.074
public administrative support	353.84
public support	379.114
law	344.076 85
special education	371.904 75
university extension	378.175

11.9   Interdisciplinary numbers are not provided for all topics in the Relative Index. They are omitted when the index entry is ambiguous, does not have a disciplinary focus, or lacks literary warrant. In such cases, there is no number opposite the unindented entry. For example:

Coagulation	
blood	573.159
human physiology	612.115
physiology	573.159
see also Cardiovascular system	
water supply treatment	628.162 2

(For more information on interdisciplinary numbers, see paragraphs 5.8, 7.16, 7.19–7.20.)

TERMS INCLUDED IN THE RELATIVE INDEX

11.10 The Relative Index contains most terms found in the headings and notes of the schedules and tables, and synonyms and terms with literary warrant for concepts represented by the schedules and tables. The Relative Index also contains terms for the broad concepts covered in Manual notes.

Inverted phrases are avoided, except for personal and geographic names (see paragraphs 11.12–11.13). Qualifiers are used for homonyms, ambiguous terms, and most initialisms and abbreviations. The most common use of the term may not be qualified. Disciplinary qualifiers are avoided.

11.11 The following types of names from Table 2 Geographic Areas are included in the Relative Index: (A) names of countries; (B) names of the states and provinces of most countries; (C) names of the counties of the United States; (D) names of capital cities and other important municipalities; and (E) names of certain important geographic features.

11.12 Also included in the Relative Index are the personal names of the following groups of persons: heads of state used to identify historical periods, e.g., Louis XIV; founders or revealers of religions, e.g., Muhammad; initiators of schools of thought when used to identify the school, e.g., Smith, Adam.

11.13 Place names and other proper names are generally given in the form specified by the second edition, 2002 revision, 2005 update, of the *Anglo-American Cataloguing Rules* (*AACR2*), based on the names established in the Library of Congress authority files. If the *AACR2* form is not the common English name, an entry is also included under the familiar form of the name.

Plants and animals are indexed under their scientific and common names.

11.14 The choice of singular form versus plural form follows ISO 999:1996, *Guidelines for the content, organization and presentation of indexes.* Count nouns are generally in the plural; noncount nouns and abstract concepts are generally in the singular. Parts of the body are in the plural only when more than one occurs in a fully formed organism (e.g., ears, hands, nose). Plants and animals follow scientific convention in the choice of singular form versus plural form, with the decision based on whether the taxonomic class has more than one member (e.g., Horses, Lion, Lipizzaner horse). Where usage varies across disciplines, the index entry reflects the form preferred in the discipline where interdisciplinary works are classified.

11.15   Terms usually not included in the Relative Index are:

(A)   Phrases beginning with the adjectival form of countries, languages, nationalities, religions, e.g., English poetry, French cooking, Italian architecture, Hindu prayer books.

(B)   Phrases that contain general concepts represented by standard subdivisions such as education, statistics, laboratories, and management; e.g., Art education, Educational statistics, Medical laboratories, Bank management.

When there is strong literary warrant for such a phrase heading as a sought term, it may be included in the Relative Index, e.g., English literature. When the phrase heading is a proper name or provides the only form of access to the topic, it may also be included, e.g., English Channel, French horns, Amharic literature.

Options

12.1   Some devices are required to enable the DDC to serve needs beyond those represented in the standard English-language edition. At a number of places in the schedules and tables, *options* are provided to give emphasis to an aspect in a library's collection not given preferred treatment in the standard notation. In some cases, options are also suggested to provide shorter notation for the aspect.

12.2   Options are provided throughout the Classification to emphasize jurisdiction, ethnic or national group, language, topic, or other characteristic.

12.3   Options described in notes appear in parentheses and begin with "Option:". Options that apply to the full entry appear at the end of the entry; options to a specific instruction in the entry are indented under the appropriate note. For example, the following option appears at the end of the entry for 420–490:

(Option B: To give local emphasis and a shorter number to a specific language, place it first by use of a letter or other symbol, e.g., Arabic language 4A0 [preceding 420], for which the base number is 4A. Option A is described under 410)

12.4   Some *optional numbers* are enumerated in the schedules and tables and appear in parentheses in the number column. A special optional arrangement (222)–(224) for books of the Bible as arranged in Tanakh appears as a subsection of the Manual note for 221.

12.5   *Arrange-alphabetically* and *arrange-chronologically notes* are not placed in parentheses, but are also options. They represent suggestions only; the material need not be arranged alphabetically or chronologically. An example of an arrange-alphabetically note is found at 005.133 Specific programming languages: "Arrange alphabetically by name of programming language, e.g., C++."

12.6   Some national libraries and central cataloging authorities assign a few optional numbers, e.g., Library and Archives Canada uses C810 for Canadian literature in English and C840 for Canadian literature in French.

12.7   Most of the time, the responsibility for implementing an option rests with the local library. Libraries should weigh the value of using an option against the loss in interoperability of numbers. The library will not be able to use numbers assigned by other libraries, and other libraries will not be able to use the optional numbers assigned by the library. In addition, unless the option is widely used in a region, users may be confused by the alternate notation.

Close and Broad Classification

13.1   The Dewey Decimal Classification provides the basic option of close versus broad classification. *Close classification* means that the content of a work is specified by notation to the fullest extent possible. *Broad classification* means that the work is placed in a broad class by use of notation that has been logically abridged. For example, a work on French cooking is classed closely at 641.5944 (641.59 Cooking by place + 44 France from Table 2), or broadly at 641.5 (Cooking).

13.2   A library should base its decision on close versus broad classification on the size of its collection and the needs of its users. For example, a work on the sociology of sibling relationships in Canadian society would be most usefully classed in 306.8750971 (306.875 Sibling relationships + 09 Geographic treatment from Table 1 + 71 Canada from Table 2) in a research library or large public library. A small school library might prefer to class the same work in the broader number (306.875) without including the geographic facet in the notation. An engineering library might prefer close classification for works in engineering, but broad classification for disciplines outside science and technology.

13.3   The classifier should never reduce the notation to less than the most specific three-digit number (no matter how small the library's collection). A number also must never be reduced so that it ends in a 0 anywhere to the right of the decimal point.

13.4   One aid to logical abridgment of DDC numbers is the segmentation device provided by the Decimal Classification Division of the Library of Congress and some other centralized cataloging services.

13.5   The abridged edition of the Dewey Decimal Classification is another source for broad classification.

More Information

14.1   Classifiers desiring a more in-depth introduction to the Dewey Decimal Classification may consult *Dewey Decimal Classification: Principles and Application*, 3rd ed., by Lois Mai Chan and Joan S. Mitchell (Dublin, Ohio: OCLC, 2003).

14.2   More information about the use and application of the DDC, plus training materials, can be found on the Dewey web site (http://www.oclc.org/dewey/) and on *025.431: The Dewey blog* (http://ddc.typepad.com/).

Glossary

The Glossary defines terms used in the Introduction and throughout the schedules, tables, and Manual. Fuller explanations and examples for many terms may be found in the relevant sections of the Introduction. An index to the Introduction and Glossary follows the Glossary.

Abridged edition: A shortened version of the Dewey Decimal Classification (DDC) system that is a logical truncation of the notational and structural hierarchy of the corresponding full edition on which it is based. The abridged edition is intended for general collections of 20,000 titles or less. *See also* **Broad classification; Full edition.**

Add note: A note instructing the classifier to append digits found elsewhere in the DDC to a given base number. *See also* **Base number.**

Add table: *See* **Tables (2).**

Application: *See* **Rule of application.**

Approximate the whole: When a topic is nearly coextensive with the full meaning of a DDC class, the topic is said to "approximate the whole" of the class. The term is also used to characterize topics that cover more than half the content of a class. When a topic approximates the whole of a class, standard subdivisions may be added. Topics that do not approximate the whole are said to be in "standing room" in the number. *See also* **Class-here note; Standard-subdivisions-are-added note; Standing room.**

Area table: An auxiliary table (Table 2) that gives geographic areas primarily, but also lists historical periods and several numbers for persons associated with a subject. Areas of the world are listed systematically, not alphabetically. Area table notation may be used with other numbers in the schedules and tables when explicit instructions permitting such use are given. *See also* **Tables.**

Arrange-alphabetically note: A note suggesting the option of alphabetical subarrangement when identification by specific name or other identifying characteristic is desired. *See also* **Option**.

Arrange-chronologically note: A note suggesting the option of chronological subarrangement when identification by date is desired. *See also* **Option.**

Artificial digit: A letter or other symbol used optionally as a substitute for digits 0–9 to provide a more prominent location or shorter notation for a jurisdiction, language, literature, religion, ethnic or national group, or other characteristic. *See also* **Option.**

Aspect: An approach to a subject, or characteristic (facet) of a subject. *See also* **Discipline; Facet; Subject.**

Attraction: *See* **Classification by attraction.**

Author number: *See* **Book number.**

Base number: A number of any length to which other numbers are appended. *See also* **Add note.**

Book number: The part of a call number that distinguishes a specific item from other items within the same class number. A library using the Cutter-Sanborn system can have D548d indicate David Copperfield by Dickens (where D stands for the D of Dickens, 548 stands for "ickens," and d stands for David Copperfield). *See also* **Call number; Cutter number; Work mark.**

Broad classification: The classification of works in broad categories by logical abridgment, even when more specific numbers are available, e.g., the use of 641.5 Cooking instead of 641.5972 Mexican cooking for a cookbook of Mexican recipes. Broad classification is the opposite of close classification. *See also* **Abridged edition; Close classification.**

Built number: A number constructed according to add instructions stated or implied in the schedules or tables. *See also* **Number building.**

Call number: A set of letters, numerals, or other symbols (in combination or alone) used by a library to identify a specific copy of a work. A call number may consist of the class number; book number; and other data such as date, volume number, copy number, and location symbol. *See also* **Book number; Class number.**

Caption: *See* **Heading.**

Category: *See* **Class** *(Noun).*

Centered entry: An entry representing a subject covered by a span of numbers, e.g., 372–374 Specific levels of education. The entry is called "centered" because the span of numbers appears in the center of the page in the print version of the DDC rather than in the number column on the left side of the page. Centered entries are identified by the symbol > in the number column.

Characteristic of division: *See* **Facet.**

Citation order: The order in which two or more characteristics (facets) of a class are to be combined in number building. When number building is not permitted or possible, instructions on preference order with respect to the choice of facets are provided. *See also* **Facet; Number building; Preference order.**

Class: (Noun) A category in the DDC formed on the basis of one or more characteristics and represented by a number. Classes explicitly provided in the tables and schedules are accompanied by a description consisting of a heading and often one or more notes. *See also* **Division; Entry (1); Main class; Section; Subdivision.** (Verb) To assign a class number to an individual work. *See also* **Classify.**

Class-elsewhere note: A note instructing the classifier about the location of interrelated topics. The note may show preference order, lead to the interdisciplinary or comprehensive number, override the first-of-two rule, or lead to broader or narrower numbers in the same hierarchical array that might otherwise be overlooked. *See also* **Comprehensive number; Interdisciplinary number; Preference order.**

Class-here note: A note that identifies topics that are equivalent to the whole of the class under which the note appears. The topic as a whole is classed in the number under which the note appears; parts of the topic are classed in the most appropriate subdivision of the number. Topics identified in class-here notes, even if broader or narrower than the heading, are said to "approximate the whole" of the number; therefore, standard subdivisions may be added for topics in class-here notes. Class-here notes also may identify the comprehensive or interdisciplinary number for a subject. *See also* **Approximate the whole; Comprehensive number; Interdisciplinary number.**

Class number: Notation used to represent a class in the DDC. *See also* **Call number; Notation.**

Classification: A logical system for the arrangement of knowledge.

Classified catalog: A catalog arranged according to the notational order of a classification system.

Classify: (1) To arrange a collection of items according to a classification system. (2) To assign a class number to an individual work.

Close classification: The classification of works to the fullest extent permitted by the notation. Close classification is the opposite of broad classification. *See also* **Broad classification; Full edition.**

Coextensive: Describes a topic equal in scope to the concept represented by the number.

Comparative table: A table provided for a complete or extensive revision that lists in alphabetical order selected topics accompanied by their number in the previous edition and their number in the current edition. *See also* **Equivalence table; Revision.**

Complete revision: *See* **Revision** *(Complete revision).*

Complex subject: A complex subject is a subject that has more than one characteristic. For example, "unemployed carpenters" is a complex subject because it has more than one characteristic (employment status and occupation). *See also* **Preference order.**

Comprehensive number: A number (often identified by a "Class here comprehensive works" note) that covers all the components of the subject treated within that discipline. The components may be in a span of consecutive numbers or distributed throughout the schedule or table. *See also* **Interdisciplinary number.**

Concept: An idea represented in full or part by a class.

Coordinate: Describes a number or topic at a level equal to another number or topic in the same hierarchy.

Cross classification: The accidental placement of works on the same subject in two different class numbers. This tends to happen when works being classified deal with two or more characteristics of a subject in the same class. Notes on preference order should prevent cross classification. *See also* **Preference order.**

Cross reference: *See* **Class-elsewhere note; See-also reference; See reference**.

Cutter number: The notation in a book number derived from the Cutter Three-Figure Author Table, the Cutter-Sanborn Three-Figure Author Table, or the OCLC Four-Figure Cutter Tables. The OCLC Four-Figure Cutter Tables are revised and expanded versions of the Cutter Three-Figure Author Table and the Cutter-Sanborn Three-Figure Author Table. *See also* **Book number.**

DDC: Dewey Decimal Classification.

DDC Summaries: A listing of the first three levels (main classes, divisions, and sections) of the Dewey Decimal Classification system. The headings associated with the numbers in the summaries have been edited for browsing purposes, and may not match the complete headings found in the schedules. *See also* **Division; Main class; Section; Summary.**

Decimal point: The dot that follows the third digit in a DDC number. In strict usage the word "decimal" is not accurate; however, common usage is followed in this edition's explanatory material.

Definition note: A note indicating the meaning of a term in the heading.

Digit: The smallest individual unit in a notational system. For example, the notation 954 has three digits: 9, 5, and 4.

Discipline: An organized field of study or branch of knowledge, e.g., 200 Religion, 530 Physics, 364 Criminology. In the DDC, subjects are arranged by disciplines. *See also* **Subject.**

Discontinuation: The shifting of a topic or the entire contents of a number to a more general number in the same hierarchy, or the complete removal of the topic or number. A topic or number is discontinued because the topic or concept represented by the number has a negligible current literature or represents a distinction that is no longer valid in the literature or common perception of the field. A note explaining its shift or removal accompanies a discontinued topic or number. Discontinued numbers appear in square brackets. *See also* **Relocation; Schedule reduction.**

Displaced standard subdivision: A standard subdivision concept moved to a special provision in the schedule in place of its regular notation from Table 1. A do-not-use note is always provided at the regular location of the standard subdivision concept. *See also* **Do-not-use note; Standard subdivisions.**

Division: The second level of subdivision in the DDC, represented by the first two digits in the notation, e.g., 64 in 640 Home and family management. *See also* **DDC Summaries; Main class; Section.**

Do-not-use note: A note instructing the classifier not to use all or part of a regular standard subdivision notation, but instead to use a special provision or standard subdivision notation at a broader number. Also used to instruct the classifier not to use all or part of an add table provision, but instead to use a special provision. *See also* **Displaced standard subdivision.**

Document: A generic term for all media capable of conveying, coding, and preserving knowledge. Documents may be books, journals, electronic resources, reports, sound recordings, motion pictures, etc.

Dual provision: The inadvertent provision of more than one place in the DDC for the same aspect of a subject.

Entry: (1) In the schedules and tables, a self-contained unit consisting of a number or span of numbers, a heading, and often one or more notes. (2) In the Relative Index, a term or phrase usually followed by a DDC number. (3) In the Manual, a self-contained unit consisting of a number or group of numbers, the associated headings or topics, and an extended instruction or discussion.

Enumerative scheme: A classification system in which numbers for complex subjects are precombined and listed.

Equivalence table: A table provided for a complete or extensive revision that lists in numerical order the classes of the current edition with their equivalent numbers in the previous edition (and vice versa). *See also* **Revision.**

Expansion: The development of a class in the schedules or tables to provide further subdivisions. *See also* **Revision.**

Extensive revision: *See* **Revision** *(Extensive revision).*

Facet: Any of the various categories into which a given class may be divided, e.g., division of the class "people" into the categories of ethnicity, age, education, and language spoken. Each category contains terms based on a single characteristic of division, e.g., children, adolescents, and adults are characteristics of division of the "ages" category. *See also* **Citation order.**

Facet indicator: A digit used to introduce notation representing a characteristic of the subject. For example, "0" is often used as a facet indicator to introduce standard subdivision concepts.

First-of-two rule: The rule instructing that works dealing equally with two subjects that are not used to introduce or explain one another are classed in the number coming first in the schedules or tables.

Footnote: An instruction that applies to many subdivisions of a class, or to a topic within a class. The affected subdivision or topic is marked with a symbol such as an asterisk. In the print version of the DDC, the footnote is located at the bottom of the page. In the electronic version, the footnote is included in the notes section of each class to which the instruction applies.

Former-heading note: A note listing the heading associated with the class number in the previous edition. The note is used when the heading has changed so much that it bears little or no resemblance to the previous heading, even though the meaning of the number has remained substantially the same.

Full edition: The complete version of the Dewey Decimal Classification (DDC) system. *See also* **Abridged edition; Close classification.**

Heading: The word or phrase used as the description of a given class. Also called "caption."

Hierarchical force: The principle that the attributes of a class as defined in the heading and in certain basic notes apply to all the subdivisions of the class, and to all other classes to which reference is made.

Hierarchy: The arrangement of a classification system from general to specific. In the DDC, the length of the notation and the corresponding depth of indention of the heading usually indicate the degree of specificity of a class. See references and centered entries are used to indicate exceptions to the notational hierarchy. *See also* **Centered entry; See reference.**

Hook number: A number in the DDC without meaning in itself, but used to introduce examples of the topic. Hook numbers have headings that begin with "Miscellaneous," "Specific," or "Other"; and do not contain add notes, including notes, or class-here notes. Standard subdivisions are always bracketed under hook numbers.

Including note: A note enumerating topics that are logically part of the class but are less extensive in scope than the concept represented by the class number. These topics do not have enough literature to warrant their own number. Standard subdivisions may not be added to the numbers for these topics. *See also* **Literary warrant**; **Standing room.**

Indention: Typographical setting of notes and subheadings below and to the right of the main entry term.

Influence: *See* **Rule of application.**

Interdisciplinary number: A number (often identified by a "Class here interdisciplinary works" note) to be used for works covering a subject from the perspective of more than one discipline, including the discipline where the interdisciplinary number is located, e.g., the interdisciplinary number for marriage is 306.81 in Sociology. *See also* **Comprehensive number.**

Literary form: A mode of literary expression such as poetry, drama, fiction, etc. Each form can be subdivided into kinds of forms, e.g., lyric poetry, comedy, science fiction, etc.

Literary warrant: Justification for the development of a class or the explicit inclusion of a topic in the schedules, tables, or Relative Index, based on the existence of a body of literature on the topic.

Main class: One of the ten major subdivisions of the DDC, represented by the first digit in the notation, e.g., 3 in 300 Social sciences. *See also* **DDC Summaries; Division; Section.**

Manual: A guide to the use of the DDC that is made up primarily of extended discussions of problem areas in the application of the DDC. In the schedules and tables, see-Manual references indicate where relevant discussions are located in the Manual. *See also* **Manual note.**

Manual note: An individual entry in the Manual. *See also* **Entry (3); Manual; See-Manual reference.**

Notation: Numerals, letters, and/or symbols used to represent the main and subordinate divisions of a classification scheme. In the DDC, Arabic numerals are used to represent the classes, e.g., notation 07 from Table 1 and 511.3 from the schedules. *See also* **Class number.**

Notational synthesis: *See* **Number building.**

Note: An instruction, definition, or reference that explains the contents and use of a class, or the relationship of the class to other classes. *See also* **Add note**; **Arrange-alphabetically note; Arrange-chronologically note; Class-elsewhere note; Class-here note; Definition note; Discontinuation; Do-not-use note; Footnote; Former-heading note; Including note; Manual note; Number-built note; Preference order; Relocation; Revision note; Scope note; See-also reference; See-Manual reference; See reference; Standard-subdivisions-are-added note; Subdivisions-are-added note; Variant-name note.**

Number building: The process of constructing a number by adding notation from the tables or other parts of the schedules to a base number. Also called "notational synthesis." *See also* **Base number; Citation order.**

Number-building note: *See* **Add note.**

Number-built note: A note that states where the number building instructions may be found for a built number that is explicitly listed in the schedules or tables. Typically, such built numbers are listed for two reasons: to provide an entry for a built number under which other notes are required; or to provide an entry for a three-digit built number.

Number column: In the print version of the DDC, the column of numbers that appears in the left margin of the schedules and tables, and to the right of the alphabetical entries in the Relative Index.

Option: An alternative to standard notation provided in the schedules and tables to give emphasis to an aspect in a library's collection not given preferred treatment in the standard notation. In some cases, an option may provide shorter notation for the aspect. *See also* **Optional number.**

Optional number: (1) A number listed in parentheses in the schedules or tables that is an alternative to the standard notation. (2) A number constructed by following an option. *See also* **Option.**

Order of preference: *See* **Preference order.**

Period table: A table giving chronological time periods with their notation. For many literatures, period tables are given in the schedules. For works not limited to a particular language, the period notation is taken from Table 1 —0901–0905. *See also* **Tables.**

Phoenix schedule: *See* **Revision** *(Complete revision).*

Preference order: The order indicating which one of two or more numbers is to be chosen when different characteristics of a subject cannot be shown in full by number building. A note (sometimes containing a table of preference) indicates which characteristic is to be selected for works covering more than one characteristic. When a notation can be synthesized to show two or more characteristics, it is a matter of citation order. *See also* **Citation order.**

Preference table: *See* **Preference order.**

Prime marks: *See* **Segmentation.**

Reduction of schedules: *See* **Schedule reduction.**

Regularization: The replacement of special developments for standard subdivision concepts by use of the regular standard subdivisions found in Table 1.

Relative Index: The index to the DDC. It is called "Relative" because it shows the connection between subjects and the disciplines in which they appear. In the schedules, subjects are arranged within disciplines. In the Relative Index, subjects are listed alphabetically. Under each subject, the disciplines in which the subject is found are listed alphabetically. In the print version of the DDC, the disciplines are indented under the subject. In the electronic version, the disciplines appear as subheadings associated with the subject.

Relocation: The shifting of a topic from one number to another number that differs from the old number in respects other than length. Notes at both ends of the relocation identify the new and former numbers. *See also* **Discontinuation.**

Retroactive citation order: In number building, the combination of characteristics (facets) of a class starting with a number coming later in the schedule as the base number, then adding as instructed from numbers earlier in the sequence.

Reused number: A number with a total change in meaning from one edition to another. Usually numbers are reused only in complete revisions or when the reused number has been vacant for two consecutive editions.

Revision: The result of editorial work that alters the text of any class of the DDC. There are three degrees of revision: *Routine revision* is limited to updating terminology, clarifying notes, and providing modest expansions. *Extensive revision* involves a major reworking of subdivisions but leaves the main outline of the schedule intact. *Complete revision* (formerly called a phoenix) is a new development; the base number remains unchanged from the previous edition, but virtually all subdivisions are changed. Changes for complete and extensive revisions are shown through comparative and equivalence tables rather than through relocation notes in the schedule or table affected. *See also* **Comparative table; Equivalence table.**

Revision note: A note that introduces a complete or extensive revision.

Routine revision: *See* **Revision** *(Routine revision).*

Rule of application: The rule instructing that works about the application of one subject to a second subject or the influence of one subject on another subject are classified with the second subject.

Rule of three: The rule instructing that works giving equal treatment to three or more subjects that are all subdivisions of a broader subject are classified in the first higher number that includes all of them.

Rule of zero: The rule instructing that subdivisions beginning with zero should be avoided if there is a choice between the 0 subdivision and subdivisions beginning with 1–9 in the same position in the notation. Similarly, subdivisions beginning with 00 should be avoided when there is a choice between 00 and 0.

Scatter note: A class-elsewhere, see-reference, or relocation note that leads to multiple locations in the DDC. *See also* **Class-elsewhere note; Relocation; See reference.**

Schedule reduction: The elimination of certain provisions of a previous edition, often resulting in discontinued numbers. *See also* **Discontinuation.**

Schedules: (1) Listings of subjects and their subdivisions arranged in a systematic order with notation given for each subject and its subdivisions. (2) The series of DDC numbers 000–999, their headings, and notes.

Scope note: A note indicating that the meaning of a class number is broader or narrower than is apparent from the heading.

Section: The third level of subdivision in the DDC, represented by the first three digits in the notation, e.g., 641 in 641 Food and drink. *See also* **DDC Summaries; Division; Main class.**

See-also reference: (1) In the schedules and tables, a note leading to classes that are tangentially related to the topic and therefore might be confused with it. (2) In the Relative

Index, a note leading to a synonym, broader term, or related term. (3) In the Manual, a note leading to related Manual notes.

See-Manual reference: A note leading from an entry in the schedules or tables to additional information about the number in the Manual.

See reference: A note (introduced by the word "for") that leads from the stated or implied comprehensive or interdisciplinary number for a subject to component parts of the subject in numbers other than direct subdivisions of the original number or span. *See also* **Class-elsewhere note.**

Segmentation: The indication of logical breaks in a number by a typographical device, e.g., slash marks or prime marks. Segmentation marks indicate the end of an abridged number.

Shelf mark: *See* **Call number.**

Standard subdivisions: Subdivisions found in Table 1 that represent frequently recurring physical forms (dictionaries, periodicals) or approaches (history, research) applicable to any subject or discipline. They may be used with any number in the schedules and tables for topics that approximate the whole of the number unless there are instructions to the contrary. *See also* **Tables.**

Standard-subdivisions-are-added note: A note indicating which topics in a multiterm heading may have standard subdivisions added to them. The designated topics are considered to approximate the whole of the number. *See also* **Approximate the whole.**

Standing room: A term characterizing a topic without sufficient literature to have its own number, and considerably narrower in scope than the class number in which it is included. Standard subdivisions cannot be added to a topic in standing room, nor are other number-building techniques allowed. Topics listed in including notes have standing room in the class number, as do minor unnamed topics that logically fall in the same place in the DDC. To have standing room is the opposite of approximating the whole. *See also* **Approximate the whole.**

Subdivision: (1) A subordinate member of a class, e.g., 518 Numerical analysis is a subdivision of class 510 Mathematics, and 518.5 Numerical approximation is a subdivision of 518. *See also* **Class** *(Noun).* (2) Notation that may be added to other numbers to make a class number appropriately specific to the work being classified. *See also* **Standard Subdivisions; Tables.**

Subdivisions-are-added note: A note used where subdivisions are provided by add instructions indicating which topics in a multiterm heading may have subdivisions added to them. The designated topics are considered to approximate the whole of the number. *See also* **Approximate the whole.**

Subject: An object of study. Also called topic. It may be a person or a group of persons, thing, place, process, activity, abstraction, or any combination of these. In the DDC, subjects are arranged by disciplines. A subject is often studied in more than one discipline, e.g., marriage is studied in several disciplines such as ethics, religion, sociology, and law. *See also* **Discipline.**

Subject catalog: An index to the contents of a collection. If access is provided alphabetically by words, it is called an alphabetical subject catalog. If access is provided by the notation of a classification system, it is called a classified catalog. *See also* **Classified catalog.**

Subordinate: Describes a number or topic at a lower (narrower) level than another number or topic in the same hierarchy. *See also* **Superordinate.**

Summary: A listing of the chief subdivisions of a class that provides an overview of its structure. *See also* **DDC Summaries**.

Superordinate: Describes a number or topic at a higher (broader) level than another number or topic in the same hierarchy. *See also* **Subordinate.**

Synthesis of notation: *See* **Number building.**

Table of preference: *See* **Preference order.**

Tables: In the DDC, lists of notation that may be added to other numbers to make a class number appropriately specific to the work being classified. The numbers found in a table are never used alone. There are two kinds of tables: (1) The six numbered auxiliary tables (Tables 1–6) representing standard subdivisions, geographic areas, languages, ethnic groups, etc. (2) Lists of special notation found in add notes under specific numbers throughout the schedules and occasionally in Tables 1–6. These lists are called add tables. *See also* **Add note.**

Terminal zero: The one or two zeros appended to the notation for a division or main class to form a three-digit number. A single zero is added to the two-digit notation for a division to form a three-digit number, e.g., 51 + 0 = 510 Mathematics. Two zeros are added to the single-digit notation for a main class to form a three-digit number, e.g., 5 + 00 = 500 Science. *See also* **Division; Main class.**

Topic: *See* **Subject.**

Unabridged edition: *See* **Full edition.**

Variant-name note: A note listing synonyms or near synonyms for a topic in a heading when it is awkward or inappropriate to include such information in the heading.

Word-by-word alphabetization: Refers to the filing of entries word by word, not letter by letter. For example, New York files before Newark in word-by-word alphabetization; Newark files before New York in letter-by-letter alphabetization.

Work: A distinct intellectual or artistic creation.

Work mark: The part of a book number that consists of a letter appended to the author (or biographee) designation to show the first letter of the title (or first letter of the surname of the biographer). *See also* **Book number.**

Index to the Introduction and Glossary

References to the Introduction are identified by paragraph numbers. References to the alphabetically arranged Glossary are identified by G.

Manual

Notes on Table Numbers

Table 1. Standard Subdivisions T1

Table 1. Standard Subdivisions

T1—01

Philosophy and theory

The term philosophy and theory is treated as a single concept, covering the general or abstract principles applied to a field of activity or thought, such as science or art. Use T1—01 for a work discussing the discipline itself as a discipline, rather than its subject matter. Do not use T1—01 where theory constitutes the bulk of the subject matter of a field, e.g., nuclear physics. In philosophy subdivisions of 100, T1—01 itself is seldom used, though its subdivisions may be, and then only in the sense of theory and method of the topic.

Criticism

Use T1—01 for techniques and principles of criticism of a discipline. However, class the criticism itself in the same number as the subject of the criticism, e.g., criticism of Browning's poetry 821.8, of Frank Lloyd Wright's architecture 720.92, of Italian cooking 641.5945.

T1—015 vs. T1—0245–0246

Scientific principles vs. The subject for people in scientific and technological occupations

Use the number for the technology plus notation 015 from Table 1 for the scientific principles of a technology, e.g., mathematical principles of engineering 620.00151. In such cases the table of contents will often be organized by concepts found in subdivisions of the technology or will follow the table of contents found in common treatises on the technology. Conversely, use the number for the science plus notation 024 from Table 1 for the science if the work is written for technologists and engineers, e.g., mathematics for engineers 510.2462. In such cases the table of contents will be organized by concepts found in subdivisions of the science or will follow the table of contents found in common treatises on the science. If in doubt between science and technology, prefer the technology number.

When not to use either subdivision

Do not use T1—015 and T1—024 in 500 and 600 when there is a direct relationship between a science and a corresponding technology, e.g., do not use 540.2466 for chemistry for chemical engineers, or 660.0154 for chemical principles in chemical engineering.

T1—0207 vs. T3B—7, T3A—8 + 02, T3B—802, T3B—8 + 02, T3A—8 + 07, T3B—807, T3B—8 + 07

Humor, satire, jokes

Any subject may be dealt with in a humorous or satirical manner. Use the number for the subject without T1—0207 for works where the humor involved is entirely incidental to the serious treatment of the subject, e.g., a joke inserted into a lecture to provide respite from a serious mood. Use the number for the subject plus notation 0207 from Table 1 for works where the author's intention is serious, but where humor or satire is used to convey the author's message, e.g., political satire grounded in genuine political criticism. Use numbers in literature, usually T3B—802 (or T3A—8 + 02 or T3B—8 + 02), only for works where the subject merely provides the occasion for humor, the author's primary concern being to amuse, e.g., a collection of jokes about cats. If in doubt between literature and the subject, prefer the subject. If in doubt whether to use T1—0207, prefer the subject without it.

Use T3B—802 (or T3A—8 + 02 or T3B—8 + 02) for jokes; use T3B—807 (or T3A—8 + 07 or T3B—8 + 07) for humorous literary works without identifiable literary form. Use T3B—7 only for collections of humor or satire in more than one literary form, including both verse and prose. (Class works in a particular literary form, e.g., drama or fiction, with the form; class works in multiple forms of literary prose with prose.)

T1—0222 vs. T1—0223

Pictures and related material vs. Maps, plans, diagrams

Use T1—0222 for charts that are basically pictures of things, T1—0223 for charts that are basically maps or diagrams. Use T1—0222 for designs that give a visual impression of what something does or will look like, e.g., architectural drawings; use T1—0223 for designs that show details on horizontal or vertical planes (often as a preliminary to construction), or the arrangement and relations of parts showing how something works. Use T1—0223 for atlases, which are usually compilations of maps, plans, or diagrams, unless they are compilations of pictorial material. Use T1—0222 for anatomical atlases, which are usually picture-like. Use 001–999 without adding either standard subdivision for atlases that are simply heavily illustrated texts on a subject.

Use T1—0222 for comprehensive works, e.g., architectural drawings and plans 720.222. If in doubt between T1—0222 and T1—0223, prefer T1—0222.

T1—024

The subject for people in specific occupations

Use T1—024 for works that emphasize special instructions for people in specific occupations that general readers would not find useful, e.g., mathematics for engineers 510.2462. Do not use T1—024 for works that draw examples from one broad discipline or for one kind of professional user, but effectively cover the subject for the general reader, e.g., use 616.12 (*not* 616.12002461073) for a textbook on cardiology for nurses that would be equally useful to patients, relatives, or social workers.

Do not use T1—024 when it is redundant, that is, when it is directed towards people who would typically be expected to study the subject, e.g., engineering for engineers 620 (*not* 620.002462).

Table 1. Standard Subdivisions   T1

T1—025 vs. T1—029

Directories of enterprises and products

Use T1—025 for directories that describe business enterprises in a manner that serves people who run businesses; who invest in or lend money to businesses; or who want to sell ideas, products, and services to businesses. These directories typically emphasize organization, officers, and financial information. Use T1—029 for directories and catalogs designed to help customers obtain or evaluate products and services. If in doubt, prefer T1—025.

Directories of business and related enterprises

The guidelines in this section apply to directories that concentrate on enterprises and provide significant information about their organization, and sometimes also their officers, finances, and line of work. Use T1—025 with numbers from 001–999 for directories of persons and organizations that do not concentrate on enterprises, or that simply supply their names, addresses, and contact persons.

Limited to specific industries

Use T1—025 with subdivisions of 338.76 and related numbers for directories of enterprises in specific industries that emphasize organization, officers, and financial information. Related numbers are subdivisions of 338.8 that are divided by industry for business combinations; 332.1–.6 for financial institutions; 333.33 for real estate businesses; 334 for cooperative enterprises; 368 for insurance enterprises; and 380 for enterprises engaged in commerce, communications, and transportation.

Because "organization" is a basic element of 338.76 and related numbers, the guidelines in the Manual note T1—025 vs. T1—0601–0609 do not apply. Use notation 025 from Table 1 with these numbers for listings of companies, even if there is significant general information on the companies.

In most cases, the arrangement of a directory by enterprises points to use of T1—025 with subdivisions of 338.76 and related numbers, unless there is a predominance of detail on products and services. In that case, use T1—029 as instructed below. If in doubt, however, prefer T1—025.

Not limited to specific industries

Use T1—025 with 338.7, 338.8, and their general subdivisions (those not limited to specific industries) for directories of enterprises that are not limited to a specific industry, e.g., directories of all business enterprises in France 338.702544, directories of multinational enterprises 338.88025.

Use 338.74025 only for directories explicitly limited to corporations. If the limitation is not explicitly stated, prefer 338.7025.

Use 338.767025 for directories of manufacturers that give financial and organizational information.

Use T1—025 with numbers in 381–382 for directories of merchants. Use 381.025 and 382.025 for chambers of commerce and boards of trade, even when the membership includes a wide cross section of business enterprises in an area.

Use T1—025 with numbers in 914–919 for telephone, city, and fax directories, and for business white pages (telephone directories largely limited to businesses) and yellow pages that are issued with general directories of people and organizations in an area. Use 338.7025, however, for business white pages and comprehensive fax directories of businesses that are not produced in connection with a directory of all people and organizations, and 338.02029 for yellow pages that are not produced in connection with a directory of all people and organizations.

Product and service directories and catalogs

Product and service directories may go by a variety of names, including trade catalogs and yellow pages. Yellow pages are usually not limited by specific industries. The guidelines in this section also apply to buyers' guides and consumer reports.

Limited to specific industries

Use T1—029 with numbers from 001–999 (other than 338.47 and related numbers) for directories of products and services in specific industries, e.g., information services 025.04029, chemical products of United States 660.02973, food and drink in Europe 664.00294. In all cases, use the number that represents making the products or producing the services, except when they are produced by three or more industries serving a single consumer industry. In such cases, use the number for the consumer industry, e.g., a directory of publishers, binders, and furniture makers serving libraries 020.29.

Not limited to specific industries

Use 338.4029 for wide-ranging product directories that emphasize products of secondary industries, or services and products of secondary industries. Use 338.02029 for wide-ranging directories that cover everything from farm produce and minerals to the output of secondary industries. If in doubt, prefer 338.4029.

Use 338.4029 (*not* 670.29) for directories of manufactured products, as they are then usefully classed with other comprehensive or wide-ranging directories.

Use 338.4700029 for comprehensive directories of services.

T1—025 vs. T1—0601–0609

Directories of persons and organizations vs. Organizations

Use T1—025 for works covering several or many organizations containing directory information, even if not called directories, i.e., works that supply addresses, key officers or contact people, phone numbers, and brief statements of purpose. These works may include directory information about component parts of individual organizations, and/or a limited amount of general information on structure and component parts. However, use T1—06 if there is significant general information (more than a page) per organization. Use T1—0601–0609 for works covering history, charters, regulations, membership lists, and administrative reports of an organization, and also for conference programs of an organization and organizational handbooks.

Use T1—06 for a combined organizational handbook and membership directory, even if the membership part predominates. However, use T1—025, plus the Table 2

Table 1. Standard Subdivisions T1

notation for the area that the organization serves, if the organizational part consists of only a few preliminary pages followed by an extensive directory of members.

Use T1—025 for a membership list that includes addresses, as that is counted as a directory.

If in doubt, prefer T1—025.

See also discussion at T1—025 vs. T1—029.

T1—0285

Computer applications

Use T1—0285 for comprehensive works on data processing applied to a subject. Also use T1—0285 if 004 is the interdisciplinary number for the applied concept, e.g., digital computers T1—0285. Do not use T1—02854 by itself, since the digit 4 simply repeats the meaning of notation 0285. However, it is not redundant to add to T1—0285 the notation for subdivisions of 004, e.g., digital personal computers T1—0285416.

Do not add the digit 4 by itself to a number divided like 004–006 if the base number is limited to data processing and computer concepts, e.g., 651.8, 658.05.

Electronic resources and programs

Use T1—028553 for programs themselves and for works about programs, regardless of form (e.g., programs in electronic form, printed program listings bound into books). Do not use T1—0285 to indicate that a work is in electronic form, e.g., use 310 (*not* 310.285) for electronic census data.

Do not use T1—028553 for items that include both programs and data files, unless the data files are clearly of minor importance, e.g., small files intended merely to help beginners learn to use the programs.

If in doubt, do not use T1—028553.

T1—0601–0609

Organizations

Use subdivisions in T1—0601–0609 primarily for membership organizations and associations, but also for a selection of nonmembership institutions, foundations, and agencies that do not belong to the categories listed in class-elsewhere notes under T1—0601–0609. However, do not use T1—06 for nonmembership organizations if "organization" is inherent in the subject. For example, except as indicated below, do not use T1—06 with most subdivisions in 360 for social services. Under such numbers, use T1—09 for the basic organizations in specific areas, and for specific basic organizations, e.g., hospitals in China 362.110951. However, use T1—06 for associations that include the basic organizations and their staffs as members, e.g., hospital associations in China 362.1106051.

Use T1—06 also for administrative (in contrast to service) histories of institutions, e.g., administrative histories of hospitals (362.1106) or police agencies (363.206).

Do not confuse these histories with how-to works on management, which are classed in T1—068.

Do not use T1—06 for membership organizations if "membership organization" is inherent in the subject, e.g., in 366 Associations or 061–068 General organizations. T1—06 is not used with numbers for a religion because of the ambiguity of membership organization in religion, e.g., 296.06 is bracketed, and a reference leads to 296.67 where membership is inherent in the organization number.

Selection of area number

For membership organizations, use the area that is the chief focus of the membership, e.g., American Medical Association 610.6073. For local affiliated associations or chapters that have their own name, use the area number of the local organization, e.g., Massachusetts Medical Association 610.60744. For offices and chapters that take the name of the parent body, use the number of the parent organization, e.g., the Washington office of the American Medical Association 610.6073 (*not* 610.60753).

For nonmembership organizations, institutions, foundations, and conferences, use the area number of the headquarters. Also use the number of the headquarters for membership organizations whose area cannot be determined.

T1—068

Management

The subdivisions of T1—068 parallel the subdivisions of 658. Use 658 as a guide to selecting the correct subdivision of T1—068, e.g., information management 658.4038, therefore information management applied to automobile manufacturing 629.2220684.

T1—068 vs. 353–354

Public administration and management in specific fields

Use numbers outside 350–354 plus notation 068 from Table 1 for the management or administration of organizations, public or private, that directly perform the work within their scope. Use numbers in 353–354 for agencies that regulate, control, or support organizations that provide the actual services. For example, use 363.2068 (*not* 353.36216) for management of city police departments; use 364.62068 (*not* 353.39) for management of parole boards; use 385.068 (*not* 354.767) for management of a nationalized railway system.

A given field may have both public administration and management aspects. For example, use 385.068 for managing railroads, but use 354.76728 for managing agencies that regulate railroads; use 025.1974 for administering public libraries, but use 353.73 for administering agencies that support public libraries.

Exceptions

Use 353–354 for administration of activities specific to government (such as licensing, taxing, and gathering census information, that is, activities found in 352 that are not also found in 658) when applied to specific fields of public administration.

Table 1. Standard Subdivisions   T1

Foreign affairs are among the few major activities for which administration of an actual operation is classed in 353–354. Use 353.13 (*not* 327.068 or numbers in 327.3–.9, plus notation 068 from Table 1) for foreign affairs management. Similarly, use 353.17 (*not* 327.12068 or numbers in 327.123–.129 plus notation 068 from Table 1) for foreign intelligence management.

If in doubt, prefer the number outside public administration.

T1—072 vs. T1—0601–0609

Research vs. Organizations

Use T1—072 for organizations that conduct research, e.g., agricultural research stations in the United States 630.72073; but use T1—06 for membership organizations that primarily promote research, e.g., the American Association for the Advancement of Science 506.073. If in doubt, prefer T1—072.

See also discussion at T1—07201–07209 vs. T1—0721.

T1—07201–07209 vs. T1—0721

Geographic treatment of research vs. Research methods

Use the geographic treatment span for works on research in progress or being planned, or for works that consist of general descriptions of research projects and do not emphasize the research method. Also use the geographic treatment span for works on research organizations that perform or sponsor all or most of the research in their fields, even if they have names like agricultural experiment stations.

Do not use notation for a specific research method when it is redundant, e.g., historical research in history, experimental research in an experimental science such as chemistry.

However, use T1—0723 for surveys and data collection projects that concentrate on specific areas and concentrate on a single survey rather than on a number of projects.

If in doubt, prefer T1—07201–07209.

T1—074 vs. T1—029

Museums, collections, exhibits vs. Commercial miscellany

Use T1—074 for catalogs whose primary purpose is to promote knowledge or art, such as catalogs of collections; use T1—029 for catalogs whose primary purpose is to promote sale or distribution of products. Use T1—074 for catalogs of replicas, duplicates, and minor items when offered for sale in museum- or exhibit-like settings by noncommercial institutions. Also use T1—074 for auction catalogs (e.g., in art), and for catalogs of temporary exhibits of groups of artists, even if a succession of such exhibits provides most of the artists with their primary source of income. If in doubt, prefer T1—074.

T1—08 and 306.2–.6

Cultural institutions and groups of people

Use the interdisciplinary number for a topic pertaining to a cultural institution plus notation 08 from Table 1 for works on groups of people in relation to a cultural institution, e.g., racism in sports 796.089 (*not* 306.483), women in science 500.82 (*not* 306.45), police discrimination against minorities 363.208 (*not* 306.28). If the interdisciplinary number for the cultural institution falls in 306.2–.6, use the number for the institution or related topic plus notation 08 from Table 1, e.g., discrimination against retired women 306.38082.

T1—081 and T1—08351, T1—08352, T1—08421, T1—08422

Men and women, Males twelve to twenty and females twelve to twenty, Young men and young women

Use subdivisions for men and women only if the works explicitly emphasize the sex of the people treated. For example, do not use 363.370811 for men as a group with respect to fire fighting unless the work makes clear that *male* fire fighters are being contrasted with *female* fire fighters, or 364.3608351 for juvenile delinquents (a term often implying young men under eighteen) unless *male* delinquents are being contrasted to *female* delinquents.

T1—0882 and 200

Religious groups and Religion

Use subdivisions of T1—0882 in 200 to represent official or semiofficial positions of denominations and sects, e.g., Catholic teachings on socioeconomic problems 261.8088282.

Do not use T1—0882 for works of an individual except in the rare cases in which an individual's view has become an official statement of a group. That is, use 261.8 (*not* 261.8088282) for writings on Christian attitudes towards socioeconomic problems by persons who happen to be Catholic.

T1—09

History and geographic treatment of subjects and disciplines

Different numbers are occasionally provided for the history and geographic treatment of a subject and for the history and geographic treatment of the discipline within which the subject is treated, e.g., 364.9 is provided for history and geographic treatment of crime and its alleviation, while 364.09 is provided for comparable treatment of criminology. Use 364.9 for geographic treatment of offenses, offenders, causes, prevention, and treatment (when all are considered together). Use 364.09 for geographic treatment of criminology and of the principles and methods used in analyzing causes and remedies of crime. If in doubt, prefer the number for the history and geographic treatment of the subject.

Use T1—09 for either or both aspects where the distinction is not made between the subject and the discipline.

Table 1. Standard Subdivisions T1

T1—09 vs. T1—089

History, geographic treatment, biography vs. Ethnic and national groups

Use T1—09, not T1—089, to identify distinguishing characteristics of a subject in an area where a specific group of people lives, e.g., Arab architecture 720.9174927 (*not* 720.89927); French desserts 641.860944 (*not* 641.8608941).

Regions where specific ethnic groups predominate

Do not use T1—09174 (regions where specific ethnic groups predominate) for treatment as groups of people since such use would practically duplicate the ethnic group numbers. For example, Arabs living in all areas where Arabs predominate constitute the overwhelming majority of all Arabs; therefore, use T1—089927 for treatment of Arabs as a group, and use T1—09174927 only for works about the area where they live, and works about styles prevailing in areas where they live.

T1—0901–0905

Historical periods

Do not use historical periods for subjects that have no significant history outside the period indicated, e.g., the history of railroads 385.09 (*not* 385.0903), but the history of railroads during the 19th century 385.09034. If in doubt, do not use periods.

Do not use the most recent period subdivision for works on current practice or the state of the art of a subject, since most users will expect to find these works in the base number. However, use the latest period number when the nature of the subject requires attention to the changing situation, e.g., 320.90511 for world political conditions in 2000–2009.

Use earlier historical periods only for retrospective works, not for contemporary works. For example, use 781.09032 for a current work on music theory of the baroque, but use 781 for a reprint of a treatise on music theory written in 1620 (when baroque music was in style).

T1—092

Biography

The following instructions apply also to notation 2 from Table 2 when numbers from Table 2 are added directly without the interposition of T1—09.

In the following notes the word "biography" is used for stylistic convenience; however, the instructions apply fully to description and critical appraisal as well as other aspects of treatment of individuals.

Do not use T1—092 for the actual works of a person except where instructed to do so at certain numbers in 700–779.

See also discussion at Table 3A: Biography; also at 170.92 vs. 171; also at 230–280; also at 200.92 and 201–209, 292–299; also at 220.92; also at 297.092; also at 300 vs. 600: Biography; also at 338.092; also at 362.1–.4 vs. 610; also at 610.92 vs. 615.534092; also at 615.53: Biography; also at 700.92; also at 709.2 vs. 381.457092; also at 779 vs. 770.92; also at 780.92 and 791.092; also at 780.92; also at 781.6; also at 784–788; also at 796.092; also at 913–919: Add table: 04: Biography; also at 920.008 vs. 305–306, 362; also at 920.009, 920.03–.09 vs. 909.09, 909.1–.8, 930–990; also at 930–990: Wars: Personal narratives; also at 930–990: Biography.

Comprehensive biography

Use the number for the subject of the person's most noted contribution for the comprehensive biography of the person. If the person made approximately equal contributions to a number of fields, use the number for the subject that provides the best common denominator, giving some extra consideration to the person's occupation. For example, use the university's area number under 378 for a physicist who became a science teacher, then head of a school of science, but went on to become a university president. Use 300.92 for a person who made significant contributions in political science, in university education, and the study of administrative and economic aspects of utility regulation, since that number provides the best common denominator for his work. However, use 610.92 for a famous woman doctor who also served as a feminist leader, wrote minor novels, and often served as a delegate to political conventions, unless there is an obvious emphasis on her avocations. Give weight to designations listed first in biographical dictionaries, but make allowances for the tendency to list occupation first even when a career transcends occupation.

If in doubt between a number for a discipline and a number for a specific subject within the discipline, prefer the number for the discipline, e.g., use 620.0092 rather than 621.092 for a mechanical engineer who also did important work in transportation and construction engineering.

Public figures

Biographies of public figures frequently present difficulties because the person may have filled several positions that are given varying emphasis by different authors, or may have filled one position that had many facets. Use 930–990 for comprehensive works on persons who held such positions. However, use a number reflecting one position or interest of a person's career if a biography emphasizes this, e.g., use 362.1092 for a biography emphasizing Wayne Morse's promotion of the National Institutes of Health, even though he was a U.S. senator. *(See also Partial biography, below.)*

A public figure may exert a wide-ranging impact upon the history of the jurisdiction served. For example, Daniel Webster is most famous as a U.S. senator, although he served twice as secretary of state and was also a lawyer and orator. In all these roles he influenced the history of his time. Use 973.5092 for his biography, rather than 328.73092 for his senatorial service, 327.730092 for his foreign relations service, or 349.73092 for his legal activities. However, if a person in a high office of general responsibility concentrated on a single important field, consider a number that identifies that field. For example, William Wilberforce's chief interest while serving as a British Member of Parliament was the abolition of slavery. Thus use

Table 1. Standard Subdivisions T1

326.8092 for his biography, rather than 941.073092 for his impact on the general history of his period or 328.41092 for his legislative work.

Give greatest weight to the highest office reached, unless there is a clear reason to do otherwise, using the following table of preference:

1. Use 930–990 for monarchs, presidents, other heads of state, prime ministers, vice presidents, and regents, using the number for the period during which they held office. Also use 930–990 for public figures of any position or combination of positions who had a significant impact upon general history, using the period numbers that best approximate their period of influence. Candidates of major parties for the highest office of a country are also assigned history numbers, generally using the number for the period during which they ran for office, e.g., use 973.68092 for Stephen Douglas, who ran against Lincoln in 1860. Sometimes a candidate defeated for party nomination made enough difference in the outcome to warrant a history number for his comprehensive biography, e.g., use 973.923092 for Eugene McCarthy, who ran unsuccessfully for the Democratic presidential nomination in 1968.

2. Use the number for the field of service for cabinet members, e.g., use 327.440092 for a foreign minister of France.

3. Use 327.3–.9 for ambassadors and pre-World War II ministers plenipotentiary.

4. Use 328.4–.9 for legislators not warranting a specific subject number, e.g., a floor leader, whip, or member noted for promoting legislative work. Biographers tend to concentrate upon legislators who left their mark on general history; so always consider the number in 900 for the area the legislature served before assigning another. Only occasionally will a work focus on a legislator's own constituency.

5. Use 327.3–.9 for diplomats below the level of ambassador or pre-World War II minister plenipotentiary; however, if associated with notable events, use the number for the events.

6. Use the number for field of service for public administrators not holding cabinet positions, if their contribution to the service was significant, e.g., use 363.25092 for J. Edgar Hoover, director of the U.S. Federal Bureau of Investigation; otherwise use 352–354.

Use the same preference for public figures of state, provincial, and local jurisdictions. Usually national office takes preference over other levels, but consider the weight of contributions. For example, DeWitt Clinton, the famous governor of New York, was briefly U.S. senator, and was a minor party candidate for president, but use 974.703092 for New York State history of his time for his comprehensive biography. Fiorello La Guardia served fourteen years as U.S. representative, and briefly as chief of the U.S. Office of Civilian Defense and as director of the United Nations Relief and Rehabilitation Administration; but use 974.71042092 for his biography, as he is best known as mayor of New York City.

Systems and laws named after people

Do not use T1—092 for a system or law named after a single individual, but *do* use it for treatment of the individual emphasizing biography, e.g., use 150.1952 for a work on Freudianism, but use 150.1952092 for a biography of Freud.

When an individual is named in a heading or notes, treat the system according to the standard rules for topics, but be liberal about adding notation 092 from Table 1 for treatment emphasizing the individual. For example, 576.52 (Laws of genetics) gives Mendel's laws in a class here note, so any subdivision may be added, e.g., use 576.5205 for serials on Mendel's laws, use 576.52092 for Mendel's biography. Conversely, 150.19434 (Neobehaviorism) gives systems of Guthrie, Hull, Skinner, Tolman in an including note, so standard subdivisions are not added, e.g., use 150.19434 for serials on systems of Skinner without addition of notation 05 from Table 1. However, use notation 092 for biographical treatment of any of these individuals, e.g., use 150.19434092 for a biography emphasizing Skinner's work on neobehaviorism.

Families and close associates of the famous

Class a history of the immediate or extended family of a famous person with the biography of that person if the work strongly emphasizes the famous person. The same rule applies to the biography of a single relative or close associate of a famous person. However, if the relative or associate is important in his or her own right, or if the famous person is not strongly featured, class the life of the relative in the subject warranted by his or her own work, e.g., use 269.2092 for a biography of evangelist Ruth Carter Stapleton, sister of President Jimmy Carter, that treats the president only incidentally. If in doubt, do not use the number assigned to a famous person for a relative or close friend; prefer a number warranted by the biographee's own activities. Class a general family history in 929.2.

Partial biography

Class each partial biography featuring a specific contribution of a person with the contribution. However, use the comprehensive biography number for a work about the portions of a person's life that preceded the activity with which the person is chiefly associated, unless the work has significant alternative subject emphasis. For example, use 796.42092 for British Member of Parliament Christopher Chataway's earlier life as an athlete; but use 954.045092 for the childhood of Indira Gandhi, the number for her period as prime minister of India.

Biography associated with place rather than subject

Class an individual biography in the number most nearly covering the history and civilization of the place and time of the activity emphasized when a work is not clearly associated with any subject but is clearly associated with a place, even in cases when a person's activity may not approximate the whole of the most specific period, e.g., use 979.46104092 for the diary of a resident of San Francisco during the Gold Rush.

See also discussion at T1—0922 vs. T1—093–099; also at 930–990: Biography.

Table 1. Standard Subdivisions   T1

T1—0922

Collected biography

Use T1—0922 for a work on two people collaborating in the same field, e.g., the Wright brothers 629.1300922, Pierre and Marie Curie 530.0922. However, use T1—092 when the focus is strongly on one of the two.

Do not use area subdivisions for collected biography of groups that have a strong collective personal identity, even though all the members are known to have come from one particular area, e.g., the Beatles 782.421660922 (*not* 782.42166092242 or 782.42166092242753).

T1—0922 vs. T1—093–099

Collected biography vs. Specific continents, countries, localities

Collected biography covers description and critical appraisal of work, and geographic treatment covers description by place, by specific instance of the subject. Prefer T1—0922 over T1—093–099 for material limited by persons but emphasizing area aspects. However, use T1—093–099 when the intent of the author or compiler is to describe works of art characteristic of an area, or simply to describe such works in an area (even though the works may be listed under their producers). When the title and front matter do not reveal the intent, any discussion of style is an important indicator. A discussion focusing on the character and style of the individual producers indicates biography; one focusing on the characteristics of the place and times indicates geographic treatment. For example, use 730.92245 for a book on the style and character of sculptures by Cellini, Donatello, and Michelangelo, but use 730.94509024 for a book illustrating Italian Renaissance sculpture by describing the work of these same men. If in doubt, prefer T1—0922.

Use the area number if the text is largely confined to concise descriptions of works of technology or art (or to identifications and illustrations of them), even if persons are indicated in the title, e.g., descriptions of the works of six famous Italian sculptors 730.945.

However, use T1—092 without further subdivision for individual persons for all description and critical appraisal of works they have produced.

T1—0940902 vs. T1—0902

Medieval period in European history vs. 6th–15th centuries, 500–1499

Use T1—0940902 for works that are clearly focused on Europe in the Middle Ages and the medieval period, but use T1—0902 for works that attempt to cover the whole world during the period. However, the medieval record of many subjects outside Europe is poorly documented, so a work attempting worldwide coverage may in fact be predominantly about the subject in Europe. If in doubt, prefer T1—0940902.

Table 2. Areas, Periods, Biography

T2—162

Oceans and seas

Use T2—163–168 (*not* T2—3–9) for parts of oceans and noninland seas limited by either country or locality, e.g., use T2—16347 (*not* T2—752 or T2—7551) for Chesapeake Bay, an arm of the Atlantic Ocean that is almost surrounded by Maryland and Virginia.

Estuaries

Use the appropriate area number in T2—3–9 for estuaries that are parts of named rivers, but use T2—16 for estuaries that are parts of oceans and noninland seas, e.g., use T2—16347 (*not* T2—7553) for the York River, an estuary of the Chesapeake Bay.

Coastal waters

Use the number in T2—163–168 that includes the majority of the waters for comprehensive works on the coastal waters of a country, e.g., coastal waters of Russia T2—1632 (*not* T2—16334 or T2—16451), of the United States T2—1634 (*not* T2—16364 or T2—1643). If the areas are approximately equal in size, use the number coming first, e.g., coastal waters of Spain T2—16338 (*not* T2—16381), of Panama T2—16365 (*not* T2—1641).

T2—163 and T2—164, T2—165

Atlantic, Indian, and Pacific Oceans

Table 2 divides the world ocean into three parts—Atlantic, Indian, and Pacific Oceans. The Arctic Ocean is considered a sea of the Atlantic. There is no Antarctic Ocean, but provision is made in T2—167 for the extreme southern portions of the three oceans.

Divisions between the oceans are as follows:

Atlantic-Pacific: north, Bering Strait; south, a line drawn southeasterly from Cape Horn to the northern tip of Palmer Peninsula, Antarctica

Pacific-Indian: north, a line from Melville Island to Timor, thence through the islands of Indonesia to Singapore Strait; south, a line drawn south from Cape Howe, Victoria, Australia, on the 150° east meridian

Indian-Atlantic: north, Suez Canal; south, a line drawn south from Cape Agulhas, South Africa, on the 20° east meridian

Use notes and references to decide where to class connecting bodies of water, e.g., Bering Strait T2—16451 (*not* T2—16325 or T2—16327).

Table 2. Areas, Periods, Biography   T2

T2—3

Ancient world

The jurisdictions that existed in the ancient world are subdivided by modern regions and jurisdictions. For example, the ancient Iranian Plateau T2—357 is subdivided by the provinces of Iran, e.g., T2—35772 Persis is built using based notation 5572 from Table 2 for Fārs province. Ancient France T2—364 is subdivided by the regions and departments of modern France, e.g., T2—36439 Germania Superior is built using notation 4439 from Table 2 for Alsace.

T2—4–9

Modern world; extraterrestrial worlds

General arrangement of Table 2

The general arrangement of Table 2 is geographic rather than by political units, e.g., Hawaii T2—969 under Oceania, separated from the rest of the United States in T2—73–79; the Asian parts of Russia T2—57, separated from the European portion of Russia in T2—471–474.

Physiographic features and regions

Class a specific feature or region not named in the area table and that is wholly or almost wholly contained within a political or administrative unit with the unit; however, do not add further notation. For example, use T2—7421 for Mount Washington, New Hampshire; T2—75793 for Lake Moultrie, South Carolina; 917.5793 (*not* 917.579304) for travel connected with Lake Moultrie.

Class a river with the political or administrative unit in which the river's mouth is located, e.g., Escanaba River, Michigan T2—77494. However, if the upper part of the river is more important politically, economically, or culturally, class the river with that part, e.g., Tigris and Euphrates Rivers T2—5674 (*not* T2—5675).

Class general treatment of a specific kind of feature or region limited to a specific continent, country or locality with the continent, country, or locality plus notation 091 from the table under T1—093–099 in Table 1, e.g., rivers of Europe T2—4091693, rivers of England T2—42091693. However, do not add notation 091 for individual features or regions, e.g., Nile River of Egypt T2—62 (*not* T2—62091693). Class treatment of a specific kind of feature or region not limited to a specific continent in T2—1, e.g., rivers T2—1693.

Cities, towns, villages

Cities are not named in Table 2, except:

1. Major world cities, either with their own numbers, e.g., Amsterdam T2—492352, or in a note, e.g., Mecca T2—538

2. Smaller cities given their own numbers early in the development of the DDC, e.g., Guelph, Ontario T2—71343

3. The capital and largest city of each state of the United States, e.g., Pierre and Sioux Falls, South Dakota, at T2—78329 and T2—783371 respectively

4. Independent cities, e.g., Alexandria, Virginia T2—755296

5. United States cities coextensive with their counties (or parishes), e.g., Philadelphia T2—74811, San Francisco T2—79461

6. Cities, towns, and villages named to indicate boundaries of units when the boundaries are not readily available in reference works, e.g., throughout Australia T2—94 and the western provinces of Canada T2—711–712

Class a metropolitan area with the central city, e.g., the metropolitan area of Chicago T2—77311. Standard subdivisions may be added if appropriate.

Class general treatment of urban regions limited to a specific continent, country or locality with the continent, country, or locality plus notation 091732 (derived from notation 091 from the table under T1—093–099), e.g., urban regions of Europe T2—4091732, urban regions of England T2—42091732. Class treatment of urban regions not limited to a specific continent in T2—1732.

See also discussion at T2—41 and T2—42; also at T2—713 and T2—714; also at T2—93.

T2—4–9 vs. T2—3

Modern world; extraterrestrial worlds vs. Ancient world

Use T2—4–9 for those parts of the world more or less known to classical antiquity (the "Ancient world") when considered after the period of "ancient history," as well as other areas such as America in both ancient and later times. Use T2—3 for only the "Ancient world" during the period of "ancient history." For example, use T2—51 for later China and T2—31 for ancient China; T2—5694 for later Palestine and T2—33 for ancient Palestine; T2—44 for France and T2—364 for ancient Gaul; but use T2—7265 for both ancient and later Yucatán. The demarcation date between "ancient" and "later" varies from place to place and can be determined by examination of the terminal dates in classes 931–939, e.g., 931 China to 420, 933 Palestine to 70, 936.4 Celtic regions to 486. If in doubt, prefer T2—4–9.

T2—41 and T2—42

Scotland and England

The lower level authorities of England and the unitary authorities of England and Scotland may be referred to by a number of different names, most commonly District, Borough, or City. The term "City" does not necessarily refer to an urban locality. The Districts, Boroughs, and Cities are often named after an urban locality either within or approximately the same as the jurisdiction. If the urban locality is approximately the same as the jurisdiction, the locality is given in a class-here note. For example, Exeter City, the jurisdiction, and Exeter, the urban locality, are coextensive; thus, the table entry:

> T2—42356   Exeter City
>
>   Class here Exeter

If the urban locality is not approximately the same as the jurisdiction, only the jurisdiction is given. The classifier can assume that were the locality to be given, it

Table 2. Areas, Periods, Biography   T2

would be in an including note. For example, Canterbury City, the jurisdiction, and Canterbury, the urban locality, are not coextensive; thus, the table entry:

    T2—42234   Canterbury City

See also discussion at T2—4–9: Cities, towns, villages.

T2—713 and T2—714

Ontario and Quebec

In Ontario and Quebec, jurisdictions have the names of District, City, County, Municipality, Regional Municipality, Regional County Municipality, or Urban agglomeration. The term "City" does not necessarily refer to an urban locality. A District, City, County, Municipality, Regional Municipality, Regional County Municipality, or Urban agglomeration can be named after an urban locality within the jurisdiction. If the urban locality is approximately the same as the jurisdiction, the locality is given in a class-here note. For example, City of Toronto, the jurisdiction, and Toronto, the urban locality, are approximately the same; thus, the table entry:

    T2—713541   City of Toronto

                       Former name: Metropolitan Toronto

                       Including East York, Etobicoke, North York, Scarborough, York

                       Class here Toronto

If the urban locality is not approximately the same as the jurisdiction, only the jurisdiction is given. The classifier can assume that were the locality to be given, the locality would be in an including note. For example, City of Gatineau, the jurisdiction, and Gatineau, the urban locality, are not approximately the same; thus, the table entry:

    T2—714221   City of Gatineau

See also discussion at T2—4–9: Cities, towns, villages.

T2—73 vs. T2—71

United States vs. Canada

Use T2—73 if works about the United States and Canada are predominantly about the United States. Use T2—71 when Canada receives fuller treatment or the United States and Canada are given equal treatment. Use T2—7 only when the work also discusses areas in T2—72, even though Canada and the United States are assigned most of the numbers in the span. If in doubt, prefer T2—73.

T2—93

New Zealand

In New Zealand, the jurisdiction directly below the Region is referred to as either District or City. The term "City" does not necessarily refer to an urban locality. Districts and Cities are often named after an urban locality either within or approximately the same as the jurisdiction. If the urban locality is approximately the same as the jurisdiction, the locality is given in a class-here note. For example, Auckland City, the jurisdiction, and Auckland, the urban locality, are approximately the same; thus, the table entry:

> T2—9324   Auckland City
>
>   Class here Auckland

If the urban locality is not approximately the same as the jurisdiction, only the jurisdiction is given. The classifier can assume that were the locality to be given, it would be in an including note. For example, Dunedin City, the jurisdiction, and Dunedin, the urban locality, are not approximately the same; thus, the table entry:

> T2—9392   Dunedin City

See also discussion at T2—4–9: Cities, towns, villages.

T2—99 vs. T2—19

Extraterrestrial worlds vs. Space

Use T2—99 for the various bodies of the universe moving through space, e.g., moon rocks 552.09991. Use T2—19 only for space itself. If in doubt, prefer T2—99.

Table 3. Subdivisions for the Arts, for Individual Literatures, for Specific Literary Forms

Number building

Examples of basic number building for works in an individual language by or about individual authors (with use of Table 3A) and by or about more than one author (with use of Table 3B) are given in this entry. Use the following elements to build the numbers: base number; form; period; kind, scope, or medium; notation 08 Collections or notation 09 Criticism (plus additional 0s in some cases); subform; additional notation from Table 3C and other tables. Detailed instructions for number building appear in Tables 3A and 3B.

Note: in the following discussion, "T3" refers to both Table 3A (individual authors) and Table 3B (more than one author).

More than one form

1. Works by or about more than one author: not restricted by period or form (Table 3B)

> Base no. + notation 08 or 09
>
> 81 + 08 = 810.8 (an anthology of American literature)

2. Works by or about more than one author: restricted to a specific period but not to a specific form (Table 3B)

> Base no. + notation 08 or 09 + period
>
> 83 + 08 + 006 = 830.8006 (a collection of 18th-century German literature)

3. Works by or about more than one author: not restricted by form or period, place of authorship emphasized (Table 3B)

Base no. + notation 080 or 09 + 9 from Table 3C + area notation from Table 2

869 + 080 + 9 + 81 = 869.080981 (an anthology of literature in Portuguese by Brazilian authors)

Forms T3—1–7

1. Works by or about an individual author: restricted to a specific form and period (Table 3A)

Base no. + form + period

82 + 1 + 3 = 821.3 (Spenser's *Faerie Queene*)

2. Works by or about more than one author: restricted to a specific form but not to a specific period (Table 3B)

Base no. + form + notation 008 or 009

82 + 2 + 009 = 822.009 (criticism of English drama)

3. Works by or about more than one author: restricted to a specific form, to a specific kind, scope, or medium, and to a specific period (Table 3B)

Base no. + form + kind, scope, or medium + notation 08 or 09 + period

84 + 3 + 01 + 08 + 07 = 843.010807 (a collection of 19th-century French short stories)

4. Works by or about more than one author: restricted to a specific form but not to a specific kind, scope, or medium; restricted to a specific period (Table 3B)

Base no. + form + period + notation 08 or 09

83 + 2 + 914 + 09 = 832.91409 (criticism of German drama of the second half of the 20th century)

Form T3—8 Miscellaneous writings

1. Works by or about an individual author: restricted to a specific form, period, and subform (T3A—8)

Base no. + form + period + subform

81 + 8 + 4 + 02 = 818.402 (a collection of quotations of an individual American author of the later 19th century)

2. Works by or about more than one author: restricted to a specific form, period, and subform (T3B—8)

Base no. + form + period + subform + notation 08 or 09

84 + 8 + 914 + 02 + 08 = 848.9140208 (a collection of quotations of several French authors of the later 20th century)

Table 3A. Subdivisions for Works by or about Individual Authors

Comprehensive numbers for authors, and numbers for individual works

Follow the criteria given below on language, national affiliation, literary form, and literary period in order to determine the comprehensive number for collected works, critical evaluation, or biography of an author. Use the same national affiliation and literary period for comprehensive works and for all individual works of an author; however, use the language and form appropriate for each individual work, even if different from the language and form selected for the author's comprehensive number.

Language

Class an author with the language in which the author writes.

If an author changes place of residence or national affiliation to a country with a different language but continues to write in the same language, use the language in which the author writes, e.g., use 891.7344 for a novel in Russian by Solzhenitsyn, even if the novel was written while he was living in the United States.

Class comprehensive works for an author who writes in more than one language with the language that the author used last, e.g., Samuel Beckett 848.91409. However, if another language is predominant, class with that language. Class individual works of such an author with the language in which they were originally written.

National affiliation

National affiliation affects the choice of number only for literature written in English (810 vs. 820) or if an option for identifying national literatures is used.

If an author changes national affiliation to a country with the same language as that in which the author has been writing, use the literature number appropriate for the author's adopted citizenship, e.g., class T. S. Eliot as a British author. Class all works of such an author, including individual works written before the change of citizenship, with the same national literature.

If an author changes place of residence, but not national affiliation, to another country with the same language as that in which the author has been writing, continue to use the literature number of the author's original country, e.g., class a Jamaican author living in London, but still retaining Jamaican citizenship, as a Jamaican author.

If information about an author's national affiliation is not readily available in the work being classed or in standard reference books, use the literature number of the author's country of origin, if known; or the literature number of the country in which the author's earlier works were published.

Literary form

For comprehensive works, use the form with which an author is chiefly identified, e.g., Jane Austen 823.7. If the author is not chiefly identified with one form, use T3A—8 Miscellaneous writings plus literary period plus notation 09 from the table at T3A—81–89, e.g., use 828.91409 for a late-20th-century English author who is equally famous as a novelist, dramatist, and poet. For an individual work, use the form in which the work is written.

Literary periods

Use only one literary period for an author and all of the author's works, including works that may have been published earlier or later than the dates covered by that period. Determine the literary period in accordance with scholarly consensus about when an author flourished. For example, class an author commonly regarded as an early-19th-century writer as such, even if the author published literary works at the end of the 18th century. In the absence of scholarly comment, use the weight of bibliographic evidence to determine when an author flourished. For example, class an author who published one novel in 1999, one novel in 2000, one in 2001, and one in 2002 in the literary period beginning with 2000. If the period when an author flourished cannot be determined, use the date of the author's earliest known separate literary publication, disregarding magazine contributions, isolated student works, and juvenilia.

If a new name is known to be a pseudonym for an author whose literary period has already been established, use the established period for works attributed to the pseudonym. For example, if an English author began publishing at the end of the twentieth century and was assigned the period notation 914 for 1945–1999, then began publishing under a new pseudonym in 2001, use the same period notation 914 for works attributed to the new pseudonym (*not* 92 for 2000–).

Make an exception to the rule of only one literary period for an author if the author wrote in more than one language and flourished during different time periods in different languages: use the appropriate literary period notation for each language. For example, if an author began to flourish as a literary author in Russian during 1917–1945, use the period notation 42 for 1917–1945 for works by that author originally written in Russian. If that same author began to flourish as a literary author in American English after 1945, use the period notation 54 for 1945–1999 for works by that author originally written in English.

Biography

Do not use notation 092 from Table 1 for biography. Class literary diaries and reminiscences in T3A—8 plus period subdivision plus subdivision 03, e.g., Hemingway's *A Moveable Feast* 818.5203.

See also discussion at Table 3B vs. Table 3A.

Number building

Examples of number building are given in the *Manual* at the beginning of Table 3. Use the following flow chart as an aid to building numbers and as a supplement to the detailed instructions at Table 3A.

Flow chart A: Works by or about an individual author

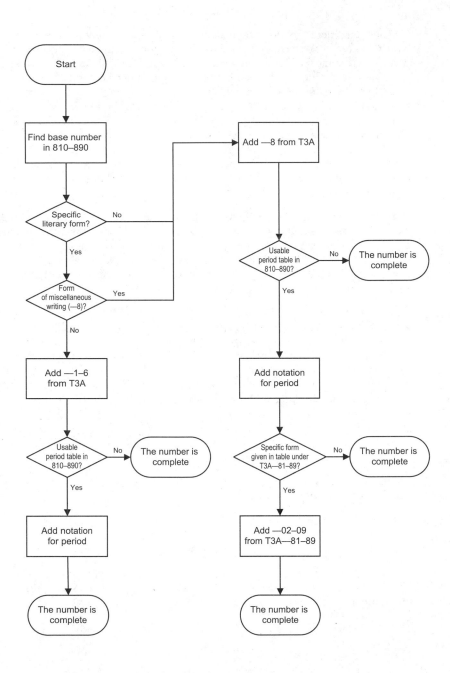

T3A—2, T3B—2 vs. T3A—1, T3B—102

Drama vs. Dramatic poetry

Use T3—2 for poetic plays intended for theatrical presentation, such as the plays of Shakespeare and Marlowe, and poetic plays designed to be read rather than acted, such as Milton's *Samson Agonistes*. Use T3A—1 and T3B—102 for poetry that employs dramatic form or some element of dramatic technique as a means of achieving poetic ends.

Use T3A—2 and T3B—2045 for monologues typically intended for use in theatrical presentations featuring only one actor. Use T3A—1 and T3B—102 for dramatic monologues that are poems in which the speaker is a fictional or historical character speaking to an identifiable but silent listener at a dramatic moment in the speaker's life, such as Robert Browning's "My Last Duchess."

If in doubt, prefer T3A—2 or T3B—2.

T3A—8 + 02, T3B—802, T3B—8 + 02 vs. 398.6, 793.735

Anecdotes, epigrams, graffiti, jokes, jests, quotations, riddles, tongue twisters vs. Anonymous riddles from the oral tradition vs. Riddles as puzzles

Use T3A—8 + 02, T3B—802, T3B—8 + 02 for interdisciplinary works on riddles and for riddles by known authors, even though they may not seem at home amid belles lettres, especially juvenile riddle jokes. Use 398.6 for anonymous riddles from the oral tradition. Use 793.735 for riddles as a type of puzzle similar to logic puzzles.

If in doubt, prefer in the following order: riddles as jokes (T3A—8 + 02, T3B—802, T3B—8 + 02), 398.6, 793.735.

T3A—8 + 03 and T3B—803, T3B—8 + 03

Diaries, journals, notebooks, reminiscences

Use T3A—8 + 03, T3B—803, and T3B—8 + 03 for diaries and reminiscences of literary authors in which the life of the author or authors as such is of key interest. However, class the diaries and reminiscences of literary authors that emphasize some other subject besides the general life of the author with the subject emphasized, e.g., use 940.5472 for a diary compiled while the author was in a prisoner-of-war camp during World War II.

Table 3B. Subdivisions for Works
by or about More than One Author

Preference order

The preference order in case of conflict between literary forms is spelled out at the beginning of the 800 schedule and in Table 3B under T3B—1–8. There are also preference orders in case of conflict among other aspects. The preference order for the four aspects expressed by means of Table 3C is as follows:

Themes and subjects	T3C—3
Elements	T3C—2
Qualities	T3C—1
Works for and by groups of people	T3C—8–9

For example, use 811.00803581 (*not* 811.00809287) for a general anthology of poetry about war written by American women poets.

The preference given to literary period in relation to the four aspects expressed by means of Table 3C varies: for works treating more than two literatures or more than one form in one literature, literary periods have a lower priority than the aspects from Table 3C; for works treating a specific form in an individual literature, literary periods have a higher priority than the aspects from Table 3C.

Specific media, scope, kinds consistently have preference over both period and the aspects from Table 3C. However, the preference given to scope in relation to kind varies: for drama, scope has a higher preference; but for fiction, kind has higher preference.

Preference orders are always the same for both collections of literary texts and criticism of the texts.

Sometimes elements low in the priority listings can be added to a number after the higher priority elements. For example, use 813.540932162 for a critical appraisal of later-20th-century American fiction about ocean travel: 813 (American fiction) + 54 (period: later 20th century) + 09 (critical appraisal) + 32162 (theme: ocean travel). The period comes first because it has higher priority than the theme; but the theme can also be expressed. Use the same preference order for these additional elements, e.g., for critical appraisal of later-20th-century American fiction about ocean travel by women, the theme of ocean travel would be expressed by means of Table 3C, but the authorship by a member of a specific group of people would not be expressed, because themes appear higher in the priority listing.

Sometimes aspects low in the priority listings can be expressed only by means of standard subdivision notation from Table 1. In the example above of a critical appraisal of later-20th-century American fiction about ocean travel by women, use notation 082 from Table 1 to express the aspect of women: 813.540932162082. For another example, use 808.83935820973209034 for a collection of 19th-century fiction of several literatures about urban life: 808.839 (collection of fiction from more than two literatures displaying specific features) + 358209732 (theme: urban life) + 09034 (standard subdivision for the historical period of the 19th century). In the priority listing, theme comes before period; and once the theme has been expressed, there is no way to express the period except by use of the standard sub-division.

See also discussion at Table 3B vs. Table 3A; also at T3B—08 and T3B—09; also at T3B—1; also at T3B—2; also at T3B—3; also at 808.8.

Number building

Examples of number building are given in the *Manual* at the beginning of Table 3. Use the following flow chart as an aid to building numbers and as a supplement to the detailed instructions at Table 3B.

Flow chart B: Works by or about more than one author

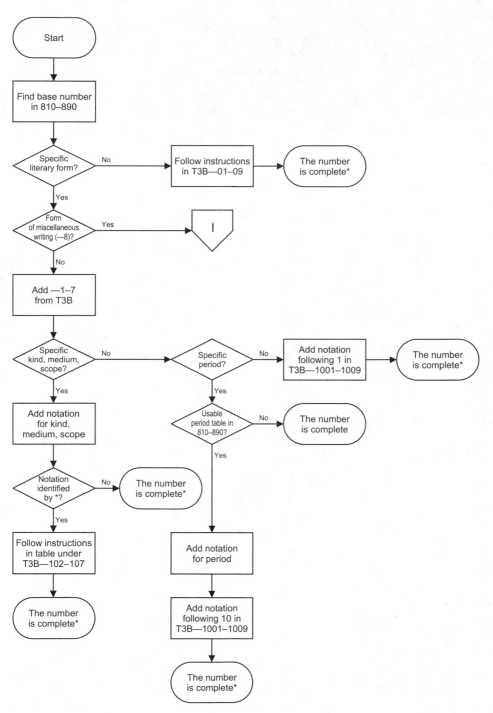

*If appropriate, standard subdivisions may be added

Flow chart B for notation 8 Miscellaneous writings

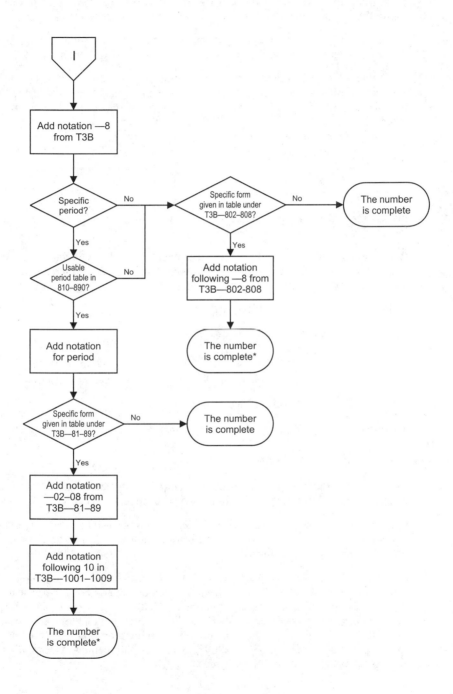

*If appropriate, standard subdivisions may be added

Table 3B vs. Table 3A

Table 3B. Subdivisions for Works by or about More than One Author vs. Table 3A. Subdivisions for Works by or about Individual Authors

Use Table 3B for an individual work by more than one author if the work is a collection where clearly defined parts are contributed by different authors.

Use Table 3A for an individual work by more than one author where the authors have collaborated so as to create a single whole and it is not easy (or at least not intended to be easy) to tell where the contribution of one author begins and the other ends. For example, use Table 3A for a play written in collaboration between Sir Francis Beaumont and John Fletcher.

If in doubt, prefer Table 3B.

T3B—08 and T3B—09

Preference order for collections and criticism of literature in more than one form

Here are examples illustrating the preference order for collections of texts (T3B—08) in more than one form from an individual literature (American literature used for the examples). The preference order is the same for criticism (T3B—09).

1. Specific themes and subjects, e.g., 810.80382 (religion)

2. Specific elements, e.g., 810.8024 (plot)

3. Specific qualities, e.g., 810.8013 (idealism)

4. Works for and by groups of people, e.g., 810.809282 (for children)

5. Period, e.g., 810.8003 (19th century)

See also discussion at Table 3B: Preference order.

T3B—091–099 vs. T3B—09001–09009

Literature displaying specific features or emphasizing subjects, and for and by specific groups of people vs. Literature from specific periods

If there is no applicable literary period table, T3B—09001–09009 cannot be used; moreover, do not add notation 0901–0905 from Table 1 to T3B—09 to show period, e.g., 20th-century Macedonian literature 891.81909 (*not* 891.81909000904).

However, the rule of zero gives T3B—091–099 priority over T3B—09001–09009. If the provisions of T3B—091–099 are used, then do not add any otherwise applicable literary period table. Instead, add notation 0901–0905 from Table 1 to indicate period, regardless of whether there is a literary period table for that literature, e.g., use 810.93580904 for 20th-century American literature in English on historical and political themes, use 891.819093580904 for 20th-century Macedonian literature on historical and political themes.

T3B—1

Preference order for poetry

Here are examples illustrating the preference order for poetry (A) from more than two literatures and (B) from one or two literatures. The preference order is the same for collections and criticism.

A. Poetry from more than two literatures

(Collections used as example)

1. Specific kinds, e.g., 808.8142 (sonnets)

2. Specific themes and subjects, e.g., 808.819353 (friendship)

3. Specific elements, e.g., 808.81922 (description)

4. Specific qualities, e.g., 808.819145 (romanticism)

5. Period, e.g., 808.81033 (18th century)

B. Poetry from one or two literatures

(Criticism of American poetry used as example)

1. Specific kinds, e.g., 811.03209 (epic)

2. Period, e.g., 811.5409 (later 20th century)

3. Specific themes and subjects, e.g., 811.009353 (friendship)

4. Specific elements, e.g., 811.00922 (description)

5. Specific qualities, e.g., 811.009145 (romanticism)

6. Works for and by groups of people, e.g., 811.0098924 (by Jews)

See also discussion at Table 3B: Preference order.

T3B—102–107, T3B—205, T3B—308 vs. T3C—1, T3C—3

Genres of poetry, drama, fiction vs. Arts and literature displaying specific qualities of style, mood, viewpoint or dealing with specific themes and subjects

Use the numbers for specific kinds of poetry, drama, and fiction for works belonging to specific literary genres, e.g., the genres of historical drama T3B—20514 and realistic fiction T3B—3083. Often the themes and other characteristics that mark specific genres can also be expressed by means of T3C—1 or T3C—3, e.g., works about historical themes T3C—358, works displaying realism T3C—12. Always prefer the genre number over the number derived from Table 3C for literary works belonging to a specific genre, e.g., a collection of historical drama T3B—2051408 (*not* T3B—20080358); criticism of realistic novels T3B—308309 (*not* T3B—300912). Add T3C—1 or T3C—3 to the genre number if it is not redundant, e.g., add T3C—358 for a discussion of historical themes in tragedy (T3B—2051209358), but not for a discussion of historical themes in historical drama.

Use T3C—1 or T3C—3 for literary works that display specific features and are not limited to a specific genre, e.g., a discussion of historical themes in serious and comic drama not limited by period T3B—2009358, a discussion of realistic elements in fiction of various kinds not limited by period T3B—300912. Use T3C—1 or T3C—3 also for literary works displaying specific features that might be regarded as marking a genre if no such genre is named for the relevant literary form in Table 3B, e.g., use T3B—200935878 for a discussion of western drama not limited by period as there is no mention of western drama under T3B—205 Specific kinds of drama. However, use genre notation 30874 from Table 3B for western fiction (*not* T3B—30095878).

If in doubt between Table 3B notation for genres and Table 3C notation, prefer the Table 3B notation.

Use notation from Table 3B only for literature (belles lettres); not for the arts, for films, or for radio or television programs. Use T3C—1 and T3C—3 to express genre for the arts, films, radio and television programs, e.g., use T3C—15 for science fiction in the arts, in films, in radio and television programs; but use T3B—308762 for science fiction as a genre of fiction. Use T3C—11 for experimental works in the arts, for experimental films, for experimental radio and television programs; but use T3B—807 for experimental literary works without identifiable literary form.

T3B—2

Preference order for drama

Here are examples illustrating the preference order for drama (A) from more than two literatures and (B) from one or two literatures. The preference order is the same for collections and criticism.

A. Drama from more than two literatures

(Criticism used as example)

     1. Specific media, e.g., 809.225 (television)

     2. Specific scope, e.g., 809.241 (one-act plays)

     3. Specific kinds, e.g., 809.2512 (tragedy)

     4. Specific themes or subjects, e.g., 809.29351 (Faust)

     5. Specific elements, e.g., 809.2925 (stream of consciousness)

     6. Specific qualities, e.g., 809.29145 (romanticism)

     7. Period, e.g., 809.204 (20th century)

B. Drama from one or two literatures

(Collections of American drama used as example)

     1. Specific media, e.g., 812.025083548 (television plays on death)

     2. Specific scope, e.g., 812.04108 (one-act plays)

3. Specific kinds, e.g., 812.051208 (tragedy)

4. Period, e.g., 812.5408 (collection of later 20th century, no focus), 812.540809287 (20th century, by women)

5. Specific themes and subjects, e.g., 812.008036 (weather)

6. Specific elements, e.g., 812.008027 (characters)

7. Specific qualities, e.g., 812.008015 (symbolism)

8. Works for and by groups of people, e.g., 812.008092827 (for girls)

See also discussion at Table 3B: Preference order.

T3B—3

Preference order for fiction

Here are examples illustrating the preference order for fiction (A) from more than two literatures and (B) from one or two literatures. The preference order is the same for collections and criticism.

A. Fiction from more than two literatures

(Collections used as example)

1. Specific kinds, e.g., 808.8383 (sociological)

2. Specific scope, e.g., 808.831 (short stories)

3. Specific themes and subjects, e.g., 808.839362 (animals)

4. Specific elements, e.g., 808.83922 (description)

5. Specific qualities, e.g., 808.83913 (idealism)

6. Period, e.g., 808.83034 (19th century)

B. Fiction from one or two literatures

(Criticism of American fiction used as example)

1. Specific kinds, e.g., 813.0876209 (science fiction)

2. Specific scope, e.g., 813.01093581 (short stories about war)

3. Period, e.g., 813.5409 (later 20th century), 813.540932162 (later 20th century, about ocean travel)

4. Specific themes and subjects, e.g., 813.009351 (about King Arthur)

5. Specific elements, e.g., 813.00927 (characters)

6. Specific qualities, e.g., 813.00912 (naturalism)

7. Works for and by groups of people, e.g., 813.009896073 (fiction by African Americans)

See also discussion at Table 3B: Preference order.

Table 3C. Additional Notation for Arts and Literature

T3C—37 vs. T3C—15

The supernatural, mythological, legendary vs. Symbolism, allegory, fantasy, myth

Use T3C—37 for mythological themes closely tied to specific mythologies of the past, e.g., Roman mythology in Renaissance poetry. Use T3C—15 for abstract myths not tied to specific mythologies of the past, e.g., the myth of a search for lost innocence. If in doubt, prefer T3C—37.

Class specific mythological persons in T3C—351, specific groups of mythological people in T3C—352, mythology as a religious theme in T3C—382013.

T3C—93–99

Residents of specific continents, countries, localities

Use notation 93–99 from Table 3C primarily for the following:

1. Literature in a language by residents of a certain area within a country, e.g., a collection of American literature by residents of Illinois 810.809773.

2. Literature in a language by residents of a country other than the traditional homeland of the dominant literature of the language, e.g., a collection of Spanish literature by Chilean authors 860.80983. The residents of a country other than the traditional homeland may be either native or nonnative residents of the country, e.g., a collection of English literature by non-Japanese residents of Japan 820.80952.

3. Literature in a language by residents of several countries on the same continent from more than one period (only for works in which the literature of one country does not predominate), e.g., French literature by residents of France, Switzerland, Belgium 840.8094; French literature by residents of Africa 840.8096.

Do not use T3C—93–99 for literature in a language by residents of the traditional homeland of the dominant literature of the language except for residents of only part of the country, e.g., a collection of Spanish literature by residents of Spain 860.8, but a collection of Spanish literature by residents of Madrid 860.8094641.

Do not use T3C—943 for German literature by residents of the Federal Republic of Germany, but use T3C—9436 for German literature by residents of Austria.

Do not use T3C—973 for literature in English by residents of the United States, but use T3C—971 for literature in English by residents of Canada.

T3C—93–99, T3C—9174 vs. T3C—8

Literature for and by residents of specific continents, countries, localities and Literature for and by residents of regions where specific ethnic and national groups predominate vs. Literature for and by ethnic and national groups

Use T3C—93–99 rather than T3C—8 for groups that predominate in an area, e.g., a collection of English literature by people of Irish ancestry in Australia 820.8089162094, but a collection of English literature by people of Irish ancestry in Ireland 820.809415; a collection of Spanish literature by Mexican-Americans 860.8086872073, but a collection of Spanish literature by Mexicans 860.80972; a collection of French literature by Arabs in France 840.808927044, but a collection of French literature by Arabs in North Africa 840.80961.

Do not use T3C—8 for the ethnic or national group so closely associated with the language that specifying the group would be redundant, e.g., a collection of Arabic literature by Arabs 892.708 (*not* 892.70808927); thus use 892.7080944 (*not* 892.70808927044) for a collection of Arabic literature by Arabs residing in France.

Do not use T3C—9174 (regions where specific ethnic and national groups predominate) for literature for and by ethnic and national groups since such use would practically duplicate the ethnic and national group numbers. For example, Arabs who are residents of all areas where they predominate taken together constitute the overwhelming majority of all Arabs, so T3C—8927 would be used for them rather than T3C—9174927. However, in most cases use of T3C—8 would be redundant. For example, most books about literature by Arabs from all areas where they predominate are about literature in Arabic, so that expressing the ethnic group Arabs with either T3C—9174 or T3C—8 would be redundant.

If in doubt, prefer T3C—93–99.

Table 4. Subdivisions of Individual Languages and Language Families

T4—1–5, T4—8 vs. T4—7

Description and analysis of the standard form of the language and Standard usage of the language (Prescriptive linguistics) vs. Historical and geographic variations, modern nongeographic variations

A language may have multiple standard forms. Use T4—1–5 and T4—8 for any of the standard forms, e.g., use 421.52 (*not* 427.994) for a work on standard Australian English pronunciation. Use 427.994 for a work on Australian English pronunciation only if it stresses the distinctive characteristics that make Australian pronunciation different from British or American pronunciation. If in doubt, prefer T4—1–5 and T4—8.

T4—3 vs. T4—81

Dictionaries of the standard form of the language vs. Standard usage of words

Use T4—3 for works intended for ready reference. Specialized dictionaries may be arranged in other ways besides alphabetically (e.g., picture dictionaries in subject order, thesauri in classified order), but the order must be appropriate for ready reference.

Use T4—81 for works intended to be read or studied in full in order to learn vocabulary. The works may be informal and entertaining, e.g., narratives for small children, or formally organized into lessons with quizzes.

If in doubt, prefer T4—3.

Historical and geographic variations, modern nongeographic variations

Use of standard subdivisions

Add notation from Table 1 to T4—7 and its subdivisions according to the usual limitations on use of standard subdivisions. For example, use notation 03 from Table 1 and notation 03 from the table under T1—093–099 in Table 1 for dictionaries, e.g., a dictionary of Old High German 437.0103, a dictionary of Northern Yemeni Arabic 492.7709533203.

Where subdivisions are provided for early versions of a language, notes are used to override the rule of zero so that geographic variants of an early version of a language class with the early version, e.g., use 427.0209428 for Middle English dialects of northeast England. Use 427.9428 for modern dialects of northeast England and comprehensive works on Middle English and modern English dialects of northeast England.

Pidgins and creoles

Class a specific pidgin or creole as a variation of the source language from which more of its vocabulary comes than from its other source language(s). Class a pidgin or creole, which is customarily associated with a specific geographic area, in T4—709 plus the area number from Table 2 or in one of the subdivisions of T4—7 for geographic variations where they are provided in 420–490, e.g., the Krio language of Sierra Leone 427.9664.

Table 5. Ethnic and National Groups

Nationality and language

Table 5 Ethnic and National Groups and Table 6 Languages are both based on the traditional sequence of languages in 420–490, and therefore most numbers are developed in parallel. But separate tables are needed because language and nationality do not always match, e.g., there are Canadian people (T5—11 in Table 5), but no Canadian language; there is a Yiddish language (T6—391 in Table 6) but no Yiddish people.

Ethnic group and nationality

The generally preferred citation order is ethnic group over nationality, as nationality is normally given a low priority, and citizens and noncitizens of a country class in the same number. However, a different and atypical citation order is given at some specific numbers in Table 5, e.g., for Canadians of French and British origin, the prescribed citation order is nationality first (T5—11 Canadians), then ethnic group: T5—112 for Canadians of British origin, T5—114 for Canadians of French origin. Use the numbers T5—21071 (T5—21 people of British Isles + 71 Canada) and T5—41071 (T5—41 French + 71 Canada) only for persons of British and French origin in Canada who are not Canadian citizens. But in the absence of specific instructions to the contrary use the citation order given at the beginning of the table, e.g., Canadians of Ukrainian descent T5—91791071 (*not* T5—11). Use this same number for both Canadians of Ukrainian descent and persons of Ukrainian descent who are in Canada but not Canadian citizens.

Table 5. Ethnic and National Groups   T5

In general, use the same number for both the majority ethnic group of a nation and the total population viewed as a national group, e.g., T5—94541 for both ethnic Finns and all citizens of Finland viewed as a national group. Usually, priority between ethnic and national affiliation is an issue only for minority ethnic groups, e.g., use T5—39704897 (T5—397 Swedes + 4897 Finland) for Finnish citizens who are ethnic Swedes, a minority ethnic group, because their ethnic group takes priority over their nationality. Use T5—94541073 (T5—94541 Finns + 73 United States) for Finnish citizens who are ethnic Finns in the United States, but use T5—397073 (T5—397 Swedes + 73 United States) for Finnish citizens who are ethnic Swedes in the United States, which is the number for all persons of Swedish descent in the United States. Their Finnish national origin is not expressed because of the low priority given to nationality. The exception to this rule occurs when the class number to which Table 5 notation is added defines the present location of the group, as in 940–999, so that it is possible to express both the present and the past location of the group, e.g., use 973.0439704897 for ethnic Swedes from Finland in United States history.

Special developments that allow expression of both ethnic and national affiliation are typically made only for the majority ethnic group in a nation, under the heading "national group," e.g., T5—6887 expresses both Spanish American ethnicity and Venezuelan nationality, while T5—9697292 expresses both African ancestry and Jamaican nationality. However, there is no special development to express both African ancestry and Venezuelan nationality because African Venezuelans are a minority in Venezuela and cannot be called a "national group." Therefore the number for African Venezuelans in England (T5—96042) is the same as the number for persons of African ancestry in general in England; and Venezuelan nationality is not expressed (*except* when it is possible to express both present and past location, e.g., African Venezuelans in English history 942.00496087). Conversely, Table 5 numbers for Venezuelans of Spanish origin in England (T5—6887042) and Jamaicans of African origin in England (T5—9697292042) always express the national origins.

In some cases, special developments for national groups lead to the number for a national group being clearly different from the number for the largest ethnic group of the country. For example, the number for the Bhutanese as a national group is T5—91418; but the Bhotia, the largest ethnic group, speak Tibetan dialects and class as an ethnic group with the Tibetans in T5—9541. In some cases, the national group number for a country may not express the ethnicity of the majority of the population. For example, the national group numbers for all the modern nations of Latin America where Spanish is at least one of the official languages express Spanish-American ethnicity, though the majority of the population in some countries is of native American origin, e.g., Bolivia. Class works that discuss all the people of a nation in the national group number specified in the table. Class works that focus on a specific ethnic group with the ethnic group. Use the national group number for a work that focuses on a specific ethnic group if it expresses the appropriate ethnicity, e.g., use T5—6884 for works that discuss all the people of Bolivia and also for works that focus on the Bolivians who speak Spanish and follow Spanish-American customs; but use T5—98323084 for works that focus on the Quechua of Bolivia, T5—98324084 for works that focus on the Aymara of Bolivia.

Adding area notation

Area notation is normally added to a Table 5 number to signify location, e.g., sociology of Italians in England 305.851042. However, area notation is omitted whenever it is redundant, e.g., 973.046872 Mexican Americans in U.S. history (*not* 973.046872073).

African Americans

An atypical development for African Americans (T5—96073) gives extra emphasis to nationality for a minority group, while still preserving the usual citation order of ethnic group before nationality. The 073 signifies U.S. nationality rather than location; so area numbers can be added to it in the usual way, e.g., use T5—960730747 for U.S. citizens with African ancestry in New York State. However, this applies only to U.S. citizens; so use T5—960747 for noncitizens of African ancestry in New York State. There are no special developments for most ethnic groups in the United States, e.g., use T5—510747 for persons of Italian descent in New York State regardless of whether they are U.S. citizens. The Table 5 number for African Americans always expresses the U.S. national origin when used for areas outside the U.S., e.g., use T5—96073042 for African Americans in England. Conversely, the number for Italian Americans in England (T5—51042) is the same as for Italians in England (with the usual exception for history, e.g., Italian Americans in English history 942.00451073).

T5—112, T5—114 vs. T5—2, T5—41

Canadians of British origin and Canadians of French origin vs. British, English, Anglo-Saxons and French

Use T5—112 for Canadian citizens of British origin and T5—114 for Canadian citizens of French origin, even with numbers that already specify Canada, e.g., use 971.004112 for Canadian citizens of British ancestry in Canadian history. Use T5—112 or T5—114 for accounts of persons of British or French ancestry becoming Canadian citizens. Also use T5—112 and T5—114 for persons of British or French origin living in the territory that later became the nation of Canada if they are regarded as among the precursors of British or French Canadians or founders of the nation, e.g., the French in Canada 1600–1867 971.004114.

Use T5—2 and T5—41 for persons of British or French ancestry who were not and never became Canadian citizens, even though they may have resided in Canada or in the territory that later became Canada. For example, the inhabitants of the French colony Acadia in what is now Nova Scotia who were expelled in 1755 and became the Cajuns of today's Louisiana were never Canadian citizens; so use T5—410763 (*not* T5—1140763) for Louisiana Cajuns.

If in doubt, prefer T5—112 and T5—114.

T5—13 vs. T5—2073, T5—21073

People of United States ("Americans") vs. British, English, Anglo-Saxons in United States and People of British Isles in United States

Use T5—13 (*not* T5—2073 or T5—21073) for U.S. citizens of British ancestry, even with a number that already means United States, e.g., British Americans in U.S. history 973.0413. Use T5—13 for comprehensive works on both U.S. citizens

Table 5. Ethnic and National Groups   T5

and non-U.S. citizens of British ancestry in the United States. Use T5—13 for accounts of persons of British ancestry becoming U.S. citizens. Use T5—2073 or T5—21073 for non-U.S. citizens of British ancestry in the United States. (Do not add 0 plus notation 73 if T5—2 or T5—21 is used with a number that already means United States, as it would be redundant, e.g., all noncitizens of British ancestry in U.S. history 973.042.) If in doubt, prefer T5—13.

T5—201–209 vs. T5—2101–2109

British, English, Anglo-Saxons by area vs. People of British Isles by area

Use T5—201–209 for people of British ancestry in an area when many of them are or have most recently been citizens of the United States, Canada, Australia, or New Zealand, e.g., people from the United Kingdom, the United States, Canada, and Australia in the Third World T5—201724. Use T5—2101–2109 for people of British ancestry in an area when they are or have most recently been citizens of the United Kingdom, e.g., people from the United Kingdom in the Third World T5—2101724. If in doubt, prefer T5—201–209.

T5—9435

Turks

Use T5—9435 for (a) the people of Turkey as a national group; and (b) people who speak, or whose ancestors spoke, Turkish (Osmanli Turks and their descendants), including those who are not Turkish nationals, e.g., Turkish Cypriots T5—943505693.

T5—96073

African Americans (United States Blacks)

The 073 in T5—96073 signifies U.S. nationality rather than location. It is never omitted even where it would be redundant if it simply signified location, e.g., 973.0496073 African Americans in U.S. history (as distinct from 973.0496 for noncitizens of African ancestry in U.S. history). Area subdivisions are added to it in the usual way, e.g., 305.8960730747 sociology of African Americans in New York (as distinct from 305.8960747 sociology of non-U.S. citizens of African ancestry in New York).

Table 6. Languages

The source of information about language families most used in recent revisions of Table 6 is *Ethnologue*, 15th edition (Dallas, Texas: SIL International, 2005; also on the Internet http://www.ethnologue.com/). However, Table 6 diverges from *Ethnologue* in many specific instances. Check Table 6 and the Relative Index first to find a specific language or group of languages. If nothing is found, consult *Ethnologue* to find the appropriate language family or group of languages.

T6—926

Linear A

It is not known what language is represented by the Linear A script used in ancient Crete (also known as Minoan Linear A). At one time the language was thought to be a West Semitic language, and works on the script have been classed in T6—926 Canaanite languages for many years. If the script is deciphered and the language identified as a non-Canaanite language, then Linear A will be moved to the appropriate place.

T6—9639

Bantu languages

Groups and zones of Bantu languages were originally based on Malcolm Guthrie's *Comparative Bantu; an Introduction to the Comparative Linguistics and Prehistory of the Bantu Languages*, 1967–1971. These groups and zones appear in a modified and updated form in *Ethnologue*, 15th edition (Dallas, Texas: SIL International, 2005; also on the Internet http://www.ethnologue.com/). Most of the time, but not always, Table 6 follows *Ethnologue*. Check Table 6 and the Relative Index first to find a specific language or group of languages. If nothing is found, consult *Ethnologue*.

Notes on Schedule Numbers

001.9 and 130

Controversial knowledge and Parapsychology and occultism

Both 001.9 and 130 cover topics that cannot be disproved or be brought into the realm of certain and verifiable knowledge. Works that belong in either 001.9 or 130 include one or more of the following indicators:

1. A claim of access to secret or occult sources

2. A rejection of established authority

3. A pronounced reverence for iconoclasts, for laypersons-become-experts

4. An uncritical acceptance of lay observation of striking phenomena

5. A fixation on the unexplained, the enigmatic, the mysterious

6. A confidence verging on certainty in the existence of conspiracies and the working of malevolent forces

7. An acknowledgment of the powers of extraterrestrial beings or intelligences (other than religious beings)

Use 001.9 for phenomena not closely linked to humans. Use 130 for phenomena closely linked to human beings—the human mind, human capabilities and powers, human happiness. In case of doubt, and for interdisciplinary works, prefer 001.9.

004–006 vs. 621.39

Computer science vs. Computer engineering

Use 004–006 for works on (a) computer hardware from the user's viewpoint, (b) software or firmware, (c) comprehensive works on assembling the physical components and installing the software of a computer system, or (d) comprehensive works on the computer science and computer engineering aspects of a computer topic.

Use 621.39 for works that (a) treat computer hardware solely from the viewpoint of engineering, manufacturing, or repair and (b) do not treat software or the program aspect of firmware. Use 621.39 for works limited to assembling the physical components of a computer system, and for works treating the physical processes of manufacturing firmware chips, not discussing the programs embodied in those chips. Use 621.39 for works treating 004–006 concepts only if the 004–006 concepts are applied to 621.39 concepts, as in computer graphics programs to assist in design of computer circuitry 621.3950285668.

If in doubt, prefer 004–006.

004 vs. 005

Computer hardware and software

Use 004 for works on computer hardware and works treating both computer hardware and the "soft" aspects of computer systems—programs, programming, and data. Use 005 for works treating only these "soft" aspects. Use 005.1–.8 together with notation 0285 from Table 1 for works on hardware applied to topics named in 005.1–.8, e.g., parallel architectures for database machines 005.740285435. However, use 004.6 (*not* 005.71) for works on hardware for interfacing and data communications. If in doubt, prefer 004.

See also discussion at 004.6 vs. 005.71.

004.0151 vs. 511.1, 511.35

Computer mathematics

Use 004.0151 for works on mathematics applied to computers, and for comprehensive works on computer mathematics.

Use 511.1 for works on branches of mathematics in which objects can only have discrete or finite values, and hence can be represented on digital computers. These branches are often collectively referred to as "discrete mathematics" or "finite mathematics."

Use 511.35 for works on the theory of computer mathematics, without reference to practical implementations on real computers. Use 511.35 for works on Turing machines, because Turing machines are a theoretical concept. This subject is also called automata theory or machine theory.

If in doubt, prefer in the following order: 004.0151, 511.1, 511.35.

004.1

Computers and processors

In 004.1, its subdivisions, and similar numbers elsewhere in 004–006 and 621.39, computers and processors (central processing units) are treated for classification purposes as if they were the same. In fact they are not, but few works about processors can avoid discussing the other parts of the computer with which the processor must interact; hence works about specific types of computers and processors are typically not different enough to justify separate numbers.

Programmable calculators

Use 510.28541 rather than 004.1 for programmable calculators because they are limited-function computers, capable of working only with numbers, not alphabetic data.

004.1 vs. 004.24

Performance evaluation

Use 004.1 for general evaluations of computers, e.g., general evaluations of personal computers 004.16, of a specific kind of personal computer 004.165. Use 004.24 only for specialized works treating performance measurement and evaluation as an aid in designing or improving the performance of a computer system. If in doubt, prefer 004.1.

Add notation 029 from Table 1 to the number in 004.1 if the emphasis is on evaluation as a consideration in purchasing, e.g., evaluation and purchasing manuals for personal computers 004.16029.

004.1 vs. 004.3

Processing modes

Many computers, processors, and computer systems can be classified either by type of computer as defined in 004.1 or by processing mode.

Use 004.1 for works that discuss a computer, processor or computer system in general. Use 004.3 only for works that emphasize the processing mode.

For example, the Intel Pentium® processor is a microprocessor that supports multiprogramming, interactive processing, and multiprocessing. Use 004.165 for works discussing the Pentium in general. Use 004.357 for Pentium-based multiprocessing computers.

If in doubt, prefer 004.1.

004.11–.16

Types of digital computers

Use 004.11–.16 and 621.3911–.3916 only for works that emphasize the specific type of computer. Use 004 and 621.39 for works that refer to a particular type as an illustration of what computers in general do. For example, use 004, not 004.12, for a general introduction to computers written at a time when the only computers were mainframes. If in doubt, prefer 004 or 621.39 without subdivision.

Specific computers

Here, "numbers for specific computers in 004–006" include 004.125, 004.145, 004.165, 005.265, and numbers in 004–006 built using these numbers, e.g., 006.7765.

Use numbers for specific computers in 004–006 for works treating more than one computer or processor only if:

1. The work treats a single series of very closely related computers or processors (e.g., the Intel Pentium® microprocessors 004.165); or

2. The work treats primarily one specific computer or processor but adds that it is also applicable to other similar machines (e.g., a work about programming the IBM PC® that says it can also be used as a guide to programming "IBM-compatible" computers 005.265).

Use numbers for specific computers in 004–006 for works that discuss a computer and its processor, e.g., a work about the Apple iMac® series of computers and the PowerPC® series of microprocessors 004.165.

If in doubt, do not use numbers for specific computers in 004–006.

004.21 vs. 004.22, 621.392

Systems analysis and design vs. Computer architecture

Use 004.21 for works on computer-based systems involving a computer, application programs, and procedures, usually also other hardware, often a database and communications network, all working together to accomplish a task for the user. Use 004.21 for comprehensive works on systems analysis and design.

Use 004.22 for works focusing on the design and structure of the computer itself and on the computer in relation to its peripheral devices. Most works on computer architecture treat software or the program aspect of firmware as well as hardware; but in the discussion of programs, the focus is on system programs, which make the computer function properly, rather than on application programs, which accomplish user tasks. Use 004.22 for comprehensive works on computer architecture.

Use 621.392 for works that treat computer hardware but do not treat software or firmware.

If in doubt, prefer in the following order: 004.21, 004.22, 621.392.

004.6 vs. 005.71

Computer communications

Use 004.6 for comprehensive works on both the "hard" and "soft" aspects of computer interfacing and communications. Use 005.71 for comprehensive works on "soft" aspects—programming, programs, and data in interfacing and communications. Use 005.7–.8 for specific data aspects of interfacing and communications, e.g., error-correcting codes 005.72, data compression 005.746, data encryption 005.82. If in doubt, prefer 004.6.

004.6 vs. 384.3

Computer communication services

Use 004.6 for works on computer communication and its hardware in office and private use, works on computer science applied to the technological aspects of computer communication, practical works explaining how to use the hardware and software involved in computer communications, and interdisciplinary works.

Use 384.3 for works on economic and related aspects of providing computer communication services to the public, and works focusing on services and service providers, on broad issues of public good in relation to computer communication.

If in doubt, prefer 004.6.

004.6 vs. 621.382, 621.3981

Digital communications

Use 004.6 for works on digital communications that do not emphasize engineering, including works dealing with telecommunications and data communications engineering plus interfacing and communications in computer science.

Use 621.382 for works on digital telecommunications, or digital aspects of both telecommunications and data communications, that emphasize engineering. Use 621.3981 for works on computer data communications that emphasize engineering.

If in doubt, prefer in the following order: 004.6, 621.382, 621.3981.

See also discussion at 004.6 vs. 005.71; also at 004.6 vs. 384.3.

004.678 vs. 006.7, 025.042, 384.33

Internet and World Wide Web

The Internet and the World Wide Web (WWW) can be written about from various disciplinary viewpoints. Because the Dewey Decimal Classification is organized by disciplines, it is necessary to decide the focus of a particular work about the Internet or the WWW in order to choose the correct number.

Use 004.678 for works about the Internet or WWW if they contain a substantial amount of computer science material and at least some information about computer hardware, or if they include a comprehensive overview of the Internet as a system of hardware, software, communications protocols, and other aspects of computer communications included in 004.6.

Use 006.7 for general works about the use of HTML and XML to create hypertext documents on the World Wide Web, and works that discuss web page design or effective web pages.

Use 025.042 for:

1. Interdisciplinary works about the Internet and WWW that do not contain enough computer science material to be classified in 004.678, but that do contain some information science material

2. Information science works that emphasize search and retrieval, including use of web browsers and web search engines to facilitate search and retrieval on the Internet

3. Works that describe information resources available on the Internet or WWW, and on how to find information there

Use 384.33 for works on Internet access providers and works on economic and public policy issues concerning the Internet.

If in doubt, prefer in the following order: 004.678, 025.042, 006.7, 384.33.

005.1–.2 vs. 005.42

Application programming vs. Systems programming

Use 005.1–.2 for works on writing application programs and comprehensive works about writing both application and systems programs, including works about writing application programs that run on specific operating systems or user interfaces, e.g., writing application programs that run on the personal computer operating system MS-DOS 005.268, writing application programs that run on the personal computer graphical user interface Microsoft Windows 005.269. Use 005.42 for works about writing systems programs, e.g., writing operating systems 005.42, writing user interfaces 005.428. If in doubt, prefer 005.1–.2.

See also discussion at 005.3, 005.5 vs. 005.43–.45.

005.1 vs. 005.3

Programming vs. Programs

In this discussion, "other programming numbers" comprise 005.2, 005.42, 005.711, 005.712, 006.336, 006.337, 006.66 and 006.67. "Other numbers for programs" comprise 005.43, 005.5, 005.713, 006.338 and 006.68.

Use 005.1 and other programming numbers for works on writing programs, on software engineering, on modifying existing programs in ways that are typically done by computer programmers. Use 005.3 and other numbers for programs for works on using programs that have already been created by others, including works on writing macros of the kind that are typically written by end users of software packages.

Use 005.1 and other programming numbers for works on programming to achieve reliability, compatibility, portability, and other ideal qualities. Use 005.3 and other numbers for programs for works that discuss whether existing programs actually have these qualities.

Use 005.10218 and 005.150218 for standards for programs and program documentation that are aimed at programmers and documentation writers, to ensure that they produce good programs and documentation. Use 005.30218 and other numbers for programs for works that discuss standards to help users in selecting from among existing programs and documentation.

Use 005.14 for works on testing and measurement as part of program development. Use 005.30287 and other numbers for programs for works that discuss ways for users to test or measure programs as an aid in selection.

Use 005.1 or 005.2 for works devoted equally to programming and programs.

If in doubt, prefer 005.1 or other programming numbers.

005.101

Logic in computer programming

Use notation 01 from Table 1 only for specialized works with an intense focus on logical analysis. Typically such works treat symbolic (mathematical) logic; use notation 015113 for these works. Do not use notation 01 from Table 1 in 005.1–.2 for general discussions of logic in programming because logic is inherent in programming and is discussed in nearly every work about programming.

005.15 vs. 808.066005

Program documentation

Use 005.15 for comprehensive works on how to prepare program documentation; works on how to prepare the technical documentation needed by the personnel who will maintain, modify, and enhance the program (including such things as program source listings, program comments, flow charts, decision logic tables, file specifications, program function descriptions, program test history records, modification logs); works on how to prepare program users' manuals that focus on content rather than form; works on policies for program documentation.

Use 808.066005 for works that emphasize effective technical writing—that is, works that emphasize such things as organizing for clarity, writing appropriately for the intended audience, using good paragraph structure, preferring the active voice, using consistent terminology. Typically such works are concerned only with users' manuals.

If in doubt, prefer 005.15.

005.268 vs. 005.265, 005.269

Programming for specific operating systems, for specific computers, and for specific user interfaces

Numbers beginning with 005.26 are limited to personal computers. Similar numbers for other types of computers, with instructions for building numbers by adding notation from 005.26 numbers, are found in 005.22–.24 and 005.27.

Use 005.268 (and similar numbers for other types of computers) for works on writing software that runs on specific operating systems. Use 005.265 (and similar numbers for other types of computers) for works on writing software that runs on specific computers. Use 005.269 (and similar numbers for other types of computers) for works on writing software that runs on specific user interfaces other than the native interface of the computer operating system. (Class Microsoft Windows® versions through 3.x in 005.269; starting with Windows NT and Windows 95, class Microsoft Windows in 005.268.)

See also discussion at 005.269 and 005.284, 005.3684, 005.384.

If two or three of these numbers are applicable to the same work, follow the preference note at 005 and class with the number coming last in the schedule (with the exception specified below). For example, if a work treats writing software that runs on a specific computer, on a specific operating system, and on a specific add-on user interface, prefer 005.269. Exception: If a specific computer has only one operating system, so that all programs that run on that computer also run on the operating system, e.g., the Apple iMac® series of computers and Mac OS X®, class writing programs that run on that computer and operating system with the computer in 005.265. Earlier and later versions of the same operating system (e.g., Macintosh System 9® and Mac OS X®) count as one operating system, even though the differences between the earliest and the latest versions may be great.

If in doubt, prefer in the following order: 005.268 and similar numbers, 005.269 and similar numbers, 005.265 and similar numbers.

005.269 and 005.284, 005.3684, 005.384

User interfaces

The native interface of an operating system is the user interface bundled inseparably with the operating system.

005.3

Programs

Class a program or programs designed to run on two types of computers with the predominant type if there is one, e.g., a program that runs on five mainframe computers and one midrange computer 005.32. If neither of two types is predominant, class with the smaller type, e.g., a program for midrange and personal computers 005.36.

Class programs for a specific application in computer science with the application in 005–006, but never in 004. Among the numbers most frequently used for software besides 005.3 and its subdivisions are 005.43 for systems software and operating systems, 005.5 for general purpose application software (such as word processing programs and spreadsheets), 005.713 for interfacing and data communications programs, 005.74 for database management systems, and 006.68 for computer graphics programs.

Programs applied to a particular subject or discipline are classed with the subject or discipline, plus notation 028553 from Table 1, e.g., programs for tax accounting 657.46028553.

See also discussion at T1—0285; also at 005.1 vs. 005.3.

005.3, 005.5 vs. 005.43–.45

Application programs vs. Systems programs

Use 005.3 for collections of or works about multiple kinds of application programs, and for comprehensive works on application programs and systems programs. Application programs are programs that do things users want done, for example, electronic spreadsheets, statistical packages, word processing programs, desktop publishing programs, computer games, educational programs, tax preparation programs, inventory control programs.

Use 005.5 for general purpose application programs, such as spreadsheets, statistical packages, word processing programs.

Use 001–999 for application programs employed in a specific discipline, e.g., application programs employed in library operations 025.0028553, computer games 794.8.

Use appropriate subdivisions of 005.3 for works about application programs that run on specific systems, e.g., application programs that run on a specific personal computer operating system 005.3682.

Use 005.43–.45 for systems programs and works about them. Systems programs are programs that enable computers to function properly; in effect, they provide life support and housekeeping for computers. Systems programs accomplish little that interests users except to make it possible for application programs to run. Examples of systems programs are operating systems, utilities packages, user interfaces, and programming language translators.

If in doubt, prefer 005.3 and its subdivisions.

See also discussion at 005.3682 vs. 005.365, 005.3684.

005.3682 vs. 005.365, 005.3684

Programs for specific operating systems, for specific computers, and for specific user interfaces

Numbers beginning with 005.36 are limited to personal computers. Similar numbers for other types of computers, with instructions for building numbers by adding notation from 005.36 numbers, are found in 005.32–.34 and 005.37.

Use 005.3682 (and similar numbers for other types of computers) for application programs that run on specific computer operating systems, and comprehensive works on application and systems programs that run on specific computer operating systems. Use 005.365 (and similar numbers for other types of computers) for application programs that run on specific computers, and comprehensive works on application and systems programs that run on specific computers. Use 005.3684 (and similar numbers for other types of computers) for application programs that run on specific user interfaces other than the native interface of the computer operating system, and comprehensive works on application and systems programs that run on specific user interfaces other than the native interface of the computer operating system. (Class Microsoft Windows® versions 3.x in 005.3684; starting with Windows NT and Windows 95, class Microsoft Windows in 005.3682.)

See also discussion at 005.269 and 005.284, 005.3684, 005.384.

If two or three of these numbers are applicable to the same work, follow the preference note at 005 and class with the number coming last in the schedule (with the exception specified below). For example, if a work treats application programs that run on a specific computer, on a specific operating system, and on a specific add-on user interface, prefer 005.3684. Exception: If a specific computer has only one operating system, so that all programs that run on that computer also run on the operating system, e.g., the Apple iMac® series of computers and Mac OS X®, class programs that run on that computer and operating system with the computer in 005.365. Earlier and later versions of the same operating system (e.g., Macintosh System 9® and Mac OS X®) count as one operating system, even though the differences between the earliest and the latest versions may be great.

If in doubt, prefer in the following order: 005.3682 and similar numbers, 005.3684 and similar numbers, 005.365 and similar numbers.

See also discussion at 005.3, 005.5 vs. 005.43–.45.

005.74 vs. 005.436

File managers and file organization

Use 005.74 or 005.75 for a file manager in the sense of software that manages data files, providing the ability to create, enter, change, query and produce reports on a data file or data files. Use 005.436 for a file manager in the sense of software that is used to manage files and directories on a computer, providing the ability to delete, copy, move, rename and view files and directories. A file manager in this latter sense may be part of an operating system or a separate utility program. Use 005.436 for comprehensive works on both kinds of file managers.

Use 005.741 for works on file organization in the sense of the structure of data within a single file that permits access to the data. Use 005.436 for works on file organization in the sense of the way that multiple files are organized on a disk or other storage medium.

If in doubt, prefer 005.74.

006.3 vs. 153

Cognitive science

Cognitive science is the interdisciplinary study of the mind and computers as information processing systems.

Use 006.3 for cognitive science if the goal is to produce computer systems with better artificial intelligence. Use 153 for cognitive science if the goal is to understand better how the human mind works. If in doubt, prefer 006.3.

006.35 vs. 410.285

Computational linguistics vs. Computer applications in linguistics

Use 006.35 for works on computational linguistics. Use 410.285 for computer applications in linguistics in general. For example, use 410.28553 for general software tools, e.g., programs that generate concordances. If in doubt, prefer 006.35.

006.37 vs. 006.42, 621.367, 621.391, 621.399

Computer vision, optical pattern recognition, and optical computers

Computer vision and optical pattern recognition

Computer vision and optical pattern recognition both involve recognition of forms, shapes, or other optical patterns for the purpose of classification, grouping, or identification; but computer vision makes extensive use of artificial intelligence for the complex interpretation of visual information, whereas optical pattern recognition involves only simple interpretation.

Use 006.37 or 006.42 for works on computer vision and optical pattern recognition that give substantial treatment to the computer programs needed to interpret optical patterns, and also for works treating computer-vision and optical-pattern-recognition devices from the user's point of view. Use 621.399 for works on designing and manufacturing the hardware for computer vision and optical pattern recognition. If in doubt, prefer 006.37 or 006.42.

Use 621.367 for works on devices that record and process optical signals while doing virtually no interpreting (either because interpretation is not needed or because interpretation is left to others—computers or humans), e.g., devices for image enhancement.

Optical computers

"Optical computers" is a term used to describe two different kinds of computers. Use 621.391 for works on optical computers that are general-purpose computers in which the central data processing mechanism is based on light (e.g., lasers). Use 006.37, 006.42, or 621.399 for works on optical computers that are special-purpose computers designed to process optical data, regardless of the type of central data processing mechanism.

011–017

Bibliographies and catalogs

The terms *bibliographies* and *catalogs* are used interchangeably in 011–017. The term *bibliographies* is more likely to be used in relation to works brought together on the basis of subject matter, authorship, time period, etc., while the term *catalogs* is more likely to be used in relation to works held in specific collections or offered for sale. The numbers in 011–017 apply equally to bibliographies and catalogs, regardless of the name given to a specific resource.

011.39 vs. 005.3029, 016.0053, 025.0422

Bibliographies of electronic resources

Use 011.39 for general bibliographies of electronic resources *not limited to computer programs (or software)*. Use 005.3029 for annotated lists of programs with lengthy reviews that are used as buyers' guides, e.g., a collection of reviews of personal computer software 005.36029. Use 016.0053 for bibliographies and lists of programs and for annotated lists if the annotations are relatively brief. Use 025.0422 for bibliographies of web sites, as they are normally indistinguishable from directories of web sites. If in doubt, prefer 011.39.

See also discussion at 011–017; also at 025.04, 025.06 vs. 005.74.

016 vs. 026, T1—07

Bibliographies and catalogs of specific subjects vs. Libraries on specific subjects vs. Table 1 notation for resources for education, research, related topics

Use 016 or 026 for works describing books, manuscripts, recordings, and the like, unless the works also describe kinds of resources not found in libraries and archives or emphasize how to use the library or archival resources for study, teaching, and research.

Use notation 07 from Table 1 for comprehensive works on resources for education, research, and related topics in a specific subject. Many of these resources are found in subdivisions of T1—07, e.g., schools and laboratories, collections of objects (such as botanical collections), and financial support.

Use 016 for works about resources in a field that describe individual works, such as books and articles. Use 016 also for inventories and calendars of archives. Use notation 07 from Table 1 in 016 if the resources being described treat education and research, e.g., a bibliography of material on education and research in mathematics 016.5107.

Use 026 for works about resources in a field that give broad descriptions of whole collections held by libraries, archives, and other information organizations. Such works often include directory information about the institutions and organizations.

If in doubt, prefer in the following order: 016, 026, T1—07.

025.04, 025.06 vs. 005.74

Data files and databases

Although there are technical differences between data files and databases, they are treated as the same for classification.

Use 025.04 or 025.06 for works on the information science aspects of the automated storage and retrieval systems that make databases available: that is, the kinds of things that users need to know about the systems in order to benefit fully from them.

Use 005.74 for computer science aspects of databases: that is, the narrowly technical issues of designing, programming, and installing databases and database management systems.

Use 001–999 for the subject content of databases (and works discussing that content) as if the databases were books, e.g., encyclopedic databases 030, bibliographic databases 010, nonbibliographic chemistry databases 540. Do not use notation 0285574 from Table 1 except for works that focus on the computer science aspects of the databases rather than the subject content.

If in doubt, prefer 025.04 and 025.06.

See also discussion at 011.39 vs. 005.3029, 016.0053, 025.0422.

080 vs. 800

General collections vs. Literature (Belles-lettres) and rhetoric

Use 080 for essays and quotations collected for nonliterary purposes, e.g., quotations collected to answer reference questions about who said something familiar. Use 080 also for collections of writings, statements or quotations on a variety of topics, e.g., a collection of quotations by Winston Churchill on various topics 082. Use 800 for a collection of quotations if all or nearly all the quotations come from works of poetry, drama, or fiction. Also use 800 for a collection of essays or quotations if the intent of the collection, as revealed in prefatory matter, is clearly literary, e.g., to exhibit literary style. If in doubt, prefer 080.

081–089

General collections in specific languages and language families

Class collections originally written in one language or language family with that language or language family. Class collections originally written in two or more languages or language families with the predominant language or language family if there is one. If no original language or language family is predominant, but the work appears in one language as a result of translation, class it with the language in which it appears. Use 080 for collections in which the material appears in multiple languages with none predominant, even if accompanied by translations into the language of the intended audience.

130 vs. 200

Parapsychology and occultism vs. Religion

Use 130 for parapsychological and occult phenomena if they are not presented as religious, or if there is doubt as to whether they have been so presented. Use 200 for works about parapsychological or occult phenomena if the author describes them as religious, or the believers and practitioners consider them to be religious. If in doubt, prefer 130.

Use 130 for knowledge reputedly derived from secret and ancient religious texts but not applied for religious purposes; however, use 200 for editions of the texts, even if annotated from an occultist viewpoint, e.g., discussion of occult traditions derived from the Zohar 135.47, but the text of the Zohar 296.162.

152–158 vs. 150.19

Specific topics in psychology vs. Psychological systems, schools, viewpoints

Certain schools and systems draw their fundamental principles from a few selected psychological topics. When such topics are used to illustrate a system, class with the system in 150.19, e.g., the subconscious, fantasies, and dreams used to illustrate psychoanalytic principles 150.195 (*not* 154). If in doubt, prefer the specific topic in 152–158.

153 vs. 153.4

Conscious mental processes and intelligence vs. Thought, thinking, reasoning, intuition, value, judgment

Many works that claim to be about thought and thinking or reasoning also cover subjects such as memory, communication, perception, motivation, and intelligence. Use 153 (*not* 153.4) for these broader works. Use 153 (*not* 153.4) also for works on "cognitive psychology." Use 153.4 only for works that focus narrowly on thought and thinking, reasoning, intuition, value, judgment. If in doubt, prefer 153.

153.7 vs. 152.1

Perceptual processes vs. Sensory perception

Use 153.7 for comprehensive works on sensory perception and perceptual processes in general, and works that focus on the active, interpretative mental processes associated with perception in general. Also use 153.7 for types of perception that involve more than one sense, e.g., space perception that involves vision and touch 153.752. Use 152.1 for works that focus on the receptive aspects of sensory perception and comprehensive works on perception by a specific sense, e.g., visual perception 152.14. If in doubt, prefer 153.7.

155

Differential and developmental psychology

Some works on the psychology of sensory perception, movement, emotions, physiological drives (152) and conscious mental processes (153) use as research populations people belonging to differential groups, or people subject to environmental influences, that are given in 155.3–.9. Use 152–153 for works in which there is clearly little or no interest in the distinctiveness of the group or influence, or in which the researcher has simply used convenient samples. This is particularly applicable to ethnic and national groups (155.8), adults (155.6), and social environment (155.92).

Sex psychology

Use 155.3 for a study on sex psychology, drawing almost exclusively upon adult middle-class whites, but showing only marginal interest in the class, age, or ethnic group of the respondents. Use 155.3 also for discussion of the social class, national, or ethnic bias of such research, as the interest is in the validity of the findings about sex psychology.

155.89 vs. 155.84

National psychology vs. Psychology of specific ethnic groups in areas where they are not predominant

Use 155.89 for the psychology of nations taken as a whole, and the psychology of ethnic groups that are predominant in an area constituting an independent nation. Use 155.84 for the psychology of ethnic groups taken as a whole and the psychology of ethnic groups in areas where they are not predominant. For example, use 155.89595 for the national psychology of Malaysia or the psychology of Malays in Malaysia; but use 155.849928 for the psychology of Malays taken as a whole, 155.8499280593 for Malays in Thailand. If in doubt, prefer 155.89.

170.92 vs. 171

Persons associated with ethics vs. Ethical systems

Use 170.92 for biography, collected works, critical appraisal of the work of an individual moral philosopher if the ethical system represented by the philosopher cannot be determined. Use 171 for biography, collected works, critical appraisal if the ethical system can be determined, e.g., critical appraisal of the ethics of Jeremy Bentham 171.5092. If in doubt, prefer 170.92.

180–190

History, geographic treatment, biography

Class single works by individual philosophers with the topic in philosophy. If there is no focus on a specific topic, class a work expressing primarily the philosopher's own viewpoint with the collected works of the philosopher in 180–190, e.g., use 193 for a general work by Hegel, such as *Phenomenology of Spirit*.

Class a work by an individual philosopher that is primarily a discussion of other philosophers' writings with the other philosophers' writings. For example, use 190 for a work by a western philosopher that is mostly a criticism of contemporary philosophers.

Use 100 for a work by an individual that takes a broad look at many questions in philosophy and does not seek to argue for the individual's own viewpoint.

200 vs. 100

Religion vs. Philosophy

Both religion and philosophy deal with the ultimate nature of existence and relationships, but religion treats them within the context of revelation, deity, worship. Philosophy of religion (210) does not involve revelation or worship but does examine questions within the context of deity.

Use 200 for any work that emphasizes revelation, deity, or worship, even if it uses philosophical methods, e.g., a philosophical proof of the existence of God 212.1. Use 180–190 for the thought of a religious tradition used to examine philosophical questions without reference to deity or religious topics, e.g., Jewish philosophy 181.06, Christian philosophy 190. However, use 200 for ethics based on a religion. If in doubt, prefer 200.

200.9 vs. 294, 299.5

Geographic treatment of religion vs. Religions of Indic and of East and Southeast Asian origin

Use 200.9 for works covering various religious traditions in an area, not just the religions that originated there, e.g., use 200.954 for the religions of India (including Christianity and Islam), use 200.951 for the religions of China (including Christianity and Buddhism). Use 294 and 299.5 for the religions that originated in particular geographic areas. Most of these religions have spread beyond the area where they originated. These areas also have adherents of religions that originated elsewhere, e.g., Buddhism (which originated in India) is present in China. If in doubt, prefer 200.9.

200.92 and 201–209, 292–299

Persons associated with religions other than Christianity

Persons associated with the religions in 292–299 are often identified with a number of religious functions and activities. For example, a Hindu guru may be thought of as a theologian, a teacher, a missionary, or a clergyman. If a religious leader cannot be identified primarily with one function, activity, or sect, class the leader's biography in the base number for the religion and add notation 092 from Table 1. Use 200.922 for collected biography of persons from many religions who are not identified with one function or activity. Use a number that corresponds to the number given in the table below for persons associated with a specific religion, e.g., a Buddhist member of a religious order 294.3657092 (corresponds to 206.57092 in the table below). Use the following table of preference for comprehensive biographies of persons primarily identified with one function, activity, or sect:

Founders of religions	206.3
Founders of sects	209
Founders of religious orders	206.57092
Religious leaders (high ranking officials)	200.92
Of specific sects	209
Theologians	202.092
Moral theologians	205.092
Missionaries	207.2092
Martyrs, heretics, saints	200.92
Of specific sects	209
Teachers	207.5092
Members of religious orders	206.57092
Clergy	200.92
Of specific sects	209

Use the subdivisions of 206 for the nature, role, and function of religious leaders. Except for founders of religions (206.3) and founders and members of religious orders (206.57092), do not use the subdivisions of 206 for biography.

Class works dealing with only one aspect of a person's career with the aspect, e.g., Muḥammad as a moral theologian 297.5092 (*not* 297.63).

201–209 and 292–299

Comparative religion

Except for 296 Judaism and 297 Islam, the subdivisions of the various religions in 292–299 are based on 201–209. All topics in 201–209 are provided for under the separate religions in 292–299, either explicitly, by synthesis, or by implication, even if the order is sometimes different. What is said about 201–209, therefore, will also be true of 292–299.

Compare the topics in 201–209 with the subdivisions of Christianity for clues to placement of specific topics. A comparative list follows:

Social theologies	201.7	261
Doctrinal theologies	202	230
Public worship	203	246–247, 263–265
Religious experience, life, practice	204	242, 248
Religious ethics	205	241
Leaders and organizations	206	250, 262, 267
Pastoral theology and work	206.1	253
Missions, religious education	207	266, 268
Sources	208	220
Denominations, sects, reform movements	209	280

Denominations and sects

Class a denomination or sect with the religion to which its own members say it belongs.

Class the early history of a specific religion before its division into sects as general history of the religion, but class a comprehensive survey of the various sects in the number for the sects of the religion, e.g., the sects and reform movements of Buddhism 294.39. Class a work dealing with both early history and sects in the general number for history of the religion.

Class religious orders in 206.5 and similar numbers in 292–299, not with any sect within the religion to which the orders may belong.

203.6, 263.9, 292–299 vs. 394.265–.267

Customs associated with religious holidays

Use 203.6, 263.9, and similar numbers in 292–299 for the religious customs associated with religious holidays, e.g., sunrise Easter services 263.93, lighting the Hanukkah lamp 296.435. Use 394.265–.267 for the secular customs associated with religious holidays, e.g., Easter egg hunts 394.2667, eating latkes and spinning the

Hanukkah top 394.267. If in doubt, prefer 203.6, 263.9, and similar numbers in 292–299.

207.5, 268 vs. 200.71, 230.071, 292–299

Religious education, Christian religious education vs. Education in religion, education in Christianity, in Christian theology

Use 207.5 (and similar numbers in 292–299, such as 294.575 Hindu religious education or 297.77 Islamic religious education) for works on how various religions educate their members (especially young members) to be good followers of their own religions, usually called "religious education." Such education stresses knowledge of the faith and living as a member of a religion, and is meant to instill the values of a particular religion, not to study it in a detached manner. Use 268 for religious education as a ministry of the Christian church for the purpose of confirming believers in Christian faith and life, and religious education programs sponsored by the local church.

Use 200.71 for works on education in and teaching of comparative religion, the religions of the world, and religion as an academic subject, usually called "religious studies." Use 230.071 for works on education in and teaching of Christianity as an academic subject, e.g., a course on Christianity in secular secondary schools 230.0712. Use a similar number in 292–299 for works on education in and teaching of another specific religion as an academic subject, e.g., a course on Hinduism in secular secondary schools 294.50712, on Islam 297.0712.

If in doubt as to which type of education is being treated, prefer 207.5 (or a similar number in 292–299) and 268.

Use 200.711 (*not* 207.5) for works on religious education at the level of higher education, and for works on the education of the clergy. Use 230.0711 (*not* 268) for works on higher education in both Christianity and Christian theology and for works on education of the clergy; all of this education usually takes place in divinity schools, theological seminaries, and graduate departments of theology or ministry in universities. Class education or training of the clergy for specialized work with the specialty, e.g., courses in Biblical studies 220.0711, programs in Christian pastoral counseling 253.50711. Use similar numbers from 292–299, e.g., university education in Islam 297.0711.

Class study and teaching of specific topics in comparative religion, Christianity, or the specific religions in 292–299, as follows:

> Class works on teaching a specific topic to children of primary-school age with works on religious education of children in general, e.g., Christian religious education courses on the Bible for children 268.432; Jewish religious education courses on the Tanakh (scriptures) for children 296.68.

> Class works on teaching a specific topic to persons of secondary-school age and older with the topic using notation 071 from Table 1, e.g., study and teaching of Christian church history in secondary schools 270.0712; study of the Tanakh in Jewish colleges and universities 221.0711.

Use 268.434 for Christian religious education of adults, other than in the setting of formal higher education, e.g., works on adult education in parish religious education programs or Sunday schools.

220.92

Biography of individual persons in Bible

Class a comprehensive biography of a Biblical person with the book or books with which the person is most closely associated, usually the historical part of the Bible in which the person's life is narrated, e.g., Solomon, King of Israel, in 1st Kings 222.53092. Solomon's association with 223 Poetic books is weaker. However, some Biblical persons are more closely associated with nonhistorical books, e.g., class Isaiah and Timothy with the books that bear their names, 224.1092 and 227.83092, respectively. Although they appear briefly in historical narratives, their lives are not narrated in full there. Use 225.92 for the apostles John, Peter, and Paul, since each is associated with a number of books in the New Testament, but use 226.092 for the other apostles, associated primarily with Gospels and Acts.

See also discussion at 230–280.

221

Optional numbers for books of Old Testament (Tanakh)

Alphabetic index

Each of the books of the Old Testament (Tanakh) and the combination of them can have one of three different numbers depending on whether one chooses the preferred arrangement at 222–224 or one of the two optional arrangements. Optional numbers showing the books in the order found in Jewish Bibles appear as the second half of this entry (Option A) and at 296.11 (Option B). The following alphabetic listing gives the three numbers for each book or combination of books:

Book	Preferred	Option A	Option B
Amos	224.8	223.63	296.1143
Canticle of Canticles	223.9	224.41	296.11641
Chronicles	222.6	224.8	296.1168
Chronicles 1	222.63	224.81	296.11681
Chronicles 2	222.64	224.82	296.11682
Daniel	224.5	224.5	296.1165
Deuteronomy	222.15	222.5	296.1125
Ecclesiastes	223.8	224.44	296.11644
Exodus	222.12	222.2	296.1122
Esther	222.9	224.45	296.11645
Ezekiel	224.4	223.5	296.1139
Ezra	222.7	224.6	296.1166
Five scrolls	221.044	224.4	296.1164
Former Prophets	222	223.1	296.1131
Genesis	222.11	222.1	296.1121
Habakkuk	224.95	223.68	296.1148
Haggai	224.97	223.72	296.1152

Hosea	224.6	223.61	296.1141
Isaiah	224.1	223.3	296.1137
Jeremiah	224.2	223.4	296.1138
Job	223.1	224.3	296.1163
Joel	224.7	223.62	296.1142
Jonah	224.92	223.65	296.1145
Joshua	222.2	223.11	296.1132
Judges	222.32	223.12	296.1133
Ketuvim	223	224	296.116
Kings	222.5	223.14	296.1135
Kings 1	222.53	223.141	296.11351
Kings 2	222.54	223.142	296.11352
Kohelet	223.8	224.44	296.11644
Lamentations	224.3	224.43	296.11643
Later Prophets	224	223.2	296.1136
Leviticus	222.13	222.3	296.1123
Malachi	224.99	223.74	296.1154
Megillot	221.044	224.4	296.1164
Micah	224.93	223.66	296.1146
Minor Prophets	224.9	223.6	296.114
Nahum	224.94	223.67	296.1147
Nehemiah	222.8	224.7	296.1167
Nevi'im	224	223	296.113
Numbers	222.14	222.4	296.1124
Obadiah	224.91	223.64	296.1144
Pentateuch	222.1	222	296.112
Prophetic books	224	223	296.113
Proverbs	223.7	224.2	296.1162
Pslams	223.2	224.1	296.1161
Qohelet	223.8	224.44	296.11644
Ruth	222.35	224.42	296.11642
Samuel	222.4	223.13	296.1134
Samuel 1	222.43	223.131	296.11341
Samuel 2	222.44	223.132	296.11342
Song of Solomon	223.9	224.41	296.11641
Song of Songs	223.9	224.41	296.11641
Torah	222.1	222	296.112
Writings	223	224	296.116
Zechariah	224.98	223.73	296.1153
Zephaniah	224.96	223.71	296.1151

Optional numbers for books of Bible as arranged in Tanakh (Jewish Bible, Hebrew Bible) (Option A)

The following schedule is an optional arrangement for books of the Bible as found in Jewish Bibles. The preferred arrangement is at 222–224 in the regular schedule. Option B is given at 296.11 in the regular schedule. The see references and footnote instructions in this optional arrangement refer to numbers in the schedules, not to other numbers found in the Manual entries.

> ### (222–224) Optional numbers for books of Bible as arranged in Tanakh (Jewish Bible, Hebrew Bible)

>> Class comprehensive works in 221

>> *For Apocrypha, pseudepigrapha, see 229*

>> *See Manual at 221: Optional numbers for books of Bible*

(222)   *Torah (Pentateuch)

(Optional number; prefer standard 222.1)

(.1)   *Genesis

(Optional number; prefer standard 222.11)

(.2)   *Exodus

(Optional number; prefer standard 222.12)

For Ten Commandments, see 222.6

(.3)   *Leviticus

(Optional number; prefer standard 222.13)

(.4)   *Numbers

(Optional number; prefer standard 222.14)

(.5)   *Deuteronomy

(Optional number; prefer standard 222.15)

For Ten Commandments, see 222.6

(.6)   *Ten Commandments (Decalogue)

(Optional number; prefer standard 222.16)

(223)   *Prophetic books (Nevi'im)

(Optional number; prefer standard 224)

(.1)   *Former Prophets (Nevi'im rishonim)

(Optional number; prefer standard 222)

(.11)   *Joshua

(Optional number; prefer standard 222.2)

(.12)   *Judges

(Optional number; prefer standard 222.32)

---

*Add as instructed under 221–229

Optional numbers for books of Bible as arranged in Tanakh
(Jewish Bible, Hebrew Bible) (Option A)

(.13)   *Samuel

>   (Optional number; prefer standard 222.4)

(.131)   *Samuel 1

>   (Optional number; prefer standard 222.43)

(.132)   *Samuel 2

>   (Optional number; prefer standard 222.44)

(.14)   *Kings

>   (Optional number; prefer standard 222.5)

(.141)   *Kings 1

>   (Optional number; prefer standard 222.53)

(.142)   *Kings 2

>   (Optional number; prefer standard 222.54)

(.2)   *Later Prophets (Nevi'im aḥaronim)

>   (Optional number; prefer standard 224)

>>   *For Isaiah, see 223.3; for Jeremiah, see 223.4; for Ezekiel, see 223.5; for Minor Prophets, see 223.6*

(.3)   *Isaiah

>   (Optional number; prefer standard 224.1)

(.4)   *Jeremiah

>   (Optional number; prefer standard 224.2)

(.5)   *Ezekiel

>   (Optional number; prefer standard 224.4)

(.6)   *Minor prophets

>   (Optional number; prefer standard 224.9)

>>   *For Zephaniah, Haggai, Zechariah, Malachi, see 223.7*

(.61)   *Hosea

>   (Optional number; prefer standard 224.6)

---

*Add as instructed under 221–229

Optional numbers for books of Bible as arranged in Tanakh (Jewish Bible, Hebrew Bible) (Option A)

(.62)   *Joel

  (Optional number; prefer standard 224.7)

(.63)   *Amos

  (Optional number; prefer standard 224.8)

(.64)   *Obadiah

  (Optional number; prefer standard 224.91)

(.65)   *Jonah

  (Optional number; prefer standard 224.92)

(.66)   *Micah

  (Optional number; prefer standard 224.93)

(.67)   *Nahum

  (Optional number; prefer standard 224.94)

(.68)   *Habakkuk

  (Optional number; prefer standard 224.95)

(.7)   *Zephaniah, Haggai, Zechariah, Malachi

  (Optional number; prefer standard 224.9)

(.71)   *Zephaniah

  (Optional number; prefer standard 224.96)

(.72)   *Haggai

  (Optional number; prefer standard 224.97)

(.73)   *Zechariah

  (Optional number; prefer standard 224.98)

(.74)   *Malachi

  (Optional number; prefer standard 224.99)

(224)   *Writings (Ketuvim)

  (Optional number; prefer standard 223)

(.1)   *Psalms

  (Optional number; prefer standard 223.2)

*Add as instructed under 221–229

224

Optional numbers for books of Bible as arranged in Tanakh
(Jewish Bible, Hebrew Bible) (Option A)

(.2)   ***Proverbs**

       (Optional number; prefer standard 223.7)

(.3)   ***Job**

       (Optional number; prefer standard 223.1)

(.4)   ***Megillot (Five scrolls)**

       (Optional number; prefer standard 221.044)

(.41)   *Song of Solomon (Canticle of Canticles, Song of Songs)

         (Optional number; prefer standard 223.9)

(.42)   *Ruth

         (Optional number; prefer standard 222.35)

(.43)   *Lamentations

         (Optional number; prefer standard 224.3)

(.44)   *Ecclesiastes (Kohelet, Qohelet)

         (Optional number; prefer standard 223.8)

(.45)   *Esther

         (Optional number; prefer standard 222.9)

(.5)   ***Daniel**

       (Optional number; prefer standard 224.5)

(.6)   ***Ezra**

       (Optional number; prefer standard 222.7)

(.7)   ***Nehemiah**

       (Optional number; prefer standard 222.8)

(.8)   ***Chronicles**

       (Optional number; prefer standard 222.6)

(.81)   *Chronicles 1

         (Optional number; prefer standard 222.63)

(.82)   *Chronicles 2

         (Optional number; prefer standard 222.64)

*Add as instructed under 221–229

230–280

Persons associated with Christianity

Use the following table of preference for comprehensive biographies:

Jesus Christ, Mary, Joseph, Joachim, Anne, John the Baptist	232.9
Other persons in the Bible	220
Founders of denominations	280
Founders of religious orders	271
Higher clergy (e.g., popes, metropolitans, archbishops, bishops) prior to 1054	270.1–.3
Higher clergy subsequent to 1054	280
Theologians	230
Moral theologians	241
Missionaries	266
Evangelists	269.2
Persons noted for participation in associations for religious work	267
Martyrs	272
Heretics	273
Saints	270
Saints prior to 1054	270.1–.3
Saints subsequent to 1054	280
Mystics	248.22
Hymn writers	264.23
Religious educators	268
Members of religious orders	271
Clergy prior to 1054	270.1–.3
Clergy subsequent to 1054	280
Members of the early church to 1054	270.1–.3
Members of denominations	280
Christian biography of persons who fall in none of the above categories	270

Add notation 092 from Table 1 as appropriate, e.g., collected biography of saints 270.0922; Pope Gregory the Great 270.2092.

Use numbers in the range 220–269 other than those listed in the table of preference above for comprehensive biographies of persons with specialized religious careers, or for works treating only one aspect of a person's life and work, e.g., a Biblical scholar 220.092.

Use subdivisions of 230 for biography and criticism of individual theologians, e.g., Saint Thomas Aquinas 230.2092. Use 230.044092 for Protestant theologians who are not connected with a specific denomination or who are important and influential enough to transcend their own denominations, e.g., Karl Barth 230.044092. Use 230.092 for theologians not connected with any specific type of theology. If in doubt, prefer 230.092. Class critical appraisal of an individual theologian's thought on a specific topic with the topic, e.g., on justification 234.7092.

Do not use 248.2 Religious experience or its subdivisions except 248.22 for comprehensive biographies, e.g., a biography of Teresa of Avila's religious life 282.092 (*not* 248.2092). However, use 248.2 for biographical accounts written for devotional purposes, not as comprehensive accounts of a person's life, e.g., the story of one's conversion 248.246092.

Do not use 253, 255, and 262.1 for biographies of persons who are members of the groups listed in the table of preference above.

Class biographies of members of specific denominations and sects with the main branch of the denomination rather than with the most specific organization or area, e.g., a biography of a member of the Lutheran Church in America 284.1092 (*not* 284.133092); a biography of a clergyman of the African Methodist Episcopal Church 287.8092 (*not* 287.83); a biography of a Russian clergyman of the Orthodox Church 281.9092 (*not* 281.947092); collected biography of Catholics in the United States 282.092273.

Use 280 without subdivision for members of nondenominational and interdenominational Christian churches. Also use 280 without subdivision if a person living after 1054 belongs to a Christian church, but it cannot be determined which denomination.

If a person does not belong to a church, or if it cannot be determined whether the person belongs to a church, use the historical period that most closely matches the individual's life span or the time period of the individual's greatest prominence in 270 and the country if known, e.g., biography of a 20th-century Christian 270.82092, biography of a 20th-century United States Christian 277.3082092.

See also discussion at 220.92.

231.7652 vs. 213, 500, 576.8

Relation of scientific and Christian viewpoints of origin of universe vs. Creation in philosophy of religion vs. Natural sciences and mathematics vs. Evolution

Evolution versus creation

Use 231.7652 for works on creation science or creationism written by Christians who assume that the Bible provides a chronology of natural history and who rely upon religious premises in responding to theories from the natural sciences. Similarly, use 231.7652 for works that attempt to refute creation science, unless they take the writings of creationists as a starting point from which to demonstrate the case for evolution. On the other hand, use 500 for works by creationist authors that attempt to refute evolution theory by examining the writings, hypotheses, and findings of scientists.

The difficulty stems from the fact that on the question of evolution the *pro* and *con* positions differ so radically that they normally belong in different disciplines, science and religion, respectively. However, when a religious author is trying to enlighten scientists on a specific scientific matter, class the work with science, while if a scientist is trying to enlighten the religious on a specific religious matter, class the work with religion. The correct classification is determined by the intent of the author, and the interest of the readers that the author is seeking to reach, not by the truth, falsity, or validity of interpretations and premises.

Use 231.7652 for comprehensive works including both religion and science.

Use 213 for works that consider the relation between divine creation and evolution as a philosophical problem, without appealing to a particular religion or scripture. If in doubt between 213 and 231.7652, prefer 231.7652.

The most common focus of interest of works belonging in 500 is on biological evolution. Use 576.8 for these works. Use 523.88 if the emphasis of a work is mainly on stellar evolution, 530 if on basic physical principles, 551.7 if on historical geology, and 560 if on paleontology. Use 500 if there is no clear emphasis on a specific branch of science.

241 vs. 261.8

Christian ethics vs. Christian social theology

Some topics are covered in both religious ethics and social theology, e.g., war and peace (241.6242, 261.873). Use 241 for works that focus on what conduct is right or wrong. Use 261.8 for works that may discuss right and wrong, but treat the topic in a broader context as a problem in society and discuss Christian attitudes toward and influence on the problem. Use 241 for works that emphasize what the individual should do. Use 261.8 for works that stress what the church's stance should be, what response the church or Christian community should make to alleviate the problem, or the church's view on problems transcending individual conduct. If in doubt, prefer 241.

260 vs. 251–254, 259

Christian social and ecclesiastical theology vs. Local church and Pastoral care of specific kinds of persons

The local church is the group in which individual believers can meet regularly face to face for worship, fellowship, and church activities—for example, a congregation, a college church group.

Among the more recent forms of the local church are the small groups called basic Christian communities or basic ecclesial communities. These are smaller than parishes or congregations, but, like other forms of the local church, are organized for the general religious welfare of their members, not just for special projects or functions. Class these in the same way as parishes, i.e., class comprehensive works in 250 (or in 262.26 when treated as part of ecclesiology), and class specific aspects with the aspect in the subdivisions of 250.

Use either 250 or 260 for activities undertaken by the church, depending on the context. Use 250 for works intended for the individual practitioner in the local setting. This may be as small as a parish youth group or as large as a counseling program that serves a metropolitan area. Use 261 for the church's attitude to cultural and social problems, and its activities regarding them, unless the context is limited to the local church, e.g., a practical work for the prison chaplain 259.5, but the church's attitude to the treatment of criminals 261.8336. If in doubt, prefer 260.

Use 260 for some activities that can be conducted by the local church, e.g., public worship (264–265), religious education (268), spiritual renewal and evangelism (269), as the context of works on these subjects is often broader than the local church.

Use 262 for church organization, unless the scope is limited to administration of the local church (254).

261.5

Christianity and secular disciplines

Use 261.5 for personal Christian views and church teachings about secular disciplines as a whole, their value, how seriously a Christian should take them, how far the disciplines should affect faith. Class Christian philosophy of a secular discipline with the discipline, e.g., a Christian philosophy of psychology 150.1. In some cases specific provision is made for use of secular disciplines for religious purposes, e.g., use of drama 246.72. If in doubt, class with the secular discipline.

270, 230.11–.14 vs. 230.15–.2, 281.5–.9, 282

Early church to 1054 vs. Eastern churches, Roman Catholic Church

Use 270.1–.3 (*not* 281.1–.4) for the history of the Church prior to 1054, because the early church is considered to be undivided by denominations until the schism of 1054. Use 274–279 for the history of specific churches prior to 1054.

Use 270.1–.3 or 274–279 for the history of the Eastern and Roman Catholic churches before 1054. Use 281.5–.9 or 282 for works on later history or works that cover both the early and later history. If in doubt for works about both Eastern and Roman Catholic churches, prefer 270. If in doubt for works about a specific denomination, prefer 281.5–.9 or 282.

Use 230.11–.14 for theology of Eastern and Roman Catholic churches before 1054. Use 230.15–.2 for later theology.

280.042 vs. 262.0011

Relations between denominations vs. Ecumenism

Use 280.042 for works on the ecumenical movement and interdenominational co-operation. Use 280.042 also for works on relations between two or more specific denominations having notation that differs in the first three digits, e.g., relations between Roman Catholics (282) and Lutherans (284.1). Class works about relations among denominations having the same notation in the first three digits in the most specific number that includes them all, e.g., relations among the various Baptist denominations, between Baptists and Disciples of Christ 286. Class works about relations between one denomination and several others with the denomination emphasized, e.g., relations between Baptists and other denominations 286. Class discussions among denominations on a specific subject with the subject, e.g., the Eucharist 234.163. Use 262.0011 for theoretical works on ecumenism. If in doubt, prefer 280.042.

283–289

Protestant and other denominations

Under the general name of some denominations, e.g., Presbyterian churches of United States origin 285.1, notation is provided for specific denominations, e.g., 285.13. The specific denominations are named church bodies uniting a number of individual local churches, e.g., the Presbyterian Church (U.S.A.) 285.137, the Associate Presbyterian Church of North America 285.13 (the latter denomination is not listed in the schedule). Along with notation for specific denominations, a span for treatment of the denomination by continent, country, or locality will also be provided, e.g., 285.14–.19. Use the notation for specific denominations if the denominations are treated with regard to all or nearly all the geographic area they cover, but use the span for treatment by continent, country, or locality for works on a specific denomination covering a smaller area, e.g., use 286.132 for the Southern Baptist Convention, but use 286.1768 for a state association of Southern Baptist churches in Tennessee (286.1 plus notation 768 for Tennessee from Table 2). Use the span for treatment by continent, country, or locality for individual local churches, regardless of the specific denomination to which they belong. Also use the span for treatment by continent, country, or locality for a work about several specific denominations in one country by area, e.g., a work describing the various Presbyterian denominations in the United States 285.173 (*not* 285.13).

Where the notation for specific denominations is limited to churches that originated in the United States or the British Commonwealth, e.g., the numbers following 284.1, 285.1, 285.2 and 287.5, use the span for treatment by continent, country, or locality for specific denominations in other areas, e.g., use 284.135 for the Evangelical Lutheran Church in America, but use 284.1485 (284.1 plus notation 485 for Sweden from Table 2) for the Lutheran Church of Sweden.

297.092

Persons associated with Islam

Use the following table of preference for comprehensive biographies of persons associated with an identifiable function, activity, or sect in Islam:

Muḥammad the Prophet	297.63
Muḥammad's family	297.64
Muḥammad's companions	297.648
Prophets prior to Muḥammad	297.246092
Other persons in Koran	297.122092
Founders of sects and reform movements	297.8
Founders of Sufi orders	297.48
Higher non-Sufi religious leaders	297.092
Of specific sects and movements	297.8
Theologians	297.2092
Moral theologians	297.5092
Da'wah workers	297.74
Leaders and members of Sufi orders	297.48
Other Sufis (mystics)	297.4
Religious educators	297.77092

Mosque officers	297.092
Of specific sects and movements	297.8
Members of sects and movements	297.8

Use 297.61 Leaders and their work for the role, function, and duties of religious leaders, not for biography of religious leaders.

Class works dealing with only one specialized aspect of a person's career or religious experience with the aspect, e.g., an account of conversion to Islam 297.574092.

Use 297.092 if a Muslim cannot be identified primarily with one function, activity, or sect.

297.26–.27

Islam and secular disciplines

Use numbers outside 200 for works that focus on issues of importance to practitioners of a secular discipline and for works that describe achievements of Muslims working within the discipline, but use 297.26–.27 for works that focus on Islamic theological issues in relation to secular disciplines. For example, class works describing achievements of Islamic arts with art, but use 297.267 for Islamic attitudes toward the arts, e.g., what kinds of music and visual arts are consistent with Islamic beliefs. Use 320.91767 (political situation and conditions in the Islamic world) or another subdivision of 320 for a work on Islam and politics that emphasizes issues primarily of concern to political scientists, but use 297.272 for a work on Islam and politics that emphasizes Islamic religious issues. If in doubt, prefer a number outside 297.

299.93

New Age religions

Class New Age perspectives on health and medicine, environmentalism, gardening, and other activities and areas of knowledge with the subject and discipline under discussion, even if the discussion rejects some of the main tenets of the discipline, e.g., using mental energy to cure illness 615.851.

Use 130 and its subdivisions for New Age literature mostly concerned with psychic and paranormal phenomena.

Use 201–209 for works on some aspects of religion from a New Age perspective if the works do not attempt to speak for a particular known religion or to establish a new religion or sect, e.g., use 204 for a New Age perspective on spirituality.

Use 299.93 for works concerned with several New Age religions, but use 200 if the work includes sects of the more established religions, e.g., sects of Buddhism, Hinduism, Native American religion, etc.

Use 299.93 for comprehensive works on the New Age as a whole or as a movement.

300–330, 355–390 vs. 342–347, 352–354

Bills, hearings, and legislative reports

Use 300–330 and 355–390 for:

General hearings and related reports, e.g., hearings on the state of the United States economy 330.973

Hearings and related reports on public policy

Oversight hearings and related reports that focus on whether present appropriations, laws, and public policies are meeting the needs of society

Hearings and related reports of legislative investigations not related to proposed legislation, e.g., investigations into political corruption 364.131

Military appropriation and authorization bills, hearings, and related reports

Use 342–347 for:

Bills, hearings, and reports relating to ordinary laws

Bills (including authorizations and appropriation bills) and related hearings and reports that establish government agencies. Use the number for the subject with which the agency deals, e.g., a bill to establish the U.S. Department of Education 344.73070262

Hearings on judicial nominations. Use numbers in 345 and 347, e.g., a hearing on a nomination to the U.S. Supreme Court 347.732634

Use 352–354 for:

Hearings and related reports on nonmilitary authorizations and appropriations that do not emphasize public policy and the needs of society. Use 352.49 plus notation 023 from the table under 352.493–.499 for general hearings and reports, e.g., hearings on appropriations in Germany that do not emphasize public policy and the needs of society 352.4943023. Use the number for a specific agency plus notation 249 from the table under 352–354 for hearings and reports on a specific agency that do not emphasize public policy and the needs of society, e.g., hearings that do not emphasize health policy on appropriations to support health facilities 353.68249, to support health care facilities in Germany 353.6824943023

Oversight hearings focusing on agency internal performance. Use the number for the agency, e.g., an oversight hearing on internal performance of the U.S. Bureau of Indian Affairs 353.53497073

If in doubt, prefer in the following order: 300–330 and 355–390; 352–354; 342–347.

See also discussion at 300, 320.6 vs. 352–354: Nomination hearings.

300, 320.6 vs. 352–354

Social sciences and policy formulation vs. Specific topics of public administration

Public policy

Use 000–199, 300–349, 355–399, 600–999 for the public policy itself (what the policy is or should be, as distinct from how it is formulated or administered) in specific fields, e.g., public policy for libraries 021.8, economic development and growth policies 338.9, welfare policy 361.61, arts policy 700; however, religious policy is classed in 322.1, language policy in 306.449, and science policy in 338.926. However, use 323 for policies with civil rights implications, e.g., citizenship policy 323.6 (*not* 303.4833 or 353.48).

Certain policies have names that suggest one discipline but actually concern another. For example, use 338.926 for technology policy, technology transfer policy, research and development (R and D) policy, and even science policy if formulated in terms of promoting economic growth and development.

Use 320.6 for interdisciplinary works on policy formulation, and works on how society as a whole makes up its mind. Governments usually, but not always, make up the leading parties in policy formulation, e.g., presidents, governors, courts, and legislatures at various levels. Use 320.6 for policy formulation led or mediated by agencies in two or more branches of government, but use 352.34 for policy formulation conducted by executive agencies, how an executive decides upon policies and gets them carried out. Class policy formulation in a specific field by "the government" or society with the policy as explained above, but class policy formulation by executive agencies in specific fields in 352–354, plus notation 234 derived from 352.34.

For example, use 323 for a work about what civil rights policies are or should be, and on how society as a whole decides what they should be; 353.48234 for a work on how a civil rights agency resolves policy issues; and 353.485 for a work on how to administer civil rights policies. Similarly, use 338.9 for a work on economic development, 354.27 for a report on an economic development agency, and 354.27234 for a work on policy making in an economic development agency.

If in doubt, prefer the number outside public administration.

Nomination hearings

Class all nomination hearings for executive officers in 352–354, because it is difficult to determine whether emphasis is on matters like personal qualifications and administrative issues or on the policies that the agency should carry out. Class nominations for the head of an agency in the field that the agency administers, plus notation 2293 from the table under 352–354, e.g., nomination hearing for an attorney general 353.42293.

See also discussion at T1—068 vs. 353–354.

300 vs. 600

Social sciences vs. Technology

Use 300 for works that discuss the social implications of a technology, e.g., the economic importance of lumbering 338.17498 (*not* 634.98). Use 300 for works on the social utilization, the social control, and the social effect of technology. Use 600 for works that discuss how to make, operate, maintain, or repair something, e.g., manufacture of motor vehicles 629.2.

Use 300 rather than 600 for the following categories of material:

1. Works that emphasize the social use of the topic rather than operating or processing it, e.g., tea drinking in England 394.12 (*not* 641.33720942 or 641.63720942)

2. Works that emphasize the overall perspective, e.g., the shift from coal to oil in American industry 333.82130973 (*not* 621.4023)

3. Works that emphasize the social control as opposed to the control exercised during the manufacturing process, e.g., standards of drug quality imposed by a government agency or a trade association 363.1946 (*not* 615.19)

4. Works that cite raw statistics, e.g., crop production, acreage, fertilizer consumption, farm size 338.1 (*not* 630)

Technical reports

Use 300 for technical and research reports that emphasize procedural technicalities and refer to economic, legal, administrative, or regulatory complexities. Consider the purpose of the writer and the mission of the agency authorizing the reports in determining the classification of a report series, and of individual reports in a series. Use 300 if the emphasis is on the exercise of social control over a process or the social aspects of technological processes, e.g., water quality monitoring systems 363.739463 (*not* 628.161), a work describing how railroads serve Argentina 385.0982 (*not* 625.100982); a report on fertilizer and rice studying production efficiency in developing countries 338.162 (*not* 633.1889).

Interdisciplinary works

Use 300 as the interdisciplinary number for a phenomenon of social significance; and as the place of last resort for general works on a subject lacking disciplinary focus, e.g., a work on industrial archaeology not emphasizing how things were made 338.47609 (*not* 609). However, use 600 for works that emphasize descriptions of products or structures, such as clocks, locomotives, and windmills.

Biography and company history

Use 600 for works on artisans, engineers, and inventors. However, use 338.7 for works on artisans, engineers, and inventors who are of more interest as entrepreneurs, e.g., Henry Ford 338.76292092.

Use 600 (or 700 if the interest is artistic) for works on the products of specific companies that emphasize the description and design of the products, e.g., Seth Thomas clocks or Ferrari automobiles. However, use 338.7 if the organization or history of the company receives significant attention, e.g., Seth Thomas clocks 681.113097461, but the Seth Thomas Clock Company and its clocks 338.7681113097461.

301–307 vs. 361–365

Sociology vs. Social problems and services

Use 301–307 only for works on social phenomena that focus on the phenomena themselves and not on actual or potential remedies to any social problems that those phenomena may cause.

Use 361–365 for works on social phenomena that focus on actual or potential remedies to the social problems that those phenomena cause.

Examples:

1. Use 306.85 for the family as a social phenomenon.

2. Use 306.88 for a work discussing the effect of the changing social roles of men and women in the dissolution of the family.

3. Use 362.82 for a work that discusses actual and potential remedies for family dissolution.

If in doubt, prefer 301–307.

302–307 vs. 150, T1—019

Social psychology vs. Psychology

Use 302–307 for works that focus on group behavior, including those that discuss the role of the individual in group behavior. Use 150 for works that focus on the individual, including those that discuss the influence of group behavior on the individual. If in doubt, prefer 302–307.

Use 302–307 without adding notation 019 from Table 1 for application of social psychology to a subject, e.g., social psychology of religion 306.6. Use the number for the subject plus notation 019 from Table 1 for the application of psychology to a subject, e.g., individual psychology of religion 200.19. If in doubt, prefer 302–307.

302–307 vs. 156

Comparative psychology

Use 302–307 for works considering the social behavior of animals as a background to human social behavior. Use 156 for works on comparative social psychology when used to shed light on the behavior of the individual. If in doubt, prefer 302–307.

302–307 vs. 320

Specific topics in sociology and anthropology vs. Political science

Use 302–307 for works on social institutions, processes, and phenomena if they emphasize how the social topics are related to and manifested in political ones, even if they have a political cast. Only use 320 for works on political institutions, processes, and phenomena in which the political aspects are emphasized. For example, use 305.42 (*not* 324.623) for a work on the relation between the feminist movement and the enfranchisement of women. If in doubt, prefer 302–307.

303.483 vs. 306.45, 306.46

Social effects of science and technology

Use 303.483 for the effects of scientific discoveries and technological innovations upon society, e.g., a work on the transformation of religious, economic, and leisure institutions stemming from the development of electronic media 303.4833. Use 306.4 for the patterns of behavior of the individuals and groups engaged in scientific or technical endeavors, e.g., a description of the milieu that seems to be conducive to technological innovation 306.46. If in doubt, prefer 303.483.

305.6 vs. 305.92, 306.6

Sociology of religion and religious groups

Use 305.6 for the sociology of a group of people who are identified as belonging to a particular religion, especially if they are a minority group in a particular place, e.g., a work on the sociology of Christians in Indonesia 305.67598.

Use 305.92 for the sociology of a group of people whose occupation is religious, e.g., a work on the sociology of shamans 305.920144, a work on the sociology of people in Christian religious orders 305.9255.

Use 306.6 for the sociology of religious institutions considered from a secular viewpoint, e.g., a work on the sociology of the Christian Church 306.66.

If in doubt, prefer in the following order: 306.6, 305.6, 305.92.

305.9 vs. 305.5

People by occupation vs. People by social and economic levels

Use 305.9 for works on an occupational group when either

> 1. there is little or no emphasis on social or economic level,

> 2. the group is well represented in two or more distinct social or economic levels, or

> 3. the group has an indefinite or transitional status.

Use 305.5 for works on an occupational group considered in terms of its specific social status. If in doubt, prefer 305.9.

306 vs. 305, 909, 930–990

Groups of people vs. Culture and institutions vs. History

Use 305 for groups of people, e.g., women as a social category 305.4. Use 306 for social institutions, e.g., the family 306.85. Use the number for the institution in 306, plus notation 08 from Table 1, for the role of a specific groups in a specific institution of society, e.g., women in the family 306.85082.

Use 909 and 930–990 for the role of groups of people in history, and for accounts of the major events shaping the history. In particular, use 909 and 930–990 for the history of ethnic and national groups.

If in doubt, prefer in the following order: 306, 305, 909, 930–990.

307

Communities

Use 307 for works on the community in a relatively restricted area as a social phenomenon and works on community planning, development, and redevelopment. These terms are used here in their ordinary meaning to imply the planning for and development of the community as a whole. Use 300 apart from 307 for works where specific subjects of community interest are addressed, e.g., economic development of the community 338.93–.99, developing hospitals for the community 362.11, planning community housing 363.5525, planning the city water supply 363.61, planning the education system 379.4–.9.

320 vs. 306.2

Politics of political institutions vs. Sociology of political institutions

Use 320 for works on the descriptive, comparative, historical, and theoretical study of political institutions and processes, in which the social environment is considered only as a background. Use 306.2 for works on the social dynamics of political institutions, the social sources (e.g., ethnic group, class, family) and the social processes of political institutions, or the impact of these institutions and their activity on the social environment. Use 306.2 also for works dealing with political institutions and processes as models for social institutions and processes. If in doubt, prefer 320.

320.557 vs. 297.09, 297.272, 322.1

Islamism and Islamic fundamentalism

Use 320.557 for works emphasizing the religiously oriented political ideologies of Islamism or Islamic fundamentalism; and for works on Islamism or Islamic fundamentalism that emphasize political aspects from a secular viewpoint.

Use 297.09 and other subdivisions of 297 only for works that emphasize religious aspects of Islamism or Islamic fundamentalism, such as a concern to maintain and hand down a pure version of the Islamic faith, a mindfulness to follow the strict letter of the Koran and Hadith, an attempt to generate a religious reawakening through preaching, teaching, and other forms of religious communication. Use 297.272 only for works that treat politics from the religious point of view.

Use 322.1 for works emphasizing the political role of Islamist or Islamic fundamentalist organizations and groups in relation to the state.

Use notation 082 Religious parties from table under 324.24–.29 for Islamist parties that function as regular political parties, e.g., Turkish Islamist parties 324.2561082, comparative studies of Islamist parties 324.2182.

If in doubt, prefer in the following order: 320.557; 322.1, 324.2; a subdivision of 297.

320.9, 320.4 vs. 351

Government vs. Public administration

Government is limited to considerations of the nature, role, goals and structure of states; their political direction and control; and how central controls are exercised and balanced against each other. Public administration concentrates on executive agencies and the procedures used to carry out their goals, policies, and actions in various fields.

Use 320.9 for works that discuss the habitual conduct and methods of people in high office, even if they appear to cover the structure and functions of government.

Use 320.4 for works on the overall structure of governments, emphasizing their chief legislative, judicial, and executive organs, or for works that discuss typical activities of the different branches, e.g., regulating safety as an illustration of the police function. Use 320.4 also for comprehensive works on government and public administration of specific areas, but not for works emphasizing the work of carrying out goals and policies. Use 320 for interdisciplinary works on government and public administration not limited to specific areas.

Use 351 for works that emphasize agencies of the executive branch, or the usual components of administration: planning, organizing, staffing, financing, and equipping agencies to do a job.

If in doubt, prefer in the following order: 320.9, 320.4, 351.

322.1 vs. 201.72, 261.7, 292–299

Politics and religion

Use 322.1 for works discussing the relationships between religious organizations or movements and states or governments from a secular perspective. Use 201.72, 261.7, and similar numbers in 292–299 for works on the position that religious people and organizations take or should take toward political affairs (including the state). If in doubt, prefer 322.1.

324 vs. 320

The political process vs. Politics and government

Use 324 for works limited to party politics, but use 320 for comprehensive works on politics. "Politics" in the caption at 320 covers the concepts of adjusting relationships among individuals and groups in a political community, guiding and influencing the policy of government, and winning and holding control of society. If in doubt, prefer 324.

See also discussion at 909, 930–990 vs. 320.

324 vs. 320.5, 320.9, 909, 930–990

Political movements

Use 324 for works on the attempts of political movements to achieve power by nonviolent means and their ventures into electoral politics (even as splinter parties with scant chance of success). Use 320.5 for works concerning the thought and internal history or dynamics of political ideological movements. Use 320.5 also for comprehensive works on specific ideological movements. Use 320.9 for the impact of these movements on the political system and their interaction with other political forces. Use 909, 930–990 for works on movements that come to power or directly affect the major events of history. If in doubt, prefer in the following order: 324, 909 and 930–990, 320.9, 320.5.

See also discussion at 909, 930–990 vs. 320.

324.2094–.2099 and 324.24–.29

Political parties in specific continents, countries, localities in modern world

Use 324.209 (or 324.21 for specific kind of party) for treatment of political parties by continent and by region larger than a specific country, e.g., political parties in Europe 324.2094; Conservative parties in Europe 324.214094.

Use 324.24–.29 for treatment of political parties by country, using area notation for country from Table 2, followed by notation to express the party, e.g., political parties in United Kingdom 324.241; the Conservative Party 324.24104.

Use the country number in 324.24–.29, followed by notation to express the party, plus notation 09 from Table 1, for treatment of political parties by locality within a country, since in most countries the local party is a branch of the national party, or, at least, a local organization of persons who regard themselves as members of a national party, e.g., the Conservative Party in Wales 324.2410409429 (*not* 324.242904). Use the same rule for works on regionalist parties, e.g., a regionalist party in Wales 324.241098409429 (*not* 324.2429084). Use the national number, plus modified standard subdivision 324.2094–.2099 and 009, for comprehensive works on parties of a specific part of a nation, e.g., parties of Wales 324.241009429, of Catalonia 324.246009467.

However, for Canada, the United States, and Australia, each of which has strong traditions of autonomy for state and provincial parties, the political parties of states and provinces are treated like "countries" rather than like "localities," e.g., political parties of New York State 324.2747 (*not* 324.27309747); the Democratic Party in New York State 324.274706 (*not* 324.273609747). Regions and localities are subordinated to national or state and provincial numbers, e.g., the Democratic Party in the Midwest 324.27360977, in New York City 324.274706097471.

330 vs. 650, 658

Business

Use 330 for works on business that present general information, economic conditions, financial information (such as interest rates), and reports on what certain companies are doing. Use 650 for works on business that emphasize practical managerial information and that cover 651 Office services as well as 658 General management. Use 658 if the work is limited to management. Use 330 for comprehensive works on 330 and 650. If in doubt, prefer 330.

331.120424 vs. 331.1377

Full employment policies vs. Prevention and relief of unemployment

Use 331.120424 for works on government labor policies and programs wider than simply combating unemployment, e.g., public service employment as a measure to provide both jobs for the unemployed and assistance to distressed areas and state and local governments. Use 331.1377 for works on government labor policies and programs that discuss them solely in terms of prevention and relief of unemployment. If in doubt, prefer 331.120424.

332, 336 vs. 339

Macroeconomics

Use 332 and 336 for works on economic topics considered in their own right, e.g., monetary activities of central banks 332.112. Use 339 if the topics are discussed in relation to the total economic picture of a country or region, since macroeconomics is the study of the economy as a whole, especially with reference to its general level of output and income and the interrelationships among sectors of the economy, e.g., activities of central banks undertaken primarily to carry out macroeconomic policy 339.53. If in doubt, prefer 332 and 336.

332 vs. 338, 658.15

Financial topics in production economics and financial management

Use 332 for works discussing financial topics from the viewpoint of people or organizations with money to invest and those who serve them—investors, bankers, stockbrokers, and the like. Use 338 for works discussing financial topics from the viewpoint of people concerned with the production of goods and services, or who are interested in capital because it is necessary for production. For example, use 332.6722 (domestic investment in specific types of enterprise) for a work discussing whether mining is a safe and profitable field of investment for the general public; but use 338.23 (financial aspects of extraction of minerals) for a work discussing whether the mining industry will attract enough investment to expand production. Use 658.15 (or the subject plus notation 0681 from Table 1) for works discussing financial topics from the viewpoint of an executive responsible for the financial management of an organization, or works that focus narrowly on managerial concerns. If in doubt, prefer 332.

332.632044 vs. 332.6323

Gilt-edged securities

Use 332.632044 for works on all types of gilt-edged securities. In American usage the term may refer to any security of exceptionally high quality, or it may refer primarily to high-quality bonds. Use 332.6323 for works only on bonds. Use 332.63232 also for British works on gilt-edged securities, as in British usage the term refers to government bonds. If in doubt, prefer 332.632044.

332.6322 vs. 332.6323

Stocks

Use 332.6322 for stocks in the sense of shares (American usage), but use 332.6323 for stocks in the sense of bonds (British usage). If in doubt, prefer 332.6322.

333.7–.9 vs. 363.1, 363.73, 577

Social aspects of ecology

Use numbers in 300 rather than 577 for works on ecology and specific natural environments that discuss public policy and resource economics rather than biology. Class works on natural resource management, environmental impacts and monitoring, risk assessment, development, conservation and biodiversity as follows:

1. Natural resource management: Use 333.7 or the number for the specific resource, e.g., management of wetlands 333.918.

2. Environmental impacts and monitoring:

A. The resource situation in general: Use 333.7 or the number for the specific resource (without adding any further subdivisions), e.g., monitoring biodiversity 333.95;

B. Environmental impacts: Use 333.714 or the number for the specific resource plus notation 14 from the table under 333.7–.9, e.g., monitoring the impact of reclamation projects on wetlands 333.91814;

C. Pollution levels: Use 363.7363 or the number for the specific kind of pollutant or environment plus notation 63 from table under 362–363, e.g., monitoring oil pollution 363.738263. (However, use 333.7–.9 as instructed under 2. B. above for the impact of pollution, e.g., monitoring the impact of oil pollution on wetlands 333.91814);

D. Potential environmental impacts: Class with the development whose impact is being studied, e.g., the potential impact of an oil pipeline on tundra ecology 388.55.

3. Risk assessment:

A. Generalized risks to the environment: Class as an impact study in 333.714 or the number for the specific resource plus notation 14 from the table under 333.7–.9, e.g., contemporary risks to wetlands of America 333.918140973;

B. Safety risks: Use the subdivision for the specific threat in 363.1 plus notation 72 from the table under 362–363, e.g., assessing the risk to humans of pesticides in food 363.19272;

C. Risks of specific developments: Class with the specific development as a study of potential impacts, e.g., assessing the risk of tourism to biodiversity in East Africa 916.7604.

4. Development: Use 333.715 or the number for the specific resource plus notation 15 from the table under 333.7–.9, e.g., hydroelectric power development 333.91415.

5. Conservation: Use 333.72 or the number for the specific resource plus notation 16 from the table under 333.7–.9, e.g., conservation of biodiversity 333.9516.

6. Biodiversity: Use 333.95 (especially for works emphasizing its value or importance).

If in doubt, prefer in the following order: 333.7–.9, 363.1, 363.73, 577.

See also discussion at 363.73 vs. 571.95, 577.27.

333.7–.9 vs. 363.6

Natural resources and energy vs. Public utilities

Use 333.7–.9 for comprehensive works on resources, projection of needs and sup-plies, development, conservation and protection of resources. Use 363.6 for works on problems and services related to utilities distributing and delivering the re-sources to users. Use 333.7–.9 for "supply" as a noun, but use 363.6 for "supply" as a verb. If in doubt, prefer 333.7–.9.

However, use 333.7932 for a work about distribution of electrical power by utilities if the work emphasizes the problems of developing the supply of electricity, says little about the problems of distributing the electricity to customers, and does not discuss prices without reference to production costs.

Use 333.717 or a number for a specific resource in 333.7–.9 plus notation 17 from the table under 333.7–.9 for works on the rationing of natural resources still in their natural state, but use 363 for works on the rationing of final products, e.g., wellhead allocation of natural gas for companies or jurisdictions 333.823317, but rationing of natural gas among consumers or classes of consumers at the other end of the line 363.63. If in doubt, prefer 333.717 and numbers for specific resources in 333.7–.9.

333.7–.9 vs. 508, 913–919, 930–990

National parks and monuments

Use 333.7–.9 for works on national parks where the main attraction is nature if the emphasis is on conservation and protection of natural resources, e.g., forest parks 333.784, game reserves 333.954916. Use 508 or other numbers in 500 if the em-phasis is on description of and guides to natural phenomena, e.g., a comprehensive guide to the natural history of Yellowstone National Park 508.78752, a guide to the geology of Yellowstone 557.8752.

Use 913–919, plus notation 04 from the table under 913–919 followed by notation for the historical period when the guidebook was written, for general guidebooks to all the national parks of an area, e.g., a 1989 general guidebook to the national parks of South America 918.0438.

Class general works about historical monuments with the events commemorated. For example, class a battlefield national park with the battle, e.g., Gettysburg Na-tional Military Park 973.7349. Class a park associated with the life of an individual in the biography number for that individual, e.g., Lyndon B. Johnson National His-torical Park 973.923092, George Washington Carver National Monument 630.92.

If in doubt, prefer in the following order: 333.7–.9; 508 and other numbers in 500; 930–990; 913–919.

See also discussion at 913–919: Historic sites and buildings; also at 913–919: Add table: 04: Guidebooks; also at 930–990: Wars; also at 930–990: Historic preservation.

333.72 vs. 304.28, 320.58, 363.7

Environmentalism

Use 333.72 for works on environmentalism discussing the broader concept of pre-serving and protecting the supply as well as the quality of natural resources and for works about the environmental movement that focus on the concerns it shares with the long established conservation movement. Use 304.28 for works that emphasize the effect upon society of overuse, misuse, or pollution of the environment. Use 320.58 for works that emphasize the political ideologies of environmentalism. Use 363.7 for works on preserving and restoring the quality of the social living space, i.e., taking care of wastes, pollution, noise, the dead, and pests. If in doubt, prefer in the following order: 333.72, 304.28, 363.7, 320.58.

333.73–.78 vs. 333, 333.1–.5

Natural resources vs. Land economics

Use 333.73–.78 for works on land as a natural resource, as a source of economic goods (chiefly agricultural and mineral), and for works on the usage of the land and its resources. Use 333.73–.78, plus notation 17 from the add table under 333.7–.9, for works on control of usage regardless of who owns the land, e.g., price control, zoning. Use 333.73 for comprehensive works on land policy.

Use 333.73–.78 for land inventories, which often focus on land as a resource and land usage.

Use 333 for comprehensive works on land and on natural resources only if the works contain substantial discussion of ownership. It is more common for compre-hensive works on land to contain substantial discussion of ownership than compre-hensive works on other natural resources. Use 333.7–.9 for comprehensive works on natural resources that treat predominantly nonownership aspects. If in doubt, prefer 333.7–.9.

Use 333.1–.5 for land as property, where the central issues are the right to posses-sion and use, and the right to transfer possession and use. Use 333.1–.5 for control of land only if the control is the kind that stems from ownership.

Use 333 for comprehensive works on both 333.1–.5 and 333.73–.78 with respect to land only if the works contain substantial discussion of ownership. Use 333.1–.5 for works on the right to use land and its resources. If in doubt, prefer in the following order: 333.73–.78, 333.1–.5, 333.

333.955–.959 vs. 639.97

Conservation and management of specific kinds of animals

Conservation and resource management are primarily economic concepts. Use 333.955–.959 for works on conservation of specific kinds of animals if the works discuss public policy and programs; give estimates or statistics of populations, abundance, harvest, catches, and kills; make appeals for resource management; and issue calls to protect an animal or save it from extinction. Use 639.97 for works that discuss agricultural methods and techniques and how to carry them out.

A few terms used in conservation work are troublesome because they may refer to either economics or technology. Use 333.955–.959 for works on rescue, reintroduction, management, and habitat improvement of specific kinds of animals, if the works are focused on programs and the rationale behind the activities. Use 639.97 only if the work is focused on hands-on activities where the animals are living.

If in doubt, prefer 333.955–.959.

335 vs. 306.345, 320.53

Socialism and related systems in economics, sociology, and political theory

Use 335 for interdisciplinary works on socialism and related systems, and works on their philosophic foundations, since they are based upon theories of how the economy does or should work. Use 335 also for wide-ranging works that do not fit within normal disciplinary boundaries but are clearly about socialism and related systems. Use 335 also for works discussing how another economic system should be reorganized into a socialist system.

Use 306.345 only for sociological studies of how socialist economic systems work out in practice.

Use 320.53 for works that emphasize how political movements intend to introduce socialism and what political forces they expect to harness to attain and keep power, or that discuss political movements and forces without in-depth discussion of the economic dynamics or theory.

Works in 320.53 and 335 may include material that is prescriptive, that says how society, the economy, or the political system ought to be organized. If in doubt, prefer 335.

337.3–.9 vs. 337.1

Foreign economic policies and relations of specific jurisdictions and groups of jurisdictions vs. Multilateral economic cooperation

Use 337.3–.9 for works on relations between a cooperative group treated as a whole and other countries or groups, e.g., economic relations of the European Union with Japan 337.4052, economic relations of the European Union with the rest of the world 337.4. Use 337.1 for works on cooperative relations among the states of multistate groups, e.g., cooperation within the European Union 337.142. If in doubt, prefer 337.3–.9.

338.091–.099 vs. 332.67309, 338.6042

Location of industry and investment

Use 338.091–.099 for works showing where industry is in fact located, i.e., for works that consider location as a condition. Use 338.6042 for works on the rationale for and the process of locating business organizations, i.e., for works that consider location as an action.

Use 332.67309 for works describing the advantages and disadvantages of making international investments, including establishing international enterprises, in particular areas.

If in doubt, prefer 338.091–.099.

338.092

Business biography

Use 338.0922 for collected biography of businesspeople in many fields. Use 338.040922 for collected biography of entrepreneurs in many fields.

Use 338.1–.4 for biographies of business leaders not limited to a specific enterprise but limited to a specific field, e.g., business leaders in the automotive manufacturing industry 338.4762920922. Use 338.6–.8 for biographies of people associated with the development and operation of specific types of enterprises but not confined to a specific industry or group of industries, e.g., small-business owners 338.6420922, people associated with trusts 338.850922. Use 338.70922 for biographies of company directors on the boards of companies in several industries or groups of industries. Use 338.76 for a biography of an entrepreneur or business leader associated with a specific business enterprise, e.g., the founder of a cosmetics manufacturing company 338.766855092.

338.1 vs. 631.558

Crop yields

Use 338.1 for works on crop yields that are compilations giving the total production of an area. Use 338.16 for works on yields per unit of area if they are taken as indicators of production efficiency, either of agricultural systems using various methods (e.g., crop rotation) or of agricultural systems prevailing in various areas. Use 631.558 only for works that have little or no economic or testing implications, e.g., lists of record yields of various crops. Class with the subject in agriculture if yield studies per unit of area are used in technical tests of varieties or specific production techniques, e.g., yield tests of fertilizer 631.80287. If in doubt, prefer 338.1.

338.926 vs. 352.745, 500

Science policy

Science policy generally focuses on what society should do to promote the utilization of science and the growth of industries and activities based on science. Use 338.926 for works on science policy regarded as a policy or program to promote economic development and growth (use similar numbers in 338.93–.99 for science policy for economic development in specific areas, e.g., Europe 338.9406). Use 352.745 (and similar numbers in 352–354, built with 352.745) for works on public administration of science policy. Use 354.274 for works that emphasize administration of economic development. In the absence of a focus on the social sciences, use 509 for natural science policy in an area. If in doubt, prefer 338.926.

340, 342–347 vs. 340.56

Civil law

Use 340 for comprehensive works that treat civil law as all law that is not law of nations or criminal law (342–344, 346–347). Contrast civil law in this sense with criminal law (345). Use 340.56 for works that treat civil law as a system of law derived from Roman law that is in use to a greater or lesser extent in most countries in the modern world, e.g., Germany, France, Japan, Brazil, and even in some subordinate jurisdictions of countries that otherwise use another system, e.g., the province of Quebec in Canada and the state of Louisiana in the United States. If in doubt, prefer 340.

340, 342–347 vs. 340.57

Common law

Use 340 and 342–347 for works that treat common law as the system of law of England and other countries, such as the United States, whose law is derived from English law, or that treat common law as the branch of English law that derives from the old English courts of common law as opposed to the branch of law known as equity that grew up in the Court of Chancery. Use 340.57 for works that treat common law as law that is not the result of legislation but rather of custom and judicial decision. If in doubt, prefer 340.

340 vs. 808.06634

Legal writing

Use the number for the subject in 340 for works on the composition of legal briefs, law reports, and other documents if the work emphasizes how to make the document comply with the law, e.g., how to draw up a legal contract 346.022. Use 808.06634 for works that emphasize techniques of composition. If in doubt, prefer 340.

340.02–.09 vs. 349

Geographic treatment of law

Use 340.02–.09 for works intended to be general in coverage, even if most examples are taken from a specific jurisdiction. Use 349 for works limiting the law to a specific jurisdiction. For example, use 340.03, general law dictionaries, (*not* 349.7303, dictionaries of American law), for *Black's Law Dictionary*, even though the majority of the cases cited are from the United States. Use 340.025752 for a directory of lawyers who can practice law not only in Maryland but also in other parts of the United States and whose place of residence is in Maryland, but use 349.752025 for a directory of lawyers who can practice in Maryland but whose place of residence need not be in Maryland. If in doubt, prefer 340.02–.09.

340.52

Law and indigenous peoples

Use 340.52 for laws of indigenous peoples that had legal systems of their own prior to their incorporation into the national systems of other groups, e.g., laws of North American native peoples before becoming a part of the United States 340.5273. Use 342–347, plus notation 089 from Table 1, for the laws of such groups on a specific subject, e.g., family law of North American native peoples 346.01508997.

Use 341 for the relations between indigenous peoples and a nation established in their territory before their incorporation into the nation, e.g., treaties between the United States and native American peoples on territorial matters 341.42026673008997.

Use the numbers of the specific jurisdiction in 342–349 for the relations between an indigenous people and a nation established in its territory after its incorporation into the nation, e.g., law regulating nursing services for Aboriginal Australians 344.9404140899915, legal status of Aboriginal Australians 346.94013.

340.9

Conflict of laws

Use 340.9 for works where the key issue is usually which jurisdiction's laws are to govern the case, e.g., whose laws will govern in the case of a Canadian citizen married in France to a citizen of Germany and later divorced in Mexico when a dispute arises as to the disposition of jointly owned personal property? Although usually called private international law, it is not the law governing the interrelationships of nations, but the law governing the conflicts and disputes between private citizens of different nations, and its material is drawn from private law.

341 vs. 327

Law of nations vs. International relations

Use 341 for works that discuss the standards and principles that it is commonly felt should govern international relations, or for works that discuss concrete events from the standpoint of the problems that they pose to this system of order. Use 341.026 for works on treaties and cases of international courts. Use 327 for works that discuss what is actually transpiring in international relations (including the theory as to why things happen as they do), and the effects of what has happened. If in doubt, prefer 341.

341.45 vs. 343.0962

Law of the sea vs. Law of ocean transportation

Use 341.45 for works emphasizing jurisdictional issues of law of the sea, i.e., works that discuss the problems that arise from the fact that the high seas are outside the jurisdiction of any nation. Use 343.0962 for works emphasizing transportation issues of maritime law or admiralty law that consider legal issues that could arise either within or outside a single national jurisdiction. If in doubt, prefer 341.45.

342–349

Geographic treatment of law

Class law limited by geographic area as follows:

1. For law limited to a specific jurisdiction: Use 349 or 342.3–.9 (and parallel numbers, e.g., 343.3–.9) plus the area number for that jurisdiction, e.g., law of Germany 349.43, railroad law of Germany 343.43095.

2. Class the laws of local jurisdictions (cities, counties, subprovincial jurisdictions) as follows:

For the laws of a specific local jurisdiction: Use 349 or 342.3–.9 (and parallel numbers, e.g., 343.3–.9) plus the area number for the local jurisdiction, e.g., tax laws of Bayreuth, Bavaria 343.4331504; by-laws relating to public parks in Sheffield, England 346.42821046783.

For the laws of all the localities of a given area: Use the area number for the jurisdiction that contains the localities, e.g., tax laws of the cities of Bavaria

343.43304, of the cities of Germany 343.4304, laws relating to the public parks of cities in the United Kingdom 346.41046783.

Do not observe the principle of approximating the whole for jurisdictions for which there is no specific area number, i.e., subdivisions may be added for a jurisdiction not having its own number, e.g., Flint, Michigan's and Mt. Morris, Michigan's ordinances governing mental health services to the addicted 344.77437044. (Flint is in an including note at T2—77437 in Table 2, which normally means subdivisions may not be added for it. Mt. Morris, a suburb of Flint, is not mentioned in the including note, but subdivisions may still be added).

3. For the application of law of a specific jurisdiction to a limited area within that jurisdiction: Use the number for the law of the jurisdiction plus notation 09 from the table under 342–347, e.g., German law as practiced in Bavaria 349.4309433, application of German railroad law in Bavaria 343.4309509433.

4. For law limited to a specific regional intergovernmental organization: Use 349.2 or 342.2 (and parallel numbers, e.g., 343.2) plus the area number for that organization, e.g., law of European Union 349.24, railroad law of European Union 343.24095.

5. Class the laws of more than one jurisdiction other than those of a specific regional intergovernmental organization as follows:

> For a collection of laws from various jurisdictions located in a particular area: Use 349 or 342.3–.9 (and parallel numbers, e.g., 343.3–.9) plus the area number for that area, e.g., law of Germany, France, Italy 349.4, railroad laws of Germany, France, Italy 343.4095.

> For laws that affect more than one jurisdiction: Use 341 or 342.3–.9 (and parallel numbers, e.g., 343.3–.9) plus the area number for the area affected, e.g., treaties among Germany, France, Italy 341.02644, international laws regulating disarmament in Germany, France, Italy 341.733094, international laws regulating railroads in Germany, France, Italy 343.4095.

See also discussion at 340.02–.09 vs. 349.

Law of countries with federal governments

In federally organized countries, e.g., the United States, Australia, Federal Republic of Germany, there are two sets of laws: those of the central jurisdiction (national laws) and those of subordinate jurisdictions (laws of the provinces or states). Use the area number for the subordinate jurisdiction for laws of an individual state or province, e.g., criminal law of Virginia 345.755, of New South Wales 345.944. However, use the area number for the federal jurisdiction for laws of the states or provinces taken as a whole, e.g., criminal laws of the states of the United States 345.73, of the states of Australia 345.94. Use the area number for the region for works on the state and provincial laws of a region, e.g., provincial criminal law of western Canada 345.712.

Use of area number for capital districts

Use the area number for the capital district if the laws are, in effect, local laws even though passed by the national legislature, e.g., use notation 753 from Table 2 for laws of Washington, D.C., even though the United States Congress passes some of these laws.

Jurisdiction in time

Class the laws of an area that was at some point not an independent jurisdiction as follows:

1. If the law is still operative in the now-independent jurisdiction, use the area number for the jurisdiction in question. For example, use notation 5491 from Table 2 for a law that is currently operative in Pakistan, even though it was enacted before Pakistan became independent, e.g., use 347.5491052 for the Limitation Act of 1908.

2. If the law is no longer operative in the now-independent jurisdiction, use the area number for the jurisdiction that was previously dominant. For example, use notation 54 from Table 2 for India for a law of 1908 no longer operative in Pakistan.

342.085 vs. 341.48

Civil rights vs. Human rights

Use 342.085 for works on the political and social rights of individuals that are recognized by the laws of a particular jurisdiction or group of jurisdictions. Use 341.48 for works on the political and social rights that are recognized by international agreements (such as the Universal Declaration of Human Rights) as the inherent and inalienable rights of all human beings. If in doubt, prefer 342.085

343.04–.06 vs. 336.2, 352.44

Tax law vs. Taxes and taxation vs. Revenue administration

Use 343.04–.06 for most works on taxes, especially popular works, because they usually explain what the law allows and prohibits, e.g., a work for taxpayers about U.S. income tax deductions 343.730523. Use 336.2 for works on the economics of taxes and interdisciplinary works on taxes, e.g., an economic and political analysis of U.S. tax policy 336.200973. Use 352.44 for works on tax administration, especially the administration of assessment and collection. If in doubt, prefer 343.04–.06.

343.078 vs. 343.08

Regulation of secondary industries and services vs. Regulation of commerce

Use 343.078 for works discussing regulations for topics such as production quotas, quality of the material produced, sizes of products specified, e.g., what services hotels are permitted to provide, how they are to provide them, and what rates they may charge 343.07864794. Use 343.08 for works discussing regulations for topics such as truth-in-labeling, advertising practices, and other aspects of marketing, e.g., how hotels may advertise 343.085564794. If in doubt, prefer 343.078.

345.02 vs. 346.03

Criminal offenses vs. Torts (Delicts)

Use 345.02 for acts considered as criminal offenses, but use 346.03 if those acts are considered as torts (a part of civil law), e.g., libel and slander considered from the standpoint of criminal law or brought as a criminal action 345.0256, but considered as a tort or brought as a civil action 346.034. Whether a particular act is regarded as a crime or as a tort or as neither will often depend on the jurisdiction, e.g., adultery may be regarded as a crime for which the offender may be prosecuted, a tort for which the offender may be sued, or merely as a fact to be adduced in evidence in a divorce case. If in doubt, prefer 345.02.

347

Jurisdiction

The location of the court does not necessarily determine the jurisdiction involved in procedure and courts, e.g., use 347.744 for procedure in a court in Boston, Massachusetts, if it is a state court, but use 347.73 if it is a United States district court.

351 vs. 352.29

Organization and structure of government agencies

Use 351 for general descriptions of administrative agencies and their work if the descriptions cover a representative sample of the agencies of a jurisdiction, e.g., a work on the ministries of the Indian government 351.54. Use 352.29 only for works emphasizing the organizational aspects of departments and agencies, e.g., a work detailing the organizational patterns of agencies of the Indian government 352.290954. If in doubt, prefer 351.

See also discussion at 352–354: Add table: 22.

351.3–.9 vs. 352.13–.19

Administration in and of subordinate jurisdictions in specific areas

Use 351.3–.9 for descriptive works on administration of individual jurisdictions regardless of kind, e.g., administration of the government of Ontario 351.713, of Cook County (Illinois) 351.7731, of Northern Highland (Scotland) 351.41152. This approach ensures consistent classification of works on administration of specific subordinate jurisdictions, since a classifier does not need to decide to which category a specific government belongs, e.g., whether Cook County is urban, or Northern Highland is rural.

Also use 351.3–.9 for works on administration of an individual jurisdiction and its subordinate jurisdictions, e.g., administration of Ontario and its local authorities 351.713. Use 352.13–.19 plus notation 09 from Table 1 only for general treatises on subordinate jurisdictions or on specific kinds of subordinate jurisdictions, e.g., provincial administration in Canada 352.130971, county administration in Illinois 352.1509773, rural administration in United Kingdom 352.170941.

The distinction between 351.3–.9 and 352.13–.19 is carried over under specific topics of public administration in 352–354. Use 352–354 plus notation 093–099 from

Table 1 for reports and practical works on the administration of a specific activity in a given jurisdiction or region, e.g., administration of social welfare in Ontario 353.509713. Use 352–354 plus notation 213–219 from the add table at 352–354 (and with notation 093–099 from Table 1) for theoretical and general descriptive works on how state (provincial) and local administration of a subject in a specific higher jurisdiction or region has been or should be conducted, e.g., local administration of social welfare in Ontario 353.521409713.

If in doubt, prefer 351.3–.9.

352–354

Specific topics of public administration

Agencies and their divisions

Use the same number for the administration of a function and the administration of an agency designated to perform that function. For example, use 354.50973 for both public administration of agriculture in the United States and administration of the United States Department of Agriculture. Also use the same number for an administrative report of a specific agency and an independent study of the functions that the agency performs. For example, use 354.5097305 for both the Annual Report of the United States Department of Agriculture and an independent journal on agricultural administration in the United States.

Use the number that best fits the responsibility of a specific agency. For example, use 352.5 for a general services agency having a wide range of miscellaneous functions, so long as the predominant duty concerns property administration (as is often the case), even if it has sections on archives and personnel training.

For works on a part of an agency, use the number that best fits the responsibility of that part of the agency, even if the number differs from the number for the agency as a whole. For example, use 352.53 for a procurement section in a general services agency, and 352.669 for a personnel training section in such an agency. For an archives section in the agency, use either 352.744 if it promotes archival activity or 026.93–.99 if it maintains general archives of the jurisdiction.

In some cases, the schedule gives a specific name of a generalized type of agency in a class-here note at a given number, referring to a typical agency with such a name. An agency with a similar name but a different function should be classed according to its function. Only when there is a conspicuous difference in the usage of different countries do notes in the schedule explain the difference. For example, at 353.3 one note reads "Class here home departments and ministries, European style interior ministries"; another note reads "See also 354.30973 for United States Department of the Interior."

Use the same number for two agencies that independently cover approximately the same field. However, use notation from the table under 352–354 for an agency that has a different relation to the subject. For example, use 354.760973 for the United States Department of Transportation, but use 354.76280973 for the former United States Interstate Commerce Commission (the ICC, which regulated transportation, not commerce). The base number for administration of transportation (354.76) and the final notation for area (T1—0973) are the same in both cases, but notation 28 for regulation is interposed between them for the ICC.

Use notation in 352–354 for agencies provided for in 352–354, even when the agencies are nominally subordinate to a nonexecutive branch of government. For example, use 352.430973 for the United States General Accounting Office, which is officially part of the legislative branch, but which performs a classical executive function of reviewing accounts and judging the effectiveness of expenditures throughout the government.

See also discussion at T1—068 vs. 353–354.

Add table

22

Organization and structure of government agencies

Use a number in 352–354 without adding notation 22 for general works on specific agencies, e.g., a work describing the Indian Home Ministry 353.30954. Use numbers in 352–354 plus notation 22 only for works emphasizing the organizational aspects of departments and agencies. If in doubt, prefer the number in 352–354 without notation 22.

See also discussion at 351 vs. 352.29.

2293

Heads of departments and agencies

Secretaries of state

Use notation 2293 for secretaries of state in the United Kingdom and countries in the Commonwealth of Nations, where the term is a generic one for heads of executive departments, often of cabinet level. (General works on this kind of secretary of state are classed in 352.293.)

Use 353.22930973 for the Secretary of State of the United States, a position equivalent to foreign minister or minister of foreign affairs in most other countries.

Do not use notation 2293 for secretaries of state in states of the United States. Most state secretaries of state may be classed in 352.387 plus notation 0974–0979 from Table 1 when their central duty is the authentication, maintenance, and preservation of important state papers and other records, and the compilation of organization manuals of the state government. When the office of a specific secretary of state has a range of duties that does not fit comfortably in the records management number, class the office in other numbers in 352–354.

Agencies named for their heads

Do not use notation 2293 from the add table with numbers in 352–354 for departments (usually quite small ones) named for their heads, e.g., offices of inspectors general or offices of ombudsmen. These agencies, and reports issued in the name of their heads, are classed in the number that most nearly approximates their duties, e.g., reports of inspectors general and ombudsmen 352.88, reports of ombudsmen in personnel agencies 352.6235.

27–28

Public administration of supporting and controlling functions of government

Use notation 27 and 28 in fields where the role of government is commonly both supportive and regulatory. For example, use notation 27 throughout 354 in the special sense of administering development, or research and development, as explained under 354.27 in the schedule. Likewise, use notation 28 in much of 354 in the special sense of controlling public utilities, as explained under 354.428 and 354.728 in the schedule.

Do not use notation 27 in fields where the primary role of government is supportive, and do not use 28 in fields where the primary role of government is regulatory. For example, use 353.78 (*not* 353.7827) for administration of recreation agencies, because most recreation agencies support recreation; and use 353.9 (*not* 353.928) for administration of safety agencies, because the primary role of safety agencies is safety regulation. Use notation 27 and 28, however, for the less common function of these agencies, e.g., works on regulating recreation 353.7828, and works on administration of programs promoting safety 353.927.

352.13 vs. 352.15

State and provincial administration vs. Intermediate units of local administration

Use 352.13 for territorial subdivisions with an extent that places them distinctly above "local administration," regardless of what they are called. The following list indicates the major territorial units that can currently be regarded as equivalent to "states and provinces" as defined in the note at 352.13:

Argentina   (provinces)
Australia   (states)
Brazil   (federal units)
Canada   (provinces)
Chile   (regions)
China   (provinces, autonomous regions)
(former) Czechoslovakia   (regions)
Ethiopia   (federal states)
France   (regions)
Germany   (states)
India   (states)
Indonesia   (provinces)
Iran   (provinces)
Italy   (regions)
Japan   (regions)
Korea   (regions)
Mexico   (states)
Nigeria   (states)
Pakistan   (provinces)
Peru   (regions)
Philippines   (regions)
Russia   (provinces, territories, autonomous republics)

South Africa   (provinces)
(former) Soviet Union   (union republics)
Spain   (autonomous communities)
Sudan   (regions)
United States   (states)
(former) Yugoslavia   (republics, autonomous provinces)

Also use 352.13 for similar units that may be created in the future, and for "territories" in the sense of areas on the road to statehood, e.g., historic treatment of administration in territories of the United States 352.13097309.

Use 352.16 for general treatment of special urban units coordinate with states and provinces, e.g., administration of nationally controlled municipalities in China 352.160951.

Use 352.15 for all other units intermediate between the national governments and the primary units of local administration.

355–359 vs. 623

Military science vs. Military and nautical engineering

Use 623 for physical description, design, manufacture, operation, and repair of ordnance; use 355–359 for procurement and deployment, and also for the units and services that use the ordnance. Histories of the development of weapons emphasizing the interplay of human and social factors are regarded as procurement history, and are classed in 355.8 and similar numbers in 356–359 (e.g., 359.8, numbers built with notation 8 from add table under 356–359). If in doubt, prefer 355–359.

355.1409

History, geographic treatment, biography

Class uniforms of several participants in a particular war in the area number corresponding to the one used for the war in general history, e.g., uniforms of the Peninsular War (part of the Napoleonic Wars classed in 940.27) 355.14094, not 355.140946.

Class uniforms of a specific branch of the armed services with the branch, e.g., uniforms of the Royal Air Force 358.41140941.

359.32 vs. 359.83

Ships as naval units vs. Ships as transportation equipment and supplies

Use 359.32 or similar numbers in 359.9 (e.g., 359.933, 359.9435, 359.9853) when a work on ships focuses on matters normally covered by analogous works on regiments and other military units, e.g., the crew and its organization, duties, effectiveness, and history. Works about a specific ship will usually consider the ship as a naval unit (unless there is only one ship of a class). Use 359.83 or similar numbers in 359.9 (e.g., 359.9383, 359.94835, 359.98583) when the work focuses on development, procurement, operation, and actual or potential combat effectiveness of the hardware, or when discussion of personnel or personalities focuses on persons responsible for development and procurement of ships, e.g., Admiral Rickover's work in developing nuclear submarines 359.93834092. Use 359.83 also for comprehensive works. If in doubt, prefer 359.32.

Use notation 09 from Table 1 plus country numbers from Table 2 for either specific ships, or a number of ships of a specific class employed by a specific nation.

361–365

Social problems and services

Problems and services are often linked terms, and, where one is spelled out, the other is implied, e.g., addiction at 362.29 implies services to the addicted, and services of extended medical care facilities at 362.16 imply the problems that require such services.

See also discussion at 300 vs. 600.

361–365 vs. 353.5

Social problems and services vs. Public administration of social welfare

Much of the material on social problems and services consists of government reports or gives considerable emphasis to the political and legal considerations related to social services. Use 361–365 for reports about welfare programs and institutions or for works that focus on the problem or the service, e.g., a discussion of political obstacles to effective poverty programs 362.5, a discussion of the political maneuvering behind the adoption of an act of the United States Congress spelling out a new housing program 363.580973. Use 353.5 for reports concentrating on the administrative activities of agencies supporting and regulating the programs and institutions. If in doubt, prefer 361–365; however, prefer 353.5 for administrative annual reports of government agencies.

361 vs. 362–363

Social problems and social welfare in general vs. Specific social problems and services

Use 361 for comprehensive works on the whole range of problems and services found in 362–363, for works on principles and methods of assessing and solving the problems when the works do not address a specific problem, and for works on the principles and methods of welfare work in general. Use the number for a specific problem in 362–363, plus notation 5 from the table under 362–363, for works on the application of the principles and methods to a specific problem, e.g., social work with poor people 362.553, housing allocation to relieve discrimination 363.55. If in doubt, prefer 361.

362–363 vs. 364.1

Specific social problems and services vs. Criminal offenses

Use 362–363 for a human activity considered as a social problem, but use 364.1 for the activity treated as a crime, e.g., drug addiction as a social problem 362.29, but illegal use of drugs 364.177; suicide as a social problem 362.28, but suicide treated as a crime 364.1522. If in doubt, prefer 362–363.

362.1–.4 and 614.4–.5

People with illnesses and disabilities and Incidence of and public measures to prevent disease

Use 362.1 and 362.4 for works on the social provision of services to people with physical illnesses or disabilities. Use 614.4–.5 for works on preventive measures, regardless of whether the emphasis is medical or social, e.g., social provision of immunization services and works on the medical aspects of immunization 614.47. Use 614.4–.5 for public measures strictly limited to preventive ones, e.g., fluoridation and programs advising people how to avoid cavities 614.5996; but programs to identify and treat people with cavities 362.19767. If in doubt, prefer 362.1.

Use 362.2 for works about the incidence and prevention of mental illness, mental illness as a social problem, and social provision of services to people with mental illness.

Use 614.4–.5 for studies of epidemics and the incidence of physical disease (including mental retardation and physical disabilities) when treated solely from the medical standpoint. Use 362.1 and 362.3–.4 for works emphasizing diseases as social problems. If in doubt, prefer 614.4–.5.

362.1–.4 vs. 610

Biographies and case histories of people with illnesses and disabilities, and biographies of medical personnel

Use 362.1–.4, plus notation 092 from Table 1, for biographies and memoirs of people who are dying and people with illnesses and disabilities if the works lack any other disciplinary focus, since such works typically illustrate the way society addresses itself to fundamental health problems and their solution. Use 001–999 for works that focus on a specific discipline, e.g., a work offering guidance in the Christian life with respect to health misfortunes 248.86, Christian meditations in times of illness 242.4. Use 362.1–.4, without adding notation 092 from Table 1, for studies of individual cases designed for the use of researchers, practitioners, and students in the social services, e.g., studies of services to patients with heart disease 362.19612. Use 616–618, plus notation 09 Case histories from the table under 616.1–.9, for studies of patients describing their illnesses in medical terms rather than their lives in social terms, e.g., case studies of heart disease 616.1209. If in doubt, prefer 362; however, prefer 616.8909, 616.890092, and similar numbers for psychiatric disorders (subdivisions of 616.852, 616.858, 616.89, 618.76), since the consideration of external circumstances is generally subordinated to the discussion of the state of mind of the patient.

Use 610 for most biographies of medical personnel, but use 362 for works on public health doctors or nurses emphasizing their influence on public health services and awareness, e.g., a biography of a doctor noted chiefly for promoting nursing homes 362.16092.

363 vs. 302–307, 333.7, 570–590, 600

Control of technology

Use 363, particularly 363.1 (safety) and 363.7 (environment), for works on control of technology addressing what must be done, regulating how it is to be done, inspecting to see whether or not it has been done, and investigating when it was not done. Use 600 only for works dealing with the technological procedures for carrying out a given operation. Use 363 for institutional breakdown (who let it break), but use 600 for machinery breakdown (finding out what broke).

Use 363 if the author or publishing agency is interested in social service and social need, 304.2 if interested in human ecology, 333.7 if interested in economics, 579 or 580–590 if interested in how organisms survive, 620–690 if interested in how to make things, 628.5 if interested in physical techniques for controlling pollution, 632–635 if interested in how crops survive.

Use 363 for comprehensive works and works oriented toward problems and their solution. Use 302–307 for works giving significant consideration to the social dynamics of the problem, use 333.7 for resource-oriented material, and use 600 for works emphasizing technology.

If in doubt, prefer in the following order: 363, other numbers in 300, 570–590, 600. Especially prefer numbers in 300 for most works produced by commercial publishers and environmental or safety advocacy groups.

See also discussion at 300 vs. 600; also at 301–307 vs. 361–365.

363 vs. 344.02–.05, 353–354

Other social problems and services vs. Law and public administration

Use 363 for the work of agencies by which the government carries out the detailed intent of the law in matters of population, safety, the environment, and provision of basic necessities, including most discussion of policy and most detailed procedures for enforcing law, policy, or regulation. Use 344.02–.05 for the law itself, draft laws, and enforcement of the law in courts with respect to these fields. Use 353–354 for the internal administration of agencies concerned with these fields, including their administrative annual reports. If in doubt, prefer 363.

Law enforcement

Use 363.23 for law enforcement by the police, but use 353–354 for enforcement of the law by government agencies in the sense of seeing that the requirements of the law are being met, e.g., activities of a department of education to ensure that the requirements of the law are being met in schools 353.8. However, use 340 for laws governing how such enforcement should be carried out, e.g., the law governing what measures police may use in enforcing the law 344.0523 (or 345.052 if the work treats matters of criminal investigation). If in doubt, prefer 363.23.

Class enforcement of the law through the courts in 342–347, plus notation 0269 from table under 342–347 where appropriate, e.g., court procedure that promotes the enforcement of tax law 343.040269.

363.1

Public safety programs

The meaning and scope of the word "safety" may vary. Use 363 if the scope covers most of the social services, or even 361 if sufficient 362 material is included. Use

363.2 if "safety" is used narrowly to comprise only the work of the police and fire departments.

Priority of safety

Use 363.1 or 363.3, rather than numbers elsewhere in 300, for those aspects of safety that society must deal with through investigations and programs (the topics in the add table at 362–363), e.g., railroad safety 363.122 (*not* 385.0289). However, use 353.9 for the public administration of safety.

363.1 vs. 600

Safety regulations

Use 363.1, plus subdivision 6 from the table under 362–363 if appropriate, for manuals written by or for safety agencies that discuss technical details useful as background for regulation and inspection of various operations while still focusing primarily on safety services. Use the 600 number for the technology involved for safety regulations that spell out operating and construction techniques in explicit detail, even if the regulations are in the form of an officially promulgated regulation by a safety authority. If in doubt, prefer 363.1.

363.31 vs. 303.376, 791.4

Censorship

Use 363.31 for censorship of movies and programs after being released or aired, e.g., use of v-chips by parents. Use 303.376 for theories of censorship and sociological studies of censorship of movies, radio, and television. Use 791.4 for censorship of films and programs as they are being produced, e.g., censorship through editing. If in doubt, prefer 363.31.

363.5, 363.6, 363.8 vs. 338

Housing, public utilities, and food supply vs. Production

363.5, 363.6, and 363.8 deal with the problems of providing the basic necessities of life, and each has economic implications. Use 363.5, 363.6, or 363.8 for social factors affecting the availability of housing, water, fuel and food, or for social measures to ensure an adequate supply. Use 338 for the effect of these topics on the economic aspects of society, or the impact of economic conditions on the availability of housing, water, fuel, or food. For example, use 363.81 for a study of the mismatch between the expected growth of the food supply and of the population, but use 338.19 for a study of the effect of a drop in farm prices on the food supply. If in doubt, prefer 363.5, 363.6, or 363.8.

363.5 vs. 307.336, 307.34

Housing

Use 363.5 for works on housing problems and solutions addressed specifically to housing. Use 307.336 for the descriptive analysis of housing patterns that treats problems in the context of the sociology of communities. Use 307.34 for works addressing housing problems in the context of restructuring whole communities. If in doubt, prefer in the following order: 363.5, 307.34, 307.336.

363.5 vs. 643.1

Housing vs. Houses

Use 363.5 for interdisciplinary works on housing that treat the social aspects of lodging, as the term "housing" normally refers to the provision of lodging considered in the abstract. Use 643.1 for interdisciplinary works on houses and their use and for the home economics aspects of either housing or houses, as the term "houses" normally refers to the buildings considered as physical objects. If in doubt, prefer 363.5.

363.61

Water reports

Use 363.61 for reports concentrating on the problem of treating and delivering water to consumers and for interdisciplinary reports on water supply. Use 333.91 for water supply reports concentrating on water used, or needed in the future; 363.7284 for reports concentrating on assuring that wastewaters are properly treated; 363.739472 for reports concentrating on protection of natural waters; and 553.7 for reports concentrating on the supply of water on hand. If in doubt, prefer 363.61.

Use 333.9116 for general works on monitoring to protect water quality; 553.7, plus notation 1–9 from Table 2 where appropriate, for reports that describe the present chemical and biological status of available water but do not not focus on a specific objective, e.g., a base-line study of the quality of French surface waters 553.780944; 363.61 for water quality monitoring reports as tools for assuring compliance with water supply standards; 363.739463 for such reports as tools for assuring compliance with wastewater pollution standards; 628.16 for reports as tools for determining plant loads and technical difficulties in water treatment; and 628.3 for reports as tools for checking the effectiveness of sewage treatment works.

363.73 vs. 571.95, 577.27

Pollution vs. Toxicology vs. Effects of humankind on ecology

Use 363.7363 or the number for the specific pollutant or environment in 363.738–.739, plus notation 63 from the table under 362–363, for pollution studies in which the growth and decline of biological indicator species is merely used to measure the extent and kind of pollution, and interpreted to suggest the need for, or sufficiency of, remedial measures, e.g., acid rain monitoring by use of indicator species 363.738663.

Use 571.95 for the pathological conditions caused by pollution and other agents in tissues of organisms. Use 577.27 or the number for the specific ecological environment (biome) in 577.3–.7, plus notation 27 derived from instructions under 577.3–.6 or notation 27 derived from instructions under 577.76–.79, for the more generalized effects of substances upon the community of organisms, e.g., the reduction of species counts (biodiversity) and the general health and vigor of surviving species.

If in doubt, prefer in the following order: 363.73, 571.95, 577.27.

See also discussion at 333.7–.9 vs. 363.1, 363.73, 577.

363.8 vs. 613.2, 641.3

Food supply vs. Dietetics vs. Food

Use 363.8 for works on meeting the food supply needs of society in general and of various social groups and for interdisciplinary works on nutrition. Use 613.2 for works emphasizing how to help individuals meet dietary requirements and maintain optimal balanced intake without gaining or losing weight, for material to help dietitians in planning diets for individuals, and for comprehensive works on personal aspects of nutrition. Use 641.3 for works emphasizing the food itself and for interdisciplinary works on food. If in doubt, prefer in the following order: 363.8, 641.3, 613.2.

371 vs. 353.8, 371.2, 379

School administration and policy

Use 371 for the basic operations and activities of schools and school systems. Use 353.8 only for administration of national and state or provincial departments of education that regulate and support local school systems. Use 371.2 for comprehensive works on school (or school-system) administration and for works covering both 371.2 and 353.8. Use 371.201–.207 and numbers to which reference is made under 371.201–.207 for specific topics in plant and system administration.

Use 379 for policy and debate on major policy issues in education, e.g., discussion of the role of government. Subdivisions are provided in 379 only for general works on support and control of public education, and for a limited selection of major, controversial issues in education. Use 370–378 for public policy and debate concerning all other issues in education (that is, all issues not specifically named in 379).

If in doubt, prefer in the following order: 371, 371.2, 379, 353.8.

371.01–.8 vs. 372–374, 378

Specific levels and topics of education

Use 371.01–.8 for specific topics relating to two or more levels of education, e.g., to primary and secondary education, to secondary and higher education. Use 372–374 and 378 for any or all topics related to a specific level of education. There is specific provision at each level for each specific topic in 371.01–.8, usually in subdivision 1 under each level, e.g., in 372.1. If in doubt about whether a work relates to only one level, or to two or more levels, prefer 371.01–.8.

371.262 vs. 371.264

Standardized tests vs. Academic prognosis and placement

Use 371.262 for works that focus on particular tests and their use. Use 371.264 for general discussions of the use of results of standardized tests in prognosis and placement. Use 371.26 for works giving substantial treatment to both the tests in general and to their use in prognosis and placement. If in doubt, prefer 371.262.

372.24 and 373.23

Specific levels of primary and secondary education

The following tables show some common combinations of grades or sublevels used in primary and secondary education. Use the pattern shown in the first table when individual grades are discussed. That table reflects the 3-3-3-3 plan used in the schedule. The other tables after the first show how other combinations of levels fit into the schedule.

Grades	Number
1–3 (Lower primary level)	372.241
4–6 (Intermediate primary level)	372.242
7–9 (Lower secondary level)	373.236
10–12 (Upper secondary level)	373.238

The 6-6 pattern:

Grades	Number
1–6 (Primary school)	372
7–12 (Secondary school)	373

The 8-4 pattern:

Grades	Number
1–8 (Primary school)	372
9–12 (Secondary school)	373

The 4-4-4 pattern:

Grades	Number
1–4 (Primary school)	372
5–8 (Lower secondary school)	373.236
9–12 (Secondary school)	373

Use the higher level for other combinations of grades unless the majority of the grades are at the lower level, e.g., a primary school covering kindergarten through second grade 372.241. Use 371 for schools extending from first to ninth grade or beyond.

These guidelines apply only to discussion of specific combinations of grades in general, e.g., junior high schools (lower level secondary schools) in the United States 373.2360973. Use the geographic span under the general number for primary or secondary education (or 371.009) for specific schools, e.g., a specific junior high school in Atlanta, Georgia 373.758231.

The source of information for comparison of international levels of education is *International Standard Classification of Education: ISCED 1997* (UNESCO 1997).

378.4–.9 vs. 355.00711

College level military schools

Use 378.4–.9 (378 plus area notation of the place where it is found) for a college level military school that is not an official training academy, that is, those whose students (*except* in wartime) usually enter civilian occupations, e.g., Virginia Military Institute (Lexington, Virginia) 378.755853, The Citadel (Charleston, South Carolina) 378.757915.

Use 355.00711 plus the area notation of the country it serves for an official military service academy (or a similar number for an academy of a specific service), e.g., the Royal Military Academy (Sandhurst, England) 355.0071141, the United States Naval Academy (Annapolis, Maryland) 359.0071173.

If in doubt, prefer 378.4–.9.

380

Commerce, communications, transportation

Since 380 is part of 330, the table of preference under 330 also applies to subjects in 380. Commerce, communications and transportation take the same position in that table as production. Therefore, use 331.1251388 for a work on the labor market in transportation, but use 388.049 for a work on production economics of transportation.

Add table

09 vs. 065

History and geographic treatment vs. Business enterprises

Use notation 09 for the system (facilities, activities, services) maintained by the company in a specific area, e.g., railroad transportation provided by the Union Pacific Railroad 385.0978. For international companies, use notation 09 only when coverage is limited to a specific area, e.g., comprehensive works on air transportation provided by United Airlines 387.7, air transportation in the United States provided by United Airlines 387.70973.

Use notation 065 for the corporate history of the company, e.g., the corporate history of the Union Pacific Railroad 385.06578. For international companies, use the area number for the country that is its home base, e.g., United Airlines 387.706573.

If in doubt, prefer 09.

384.54, 384.55, 384.8 vs. 791.4

Radio, television, and motion pictures

Use 384.54, 384.55, and 384.8 for interdisciplinary works and for the various aspects of presenting a program to the general public, e.g., selecting the correct day and time to broadcast a television variety show 384.5531. Use 791.4 for the various aspects of producing an individual program, e.g., arranging the various acts of a television variety show 791.450232. If in doubt between 384 and 791.4, prefer 384.

Class the history of a radio, television, or motion picture company as follows:

1. Use 384, plus notation 09 from Table 1, for a general history of the enterprise, e.g., a history of NBC (National Broadcasting Company) Television Network 384.5540973, and the history of the system (facilities, activities, services) main-

tained by the enterprise, e.g., stations broadcasting NBC television programs 384.554530973.

2. Use 384, plus notation 065 from the add table under 380, for the corporate history of the enterprise, e.g., the corporate history of the NBC Television Network 384.55406573.

3. Use 791.4, plus notation 09 from Table 1, for the history and critical appraisal of the products of the enterprise, e.g., the history of the television programs provided by NBC 791.450973.

391 vs. 646.3, 746.92

Costume vs. Clothing

Use 391 for clothing customs, such as what was worn, what is now fashionable, national costumes, e.g., Edwardian fashion 391.0094109041, Lithuanian national costumes 391.0094793. Use 646.3 for home economics aspects of clothing, such as how to dress on a limited budget, select the best quality clothing, dress correctly for the business world. Use 746.92 for artistic aspects of clothing, such as clothing considered as a product of the textile arts, fashion design. If in doubt, prefer in the following order: 391, 746.92, 646.3.

The source of information about kinds of costume and clothing is *The Fairchild Dictionary of Fashion*, 3rd ed. (New York: Fairchild Publications, 2003).

398.2

Folk literature

Literary collections cannot be specified for folk literature in 398.2. Disregard this aspect in classifying, and use the most specific number available.

Use notation 09 from Table 1 to distinguish literary criticism of collections of tales and lore, e.g., criticism of ghost stories 398.2509, criticism of French ghost stories 398.209440509. However, do not add notation 09 for individual tales or lore, e.g., literary criticism of a ghost story from France 398.2094405.

398.2 vs. 201.3, 230, 270, 292–299

Myths and legends

Use 398.2 for myths or mythology presented in terms of cultural entertainment or, especially, as representative of the early literary expression of a society, even if they are populated by gods and goddesses. Use 201.3 and similar numbers elsewhere in 200 for mythology presented from a strictly theological point of view or presented as an embodiment of the religion of a people. For example, use 398.2 for Greco-Roman myths retold for a juvenile audience; but use 294.382325 for Jataka tales illustrating the character of the Buddha.

Use 398.2 for mythology having a nonreligious basis that deals with beliefs and stories that can be referred to as superstitions, legends, fairy tales, etc., where the religious content or interest is not apparent. Use 201.3 and similar numbers elsewhere in 200 for mythology having a religious basis that deals with the most basic beliefs of people and with religious beliefs and practices.

Class specific myths and legends presented as examples of a people's religion with the subject in religion, e.g., legends of Jesus' coming to Britain 232.9.

Use 398.2 for interdisciplinary works on mythology, since this number includes folk narratives with a broader focus than religion alone. If in doubt, prefer 398.2.

398.2 vs. 398.3–.4

Folk literature

Use 398.2 for a folk tale on a specific subject and literary criticism of that tale. Use 398.3–.4 for comprehensive works on the history and criticism of the tale, e.g., tales of witches and wizards 398.21, a treatise on why in the tales witches are usually evil and wizards are usually good 398.45. If in doubt, prefer 398.2.

401.43 vs. 306.44, 401.45, 401.9, 412, 415

Meaning

Use 401.43 for works on semantics dealing with meaning in language, covering topics such as synonymy, ambiguity, and semantic truth (metalinguistic truth). Semantics is particularly concerned with the underlying logical structure of natural language, i.e., what elements are necessary beyond correct grammar for statements to make sense. Use 412 for works on etymology that study the history of the meanings of individual words. Use 415 for works on grammar that are concerned with meaning only in relation to morphology and syntax. If in doubt, prefer 401.43.

Use 401.45 for interdisciplinary works on linguistic pragmatics. Use 306.44 for works on the sociology of language concerned with meaning as affected by sociocultural context. Use 306.44 also for works on linguistic pragmatics that deal with language in its sociocultural context, but use 401.9 for works on pragmatics that focus on the individual psychological context. If in doubt, prefer 401.45.

407.1, T1—071 vs. 401.93, T4—019, 410.71, 418.0071, T4—80071

Education in language vs. Language acquisition

Use 407.1 for broad works on language education not limited to the prescriptive approach and comprehensive works on the study and teaching of both language and literature. Use 410.71 for works on the study and teaching of linguistics. Use 418.0071 for works on how to study or teach language using a prescriptive approach. The basic distinction between prescriptive and nonprescriptive linguistics is explained in the Manual note at 410. If in doubt, prefer 407.1.

Use notation for the specific language, plus notation 071 from Table 1 (which is incorporated in Table 4), for works on studying and teaching the linguistics of that language, broad works on studying and teaching the language that are not limited to the prescriptive approach, and comprehensive works on studying and teaching both the language and its literature, e.g., comprehensive works on studying and teaching French language and literature 440.71. Use notation 80071 from Table 4 for works on how to study or teach a specific language using a prescriptive approach, e.g., how to teach basic French 448.0071. If in doubt, prefer T1—071.

Use 401.93 for works on the psychology of learning language informally, as a child learns from its parents. Use T4—019 for the psychology of learning a specific language informally. Use 418.0071, or T4—80071 for a specific language, for the psychology of formal study and teaching of language. Use 401.93, or T4—019 for a specific language, for comprehensive works on the psychology of learning language both formally and informally. If in doubt, prefer 401.93 or T4—019.

410

Linguistics

Prescriptive linguistics

Use 410, 411–417, 419, and 420–490 plus notation 1–7 from Table 4 for works on nonprescriptive approaches to linguistics (e.g., descriptive and theoretical linguistics), which are concerned with describing or explaining language usage as it does or did exist, without regard to an ideal of correct usage. Use 418 and 419–490 plus notation 8 from Table 4 for works on prescriptive approaches, which are concerned with promoting standard or correct usage of language, i.e., trying to learn to speak or write like educated native users of a standard form of a language. For example, use 415 and notation 5 from Table 4 for descriptive works about grammar, but use 418 and notation 82 from Table 4 for prescriptive works about grammar, e.g., descriptive works on French grammar 445, prescriptive works on French grammar 448.2. However, use 413 and notation 3 from Table 4 for dictionaries, regardless of whether they are prescriptive or descriptive, e.g., French dictionaries 443.

Use the number for nonprescriptive approaches for comprehensive works containing both nonprescriptive and prescriptive linguistics, e.g., a collection containing both descriptive and prescriptive papers about grammar in general or the grammar of many different languages 415. If in doubt, prefer the number for nonprescriptive approaches.

Contrastive linguistics

Use 410 or other numbers not limited to applied linguistics for works of contrastive linguistics that are purely descriptive or theoretical, or a combination of applied and nonapplied linguistics. Use 418 and notation 8 from Table 4 for works of contrastive linguistics that focus on finding ways to prevent errors caused by interference or negative transfers from a first language in learning a second language or in translating into a second language. If in doubt, prefer the number not limited to applied linguistics.

Historical linguistics

Use 417.7 for works on general historical (diachronic) linguistics. Use notation 09 from Table 1 for general historical linguistics of a specific language, or for historical linguistics of a specific topic, if the work gives a history, but not if the work merely discusses the processes of change in a general way. For example, use 415 for a general description of grammatical change, 425.09 for a history of grammatical changes in the English language, and 420.9 for a history of all kinds of changes in the English language. Although no provision comparable to 417.7 exists for individual languages in Table 4, notation 7 is provided under specific languages for works that focus on the distinctive characteristics of specific early forms of the language, e.g., 427.02 Middle English.

Comparative linguistics

Class a comparison of two languages with the language requiring local emphasis (usually the language that is less common in the particular setting). For example, libraries in English-speaking countries will use 495.6 for a work comparing English and Japanese, but libraries in Japan will use 420. If no emphasis is required, class the work with the language coming later in Table 6.

Class a comparison of three or more languages in the most specific number that will contain them all; e.g., use 430 for a comparison of Dutch, German, and English, since all are Germanic languages; use 491.6 for a comparison of Gaelic, Welsh, and Breton, since all are Celtic languages.

Use 410 if there is no number that will contain all the languages, e.g., a comparison of French, Hebrew, and Japanese.

Use the same criteria for comparisons of just one feature of various languages, but do not add notation from Table 4 to the number for language families unless there are special instructions to do so. For example, libraries in English-speaking countries will use 495.65 for a comparison of English and Japanese grammar, but libraries in Japan will use 425. Use 415 for a comparison of French, Hebrew, and Russian grammar; use 430.045 for a comparison of Dutch, German, and English grammar (because at 430.04 there are instructions to add); but use 491.6 for a comparison of Gaelic, Welsh, and Breton grammar.

See also discussion at 407.1, T1—071 vs. 401.93, T4—019, 410.71, 418.0071, T4—80071.

420–490

Specific languages

Dialects

Sources may differ as to whether a particular tongue is a language or a dialect. Treat a tongue as a dialect if it is shown as such in the Dewey Decimal Classification even if it is treated as a language in the work being classified, and vice versa.

Language vs. subject

Class examples and collections of "text" whose purpose is to display and study a language with the language, even if limited to a specific subject, e.g., a grammar of scientific English 425. Class language analysis of a specific work with the number for the work. If in doubt, prefer the specific subject or work.

471–475, 478 vs. 477

Classical vs. Old, postclassical, Vulgar Latin

The dates of the Classical Age of Latin are 80 B.C. to 130 A.D. (the Ciceronian Age 80 B.C. to 43 B.C., the Golden Age of Augustan literature 43 B.C. to 18 A.D., the Silver Age 18 A.D. to 130 A.D.). Use 471–475 and 478 for formal or literary Latin written at any time after the Classical Age that conforms to the standards of that age, e.g., a linguistic study on Latin manuscripts of the monks of Iona. However, use 477 for works on Vulgar Latin, on Old Latin (80 B.C. or earlier), or on postclassical Latin. The phrase "postclassical Latin" refers to the nonclassical or vulgarized Latin used from the death of Juvenal (140 A.D.) until the period of renewed interest in the "pure" Latin of the Classical Age in the 11th and 12th centuries, and from the 14th century onward. If in doubt, prefer 471–475 and 478.

500 vs. 001

Natural sciences and mathematics vs. Knowledge

Use 500 for works about "science" that clearly imply emphasis on the natural sciences and mathematics. Use 001 for works that use the word "science" without implying emphasis on "natural science," for example, works that also cover the social sciences and the analytical aspects of other disciplines. Use 001.2 Scholarship and learning when the word "science" is used to cover disciplines outside 500. Use 001.4 Research rather than 507.2 for works on scientific method and scientific research with no clear emphasis on "natural science." However, use 509 for "history of science," as that term normally relates to the natural sciences and mathematics. If in doubt, prefer 500.

510

Mathematics

Primary and secondary school topics

Use the following numbers for the mathematical topics presently taught in primary and secondary schools of the United States:

Arithmetic	513
Algebra	512.9
Geometry	516.2
Trigonometry	516.24

Use caution, however, when classifying works with "precalculus" in the title. Use 510 for works that cover three or more of algebra, arithmetic, elementary calculus, geometry and trigonometry. Use 512 for works that predominantly cover algebra, or cover algebra and arithmetic. Use 515 for works that predominantly cover elementary calculus. If in doubt, prefer 510.

Combination of topics

Use the following instructions when classing in 512.1 Algebra combined with other branches of mathematics, 513.1 Arithmetic combined with other branches of mathematics, and 515.1 Analysis and calculus combined with other branches of mathematics and when using "Class here linear algebra combined with analytic geometry" at 512.5 Linear algebra:

1. Use these numbers for works that deal basically with one subject but have some information on another subject either added at the end of the work or interspersed throughout it. For example, use 512.12 Algebra and Euclidean geometry for a textbook with ten chapters on algebra and two on Euclidean geometry.

2. Use these numbers only for works that are predominantly about the branch first named. For example, use 512.13 only for works about algebra with some

trigonometry added; use 516.24 for works about trigonometry with some algebra added.

510, T1—0151 vs. 003, T1—011

Systems

Use 510 for works about purely mathematical systems, e.g., systems of equations. Careful examination may be required to determine whether a work is limited to purely mathematical systems, because the same or similar terms may be applied to both mathematical systems and mathematical descriptions of real-world systems; for example, a work on dynamical systems may discuss either mathematics (515.39) or real-world systems (003.85).

Use 003 for works on mathematics applied to real-world systems, even though they are highly mathematical, and even though a significant part is organized according to mathematical concepts. Use 003 if the work makes clear that the mathematics is intended as background for systems theory, and the systems part of the work will typically be organized according to specific applications, types of systems, or systems concepts such as control, stability, input-output, feedback, observability, or state estimation.

If in doubt, prefer 510.

Use notation 011 from Table 1 for works that clearly stress systems, modeling, forecasting, or other topics named in 003. Use notation 0151 from Table 1 for works lacking such stress. If in doubt, prefer T1—0151.

See also discussion at 519.5, T1—015195 vs. 001.422, T1—0727.

510, T1—0151 vs. 004–006, T1—0285

Mathematics and computer applications

Use 510 plus notation 0285 from Table 1 for the use or application of computers in mathematics, e.g., computer programs used for the numerical solution of ordinary differential equations 518.63028553. Use 004–006 plus notation 0151 from Table 1 for mathematics applied to computers, e.g., recursive functions used to explain how computers work 004.0151135. If in doubt, prefer 510 plus notation 0285 from Table 1.

If the application is in a third discipline, use notation 0285 from Table 1 for works that involve both the use of computers and the use of mathematics, e.g., a computer program for solving structural engineering calculations 624.1028553.

519.5, T1—015195 vs. 001.422, T1—0727

Statistics

The subject of statistics can be divided into three parts:

  1. How to obtain and arrange statistical data

  2. How to manipulate the data by mathematical means to produce information regarding the topic being examined

3. How to interpret the statistical results

Use 519.5, or the number in 001–999 for the subject, plus notation 015195 from Table 1, for works containing only 2, or 2 with 1 or 3 or both as incidental information. Use 001.422, or the number in 001–999 for the subject, plus notation 0727 from Table 1, for works giving equal treatment to 1, 2, and 3, or containing information about only 1 or 3 or both 1 and 3.

In many disciplines a word derived from the discipline name combined with -metrics or -statistics is used for statistical work, e.g., sociometrics, econometrics, biometrics, biostatistics. Commonly works on these subjects concentrate on 2 from the above list, with secondary treatment of 3 or 1 or both. Use the number in 001–999 for the subject plus notation 015195 from Table 1 for these works. Use the number in 001–999 for the subject plus notation 0727 from Table 1 for works of broader treatment, emphasizing 1 or 3 or both 1 and 3.

If in doubt, prefer 519.5 or T1—015195.

See also discussion at 510, T1—0151 vs. 003, T1—011.

520 vs. 500.5, 523.1, 530.1, 919.9

Outer space

Use 520 for popular works on astronomy that use the terms "space" and "outer space" while discussing the various interesting astronomical bodies and phenomena of the universe, and use 523.1 for works that use the terms as synonymous with the universe treated as a single unit.

Use 520 for works on exploring space or outer space that emphasize astronomical findings (or use a specific number in 523 if the work is limited to specific bodies, e.g., the solar system 523.2). Use 919.9 plus notation 04 from the table under 913–919 when the works refer to geographic exploration, that is, live humans going out on real or imaginary visits to the planets or stars.

Use 500.5 for a work on space sciences in general that has no particular reference to astronomical bodies. Use 530.1, where an including note mentions space, if the work refers simply to space with nothing in it.

If in doubt, prefer in the following order: 520, 523.1, 530.1, 500.5, 919.9.

520 vs. 523.1, 523.112, 523.8

Astronomy and allied sciences vs. The universe, galaxies, quasars vs. Galaxies vs. Stars

Use 520 for works describing the universe in its several distinct components, e.g., as individual planets, stars, galaxies. Use 523.1 for works treating the universe as a single unit. If in doubt, prefer 520.

Stars and galaxies

Use 523.8 for comprehensive works on stars and galaxies when they are treated as individual astronomical bodies. However, use 523.112 when the work considers stars primarily as components of galaxies. Use 523.1 if the work considers galaxies and stars primarily in the context of cosmological theories, with little discussion of individual stars or galaxies. Use 520 for works that discuss other astronomical bodies, e.g., planets and comets, as well as stars and galaxies.

If in doubt between 523.8 and 523.112, prefer 523.8.

523 vs. 550

Earth sciences in extraterrestrial worlds

Use 523 for phenomena of celestial bodies when the celestial body has no distinct lithosphere, since in such cases hydrosphere and meteorology are moot concepts, and thus the phenomena are not directly comparable to terrestrial phenomena. Use 559.9 and notation 0999 from Table 1 in 551–553 for phenomena of celestial bodies that have distinct lithospheres when the phenomena are directly comparable to terrestrial phenomena. For example, use 551.5099923 for the atmosphere of Mars (which has a lithosphere), but use 523.86 for the atmosphere of stars (which do not); use 523.45 for the red spot of Jupiter (a planet without a distinct lithosphere). If in doubt, prefer 523.

530.416 vs. 539.75

Responsive behavior and energy phenomena vs. Nuclear activities and interactions

Use 530.416 for works that study topics in responsive behavior, energy phenomena, nuclear activities, nuclear interactions in the context of the condensed (solid and liquid) state, i.e., in answer to the question, what is taking place in condensed matter that makes it behave the way it does. Use 539.75 for works that study these topics in the abstract, or in the context of nuclear structure, i.e., in answer to the question, what makes the atom and its particles behave the way they do. If in doubt, prefer 530.416.

530.475 vs. 530.12, 531.16

Brownian motion and particle mechanics

Use 530.475 (or the similar numbers 530.415, 530.425, 530.435) for treatment of particles in diffusion within various states of matter. Use 530.12 for comprehensive works on particle mechanics. Particle mechanics is a subject that exists in both classical and quantum physics, but is far more basic to the study of quantum physics, where the quanta can be considered particles. Use 531.16 only if the emphasis is clearly on classical mechanics. Use other numbers in modern physics if appropriate, e.g., orbits of subatomic particles 539.725. If in doubt, prefer in the following order: 530.475, 530.12, 531.16.

Use 530.475 for interdisciplinary works on Brownian motion, which usually refers to the random motion of microscopic particles. However, class with the subject the extension by analogy of the concept to a variety of similar random movements, e.g., of prices, of biological populations, of instrumental recordings.

Use 530.425 for works on Brownian motion with an emphasis (often unstated) on such motion in fluids.

541 vs. 546

Physical chemistry of specific chemicals

Use a subdivision of 546 for physical chemistry of a specific element or compound; however, use a subdivision of 541 when one or two examples drawn from large groupings like metals (546.3) or nonmetals (546.7) are used primarily to study or explain a specific topic in physical chemistry, e.g., hydrogen-ion concentration 541.3728 (*not* 546.2).

If in doubt, prefer 541.

548 vs. 530.41

Crystallography vs. Solid-state physics

Use 548 for works on crystals and crystallography when these terms are used to refer to discrete objects and abstract lattice patterns. Use 530.41 for works on crystallography and the crystalline state in their broad senses, i.e., when the terms are used to cover atomic arrangement in metals, ceramics, amorphous materials, or polymers. Use 530.41 as the comprehensive number. If in doubt, prefer 548 for works clearly emphasizing ordinary crystals.

549 vs. 546

Mineralogy vs. Inorganic chemistry

Use 549 numbers for topics of physical and theoretical chemistry pertaining to the structure and behavior of homogeneous crystalline solids. Use 546 numbers for comprehensive works on the chemistry and mineralogy of specific chemical types. If in doubt, prefer 549.

549 vs. 548

Mineralogy vs. Crystallography

Use 549 for the crystallography of specific minerals unless the minerals are used to study or explain a topic in 548, e.g., quartz, feldspar, and related crystals 549.68, but a study of isomorphism using quartz, feldspar, and related crystals 548.3. If in doubt, prefer 549.

550 vs. 910

Earth sciences vs. Geography and travel

Geophysics (550) is the analysis of the structure of the earth and the forces shaping it; physical geography (910.02) is the description of the resulting landscape. Use the number for a specific force or process in 551 for descriptions of the results of the specific force or process, e.g., earthquakes in Myanmar 551.2209591. Use the number for a specific land form in 551.41–.45 for the operation of all forces and processes that combined to create a specific topographic land form, e.g., formation of mountains in Myanmar 551.43209591. Use 554–559 for the operation of all the forces and processes taken as a whole in a specific area, especially if the work emphasizes solid geology, e.g., geophysical processes operating in Myanmar or the geology of Myanmar 555.91. However, use 910.02 or the specific area number in 913–919, plus notation 02 from the table at 913–919, when a work treats the geographic landscape with only minor consideration of geophysical processes, e.g., graphical description of surface features in Myanmar 915.9102. If in doubt, prefer 550.

Use 910 or the specific area number in 913–919, plus notation 04 from the table at 913–919, for descriptions of surface features for travelers. Such descriptions usually cover resort accommodations and the ambience as well as geographic features, e.g., contemporary tourist beaches in Myanmar 915.91045.

551.302–.307 vs. 551.35

Erosion and weathering, sediments and sedimentation, soil formation, mass movement vs. Geologic work of water

Use 551.302–.304 for works giving due coverage to the work of wind, glaciers, or frost, even if agents other than water take up only a small part of the text, since water is by far the most important agent in the erosion, transport, and deposit of geologic materials. Use 551.352–.354 only for works limited to the work of water or to materials transported by water.

Use 551.305 for the work of water in soil formation and 551.307 for the work of water in mass movement. Water is also the most important agent in these processes, but it almost always acts in conjunction with other agents to produce the processes, e.g., action of dissolved chemicals, temperature changes, or earthquake vibrations.

551.5 vs. 551.6

Meteorology vs. Climatology and weather

Meteorology analyzes and describes the properties and phenomena of the atmosphere, and thus explains climate and weather. Meteorology is also the comprehensive subject, encompassing consideration of climatology and weather. Use 551.5 for works called "climatology," "climate and weather," or simply "climate" or "weather," if they cover topics in meteorology. Use 551.6 only when the words are limited to four senses:

1. The description of phenomena of the atmosphere taken as a whole, weather usually being the short-range description, and climate the long-range description

2. The prediction of weather, climate, or specific meteorological phenomena, that is, weather forecasting and forecasts (551.63–.65)

3. The study of climate or meteorology in small areas, that is, microclimatology or micrometeorology (551.66)

4. The attempt to modify weather or any specific meteorological phenomena (551.68), which is actually a technology

Use 551.5 numbers for all other aspects, including description (weather reports) of specific phenomena, regardless of the terms used in the work in hand, e.g., a discussion of the factors that produce weather 551.5, reports of rainfall 551.577, a description of climate types of Asia 551.62095, forecasts of rainfall 551.6477, a forecast of a rainy day in Singapore 551.655957.

If in doubt, prefer 551.5.

551.7 vs. 560

Historical geology vs. Paleontology

Use 551.7 for works on historical geology, which studies the rocks and their strata, using paleontological facts to help date and interpret deposition, movement, and erosion. Use 560 for works on paleontology, which studies life in former geological ages through the interpretation of fossils. Paleontology utilizes the same material as historical geology, i.e., the geologic record, but only as a record of life and the environment in which life evolved. If in doubt, prefer 551.7.

571–575 vs. 630

Physiology, anatomy, and pathology of agricultural plants and animals

Use 571–575 for results of experimental work on basic physiology and pathology that utilize domestic plants and animals as models.

When domestic plants and animals are studied for agricultural purposes, observe the following guidelines:

Use 571.2 and 571.32 and similar numbers in 571.5–.8 and 575 for physiology and anatomy of agricultural plants, but use 636.0891–.0892 and similar numbers in 636.1–.8 for physiology and anatomy of agricultural animals.

Use 632 for comprehensive works on pathology and diseases of agricultural plants and animals, or for comprehensive works on pathology and diseases of plants. Use 633–635 plus notation 9 from the table under 633–635 for pathology and diseases of specific agricultural plants, e.g., diseases of cotton 633.519. Use 636.0896 for comprehensive works on pathology and diseases of agricultural animals. Use 636.1–.8 for pathology and diseases of specific kinds of agricultural animals plus notation 39 in add table under 636.1–.8 or notation 0896 as instructed in certain entries in the schedule, e.g., diseases of race horses 636.1239, diseases of horses 636.10896.

If in doubt, prefer 571–575.

See also discussion at 571–573 vs. 610.

571–573 vs. 610

Results of research in biology and medicine

Use 571–573 for results of physiological and anatomical research with animal models in 571–573. Use 615–618 for results of pharmacological, therapeutic, and pathological research if the medical relevance for humans is either stated or implied. If in doubt, prefer 571–573.

571.629 vs. 571.29

Cell biology vs. Physiology of microorganisms

Use 571.629 for works on microorganisms that go into details of internal structures, e.g., membranes and organelles, without also discussing details of reproduction. Use 571.29 for works that discuss only generalities of microorganisms or discuss cell reproduction of microorganisms in addition to their general cell biology. If in doubt, prefer 571.629.

571.8 vs. 573.6, 575.6

Reproduction, development, and growth vs. Reproduction in animals and in plants

Use 571.8 for comprehensive works on reproduction, development, and growth, and for works covering reproduction of both animals and plants. Use 571.81 for comprehensive works on reproduction, development, and growth in animals, but not for reproduction alone in animals. Use 571.82 for comprehensive works on reproduction, development, and growth in plants, but not for reproduction alone in plants. Use 573.6 for reproduction in animals as well as reproductive system in animals, and 575.6 for reproduction in plants as well as reproductive organs in plants. If in doubt, prefer 571.8.

Reproduction in other organisms

Use 571.829 for reproduction of fungi and algae. Although some fungi and algae have reproductive organs, e.g., mushrooms and seaweeds, most do not, and the organs are poorly developed at best.

Use 571.8429 (*not* 571.829) for reproduction of unicellular microorganisms, and 571.84529 for the sexual reproduction of unicellular microorganisms.

Vegetative reproduction

Use 571.89 for comprehensive works on vegetative reproduction. Use 571.829 for vegetative reproduction of microorganisms, and 575.49 for vegetative reproduction of plants.

573.44 vs. 571.74

Hormones

Use 573.44 for works that emphasize endocrine hormones or hormones in animals while giving relatively limited treatment to hormones outside the animal kingdom. Use 571.74 only for truly comprehensive works on hormones, e.g., works that give balanced treatment to hormones in plants and microorganisms as well as animals. If in doubt, prefer 573.44.

576.5 vs. 572.8

Genetics vs. Biochemical genetics

Use 576.5 for comprehensive works on genetics, for works that emphasize the somatic manifestations of genes, and works that do not emphasize the DNA-based chemical structure of genetic material. Use 572.8 for works on genetics that emphasize the chemical structure and processes, e.g., DNA, RNA, replication, errors in transcription, and crossing over. If in doubt, prefer 576.5.

576.8 vs. 560

Evolution vs. Paleontology

Use 576.8 for works that emphasize how paleontological findings are evidence for evolution and works that include significant nonpaleontological evidence. Use 560 for works on the evolution of extinct organisms and works on the history of life that emphasize the description of extinct organisms and ancient environments. If in doubt, prefer 576.8.

577.3–.7 vs. 578.73–.77

Ecology of specific kinds of environments vs. Biology of specific kinds of environment

Use 577.3–.7 for works emphasizing either the nature of an environment or the interrelationships among various kinds of organisms found in the environment. Use 578.73–.77 for descriptive accounts of organisms found in a specific kind of area, e.g., plants and animals found in wetlands 578.768; and for comprehensive works on the biology of a specific kind of area, e.g., marine biology 578.77. If in doubt, prefer 577.3–.7.

577.3–.7 vs. 579–590

Ecology of dominant organisms in a specific kind of environment

Use 577.3–.7 for the ecology of dominant organisms (usually plants) of a specific ecological environment (biome). For example, use 577.4 (*not* 584.917) for the role of grass in grasslands. Similarly, use 577.3 for the ecology of specific forest associations, e.g., ecology of coniferous forest associations in Canada 577.30971 (*not* 585.0971 or 585.170971); and use 577.686 (*not* 597.17686) for fishpond ecology.

Use 579 or 580–590 only for works that emphasize the biology of the dominant kind of organism, e.g., the biology of grass in grasslands 584.9 (*not* 584.917), the biology of fish found in fishponds 597.17636.

If in doubt, prefer 577.3–.7.

578 vs. 304.2, 508, 910

Natural history vs. Human ecology vs. Geography

Use 578 for works on nature that concentrate on nonhuman living organisms and their settings. Use 304.2 for works that emphasize the relationship between natural phenomena and human institutions. Use 508 for works on nature that give significant treatment to earth sciences phenomena, e.g., weather, water features, and mountains. Use 910 for works that describe human settlement as well as natural phenomena. If in doubt, prefer in the following order: 578, 508, 910, 304.2.

578.76–.77 vs. 551.46, 551.48

Biology of aquatic environments vs. Oceanography and hydrology

Use 578.76–.77 for works on aquatic and marine biology, including comprehensive works on biology and ecology of water bodies. These works may include significant consideration of land and sea waters as part of the lives of aquatic organisms, but do not usually include detailed physical description of water bodies. Use 551.46 and 551.48 for works limited to nonliving natural phenomena, and for comprehensive treatment of biological and physical phenomena of water bodies. If in doubt, prefer 578.76–.77.

579–590

Taxonomic nomenclature and sources of information

Taxonomic nomenclature

The notes below mention several of the commonly recognized taxonomic levels used in classifying organisms. The broadest is kingdom, followed (in order of increasing specificity) by phylum or division, class, order, family, genus, species.

In the schedules for specific kinds of organisms, scientific terms are preferred in headings for taxonomic numbers below the kingdom level. If there is an alternative scientific name still in current use, it is given in the heading in parentheses following the preferred term. If there are two or more alternative scientific names in current use, the preferred term is given in the heading, and the alternative names are given in a variant-name note. For example, Mycetozoa, Myxomycetes, Myxomycophyta, Myxomycota are given as variant names for Myxomycotina (slime molds) at 579.52. Most obsolete names have been dropped. If a common name is well established in the literature but does not have a clear-cut corresponding scientific term (or terms), the common name may be used alone, e.g., 598.412–.415 Ducks.

A scientific name given in a class-here note is usually that of a subordinate taxon that comprises all or most of the members of the group in the heading. For example, under 583.99 Asterales, the class here note gives Asteraceae (Compositae), the only family in the order.

Common names are linked to scientific names by parentheses when they are generally understood to be exact equivalents. When two common names are linked to a scientific name, a comma between them means that they are alternative common names, e.g., "(doves, pigeons)" after Columbidae in the class-here note at 598.65. An "and" means that the two groups with common names together comprise the scientific group, e.g., "(poplars and aspens)" after Populus in the including note at 583.65. Common names that simply refer to well-known members of a scientific class, however, are listed alphabetically in an including note.

With plants (and occasionally with animals), the familiar name for families consists of the name of a typical member or members plus the word "family," e.g., Ranunculaceae (buttercup family) at 583.34. The typical member may be a single species or a large genus with hundreds of species, but seldom approximates the whole of the family. Classifiers must not assume that if the family approximates the whole of an order, the typical members do also.

An illustration of two terminology problems appears at 583.23 Laurales. The main family of this order is Lauraceae, the laurel family, which encompasses over 85 percent of the species of the order. The family is therefore given in a class here note, signifying that subdivisions can be added to the number for works on the family because it approximates the whole of the order.

Only a few species of the laurel family, however, are individually known as laurels, while several plants of other orders are also called laurels. Since it is useful to know where to class comprehensive works on laurels, the including note reads, in part: "Including ... comprehensive works on laurels." Being listed in an including note means that laurels (even in its broadest sense encompassing all plants called laurels) do not approximate the whole of the 2800 species in the order Laurales.

Some large classes of organisms have two including notes, for classifier convenience. The first including note lists the scientific names of families or higher taxa and their corresponding common names, the second the common names that do not correspond with the given scientific names. Genera are listed with the common names because so many have become common names.

Sources of taxonomic information

Taxonomic schedules usually follow the arrangement accepted in *The New Encyclopaedia Britannica*, 1989. Other works that often prove helpful are *Synopsis and Classification of Living Organisms* edited by Sybil P. Parker (McGraw-Hill, 1982), and *Webster's Third New International Dictionary*.

See also discussion at 579.24–.25; also at 579.3; also at 599.

579–590 vs. 571–575

Biology of whole organisms vs. Biology of internal processes

Use 579 or 580–590 for general and external biological phenomena of specific kinds of organisms. Use 571–575, plus notation 1 (for animals) or 2 (for plants and microorganisms) from various add instructions in 571–575, for internal biological processes and structures of specific kinds of organisms.

The distinction between the biology of whole organisms in 579 or 580–590 (the first biology) and the biology of internal processes in 571–575 (the second biology) is based upon the recognition of fundamental differences between the literature of the two biologies. While the distinction between the two is not absolute, there are a number of basic differences:

1. The first biology requires the study of whole organisms or taxonomic groups and their relationships to each other and the environment; the second requires the study of parts of organisms to find out how the various processes work.

2. The first biology is studied primarily in the field, where it usually involves descriptive research; the second is studied primarily in laboratories, where it usually involves experimental research. (Either kind of research, however, can be used in either biology.)

3. In the first biology, topics are usually seen as typical only of the specific kind of organism being studied, e.g., snail shells, reproductive behavior of sticklebacks, weaverbird nests. In the second biology, the process studied in one organism is usually seen as typical of all living organisms (or as typical of a large class of organisms such as animals, vertebrates, or mammals), e.g., cell division, blood circulation, immune reactions.

4. Natural history is at the core of the first biology, and approximates the whole of it; physiology is at the core of the second, and approximates the whole of it.

5. Most of the literature in the first biology is written by specialists named after kinds of organisms, e.g., ornithologists and ichthiologists, while most of the lit-

erature on the second biology is written by specialists named after the processes and structures they study, e.g., biochemists and cytologists. The biggest exception is ecology (a study of processes involving whole organisms, counted here in the first biology), where the specialists tend to concentrate on the ecology of different kinds of environments.

6. Finally, the first biology dominates the collections of general and small libraries, while the second is collected much more heavily in academic and research libraries.

If in doubt, prefer 579 or 580–590.

579.165 vs. 616.9041

Harmful organisms vs. Medical microbiology

Use 579.165 for the biology of pathogenic microorganisms. Use 616.9041 for the study of the microorganisms in relation to human diseases. If in doubt, prefer 579.165.

579.24–.25

Virus classification

Subdivisions for specific kinds of viruses in 579.24–.25 are based upon *Classification and Nomenclature of Viruses* by the International Committee on Taxonomy and Viruses, 1982.

579.3

Classification of bacteria

Subdivisions for specific kinds of bacteria in 579.3 are based upon sections of *Bergey's Manual of Systematic Bacteriology*, 1984–1989. In most cases the sections have names that are English phrases defining exactly what the section contains, e.g., "Anaerobic Gram-Negative Straight, Curved and Helical Rods." *Bergey's* does use some traditional Latin or Greek names. At 579.39, where it is clear that one of *Bergey's* names (Oxygenic photosynthetic bacteria) corresponds to two traditional names, the traditional names (Cyanobacteria and Prochlorales) are preferred in the heading, and *Bergey's* name is given as a definition.

Minor kinds of bacteria

Use 579.32 for bacteria described in sections 1–3, 6–11, 20–25, and 33 of *Bergey's Manual*.

Actinomycetes and related orders

Use 579.37 for bacteria described in sections 14–17 and 26–32 of *Bergey's Manual*.

580 vs. 582.13

Angiospermae (Flowering plants) vs. Plants noted for their flowers

Use 580 for works on the taxonomic group called "flowering plants," as found in 583–585. This group includes most plants that will be found in a typical vegetable garden. Use 582.13 for works largely limited to nondomesticated plants with attractive flowers. These are the kind of plants that are found in nature, but that might also find a place in flower gardens or flower books. If in doubt, prefer 580.

583–585 vs. 600

Interdisciplinary works on specific kinds of seed plants

Use 583–585 for works limited to the botany of useful plants, and for works giving significant treatment to species of no particular economic value. For example, use 583.34 for a work covering the 300 species of the buttercup family, and 583.952 for a work on peppers that covers all the species of Capsicum and other genera that are called peppers. Also use 583–585 when there are two or more uses in technology, or one such use offset by an obvious botanical interest, e.g., 583.46 for oaks because oaks are useful as ornamental trees as well as lumber trees, and 583.23 for laurels because the many wild species of interest to botanists usually outweigh the few species that are well known as ornamentals.

Use numbers in 600 for interdisciplinary works on most kinds of seed plants that have a single dominant use. For example, use 615.321 for medicinal plants, 633.2–.3 for forage plants, 635.9 for ornamental plants (635.933734 for roses), 641.33–.35 for food plants (641.3411 for apples), 674 for lumber plants, and 677 for textile plants (677.21 for cotton).

The interdisciplinary number for most common plants is given in the Relative Index as the number opposite the unindented term. Use 583–585 for interdisciplinary works on plants that are not indexed, unless they belong in categories like those mentioned in the preceding paragraph. If in doubt, prefer 583–585.

583–584

Classification and common names of Angiospermae (flowering plants)

The arrangement for specific kinds of dicotyledons in 583 is based upon the arrangement found in the article "Angiosperms" in *The New Encyclopedia Britannica*, 1989, volume 13, pages 627–835.

The subdivisions of monocotyledons in 584 are defined by reference to the same article in *The New Encyclopaedia Britannica*, but the basic outline from early editions of the Dewey Decimal Classification is retained.

Exercise caution in identifying orders and families of flowering plants by common names; many such names are used for plants in several unrelated taxonomic groups. Notes in the schedule linking the common names are not exhaustive.

598.824–.88

Families and common names of Oscines (Passeres, songbirds)

Use 598.8 for songbird families not given in 598.824–.88. Exercise caution in identifying families of songbirds by common names; many such names are used for birds of several different families.

599

Classification of mammals

In addition to the general sources of taxonomic information used throughout 579–590, *Walker's Mammals of the World*, 1991, is particularly helpful for genera and families.

See also discussion at 579–590.

599.94 vs. 611

Anthropometry vs. Human anatomy

Use 599.94 for works emphasizing variations of external features, shapes, and gross bone structure (e.g., the comparison of heavy-boned and thin-boned people, indexes of length and breadth of skeletal features). Use 611 for works emphasizing norms of overall structure, for detailed structure of bones, and for works on all other internal organs and structures. If in doubt, prefer 599.94.

604.7 vs. 660.2804

Hazardous chemicals

Use 604.7 for comprehensive consideration of hazardous chemicals that includes handling, transporting, and utilization outside the chemical industry. Use 660.2804 for consideration of hazardous chemicals during chemical engineering. If in doubt, prefer 604.7.

However, use numbers in 660 as comprehensive technology numbers for specific hazardous chemicals, e.g., processing, transportation, utilization of natural gas 665.73.

610 vs. 616

Medicine and health vs. Diseases

Use 610 for works containing separate treatment of health, pharmacology, and therapeutics, as well as of diseases. Use 616 for comprehensive works on the diseases listed in 616–618.

Use the table of contents as a guide in deciding whether a work belongs in 610 or 616. Use 610 if it reads like a summary of topics in 610.73–618; use 616 if it reads like a summary of topics in 616.02–.99 or in 616–618. Use 616 also if the whole of medicine is brought to bear on the concept of diseases in a single treatise that discusses group after group of diseases.

If in doubt, prefer 610.

Standard subdivisions

Use notation from Table 1 under 616 only for works clearly limited to the concept of diseases or works focusing on topics named in the class-here note at 616: clinical medicine, evidence-based medicine, internal medicine. Use 610.3 for medical dictionaries, 610.711 for medical schools, 610.92 for doctors not having a distinct specialty. If in doubt, prefer 610 plus notation from Table 1.

610.92 vs. 615.534092

Biographies of chiropractors

Use 610.92 for biographies of chiropractors who do not limit their practice. Use 615.534092 for biographies of chiropractors who limit their practice to therapeutic manipulation (615.82) or to manipulation for diseases of the musculoskeletal system (616.7062). If in doubt, prefer 610.92.

612 vs. 611

Human physiology vs. Human anatomy, cytology, histology

Physiology deals with how organs work, while anatomy concerns their form and structure. Use 612.1–.9 for works bearing the names of organs or regions that (1) emphasize their physiology, (2) treat physiology as well as anatomy, (3) treat tissue structure as well as gross anatomy, (4) treat cytology (cell biology), or (5) treat histology (tissue biology). Use 611.1–.9 for works bearing the names of organs or regions that emphasize gross anatomy. Use 611.018 for treatment of anatomy, physiology, and pathology at the cytological and histological level if not limited to specific organs or regions. If in doubt, prefer 612.

612.1–.8

Physiology of specific functions, systems, organs

612.1–.8 contains the basic division of the human body into physiological systems. Parallel subdivisions 1–8 appear in shortened or slightly altered form under 611 for human anatomy; under 615.7 for pharmacokinetics; under 616 for diseases; and under 617.4 for surgery by system.

Use 612.1–.8 as a guide to classing an organ or function not provided for in one of the parallel arrays, e.g., use 615.74 Drugs affecting lymphatic and glandular systems for pharmacokinetics of the pituitary gland, as this is parallel to 612.4 Hematopoietic, lymphatic, glandular, urinary systems, where the pituitary gland is named at 612.492; use 615.73 Drugs affecting digestive system and metabolism for pharmacokinetics of the pancreas, as this is parallel to 612.3 Digestion, where the pancreas is named at 612.34. However, use 615.761, where the urinary system is given, for pharmacokinetics of the kidneys, even though kidney physiology is at 612.463, under 612.46, where the urinary system appears in the 612 schedule.

612.8 vs. 152

Physiology of nervous system vs. Psychology of sensory perception, movement, emotions, physiological drives

Use 612.8 for works that emphasize the physical and chemical mechanisms and pathways of sensations, emotions, and movements, e.g., 612.8232 for studies using electrodes to determine how the brain processes emotions. Use 152 for works that emphasize awareness, sensation, intentions, meanings, and actions as experienced by the individual or observed and described without reference to the physics or chemistry of the nervous system, e.g., 152.47 for feeling anger. Use 152 for comprehensive works. If in doubt, prefer 612.8.

613 vs. 612, 615.8

Personal health and safety vs. Human physiology vs. Specific therapies and kinds of therapies

Topics in 613 also appear in 612, e.g., exercise 612.044 and 613.71, rest 612.76 and 613.79. Use 613 numbers for works on applied or "how to stay healthy" aspects; use 612 numbers for works on descriptive physiology or "how the body works" aspects. Use 612 for comprehensive treatment of descriptive physiology and promotion of personal health. Use 613 for works that give information about physiology as background for an emphasis on promotion of personal health. If in doubt, prefer 613.

Topics in 613 also appear in 615.8, e.g., breathing 613.192 and 615.836, diet 613.2 and 615.854, exercise 613.71 and 615.82. Use 613 numbers for works on preventive or "staying healthy" aspects; use 615.8 numbers for works on therapeutic or "regaining health" aspects. Use 613 for comprehensive works. If in doubt, prefer 613.

614.4

Epidemiology

The term "epidemiology" sometimes refers to a research technique with application outside 614, e.g., in determining etiologies, such as smoking as a cause of cancer 616.994071; in determining the dimensions of social service requirements, such as the incidence, extent, severity of mental retardation 362.32; in exploring the possible effectiveness of proposed preventive measures, such as in reducing traffic accidents 363.1257.

615.1 vs. 615.2–.3

Drugs (Materia medica) vs. Specific drugs and groups of drugs

Most drugs are organic (615.3). Use 615.1 for comprehensive works on drugs even if there is a strong predominance of organic drugs, as long as coverage of inorganic drugs is in proportion to their importance. However, use 615.321 for comprehensive works on crude drugs and simples (products that serve as drugs with minimal processing, e.g., medicinal teas). If in doubt, prefer 615.1.

615.1 vs. 615.7

Drugs (Materia medica) vs. Pharmacokinetics

The term "pharmacology" may be used in the titles of works mainly limited to pharmacokinetics. Use 615.1 if the table of contents is arranged by types of drugs. Also use 615.1 for comprehensive works on drugs. Use 615.7 if the table of contents is arranged by physiological systems or if the work emphasizes the physiological and therapeutic action of drugs. If in doubt, prefer 615.1.

615.2–.3 vs. 615.7

Specific drugs and groups of drugs vs. Pharmacokinetics

Use 615.2–.3 for drugs that have an effect on several physiological systems or are not known primarily for their effect on a single system, e.g., antibiotics 615.329.

Use 615.7 for drugs known primarily for their effect on a single system, e.g., digitalis 615.711 Cardiotonic agents, or 616.129061 Drug therapy for heart failure (*not* 615.32395 Drugs derived from Scrophulariales); alcohol 615.7828 (*not* 615.32). If in doubt, prefer 615.2–.3.

615.53

General therapeutic systems

Use 615.53 only for historical or theoretical works about general therapeutic systems, e.g., a discussion of the theory of chiropractic 615.534. Use therapy numbers for works that discuss the application of these systems to therapy, e.g., the application of chiropractic 615.82. Use numbers in 616–618 when the therapies are applied to specific conditions, e.g., chiropractic in musculoskeletal diseases 616.7062.

Biography

Class biographies of founders of therapeutic systems with the system, e.g., use 615.533092 for a biography of Andrew Taylor Still, the founder of osteopathy. However, use 610.92 for other practitioners of a specific system.

See also discussion at 610.92 vs. 615.534092.

615.7 vs. 615.9

Pharmacokinetics vs. Toxicology

Use 615.704, or the number in 615.71–.78 for the system affected, for toxic effects and interactions of drugs primarily of pharmacokinetic interest. However, use 615.9 when a drug primarily of pharmacokinetic interest is considered a poison because it is so toxic that a single inadvertent ingestion would cause serious complications or death, e.g., the pharmacokinetics of atropine (belladonna) 615.7 (*not* in any specific subdivision because it affects several systems), but the toxicology of belladonna 615.9523952. If in doubt, prefer 615.7.

615.8

Specific therapies and kinds of therapies

Class the application of therapies listed in 615.8 to certain specific types of disorders with the disorder, even if the work takes the application for granted without highlighting it in the title, e.g., use 616.9940642 (*not* 615.842) for radiotherapy emphasizing cancer treatment; use 616.891654 (*not* 615.85154) for music therapy emphasizing psychiatric uses.

615.852 vs. 203.1, 234.131, 292–299

Religious and psychic therapies vs. Religious healing and Christian gift of healing

Use 615.852 for works on healing and medicine that focus on religious practices as a part of the medical practice. Use 203.1, 234.131, and similar numbers in 292–299 for works on healing as a religious practice, including such topics as religious beliefs about illness, rituals and prayers for healing, miraculous cures by charismatic leaders or saints, e.g., healing in religions of North American native peoples

299.7131 (number built with 31 from 203.1). Works on healing as a religious practice may also be concerned with emotional or spiritual healing as well as physical healing, or in place of physical healing. Use 615.8528 for works on the use of psychic powers in healing that do not mention a religious context. If in doubt, prefer 615.852.

Class other works concerning illness or medicine and religion as follows:

Religion and the art and science of medicine	201.661
Christianity	261.561
Other religions	292–299
Religion and health and illness and the social questions and programs concerning them	201.7621
Christianity	261.8321
Other religions	292–299
Discussion of whether cures are miracles	202.117
Christianity	231.73
Philosophy of religion	212

616 vs. 612

Diseases vs. Human physiology

Use 616 for comprehensive works on diseases that move from a discussion of physiology to a more general consideration of causes of disease, complications, prevention, and therapy. Use 612 for comprehensive works on physiology (612) and pathological physiology (616.07). For example, use 616.1 for the physiology, pathology, and therapeutics of the circulatory system, but use 612.1 for the normal and pathological conditions of the circulatory system. If in doubt, prefer 616.

616 vs. 616.075

Clinical medicine

Use 616 for works on clinical medicine covering the application of all branches of medicine to the treatment of various diseases. Use 616.075 for works on clinical medicine limited to diagnosis or to the work of a clinical diagnostic laboratory. If in doubt, prefer 616.

616 vs. 617.4

Nonoperative therapies

Use numbers in 616 for most works on nonoperative therapies, e.g., therapeutic manipulations of muscles 616.74062 (*not* 617.473062). Use 617.4, which is primarily limited to operative surgery of systems, for nonoperative therapies only if they have some connection with operative surgery, e.g., electrotherapy by heart pacer 617.4120645, since the pacer must be surgically implanted (617.4120592). If in doubt, prefer 616.

616 vs. 618.92

Diseases vs. Pediatrics

Use 616 for diseases that are most often treated in children, but that remain lifetime problems or threats, e.g., congenital diseases 616.043, mumps 616.313. Use 618.92

only if the work in hand is limited to the occurrence of the disease in children, e.g., mumps in children 618.92313. If in doubt, prefer 616.

616.1–.9

Specific diseases

Add table

071 vs. 01

Etiology vs. Microbiology

Use notation 071 when a work considers multiple possible causes for a disease, e.g., genetic factors, environmental factors, and viruses as causes of cancer 616.994071. Use notation 01 or one of its subdivisions if the emphasis is on microorganisms or a specific type of microorganism, even when the cause of a disease is complex and not yet fully understood, e.g., oncogenic viruses 616.994019. If in doubt, prefer notation 071.

Use notation 01 without further subdivision when the etiological agent for a specific disease is known to be a single type of microorganism, unless predisposing and contributing factors are emphasized, e.g., Treponema pallidum causing syphilis 616.951301, but predisposing factors leading to severity of syphilis 616.9513071.

616.8583

Homosexuality

Use 616.8583 for homosexuality only when the work treats homosexuality as a medical disorder, or focuses on arguing against the views of those who consider homosexuality to be a medical disorder. Class works about gay men and lesbians in relation to other topics in medicine with the topic plus notation 08664 from Table 1, e.g., advice to gay men and lesbians about finding psychotherapy for a variety of psychiatric problems 616.891408664. Class most works about gay men and lesbians outside medicine, e.g., Christian attitudes to homosexuality 270.08664, interdisciplinary works on homosexuality 306.766, gay men and lesbians in armed forces 355.008664. If in doubt, prefer a number other than 616.8583.

616.86 vs. 158.1, 204.42, 248.8629, 292–299, 362.29

Recovery from addiction

Use 616.86 for self-help programs for individuals recovering from substance abuse and interdisciplinary works about recovery programs that focus on the individual's life with addiction, covering the individual's experience with both social and medical aspects. Use 204.42, 248.8629, and similar numbers in 292–299 for religious guides and inspirational works for the recovering addict. Use 362.29 for works on organizations providing recovery programs, including administration of the program, and interdisciplinary works that cover both organizational and therapeutic aspects of recovery programs. If in doubt, prefer 616.86.

Class works that treat recovery programs for people recovering from a specific kind of substance abuse as a medical service with the substance in 616.86, plus notation 06 Therapy or notation 03 Rehabilitation from the table under 616.1–.9, whether the programs are run by professionals, such as psychiatrists or clinical psychologists, or whether they are self-help programs run by laypeople. Use notation 06 for programs to arrest the illness and begin recovery, e.g., twelve step programs. Use notation 03 for programs to help the individual remain in recovery. If in doubt, prefer notation 06.

Class works that treat recovery programs for those recovering from a specific kind of substance abuse as a social service, with the substance in 362.29, plus notation 86 Counseling and guidance from the table under 362–363. Such works typically emphasize the organizational or institutional aspects of the program.

For example, use 616.86103 for interdisciplinary works on life as a recovering alcoholic; 616.86106 for the twelve step Alcoholics Anonymous program; 204.42 for a general guide for a recovering alcoholic on how to live a religious life; 248.86292 for a guide for a recovering alcoholic on how to live a Christian life; 362.29286 for comprehensive works on Alcoholics Anonymous, the organization that provides the twelve step program and places for individuals in the program to meet.

Do not use 158.1 for works on recovery from addiction, because psychology applied to a medical problem is classed with the medical problem, not in 150.

616.89 vs. 150.195

Mental disorders vs. Psychoanalytic systems

Use 616.89 and similar numbers (616.852, 616.858, 618.76) for applications of a psychoanalytic system in psychiatry, e.g., 616.8917 for psychoanalytic treatment of mental illness. Use the appropriate subdivision of 150 for applications of a psychoanalytic system to specific topics or branches of normal psychology, or to specific topics or branches of both normal and abnormal psychology, e.g., 154.63 for Freudian theories of dream analysis. Use 150.195 for comprehensive works on a psychoanalytic system or its founder, e.g., 150.1952 for Freudian system. If in doubt, prefer 616.89.

617

Surgery, regional medicine, dentistry, ophthalmology, otology, audiology

Add table

06

Therapy

Do not use notation 06 by itself with numbers whose meaning is limited to surgery, since surgery is a therapy. Add subdivisions of 06 to surgery numbers for specific physical therapies used in preparation for or rehabilitation from operative surgery, or for branches of surgery not limited to operative surgery, e.g., drug therapy in treatment of burns 617.11061. Use notation 06 freely under numbers not limited to surgery, e.g., ophthalmologic therapy 617.706.

617.5

Regional medicine

This number brings together two different concepts: (1) regions, which incorporate parts of several physiological systems, e.g., the abdominal region 617.55; and

(2) organs, which are parts of single systems, e.g., the stomach 617.553. Use numbers for regions in 617.5 for works covering regional medicine as well as regional surgery, but use notation 059 from the table under 617 for works limited to regional surgery, e.g., diseases of abdomen 617.55, abdominal surgery 617.55059. Use numbers for specific organs in 617.5 only for surgery, since nonsurgical treatment is given with the system in 616.1–.8, and do not add notation 059 by itself except for surgery utilizing specific instruments or techniques, e.g., diseases of stomach 616.33, cryosurgery of stomach 617.553059, but stomach surgery 617.553. Use notation 0592–0598 from the table under 617 with numbers for specific organs for plastic surgery, transplantation of tissue and organs, implantation of artificial organs, implantation and removal of assistive devices for organs, endoscopic surgery, and laser surgery, e.g., liver transplantation 617.55620592. If in doubt for organs, prefer 616, or 617.6–.8 for teeth, eyes, and ears. If in doubt for regions, prefer 617.5.

618.92097 vs. 617

Regional medicine, ophthalmology, otology, audiology in pediatrics vs. Surgery, regional medicine, dentistry, ophthalmology, otology, audiology

Use 618.92097 for nonsurgical specialties given in 617.5 (regional medicine) and 617.7–.8 (ophthalmology, otology, audiology) when applied to children. Use 617.98 for comprehensive works on surgical specialties applied to children. Use the number for the subject in 617, plus notation 0083 from the table under 617 if appropriate, for works on surgery of a specific organ, system, disorder applied to children, e.g., medicine of the back for children 618.9209756, but surgery of the back for children 617.560083.

Use 617 for both nonsurgical and surgical aspects of topics given in 617.1–.2 when applied to children, e.g., pediatric sports medicine 617.1027083. Use 617.6 for both medical and surgical aspects of dentistry for children, e.g., comprehensive works 617.645, diseases of the teeth and gums 617.630083, dental surgery 617.605083.

If in doubt, prefer 618.92097.

618.977 vs. 617

Special branches of geriatric medicine vs. Surgery, regional medicine, dentistry, ophthalmology, otology, audiology

Use 618.9775–.9778 for nonsurgical specialties given in 617.5–.8 (regional medicine, dentistry, ophthalmology, otology, audiology) when applied to people in late adulthood. Use 617.97 for comprehensive works on surgical specialties applied to people in late adulthood. Use the number for the subject in 617, plus notation 00846 from the table under 617 if appropriate, for works on surgery of a specific organ, system, disorder applied to people in late adulthood, e.g., medicine of the back for people in late adulthood 618.97756, but surgery of the back for people in late adulthood 617.5600846; diseases of the teeth and gums 618.97763, but dental surgery 617.6050846.

Use 617 for both nonsurgical and surgical aspects of topics given in 617.1–.2 when applied to people in late adulthood, e.g., injuries in late adulthood 617.100846.

If in doubt, prefer 618.977.

622.22, 622.7 vs. 662.6, 669

In-situ processing and ore dressing vs. Chemical engineering of fuels and metallurgy

Use 622.22 or the number for the specific material in 622.3 for in-situ processing, which uses chemical techniques to get the target materials (or compounds containing the target materials) out of the ground and is usually considered as mining, e.g., solution mining of uranium 622.34932. However, class in-situ processing of a fossil fuel in the chemical engineering number for the material produced, as this usually transforms the fuel into another form, e.g., coal gasification 665.772.

Use 622.7 for ore dressing, which refers to physical means of separating more usable ore from the low-grade materials that are dug out of the ground, e.g., magnetic separation of iron ore 622.77. However, use a number in chemical engineering (usually metallurgy, 669) when physical means that effect substantial chemical change are applied, e.g., electrodeposition of iron from ores 669.14.

Class use of high temperatures that cause drastic chemical changes in chemical engineering, e.g., pyrometallurgy 669.0282.

If in doubt, prefer 622.22 or 622.7.

624 vs. 624.1

Civil engineering vs. Structural engineering

Use 624 for basic texts on civil engineering that discuss both (1) structural engineering (which treats the specific subdisciplines of civil engineering that have general applicability to all kinds of structures) and (2) the various types of structures to which the engineering is applied. Use 624.1 only for works that take a narrow view of structural engineering, and do not discuss the various types of structures. If in doubt, prefer 624.

624 vs. 690

Civil engineering vs. Construction of buildings

Use 624 for works about "building" or "construction" covering construction of all types of structures. Use 690 only for works limited to discussion of habitable structures (buildings). If in doubt, prefer 624.

629.046 vs. 388

Transportation equipment vs. Transportation

Use 629.046 and other vehicle numbers in 600 (e.g., 623.74, 623.82, 625.2, 629.1–.4, and 688.6) for:

    1. Description of the vehicle, e.g., steam locomotives of the 1930s 625.26109043

    2. Technology of the vehicle, e.g., design tests for ships 623.810287

    3. Operation (technical) of the vehicle, e.g., piloting spacecraft 629.4582

    4. Maintenance and repair of the vehicle, e.g., repairing motorcycles 629.28775

Use 385–388 for:

1. Services provided by the vehicle, e.g., transportation of passengers by trains 385.22

2. Operation (general) of the vehicle, e.g., duties of the ship's captain 387.54044

3. Economic and social aspects of the vehicle, e.g., a register of the airplanes owned by a company 387.73340216

Use 385–388 for interdisciplinary works. If in doubt, prefer 629.046 and other vehicle numbers in 600.

629.1366 vs. 387.740426

Air traffic control

Use 629.1366 for the equipment needed for air traffic control, e.g., radar devices, and the duties of the air traffic controllers. Use 387.740426 for general operational aspects, e.g., determining how many controllers are needed per airport; for economic and social aspects, e.g., the radio call letters of the control tower; and for interdisciplinary works. If in doubt, prefer 629.1366.

629.43, 629.45 vs. 559.9, 919.904

Space flight vs. Earth sciences of, geography of, and travel in extraterrestrial worlds

Use 629.43 and 629.45 for traveling to an extraterrestrial world and exploring it from space, e.g., Viking Mars Program 629.43543. Use 559.9 and notation 0999 from Table 1 in 551–553 for discoveries in extraterrestrial worlds emphasizing the "earth sciences" of the world, e.g., volcanic activity of Mars 551.21099923. Use 919.904 only for projected accounts about exploring the world, e.g., astronautics on Mars 919.92304. If in doubt, prefer 629.43 and 629.45.

630 vs. 579–590, 641.3

Agriculture and related technologies vs. Natural history of specific kinds of organisms vs. Food

Interdisciplinary numbers

Use numbers in 630 for interdisciplinary works on domestic plants and animals, or works discussing species known almost exclusively in agriculture. Use numbers in 630 as the interdisciplinary numbers for species if the work discusses varieties not known in nature. Use numbers in 579 or 580–590 for interdisciplinary works on plants and animals in general.

Use numbers in 630 for works that have material on where to find species in the wild, but concentrate on how to grow them, e.g., finding and growing wild flowers 635.9676 (*not* 582.13); where aquarium fishes are found and how to raise them 639.34 (*not* 597). Use numbers in 579 or 580–590 as the interdisciplinary numbers for species harvested in the wild, e.g., mushrooms, trees, and fishes, unless the species is best known for a single product, e.g., teak for lumber 674.144 (*not* 583.96).

Use 641.3 for interdisciplinary works on food. Use 641.3 (*not* 579, 580–590 or 630) for works that discuss the utilization and food value as well as the agriculture and biology of edible plants and animals.

If in doubt, prefer in the following order: 630, 641.3, 579 or 580–590.

632.95 vs. 632.2–.8

Pesticides vs. Specific diseases and pests

Pesticides are an exception to the general rule that control of specific pests and diseases is classed with the disease or pest. Use 632.95 if a work concentrates on a pesticide, discussing the mechanism of action, the on-farm environmental effects, or the safety aspects, even if the pesticide is used only on a single kind of pest or disease.

Use 632.2–.8 if the work treats control of the pest or disease in crops, rather than emphasizing the pesticide and its toxicity. For example, use 632.951 for a work on how a rodenticide kills rats, or how it is a danger to local wildlife that eats poisoned rats, 632.9540289 for the safety hazards of herbicides; but use 632.69352 for a work on how to control rats by laying out rodenticides, 632.5 for a work on how to control weeds by spraying herbicides. If in doubt, prefer 632.95.

Use 632.95 for on-farm environmental effects of pesticides only if the work is limited to technical aspects. Use 363.7384 for interdisciplinary works on environmental effects of pesticides.

633–635

Specific plant crops

Certain plants have more than one number if they are important for two or more quite different crops. Some of the more important distinctions are:

Cereals versus cereal grasses (633.1 vs. 633.25)

Use 633.1 if the cereal is grown for grain (even if the fodder is an important by-product), but use 633.25 if the whole plant is to be consumed by livestock (even if the grain is allowed to ripen).

Legumes (633.3 vs. 635.65)

Use 633.3 if the legume is grown for either the ripened seed or forage, but use 635.65 if the pod is to be picked green or unripened for human consumption.

Other crops

For crops that are listed in only one number, use that number if the difference in production techniques and the appearance of the crop produced by the farmer is minor, e.g., use 635.21 for potatoes whether grown for food, feed, or starch, as they are all grown in the same manner and look alike. However, use 634.9753 for hemlocks grown for lumber, but 635.97752 for hemlocks grown for landscaping, as they are grown in a quite different manner and look quite different when shipped. If the crop described in a work does not fit existing numbers where the plant is named, use the closest suitable number, e.g., a legume grown for hard fibers 633.58. If in doubt, prefer the existing number coming first in the schedule.

635.9 vs. 582.1

Flowers and ornamental plants in agriculture vs. Herbaceous and woody plants, plants noted for their flowers

Use 635.9 (often 635.97 Other groupings of ornamental plants) for works that emphasize plants to be cultivated or appreciated in human-made settings. Use 582.1 for works that emphasize the plants in nature or their biology. If in doubt, prefer 635.9.

See also discussion at 630 vs. 579–590, 641.3.

636.1–.8 vs. 636.088

Specific kinds of domestic animals vs. Animals for specific purposes

Use numbers in 636.1–.8 for terms used in subdivisions of 636.088 applied to specific kinds of domestic animals. Terms listed in 636.088 may apply to only one or a few kinds of animals provided for in 636.1–.8 and are therefore used primarily for number building. For example, the numbers for raising cows for milk and raising poultry for eggs are both derived in part from the eggs and milk number 636.08842. Notation 42 is added to 636.21 (cattle for specific purposes), giving 636.2142 for dairy farming, and to 636.51 (poultry for specific purposes), giving 636.5142 for egg production. 636.08842 itself will seldom be used, because there are few works on producing both milk and eggs or on producing milk from several kinds of animals. Use 636.5142 for works on producing eggs from several kinds of birds. If in doubt between a subdivision of 636.088 and a derived subdivision under 636.1–.8, prefer the latter.

636.70886, 636.70888 vs. 636.73, 636.752

Dogs for work and sport vs. Working and sporting dogs

Use 636.70886 and 636.70888 for works that cover dogs used as work animals (e.g., disaster search and rescue dogs, guide dogs) or dogs used as sport animals (e.g., fighting dogs) without limitation to a specific breed or group of dogs. Dogs as work animals also include dogs used in the movies, on television, and on stage. Sled dogs and watchdogs are explicit exceptions to the general rule, in that, although they are dogs used as work animals, they are classed in 636.73, since nearly all these dogs belong to the group of breeds recognized as working dogs.

Use 636.73 and 636.752 for works on specific breeds and groups of breeds of dogs, recognized by the American Kennel Club (AKC) as "working dogs" or as "sporting dogs."

If in doubt, prefer 636.70886 and 636.70888.

636.72–.75

Specific breeds and groups of dogs

The main groupings used are those recognized by the American Kennel Club (AKC) in *The Complete Dog Book*, 1997. The roughly corresponding groupings of the Kennel Club of United Kingdom (KC) are given in class-here notes when the names differ materially. Most, but not all, of the breeds listed in the schedule are those recognized by the AKC. Class other breeds having pedigrees recognized in other nations that fit within the AKC or KC groupings with the groupings, e.g., European gundogs 636.752.

If in doubt about a breed not named in the schedule, class it in 636.7 (*not* 636.71).

Hounds

Use *Encyclopedia Americana* for help in separating gazehounds (636.7532) from scent hounds (636.7536).

636.82–.83

Specific breeds and kinds of domestic cats

Use David Taylor's *The Ultimate Cat Book*, 1989, for help in determining where a specific breed of cats should be classed.

643.29, 690.879, 728.79 vs. 629.226

Mobile and motor homes

Use 643.29 for interdisciplinary works on mobile homes and for mobile homes meant to serve as permanent homes. Use 629.226 (where campers, motor homes, trailers [caravans] are presented as types of motor land vehicles) only for what are essentially either automobiles with living accommodation, collapsible living accommodation to be used with trucks or trailers, or trailers with such limited living accommodation that they would not (even when hooked up) serve as permanent homes. Do not use 629.226 for mobile homes that must be towed and are meant to stay in one location for a long time. Use 690.879 for works on building mobile homes, and use 728.79 for works on the architecture of mobile homes. If in doubt, prefer 643.29.

647 vs. 647.068, 658.2, T1—0682

Institutional housekeeping vs. Plant management

Use 647 and subdivisions of 647.9 without the addition of the management notation from Table 1 for most works on the management of institutional households, because the term "management" often refers to the basic techniques of operating an establishment, i.e., to the topics found in 642–646 and 648 taken as a whole, when they apply to public facilities. Use 647.068 (or 647.94068, 647.95068, etc.) only when the work treats the kind of management topics found in 658.1–.8, e.g., financial management and marketing. If in doubt between 647 and 647.068, prefer 647.

Plant management covers some of the same topics as institutional housekeeping, e.g., utilities, equipment, maintenance. Use 647 (or other 640 numbers for specific aspects) if the emphasis is on doing the actual work, but use 658.2 if the emphasis is on making sure that the work is done, e.g., a how-to work on running utilities for restaurants 644, on hospital housecleaning 648.5; but a work on managing restaurant utilities 647.950682, on managing hospital housecleaning services 362.110682. If in doubt between 647 (or other 640 numbers for specific aspects) and 658.2 (or T1—0682), prefer 647.

658.04 vs. 658.114, 658.402

Management of enterprises of specific forms vs. Initiation of business enterprises by form of ownership organization vs. Internal organization

Use 658.04 for comprehensive works on management of enterprises of specific legal or ownership forms (e.g., corporations, partnerships). Use 658.114 for works that focus on initiating enterprises of specific legal or ownership forms—either starting a new business or converting an existing business to a new form, e.g., starting up a new individual proprietorship 658.1141, converting an individual proprietorship to a corporation 658.1145.

Use 658.402 for works on the internal managerial organization of an enterprise (how authority and responsibility are apportioned), not its legal or ownership organization. For example, in a line organization a single manager exercises final authority, either directly over production workers or over several supervisors who in turn supervise workers.

If in doubt, prefer in the following order: 658.04, 658.114, 658.402.

658.45 vs. 651.7, 808.06665

Communication in management vs. Communication as an office service vs. Business writing

Use 658.45 for works that focus on use of communication to achieve management goals. These works often emphasize the personal relations aspects of management communication.

Use 651.7 for works emphasizing such topics as the use of the telephone, techniques of dictation, how to use microcomputer software for form letters, mail-handling techniques—in short, the mechanics of communication. Do not use 651.7 for works that emphasize effective business writing style.

Use 808.06665 for style manuals on business writing and works on how to do effective business writing, whether aimed at secretaries or executives. Use 808.066651 for works on how to write a specific type of communication (e.g., business letters) and for model collections of a specific type intended to illustrate good writing style.

If in doubt, prefer in the following order: 658.45, 808.06665, 651.7.

669

Alloys

Use 669 for comprehensive works on alloys of a variety of metals. Use 669.1–.7 for comprehensive works on a specific alloy, or the alloys of a specific metal. Use 669.9 for the physical and chemical metallurgy of alloys, and the process of forming alloys.

Use the number for the chief constituent metal (if readily ascertainable) for an alloy not listed in 669, e.g., Monel®, a nickel alloy of about 67 percent nickel and 30 percent copper 669.7332 (*not* 669.3). If the chief constituent is not readily ascertainable, use the number for the metal coming first in the schedule, except use 669.142 for all alloys of steel.

671–679 vs. 680

Manufacture of products from specific materials vs. Manufacture of products for specific uses

In general, use 671–679 for primary products, and use 680 for final products from a given material, e.g., textiles 677, clothing 687. The distinction between 671–679 and 680 cannot be drawn consistently because some products from specific materials are in 680, e.g., leather and fur goods 685; and some products for specific uses are in 671–679, e.g., paper plates and cups 676.34. If in doubt, prefer 671–679.

680 vs. 745.5

Handicrafts

Use 680 for crafts in the sense of country crafts, and cottage industries and trades, such as those of the blacksmith (682) or harness maker (685.1). Also use 680 for handicrafts treated as the routine way of manufacturing secondary and final products. Use 745.5 for handicrafts when limited to artistic work. If in doubt, prefer 680.

690 vs. 643.7

Construction of buildings vs. Renovation, improvement, remodeling in home economics

Use 690.80286 or other numbers in 690 for works on home renovation and remodeling for professional builders. (Use the special standard subdivision notation 0286 for remodeling in 690 only with numbers drawn from 725–728; do not use a standard subdivision for this subject elsewhere in 690.) Use 643.7 and other numbers in 643 for a broad range of material intended for the do-it-yourself enthusiast, as indicated by the scope note at 643 reading "works for owner-occupants or renters covering activities by members of household." If in doubt, prefer 690.

700.92

Persons in the arts

The instructions for the classification of artists vary, either between major areas of the arts or within one division, e.g., use 730.92 for a sculptor, 730.092 for a sculptor who has also worked in one or more of the other plastic arts, 738.092 for a potter regardless of material or product.

Use either notation 092 from Table 1 or notation for period or place for works of an artist or artists as instructed under specific numbers, e.g., use 730.92 for works of a French sculptor, but use 741.944 for drawings by a French artist.

704.9 and 753–758

Iconography

Prefer iconography over history and geographic treatment, e.g., a general work on Romanesque art 709.0216, Romanesque painting 759.0216, Romanesque art of Normandy 709.44209021, Romanesque painting of Normandy 759.4209021, but the Virgin Mary and Child in Romanesque art of Normandy 704.948550944209021, the Virgin Mary and Child in Romanesque painting of Normandy 755.550944209021. However, care should be taken in classifying schools and styles that are usually limited in subject matter, such as early Christian, Byzantine, and Romanesque schools, which usually treat religious themes. Use 704.9 or 753–758 only if a point is made that iconography or one of its aspects is the focus of the work.

Use of standard subdivisions

Add standard subdivisions to iconography numbers even if the topic does not approximate the whole of the heading. There are four exceptions: 704.9428 and 757.8 Pornography, 704.9434 and 758.5 Plants, 758.3 Animals, and notation from Table 2. For instance, if a work covers only roses in art or dogs in painting, a standard subdivision should not be added.

Add notation 09 from Table 1 plus notation 3–9 from Table 2 to show the nationality or locality of the artists rather than the location of the subject, e.g., Canadian portraits of British royal children 704.94250971, Canadian portrait paintings of British royal children 757.50971. Do not add notation 074 from the table under T1—093–099 in Table 1 unless the area covered by the work being classed approximates the whole of the area indicated by the notation from Table 2.

709.012–.015, 709.02–.05 vs. 709.3–.9

Fine and decorative arts by periods of development vs. Fine and decorative arts by specific continents, countries, localities

Class the works produced by an artistic school or in a particular style as follows:

1. From the same locality, with the locality in 709.3–.9

2. From various localities within a specific country, with the country in 709.3–.9

3. From two countries, with the country coming first in Table 2 in 709.3–.9

4. From three or more European countries, with the period when the school or style flourished in 709.012–.015 or 709.02–.05

5. From three or more non-European countries within the same continent, with the continent in 709.3–.9

6. From three or more countries not within the same continent, with the period when the school or style flourished in 709.012–.015 or 709.02–.05

If in doubt, prefer in the following order: 709.012–.015 and 709.02–.05, the country number in 709.3–.9, the locality number in 709.3–.9.

709.2 vs. 381.457092

Art dealers

Use 709.2 for art dealers as a part of the art world, e.g., the artists the dealers knew and works of art they handled. Use 381.457092 for works about art dealers that focus on the economics of trading in art. If in doubt, prefer 709.2.

729

Design and decoration of structures and accessories

Use 729 only for general works that focus specifically on architectural design. Use 690 for works that treat construction alone, and use 721 for works that treat design and construction together. Use 729 for works on decoration only when the subject is being treated as an aspect of architectural decoration rather than as an art object in itself, e.g., the use of murals as architectural decoration 729.4, but comprehensive works on murals 751.73.

731–735 vs. 736–739

Sculpture vs. Other plastic arts

Use 731–735 for products and techniques of sculpture. Use 736–739 for products and techniques of the plastic arts. For example, use 731.74 for a bronze figure that is a sculptured bust, but use 739.512 for a bronze figure that is part of a larger decorative work (such as a finial or handle). If in doubt, prefer 731–735.

741.5

Choice between comic books, graphic novels, fotonovelas, cartoons, caricatures, comic strips and subject

Use 741.5 and its subdivisions for works of the imagination in comic book, graphic novel, fotonovela, cartoon, caricature, or comic strip forms that are primarily intended to delight. Use 001–999 plus notation 0207 or notation 0222 from Table 1 for works in these forms that are primarily intended to inform or persuade. Use notation 0207 Humorous treatment for works where the author's intention is serious, but where humor is used to convey the author's message; use notation 0222 Pictures and related illustrations for works where humor is not apparent. For example, use 900 plus notation 0207 from Table 1 for cartoon histories that are primarily intended to inform the reader about history, while using humor to convey the message, e.g., a cartoon history of the United States 973.0207; however, use 741.5 and its subdivisions for works that are primarily humorous in intent and merely use snatches of history as an occasion for humor. Use 510 plus notation from Table 1 for a work primarily intended to teach math, even if it has a thin fictional framework. Use 001–999 plus notation from Table 1 for works presented as cartoon textbooks, journalism, biographies or autobiographies about nonfiction topics, e.g., Larry Gonick's *The Cartoon Guide to Physics* 530.0207, Joe Sacco's *Safe Area Goražde* ["the War in Eastern Bosnia, 1992–95"] 949.742, *Our Cancer Year* (by Joyce Brabner and Harvey Pekar; illustrations by Frank Stack) 362.1969940092; however, use 741.5 and its subdivisions for works presented as factual that are known to be fictional, e.g., fictional autobiography. If in doubt about a work presented as a cartoon textbook, journalistic, biographical or autobiographical account about a nonfiction topic, prefer the number for the topic.

See also discussion at T1—0207 vs. T3B—7, T3A—8 + 02, T3B—802, T3B—8 + 02, T3A—8 + 07, T3B—807, T3B—8 + 07.

Use 741.5 and its subdivisions for works in comic book, graphic novel, fotonovela, cartoon, caricature, or comic strip forms that present fictional narratives comparable to short stories or novels in literature. Difficulties arise with nonfiction novels that use the techniques of fiction writing to tell the story of actual people and actual events. Class an account of a true event or series of events using the names of the people involved, not inventing characters or distorting facts to enhance an intended artistic effect, and not going beyond the information available to the author from investigation and interviews, in the discipline appropriate to the facts described, e.g., Rick Geary's *The Beast of Chicago: An Account of the Life and Crimes of Herman W. Mudgett Known to the World as H. H. Holmes* 364.1523092. If, however, the author goes beyond what is learned from investigation and interviews in describing conversations, feelings, thoughts, or states of mind of the people depicted in the book, use 741.5 and its subdivisions. If in doubt about a work that uses techniques of fiction writing, prefer 741.5 and its subdivisions.

Use 741.5 and its subdivisions for adaptations in comic book, graphic novel, fotonovela, cartoon, caricature, or comic strip forms of other works of the imagination, such as literary works, operas, dramatic films, e.g., an adaptation of Kafka's *Metamorphosis* as a graphic novel by Peter Kuper, an American 741.5973. Adaptations of works of the imagination are classed in the number appropriate to the adaptation, not the work being adapted. (Do not regard a translation as an adaptation unless the changes are much greater than is common with translations; for example, use 741.59519 for a graphic novel translated from Korean into English.) Adaptations of nonfiction works, however, are classed with the subject, e.g., *The Picture Bible* (script by Iva Hoth; illustrations by Andre Le Blanc) 220.9505.

741.5 vs. 741.56

Comic books, graphic novels, fotonovelas vs. Cartoons, caricatures, comic strips

Use 741.5 and 741.59 for comic books, graphic novels, fotonovelas, e.g., *Astérix* (by Uderzo and Goscinny), *Astro Boy* (by Osamu Tezuka), *Contract with God and Other Tenement Stories* (by Will Eisner), *Fantastic Four*, *Nikopol Trilogy* (by Enki Bilal), *Strangers in Paradise* (by Terry Moore), *Tintin* (by Hergé), *Wonder Woman*. These are multi-panel works written to be read in relatively long segments, like short stories or novels. If they were originally published in parts, the parts are likely to have been issued monthly or less frequently (occasionally weekly or biweekly as part of serial anthologies), not daily.

Use 741.56 and 741.569 for cartoons, caricatures, comic strips, e.g., caricatures by Max Beerbohm, Al Hirschfeld, and David Levine; *New Yorker* and *Punch* cartoons; cartoons by Michael Leunig; *Andy Capp* (by Reg Smythe), *Doonesbury* (by G. B. Trudeau), *The Far Side* (by Gary Larson), *For Better or for Worse* (by Lynn Franks Johnston), *Garfield* (by Jim Davis), *Peanuts* (by Charles M. Schulz). These were written to be read in brief segments, like jokes or anecdotes. They have a single panel, or a few panels issued daily or weekly online or in a newspaper; consequently, they have an anecdotal quality even when the same characters appear in many segments brought together in collected works.

Use 741.56 and 741.569 for works originally published as comic strips, unless the same main characters also appear frequently in comic books, graphic novels, fotonovelas. Avoid separating works about the same characters between 741.569 and 741.59; use the number for the form in which the characters most commonly appear, regardless of whether the content of the work in hand was originally issued as comic strips or comic books, e.g., 741.56973 for works about Dick Tracy (most commonly issued as comic strips), but 741.5973 for works about Spider-Man or Star Wars (most commonly issued as comic books). If in doubt, prefer 741.59.

Use 741.5 and 741.59 for comprehensive works on both kinds of graphic works. Use 741.59 for graphic artists and writers who are equally well known for doing both kinds of graphic works.

If in doubt, prefer 741.5 and 741.59.

Use 741.51 Techniques, procedures, apparatus, equipment, materials and 741.53 Special aspects of comic books, graphic novels, fotonovelas, cartoons, caricatures, comic strips for both kinds of graphic works.

741.593–.599 and 741.5693–.5699

Specific continents, countries, localities

Use the same guidelines for selecting geographic notation for cartoons, caricatures, comic strips as for comic books, graphic novels, fotonovelas.

Use notation for the country of the artist or writer for a work or a collection that features a particular artist or writer, e.g., a collection of comic books by a single Japanese artist 741.5952. Use the same number for biography or critical appraisal of a single writer or artist, e.g., a biography of the Japanese artist 741.5952. If an artist or writer changes place of residence to another country but does not change citizenship, use the area notation for the country of origin. If the artist or writer does change citizenship, however, use the area notation for the country of adopted citizenship. If information about an artist's or writer's national affiliation is not readily available in the work being classed or in standard reference books, use the area notation for the country of origin, if known; or the notation for the country in which the person's earlier works were published.

Use notation for the country where first published for a work or a collection where multiple hands (e.g., writers, pencilers, inkers, colorists, letterers) have contributed and no one artist or writer is featured, if the work reflects the culture of that country, e.g., a graphic novel first published in the United States 741.5973, a graphic novel first published in Japan then translated into English and published in the United States 741.5952 (*not* 741.5973).

If in doubt, try to determine what area's cultural tradition the work primarily reflects or was originally aimed at, and use the notation for that area. If still in doubt, prefer notation for the area that comes later in Table 2.

741.6 vs. 800

Illustrations

Use 741.6 for illustration in general. Class a specific type of illustration with the art form represented if the type is emphasized, e.g., etchings. Use 800 for illustrations that merely accompany or enhance the literary text. If in doubt, prefer 741.6.

745.1

Antiques

Use the available number in 700 for a specific type of antique, e.g., gold coins 737.43, antique New England furniture 749.0974.

If there is no available number in 700–779, use the 600–699 number for a specific type of antique, e.g., antique passenger automobiles 629.222. If there are separate numbers in 600–699 for the use of the object and for its manufacture, prefer the use number, e.g., thimbles 646.19 (*not* 687.8).

If there is no available number in either 600–699 or 700–779 for a specific antique or collectible, class it with the subject with which it is most closely associated, e.g., Shirley Temple collectibles 791.43028092.

745.5928

Handcrafted models and miniatures

Class handcrafted miniatures and models as follows:

Use 700 for handcrafted models:

1. If there is a specific number in 700 for the model, e.g., paper airplanes 745.592.

2. If there is a specific number in 700 for the subject illustrated by the model, e.g., handcrafted miniature furniture 749.0228. (Use notation 0228 from Table 1 to indicate the model or miniature.)

3. If there is no number in 600 for the model or the subject illustrated by the model. In this case the most specific number possible is chosen.

Use 600 for handcrafted models and miniatures if there is no specific number in 700 *and* either of the following conditions is met:

1. If there is a specific number in 600 for the model, e.g., handcrafted model airplanes 629.133134.

2. If there is a specific number for the subject illustrated by the model, e.g., handcrafted miniature reciprocating steam engines 621.1640228. (Use notation 0228 from Table 1 to indicate the model or miniature.)

769.9

History, geographic treatment, biography of printmaking and prints

Use 769.92 for both printmakers who copy other artists and the artists being copied (if only prints are being discussed), e.g., prints after Gainsborough 769.92. Use 769.93–.99 for prints produced by a print workshop or a studio. If in doubt, prefer 769.92.

776 vs. 006.5–.7

Computer art

Use 776 for comprehensive works on computer art and for works on computer art where the computer itself displays the art object or creates the final art object. Use 700–780 plus notation 0285 from Table 1 or specific provisions in the schedule for works on computers used as tools or devices to create art objects, e.g., computers and the arts 700.285, computers in the graphic arts 760.0285, computer composition of music 781.34.

Use 006.5–.7 for works on the computer hardware and software used in computer arts, e.g., computer sound 006.5, computer graphics 006.6, multimedia systems 006.7. Such works will typically tell how to use the hardware or the software, and may include information on such topics as file compression.

If in doubt, prefer 776.

779 vs. 770.92

Photographic images vs. Biography

Use 779 and its subdivisions, plus notation 092 from Table 1, for collections and critical appraisals of photographic images by individuals. Use 779 and its subdivisions, plus notation 09 from Table 1 and notation 1–9 from Table 2, for collections and critical appraisals of photographic images by several artists from the same area to show the area where the photographers originated, e.g., collections of portrait photographs by French photographers 779.20944. In both cases, the collection may contain one or more type of photographic images, e.g., photographs, prints, digital images, filmstrips, slides, transparencies. Use 770.92 for biographies and critical appraisals of the body of the photographers' works, which may also contain some photographic images. If in doubt, prefer 779.

780

Music

Building numbers

Building a number for a work that is classed in 780 is a four-step process:

   1. Determine the various facets of the work.

   2. Arrange the facets in the proper order.

   3. Determine whether or not the topics belonging to the facets can be indicated.

   4. Follow the add instructions.

For example, in building the number for a work entitled *Harmony in Beethoven's piano sonatas*, one takes the following steps:

   1. *Determine the various facets of the work*: For the work being classed, there are four facets, or aspects: a general musical topic, harmony; the composer, Beethoven; the instrument, piano; and a musical form, sonata.

2. *Arrange the facets in proper order*: The usual arrangement is the executant (the voice or instrument that produces the music), here the piano at 786.2; the music form, here the sonata at 784.183; general principles, here harmony at 781.25; standard subdivisions, here a person associated with the music at 780.92 (in this case Beethoven). This arrangement obeys the general instruction at 780, which states: unless other instructions are given, class subjects with aspects in two or more subdivisions of 780 in the one coming last. The major exception to executant before form occurs with vocal music *(see 782 for complete details)*. If one decided to follow the option of classing all works related to a composer in 789, the arrangement would then be composer, the executant, the musical form, general principles, other standard subdivisions.

3. *Determine whether or not the topics belonging to the facets can be indicated*: If the topic is given in a class-here note or is the same or approximately the same as a number's heading, a topic from another facet can be indicated. If the topic is given in an including note, topics in other facets cannot be indicated. Since the topics, piano, sonata, and harmony, are the headings at 786.2, 784.183, and 781.25, respectively, further topics can be indicated. (For *Harmony in Chopin's mazurkas for piano*, the topics harmony and Chopin cannot be indicated because mazurka is a part of the including note at 784.1884.)

4. *Follow the add instructions*: At 786.2 *Pianos, the * refers to the footnote, which instructs one to add as instructed in the add table under the centered entry at 784–788. The add instruction in the add table says that musical forms and instruments are shown by adding 1, then the numbers following 784.1 in 784.18–.19. Thus, facet indicator 1 plus 83 from 784.183 †Sonata form and sonatas added to 786.2 produces 786.2183 Piano sonatas. At 784.183, the † refers to the footnote, which instructs one to add as instructed in the add table under the centered entry at 781.2–.8, which says that in order to show general principles add 1 and then the numbers following 781 in 781.1–.7. The result of adding 1 and then 25 from 781.25 *Harmony is 786.2183125 harmony in piano sonatas. Even though the * at 781.25 indicates that further additions are possible, i.e., adding 092 to indicate Beethoven, the general add instruction at 780 forbids using 0 or 1 (alone or in combination) more than twice. (An option does allow further additions.) Thus, the class number for *Harmony in Beethoven's piano sonatas* is 786.2183125.

Examples

Works about music

New music vocabulary: a guide to notational signs	780.148
Music notation	780.148
Sound structure in music	781.234
Timbre	781.234
New life in country music	781.642
Western popular music	
Country	781.642

Wagner as man and artist	782.1092
Opera	782.1
General biography and criticism	092 (from Table 1)
Voice production in choral technique	782.5143
Choral music	782.5
Facet indicator	1
Performance technique	43 (from 781.43)
Bartok orchestral music [criticism]	784.2092
Orchestra	784.2
Composer	092 (from Table 1)
Bartok. Concerto for orchestra [criticism]	784.2186
Orchestra	784.2
Facet indicator	1
Concerto form	86 (from 784.186)
Scoring for brass band	784.9138
Brass band	784.9
Facet indicator	1
Arrangement	38 (from 781.38)
Beethoven string quartets [criticism]	785.7194092
Chamber group-strings	785.7
Size of ensemble	19
Quartet	4 (from 785.14)
Composer	092 (from Table 1)
The fugue in piano music	786.21872
Piano	786.2
Facet indicator	1
Fugue	872 (from 784.1872)
Scientific piano tuning and servicing	786.21928
Piano	786.2
Facet indicator	1
Tuning	928 (from 784.1928)
The origins of bowing	787.1936909
Bowed stringed instruments	787
Facet indicator	1
Bowing	9369 (from 784.19369)
History	09 (from Table 1)
Pablo Casals; a biography	787.4092
Cello	787.4
Performers	092 (from Table 1)

Discography of zither music	016.78770266
Subject bibliography	016
Zither	787.7
Recordings	0266 (from 780.266)
The organs of London	786.519421
Organ	786.5
Facet indicator	19
London	421 (from Table 2)
The Story of "Silent Night"	782.281723
Carols	782.28
Facet indicator	1
Christmas music	723 (from 781.723)

Scores

Hymns for choirs, arranged for mixed voices and organ by David Willcocks	782.527
Choral music for mixed voices	782.5
Hymns	27 (from 782.27)
Lees. Breathe on me, breath of God; anthem for 3-part female voice choir unaccompanied	782.6265
Choral music-women's voices	782.6
Anthems	265 (from 782.265)
Schubert song cycles	783.247
Solo voice	783.2
Song cycle	47 (from 782.47)
Brahms. Variations on the St. Anthony Chorale	784.21825
Orchestra	784.2
Facet indicator	1
Variations	825 (from 784.1825)
Berlioz. Romeo and Juliet; a dramatic symphony	784.22184
Orchestra with vocal parts	784.22
Facet indicator	1
Symphony form	84 (from 784.184)
Schuller. Trio: oboe, horn, viola	785.42193
Ensembles of woodwind, brass, strings	785.42
Size of ensemble	19
Trios	3 (from 785.13)
Chopin. Mazurka, piano	786.21884
Piano	786.2
Facet indicator	1
Mazurka form	884 (from 784.1884)

780.079 vs. 790.2

Music and the performing arts vs. The performing arts in general

Use 780.079 for works focusing on music in relation to the other performing arts. Use 790.2 for works on the performing arts as a whole. If in doubt, prefer 780.079.

780.26

Texts; treatises on music scores and recordings

Within 780, add 026 (from 780.26) to the number in 781–788 to indicate treatises about scores and recordings. (To distinguish scores and recordings themselves within 780, apply the optional provision given at 780.) However, when 780 and 781–788 numbers are added elsewhere in the schedules, add 026 for scores and recordings, as well as for treatises about them. For example:

Number	Used for
787.2	A treatise on violin music
787.2	Violin scores
787.2	Recordings of violin music
787.2026	A treatise on violin scores
787.20266	A treatise on recordings of violin music
016.7872	A bibliography of treatises on violin music
016.7872026	A bibliography of violin scores
016.7872026	A bibliography of treatises on violin scores
016.78720266	A discography of recordings of violin music
016.78720266	A bibliography of treatises on recordings of violin music

780.92 and 791.092

Biography of persons associated with public performances

Use the number for the activity with which the person's career is chiefly identified for the biography of a performer, e.g., the biography of an opera singer 782.1092. If the person's career involves more than one kind of public performance with no particular predominance, use the activity that comes first in the following table of preference:

Music	780
Dancing	792.8
Stage	792
Motion pictures	791.43
Television	791.45
Radio	791.44

For example, use 792.028092 for the biography of a stage actor who has also done considerable work in television. Give preference to activities listed in the above table over all other activities listed in 791.

780.92

Musicians and composers

Musicians

Comprehensive works on musicians are classed in the most specific number that describes their careers. Use 780.92 only for musicians who are equally known for both their vocal and instrumental work, e.g., Ludwig van Beethoven 780.92. Use 782–783 for musicians known primarily for vocal music, e.g., Richard Wagner, an opera composer, 782.1092; Elvis Presley, a rock singer, 782.42166092. Use 784–788 for musicians known primarily for instrumental music, e.g., Sir Thomas Beecham, a conductor, 784.2092; Nicolò Paganini, a violinist, 787.2092. *(See also 781.6 for discussion of musicians associated with traditions of music other than classical.)*

See also discussion at 784–788: Add table: 092.

Composers

Use notation 092 from Table 1 to indicate a biography, a general criticism of the composer, an analysis of a composer's contribution to the development of some aspect of music (such as Haydn's role in the development of the concerto form), critical works on the body of a composer's work (such as a critique of the piano music of Ravel), and a collection of analyses of the individual pieces of music. Do not use notation 092 for criticism of an individual work by a composer.

The citation order for music requires that general criticism of a composer's works in a specific form and criticism of a single aspect of the works be separated because the aspect is shown by adding from 781. For example, use 784.2184092 for general criticism of Brahms's symphonies, but use 784.2184125 for criticism of harmony in Brahms's symphonies. However, if a library wishes to keep all criticism of a composer's works in the same number, it is optional not to add from 781, e.g., criticism of Brahms's symphonies and of harmony in Brahms's symphonies both 784.2184092.

See also discussion at 784–788: Add table: 092.

781.38

Arrangements

Add 138 (the arrangement notation derived from 781.38) to the number in 782–788 for a voice, instrument, or ensemble to indicate arrangements in general either of or for the voice, instrument, or ensemble. For example, use 787.2138 for both violin music arranged for various instruments and music of several instruments arranged for the violin, 787.2 (violin music) plus 138 (arrangements).

Add 1382–1388 (the arrangement notation derived from 781.382–.388) to the number in 782–788 for a voice, instrument, or ensemble for which the music was arranged in order to indicate the original voice, instrument, or ensemble. Use 781.382–.388 only for building other numbers; never use these numbers by themselves. For example, use 786.213872 for an arrangement of violin music for piano, that is, 786.2 (piano music) plus 13872 (arrangements of violin music).

781.47

Accompaniment

For treatises, add 147 (the accompaniment notation derived from 781.47) to indicate how to accompany the work, e.g., how to accompany violin music 787.2147.

(Option: For scores, add notation 147 to indicate the presence of accompaniment, e.g., accompanied violin music 787.2147, unaccompanied violin music 787.2.)

781.6

Traditions of music

Hybrid styles

Use 781.621–.629 for a hybrid style (a blending or fusion of two or more styles from different traditions of music to create a new style) that originates within and is associated with an ethnic or national group, e.g., a Nigerian style that blends Nigerian folk music and jazz 781.629669. Use the number coming last in 781.63–.69 for other hybrid styles, plus notation 17 from the table under 781.63–.69 if appropriate, e.g., blues-rock 781.661743, third stream music 781.68175.

Nonclassical musicians

Comprehensive works on nonclassical musicians (musicians of a tradition other than classical music) are classed in the most specific number that describes their careers. Use numbers in 781.62–.66 and in 781.69 for musicians that are equally known for both their vocal and instrumental work, e.g., Louis Armstrong, a jazz trumpeter, singer, and band leader, 781.65092. Use 782–783 for musicians known primarily for vocal music, e.g., Ella Fitzgerald, a jazz singer, 782.42165092. Use 784–788 for musicians known primarily for instrumental music, e.g., John Coltrane, a jazz tenor-saxophonist, 788.7165092. Add 162–166 or 169 (the traditions-of-music notation derived from 781.62–.66 and 781.69) to the number in 782–788 before adding notation 092 from Table 1.

See also discussion at 784–788: Add table: 092.

781.6 vs. 780, 780.9

World music

Use 781.6 for music emphasizing specific traditions, e.g., folk music around the world 781.62. Use 780 for music of various traditions from around the world, e.g., an encyclopedia of world music 780.3. Use 780.9 for the music of specific places in the world, e.g., comprehensive works on music of Brazil 780.981. If in doubt, prefer 781.6, 780.9, 780.

781.62 vs. 780.89

Folk music vs. Music with respect to ethnic and national groups

Use 781.62 for music that originates within and is associated with an ethnic or national group, e.g., African American music 781.6296073. Use 780.89 for the group in relation to music in general, e.g., a work about African American composers, opera singers, jazz conductors 780.8996073. If in doubt, prefer 781.62.

781.62 vs. 781.63–.66

Folk and popular music

Use 781.62 for folk music or popular music that originates within and is associated with an ethnic or national group. Use 781.63–.66 for other popular music. If in doubt, prefer 781.62.

Use allmusic.com (http://www.allmusic.com/) or a similar online source for help in determining the style of western popular music.

782

Vocal music

Use 782.1 for dramatic vocal scores, e.g., opera scores 782.1, scores of musical plays 782.14. Use 782.5–.9 and 783 for nondramatic vocal scores. (Use 792.5 for staging dramatic music.)

For nondramatic vocal music (782.2–.9 and 783), classification is determined by whether an item is a treatise or a recording, on the one hand, or a score, on the other. A person interested in reading about or listening to a singer or a piece of music will usually not know the singer's vocal range or the vocal requirements of that piece of music. In contrast, a person interested in scores will know the type of voice or voices involved, e.g., a song cycle sung by a soprano, or a mass sung by a tenor and male chorus. Therefore, use 782.2–.4 for treatises about and recordings of singers and nondramatic vocal forms, but use 782.5–.9 and 783 for scores and texts.

The following flow chart will help users select the correct section of vocal music.

Flow chart for vocal music

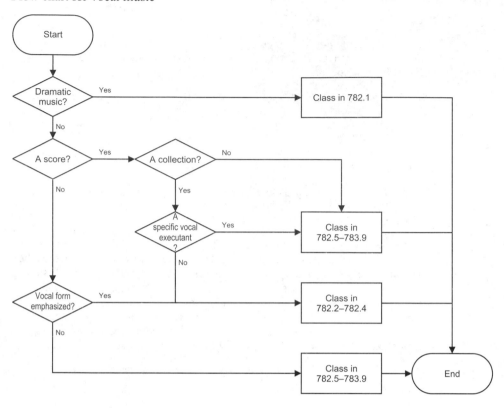

Examples (from applying the flow chart):

Soprano arias from opera [scores]	782.1
Soprano airs not from opera [scores]	783.66
Sacred songs by sopranos [recordings]	782.25
Women's soprano voice [treatise]	783.66

Vocal scores

With scores, kind of voice and size of vocal ensemble must be considered. The distinction between 782.5–.9 and 783 is based upon the number of voices per part. Use 782.5–.9 for music having several voices per part (what is usually meant by choral music). Use 783 for music having one voice per part (part songs and solos). Observe the following preference order for scores and parts of nondramatic vocal music:

Size of vocal ensemble (including solos)
Type of voice, e.g., male, high, soprano, child's
Vocal forms

Size of vocal ensemble parallels the primary division in the instrument portion of the schedule. Choral music is analogous to orchestral music (more than one voice/instrument per part in some parts); music for single voices in combination is analogous to chamber music (only one voice/instrument per part); and music for solo voice is analogous to music for solo instrument.

Type of voice also parallels the instrument portion of the schedule, in that specifying the sex and range of the voice is analogous to specifying the kind and type of instrument. Different kinds of voice are distinguished first by sex and age (women, children, men) and second by range.

For example:

Secular song for male voice choir	782.842
Male voice choir	782.8
Secular song	42 (from 782.42)
Carols for single voices in combination	783.11928
Single voices in combination	783.1
Nondramatic vocal forms	19
Carols	28 (from 782.28)

782.1 vs. 792.5, 792.6

Dramatic vocal forms

Use 782.1 for dramatic vocal forms as a type of vocal music, including such topics as tempos, plots, singers, conducting. Use 792.5 and 792.6 for dramatic vocal forms as a type of stage presentation, including such topics as costumes, sets, direction. For example, use 782.1 for operas as vocal music, 792.5 for staging of operas; use 782.14 for musical plays as vocal music, 792.6 for staging of musical plays. Use 792.509 for an opera house and its productions, e.g., a history of La Scala, Milan 792.5094521. If in doubt, prefer 782.1.

784–788

Instruments and their music

Add table

092

Biography

For persons associated with an instrument and its music <u>and</u> for persons associated with the music for the instrument, add notation 092 from Table 1 directly to the number for the instrument and its music, e.g., Nicolò Paganini (a violinist and composer) <u>and</u> Isaac Stern (a violinist) 787.2092. However, for persons interested only in the instrument, add 19 (the instrument notation derived from 784.<u>19</u>) before adding notation 092 from Table 1, e.g., Antonio Stradivari (a violin maker) 787.2<u>19</u>092.

For persons associated with a specific tradition of music other than western art music, add 162–166 or 169 (the traditions-of-music notation derived from 781.62–.66 and 781.69) before adding notation 092 from Table 1, e.g., a country music violinist 787.21<u>64</u>2092. If the person is associated with more than one tradition, do not add to show the tradition.

791.43, 791.45 vs. 777

Motion pictures and television

Use 791.43 and 791.45 for motion pictures and television as art forms and for comprehensive works on producing them. Use 777 for the technical aspects of making motion pictures and videos. For example, use 791.43025 for the use of lighting techniques to enhance the mood of the scene and for a comprehensive work on lighting, but use 777.52 for how to determine what kind of lighting apparatus to use while filming in bright sunlight. If in doubt, prefer 791.43 and 791.45.

791.43 vs. 791.45

Motion pictures vs. Television

Use the Internet Movie Database (http://www.imdb.com/) or a similar online source for help in determining if a production should be treated as a motion picture or a television program. If in doubt, prefer 791.43.

791.437 and 791.447, 791.457, 792.9

Films, radio programs, television programs, stage productions

A production recorded in a different medium than the original production is classed with the recording, not with the production, e.g., a staged opera recorded for television 791.4572 (a television program), not 792.542 (a staged opera).

793.932 vs. 794.822

Computer adventure games vs. Arcade games

Use 793.932 for computer adventure games that present the player with a situation and a goal (or goals). These goals may involve solving a mystery or problems and accumulating points. The player must think as opposed to making reflex actions, and is projected into an interactive story. An example is *Myst*®.

Use 793.932 also for computer fantasy role-playing games that involve reaching a goal by solving intellectual problems, but require reflex actions because of the fighting or athletic action, and in which outcomes are decided by the computer. Examples are *Final Fantasy*® and *SimCity*®.

Use 794.822 for arcade games that emphasize quick reflexes, as opposed to intellectual decisions. The term refers to a type of game, not just those games played in video arcades, and may include fighting, space flight, shooting, pinball, mazes, space shootouts, and strategy. Examples are *Tekken*® and *PacMan*®.

If in doubt, prefer 793.932.

795.015192 vs. 519.27

Games of chance

Use 795.015192 for the probabilities, or "odds," of winning "games of chance" in the recreational sense, i.e., any games in which chance, not skill, is the most important factor in determining the outcome, e.g., craps, poker, solitaire. Use 519.27 for "games of chance" in the mathematical sense, which are limited to games played by a single player to determine the optimal policy or strategy of winning the games and are a part of the theory of controlled probabilities. If in doubt, prefer 795.015192.

796.08 vs. 796.04

Groups of people vs. General kinds of sports and games

Use numbers in 796.08 or notation 08 from Table 1 added to numbers for specific sports or games for works on the participation of specific groups of people if the sports or games are not modified to allow their participation. Use either 796.04 or the number for the modified version if the sports or games have been modified to allow participation of specific groups of people. Numbers for the modified versions of a sport are usually given in the "specific types" or "variants" subdivisions of the sport, e.g., baseball 796.357, Little League baseball 796.35762, indoor baseball 796.3578. If these subdivisions are not provided, use the number for the type of sport as a whole. For example, use 796.3520873 for works on how people who have lost a leg can play golf, as they can usually play without a major change to the rules of golf. However, in order to participate in other sports, the person who has lost a leg may require a wheelchair. Use 796.0456 for comprehensive works on wheelchair sports. Class the wheelchair version of a specific sport with variants of the sport, e.g., wheelchair basketball 796.3238. If in doubt, prefer 796.08 or the number for the specific sport or game with use of notation 08 from Table 1.

The name of a variant of the sport may give the impression that it is for only one type of person when any type can play it. For example, women's basketball before 1971 was a variant of basketball in which there were six players per team and the three forwards played in the forecourt. Use 796.3238 (*not* 796.323082) for this variant because it can be played by either men or women.

Some sports and games have similar sounding names, but the rules are so different as to create separate, though related, sports and games. For example, American football, Canadian football, and Australian-rules football are similar sports, but they each have their own separate rules and are classed in 796.332, 796.335, and 796.336, respectively.

796.092

Sports personnel

Use the general number for the sport for the biography of sports personnel, regardless of position played or type of game, e.g., a quarterback in American professional football 796.332092 (*not* 796.33225092 or 796.33264092).

796.15 vs. 629.0460228

Play with remote-control vehicles; play with kites vs. Models and miniatures of transportation equipment

Use 796.15 for both play with remote-control model vehicles and for comprehensive works on remote-control model vehicles, e.g., flying and building remote-control model airplanes 796.154. Use 629.0460228 and similar numbers in 620 for the design and construction of model vehicles, e.g., building model airplanes 629.133134. If in doubt, prefer 796.15.

Use 790.133 for comprehensive works on play with all types of model railroads and trains, because most play with model railroads and trains does not involve remote-control vehicles.

800

Literature (Belles-lettres)

This entry uses notation from Table 3 to illustrate the application of principles to various literatures, e.g., "T3—1" is used to discuss poetry in specific literatures rather than " 811, 821, 831, 841, etc." The notation "T3—1" refers to both T3A—1 from Table 3A (individual authors) and T3B—1 from Table 3B (more than one author). Difficulties arise with the notation for T3—8 Miscellaneous writings because the literary period comes between T3—8 and its various subdivisions. In the entry this form is expressed as T3—8 + the notation for the subdivision, e.g., diaries T3—8 + 03.

Choice between literature and nonliterary subject

The discipline of literature is restricted to: (1) works of the imagination that are written in the various literary forms, e.g., fiction, poetry; (2) literary criticism and description; (3) literary history and biography. Class works of the imagination intended to delight in 800, but class works that are essentially informational with the subject in other disciplines, regardless of their literary form. For example, class Jonathan Swift's *The Drapier's Letters* as a work on monetary policy in 332.49415 (*not* as a collection of the author's letters).

Essays, speeches, letters, and diaries are commonly used for nonliterary purposes. If in doubt whether to class a work in one of these forms as literature in 800 or with a subject elsewhere in the schedule, prefer the subject.

Class nonfiction novels that use the techniques of fiction writing to tell the story of actual people and actual events as follows. Class an account of a true event or series of events using the names of the people involved, not inventing characters or distorting facts to enhance an intended artistic effect, and not going beyond the information available to the author from investigation and interviews, in the discipline appropriate to the facts described. For example, class Truman Capote's *In Cold Blood*, a true account of a multiple murder, in 364.1523. If, however, the author goes beyond what is learned from investigation and interviews in describing conversations, feelings, thoughts, or states of mind of the people depicted in the book, class the work as fiction, e.g., Norman Mailer's *The Executioner's Song* 813.54. If in doubt, class as fiction.

Other kinds of fiction, and poetry and drama, are sometimes used as vehicles for conveying factual information, e.g., biographies written in verse, fiction employed to teach the fundamentals of mathematics. Use 800 for poetry, drama, and fiction unless the form is incidental to the explanation of a specific subject, e.g., Harvey's *Circulation of the Blood* (written in Latin verse) 612.13 (*not* 871.04). Make an exception for certain ancient works that have long been classed as literature regardless of their content, e.g., Hesiod's *Works and Days* 881.01 (*not* 630), even though it deals with practical agriculture.

Class a collection of literary texts or excerpts from literary texts that is meant to serve as a model for studying another discipline with the discipline illustrated. For example, use 307 for a collection meant to explain what a community is.

Class a literary study of nonliterary works in 809.935, e.g., the Bible as literature 809.93522.

Language

Class literary works by language, not by country of origin. However, class works in English originating in North America, South America, Hawaii, and geographically associated islands in 810 (*not* 820). Class works in English from Europe, Africa, Asia, Australia, and New Zealand, and comprehensive works on English literature in 820. In certain cases, use Table 3C to indicate country of origin. *(See also discussion at T3C—93–99.)*

Class literary works in the language in which they were originally written, e.g., an English translation of a work originally written in Spanish 860 (*not* 820).

Literature of two or more languages

Works treating literature of two or more languages are usually collections or works of criticism. If two languages are involved, use the number coming first in 820–890, except where there are different instructions. For example, use 820 (*not* 860) for English and Spanish, but use 880 (*not* 870) for Greek and Latin. If more than two languages are involved, but the languages all belong to a particular language family, use the most specific number that will contain all the languages. For example, use 830 for a work covering English, German, and Dutch, since they are all Germanic languages. Do not use 820–890 for broad groupings such as Indo-European literature. For example, use 808 for collections covering English, French, and Russian (all Indo-European languages), 809 for criticism, 800 for a combination of collections and criticism. Similarly, use 800, 808, or 809 for a work about literature in more than two languages when the languages are unrelated except that they belong to a broad grouping such as nonwestern or Asian languages. For example, use 808 (*not* 890) for a collection of Arabic, Persian, and Turkish literary texts. If any one language is predominant, class with that language.

Literary form

In literature there are two basic modes of expression: poetry and prose. Class drama, whether in poetry or prose, with drama in T3—2. Class epigrams with miscellaneous writings in T3—8 + 02, regardless of mode. Class works in other forms with poetry in T3—1 if written in verse. Class prose works in T3—3 Fiction, T3—4 Essays, T3—5 Speeches, T3—6 Letters, and T3—8 Miscellaneous writings. Use the subdivision for prose literature, T3—8 + 08, only for prose works in more than one literary form. Class prose works in a specific form with the form.

Use notation 7 Humor and satire only for collections in, or works of criticism about, two or more forms including both verse and prose, because humor and satire are categories of writing rather than a form or mode. Class literary works exhibiting humor and satire in a particular form (T3—1–6 and T3—8) with the form. Table 3A for individual authors has no notation parallel to T3B—7; class a collection of works by an individual author in more than one form exhibiting humor and satire in T3A—8 + 09.

Literary period

Use the period tables supplied under various languages for the literature of that language from throughout the world and for the literatures of individual countries. For example, use 843.912 for French-language fiction of the early 20th century from throughout the world and for French-language fiction of the early 20th century from France. Use the same periods for affiliated literatures (literatures in the same language, but from countries other than the traditional homeland), e.g., use 843.912 for Belgian, Swiss, Canadian, and Senegalese French-language fiction of the early 20th century. (Optional periods are sometimes provided for use with a country other than the traditional homeland of the literature if some special device is used to set such literature apart from the literature in general. The options are described at 810–890 in the schedule.) In certain cases, use Table 3C to indicate country of origin of affiliated literatures. *(See also discussion at T3C—93–99.)*

In literary period tables, the name for a particular century is given if the span of years in the heading is less than 75 years, e.g., the 19th century in English literature is given in a class-here note under notation 8 Victorian period, 1837–1899, in the period table for English literature at 821–828. The name for the century is usually not given if the span of years in the heading is 75 or more years, e.g., the 20th century in English literature is not given under notation 91, which covers the span 1900–1999, in the period table for English literature.

Other elements

If appropriate, add notation 08 from Table 3B (or notation 08 or 008 from T3B—1008, notation 08 from table under T3B—102–107) for collections of works by or about more than one author, and notation 09 from Table 3B (or notation 09 or 009 from T3B—1009, notation 09 from table under T3B—102–107) for history, description, and critical appraisal of works of more than one author. Use this notation both on its own and also in order to add notation from Table 3C, to express features such as literary themes or subjects, literary elements (e.g., dialogue), literary qualities (e.g., romanticism), and specific kinds of persons for whom or by whom the literature is written.

Literary criticism

Class criticism with the literature being criticized. Class criticism of a specific work in the same number as the work itself, e.g., a critical analysis of Hemingway's *For Whom the Bell Tolls* 813.52. Class general criticism of the work of an author in the comprehensive number for the author, e.g., criticism of Hemingway 813.52.

Use 809 and notation 09 from Table 3B (or notation 09 or 009 from T3B—1009, notation 09 from table under T3B—102–107) for criticism of all kinds of literature except the works of individual authors. Use 809 for criticism of several literatures as a whole, 809.3 for criticism of fiction from several literatures. Use 810.9 for criticism of the English-language literature of the United States in general, 813.009 for criticism of English-language fiction of the United States in general, 813.5209 for criticism of early 20th-century American fiction in English.

Use 809.1–.7 for criticism of literature in a specific form from more than two literatures. Use 808.1–.7 for critical works in which the emphasis is on the various forms of literature as such, not on the various authors and literatures that may be used as examples. If in doubt between 808.1–.7 and 809.1–.7, prefer 809.1–.7.

Use 801.95 for the theory and technique of literary criticism. Use 808.1–.7 for the theory and technique of criticism of specific literary forms. If in doubt between 801.95 and 808.1–.7, prefer 801.95.

Class appreciation of literature in the same manner as other criticism.

Class textual criticism of literature in the same manner as other criticism. However, use 801.959 (*not* 808.1–.7) for the theory and technique of textual criticism of specific literary forms.

Class criticism of criticism with the criticism being criticized and hence with the original subject of criticism, e.g., criticism of Hemingway and a criticism of that criticism by a third person, both 813.52.

Class works about critics in the same manner as works about other authors, i.e., class critics with the kind of literature that they chiefly criticize, e.g., a man who devoted the major part of his life to criticizing the works of Hemingway 813.52; a critic of Spanish literature 860.9.

Class criticism and critics with the language of the literature they are criticizing, not with the language in which the criticism is written, e.g., a French critic writing in French but criticizing American literature 810.9.

Adaptations

An adaptation may alter the form of a work or modify the content to such an extent in language, scope, or level of presentation that it can no longer be considered a version of the original. Class an adaptation in the number appropriate to the adaptation, e.g., Lamb's *Tales from Shakespeare* 823.7.

However, class a prose translation of poetry (which is merely a change in mode) in the number for the original work, e.g., Dante's *Divine Comedy* translated into German prose 851.1.

Excerpts

Class a collection of excerpts from different literary works as a collection.

800, T3C—362 vs. 398.245, 590, 636

Literature (Belles-lettres) and pets as specific subjects in literature vs. Folk literature of animals vs. Animals vs. Animal husbandry

Class literary accounts of animals, whether fictional or true, with the appropriate form in literature, e.g., poetry. Use subdivisions of T3—8 Miscellaneous writings for literary accounts of actual animals in the form of anecdotes or personal reminiscences, T3—8 + 02 for anecdotes, T3—8 + 03 for reminiscences, diaries, journals; or T3—8 + 07 for works without identifiable literary form.

Use T3C—362 for collections of literary works that treat pets as a specific subject or theme, e.g., a collection of English fiction about cats 823.00803629752.

Class works about animals intended to contribute to some discipline other than literature in the relevant discipline. Use 398.245 for folk literature of animals. Use 590 for animal stories in which the author's emphasis is on the habits and behavior of the animal. Use 636 where the emphasis is on the care and training of the animal.

If in doubt, prefer 800.

800 vs. 398.2

Literature (Belles-lettres) vs. Folk literature

Folk literature is anonymous, having been handed down by word of mouth from one generation to the next. In other words, folk literature is anonymous because it comes from an oral tradition. Folk literature can be collected and retold, e.g., folk tales collected and retold by Jacob and Wilhelm Grimm; but those who collect and retell are not the authors of the literature. Use 398.2 for folk literature.

Works whose authors are unknown only because the authors chose to publish under a pseudonym are not considered to be folk literature. Use 800 for literary works by pseudonymous authors.

Anonymous classics are not considered to be folk literature. Although their authorship is unknown and many of them came from an oral tradition, such works have a recognized literary merit and form part of the literary canon. Use 800 for them, e.g., *Njáls Saga* 839.63, *Mort le Roi Artu (Mort Artu)* 843.1, *Mabinogion* 891.6631. An aid in identifying anonymous classics in European literatures is *Anonymous Classics: A List of Uniform Headings for European Literatures*, 2nd ed. revised by the IFLA Working Group on Anonymous Classics (http://bibpurl.oclc.org/web/9557). Not all of these anonymous classics are literary; some need to be classed with the subject, especially in religion.

Works by known authors, even if in a genre that is traditional for folk literature or about typical folk literary topics, are not considered to be folk literature. Use 800 for them, e.g., fairy tales by Hans Christian Andersen 839.8136; *Inner City Nursery Rhymes* by Barbara Sillars Harvey 811.54, novels by Keri Arthur about werewolves and vampires 823.92.

Some legendary or historical events or themes form the basis for original works in many literatures, periods, and forms, e.g., the search for the Holy Grail or the battle of Roland with the Saracens. Medieval works involving them are often anonymous. Class each retelling of the event or theme with the literature, form, and period in which it was written, e.g., Mary Stewart's Merlin trilogy 823.914. Use 809.933 for works about a specific theme treated in several literatures.

If in doubt, prefer 800.

808.8

Collections of literary texts from more than two literatures

Here are examples illustrating the preference order for collections of texts in more than one form from more than two literatures. The preference order is the same for criticism (809).

1. Specific themes and subjects, e.g., 808.80382 (religion)

2. Specific elements, e.g., 808.8024 (plot)

3. Specific qualities, e.g., 808.8013 (idealism)

4. For and by specific kinds of persons, e.g., 808.899282 (children)

5. Period, e.g., 808.80033 (18th century)

See also discussion at Table 3B: Preference order.

808.81–.88 and 809.1–.7

Specific kinds of poetry, drama, fiction, speeches

The add instructions at 808.812–.818 Specific kinds of poetry, which allow the addition of the numbers following —10 in notation 102–107 from Table 3B, also permit further addition at that point, since numbers in the range T3B—102–107 have a footnote that leads to an add table under a centered entry: "Add as instructed under T3B—102–107."

Do not add notation 08 Collections of literary texts from the add table under T3B—102–107 by itself, since it would be redundant because 808.8 already means collections of literary texts, e.g., collections of narrative poetry 808.813 (*not* 808.81308). However, add notation 08 if it serves as a link for adding further notation from Table 3C, e.g., collections of narrative poetry about political themes 808.813083581.

Apply the same policy for collections of specific kinds of drama, fiction, and speeches, e.g., a collection of short stories 808.831 (*not* 808.83108), but a collection of short stories about political themes 808.831083581.

Apply a similar policy for history and criticism of specific kinds of poetry, drama, fiction, speeches. Do not add notation 09 History, description, critical appraisal by itself to numbers in 809 History, description, critical appraisal of more than two literatures, e.g., history and criticism of narrative poetry 809.13 (*not* 809.1309). However, add notation 09 if it serves as a link for adding further notation from Table 3C, e.g., history and criticism of narrative poetry about political themes 809.13093581.

808.82 vs. 791.437, 791.447, 791.457, 792.9

Texts of plays vs. Production scripts

Use 808.82 and similar numbers built with T3A—2 or T3B—2 for texts of plays. Use 791.437, 791.447, 791.457, and 792.9 for production scripts. A production script contains a variety of directions, e.g., where the furniture is to be placed, where the actors are to stand. For example, use 812.52 for the text of Thornton Wilder's

Our Town, but use 792.92 for the production script for a staged production of *Our Town*. If in doubt, prefer 808.82 and similar numbers.

900

History

Use 900 for the story of events that have transpired, or an account of the conditions that have prevailed, in a particular place or region. Use 001–899 for the history of a specific subject, e.g., a history of political developments (such as internal developments in government) without respect to their effect upon the larger society and place where they occur 320.9, history of economic events in France 330.944, history of warfare 355.0209, history of clocks 681.11309.

The general arrangement of Table 2, which determines the number assigned to the history of a particular place, is geographic rather than by political units, because although political affiliation may change, position on the earth's surface does not, e.g., history of Hawaii 996.9 under Oceania (*not* under United States history).

History includes the present (situation and conditions), but not the future (projected events). Use 303.49 for projected events.

Historic events vs. nonhistoric events

Depending upon their impact, class specific events either in 900 or in specific disciplines in 001–899. Use 930–990 for events that are important enough to affect the general social life and history of the place, regardless of any discipline involved, e.g., the sinking of the Lusitania 940.4514; the assassination of Abraham Lincoln 973.7092; the 1906 San Francisco earthquake 979.461051.

Use 001–899 for the history of the discipline for other specific events. For example, use 364 for the history of a crime, e.g., the Whitechapel murders committed by Jack the Ripper 364.1523. Use 796–799 for a sporting accident, e.g., a fatal accident during an automobile race 796.72.

If in doubt about the impact of the event, prefer 900.

However, take into account the author's purpose or point of view. For example, use 364.1524092 (*not* 973.922092) for a work about the assassination of John F. Kennedy that focuses on the modus operandi of the crime, the detective work involved in solving it, or both.

Use 300 for events that emphasize social aspects. Use 363 (*not* any other discipline involved) if safety factors are stressed, e.g., use 363.12365 for a study of the wreck of the Andrea Doria to determine what the causes of the accident were or what preventive measures might be mandated as a result of the incident.

Use 001–899 for collected accounts of events pertaining to one discipline, e.g., scientific travel 508. Use 904 for collected events without such focus.

909, 930–990 vs. 320

History and politics

Political history

Use 909 and 930–990 for political history that emphasizes major political events typified by the "battles, kings, and dates" school of history. Use 320.9 for political history that emphasizes the mechanics of give and take of political forces and movements and their internal development. Use 909 and 930–990 if the forces and movements come to power or bring about major changes in society. If in doubt, prefer 909 and 930–990.

See also discussion at 909, 930–990 vs. 320.4, 321, 321.09.

Political activities

Use 909 and 930–990 for the sum total of political activity of a specific period or place. Use 320 for specific important political activities presented in terms of the discipline political science, but consider 909 and 930–990 whenever an activity is discussed in a manner that highlights its influence on general events. Use 909 and 930–990 for important events and leaders with wide-ranging responsibilities, unless considered primarily in the context of a specific subject. If in doubt, prefer 909 and 930–990.

Special consideration of 320.9, 324, and 328 follows:

320.9: Use 320.9 for habitual activities and styles of leading political figures as a group, and activities reflecting the adjustment of political forces or the status of political parties and movements. Use 909 and 930–990 for the activities analyzed in terms of their effect on general events.

324: Use 324.2 for party histories; use 324.5 and 324.24–.29, plus notation 015, for histories of nomination campaigns; and use 324.9 for histories of election campaigns, but only when they treat largely internal events of the parties and campaigns, or report winners, losers, and votes. Use 930–990 for the history of how a party or candidate came to power (or almost did), or how party and campaign events move nations (or other areas) in certain directions.

328: Use 328.4–.9 for histories of specific legislative bodies, but only when they are largely limited to what happened within or to the bodies, without significant consideration of what the legislative body did for the political unit it served. Use 328 for reports of proceedings of a legislature (i.e., its motions, debates, actions). Use 930–990 for the accomplishments of a given legislative session, but use 328 if the work concentrates on the body's internal history.

909, 930–990 vs. 320.4, 321, 321.09

Change of government

Use 909 and 930–990 for the history of changes in government or for particular coups and revolutions in specific areas, e.g., revolutions in the 20th century 909.82, the Russian Revolution 947.0841. Use 320.4 for political treatment of systems of government that precede or follow changes in a specific country, e.g., the government of the Soviet Union after the 1917 revolution 320.4470904. Use 321 numbers other than 321.09 for works on particular systems or kinds of systems and general political treatment of a specific system of government preceding or following changes, e.g., new republics 321.86. Use 321.09 primarily for studies of *the process* of change, rather than for works on particular changes. If in doubt, prefer in the following order: 909 or 930–990; 320.4; all subdivisions of 321 except 321.09; 321.09.

909, 930–990 vs. 910

History vs. Geography and travel

Use 909 or 930–990 if a work deals with both geography and civilization or with both travel and civilization. However, use 910 if the treatment of geography or travel is predominant. If in doubt, prefer 909 or 930–990

Use 910.02 or 913–919, plus notation 02 from table under 913–919, if the work deals only with the description of the physical earth.

913–919

Geography of and travel in ancient world and specific continents, countries, localities in modern world; extraterrestrial worlds

Historic sites and buildings

Works describing historic sites and buildings should be classed with the discipline that is emphasized.

Class a work about a building or historic site that has or had a specific purpose with the purpose of the building or site unless some other discipline is emphasized, e.g., a work about a Benedictine monastery in Lower Austria that emphasizes the history of the religious order in that place 271.1043612, a guide to the New York Stock Exchange building 332.64273. Class works about buildings that are associated with the life of an individual with the biography number for that person, e.g., the home of Thomas Wolfe in Asheville, North Carolina 813.52. Class works about a site that is famous for a historic event with the history of the event, e.g., Gettysburg National Military Park 973.7349.

Use 720.9 or 725–728 for works on a building or buildings in an area that emphasize the architecture of the building or buildings, e.g., a work on a church in Paris that emphasizes architectural history 726.50944361. Also use 725–728 for comprehensive works on the art history of a building and its contents, including the architecture of the building and the art works it contains.

Use 930–990 for a work that describes the buildings in an area for the purpose of illustrating the history of the area. (See the discussion at 930–990: Historic preservation.)

Use 913–919 for works when no specific purpose or discipline is evident. (See the discussion below under 04 Travel on Guidebooks.)

See also discussion at 333.7–.9 vs. 508, 913–919, 930–990.

Add table

The following flow chart is offered as an aid to building numbers and as a supplement to the detailed directions at 913–919.

Flow chart for geography and travel

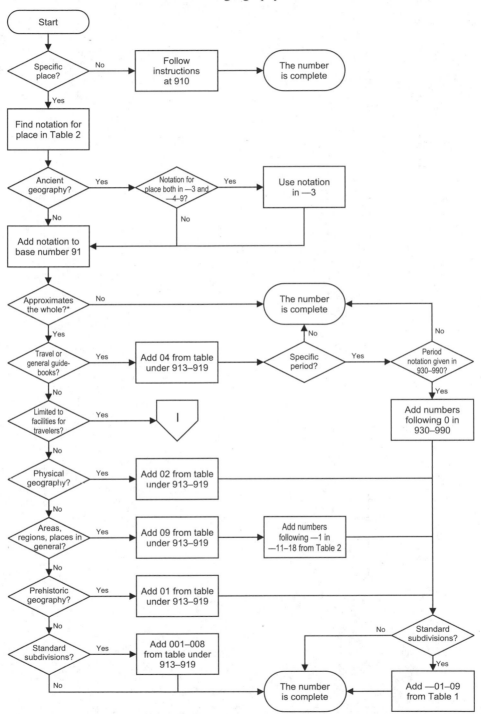

*See also Introduction and Glossary for information about "Approximates the whole"

Flow chart for travelers

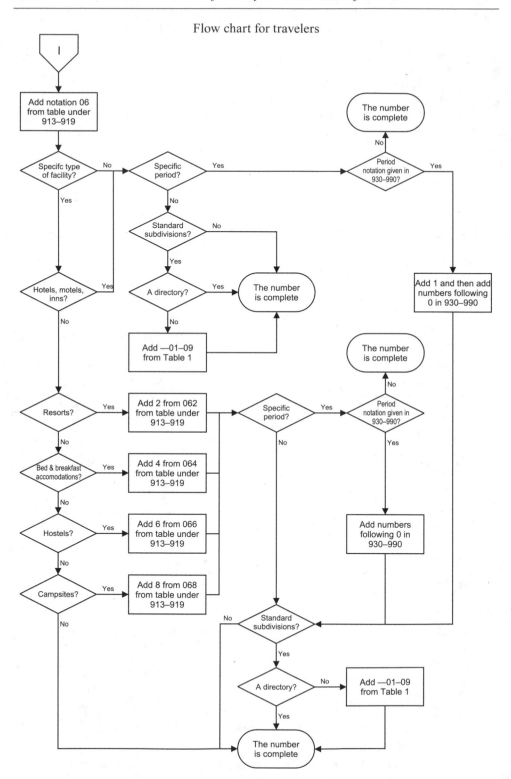

04

Travel

Use 04 for accounts of travel that emphasize events of the trip, places stopped at, accommodations, modes of transportation. If the work is purely a description of the area visited, with none, or very few, of these accompaniments, use subdivision 02 for physical geography. Use 930–990 for civilization and social conditions of the place visited and for works by a person who has lived in the area for several years.

Works on travel normally do not cover the whole of any given area. Class accounts according to the widest span covered, e.g., travel from Marseilles to Paris 914.404, travel from New York to San Francisco 917.304, travel in 1981 from New York City to Buffalo, New York 917.470443. Standard subdivisions may be added.

Discovery and exploration

Use 04 for works describing excursions into previously unknown or little known areas, e.g., the Lewis and Clark expedition 917.8042, Byrd's expedition to the South Pole 919.8904. However, use 930–990 if the initial exploration of a place forms an important part of its early history, e.g., early exploration of North America 970.01.

Use 930.1 for accounts of archaeological expeditions.

Guidebooks

A guidebook can be either a residential guidebook (i.e., a guide for the permanent resident or long-term visitor) or a tourist guidebook (i.e., a guide for the short-term visitor). Residential guidebooks cover not only the tourist attractions but also the other parts of the area, such as banks, churches, grocery stores, real estate agencies, and residential neighborhoods, and normally give a snapshot view of the history of the area. Use 940–990, plus the notation for the period during which it was written, for a residential guidebook, e.g., use 975.3042 for a residential guidebook to Washington, D.C., written in 2003. Tourist guidebooks provide detailed information about the area through which tourists travel, telling them what to see, where to stay, and where to eat. If in doubt whether the book is a residential or a tourist guidebook, class it as a tourist guidebook.

Use 913–919, plus notation 04 from the table at 913–919, for tourist guidebooks, e.g., guidebooks to the United States 917.304. For individual guidebooks, add the notation for the historical period during which it was written, e.g., use 917.530442 for a tourist guidebook to Washington, D.C., written in 2003. Use 913 for guidebooks written before ca. 499, e.g., use 913.85049 for Pausanias' guide to Attica written ca. 130. Use the corresponding number in 914–919 for modern guidebooks to ancient areas, e.g., a 2003 guide to the ruins of Rome 914.56320493.

A guidebook that is limited to an aspect of the trip is classed with that aspect, e.g., a guide to London's underground rail system 388.4209421, restaurants of Hawaii 647.95969, lodgings for tourists in London 914.2106, bed and breakfast establishments of London 914.21064. In addition, guidebooks emphasizing a specific subject are classed with the subject, e.g., a guidebook to holy places in Spain

263.04246, a skiing guide to Aspen, Colorado 796.930978843. (For guidebooks to historic sites and buildings, see the discussion in the section above, Historic sites and buildings.)

Use the number for the attraction in 001–999 for a guidebook to a locality that is usually visited for only one type of attraction. For example, most people go to Orlando, Florida, in order to visit its theme parks: Walt Disney World, Sea World of Florida, and Universal Studios Florida. Therefore, use 791.06875924 for both guidebooks to the theme parks and to Orlando in general. However, use 913–919, plus notation 04 from the table at 913–919, for a guidebook that covers more than one locality, e.g., a guide to central Florida that covers not only Orlando but also Cape Canaveral, Daytona Beach, and Tampa 917.59204.

See also discussion at 333.7–.9 vs. 508, 913–919, 930–990; also at 913–919 vs. 796.51.

Biography

Add notation 092 from Table 1 to subdivisions 041–049 for biographies of discoverers, explorers, and travelers, but not for general geographers nor for first-person accounts of travel. Use the area without further subdivision for biographies of general geographers. Use subdivisions 041–049 for first-person accounts of travel, but do not add notation 092.

913–919 vs. 796.51

Walkers' guides

Walkers' guides can be written for either the hiker or the tourist. Both types of guides give detailed instructions on how to get from point A to point B, e.g., at the fork turn left, and a general description of the route to help the walker to choose one route over another, such as distance, what can be seen. Guides for the tourist also give detailed description of things en route, e.g., the type of vegetation, the history of the wayside shrine. Use 913–919, plus notation 04 from the table at 913–919, for guides for the tourist and for walking guides to an urban area, e.g., walking guides to San Francisco 917.946104. Use 796.51 for guides for the hiker in non-urban areas. If in doubt, prefer 913–919.

Use 001–999 for a guide limited to one topic, e.g., a walker's guide to the geology of Yosemite National Park 557.9447, a walking tour of the skyscrapers of San Francisco 720.4830979461.

920.008 vs. 305–306, 362

History and description of biography as a discipline with respect to kinds of persons; general collections of biography by kind of person vs. Social groups and social welfare problems and services

Use 920.008 for collected biographies of a social group. However, use 305 or 306, plus notation 0922 from Table 1, for biographies that focus on the sociological aspects of the group. Use 362, plus notation 0922 from Table 1, for biographies that focus on the social problems of a group and their solutions. If in doubt, prefer 920.008.

For example, use 920.0086642 for a collection of biographies of gay men. However, use 306.76620922 if the biographies focus on these men as leaders in the gay-rights movements and or on other sociological aspects. Use 920.00871 for a collection of biographies of famous persons who are blind. However, use 362.410922 if the biographies focus on the problems of being blind and social services provided.

Apply the same policy for collected biographies of members of a specific ethnic or national group; however, use 920.0092 (*not* 920.0089). Apply the same policy also for collected biographies of men and of women; however, use 920.71 and 920.72, respectively (*not* 920.00811 or 920.0082).

920.009, 920.03–.09 vs. 909.09, 909.1–.8, 930–990

Biography vs. History

Use 920.009 and 920.03–.09 for collected biographies that contain both (a) biographies of historians and public figures who had a significant impact upon the general history of the place or time and (b) biographies of other public figures and/or biographies of persons of various occupations. Use 909.09, 909.1–.8, and 930–990 for collected biographies limited to biographies of historians and public figures who had a significant impact upon the general history of the place or time. For example, use 920.009033 for a collected biography of the famous persons of the 18th century that includes not only biographies of the kings and queens but also biographies of the bishops, scientists, artists, and athletes; 920.04 for a similar biography limited to Europe; and 920.044 for one limited to France. However, use 909.70922 for a collected biography of the heads of state of the 18th century; 940.099 for a collected biography of the kings and queens of Europe; and 944.0099 for a collected biography of the kings and queens of France. If in doubt, prefer 920.009 and 920.03–.09.

929.2

Family histories

Do not use numbers that are too specific for family histories, since families disperse from their place of origin. Use the area number for the country in which the family lives, not for the state, province, or smaller area, e.g., the history of a Florida family 929.20973 (*not* 929.209759). Treat England, Scotland, Wales, and Northern Ireland as separate countries.

Class a family history with the country in which the family presently lives, not with the country from which the family's ancestors came, e.g., the Duponts, a United States family of French origin, 929.20973 (*not* 929.20944).

Class family histories that give historical information about the area in which the family is located with the history of the area, e.g., prominent families in New York City 974.71.

930–990

History of ancient world; of specific continents, countries, localities; of extraterrestrial worlds

Wars

If most of a war's fighting took place in one region or country, use the number for the history of the region or country. For example, class the War of the Austrian

Succession with the history of Europe in 940.2526; class the Vietnam War with the history of Vietnam in 959.7043. Use the number for the history of the country as a whole, even when the war was fought within a limited portion of a country. For example, class the Second Seminole War, which was fought against the Seminole Indians in Florida, with the history of the United States in 973.57 (*not* with the history of Florida in 975.904).

If most of the fighting took place on the high seas, use the number for the history of the participant in whose territorial waters the majority of the battles took place (*not* with the body of water in 909.096). If the majority of the battles took place on the high seas or in territorial waters of a non-participating country or if in doubt as to where the majority took place, use the number for the history of the participant whose number comes later in 930–990. For example, class the Anglo-Dutch Wars, which consisted of naval battles in the North Sea and English Channel between England and the Netherlands, with the history of the Netherlands in 949.204 (*not* with the history of the North Sea and English Channel in 909.096336 or the history of England in 941.06).

If there was no one place where the majority of the fighting occurred, but the war was fought in the colonies of one or more of the principal participants, use the number for the history of the participant that owned or controlled all or most of the colonies at the end of the war, either the "mother" country of the colonies or the victor of the war. For example, class the Anglo-Spanish War (War of Jenkins' Ear), which was fought in the Spanish colonies of Panama, Colombia, Cuba, and Florida and in the English colony of Georgia, with the history of Spain in 946.055. Class the Spanish-American War, which was fought in the Spanish colonies of the Philippines, Cuba, and Puerto Rico, which were all owned or controlled by the United States at the end of the war, with the history of the United States in 973.89 (*not* with the history of Spain in 946.074).

If none of the previous rules apply, use the number for the history of the region or country where the war began.

The following wars are exceptions to the above rules:

Franco-German War, 1870–1871, is classed with the history of Germany in 943.082 (*not* with the history of France in 944.07). The war was fought in France between France and Prussia. The political results of the war were the creation of the Third Republic of France (during the war) and the German Empire (at end of the war).

Livonian War, 1557–1582, is classed with the history of Russia in 947.043 (*not* with the history of the Baltic States in 947.9). The war was fought between Russia and the coalition of Denmark, Grand Duchy of Lithuania, Kingdom of Poland (later the Polish-Lithuanian Commonwealth), and Sweden for control of Greater Livonia (the territory of the present-day Estonia and Latvia), where the fighting took place.

Russo-Japanese War, 1904–1905, is classed with the history of Japan in 952.031 (*not* with the history of Russia in 947.083). The war was fought in Manchuria, China, over Russia's influence in Korea.

See also discussion at 333.7–.9 vs. 508, 913–919, 930–990; also at 930–990 vs. 355.009, 355–359.

Wars: Ongoing wars

For an ongoing war, use the number for the history of the region or country in which most of the fighting has occurred. For example, when World War II was introduced in Edition 14, most of the fighting had been in Europe; thus, World War II was classed with the history of Europe in 940.53 (*not* with world history in 909.824). If there is no one region or country in which most of the fighting has occurred, use the number for the history of the region or country where the war began.

Wars: Collections of wars

Use the number for the history of the region or the number for the general world history time period for a group of wars discussed together. For example, class comprehensive works on the Crusades with the general historical period of ca. 500–1450/1500 in 909.07. However, class an individual crusade with the history of the region or country where most of the fighting took place. For example, class the First Crusade with the history of the Middle East in 956.014.

Wars: Battles and other military actions

For specific battles or military actions of a war, use the number for the war, not the number for the place where the action occurred, e.g., class a battle occurring in the Philippines during the Spanish-American War in 973.8937 (*not* with the history of the Philippines in 959.9031), air raids on Tokyo in World War II 940.54252135 (*not* with the history of Tokyo in 952.135033).

Use the number for the overall war even when a series of battles or other military actions of that war can be considered as a war unto themselves, e.g., class the war in Spain (Peninsular War), which is one of the Napoleonic Wars, with the Napoleonic Wars in 940.27 (*not* with the history of Spain in 946.06).

> However, use the numbers in the history of the United States, not the numbers in the history of Europe, for the various battles and other military actions in the North American colonies of England and France that are called wars but are aspects of European wars, e.g., class King William's War (North American aspect of the War of the League of Augsburg) with the history of the United States in 973.25 (*not* with the War of the League of Augsburg in 940.2525 or the history of England in 941.068).

When a battle or other military action occurs during the same time period and region of a major war but is not part of that war, use the number for the history of the country in which the fighting took place. For example, class the attempted French invasion of Sardinia in 1793, which took place during the time of the Napoleonic Wars but is not considered part of those wars, with the history of Sardinia in 945.9082 (*not* with the period of the Napoleonic Wars in 940.27). (Note: In 1793, Italy was not a unified country; thus, class this action in the history of Sardinia, not in the history of Italy.)

Wars: Military units

Use the numbers for military units under history of the particular war for the history of specific military units in that war, e.g., military units in World War I

940.412–.413. Use the number for military operations if there is no specific number for military units, e.g., military units in the Vietnam War 959.70434.

Use 355.3 (or similar numbers in 355–359, e.g., 358.4131, 359.31, 359.933) for comprehensive works on specific military units and for military units in peacetime.

Wars: Personal narratives

Class personal narratives of participants in a war in the appropriate subdivision of the history numbers for the specific war, e.g., personal narratives of American soldiers in World War II 940.548173. Class narratives that focus on a specific campaign, battle, or other subject with the subject, e.g., a personal account of the Battle of Berlin 940.54213155092, of Axis intelligence operations in World War II 940.5487092.

Class the narrative of a person's experiences during time of war, if it does not focus on the war as such, as biography and not in the number for the war, e.g., an actor's personal experiences of performing during 1940–1942 in Scotland 792.092 (*not* 940.53088792092).

See also discussion at 930–990: Biography; also at 930–990 vs. 355.009, 355–359.

Wars: Occupied countries

Use the war number for the history of the occupation of a country during the time of the war, e.g., occupation of countries in World War II 940.5336. Use 355.49 for military administration of the government of an occupied country during or following the war. Use 341.66 for international law concerning occupation.

Wars: History of an area not with the history of the war

Three kinds of wartime history are not classed with the history of the war (unless the number for the area covered coincides with the number for the war).

1. Use the number for the area for routine history of the everyday events of an area, even if during wartime, e.g., the history of Maryland during the Civil War 975.203 (*not* 973.709752).

2. Use the number for the history of a place for the effect of military action on the everyday life and civilization of the place, e.g., the effect of Civil War military actions on Maryland 975.203 (*not* 973.709752). However, use the war number for the participation of an area in that war, e.g., Maryland's participation in the Civil War 973.709752 (*not* 975.203).

3. Use the country's history number if there is no emphasis on the country's participation in the war, e.g., a history of Britain during George VI's reign 941.084. However, use the war number if the country's participation is emphasized, e.g., British participation in World War II 940.5341.

Other subjects called "wars"

The term "war" is sometimes applied to a sustained campaign against a problem, or to a period of conflict, tension, and competition between regions or countries. Use the following to class interdisciplinary works on these subjects:

1. A sustained campaign against a problem: Use the number for the problem, e.g., class the War on Crime with crime prevention in 364.4.

2. A period of conflict, tension, and competition between regions or countries: If there are only two countries involved and the countries are within the same region, use the number of the country coming last. If there are more than two countries but all are in the same region, use the number for the region. Otherwise, use the general world history number for the time of the hostility. For example, class the Cold War period of 1947–1991 (the period of conflict, tension, and competition between the United States and the Soviet Union and their allies) with the post World War II period in 909.825.

Also use this instruction to class interdisciplinary works on a war that is both a sustained campaign and a period. For example, class the War on Terrorism (the various military, political, and legal actions taken by the United States and its allies to end international terrorism) with the 2000–2019 period in 909.831.

Unlike military wars, class a specific aspect of this kind of war with the aspect, not with the comprehensive number for the war. For example, class foreign relations between the Soviet Union and the United States during the Cold War with foreign relations in 327.4707309045; class the Korean War with the history of Korea in 951.9042. Class terrorism as a type of social conflict with terrorism as a social problem in 363.325; class the Iraq War, 2003– , with the history of Iraq in 956.70443.

Historic preservation

Use 363.69 for comprehensive works on historic preservation and lists of preservation projects to be undertaken. However, use 930–990 if the list is primarily devoted to inventorying or describing the sites; use 720 if the list is primarily a description of buildings at the site.

Use 353.77 for administrative annual reports of agencies promoting the preservation of historical sites.

Use 720.288 (or numbers in 721–729, plus notation 0288 from Table 1) for works on historic preservation in an architectural context.

See also discussion at 333.7–.9 vs. 508, 913–919, 930–990.

Biography

Add notation 092 from Table 1 to subdivisions 01–09 for biographies of persons who lived during the historical period and also for biographies of historians and historiographers of that period, e.g., biographies of Abraham Lincoln and of Bruce Catton, Civil War historian, 973.7092. Add notation 092 even if the life span of the person or the time during which the person impacted upon the history of the country or locality does not approximate the whole of the period, e.g., biography of Rajiv Gandhi 954.052092. Use subdivision 0099 (which is limited to collected treatment) *only* for works not limited to a specific period, e.g., biographies of the kings and queens of Great Britain 941.0099. If subdivisions 01–09 for historical periods are not given in the schedule, do not add subdivision 0099 either for collected biographies limited to a specific period or for individual biographies, e.g., biographies of the 20th-century princes and princesses of Monaco and a biography of Grace, Princess of Monaco 944.949 (*not* 944.9490099). However, add subdivision 0099 for collected biographies not limited to a specific period, e.g., biographies of the princes and princesses of Monaco 944.9490099. Use subdivision 007202 for biographies of historians and historiographers whose works are not limited to a specific period, e.g., biographies of historians of British history 941.007202.

See also discussion at T1—092: Comprehensive biography: Public figures; also at 920.009, 920.03–.09 vs. 909.09, 909.1–.8, 930–990.

Add table

The following flow chart is offered as an aid to building numbers and as a supplement to the detailed instructions at 930–990.

Flow chart for history

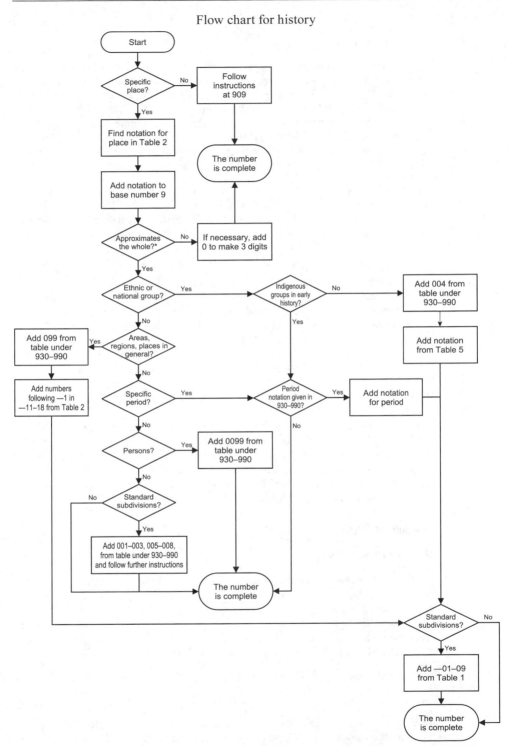

*See also Introduction and Glossary for information about "Approximates the whole"

01–09

Historical periods

The starting and finishing dates of historical period subdivisions usually mark significant events, which rarely occurred on either January 1 or December 31. The year during which the event occurred will therefore normally be given as both the finishing date of one period and the starting date of the next period. For example, 1861, the year when Kansas became a state, appears at both 978.102 Territorial period, 1803–1861 and 978.103 Statehood period, 1861–. Similarly, 1945, the year when World War II ended, appears at both 978.1032 [Kansas during] 1918–1945 and 978.1033 [Kansas during] 1945–.

When adding standard subdivisions to the historical periods, use notation 01–09 from Table 1 (*not* 001–009 from the table under 930–990). However, do not use T1—089 and T1—091, since the provisions for them given at 004 and 0091–0098 in the table under 930–990 take precedence over provisions for historical periods.

Add table: Centuries

The starting and finishing dates of historical period subdivisions may mark centuries or decades rather than significant events in the history of the area. Since such periods start on January 1 and end on December 31, the year either beginning or ending the period will appear in only one heading, e.g., 978.02 [Western United States during] 1800–1899 and 978.03 [Western United States during] 1900–. (The DDC uses the convention that a century begins with the year 00 and ends with the year 99.) In 940–990, the name for a particular century is given if the span of years in the heading is less than 75 years, e.g., the 15th century in German history is given in a class-here note at 943.028 Reigns of Albert II and Frederick III, 1438–1493. The name for the century is not usually given if the span of years in the heading is 75 or more years, e.g., the 17th century is not given at 943.04 [Germany during] 1618–1705. However, if the span in the heading covers three centuries, and the first and third century are given in the including note, the middle century is given in the class-here note, e.g., the 947.03 entry of Russian history has 1240–1462 in the heading, the 13th and 15th centuries in the including note, and the 14th century in the class here note.

930–990 vs. 355.009, 355–359

Military topics and war

Use 930–990 for works on military history that deal with the outcome of significant events in wars, e.g., the use of tanks on the Eastern Front and how their use affected various battles 940.54217. Use the history standard subdivisions in 355–359 for works emphasizing military history or topics without consideration of the general course of a war, e.g., changes in tank tactics during the course of World War II 358.18409044. If in doubt between 930–990 and 355–359, prefer 930–990.

See also discussion at 930–990: Wars.

Persons

Use 930–990 for comprehensive works on soldiers chiefly associated with the history of a specific war, e.g., William Tecumseh Sherman 973.73092. Use 355.0092 for comprehensive works on soldiers associated with more than one war, or who had long and varied careers, e.g., Douglas MacArthur. If in doubt, prefer 930–990.

941

History of the British Isles

Use 941 for works on the United Kingdom (England, Wales, Scotland, and Northern Ireland), a political entity, and on Great Britain (England, Wales, and Scotland), a geographic entity. Use 942 only for works dealing with England alone, or with England and Wales. Histories of the period since 1603 (or including this period) will seldom deal with England or England and Wales alone. Histories of the period before 1603 may deal with England or England and Wales alone. Works on the civilization of this area may deal with any combination. Use 941 for the following combinations of two areas: England and Scotland, England and Ireland, Ireland and Wales.

Tables

Table 1. Standard Subdivisions

The following notation is never used alone, but may be used as required with any regular schedule number, e.g., workbooks (—076 in this table) in arithmetic (513): 513.076. When adding to a number from the schedules, always insert a decimal point between the third and fourth digits of the complete number. Unless other instructions are given, the terminal zeros in a main class or division number should be dropped before adding a standard subdivisions, e.g., journals (—05 in this table) in mathematics (510 minus the final zero): 510.5. (Full instructions on the use of standard subdivisions are found in the Introduction to the Dewey Decimal Classification)

Standard subdivisions should be added only when the work in hand covers the whole, or approximately the whole, subject of the number in the schedules

When standard subdivision notation from Table 1 is listed in Tables 2 through 6 and in the schedules, all of the notation's notes and subdivisions as given in this table are applicable unless other instructions are given. Other Table 1 notation that is not listed in the schedules may also be used. For example, the fact that 610.7 is listed, but not 610.8 or the subdivisions of 610.7, does not exclude the use of 610.8 or 610.71

Do not add one standard subdivision to another standard subdivision unless specifically instructed. Standard subdivisions may be added to special notation listed in the regular standard subdivision sequence, to subdivisions of —04 Special topics that are specifically listed in the schedules, and to displaced standard subdivisions wherever they appear. Numbers in the schedules that look as though they were built with notation from this table but are outside the regular sequence of standard subdivisions are not considered "standard" subdivisions. Hence notation from Table 1 may be added to such schedule numbers

Never use more than one zero in applying a standard subdivision unless instructed to do so. If more than one zero is needed, the number of zeros is always indicated in the schedules. If the 0 subdivisions of a number in a schedule are used for special purposes, use notation 001–009 for standard subdivisions; if the 00 subdivisions also are used for special purposes, use notation 0001–0009 for standard subdivisions

(continued)

Table 1. Standard Subdivisions (continued)

Unless other instructions are given, observe the following table of preference, e.g., communication in education and research —07 (*not* —014):

Special topics	—04
Biography	—092
Auxiliary techniques and procedures; apparatus, equipment, materials	—028
Education, research, related topics	—07
(*except* —074, —075)	
Management	—068
Philosophy and theory	—01
The subject as a profession, occupation, hobby	—023
The subject for people in specific occupations	—024
Directories of persons and organizations	—025
Patents and identification marks	—027
Commercial miscellany	—029
Organizations	—0601–0609
Organizations (without subdivision)	—06
Groups of people	—08
Specific continents, countries, localities; extraterrestrial worlds	—093–099
Areas, regions, places in general	—091
Historical periods	—0901–0905
Museums, collections, exhibits	—074
Museum activities and services	—075
Illustrations, models, miniatures	—022
Tabulated and related materials	—021
Synopses and outlines	—0202
Humorous treatment	—0207
Audiovisual treatment	—0208
Dictionaries, encyclopedias, concordances	—03
History and geographic treatment (without subdivision)	—09
Serial publications	—05

SUMMARY

—01	**Philosophy and theory**
—02	**Miscellany**
—03	**Dictionaries, encyclopedias, concordances**
—04	**Special topics**
—05	**Serial publications**
—06	**Organizations and management**
—07	**Education, research, related topics**
—08	**Groups of people**
—09	**History, geographic treatment, biography**

—01   Philosophy and theory

Including value

Class here methodology, schools of thought

Class interdisciplinary works on philosophy in 100

See Manual at T1—01

—011   Systems

> Class here models (simulations), operations research

> Add to base number —011 the numbers following 003 in 003.1–003.8, e.g., computer modeling and simulation —0113, forecasting and forecasts —0112; however, for forecasts concerning a specific group of people, see —081–089, plus notation 01 from table under —08, e.g., forecasts concerning retired people —0869601; for short term forecasts (ten years or less) in a specific historical period, see —0901–0905, plus notation 01 from table under —0901–0905, e.g., forecasts for 2010–2019 —09051201; for forecasts in a specific continent, country, locality, see —093–099, plus notation 01 from table under —093–099, e.g., forecasts for United States —097301

> Class models (simulations) in study and teaching in —078

> *See Manual at 510, T1—0151 vs. 003, T1—011*

—012   Classification

> Class classification of bibliographic material in 025.42; class classification of bibliographic material on a specific subject in 025.46; class interdisciplinary works on classification in 001.012

—014   Communication

> Including etymology; pronunciation, spelling

> Class here language, terminology; content analysis, semiotics

> Class subject headings and thesauri in information retrieval in 025.49001–025.49999; class interdisciplinary works on communication, semiotics in 302.2; class interdisciplinary works on language in 400; class interdisciplinary works on terminology in 401.4; class interdisciplinary works on etymology in 412. Class aspects of linguistics not provided for here with the aspect in 400, e.g., translating 418.02; class readers for nonnative speakers of a specific language intended to instill a knowledge of the special vocabulary of that language for a specific subject with the language in 400, plus notation 864 from Table 4, e.g., engineering readers (in a language other than Spanish) for Spanish-speaking people —8646102462, English-language engineering readers for Spanish-speaking people 428.646102462

> *For dictionaries, see —03*

—014 1   Discourse analysis

—014 8   Abbreviations, acronyms, symbols

> Symbols classed here are limited to conventional or standard signs such as those used in mathematics, chemistry, flow charts, circuit diagrams, maps, road signs

> Including dictionaries of abbreviations, acronyms, symbols

> Class interdisciplinary works on symbols in 302.2223; class interdisciplinary works on abbreviations and acronyms in 411; class interdisciplinary dictionaries of abbreviations, acronyms, symbols in 413.15

—015   Scientific principles

Use of science to analyze and describe the subject, to support or attack its validity, to carry out operations in the subject, to provide information needed in a subject

Add to base number —015 the numbers following 5 in 510–590, e.g., mathematics —0151, meteorology —015515

Class scientific method in —0721; class statistical methods in —0727; class interdisciplinary works on natural sciences and mathematics in 500

For psychological principles, see —019

See Manual at T1—015 vs. T1—0245–0246; also at 510, T1—0151 vs. 003, T1—011; also at 510, T1—0151 vs. 004–006, T1—0285; also at 519.5, T1—015195 vs. 001.422, T1—0727

—(016)   Bibliographies, catalogs, indexes

(Optional number; prefer 016)

—019   Psychological principles

Use for applications of individual psychology only, not for applications of social psychology

Including psychology of learning specific subjects

Class social psychology in 302; class psychology of learning a specific subject at primary level in 372.3–372.8; class interdisciplinary works on psychology in 150

See Manual at 302–307 vs. 150, T1—019

—02   **Miscellany**

SUMMARY

—020 2   Synopses and outlines

Including chronologies

Class works called synopses and outlines that are regular treatises or introductions to a subject in 001–999 without use of notation 0202 from Table 1; class interdisciplinary chronologies in 902.02

—020 7   Humorous treatment

See Manual at T1—0207 vs. T3B—7, T3A—8 + 02, T3B—802, T3B—8 + 02, T3A—8 + 07, T3B—807, T3B—8 + 07

—020 8   Audiovisual treatment

—021   Tabulated and related materials

           Including statistics, statistical graphs

           Class interdisciplinary collections of statistics in 310

           See also —0727 for analysis of statistical data; also —0728 for methods of presenting statistical data

—021 2   Formulas and specifications

           Class here tables of values for use in formulas and specifications

—021 6   Lists, inventories, catalogs

           Not provided for elsewhere

           Class directories of persons and organizations in —025; class lists and catalogs of products and services offered for sale, lease, or free distribution in —029; class catalogs of collections and exhibits in —074; class price trends for collectors in —075; class bibliographic catalogs on specific subjects in 016; class directories of databases on specific subjects in 016.02506

—021 8   Standards

           Class here standardization

           Add to base number —0218 notation 1–9 from Table 2, e.g., standards in Israel —02185694; however, for biography, see —092

           Class interdisciplinary works on standardization, standards in 389.6; class collections of technical standards in 602.18

           For specifications, see —0212

—022   Illustrations, models, miniatures

           Including graphs

           Class statistical graphs in —021

—022 2   Pictures and related illustrations

           Class here cartoons, drawings, pictorial charts and designs, sketches

           Class interdisciplinary works on cartoons in 741.5

           For humorous cartoons, see —0207

           See Manual at T1—0222 vs. T1—0223

—022 3   Maps, plans, diagrams

           Class comprehensive works on historical maps and atlases in 911; class interdisciplinary works on maps, plans, diagrams; on maps, plans, diagrams of geography, travel, and roads in general and in specific areas in 912

           See Manual at T1—0222 vs. T1—0223

—022 8   Models and miniatures

           Class simulation models in —011; class model and miniature educational exhibits in —074; class interdisciplinary works in 688.1

—023   The subject as a profession, occupation, hobby

> Class here vocational guidance, choice of vocation, career opportunities, occupational specialties, professional relationships; the subject as a profession, occupation, hobby for specific groups of people

> Add to base number —023 notation 1–9 from Table 2, e.g., the subject as a profession in Great Britain —02341; however, for biography, see —092

> Class interdisciplinary works on professional relationships in 331.7; class interdisciplinary works on vocational guidance, choice of vocation, career opportunities, occupational specialties in 331.702; class interdisciplinary works on hobbies in 790.13

—024   The subject for people in specific occupations

> Add to base number —024 notation 001–999, e.g., the subject for engineers —02462

> *See Manual at T1—024; also at T1—015 vs. T1—0245–0246*

—025   Directories of persons and organizations

> Class here directories of public officials and employees; membership lists containing directory information, e.g., employment and education

> Add to base number —025 notation 1–9 from Table 2, e.g., directories of Ohio —025771; however, for biography, see —092

> Class directories giving biographical information in —0922

>> *See also —029 for directories of products and services; also 016.02506 for directories of databases on specific subjects*

>> *See Manual at T1—025 vs. T1—029; also at T1—025 vs. T1—0601–0609*

—(026)   Law

> (Optional number; prefer 341–347)

> Add to base number —026 notation 1–9 from Table 2, e.g., law of Australia —02694; however, for biography, see —092

> A special development of —026 covering treaties and cases in law of nations is given in centered entry at 341.2–341.7 for use with subdivisions in 341.2–341.7; another special development of —026 covering laws, regulations, cases, procedures, courts in the rest of law is given in centered entry at 342–347 for use with subdivisions in 342–347

—027   Patents and identification marks

—027 2   Patents

> Add to base number —0272 notation 1–9 from Table 2, e.g., patents of Japan —027252; however, for biography, see —092

> Class interdisciplinary works on patents in 346.0486; class interdisciplinary collections of patents in 608

> —027 5–027 8 Identification marks

    Class comprehensive works in —027

—027 5   Trademarks and service marks

    Class comprehensive works on trademarks generally found on products rather than identifying services in 602.75; class interdisciplinary works on trademarks and service marks in 929.95

—027 7   Ownership marks

—027 8   Artists' and craftsmen's marks

    Class interdisciplinary works in 700.278

—028   Auxiliary techniques and procedures; apparatus, equipment, materials

—028 4   Apparatus, equipment, materials

    Limited to apparatus, equipment, materials used in a subject

    Class here instruments, instrumentation

    Class apparatus, equipment, materials used in a specific auxiliary technique or procedure in —0285–0289; class collectibles, memorabilia in —075; class use of apparatus and equipment in study and teaching in —078; class products of a subject in 001–999 without adding notation 0284 from Table 1

> —028 5–028 9 Auxiliary techniques and procedures

    Class laboratory manuals in —078; class comprehensive works in —028

    For research methods, see —0721

—028 5   Computer applications

    Class here computer applications in research; data processing

    Unless it is redundant, add to base number —0285 the numbers following 00 in 004–006, e.g., digital personal computers —0285416, but digital computers as a whole —0285 (*not* —02854)

    Class computer modeling and simulation in —0113; class interdisciplinary works on data processing in 004

    See Manual at T1—0285; also at 510, T1—0151 vs. 004–006, T1—0285

—028 6   Green technology (Environmental technology)

> Former heading: Waste technology
>
> Including pollution control technology, waste technology
>
> Class here environmental engineering (environmental health engineering, environmental protection engineering), sustainable engineering
>
> Class interdisciplinary works on environmental engineering, green technology, sustainable engineering in 628; class interdisciplinary works on waste technology in 628.4; class interdisciplinary works on pollution control technology in 628.5
>
> > *See also 621.042 for engineering of alternative and renewable energy resources*

—028 7   Testing and measurement

> Use this subdivision only with numbers denoting fabrication, manufacture, construction, installation, not with numbers denoting use, operation, or application when these are different, e.g., testing and measurement of textile manufacturing machinery 681.76770287 (*not* 677.02850287), of tools 621.900287
>
> Class here laboratory manuals for testing, mensuration
>
> Class aptitude tests in a specific field in 153.94; class technology of testing and measuring instruments in 681.2; class interdisciplinary works on measurement and mensuration in 530.8
>
> > *For educational testing, see —076*

—028 8   Maintenance and repair

> Use this subdivision only with numbers denoting fabrication, manufacture, construction, installation, not with numbers denoting use, operation, or application when these are different, e.g., maintenance and repair of textile manufacturing machinery 681.76770288 (*not* 677.02850288), of tools 621.900288
>
> Class here conservation, preservation, restoration
>
> Class maintenance and repair in specific areas in —09; class interdisciplinary works on maintenance and repair in 620.0046; class interdisciplinary works on artistic conservation, preservation, restoration in 702.88
>
> > *See also —0286 for green technology; also —0682 for management of maintenance*

—028 9   Safety measures

> Use only for personal safety and safety engineering
>
> Class interdisciplinary works on safety in 363.1; class interdisciplinary works on personal safety in 613.6; class interdisciplinary works on safety engineering in 620.86
>
> > *See Manual at 363.1*

—029 Commercial miscellany

Including estimates of labor, time, materials; price trends

Class here listings of products and services offered for sale, lease, or free distribution

Add to base number —029 notation 1–9 from Table 2, e.g., commercial miscellany of Japan —02952; however, for biography, see —092

Class house organs in —05; class interdisciplinary commercial miscellany in 381.029; class noncurrent offers for sale used primarily to illustrate civilization and customs of an earlier period in 900

For price trends for collectors, see —075; for catalogs of bibliographic materials on specific subjects, see 016

See also —074 for listings of noncommercial collections and exhibits

See Manual at T1—025 vs. T1—029; also at T1—074 vs. T1—029

—03 **Dictionaries, encyclopedias, concordances**

Including thesauri (synonym dictionaries)

Class dictionaries of abbreviations, acronyms, symbols in —0148; class biographical dictionaries in —0922; class interdisciplinary encyclopedias in 030; class interdisciplinary dictionaries in 413

See also 025.49 for thesauri (controlled vocabularies)

—04 **Special topics**

Use this subdivision only when it is specifically set forth in the schedules. Add other standard subdivisions —01–09 to it and its subdivisions as required, e.g., participatory democracy in France 323.0420944

—05 **Serial publications**

Regardless of form (print or electronic) or frequency

Class here house organs, magazines, newspapers, yearbooks

Class monographic series in 001–999 without adding notation 05 from Table 1; class interdisciplinary serial publications in 050; class interdisciplinary newspapers in 071–079

For a special kind of serial publication, see the kind, e.g., directories in serial form —025, administrative reports of organizations —06

—06 **Organizations and management**

> —060 1–060 9 Organizations

Class here Greek-letter societies, student organizations; history, charters, regulations, membership lists, administrative reports

Class directories of organizations, membership lists with directory information in —025; class organizations engaged in education, research, related topics in —07; class business enterprises in 338.7; class government administrative and military organizations in 350; class nonadministrative proceedings and reports in 001–999 without adding notation 06 from Table 1; class comprehensive works on organizations active in a subject in —06; class interdisciplinary works on organizations in 060

> *See Manual at T1—0601–0609; also at T1—025 vs. T1—0601–0609; also at T1—072 vs. T1—0601–0609*

—060 1   International organizations

Class guides to national organizations of the world in —06

—060 3–060 9   National, state, provincial, local organizations

Add to base number —060 notation 3–9 from Table 2, e.g., national organizations in France —06044

—068   Management

Class a routine activity called management associated with a profession, occupation, hobby in 001–999 without adding notation 068 from Table 1, e.g., management of patients 616 (*not* 616.0068); class interdisciplinary works in 658

> *See Manual at T1—068; also at T1—068 vs. 353–354*

(Option: Class management of specific enterprises in 658.9)

—068 1   Organization and financial management

Including fund raising for festivals [*formerly* —079], fund raising, initiation of business enterprises

> *For internal organization, see —0684*

> *See also —079 for fund raising for competitions, awards, financial support*

—068 2   Plant management

Including equipment and utilities; maintenance

Class here comprehensive works on energy management

> *For a specific aspect of energy management, see the aspect, e.g., energy conservation in production management —0685*

> *See also —0288 for technology of maintenance*

> *See Manual at 647 vs. 647.068, 658.2, T1—0682*

—068 3   Personnel management (Human resource management)

Including management of employee benefits, of in-service training and residency, of wages and salaries

Class comprehensive works on in-service training and residency in —07155; class interdisciplinary works on labor relations in 331

For management of executive personnel, see —0684

See also 331.21 for wages; also 331.255 for employee benefits

—068 4   Executive management

Including contracting out, internal organization, safety management

For contracting out a specific activity in management, see the activity, e.g., contracting out financial management —0681; for a specific aspect of safety management, see the aspect, e.g., personnel safety —0683

—068 5   Management of production

Class factory operations engineering in 670.42

—068 7   Management of materials

Including physical distribution, procurement of office equipment

See also —029 for evaluation and purchasing manuals

—068 8   Management of distribution (Marketing)

Including market research, personal selling

Class financial aspects of marketing management in —0681; class results of market research in 381

For physical distribution, see —0687; for advertising, see 659.1

—07   **Education, research, related topics**

Including programmed texts

Class here subject-oriented study programs; comprehensive works on education and research, on resources for education and research

Class psychology of learning specific subjects in —019

For a specific resource not provided for here, see the resource, e.g., directories —025, bibliographies 016, libraries 026

See Manual at 016 vs. 026, T1—07

SUMMARY

—070 1–070 9   Geographic treatment

> Add to base number —070 notation 1–9 from Table 2, e.g., education and research in France —07044

—071   Education

> Class here curricula, study (education), teaching, vocational education

> Class student organizations in —0601–0609; class textbooks, school activities in a subject in 001–999 without adding notation 071 from Table 1; class comprehensive works on education and research in —07; class interdisciplinary works on education in 370; class interdisciplinary works on teaching in 371.102

> > *For review and exercise, see —076; for use of apparatus and equipment in education, see —078; for competitions, awards, financial support in education, see —079; for special education in specific subjects, see 371.9*

> > *See Manual at 407.1, T1—071 vs. 401.93, T4—019, 410.71, 418.0071, T4—80071*

—071 01–071 09   Geographic treatment

> Class here geographic treatment of any two levels of education, e.g., secondary and higher education

> Add to base number —0710 notation 1–9 from Table 2, e.g., education in Argentina —071082

>   —071 1–071 5   Specific levels of education

> Class comprehensive works in —071

> *For education in specific subjects at primary level, see 372.3–372.8*

—071 1   Higher education (Tertiary education)

> Class here professional education

> Add to base number —0711 notation 1–9 from Table 2, e.g., universities in Japan —071152; however, for biography, see —092

> > *For extension departments and services, see —0715*

—071 2   Secondary education

> Add to base number —0712 notation 1–9 from Table 2, e.g., secondary schools in rural regions —07121734; however, for biography, see —092

—071 5   Adult education and on-the-job training

> Class here continuing, further, lifelong, permanent, recurrent education; correspondence schools and courses, distance education; extension departments and services; institutes and workshops; occupational and vocational training; radio and television classes

—071 55   On-the-job training

> Class here apprenticeship, in-service training, residency

> Class management of on-the-job training by employers in —0683; class interdisciplinary works in 331.2592

—072   Research

> Class here action research, evaluation research

> Class operations research in —011; class financial support of research in —079; class results of research in 001–999 without adding notation 072 from Table 1; class interdisciplinary works on research in 001.4

> *See Manual at T1—072 vs. T1—0601–0609*

—072 01–072 09   Geographic treatment

> Add to base number —0720 notation 1–9 from Table 2, e.g., research in England —072042

> *See Manual at T1—07201–07209 vs. T1—0721*

—072 1   Research methods

> Class here laboratory manuals used in research; qualitative research, quantitative research, scientific method; research and scientific techniques not provided for elsewhere in Table 1

> Avoid notation for a specific research method when it is redundant, e.g., historical research in history 907.2 (*not* 907.22)

> *For specific research methods, see —0722–0727; for scientific method used in systems analysis, see —011. For a specific research or scientific technique provided for elsewhere in Table 1, see the technique, e.g., mathematical techniques —0151, data processing —0285, testing —0287*

> *See Manual at T1—07201–07209 vs. T1—0721*

—072 2   Historical research

> Including oral history

> Class here historiography

> It is redundant to use the final digit of —0722 in history (900); stop at —072, e.g., historical research in European history 940.072

> Class interdisciplinary works on historical research, on historiography in 907.2

> Case studies relocated to —0723

—072 3   Descriptive research

Including case studies [*formerly* —0722]; sampling techniques; surveys, questionnaires, field work, observation, interviews

Class here data collection

Class management of information collection in —0684; class collection of operational data in 001–999 without adding notation 0723 from Table 1; class interdisciplinary works on data collection in research in 001.433

For analysis of statistical data, see —0727; *for presentation of statistical data, see* —0728

See also —075 *for collection of objects*

—072 4   Experimental research

Class models (simulations) in —011

—072 7   Statistical methods

Class statistical methods used in systems analysis in —011; class interdisciplinary works on statistical methods in 001.422

For data collection, see —0723; *for presentation of statistical data, see* —0728

See also —021 *for works containing the statistics themselves*

See Manual at 519.5, T1—015195 vs. 001.422, T1—0727

—072 8   Presentation of statistical data

Class here graphic presentation

Class the statistics themselves (no matter how presented) in —021

—074   Museums, collections, exhibits

Class here festivals [*formerly* —079], exhibitions, fairs; catalogs, lists regardless of whether or not articles are offered for sale; guidebooks, history and description

Add to base number —074 notation 1–9 from Table 2 for the area in which museums, collections, exhibits are found, e.g., museums in Pennsylvania —074748, festivals in New York City —0747471

Class comprehensive works on museology of a subject in —075; class interdisciplinary works on museums, collections, exhibits in 069; class interdisciplinary works on festivals in 394.26; class interdisciplinary works on exhibitions, fairs in 907.4

For collections of books and related informational materials in specific subjects, see 016

See Manual at T1—074 vs. T1—029

—075   Museum activities and services

Class here museology, collecting, collectibles, memorabilia, price trends for collectors

Class interdisciplinary works on museum activities and services in 069; class interdisciplinary works on museum collecting in 069.4; class interdisciplinary works on recreational collecting in 790.132

For activities and services of or relating to specific museums, collections, exhibits, see —074. For a specific museological technique not provided for here, see the technique in —028, e.g., maintenance and repair of collected objects —0288

—076   Review and exercise

Including workbooks with problems, questions, answers; civil service examinations; testing, test construction and evaluation

Class programmed texts with problems, questions, answers in —07; class interdisciplinary works on civil service examinations in 351.076; class interdisciplinary works on examinations and tests in 371.26

For review and exercise using apparatus and equipment, see —078

See also 153.94 for aptitude tests in a specific field

(Option: Class civil service examinations in specific subjects in 351.076)

—078   Use of apparatus and equipment in study and teaching

Class here laboratory manuals, student projects and experiments

Class interdisciplinary works on teaching aids in 371.33

For laboratory manuals used in testing, see —0287; for laboratory manuals used in research, see —0721

—078 5   Computer-assisted instruction

Unless it is redundant, add to base number —0785 the numbers following 00 in 004–006, e.g., use of digital personal computers —0785416, but digital computers —0785 (*not* —07854); interactive video —078567

Class interdisciplinary works on computer-assisted instruction in 371.334

—079   Competitions, awards, financial support

Including fund raising to support such activities; judging competitions

Class here bursaries, certificates, contests, fellowships and scholarships, grants, honors, medals, prizes

Add to base number —079 notation 4–9 from Table 2 for geographic eligibility only, e.g., competitions open to contestants from Italy —07945, awards open to entrants from the United States —07973, fellowships limited to residents of California —079794
    Subdivisions are added for any or all topics in heading

Class description of works that are entered into competitions, that receive awards, or that are the results of financial support in 001–999 without adding notation 079 from Table 1; class interdisciplinary works on orders and decorations in 929.81

See also —0681 for financial management aspects of fund raising

Fund raising for festivals relocated to —0681; festivals relocated to —074

—08   **Groups of people**

Class here discrimination, group identity, minorities

The subdivisions listed in the add table below are special notation, not standard subdivisions

Unless other instructions are given in the add table below, observe the following table of preference, e.g., a periodical of statistics —021 (*not* —025):

Forecasting and forecasts	—01
Specific continents, countries, localities	—093–099
Areas, regions, places in general	—091
Historical periods	—0901–0905
Museums, collections, exhibits	—074
Collecting objects	—075
Illustrations	—022
Statistics	—021
Dictionaries, encyclopedias, concordances	—03
History and geographic treatment (without subdivision)	—09
Serial publications	—05

(continued)

—08   **Groups of people (continued)**

Add to each subdivision identified by * as follows:

01	Forecasting and forecasts
02	Statistics and illustrations
021	Statistics
022	Illustrations

         Including cartoons, drawings, pictures, pictorial charts and designs, sketches; graphs; maps, plans, diagrams

         Class statistical graphs in 021; class humorous cartoons in —08 without adding from this table

03	Dictionaries, encyclopedias, concordances

         Class here thesauri (synonym dictionaries)

05	Serial publications

         Regardless of form (print or electronic) or frequency

         Class here house organs, magazines, newspapers, yearbooks

07	Museums, collections, exhibits; collecting objects
074	Museums, collections, exhibits

         Class here exhibitions, fairs, festivals; catalogs, lists regardless of whether or not articles are offered for sale; guidebooks, history and description

         Add to 074 notation 4–9 from Table 2, e.g., collections in Pennsylvania 074748

075	Collecting objects

         Class here collectibles, memorabilia, price trends for collectors

09	History and geographic treatment
0901–0905	Historical periods

         Add to 090 the numbers following —090 in notation 0901–0905 from Table 1, e.g., the group in the 20th century 0904

091	Areas, regions, places in general

         Add to 091 the numbers following —1 in notation 11–18 from Table 2, e.g., the group in urban regions 091732

093–099	Specific continents, countries, localities

         Add to 09 notation 3–9 from Table 2, e.g., the group in Japan 0952

Class ethnic and national minorities in —089; class biography in —092

See Manual at T1—08 and 306.2–306.6

SUMMARY

—080 1–080 9	**Forecasting, statistics, illustrations, dictionaries, encyclopedias, concordances, serials, museums and collecting, history and geographic treatment**
—081	**People by gender or sex**
—082	**Women**
—083	**Young people**
—084	**People in specific stages of adulthood**
—085	**Relatives**
—086	**People by miscellaneous social attributes**
—087	**People with disabilities and illnesses, gifted people**
—088	**Occupational and religious groups**
—089	**Ethnic and national groups**

—080 1–080 9   Forecasting, statistics, illustrations, dictionaries, encyclopedias, concordances, serials, museums and collecting, history and geographic treatment

> Add to base number —080 the numbers following 0 in notation 01–09 from table under —08, e.g., statistics —08021

\>   —081–088 Groups of people by specific attributes

> Unless other instructions are given, class a subject with aspects in two or more subdivisions of —081–088 in the number coming last, e.g., children with disabilities —087 (*not* —083)

> Class comprehensive works on ethnic and national groups in —089. Class members of an ethnic or national group with a specific attribute, other than people with status defined by change in residence, with the attribute in —081–088, e.g., Chinese women —082

—081   *People by gender or sex

> Class here gender identity, gender role, sex role

> Subdivisions are added for either or both topics in heading

> *For women, see —082; for transgender and intersex people, see —0867*

> *See Manual at T1—081 and T1—08351, T1—08352, T1—08421, T1—08422*

—081 1   *Men

> Class here males

> *See Manual at T1—081 and T1—08351, T1—08352, T1—08421, T1—08422*

—082   *Women

> Class here females; feminist views of a subject, e.g., feminist Christian theology 230.082

> *See Manual at T1—081 and T1—08351, T1—08352, T1—08421, T1—08422*

—083   *Young people

> Class here children

—083 2   *Infants

> Children from birth through age two

—083 3   *Children three to five

> Class here preschool children

*Add as instructed under —08

—083 4   *Children six to eleven

                           Class here school children

                               For school children over eleven, see —0835

—083 41   *Boys six to eleven

—083 42   *Girls six to eleven

—083 5   *Young people twelve to twenty

                               Variant names: adolescents, teenagers, young adults, youth

                               Class youth twenty-one and over, comprehensive works on young adults in —0842

—083 51   *Males twelve to twenty

                                     See Manual at T1—081 and T1—08351, T1—08352, T1—08421, T1—08422

—083 52   *Females twelve to twenty

                                     See Manual at T1—081 and T1—08351, T1—08352, T1—08421, T1—08422

—084   People in specific stages of adulthood

                               Class comprehensive works on adults in 001–999 without adding notation 084 from Table 1

—084 2   *People in early adulthood

                               Class here comprehensive works on young adults

                               For young adults under twenty-one, see —0835

—084 21   *Young men

                                     See Manual at T1—081 and T1—08351, T1—08352, T1—08421, T1—08422

—084 22   *Young women

                                     See Manual at T1—081 and T1—08351, T1—08352, T1—08421, T1—08422

—084 4   *People in middle adulthood

—084 6   *People in late adulthood

—085   *Relatives

                               Class here parents, adoptive and foster parents, stepparents

—085 1   *Fathers

—085 2   *Mothers

                               For unmarried mothers, see —086947

*Add as instructed under —08

—085 3   *Grandparents

                     Including great grandparents of any degree (ancestors)

—085 4   *Progeny

                     Class here children considered in relation to parents

—085 5   *Siblings

                     Brothers and sisters by blood, adoption, foster care, remarriage of parents

—086   *People by miscellaneous social attributes

                     Not provided for elsewhere

—086 2   *People by social and economic levels

                     Class here people by level of cultural development [*formerly* —0863], social classes

                         For people with social disadvantages, see —08694

—086 21   *Upper classes

                     Including nobility, royalty, wealthy

                     Class here elites

                         For reigning monarchs and their regents, see —08835223

—086 22   *Middle classes (Bourgeoisie)

                     Including entrepreneurs, managers, professionals

                     Class here moderately well-to-do people

                         For lower middle classes, see —08623

—086 222   *Intelligentsia [*formerly* —08631]

                       Class here intellectual elites

—086 23   *Lower middle classes

                     Class here moderate-income people, working class in developed areas, blue collar workers

—086 24   *Lower classes

                     Including migrant workers, unskilled workers

                     Class blue collar workers in —08623; class peasants, sharecroppers in —08863

                         For slaves, serfs, peons, see —08625; for poor people, see —086942

—086 25   *Slaves, serfs, peons

*Add as instructed under —08

—[086 3]	People by level of cultural development
	Relocated to —0862
—[086 31]	Intelligentsia
	Relocated to —086222
—[086 33]	People with cultural disadvantages
	Relocated to —08694
—086 5	*People by marital status
—086 52	*Single people

For separated and divorced people, see —08653; for widowed people, see —08654

—086 523	*Engaged people
—086 53	*Separated and divorced people

Subdivisions are added for either or both topics in heading

—086 54	*Widowed people
—086 55	*Married people

For polygamists, see —08659

People in common-law marriages relocated to —08656

—086 56	*People in partnerships and unions

Class here people in common-law marriages [*formerly* —08655], civil unions, de facto relationships, domestic partnerships, registered partnerships; unmarried couples living together (cohabitation)

Subdivisions are added for either or both topics in heading

—086 59	*Polygamists
—086 6	*People by sexual orientation

Including asexuals

Transsexuals relocated to —0867

—086 62	*Heterosexuals
—086 63	*Bisexuals
—086 64	*Gays
—086 642	*Gay men
—086 643	*Lesbians

*Add as instructed under —08

—086 7   *Transgender and intersex people

                    Including female-to-male transgender people, male-to-female transgender people

                    Class here transsexuals [*formerly* —0866], transgenderists

                    Subdivisions are added for transgender and intersex people together, for transgender people alone

—086 75   *Intersex people

—086 9   *People by miscellaneous social statuses

—086 91   *People with status defined by changes in residence

                    Class here aliens, expatriates, foreigners

                    Class migrant workers in —08624; class runaway children in —086923; class tramps in —086942; class people of a specific ethnic or national group in —089

—086 912   *Immigrants

                    Class displaced persons, refugees in —086914

—086 914   *Displaced persons

                    Class here exiles, refugees, stateless persons

—086 918   *Nomads

—086 92   *Antisocial and asocial people

                    Subdivisions are added for either or both topics in heading

                    See also —086942 for tramps

—086 923   *Juvenile delinquents and predelinquents

                    Subdivisions are added for either or both topics in heading

—086 927   *Offenders

                    Class here convicts, criminals

                    Class juvenile delinquents in —086923

—086 93   *Nondominant groups

                    Class a specific nondominant group with the group, e.g., serfs —08625

—086 94   *People with social disadvantages

                    Class here people with cultural disadvantages [*formerly* —08633], alienated and excluded classes

                    Class people with a specific social disadvantage not provided for here with the disadvantage, e.g., addicts in recovery —0874

*Add as instructed under —08

—086 941   *Unemployed people

                    Class poverty-stricken and destitute unemployed people in
                      —086942

—086 942   *Poor people

                    Including homeless people, tramps

—086 945   *Abandoned children, abused children, children of unmarried parents, orphans

                    See also —086923 for runaway children

—086 947   *Unmarried mothers

—086 949   *Victims of war and crime

                    Including inmates of concentration or internment camps

—086 96   *Retired people

—086 97   *Veterans of military service

—087   *People with disabilities and illnesses, gifted people

                  Including people with learning disabilities

                  Class here people with physical disabilities

—087 1   *People with blindness and visual impairments

                  Class here people who are blind-deaf

                  Subdivisions are added for either or both topics in heading

—087 2   *People with hearing impairments

                  Class here people who are deaf

                  Class people who are deaf-blind in —0871

—087 3   *People with mobility impairments

                  Class people with mobility impairments resulting from developmental disabilities in —0875

—087 4   *People with mental illness and disabilities

                  Including addicts, addicts in recovery, alcoholics

—087 5   *People with developmental disabilities

                  Class people with congenital visual disabilities in —0871; class people with congenital hearing disabilities in —0872

                  For people with mental developmental disabilities, see —0874

—087 7   *People with physical illnesses

                  For people with a specific disability, illness, or impairment provided for elsewhere, see the disability, illness, or impairment, e.g., people with developmental disabilities —0875

*Add as instructed under —08

—087 9   *Gifted people

—088   Occupational and religious groups

> Add to base number —088 notation 001–999, e.g., nondominant religious groups —0882, Catholic teachings on socioeconomic problems 261.8088282

> Class works on the subject for people in specific occupations in —024

> *See Manual at T1—0882 and 200*

—089   Ethnic and national groups

> Class here ethnic and national minorities; racial groups, racism

> Class biography of members of a specific ethnic or national group in —0923; class treatment with respect to specific ethnic and national groups in places where they predominate in —091–099. Class members of an ethnic or national group with a specific attribute, other than people with status defined by change in residence, with the attribute in —081–088, e.g., Chinese women —082

> *See Manual at T1—09 vs. T1—089*

—089 001–089 009   Forecasting, statistics, illustrations, dictionaries, encyclopedias, concordances, serials, museology, history and geographic treatment

> Add to base number —08900 the numbers following 0 in notation 01–09 from table under —08, e.g., statistics —0890021

—089 05–089 09   Specific ethnic and national groups with ethnic origins from more than one continent, of European descent

> Add to base number —0890 the numbers following 0 in notation 05–09 from Table 5, e.g., ethnic groups of European descent —08909, ethnic groups of European descent in Namibia —0890906881

—089 1–089 9   Specific ethnic and national groups

> Add to base number —089 notation 1–9 from Table 5, e.g., groups of Italian descent —08951, groups of Italian descent in United States —08951073

—09   **History, geographic treatment, biography**

> Class historiography in —0722; class history and geographic treatment of museums, collections, exhibits representing the whole subject in —074; class history and geographic treatment of museum activities and services representing the whole subject in —075

> *See Manual at T1—09; also at T1—0601–0609: Selection of area number; also at T1—09 vs. T1—089*

---

*Add as instructed under —08

SUMMARY

—090 05		**Serial publications**
—090 1–090 5		**Historical periods**
—091		**Areas, regions, places in general**
—092		**Biography**
—093–099		**Specific continents, countries, localities; extraterrestrial worlds**

—090 05   Serial publications

>   —090 1–090 5   Historical periods

The subdivisions listed in the add table below are special notation, not standard subdivisions

Unless other instructions are given in the add table below, observe the following table of preference, e.g., a periodical of statistics —021 (*not* —05):

Short term forecasts	—01
Museums, collections, exhibits	—074
Collecting objects	—075
Illustrations	—022
Statistics	—021
Dictionaries, encyclopedias, concordances	—03
Serial publications	—05

Add to each subdivision identified by * as follows:

01	Short term forecasts
	Ten years or less
	Class long term forecasts (more than ten years) in —0112
02	Statistics and illustrations
021	Statistics
022	Illustrations
	Including cartoons, drawings, pictures, pictorial charts and designs, sketches; graphs; maps, plans, diagrams
	Class statistical graphs in 021; class humorous cartoons in —0901–0905 without adding from this table
03	Dictionaries, encyclopedias, concordances
	Including thesauri (synonym dictionaries)
05	Serial publications
	Regardless of form (print or electronic) or frequency
	Class here house organs, magazines, newspapers, yearbooks
07	Museums, collections, exhibits; collecting objects
074	Museums, collections, exhibits
	Class here exhibitions, fairs, festivals; catalogs, lists regardless of whether or not articles are offered for sale; guidebooks, history and description
	Add to 074 notation 4–9 from Table 2, e.g., collections in Pennsylvania 074748, collections of ancient objects in Pennsylvania —0901074748
075	Collecting objects
	Class here collectibles, memorabilia, price trends for collectors

(continued)

>   —090 1–090 5 Historical periods (continued)

Class historical periods in specific areas, regions, places in general in —091; class historical periods in specific continents, countries, localities in —093–099; class comprehensive works in —09

See Manual at T1—0901–0905

—090 1   *To 499 A.D.

The ancient period when the coverage is not limited to areas provided for in —093

—090 12   *To 4000 B.C.

Class here comprehensive works on prehistoric periods

For a specific prehistoric period not provided for here, see the period, e.g., 3999–1000 B.C. —09013

—090 13   *3999–1000 B.C.

—090 14   *999–1 B.C.

—090 15   *1st–5th centuries, 1–499

—090 2   *6th–15th centuries, 500–1499

Class here Middle Ages (Medieval period)

See Manual at T1—0940902 vs. T1—0902

—090 21   *6th–12th centuries, 500–1199

—090 22   *13th century, 1200–1299

—090 23   *14th century, 1300–1399

—090 24   *15th century, 1400–1499

—090 3   *Modern period, 1500–

For 20th century, see —0904; for 21st century, see —0905

—090 31   *16th century, 1500–1599

—090 32   *17th century, 1600–1699

—090 33   *18th century, 1700–1799

—090 34   *19th century, 1800–1899

—090 4   *20th century, 1900–1999

—090 41   *1900–1919

Class here early 20th century

For 1920–1929, see —09042; for 1930–1939, see —09043; for 1940–1949, see —09044

---

*Add as instructed under —0901–0905

—090 42	*1920–1929
—090 43	*1930–1939
—090 44	*1940–1949

Class here period of World War II

For 1939, see —09043

—090 45	*1950–1959

Class here late 20th century, post World War II period

For 1945–1949, see —09044; for 1960–1969, see —09046; for 1970–1979, see —09047; for 1980–1989, see —09048; for 1990–1999, see —09049

—090 46	*1960–1969
—090 47	*1970–1979
—090 48	*1980–1989
—090 49	*1990–1999
—090 5	*21st century, 2000–2099
—090 51	*2000–2019
—090 511	*2000–2009
—090 512	*2010–2019
—091	Areas, regions, places in general

History and description

Add to base number —091 the numbers following —1 in notation 11–19 from Table 2, e.g., Torrid Zone —0913; then add further as instructed under —093–099, e.g., conservation and preservation in tropical areas —0913028

*Add as instructed under —0901–0905

205

—092   Biography

Autobiography, description and critical appraisal of work, diaries, reminiscences, correspondence of people regardless of area, region, or place who are part of the subject or who study the subject, e.g., biographers, collectors, leaders and followers, practitioners and clients, scholars

Class here treatment of individuals

Class nonbiographical treatment of groups of people in —08; class biography not clearly related to any specific subject in 920; class belletristic diaries, reminiscences, correspondence in 800

Observe instructions not to use —092 that apply to 180–190, 759, 809, 810–890. (The instructions for 810–890 are found under notation 09 from Table 3B)

Do not use —092 for a person whose name is used in a schedule heading, e.g., class Muḥammad the Prophet in 297.63 (*not* 297.63092)

> *See Manual at T1—092; also at 913–919: Add table: 04: Biography; also at 930–990: Wars: Personal narratives; also at 930–990: Biography*

(Option A: Class biography in 920.1–928

(Option B: Class individual biography in 92, or B

(Option C: Class all individual biography of men in 920.71, of women in 920.72)

—092 2   Collected biography

Class here comprehensive works

Add to base number —0922 notation 3–9 from Table 2, e.g., collected biography of a subject in Italy —092245

Class collectibles and memorabilia related to more than one person in —075; class collected biography of specific continents, countries, localities when not limited to a specific subject in 920.03–920.09

> *For collected biography of members of specific ethnic and national groups, see —0923*

> *See Manual at T1—0922; also at T1—0922 vs. T1—093–099*

(Option: Class collected biography in 92, 920, or B without subdivision)

Collected biography of people by specific gender or sex; age groups; relationships relocated to —0925; collected biography of people by miscellaneous social attributes relocated to —0926; collected biography of people with disabilities and illnesses, gifted people relocated to —0927; collected biography of members of specific religious groups relocated to —0928

>   —092 3–092 8   Collected biography of specific groups of people

Unless other instructions are given, class a subject with aspects in two or more subdivisions of —0923–0928 in the number coming last, e.g., biography of African American women from Texas —0925209764 (*not* —0922764 or —0923960730764)

Class comprehensive works in —0922

—092 3   Collected biography of members of ethnic and national groups

Class collected biography of members of specific ethnic and national groups in areas where they predominate with the group in a specific area in —0922, e.g., biography of Italians in Italy —092245

Collected biography of people by specific gender or sex; age groups; relationships relocated to —0925; collected biography of people by miscellaneous social attributes relocated to —0926; collected biography of people with disabilities and illnesses, gifted people relocated to —0927; collected biography of members of specific religious groups relocated to —0928

—092 305–092 309   Collected biography of members of ethnic and national groups with ethnic origins from more than one continent, of European descent

Add to base number —09230 the numbers following 0 in notation 05–09 from Table 5, e.g., biography of members of ethnic groups of European descent —092309, biography of members of ethnic groups of European descent in Australia —092309094

—092 31–092 39   Collected biography of members of specific ethnic and national groups

Add to base number —0923 notation 1–9 from Table 5, e.g., biography of people of Italian descent —092351, biography of people of Italian descent in United States —092351073

—092 5   Collected biography of people by specific gender or sex; age groups; relationships [*all formerly* —0922, —0923]

Add to base number —0925 the numbers following – 08 in notation 081–085 from Table 1, e.g., biography of women —09252

For collected biography of transgender and intersex people, see —09267

—092 6   Collected biography of people by miscellaneous social attributes [*formerly* —0922, —0923]

Add to base number —0926 the numbers following —086 in Table 1, e.g., biography of gays —092664

—092 7   Collected biography of people with disabilities and illnesses, gifted people [*all formerly* —0922, —0923]

Add to base number —0927 the numbers following —087 in Table 1, e.g., biography of blind people —09271

—092 8   Collected biography of members of specific religious groups
              [*formerly* —0922, —0923]

              Add to base number —0928 the numbers following 2 in 230–290, e.g.,
              biography of Muslims —092897

—092 9   Biography of animals and plants

              Use this number for animals and plants treated as individuals, e.g., a
              biography of Secretariat 798.400929

—093–099   Specific continents, countries, localities; extraterrestrial worlds

              History and description by place, by specific instance of the subject

              The subdivisions listed in the add table below are special notation, not
              standard subdivisions

              Unless other instructions are given in the add table below, observe the
              following table of preference, e.g., a periodical of statistics —021 (*not*
              —05):

Maintenance and repair	—028
Forecasts	—01
Specific continents, countries, localities	—093–099
Areas, regions, places in general	—091
Historical periods	—0901–0905
Museums, collections, exhibits	—074
Collecting objects	—075
Illustrations	—022
Statistics	—021
Dictionaries, encyclopedias, concordances	—03
History and geographic treatment (without subdivision)	—09
Serial publications	—05

              Add to base number —09 notation 3–9 from Table 2, e.g., the subject in
              North America —097, in Brazil —0981; then add further as follows:

              01   Forecasts
              02   Statistics, illustrations; maintenance and repair
              021   Statistics
              022   Illustrations
                              Including cartoons, drawings, pictures, pictorial charts
                              and designs, sketches; graphs; maps, plans, diagrams
                              Class statistical graphs in 021; class humorous cartoons
                              in —093–099 without adding from this table
              028   Maintenance and repair
                              Class here conservation, preservation, restoration
              03   Dictionaries, encyclopedias, concordances
                              Including thesauri (synonym dictionaries)
              05   Serial publications
                              Regardless of form (print or electronic) or frequency
                              Class here house organs, magazines, newspapers,
                              yearbooks

                                                              (continued)

208

—093–099   Specific continents, countries, localities; extraterrestrial worlds (continued)

07   Museums, collections, exhibits; collecting objects

074   Museums, collections, exhibits

Class here exhibitions, fairs, festivals; catalogs, lists regardless of whether or not articles are offered for sale; guidebooks, history and description

Add to 074 notation 4–9 from Table 2, e.g., collections in Pennsylvania 074748, collections of Brazilian objects in Pennsylvania —0981074748

075   Collecting objects

Class here collectibles, memorabilia, price trends for collectors

09   History and geographic treatment

0901–0905   Historical periods

Add to 090 the numbers following —090 in notation 0901–0905 from Table 1, e.g., 20th century 0904; however, for museums, collections, exhibits of the subject in an area regardless of historical period, see 074, e.g., collections of 20th-century Brazilian art 709.81074 (*not* 709.810904)

091   Areas, places, regions in general

Add to 091 the numbers following —1 in notation 11–19 from Table 2, e.g., rural regions 091734

093–099   Specific continents, countries, localities; extraterrestrial worlds

Add to 09 notation 3–9 from Table 2, e.g., Poland 09438

Use 093–099 to add notation for a specific continent, country, locality when first area notation is used to specify area of origin, while second one identifies area in which subject is found or practiced, e.g., Polish political refugees 325.2109438, Polish political refugees in Canada 325.21094380971

(Option: Add historical period numbers that appear in subdivisions of 930–990, using one 0 in all cases except 00 for North America and South America, e.g., United States during Reconstruction —097308, Brazil during Empire —098104, North America in 20th century —097005. If option is used, do not use notation 090 from table above. An extra zero is used for the balance of notation from table above, e.g., statistics of Brazil —09810021)

See Manual at T1—0922 vs. T1—093–099; also at T1—0940902 vs. T1—0902

Table 2. Geographic Areas, Historical Periods, Biography

The following numbers are never used alone, but may be used as required (either directly when so noted or through the interposition of notation 09 from Table 1) with any number from the schedules, e.g., wages (331.29) in Japan (—52 in this table): 331.2952; railroad transportation (385) in Brazil (—81 in this table): 385.0981. They may also be used when so noted with numbers from other tables, e.g., notation 025 from Table 1. When adding to a number from the schedules, always insert a decimal point between the third and fourth digits of the complete number

SUMMARY

—001–009	Standard subdivisions
—01–05	Historical periods
—1	Areas, regions, places in general; oceans and seas
—11	Frigid zones
—12	Temperate zones (Middle latitude zones)
—13	Torrid zone (Tropics)
—14	Land and landforms
—15	Regions by type of vegetation
—16	Air and water
—17	Socioeconomic regions
—18	Other kinds of terrestrial regions
—19	Space
—2	Biography
—3	Ancient world
—31	China to 420
—32	Egypt to 640
—33	Palestine to 70
—34	South Asia to 647
—35	Mesopotamia to 637 and Iranian Plateau to 637
—36	Europe north and west of Italian Peninsula to ca. 499
—37	Italian Peninsula to 476 and adjacent territories to 476
—38	Greece to 323
—39	Other parts of ancient world
—4	Europe
—41	British Isles
—42	England and Wales
—43	Germany and neighboring central European countries
—44	France and Monaco
—45	Italy, San Marino, Vatican City, Malta
—46	Spain, Andorra, Gibraltar, Portugal
—47	Russia and neighboring east European countries
—48	Scandinavia
—49	Other parts of Europe

—5	Asia
—51	China and adjacent areas
—52	Japan
—53	Arabian Peninsula and adjacent areas
—54	India and neighboring south Asian countries
—55	Iran
—56	Middle East (Near East)
—57	Siberia (Asiatic Russia)
—58	Central Asia
—59	Southeast Asia
—6	Africa
—61	Tunisia and Libya
—62	Egypt and Sudan
—63	Ethiopia and Eritrea
—64	Morocco, Ceuta, Melilla, Western Sahara, Canary Islands
—65	Algeria
—66	West Africa and offshore islands
—67	Central Africa and offshore islands
—68	Republic of South Africa and neighboring southern African countries
—69	South Indian Ocean islands
—7	North America
—71	Canada
—72	Mexico, Central America, West Indies, Bermuda
—73	United States
—74	Northeastern United States (New England and Middle Atlantic states)
—75	Southeastern United States (South Atlantic states)
—76	South central United States
—77	North central United States
—78	Western United States
—79	Great Basin and Pacific Slope of United States
—8	South America
—81	Brazil
—82	Argentina
—83	Chile
—84	Bolivia
—85	Peru
—86	Colombia and Ecuador
—87	Venezuela
—88	Guiana
—89	Paraguay and Uruguay
—9	Australasia, Pacific Ocean islands, Atlantic Ocean islands, Arctic islands, Antarctica, extraterrestrial worlds
—93	New Zealand
—94	Australia
—95	New Guinea and neighboring countries of Melanesia
—96	Polynesia and other Pacific Ocean islands
—97	Atlantic Ocean islands
—98	Arctic islands and Antarctica
—99	Extraterrestrial worlds

—001–008   Standard subdivisions

—009   History

> If "history" or "historical" appears in the heading for the number to which notation 009 could be added, this notation is redundant and should not be used

—[009 01–009 05]   Historical periods

> Do not use; class in —01–05

—[009 1–009 9]   Geographic treatment and biography

> Do not use; class in —1–9

—01–05   Historical periods

> Add to base number —0 the numbers following —090 in notation 0901–0905 from Table 1, e.g., 20th century —04

—1   Areas, regions, places in general; oceans and seas

> Not limited by continent, country, locality
>
> Class biography regardless of area, region, place in —2; class specific continents, countries, localities in —3–9
>
> (Option: Add to each number in —1 as follows:
>   03–09   Specific continents, countries, localities
>   Add to 0 notation 3–9 from Table 2, e.g., Asia 05, Torrid zone of
>   Asia —1305, rivers of Asia —169305, cities of Asia —173205
>   Prefer —3–9)

SUMMARY

—11	Frigid zones
—12	Temperate zones (Middle latitude zones)
—13	Torrid zone (Tropics)
—14	Land and landforms
—15	Regions by type of vegetation
—16	Air and water
—17	Socioeconomic regions
—18	Other kinds of terrestrial regions
—19	Space

>   **—11–17   Zonal, physiographic, socioeconomic regions**
>
> Unless other instructions are given, class a subject with aspects in two or more subdivisions of —11–17 in the number coming last, e.g., forested plateaus in north temperate zone —152 (*not* —123 or —143)
>
> Class comprehensive works in —1

—11   Frigid zones

> Class here polar regions

—113   North frigid zone

—116   South frigid zone

—12   Temperate zones (Middle latitude zones)

—123   North temperate zone

—126   South temperate zone

—13   **Torrid zone (Tropics)**

—14   **Land and landforms**

—141   Continents

Including continental shelves

—142   Islands

Including atolls, coral reefs

—143   Elevations

Including mountains, plateaus, hills, slopes

—144   Depressions and openings

Including canyons, chasms, gorges, gulches, ravines, valleys; craters; caves, karsts

—145   Plane regions

Including plains

—146   Coastal regions and shorelines

Including beaches, deltas

—148   Soil

—15   **Regions by type of vegetation**

—152   Forests

—153   Grasslands

Class here grassland plains (pampas, prairies, steppes, tundras, savannas)

—154   Deserts

Class here semiarid lands

—16   **Air and water**

SUMMARY

—161	**Atmosphere**
—162	**Oceans and seas**
—163	**Atlantic Ocean**
—164	**Pacific Ocean**
—165	**Indian Ocean**
—167	**Antarctic waters**
—168	**Special oceanographic forms and inland seas**
—169	**Fresh and brackish waters**

—161   Atmosphere

—161 2   Troposphere

—161 3   Stratosphere

—161 4   Ionosphere

—162   Oceans and seas

> *For Atlantic Ocean, see —163; for Pacific Ocean, see —164; for Indian Ocean, see —165; for Antarctic waters, see —167; for special oceanographic forms and inland seas, see —168*
>
> *See also —182 for ocean and sea basins*
>
> *See Manual at T2—162*

—163   Atlantic Ocean

> *See Manual at T2—162; also at T2—163 and T2—164, T2—165*

—163 1   North Atlantic Ocean

Area north of a line drawn from Strait of Gibraltar to Straits of Florida

> *For Arctic Ocean, see —1632; for northeast Atlantic Ocean, see —1633; for northwest Atlantic Ocean, see —1634*

—163 2   Arctic Ocean (North Polar Sea)

—163 24   European sector

> Including Denmark Strait; Barents Sea, Greenland Sea, Norwegian Sea, White Sea

—163 25   Asian sector

> Including Chukchi Sea, East Siberian Sea, Kara Sea, Laptev Sea
>
> *For Bering Strait, see —16451*

—163 27   American sector

> Including Beaufort Sea, Lincoln Sea; seas of Canadian Arctic Archipelago; Baffin Bay, Hudson Bay
>
> *For Bering Strait, see —16451*

—163 3   Northeast Atlantic Ocean

—163 34   Baltic Sea

> Including Gulf of Bothnia, Gulf of Finland, Gulf of Riga; Great Belt, Little Belt; Kattegat, Oresund

—163 36   North Sea and English Channel

> Including Firth of Forth, Skagerrak, Strait of Dover

—163 37   Western waters of British Isles

> Including Firth of Clyde, Irish Sea, North Channel, Saint George's Channel, Solway Firth

—163 38   French coastal waters, Spanish coastal waters, and Portugese coastal waters to Strait of Gibraltar

> Including Bay of Biscay
>
> *For Strait of Gibraltar, see —16381*

—163 4   Northwest Atlantic Ocean

—163 42	Davis Strait
—163 43	Labrador Sea
—163 44	Gulf of Saint Lawrence, coastal waters of Newfoundland, coastal waters of eastern Nova Scotia
—163 45	North American coastal waters from Bay of Fundy to Massachusetts Bay

Including Cape Cod Bay

| —163 46 | United States coastal waters from Cape Cod to Cape Charles |

Including Long Island Sound, Nantucket Sound, Rhode Island Sound; Buzzards Bay, Delaware Bay, Narragansett Bay, New York Bay

| —163 47 | Chesapeake Bay |
| —163 48 | United States coastal waters from Cape Henry to Straits of Florida |

Including Albemarle Sound, Pamlico Sound; Biscayne Bay; Biscayne National Park

For Straits of Florida, see —16363

| —163 5 | South Atlantic Ocean |

Area south of a line drawn from Strait of Gibraltar to Straits of Florida

For southwest Atlantic Ocean, see —1636; for southeast Atlantic Ocean, see —1637; for Atlantic sector of Antarctic waters, see —1673

| —163 6 | Southwest Atlantic Ocean |

Class here west Atlantic Ocean

For northwest Atlantic Ocean, see —1634

| —163 62 | Sargasso Sea |
| —163 63 | Bahama waters |

Including Straits of Florida

| —163 64 | Gulf of Mexico |

Including Yucatán Channel

For Straits of Florida, see —16363

| —163 65 | Caribbean Sea |

Including Gulf of Darien, Gulf of Honduras, Gulf of Venezuela

For Yucatán Channel, see —16364

—163 66	South American coastal waters from Gulf of Paria to Cape São Roque
—163 67	Brazilian coastal waters southward from Cape São Roque
—163 68	Uruguayan coastal waters and Argentine coastal waters

Including Bahía Blanca Estuary, Rio de la Plata

—163 7   Southeast Atlantic Ocean

                 Class here east Atlantic Ocean

                 For northeast Atlantic Ocean, see —1633; for Mediterranean Sea,
                 see —1638

—163 72   African coastal waters from Cape of Good Hope to Congo River

—163 73   Gulf of Guinea

                 African coastal waters from Congo River to Cape Palmas

—163 75   West African coastal waters from Cape Palmas to Strait of Gibraltar

                 For Strait of Gibraltar, see —16381

—163 8   Mediterranean Sea

—163 81   Western Mediterranean

                 Strait of Gibraltar to Strait of Sicily

                 For waters between Spain and Sardinia-Corsica, see —16382;
                 for Tyrrhenian Sea, see —16383

—163 82   Waters between Spain and Sardinia-Corsica

                 Including Balearic Sea, Ligurian Sea; Gulf of Lions

—163 83   Tyrrhenian Sea

                 For Strait of Messina, see —16386

—163 84   Eastern Mediterranean

                 East of Strait of Sicily

                 For Adriatic Sea, see —16385; for Ionian Sea, see —16386; for
                 Mediterranean east of Crete, see —16387; for Sea of Crete and
                 Aegean Sea, see —16388; for Black Sea, see —16389

—163 85   Adriatic Sea

                 Including Gulf of Venice

—163 86   Ionian Sea

                 Including Strait of Messina, Gulf of Taranto

                 For Strait of Otranto, see —16385

—163 87   Mediterranean east of Crete

—163 88   Sea of Crete and Aegean Sea

                 For Dardanelles, see —16389

—163 89   Black Sea

                 Including Bosporus, Dardanelles, Sea of Azov, Sea of Marmara

—164   Pacific Ocean

                 See Manual at T2—162; also at T2—163 and T2—164, T2—165

—164 1   Southeast Pacific Ocean

        American coastal waters from Strait of Magellan to Mexico-United States boundary

        Including Gulf of California, Gulf of Guayaquil, Gulf of Panama, Gulf of Tehuantepec

        For Strait of Magellan, see —1674

—164 2   East Pacific Ocean

        For southeast Pacific Ocean, see —1641; for northeast Pacific Ocean, see —1643

—164 3   Northeast Pacific Ocean

        North American coastal waters from California to tip of Alaska

—164 32   United States waters

        Including Monterey Bay, San Francisco Bay, Puget Sound, Strait of Juan de Fuca

        For Alaskan waters, see —16434

—164 33   Canadian waters

        Including Dixon Entrance; Hecate Strait, Queen Charlotte Strait, Strait of Georgia; Queen Charlotte Sound

        Class here Inside Passage

        For Strait of Juan de Fuca, see —16432

—164 34   Alaskan waters

        Including Bristol Bay, Cook Inlet, Gulf of Alaska, Norton Sound, Shelikof Strait

        For Dixon Entrance, see —16433

—164 4   North Pacific Ocean

        American coastal waters and Asian coastal waters located in an arc from Mexico-United States boundary to southern tip of Philippines, excluding South China Sea and inner seas of the Philippines

        For northeast Pacific Ocean, see —1643; for northwest Pacific Ocean, see —1645

—164 5   Northwest Pacific Ocean

—164 51   Bering Sea

        Including Bering Strait

—164 52   Coastal waters of southeast Kamchatka

—164 53   Sea of Okhotsk

        Including La Perouse Strait

—164 54	Sea of Japan
	Including Korea Strait, Tatar Strait, Tsugaru Strait
	For La Perouse Strait, see —16453
—164 55	Eastern coastal waters and inner seas of Japan
	Including Inland Sea (Seto-naikai)
—164 56	Yellow Sea
—164 57	East China Sea
	Including Formosa Strait
	For Korea Strait, see —16454
—164 58	Philippine Sea
	Including Luzon Strait
—164 6	West Pacific Ocean
	For northwest Pacific Ocean, see —1645; for southwest Pacific Ocean, see —1647
—164 7	Southwest Pacific Ocean
—164 71	Inner seas of Philippines
	For Sulu Sea, see —16473
—164 72	South China Sea
	Including Gulf of Thailand, Singapore Strait
	For Formosa Strait, see —16457; for Luzon Strait, see —16458
—164 73	Inner seas of Malay Archipelago
	Including Celebes Sea, Ceram Sea, Molucca Sea, Sulu Sea; Makasar Strait
	For seas adjoining southern Sunda Islands, see —16474
—164 74	Seas adjoining southern Sunda Islands
	Including Bali Sea, Banda Sea, Flores Sea, Java Sea, Savu Sea
	For Karimata Strait, see —16472
—164 75	Arafura Sea
	For Torres Strait, see —16476
—164 76	Coral Sea and seas adjoining Melanesia
	Including Bismarck Sea, Solomon Sea; Torres Strait; eastern Queensland coastal waters
—164 77	Fiji Sea

—164 78   Tasman Sea

Including New South Wales coastal waters, Cook Strait

For Tasmanian coastal waters, see —16576

—164 79   Eastern coastal waters of New Zealand

—164 8   South Pacific Ocean

American coastal waters from Mexico-United States boundary to Strait of Magellan; coastal waters of Antarctica; coastal waters of New Zealand; coastal waters of Australia; coastal waters of New Guinea; waters of Melanesia; coastal waters west and south of Philippines, including South China Sea and inner seas of Philippines

For southeast Pacific Ocean, see —1641; for southwest Pacific Ocean, see —1647; for Pacific sector of Antarctic waters, see —1674

—164 9   Central Pacific Ocean

American non-coastal waters, Asian non-coastal waters; waters of Polynesia, waters of isolated islands of Pacific, such as Wake and Easter Island

Including coastal waters of Hawaii

—165   Indian Ocean

For Indian Ocean sector of Antarctic waters, see —1675

See Manual at T2—162; also at T2—163 and T2—164, T2—165

—165 2   Southwest Indian Ocean

Class here west Indian Ocean

For northwest Indian Ocean, see —1653

—165 23   Eastern coastal waters of Madagascar

—165 24   Coastal waters of south Africa and coastal waters of southeast Africa

From Cape of Good Hope to and including Delagoa Bay

—165 25   Mozambique Channel

—165 26   Coastal waters of east Africa

From Cape Delgado to Cape Guardafui (tip of the "Horn")

—165 3   Northwest Indian Ocean

—165 32   Gulf of Aden

Including 'Bab el Mandeb

—165 33   Red Sea

Including Gulf of Aqaba, Gulf of Suez

For 'Bab el Mandeb, see —16532

—165 35	Persian Gulf
	Including Strait of Hormuz
—165 36	Gulf of Oman
	For Strait of Hormuz, see —16535
—165 37	Arabian Sea
	Including Laccadive Sea
—165 6	Northeast Indian Ocean
—165 64	Bay of Bengal
—165 65	Andaman Sea
	Including Gulf of Martaban, Strait of Malacca
	For Singapore Strait, see —16472
—165 67	Coastal waters of southern Sumatra, coastal waters of Java, coastal waters of Lesser Sunda Islands
	For Timor Sea, see —16574
—165 7	Southeast Indian Ocean
	Class here east Indian Ocean
	For Arafura Sea, see —16475; for northeast Indian Ocean, see —1656
—165 74	Northwest Australian coastal waters
	From Melville Island to Northwest Cape
	Including Timor Sea
—165 75	West Australian coastal waters
	From Northwest Cape to Cape Leeuwin
—165 76	South Australian coastal waters
	From Cape Leeuwin to Cape Howe
	Including Bass Strait, Great Australian Bight, Tasmanian coastal waters
—167	Antarctic waters
	See Manual at T2—162; also at T2—163 and T2—164, T2—165
—167 3	Atlantic sector
	Including Drake Passage, Scotia Sea, Weddell Sea
	For Strait of Magellan, see —1674
—167 4	Pacific sector
	Including Amundsen Sea, Bellingshausen Sea, Ross Sea; Strait of Magellan
—167 5	Indian Ocean sector

—168	Special oceanographic forms and inland seas
	Including coastal pools, saltwater lagoons
	Class specific inland seas in —4–9
	See Manual at T2—162
—169	Fresh and brackish waters

>	—169 2–169 4 Surface waters
	Class comprehensive works in —169
—169 2	Lakes, ponds, freshwater lagoons
—169 3	Rivers and streams
—169 4	Waterfalls
—169 8	Groundwaters (Subsurface waters)
—17	**Socioeconomic regions**
—171	Socioeconomic regions by political orientation
—171 2	Noncontiguous empires and political unions
	Add to base number —1712 notation 3–9 from Table 2 for mother country, e.g., French Community —171244
	Class Roman Empire in —37
—171 3	Western bloc
—171 6	Unaligned blocs
—171 65	Afro-Asian bloc
—171 7	Former communist bloc
—171 8	Wartime groupings
—171 82	Belligerents
—171 83	Nonbelligerents and neutrals
—171 9	Non-self-governing territories
—172	Socioeconomic regions by degree of economic development
—172 2	Developed regions
—172 4	Developing regions
—173	Socioeconomic regions by concentration of population
—173 2	Urban regions
—173 3	Suburban regions
—173 4	Rural regions
	Including rural villages

—174 Regions where ethnic and national groups predominate

—174 05–174 09 Regions where groups with mixed ancestry with ethnic origins from more than one continent predominate, regions where groups of European descent predominate

Add to base number —174 notation 05–09 from Table 5, e.g., regions where groups of European descent predominate —17409

—174 1–174 9 Regions where specific ethnic and national groups predominate

Add to base number —174 notation 1–9 from Table 5, e.g., regions where Arabs predominate —174927

—175 Regions where specific languages predominate

Add to base number —175 notation 1–9 from Table 6, e.g., regions where Spanish language predominates —17561

—176 Regions where specific religions predominate

—176 1 Christianity

—176 12 Catholicism

—176 14 Protestantism

—176 2–176 9 Other religions

Add to base number —176 the numbers following 29 in 292–299, e.g., regions where Islam predominates —1767

—177 Nations belonging to specific international organizations

Including nations belonging to Organization of Petroleum Exporting Countries

Arrange alphabetically by name of organization

—18 **Other kinds of terrestrial regions**

—181 Hemispheres

Class zonal, physiographic, socioeconomic regions in a specific hemisphere in —11–17

—181 1 Eastern Hemisphere

—181 2 Western Hemisphere

Portion of world between 20° west longitude and 160° east longitude, including North and South America, most of North Atlantic Ocean (excluding northeastern portion), Southwest Atlantic Ocean, Northeast Pacific Ocean, and most of South Pacific Ocean (excluding southwestern portion)

Class land portion of North and South America in —7; class geography of Western Hemisphere in 917; class history of Western Hemisphere in 970

—181 3 Northern Hemisphere

—181 4 Southern Hemisphere

—182   Ocean and sea basins

                 The totality of continents facing and islands in specific major bodies of water

                 Class ocean and sea waters in —162; class zonal, physiographic, socioeconomic regions in a specific ocean or sea basin in —11–17

                     For a specific part of an ocean or sea basin not provided for here, see the part, e.g., Aegean region —4958, Pacific Ocean islands —9

—182 1   Atlantic region

                 Class here occident, western world

                     See also —729 for Caribbean Area

—182 2   Mediterranean region

                 (Option: Class here Mediterranean region to 476; prefer —37)

—182 21   Western Mediterranean region

                 (Option: Class here western Mediterranean region to 476; prefer —37)

—182 24   Eastern Mediterranean region

                 (Option: Class Eastern Mediterranean region to 323; prefer —38)

                     See also —56 for Middle East

—182 29   Black Sea region

                 (Option: Class here Black Sea region to 640; prefer —395)

                     See also —56 for Middle East

—182 3   Pacific region

—182 4   Indian Ocean region

—19   **Space**

                 Class extraterrestrial worlds in —99

                     See Manual at T2—99 vs. T2—19

—2   **Biography**

                 Autobiography, description and critical appraisal of work, diaries, reminiscences, correspondence of people regardless of area, region, or place who are part of the subject or who study the subject, e.g., biographers, collectors, leaders and followers, practitioners and clients, scholars

                 Class here treatment of individuals

                 Add to base number —2 the numbers following —092 in notation 0922–0929 from Table 1, e.g., collected biography —22, collected biography of Italians in Italy —2245

                 Class belletristic diaries, reminiscences, correspondence in 800

                     See Manual at T1—092

> ## —3–9 Specific continents, countries, localities; extraterrestrial worlds

Class here specific instances of the subject

An area is classed in its present number even if it had a different affiliation at the time under consideration, e.g., Arizona under Mexican sovereignty —791 (*not* —72)

Class areas, regions, places not limited by continent, country, locality in —1; class parts of oceans and noninland seas limited by country or locality in —163–168; class biography regardless of area, region, place in —2; class comprehensive works in 001–999, without adding notation from Table 2

> *See Manual at T2—162; also at T2—4–9 vs. T2—3*

(Option: Class areas and regions limited by continent, country, locality in —1)

—3   Ancient world

Class a specific part of ancient world not provided for here in —4–9

Class comprehensive works on a specific jurisdiction extending over more than one country, province, or other unit and identified by * with the jurisdiction where noted in this table, e.g., Roman Empire —37. For works on a part of such a jurisdiction, see the specific unit where the part is located, e.g., Britain —361, Rome —3763

> *See Manual at T2—3; also at T2—4–9 vs. T2—3*

(Option: Class specific parts in —4–9 as detailed below)

SUMMARY

—31	China to 420
—32	Egypt to 640
—33	Palestine to 70
—34	South Asia to 647
—35	Mesopotamia to 637 and Iranian Plateau to 637
—36	Europe north and west of Italian Peninsula to ca. 499
—37	Italian Peninsula to 476 and adjacent territories to 476
—38	Greece to 323
—39	Other parts of ancient world

—31   China to 420

Add to base number —31 the numbers following —51 in —511–516, e.g., Sichuan Province —3138

(Option: Class in —51)

—32   **Egypt to 640**

Add to base number —32 the numbers following —62 in —621–623, e.g., Alexandria —321, Giza, Memphis —322, Abydos, Karnak, Luxor, Thebes —323

See also —3948 for Sinai Peninsula

(Option: Class Egypt to 640 in —62; class lower Egypt to 640, Alexandria to 640 in —621; class Middle Egypt to 640, Giza, Memphis in —622; class upper Egypt to 640, Abydos, Karnak, Luxor, Thebes in —623)

—33   **Palestine to 70**

(Option: Class in —5694)

—334   Israel to 70

Add to base number —334 the numbers following —5694 in —56944–56949, e.g., Jerusalem —33442, Galilee —3345, Judah, Judaea —3349; however, for Darom district in Edom, see —39464; for Darom district in Arabia Petraea, see —3948

(Option: Class Israel to 70 in —5694; class Jerusalem district to 70 in —56944; class Jerusalem to 70 in —569442; class Tsafon district to 70, Galilee to 70 in —56945; class Haifa district to 70 in —56946; class Merkaz district to 70 in —56947; class Tel Aviv district to 70, Tel Aviv to 70 in —56948; class Darom district to 70, Judah, Judaea in —56949)

—335   Jordan to 70 and West Bank to 70

Subdivisions are added for Jordan to 70 and West Bank to 70 together, for Jordan to 70 alone

For Ma'dabā Province to 70, Karak Province to 70, Moab, see —39462; for Ṭafīlah Province to 70, 'Aqabah Province to 70, Edom, see —39464; for 'Aqabah Province to 622, Ma'ān Province to 622, Arabia Petraea in Jordan, Petra, see —3948

(Option: Class Jordan to 70 in —5695)

—335 1–335 5   West Bank to 70; Irbid Province to 70, 'Ajlūn Province to 70, Jarash Province to 70, Balqā' Province to 70

Add to base number —335 the numbers following —5695 in —56951–56955, e.g., Samaria —3353

(Option: Class West Bank to 70, Nablus district to 70, Samaria in —56953; class Irbid Province to 70 in —569542; class 'Ajlūn Province to 70 in —569546; class Jarash Province to 70 in —569548; class Balqā' Province to 70 in —56955)

—335 8   Amman Province to 70

(Option: Class in —56958)

—335 9   Zarqā' Province to 70 and Mafraq Province to 70

(Option: Class in —56959)

—335 93   Zarqā' province to 70

(Option: Class in —569593)

—335 97   Mafraq Province to 70

                          (Option: Class in —569597)

—34   **South Asia to 647**

                 Class here India to 647

                 Add to base number —34 the numbers following —54 in —541–549, e.g.,
                 western India —347, Indus River valley —3491; however, for Sri Lanka, see
                 —5493; for Maldives, see —5495; for Nepal, see —5496; for Bhutan, see
                 —5498

                 For southeast Asia, see —59

                 (Option: Class India to 647, South Asia to 647 in —54; class Pakistan to 647 in
                 —5491; class Bangladesh to 647 in —5492)

—35   **Mesopotamia to 637 and Iranian Plateau to 637**

                 Class here *Assyria, *Chaldean Empire, *Persian Empire, *Sassanian Empire,
                 *Seleucid Empire

                 Subdivisions are added for Mesopotamia and Iranian Plateau together; for
                 Mesopotamia alone

                 Class central Asia in —396

                 (Option: Class in —567)

                 _____

>   —352–355 Mesopotamia to 637

                 Class here Iraq to 637

                 Class comprehensive works in —35

—352   Kurdish Autonomous Region of Iraq to 637

                      (Option: Class in —5672)

—354   Upper Mesopotamia to 637

                      Including Upper Mesopotamian portion of Arabia Deserta to 637 [*formerly*
                      —3947]; Ashur, Nineveh

                      (Option: Class in —5674)

—355   Lower Mesopotamia to 637

                      Including Lower Mesopotamian portion of Arabia Deserta to 637 [*formerly*
                      —3947]; Babylon

                      Class here Akkad, Babylonia, Sumer, Ur

                      (Option: Class in —5675)

*For a specific part of this jurisdiction, region, or feature, see the part and follow instructions under
—3

—357   Iranian Plateau to 637

Class here Iran to 637, Persia to 637

Add to base number —357 the numbers following —55 in —551–559, e.g., Media —3575, Ecbatana —35752, Elam, Susa —35766, Persis, Pasargadae, Persepolis —35772

See also —396 for Hyrcania

(Option: Class Iranian Plateau to 637, Iran to 637, Persia to 637 in —55; class Hamadān province to 637, Kordestān province to 637, Kermānshāhān province to 637, Īlām province to 637, Media in —555; class Hamadān province to 637, Ecbatana in —5552; class Khūzestān province to 637, Elam, Susa in —5566; class Fārs province to 637, Persis, Pasargadae, Persepolis in —5572)

—36   **Europe north and west of Italian Peninsula to ca. 499**

Including *western Mediterranean region to ca. 499

Class here *Europe to ca. 499, *western Europe to ca. 499

(Option: Class western Mediterranean region to ca. 499 in —18221; class Europe to ca. 499, Europe north and west of Italian Peninsula to ca. 499, western Europe to ca. 499 in —4)

—361   British Isles to 410

Class here United Kingdom to 410, Great Britain to 410

Add to base number —361 the numbers following —41 in notation 411–419 of this table, e.g., Border Country to 410 —36137, Ireland to 410 —3615

For England to 410 and Wales to 410, see —362

(Option: Class British Isles to 410, United Kingdom to 410, Great Britain to 410 in —41; class Scotland to 410, northern Britain to 410 in —411; class Ireland to 410 in —415; class Northern Ireland to 410 in —416; class Republic of Ireland to 410 in —417)

—362   England to 410 and Wales to 410

Class here Brittania (Roman province)

Add to base number —362 the numbers following —42 in notation 421–429 of this table, e.g., Chester —362714

Subdivisions are added for England and Wales together, for England alone

Class comprehensive works on British Isles in —361

(Option: Class England to 410, southern Britain to 410 in —42; class Wales to 410 in —429)

*For a specific part of this jurisdiction, region, or feature, see the part and follow instructions under —3

—363   Germanic regions to 481 and Pannonia

Class here Germania Magna

Subdivisions are added for Germanic regions to 481 and Pannonia together, for Germanic regions to 481 alone

For British Isles, see —361; for Czech Republic and Slovakia, see —437; for Poland, see —438

(Option: Class Germanic regions to 481, Germany to 481, Germania Magna in —43)

Scandinavia to 481 relocated to —368; Germanic regions in Netherlands relocated to —36921; Alpine region cantons to 486, Raetia relocated to —36947

—363 1–363 6   Specific parts of Germanic regions to 481

Add to base number —363 the numbers following —43 in —431–436, e.g., Vindelicia —3633, Noricum —3636, Raetia in Austria —36364; however, for Austria, 476–481, see —436; for Liechtenstein, 476–481, see —43648

(Option: Class Bavaria to 481, Vindelicia in —433; class Austria to 476, Noricum in —436; class western Austria to 476, Raetia in Austria in —4364; class Liechtenstein to 476 in —43648)

—363 9   Pannonia [*formerly* —398]

Class here Hungary to ca. 640 [*formerly* —398]

(Option: Class in —439)

—364   Celtic regions to 486

Class here France to 486, Gaul (Gallia Transalpina)

Add to base number —364 the numbers following —44 in —441–444, e.g., Germania Superior —36439, Lugdunensis —3645, Aquitania —3647, Narbonensis —3648

For British Isles, see —361

See also —372 for Gallia Cisalpina

(Option: Class Celtic regions to 486, France to 486, Gaul [Gallia Transalpina] in —44; class Alsace to 486, Germania Superior in —4439; class central France to 486, Lugdunensis in —445; class southwestern France to 486, Aquitania in —447; class Languedoc-Roussillon to 486, Narbonensis in —448)

Netherlands to 486, Germania Inferior relocated to —3692; Belgium to 486, Belgica relocated to —3693; Luxembourg to 486 relocated to —36935; Switzerland to 486 relocated to —3694; Jura region cantons to 486, Helvetia relocated to —36943

—366   Iberian Peninsula to 415 and adjacent islands to 415

      Class here Spain to 415, Tarraconensis

      Subdivisions are added for Iberian Peninsula to 415 and adjacent islands to 415 together, for Iberian Peninsula to 415 alone

      Add to base number —366 the numbers following —46 in —461–469, e.g., Baetica —3668, Lusitania —3669

      (Option: Class Spain to 415, Iberian Peninsula to 415, Tarraconensis in —46; class Andalusia autonomous community to 415, Baetica in —468; class Portugal to 415, Lusitania in —469)

—368   Scandinavia to 481 [*formerly* —363]

      Add to base number —368 the numbers following —48 in —481–489, e.g., Denmark —3689; however, for Finland, see —4897

      (Option: Class Scandinavia to 481 in —48; class Norway to 481 in —481; class Sweden to 481 in —485; class Denmark to 481 in —489)

—369   Netherlands to 486, Belgium to 486, Luxembourg to 486, Switzerland to 486

      Add to base number —369 the numbers following —49 in —492–494, e.g., Netherlands to 486, Germania Inferior —3692 [*both formerly* —364], Germanic regions in Netherlands —36921 [*formerly* —363], Belgium to 486, Belgica —3693 [*both formerly* —364], Luxembourg to 486 —36935 [*formerly* —364], Switzerland to 486 —3694 [*formerly* —363], Jura region cantons to 486, Helvetia —36943 [*both formerly* —364], Alpine region cantons to 486, Raetia —36947 [*both formerly* —363]

      For Raetia in Austria, see —36364

      (Option: Class Netherlands to 486, Germania Inferior in —492; class Belgium to 486, Belgica in —493; class Luxembourg to 486 in —4935; class Switzerland to 486 in —494; class Jura region cantons to 486, Helvetia in —4943; class Alpine region cantons to 486, Raetia in —4947)

—37   **Italian Peninsula to 476 and adjacent territories to 476**

      The subdivisions of this table are based upon the territorial organization that was developed by Emperor Augustus at the end of the 1st century B.C. and lasted until the early 4th century A.D.

      Class here *Mediterranean region to 476, *Roman Empire

      Subdivisions are added for Italian Peninsula to 476 and adjacent territories to 476 together, for Italian Peninsula to 476 alone

      (Option: Class Mediterranean region to 476 in —1822; class Italian Peninsula and adjacent territories to 476, Roman Empire in —45)

---

*For a specific part of this jurisdiction, region, or feature, see the part and follow instructions under —3

SUMMARY

—371	Liguria
—372	Gallia Cisalpina (Cisalpine Gaul)
—373	Venetia and Istria
—374	Umbria and Picenum
—375	Etruria
—376	Latium
—377	Southern Italy to 476
—378	Sicily to 476 and Malta to 476
—379	Sardinia to 453 and Corsica to 453

—371   Liguria

Class here Liguria region to 476

(Option: Class in —4518)

—371 1   La Spezia province to 476

(Option: Class in —45183)

—371 2   Genoa (Genova) province to 476

(Option: Class in —45182)

—371 21   Genua (Genoa) to 476

(Option: Class in —451821)

—371 3   Savona province to 476

(Option: Class in —45184)

—371 4   Imperia province to 476

(Option: Class in —45187)

—371 6   *Cuneo province to 476

(Option: Class in —4513)

—371 7   Asti province to 476

(Option: Class in —4515)

—371 8   Alessandria province to 476

(Option: Class in —4514)

—372   Gallia Cisalpina (Cisalpine Gaul)

(Option: Class in —451)

—372 2   Gallia Transpadana (Transpadane Gaul)

Class here *Lombardy (Lombardia) region to 476

(Option: Class northwestern Italy to 476 in —451; class Lombardy region to 476, Gallia Transpadana [Transpadane Gaul] in —452)

*For a specific part of this jurisdiction, region, or feature, see the part and follow instructions under —3

—372 21   Valle d'Aosta region to 476

        (Option: Class in —4511)

—372 211   Augusta Praetoria (Aosta) to 476

        (Option: Class in —45111)

—372 22   *Turin (Torino) province to 476

        Class here *Piedmont (Piemonte) region to 476

        (Option: Class Piedmont region to 476 in —451; class Turin province to 476 in —4512)

—372 221   Augusta Taurinorum (Turin) to 476

        (Option: Class in —45121)

—372 23   Vercelli province to 476 and Biella province to 476

        Subdivisions are added for Vercelli province to 476 and Biella province to 476 together, for Vercelli province to 476 alone

        (Option: Class in —4517)

—372 236   Biella province to 476

        (Option: Class in —45176)

—372 24   Novara province to 476 and Verbania province to 476

        Subdivisions are added for Novara province to 476 and Verbania province to 476 together, for Novara province to 476 alone

        (Option: Class in —4516)

—372 245   Verbania (Verbano-Cusio-Ossola) province to 476

        (Option: Class in —45165)

—372 25   Varese province to 476

        (Option: Class in —4522)

—372 26   Monza-Brianza province to 476, Como province to 476, Lecco province to 476, Sondrio province to 476, Bergamo province to 476

—372 262   Monza-Brianza province to 476

        (Option: Class in —45228)

—372 264   Como province to 476

        (Option: Class in —4523)

—372 264 1   Comum (Como) to 476

        (Option: Class in —45231)

*For a specific part of this jurisdiction, region, or feature, see the part and follow instructions under
—3

—372 265	Lecco province to 476
	(Option: Class in —45237)
—372 266	Sondrio province to 476
	(Option: Class in —4525)
—372 268	Bergamo province to 476
	(Option: Class in —4524)
—372 268 1	Bergomum (Bergamo) to 476
	(Option: Class in —45241)
—372 27	Milan (Milano) province to 476
	(Option: Class in —4521)
—372 271	Mediolanum (Milan) to 476
	(Option: Class in —45211)
—372 28	Lodi province to 476
	(Option: Class in —45219)
—372 29	*Pavia province to 476
	Including Ticinum (Pavia) to 476
	(Option: Class in —4529)
—372 6	Gallia Cispadana (Cispadane Gaul)
	Class here Emilia-Romagna region to 476
	Add to base number —3726 the numbers following —454 in —4541–4549, e.g., Ravenna province to 476 —37267
	(Option: Class in —454)
—373	Venetia and Istria
	Class here Veneto region to 476, northeastern Italy to 476
	Subdivisions are added for Venetia and Istria together, for Venetia alone
	(Option: Class in —453)
—373 1	Brescia province to 476, Cremona province to 476, Mantua province to 476
—373 12	Brescia province to 476
	(Option: Class in —4526)
—373 121	Brixia (Brescia) to 476
	(Option: Class in —45261)

*For a specific part of this jurisdiction, region, or feature, see the part and follow instructions under —3

—373 15	*Cremona province to 476
	(Option: Class in —4527)
—373 18	Mantua (Mantova) province to 476
	(Option: Class in —4528)
—373 181	Mantua to 476
	(Option: Class in —45281)
—373 2	Verona province to 476
	(Option: Class in —4534)
—373 21	Verona to 476
	(Option: Class in —45341)
—373 3	Rovigo province to 476
	(Option: Class in —4533)
—373 4	Padua (Padova) province to 476
	(Option: Class in —4532)
—373 41	Patavium (Padua) to 476
	(Option: Class in —45321)
—373 5	Venice (Venezia) province to 476
	Including Venice to 476
	(Option: Class Venice (Venezia) province to 476 in —4531. Class Venice to 476 in —45311)
—373 6	Vicenza province to 476, Treviso province to 476, Belluno province to 476
—373 62	Vicenza province to 476
	Including Vicenza to 476
	(Option: Class Vicenza province to 476 in —4535. Class Vicenza to 476 in —45351)
—373 65	Treviso province to 476
	(Option: Class Treviso province to 476 in —4536. Class Treviso to 476 in —45361)
—373 68	Belluno province to 476
	(Option: Class in —4537)
—373 7	Trentino-Alto Adige region to 476
	(Option: Class in —4538)

*For a specific part of this jurisdiction, region, or feature, see the part and follow instructions under —3

—373 73   Bolzano province to 476

                          (Option: Class in —45383)

—373 75   Trento province to 476

                          (Option: Class in —45385)

—373 8   Friuli-Venezia Giulia region to 476

                          For Trieste province, see —3739

                          (Option: Class in —4539)

—373 81   Udine province to 476

                          Including Aquileia to 476

                          (Option: Class in —45391)

—373 82   Gorizia province to 476

                          (Option: Class in —45392)

—373 9   Istria

                          (Option: Class Trieste province of Italy to 476 in —45393; class Istria in
                          Slovenia to 476 in —4973; class Istria in Croatia to 476, comprehensive
                          works on Istria in —4972)

—373 91   Tergeste (Trieste) to 476

                          (Option: Class in —453931)

—373 94   Pordenone province to 476

                          (Option: Class in —45394)

—374   Umbria and Picenum

                          (Option: Class in —4565)

                          Volsinii Veteres (Orvieto) to 476 relocated to —37576

>   —374 2–374 4 Umbria

                     Class comprehensive works in —3742

—374 2   Pesaro e Urbino province to 476

                          Including Pisaurum (Pesaro) to 476

                          Class here *Umbria, *Umbria region to 476

                          (Option: Class Umbria region to 476 in —4565; class Pesaro e Urbino
                          province to 476 in —45677)

---

*For a specific part of this jurisdiction, region, or feature, see the part and follow instructions under
—3

—374 3   *Perugia province to 476

> (Option: Class Perugia province to 476 in —45651. Class Perugia to 476 in —456511)

—374 4   *Terni province to 476

> (Option: Class in —45652)

\>   —374 5–374 9   Picenum

Class comprehensive works in —3745

—374 5   *Ancona province to 476

> Class here *Marches (Marche) region to 476, *Picenum

> (Option: Class Marches region to 476, Picenum in —4567; class Ancona province to 476 in —45671)

—374 6   *Macerata province to 476

> (Option: Class in —45673)

—374 7   Fermo province to 476

> (Option: Class in —45674)

—374 8   Ascoli Piceno province to 476

> (Option: Class in —45675)

—374 9   Teramo province to 476

> (Option: Class in —45715)

—375   Etruria

> Class here Tuscany (Toscana) region to 476

> (Option: Class in —455)

—375 1   Florence (Firenze) province to 476 and Prato province to 476

> Including Faesulae (Fiesole) to 476

> Subdivisions are added for Florence (Firenze) province to 476 and Prato province to 476 together, for Florence (Firenze) province to 476 alone

> (Option: Class in —4551)

—375 11   Florentia (Florence) to 476

> (Option: Class in —45511)

—375 19   Prato province to 476

> (Option: Class in —45519)

---

*For a specific part of this jurisdiction, region, or feature, see the part and follow instructions under —3

—375 2   Pistoia province to 476

           (Option: Class in —4552)

—375 3   Lucca province to 476

           (Option: Class in —4553)

—375 4   Massa-Carrara (Massa e Carrara) province to 476

           (Option: Class in —4554)

—375 5   Pisa province to 476

           Including Pisa to 476, Velathri (Volterra) to 476

           (Option: Class Pisa province to 476, Velathri (Volterra) to 476 in —4555. Class Pisa to 476 in —45551)

—375 6   Livorno province to 476, Grosseto province to 476, Siena province to 476, Arezzo province to 476

—375 62   Livorno province to 476

           (Option: Class in —4556)

—375 64   Grosseto province to 476

           (Option: Class in —4557)

—375 66   Siena province to 476

           Including Siena to 476

           (Option: Class Siena province to 476 in —4558. Class Siena to 476 in —45581)

—375 68   *Arezzo province to 476

           Including Arretium (Arezzo) to 476, Clusium (Chiusi) to 476, Corito (Cortona) to 476

           (Option: Class in —4559)

—375 7   Umbria region in Etruria to 476

           Class comprehensive works on Umbria region to 476 in —3742

           (Option: Class in —4565)

—375 73   Perugia province in Etruria to 476

           Class comprehensive works on Perugia province to 476 in —3743

           (Option: Class in —45651)

—375 731   Perusia (Perugia) to 476

           (Option: Class in —456511)

---

*For a specific part of this jurisdiction, region, or feature, see the part and follow instructions under
—3

—375 76   Terni province in Etruria to 476

         Including Volsinii Veteres (Orvieto) to 476 [*formerly* —374]

         (Option: Class in —45652)

—375 8   Viterbo province to 476

         Including Tarquinia to 476, Viterbo to 476

         (Option: Class Viterbo province to 476, Tarquinia to 476 in —45625. Class Viterbo to 476 in —456251)

—375 82   Vulci

         (Option: Class in —45625)

—375 83   Volsinii Novi [*formerly* —376]

         (Option: Class in —45625)

—375 9   Rome (Roma) province in Etruria to 476

         Including Caere (Cerveteri) to 476

         Class comprehensive works on Rome province in —3763

         (Option: Class in —4563)

—375 95   Veii [*formerly* —376]

         (Option: Class in —4563)

—376   Latium

       Class here *Lazio region to 476

       (Option: Class in —4562)

       Volsinii Novi relocated to —37583; Veii relocated to —37595

—376 3   Rome (Roma) province to 476

         Including Ostia to 476, Praeneste (Palestrina) to 476, Vatican City to 476

         Class here Rome to 476

          For Etrurian part of Rome province to 476, see —3759

         (Option: Class Rome province to 476, Ostia to 476, Praeneste (Palestrina) to 476 in —4563; class Rome to 476 in —45632; class Vatican City to 476 in —45634)

—376 5   Latina province to 476

         (Option: Class in —45623)

—376 7   Frosinone province to 476

         (Option: Class in —45622)

---

*For a specific part of this jurisdiction, region, or feature, see the part and follow instructions under —3

—377 Southern Italy to 476

Class here Magna Graecia

(Option: Class in —457)

SUMMARY

—377 2	**Campania**
—377 3	**Samnium**
—377 5	**Apulia**
—377 6	**Calabria**
—377 7	**Lucania**
—377 8	**Bruttium**

—377 2 Campania

Class here *Campania region to 476

(Option: Class in —4572)

—377 23 *Caserta province to 476

(Option: Class in —45725)

—377 25 Naples (Napoli) province to 476

Including Puteoli (Pozzuoli) to 476

(Option: Class in —4573)

—377 251 Neapolis (Naples)

(Option: Class in —45731)

—377 252 Cumae

(Option: Class in —4573)

—377 255 Nola to 476

(Option: Class in —4573)

—377 256 Herculaneum and Pompeii

(Option: Class in —4573)

—377 256 4 Herculaneum

(Option: Class in —4573)

—377 256 8 Pompeii

(Option: Class in —4573)

—377 258 Stabiae

(Option: Class in —4573)

*For a specific part of this jurisdiction, region, or feature, see the part and follow instructions under
—3

—377 27   *Salerno province to 476

            (Option: Class in —4574)

—377 271   Salernum (Salerno) to 476

            (Option: Class in —45741)

—377 3   Samnium

            Class here *Abruzzo region to 476

            (Option: Class in —4571)

—377 31   Avellino province to 476

            (Option: Class in —45721)

—377 32   Benevento province to 476

            Including Beneventum (Benevento) to 476

            (Option: Class in —45723)

—377 33   Isernia province to 476

            Class here Molise region to 476

            For Campobasso province to 476, see —37738

            (Option: Class Molise region to 476 in —45719, class Isernia province to 476 in —457194)

—377 34   Aquila (L'Aquila) province to 476

            (Option: Class in —45711)

—377 35   Rieti province to 476

            Class here *Sabina to 476

            (Option: Class in —45624)

—377 36   Pescara province to 476

            (Option: Class in 45717)

—377 37   Chieti province to 476

            (Option: Class in —45713)

—377 38   Campobasso province to 476

            (Option: Class in —457192)

—377 5   Apulia

            Class here Puglia region to 476

            For Calabria, see —3776

            (Option: Class Puglia region to 476 in —4575; class Apulia in —45757)

*For a specific part of this jurisdiction, region, or feature, see the part and follow instructions under —3

—377 53	Foggia province to 476
	(Option: Class in —45757)
—377 56	Barletta-Andria-Trani province to 476
	(Option: Class in —45759)
—377 58	Bari province to 476
	(Option: Class in —45751)
—377 581	Barium (Bari) to 476
	(Option: Class in —457511)
—377 6	Calabria

See also —3778 for modern Calabria region

(Option: Class in —45754)

—377 63	Brindisi province to 476
	(Option: Class in —45754)
—377 631	Brundusium (Brindisi) to 476
	(Option: Class in —457541)
—377 65	Lecce province to 476
	(Option: Class in —45753)
—377 67	*Taranto province to 476

Including Tarentum (Taranto) to 476

(Option: Class in —45755)

—377 7	Lucania

Class here Basilicata region to 476

(Option: Class in —4577)

—377 73	Matera province to 476

Including Metaponto to 476

(Option: Class in —45772)

—377 75	Potenza province to 476
	(Option: Class in —45771)
—377 77	Salerno province in Lucania to 476

Class comprehensive works on Salerno province to 476 in —37727

(Option: Class in —4574)

*For a specific part of this jurisdiction, region, or feature, see the part and follow instructions under
—3

—377 773	Paestum
	(Option: Class in —4574)
—377 8	Bruttium

Class here Calabria region to 476

Add to base number —3778 the numbers following —4578 in —45781–45787, e.g., Reggio di Calabria province to 476 —37783

See also —3776 for ancient Calabria

(Option: Class in —4578)

—378	Sicily to 476 and Malta to 476

Subdivisions are added for Sicily to 476 and Malta to 476 together, for Sicily to 476 alone

(Option: Class in —458)

>	—378 1–378 2 Sicily region to 476

Class comprehensive works in —378

—378 1	Eastern Sicily to 476

Add to base number —3781 the numbers following —4581 in —45811–45815, e.g., Syracuse province to 476 —37814

(Option: Class in —4581)

—378 2	Western Sicily to 476

Add to base number —3782 the numbers following —4582 in —45821–45824, e.g., Agrigento province to 476 —37822

(Option: Class in —4582)

—378 5	Malta to 476
	(Option: Class in —4585)
—379	Sardinia to 453 and Corsica to 453

Subdivisions are added for Sardinia to 453 and Corsica to 453 together; for Sardinia to 453 alone

(Option: Class Sardinia to 453 in —459)

—379 1–379 8	Provinces of Sardinia to 476

Add to base number —379 the numbers following —459 in —4591–4598, e.g., Cagliari province to 476 —3791

—379 9	Corsica to 453
	(Option: Class in —4499)
—379 92	Corse-de-Sud department to 453
	(Option: Class in —44992)

—379 96   Haute-Corse department

                   (Option: Class in —44996)

—38   *Greece to 323

                   Class here comprehensive works on Greece and Roman Empire; the *Eastern
                   Mediterranean region to 323; the *Hellenistic World; *southern Europe to 323

                   For Roman Empire, see —37

                   (Option: Class Eastern Mediterranean region to 323 in —18224; class southern
                   Europe to 323 in —4; class Greece to 323 in —495)

—381   Macedonia to 323

                   For modern country of Macedonia to ca. 640, see —39876

                   (Option: Class Macedonia to 323 in —4956. Class Western Macedonia
                   region to 323 in —49562. Class Central Macedonia region to 323 in
                   —49565. Class Eastern Macedonia and Thrace region to 323 in —4957)

—382   Thessaly to 323, Epirus to 323, adjacent Ionian Islands to 323

                   Class here comprehensive works on Ionian Islands to 323

                        *For Ithaca Island to 323, see —383; for southern Ionian Islands to 323,
                        see —386*

                   (Option: Class Epirus to 323 in —4953; class Thessaly to 323 in —4954;
                   class Ionian Islands to 323, northern Ionian Islands to 323 in —4955)

—383   Aetolia to 323, Acarnania to 323, Doris to 323, Locris to 323, Malis to
                   323, Phocis to 323; Ithaca Island to 323

                   Including Aetolia and Acarnania department to 323, Eurytania department
                   to 323, Phocis department to 323, Phthiōtis department to 323; Amphissa,
                   Delphi

                   (Option: Class Eurytania department to 323, Phocis department to 323,
                   Phthiōtis department to 323, Doris, Locris, Malis, Phocis, Amphissa,
                   Delphi in —49515; class Aetolia and Acarnania department to 323, Aetolia,
                   Acarnania in —49518; class Ithaca Island to 323 in —4955)

—384   Boeotia to 323, Megaris to 323; Euboea Island to 323

                   Including Eurytania department to 323; Chalcis, Thebes

                   (Option: Class Eurytania department to 323, Boeotia to 323, Euboea Island
                   to 323, Chalcis, Thebes in —49515; class Megaris in —49522)

—385   Attica to 323

                   Including Marathon

                   Class here Athens to 323

                   (Option: Class Attica to 323, Athens to 323, Marathon in —49512)

*For a specific part of this jurisdiction, region, or feature, see the part and follow instructions under
—3

—386   Peloponnesus to 323 and adjacent Ionian Islands to 323

> Subdivisions are added for Peloponnesus to 323 and adjacent Ionian Islands to 323 together, for Peloponnesus to 323 alone

> *For divisions of Peloponnesus to 323, see —387–389*

> (Option: Class Peloponnesus to 323 in —4952; class southern Ionian Islands to 323 in —4955)

\>   —387–389   Divisions of Peloponnesus to 323

> Class comprehensive works in —386

—387   Achaea to 323 and Corinth to 323

> (Option: Class Corinth to 323 in —49522; class Achaea to 323 in —49527)

—388   Arcadia to 323, Argolis to 323, Elis to 323

> Including Mycenae, Olympia, Phigalia, Tiryns

> (Option: Class Arcadia to 323, Argolis to 323, Mycenae, Tiryns in —49522; class Elis to 323, Olympia, Phigalia in —49527)

—389   Laconia to 323 and Messenia to 323

> Class here Sparta to 323

> (Option: Class in —49522)

—39   **Other parts of ancient world**

SUMMARY

—391	**Aegean Islands to 323**
—392	**Diocese of Asia (Dioecesis Asiana)**
—393	**Eastern Asia Minor to 640 and Cyprus to 640**
—394	**Middle East to 640**
—395	**Black Sea region to 640 and Caucasus to 640**
—396	**Central Asia to ca. 640**
—397	**North Africa to ca. 640**
—398	**Southeastern Europe to ca. 640**

—391   Aegean Islands to 323

> Class here Sporades to 323

> (Option: Class in —4958)

—391 1   Northern Aegean Islands to 323

> Including Bozca (Tenedos) Island to 323, Gökçeada (İmroz, Imbros) Island to 323, Lemnos Island to 323, Northern Sporades (including Skyros Island) to 323, Samothrace Island to 323, Thasos Island to 323

> (Option: Class Skyros Island to 323 in —49515; class Northern Sporades to 323 in —4954; class Samothrace Island to 323, Thasos Island to 323 in —4957; class Lemnos Island to 323, Northern Aegean Islands to 323 in —49582; class Bozca (Tenedos) Island to 640, Gökçeada (İmroz, Imbros) Island to 640 in —5622)

—391 2   Lesbos Island to 323

                (Option: Class in —49582)

—391 3   Chios Island to 323

                (Option: Class in —49582)

—391 4   Samos Island to 323

                (Option: Class in —49582)

—391 5   Cyclades to 323

                (Option: Class in —49585)

—391 6   Southern Sporades to 323

                Including Dodecanese to 323, Rhodes to 323

                For Karpathos to 323, see —3917

                (Option: Class in —49587)

—391 7   Karpathos Island to 323

                (Option: Class in —49587)

—391 8   Crete to 323

                Including Knossos

                (Option: Class in —4959)

—392   Diocese of Asia (Dioecesis Asiana)

                Former heading: Western Asia Minor

                Class here *Turkey to 640, *Asia Minor to 640, *western Asia Minor to 640

                For Aegean Islands to 323, see —391; for Aegean Islands 323–640, see —4958

                (Option: Class in —561)

—392 1   Hellespontus Province

                Former heading: Mysia and Troas

                Including Balıkesir province to 640, Çanakkale province to 640; Cyzicus, Mysia, Troas, Troy

                (Option: Class Çanakkale province to 640, Hellespontus Province, Troas, Troy in —5622; class Balıkesir province to 640, Cyzicus, Mysia in —5623)

                Pergamum relocated to —3923

---

*For a specific part of this jurisdiction, region, or feature, see the part and follow instructions under
   —3

—392 2   Lydia Province

              Including Sardis

              Class here Manisa Province to 640

              (Option: Class in —5624)

—392 3   Asia Province

              Former heading: Ionia

              Including Pergamum [*formerly* —3921]; Aydın Province to 640;
              Ephesus, Magnesia ad Maeandrum, Miletus, Smyrna

              Class here İzmir province to 640; Ionia

              (Option: Class İzmir Province to 640, Asia Province, Ionia, Ephesus,
              Pergamum, Smyrna in —5625; class Aydın Province to 640, Magnesia
              ad Maeandrum, Miletus in —5626)

—392 4   Caria Province

              Including Burdur Province to 640, Denizli Province to 640, Muğla
              Province to 640, Halicarnassus

              (Option: Class in —5627)

—[392 5]   Bithynia Province

              Relocated to —39313

—392 6   Phrygia

              Including Afyon Province to 640, Eskişehir Province to 640, Kütahya
              Province to 640, Uşak Province to 640; Phrygia Pacatiana Province,
              Phrygia Salutaris Province

              (Option: Class Afyon Province to 640, Kütahya Province to 640, Uşak
              Province to 640, Phrygia Province, Phrygia Pacatiana Province in
              —5628; class Eskişehir Province to ca. 640, Phrygia Salutaris Province
              in —5635)

—392 7   Lycaonia Province and Pisidia Province

              Former heading: Pisidia

              Including Isparta Province to 640, Karaman Province to 640, Konya
              Province to 640

              (Option: Class Konya Province to 640, Lycaonia Province, Pisidia
              Province in —5642; class Isparta Province to 640 in —5643; class
              Karaman Province to 640 in —5645)

—392 8   Lycia

              Class here western part of Antalya Province to 640, comprehensive
              works on Antalya Province to 640

                  For eastern part of Antalya Province to 640, see —3929

              (Option: Class in —5644)

—392 9   Pamphylia

Class here eastern part of Antalya Province to 640

(Option: Class in —5644)

—393   Eastern Asia Minor to 640 and Cyprus to 640

Subdivisions are added for eastern Asia Minor to 640 and Cyprus to 640 together, for eastern Asia Minor to 640 alone

Class here Diocese of Pontus (Dioecesis Ponticus)

For Armenia, see —3955

(Option: Class eastern Asia Minor to 640, Diocese of Pontus in —561)

\>   —393 1–393 6   Eastern Asia Minor to 640

Class comprehensive works in —393

—393 1   Bithynia Province, Honorias Province, Paphlagonia Province

Former heading: Paphlagonia

—393 13   Bithynia Province [*formerly* —3925]

Including Asian portion of İstanbul Province to 640; Bursa Province to 640, Kocaeli Province to 640, Yalova Province to 640

(Option: Class Bithynia Province to 640 in —563; class Bursa Province to 640 in —5631; class Asian portion of İstanbul Province to 640 in —5632; class Kocaeli Province to 640, Yalova Province to 640 in —5633)

—393 15   Honorias Province

Including Bilecik Province to 640, Bolu Province to 640, Düzce Province to 640, Sakarya Province to 640

(Option: Class in —5634)

—393 17   Paphlagonia Province

Including Bartın Province to 640, Çankırı Province to 640, Karbük Province to 640, Kastamonu Province to 640, Zonguldak Province to 640

(Option: Class in —5637)

—393 2   Galatia Prima Province and Galatia Salutaris Province

Former heading: Galatia

Including Ankara Province to 640, Kırıkkale Province to 640

Class here Galatia

(Option: Class Ankara Province to 640, Galatia Prima and Galatia Salutaris provinces, Galatia in —5636; class Kırıkkale Province to 640 in —5638)

—393 3   Helenopontus Province and Pontus Polemoniacus Province

Former heading: Pontus

Class here Pontus (Roman province)

(Option: Class Pontus in —565)

—393 32   Helenopontus Province

Including Amasya Province to 640, Çorum Province to 640, Samsun Province to 640, Sinop Province to 640, Yozgat Province to 640

(Option: Class Amasya Province to 640, Samsun Province to 640, Sinop Province to 640, Yozgat Province to 640, Helenopontus Province in —5638; class Çorum province to 640 in —56383)

—393 37   Pontus Polemoniacus Province

Including Ardahan Province to 640, Artvin Province to 640, Bayburt Province to 640, Giresun Province to 640, Gümüşhane Province to 640, Ordu Province to 640, Rize Province to 640, Tokat Province to 640, Trabzon Province to 640

(Option: Class Pontus Polemoniacus Province in —565; class Ordu Province to 640, Tokat Province to 640 in —5656; class Bayburt Province to 640, Giresun Province to 640, Gümüşhane Province to 640 in —5657; class Trabzon Province to 640 in —5658; class Ardahan Province to 640, Artvin Province to 640, Rize Province to 640 in —56622)

—393 4   Cappadocia to 640

Including Aksaray Province to 640, Kayseri Province to 640, Kırşehir Province to 640, Nevşehir Province to 640, Niğde Province to 640; Cappadocia Prima Province, Cappadocia Secunda Province

(Option: Class Aksaray Province to 640, Kırşehir Province to 640, Niğde Province to 640, Cappadocia to 640, Cappadocia Prima Province, Cappadocia Secunda Province in —5641; class Kayseri Province to 640 in —56412; class Nevşehir Province to 640 in —56414)

—393 5   Cilicia Prima Province, Cilicia Secunda Province, Isauria Province

Former heading: Cilicia

Including Adana Province to 640, Mersin Province to 640, Osmaniye Province to 640

(Option: Class Mersin Province to 640, Cilicia Prima Province, Isauria Province in —5646; class Adana Province to 640, Osmaniye Province to 640, Cilicia Secunda Province in —5647)

—393 6   Northern part of Euphratensis Province

Former heading: Commagene

The part of Euphratensis Province in present-day Turkey

Including Adıyaman province to 640, Gaziantep province to 640, Kahramanmaraş province to 640, Kilis province to 640, Malatya province to 640; Cyrrhestica

Class here Commagene; comprehensive works on Euphratensis Province

> *For southern part of Euphratensis Province, southern part of Cyrrhestica, see —39432*

(Option: Class Gaziantep Province to 640, Kilis Province to 640, Cyrrhestica in —5649; class Adıyaman Province to 640, Commagene in —5652; class Kahramanmaraş Province to 640, comprehensive works on Euphratensis Province in —5653; class Malatya Province to 640 in —5654)

—393 7   Cyprus to 640

(Option: Class in —5693)

—394   *Middle East to 640

(Option: Class in —56)

—394 2   Southeast central Turkey to 640

Including Batman Province to 640, Bingöl Province to 640, Bitlis Province to 640, Diyarbakır Province to 640, Elazığ Province to 640, Erzincan Province to 640, Mardin Province to 640, Muş, Province to 640, Şanlıurfa Province to 640, Siirt Province to 640, Şirnak Province to 640, Tunceli Province to 640

Class here Osroene

(Option: Class Şanlıurfa Province to 640, Osroene in —5651; class Southeast central Turkey to 640 in —5667; class Bitlis Province to 640, Muş Province to 640 in —56672; class Bingöl Province to 640 in —56673; class Erzincan Province to 640 in —56674; class Tunceli Province to 640 in —56675; class Elazığ Province to 640 in —56676; class Diyarbakır Province to 640 in —5667; class Batman Province to 640, Mardin Province to 640, Siirt Province to 640, Şirnak Province to 640 in —56678)

—394 3   Syria to 640

> *For Phoenicia, see —3944*

(Option: Class in —5691)

—394 31   Hatay Province of modern Turkey to 640

Class here Antioch to 640

(Option: Class —5648)

---

*For a specific part of this jurisdiction, region, or feature, see the part and follow instructions under —3

—394 32	Desert provinces of modern Syria to 640
	Including southern part of Euphratensis Province, southern part of Cyrrhestica
	Class here Palmyra
	(Option: Class —56912)
—394 33	Northwest provinces of modern Syria to 640
	Including Ebla, Ugarit
	(Option: Class —56913)
—394 34	Southwest provinces of modern Syria to 640 and city of Damascus to 640
	(Option: Class in —56914)
—394 344	City of Damascus
	(Option: Class —569144)
—394 4	Phoenicia
	Including Coelesyria; Baalbek, Byblos, Sidon, Tyre
	Class here Lebanon to 640
	(Option: Class in —5692)
—394 6	Moab and Edom
—394 62	Moab
	(Option: Class Ma'dabā Province in Moab to 70 in —569562; class Karak Province to 70, Moab in —569563)
—394 64	Edom
	(Option: Class Darom district of Israel in Edom to 70, Edom in —56949; class Ṭafīlah Province of Jordan in Edom to 70 in —569567; class 'Aqabah Province of Jordan in Edom to 70 in —569572)
—[394 7]	Arabia Deserta
	Upper Mesopotamian portion of Arabia Deserta to 637 relocated to —354; Lower Mesopotamian portion of Arabia Deserta to 637 relocated to —355; Arabia Deserta to 622 relocated to —3949; Arabia Deserta, 622–637 relocated to —53
—394 8	Arabia Petraea
	Including Sinai Peninsula to 622; Petra, Philistia
	(Option: Class Arabia Petraea in —53; class Sinai Peninsula to 622, Philistia in —531; class Darom district of Israel to 622 in —56949; class 'Aqabah Province of Jordan to 622 in —569572; class Ma'ān Province of Jordan to 622, Petra in —569577)

—394 9   Arabian Peninsula to 622

Including Bahrain to 622, Kuwait to 622, Oman to 622, Qatar to 622, Saudi Arabia to 622, United Arab Emirates to 622, Yemen to 622

Class here *Arabia Deserta to 622 [*formerly* —3947]; Arabia Felix; *Persian Gulf region to 622

For Arabia Petraea, see —3948

(Option: Class Arabia Deserta, Arabia Felix, Arabian Peninsula to 622, Persian Gulf region to 622 in —53; class Yemen in —533; class Oman to 622 in —5353; class United Arab Emirates to 622 in —5357; class Qatar to 622 in —5363; class Bahrain to 622 in —5365; class Kuwait to 622 in —5367; class Saudi Arabia to 622 in —538)

—395   *Black Sea region to 640 and Caucasus to 640

Subdivisions are added for Black Sea region to 640 and Caucasus to 640 together, for Black Sea region to 640 alone

(Option: Class Black Sea region to 640 in —18229)

—395 1   Scythia

Class here Black Sea area of Romania to 640

(Option: Class in —4983)

—395 2   Sarmatia

Class here *Ukraine to 640

(Option: Class Ukraine to 640, Black Sea area of Commonwealth of Independent States to 640, Sarmatia in —477)

—395 3   Caucasus to 640

For Armenia, see —3955

(Option: Class in —475)

—395 34   Albania

A part of what is now modern Azerbaijan, not modern Albania

Variant name: Caucasian Albania

Class here *Azerbaijan to 640

(Option: Class in —4754)

—395 36   Iberia

Class here Georgia to 640

For Georgia in Colchis to 640, see —39538

(Option: Class in —4758)

*For a specific part of this jurisdiction, region, or feature, see the part and follow instructions under —3

—395 38   Colchis

                 (Option: Class in —4758)

—395 5   Armenia

                 Including modern country of Armenia to 640, Ağrı Province of Turkey to 640, Erzurum Province of Turkey to 640, Hakkâri Province of Turkey to 640, Iğdır Province of Turkey to 640, Kars Province of Turkey to 640, Sivas Province of Turkey to 640, Van Province of Turkey to 640

                 Class here Armenia region to 640

                 (Option: Class modern country of Armenia to 640 in —4756; class Sivas Province to 640 in —5655; class Armenia region to 640, Armenia [ancient kingdom] in —5662; class Erzurum Province to 640 in —56624; class Ağrı Province to 640, Iğdır Province to 640, Kars Province to 640 in —56626; class Hakkâri Province to 640, Van Province to 640 in —56628)

—396   Central Asia to ca. 640

                 Including Afghanistan to ca. 640, Māzandarān province of Iran to 637, Tajikistan to ca. 640, Turkmenistan to ca. 640, Uzbekistan to ca. 640; Ariana, Bactria, Hyrcania, Margiana, Parthia, Sogdiana

                 For Kyrgyzstan to ca. 640, see —5843; for Kazakhstan to ca. 640, see —5845

                 (Option: Class Māzandarān province of Iran to 637, Hyrcania in —5523; class Central Asia to ca. 640 in —58; class Afghanistan to ca. 640, Ariana, Bactria, Parthia in —581; class Turkmenistan to ca. 640, Margiana in —585; class Tajikistan to ca. 640 in —586; class Uzbekistan to ca. 640, Sogdiana in —587)

—397   North Africa to ca. 640

                 For Egypt to 640, see —32

                 (Option: Class in —61)

—397 1   Mauretania

                 (Option: Class in —65)

—397 12   Mauretania Tingitana

                 Including Ceuta to 647, Melilla to 647

                 Class here Morocco to 647

                 (Option: Class Morocco to 647, Mauretania Tingitana in —64; class Ceuta to 647, Melilla to 647 in —641)

—397 14   Mauretania Caesariensis

                 Class here Algeria to 647

                 (Option: Class in —65)

—397 2   Numidia

                 Class here northeastern provinces of Algeria to 647

                 (Option: Class in —655)

—397 3	Carthage
	Including Byzacium
	Class here Tunisia to 647, *Proconsular Africa (Africa proconsularis)
	(Option: Class in —611)
—397 4	Tripolis to 644
	Including Leptis Magna, Oea, Sabrata
	Class here *Libya to 644
	(Option: Class in —612)
—397 5	Cyrenaica
	(Option: Class in —612)
—397 6	Marmarica to 642
	(Option: Class in —612)
—397 7	Gaetulia
	Class here Sahara provinces of Algeria to 647
	(Option: Class —657)
—397 8	Nubia
	Class here northern states of Sudan to 500, Ethiopia (a part of what is now modern Sudan, not modern Ethiopia), Kush
	Class comprehensive works on the Sudan to 500 in —624
	(Option: Class in —625)

*For a specific part of this jurisdiction, region, or feature, see the part and follow instructions under —3

—398   Southeastern Europe to ca. 640

> Add to base number —398 the numbers following —49 in —496–499, e.g., Thrace —39861, Constantinople —398618, Illyria, Illyricum —3987, Moesia —3989; however, for Thrace, 323–ca. 640, see —4957; for Turkey in Europe (Eastern Thrace), 323–ca. 640, see —4961; for Constantinople, 323–ca. 640, see —49618

> *For Greece to 323, see —38*

> *See also —395 for Black Sea region*

> (Option: Class Thrace to 323 in —4957; class southeastern Europe to ca. 640 in —496; class Turkey in Europe (Eastern Thrace) to 323 in —4961; class İstanbul Province to 323, Constantinople to 323 in —49618; class Albania to ca. 640 in —4965; class former Yugoslavia to ca. 640, Illyria, Illyricum in —497; class Serbia to ca. 640 in —4971; class Croatia to ca. 640 in —4972; class Slovenia to ca. 640 in —4973; class Bosnia and Hercegovina to ca. 640 in —49742; class Montenegro to ca. 640 in —49745; class Macedonia to ca. 640 in —4976; class Bulgaria to ca. 640, Moesia in —499)

> Hungary to ca. 640, Pannonia relocated to —3639

—398 8   Dacia

> Number built according to instructions under —398

> Including Moldova to ca. 640 [*formerly* —476]

> Class here Romania to ca. 640

> (Option: Class Moldova to ca. 640 in —476; class Romania to ca. 640, Dacia in —498)

>   **—4–9 Modern world; extraterrestrial worlds**

Class comprehensive works on specific jurisdictions, regions, or features extending over more than one country, state, county, or other unit and identified by * with the unit where noted in this table, e.g., Rocky Mountain National Park —78869, Lake Huron —774, Appalachian Mountains —74. For works on a part of such a jurisdiction, region, or feature, see the specific unit where the part is located, e.g., Rocky Mountain National Park in Larimer County —78868, Lake Huron waters and shores in Ontario —7132, Cumberland Mountains —7691, Cumberland Mountains in Bell County, Kentucky —769123

Class comprehensive works in 001–999 without adding notation from Table 2

> *See Manual at T2—4–9; also at T2—4–9 vs. T2—3*

(Option: Class here specific parts of ancient world; prefer —3)

(Option: To give local emphasis and a shorter number to a specific country, place it first under its own continent or major region by use of a letter or other symbol, e.g., Pakistan —5P [preceding —51]; then subarrange each such number like the corresponding number in this table, e.g., Peshawar —5P23. Apply like any other area notation, e.g., geology of Peshawar 555.P23, history of Pakistan since 1971 95P.05, history of medical sciences in Pakistan 610.95P)

—4   Europe

Class here nations belonging to the Council of Europe; southern, western Europe

Class Eurasia in —5

(Options: Class here Europe to ca. 499, Europe north and west of Italian Peninsula to ca. 499, western Europe to ca. 499; prefer —36. Class here southern Europe to 323; prefer —38)

SUMMARY

—41	**British Isles**
—411	Scotland
—412	Northeastern Scotland
—413	Southeastern Scotland
—414	Southwestern Scotland
—415	Ireland
—416	Northern Ireland; Donegal County, Monaghan County, Cavan County of Republic of Ireland
—417	Republic of Ireland (Eire)
—418	Leinster
—419	Munster
—42	**England and Wales**
—421	Greater London
—422	Southeastern England
—423	Southwestern England and Channel Islands
—424	Midlands of England
—425	East Midlands of England
—426	Eastern England
—427	Northwestern England and Isle of Man
—428	Northeastern England
—429	Wales
—43	**Germany and neighboring central European countries**
—431	Northeastern Germany
—432	Saxony and Thuringia
—433	Bavaria (Bayern)
—434	Southwestern Germany
—435	Northwestern Germany
—436	Austria and Liechtenstein
—437	Czech Republic and Slovakia
—438	Poland
—439	Hungary
—44	**France and Monaco**
—441	Brittany (Bretagne) and Pays de la Loire
—442	Basse-Normandie, Haute-Normandie, Picardie, Nord-Pas-de-Calais
—443	Champagne-Ardenne, Ile-de-France, Lorraine, Alsace
—444	Burgundy and Franche-Comté
—445	Centre, Rhône-Alpes, Auvergne
—446	Poitou-Charentes and Limousin
—447	Aquitaine and Midi-Pyrénées
—448	Languedoc-Roussillon
—449	Provence-Alpes-Côte d'Azur, Monaco, Corsica

—45	Italy, San Marino, Vatican City, Malta
—451	Northwestern Italy
—452	Lombardy (Lombardia) region
—453	Northeastern Italy
—454	Emilia-Romagna region and San Marino
—455	Tuscany (Toscana) region
—456	Central Italy and Vatican City
—457	Southern Italy
—458	Sicily and adjacent islands
—459	Sardinia
—46	Spain, Andorra, Gibraltar, Portugal
—461	Northwestern Spain
—462	Western Spain
—463	Castile
—464	New Castile region
—465	Northeastern Spain
—466	País Vasco autonomous community
—467	Eastern Spain and Andorra
—468	Andalusia autonomous community and Gibraltar
—469	Portugal
—47	Russia and neighboring east European countries
—471	Northern area of European Russia
—472	Western area of Russia
—473	West central area of Russia
—474	Eastern area of European Russia
475	Caucasus
—476	Moldova
—477	Ukraine
—478	Belarus
—479	Lithuania, Latvia, Estonia
—48	Scandinavia
—481	Norway
—482	Southeastern Norway (Østlandet)
—483	Sørlandet and Vestlandet
—484	Trøndelag and Nord-Norge
—485	Sweden
—486	Southern Sweden (Götaland)
—487	Central Sweden (Svealand)
—488	Northern Sweden (Norrland)
—489	Denmark and Finland
—49	Other parts of Europe
—491	Northwestern islands
—492	Netherlands
—493	Belgium and Luxembourg
—494	Switzerland
—495	Greece
—496	Balkan Peninsula
—497	Serbia, Croatia, Slovenia, Bosnia and Hercegovina, Montenegro, Macedonia
—498	Romania
—499	Bulgaria

—41   **British Isles**

Class here Great Britain, United Kingdom

For England and Wales, see —42

See Manual at T2—41 and T2—42

(Option: Class here British Isles to 410; prefer —361)

SUMMARY

—411	**Scotland**
—412	**Northeastern Scotland**
—413	**Southeastern Scotland**
—414	**Southwestern Scotland**
—415	**Ireland**
—416	**Northern Ireland; Donegal County, Monaghan County, Cavan County of Republic of Ireland**
—417	**Republic of Ireland (Eire)**
—418	**Leinster**
—419	**Munster**

—411   Scotland

For northeastern Scotland, see —412; for southeastern Scotland, see —413; for southwestern Scotland, see —414

(Option: Class here Scotland to 410, northern Britain to 410; prefer —3611)

—411 1   Northern Scotland

For divisions of northern Scotland, see —4113–4115

\>   **—411 3–411 5   Divisions of northern Scotland**

Class comprehensive works in —4111

—411 3   Orkney Islands and Shetland Islands

Class here comprehensive works on Islands authorities

For Eilean Siar, see —4114

—411 32   Orkney Islands

—411 35   Shetland Islands

—411 4   Eilean Siar (Outer Hebrides)

Class here comprehensive works on Hebrides

For Inner Hebrides, see —41154

—411 5   Highland

Class here *Scottish Highlands

---

*For a specific part of this jurisdiction, region, or feature, see the part and follow instructions under —4–9

—411 52	Northern Highland

        Area north of Dornoch Firth, Carron River, Loch Broom; all islands in Dornoch Firth and Loch Broom

        Including former Caithness District, former Sutherland District

           See also —16336 for Dornoch Firth; also —16337 for Loch Broom

—411 54	Skye and adjacent islands

        Class here Inner Hebrides

        Subdivisions are added for Skye and adjacent islands together, for Skye alone

—411 56	Western Highland

        Great Glen and area westward; south of Dornoch Firth, Carron River, Loch Broom; excluding Skye and adjacent islands

        Including former *Inverness District, former *Lochaber District, former *Ross and Cromarty District; Great Glen, Loch Ness

           See also —16336 for Dornoch Firth; also —16337 for Loch Broom

—411 58	Eastern Highland

        Area east of Great Glen

        Including former Badenoch and Strathspey District, former Nairn District; *Grampian Mountains; *Spey River

           For Fort William, see —41156

—412	Northeastern Scotland
—412 2	Moray
—412 3	Aberdeen City

        Class here Aberdeen

—412 4	Aberdeenshire

        Including former Banff and Buchan District, former Gordon District, former Kincardine and Deeside District; *Cairngorm Mountains; *Dee River, *Deveron River

        Class here former *Grampian Region

—412 6	Angus

        Class here *Strathmore

—412 7	Dundee City

        Class here Dundee

---

*For a specific part of this jurisdiction, region, or feature, see the part and follow instructions under —4–9

—412 8   Perth and Kinross

      Class here former *Tayside Region; *Ochil Hills; *Tay River

—412 9   Fife

      Including former Dunfermline District, former Kirkcaldy District, former North East Fife District

—413   Southeastern Scotland

      Class here *Lowlands

—413 1   Stirling, Clackmannanshire, Falkirk

      Former name: Central Region

      Class here *Forth River

      See also —16336 for Firth of Forth

—413 12   Stirling

      Class here *Lennox Hills

—413 15   Clackmannanshire

—413 18   Falkirk

—413 3   West Lothian

      Class here former *Lothian Region

—413 4   Edinburgh City

      Class here Edinburgh

—413 5   Midlothian

      Class here *Pentland Hills

—413 6   East Lothian

      Class here *Lammermuir Hills

—413 7   Scottish Borders

      Including former Berwickshire District, former Ettrick and Lauderdale District, former Roxburgh District, former Tweeddale District

      Class here *Border Country, *Southern Uplands; *Tweed River

—414   Southwestern Scotland

      Class here former Strathclyde Region; *Clyde River

      See also —16337 for Firth of Clyde

—414 2   Argyll and Bute

      Including western part of former Dumbarton District; Campbeltown, Dunoon, Helensburgh, Oban; Loch Lomond

*For a specific part of this jurisdiction, region, or feature, see the part and follow instructions under —4–9

—414 3   Inverclyde, West Dunbartonshire, East Dunbartonshire,
              Renfrewshire, East Renfrewshire

—414 31   Inverclyde

—414 32   West Dunbartonshire

                      Including former Dumbarton District

                      Class here former Clydebank District

                          For western part of former Dumbarton District, see —4142

—414 36   East Dunbartonshire

                      Including former Bearsden and Milngavie District; Kirkintilloch

                      Class here former *Strathkelvin District

—414 37   Renfrewshire

—414 39   East Renfrewshire

                      Class here former Eastwood District

—414 4   Glasgow City

                  Class here Glasgow

—414 5   North Lanarkshire and South Lanarkshire

—414 52   North Lanarkshire

                      Including former Cumbernauld and Kilsyth District, former
                      Monklands District, former Motherwell District

—414 57   South Lanarkshire

                      Including former Clydesdale District, former East Kilbride District,
                      former Hamilton District

—414 6   North Ayrshire, South Ayrshire, East Ayrshire

—414 61   North Ayrshire

                      Former name: Cunninghame District

—414 64   South Ayrshire

                      Former name: Kyle and Carrick District

—414 67   East Ayrshire

                      Including former Cumnock and Doon Valley District, former
                      Kilmarnock and Loudoun District

*For a specific part of this jurisdiction, region, or feature, see the part and follow instructions under
 —4–9

—414 7	Dumfries and Galloway

Including former Annandale and Eskdale District, former Nithsdale District, former Stewartry District, former Wigtown District; *Nith River

See also —16337 for Solway Firth

—415	Ireland

For divisions of Ireland, see —416–419

(Option: Class here Ireland to 410; prefer —3615)

>	—416–419 Divisions of Ireland

Class comprehensive works in —415

—416	Northern Ireland; Donegal County, Monaghan County, Cavan County of Republic of Ireland

Class here *Bann River, *Lough Neagh

Subdivisions are added for Northern Ireland, Donegal, Monaghan, Cavan counties together; for Northern Ireland alone

(Option: Class here Northern Ireland to 410; prefer —3616)

>	—416 1–416 7 Northern Ireland

Class comprehensive works in —416

—416 1	Northeast area of Northern Ireland

Class here former *Antrim county

—416 12	Antrim Borough
—416 13	Ballymena Borough
—416 14	Ballymoney Borough
—416 15	Moyle District
—416 16	Larne Borough
—416 17	Carrickfergus Borough
—416 18	Newtownabbey Borough
—416 19	Lisburn Borough

---

*For a specific part of this jurisdiction, region, or feature, see the part and follow instructions under —4–9

>	—416 2–416 4 Western area of Northern Ireland
	Class comprehensive works in —4162
—416 2	Western area of Northern Ireland

Class here former Londonderry (Derry) county; *Sperrin Mountains

For Fermanagh District, see —4163; for west central area, see —4164

—416 21	City of Derry

Class here Derry (Londonderry)

—416 25	Limavady District
—416 27	Coleraine Borough
—416 29	Magherafelt District
—416 3	Fermanagh District
—416 4	West central area of Northern Ireland

Class here former Tyrone county

—416 41	Strabane District
—416 43	Cookstown District
—416 45	Dungannon District
—416 47	Omagh District
—416 5	Southeast area of Northern Ireland

Class here former Down county

—416 51	Castlereagh Borough
—416 53	North Down Borough
—416 54	Ards Borough

Class here *Strangford Lough

—416 56	Down District
—416 57	Banbridge District
—416 58	Newry and Mourne District

Class here *Mourne Mountains

—416 6	Southern area of Northern Ireland

Class here former *Armagh county

—416 61	Armagh District

*For a specific part of this jurisdiction, region, or feature, see the part and follow instructions under —4–9

—416 64	Craigavon Borough
—416 7	City of Belfast
	Class here Belfast, *Greater Belfast
—416 9	Donegal County, Monaghan County, Cavan County of Republic of Ireland
—416 93	Donegal County
—416 97	Monaghan County
—416 98	Cavan County
—417	Republic of Ireland (Eire)
	Class here *Shannon River
	For counties in Ulster, see —4169; for Leinster, see —418; for Munster, see —419
	(Option: Class here Republic of Ireland to 410; prefer —3617)
—417 1	Connacht
	For divisions of Connacht, see —4172–4176

>	—417 2–417 6 Divisions of Connacht
	Class comprehensive works in —4171
—417 2	Sligo County
—417 25	Sligo
—417 3	Mayo County
—417 4	Galway County
—417 45	Galway
—417 48	Aran Islands
—417 5	Roscommon County
—417 6	Leitrim County
—418	Leinster
	Class here *Barrow River
—418 1	Northwest Leinster
—418 12	Longford County
—418 15	Westmeath County
—418 2	Northeast Leinster

*For a specific part of this jurisdiction, region, or feature, see the part and follow instructions under —4–9

—418 22	Meath County
	Class here *Boyne River
—418 25	Louth County
—418 256	Drogheda
—418 3	Dublin County
	Class here *Liffey River
—418 35	Dublin
—418 38	Dún Laoghaire
—418 4	Wicklow County
—418 5	Kildare County
	Class here *Bog of Allen
—418 6	Offaly County
—418 7	Laois County
—418 8	Southeast Leinster
—418 82	Carlow County
—418 85	Wexford County
—418 856	Wexford
—418 9	Kilkenny County
	Class here *Nore River
—419	Munster
—419 1	Waterford County
	Class here *Suir River
—419 15	Waterford
—419 2	Tipperary County
—419 25	Clonmel
—419 3	Clare County
—419 4	Limerick County
—419 45	Limerick
—419 5	Cork County
	Class here *Blackwater River
—419 56	Cork

*For a specific part of this jurisdiction, region, or feature, see the part and follow instructions under
  —4–9

| —419 6 | Kerry County |
| —419 65 | Killarney |

—42   England and Wales

Subdivisions are added for England and Wales together, for England alone

See Manual at T2—41 and T2—42

(Option: Class here England to 410, southern Britain to 410; prefer —362)

SUMMARY

—421	Greater London
—422	Southeastern England
—423	Southwestern England and Channel Islands
—424	Midlands of England
—425	East Midlands of England
—426	Eastern England
—427	Northwestern England and Isle of Man
—428	Northeastern England
—429	Wales

>	—421–428 England
	Class comprehensive works in —42
—421	Greater London
—421 2	City of London
—421 3	West London
—421 32	Westminster City
—421 33	Hammersmith and Fulham London Borough
—421 34	Kensington and Chelsea Royal Borough
—421 4	North London
—421 42	Camden London Borough
—421 43	Islington London Borough
—421 44	Hackney London Borough
—421 5	Tower Hamlets London Borough
—421 6	South London
—421 62	Greenwich London Borough
—421 63	Lewisham London Borough
—421 64	Southwark London Borough
—421 65	Lambeth London Borough
—421 66	Wandsworth London Borough

—421 7	Eastern Outer London

Class here Outer London

For northwestern Outer London, see —4218; for southwestern Outer London, see —4219

—421 72	Waltham Forest London Borough
—421 73	Redbridge London Borough
—421 74	Havering London Borough
—421 75	Barking and Dagenham London Borough
—421 76	Newham London Borough
—421 77	Bexley London Borough
—421 78	Bromley London Borough
—421 8	Northwestern Outer London

Class here former Middlesex

—421 82	Hounslow London Borough
—421 83	Hillingdon London Borough
—421 84	Ealing London Borough
—421 85	Brent London Borough
—421 86	Harrow London Borough
—421 87	Barnet London Borough
—421 88	Haringey London Borough
—421 89	Enfield London Borough
—421 9	Southwestern Outer London
—421 91	Croydon London Borough
—421 92	Sutton London Borough
—421 93	Merton London Borough
—421 94	Kingston upon Thames London Borough
—421 95	Richmond upon Thames London Borough
—422	Southeastern England

Class here *Home Counties; *Thames River; comprehensive works on southern England

For Greater London, see —421; for southwestern England and Channel Islands, see —423

—422 1	Surrey

*For a specific part of this jurisdiction, region, or feature, see the part and follow instructions under —4–9

—422 11	Runnymede Borough
—422 12	Spelthorne Borough
—422 13	Surrey Heath Borough
—422 14	Woking Borough and Elmbridge Borough
—422 142	Woking Borough

Class here Woking

—422 145	Elmbridge Borough
—422 15	Epsom and Ewell Borough
—422 16	Guildford Borough and Mole Valley District
—422 162	Guildford Borough
—422 165	Mole Valley District
—422 17	Reigate and Banstead Borough
—422 18	Tandridge District
—422 19	Waverley Borough
—422 3	Kent and Medway Borough

Class here *North Downs

Subdivisions are added for Kent and Medway Borough together, for Kent alone

—422 31	Dartford Borough and Gravesham Borough
—422 312	Dartford Borough
—422 315	Gravesham Borough
—422 32	Medway Borough

Unitary authority

Including former Rochester upon Medway City, former Gillingham Borough

—422 33	Swale Borough
—422 34	Canterbury City
—422 35	Dover District and Thanet District
—422 352	Dover District

Class here *Cinque Ports

—422 357	Thanet District
—422 36	Sevenoaks District

*For a specific part of this jurisdiction, region, or feature, see the part and follow instructions under —4–9

—422 37	Tonbridge and Malling Borough and Maidstone Borough
—422 372	Tonbridge and Malling Borough
—422 375	Maidstone Borough
—422 38	Tunbridge Wells Borough
—422 39	Ashford Borough and Shepway District
—422 392	Ashford Borough
—422 395	Shepway District
—422 5	East Sussex, and Brighton and Hove

Class here former Sussex; the *Weald

Subdivisions are added for East Sussex, and Brighton and Hove together; for East Sussex alone

For West Sussex, see —4226

—422 51	Wealden District
—422 52	Rother District
—422 56	Brighton and Hove

Unitary authority

Class here Brighton

—422 57	Lewes District
—422 58	Eastbourne Borough

Class here Eastbourne

—422 59	Hastings Borough

Class here Hastings

—422 6	West Sussex

Class here *South Downs

—422 61	Crawley Borough

Class here Crawley

—422 62	Chichester District
—422 64	Horsham District
—422 65	Mid Sussex District
—422 67	Arun District
—422 68	Worthing Borough

Class here Worthing

*For a specific part of this jurisdiction, region, or feature, see the part and follow instructions under —4–9

—422 69	Adur District
—422 7	**Hampshire, Southampton City, Portsmouth City**

Subdivisions are added for Hampshire, Southampton City, Portsmouth City together; for Hampshire alone

—422 71	Basingstoke and Deane Borough
—422 72	Hart District and Rushmoor Borough
—422 723	Hart District
—422 725	Rushmoor Borough
—422 73	Test Valley Borough and Winchester City
—422 732	Test Valley Borough

Class here *Test River

—422 735	Winchester City
—422 74	East Hampshire District
—422 75	New Forest District
—422 76	Southampton City

Unitary authority

Class here Southampton

—422 77	Eastleigh Borough and Fareham Borough
—422 772	Eastleigh Borough
—422 775	Fareham Borough

Including Fareham

—422 78	Gosport Borough

Class here Gosport

—422 79	Portsmouth City and Havant Borough
—422 792	Portsmouth City

Unitary authority

Class here Portsmouth

—422 795	Havant Borough
—422 8	**Isle of Wight**

Unitary authority

Including former Medina Borough, former South Wight Borough

*For a specific part of this jurisdiction, region, or feature, see the part and follow instructions under —4–9

—422 9	Reading and neighboring unitary authorities
	Class here former Berkshire
—422 91	West Berkshire District
	Former name: Newbury District
	Unitary authority
—422 93	Reading Borough
	Unitary authority
	Class here Reading
—422 94	Wokingham District
	Unitary authority
—422 96	Windsor and Maidenhead Royal Borough
	Unitary authority
—422 97	Slough Borough
	Unitary authority
	Class here Slough
—422 98	Bracknell Forest Borough
	Unitary authority
—423	Southwestern England and Channel Islands
—423 1	Wiltshire and Swindon Borough
	Subdivisions are added for Wiltshire and Swindon Borough together, for Wiltshire alone
—423 12	North Wiltshire District
—423 13	Swindon Borough
	Former name: Thamesdown Borough
	Unitary authority
—423 15	West Wiltshire District
—423 17	Kennet District
—423 19	Salisbury District
	Class here *Salisbury Plain; *East Avon River

*For a specific part of this jurisdiction, region, or feature, see the part and follow instructions under
—4–9

—423 3	Dorset, Poole Borough, Bournemouth Borough

        Class here *Stour River

        Subdivisions are added for Dorset, Poole Borough, Bournemouth Borough together; for Dorset alone

—423 31	West Dorset District
—423 32	North Dorset District
—423 34	East Dorset District
—423 35	Weymouth and Portland Borough
—423 36	Purbeck District
—423 37	Poole Borough

        Unitary authority

        Class here Poole

—423 38	Bournemouth Borough

        Unitary authority

        Class here Bournemouth

—423 39	Christchurch Borough
—423 4	Channel Islands
—423 41	Jersey

        For Minquiers, see —42348; for Dirouilles, Ecrehous, Paternosters, see —42349

—423 42	Guernsey

        For Jethou, see —42347; for Lihou, Lihoumel, see —42349

—423 43	Alderney

        For Burhou, see —42347; for Casquets, see —42348

—423 45	Sark

        For Brecqhou, see —42347

—423 46	Herm
—423 47	Brecqhou, Burhou, Jethou
—423 48	Casquets, Chausey Islands, Minquiers

        Chausey Islands are under French jurisdiction

*For a specific part of this jurisdiction, region, or feature, see the part and follow instructions under —4–9

—423 49   Other islands

                        Including Barnouic, Dirouilles, Ecrehous, Lihou, Lihoumel,
                        Paternosters, Roches Douvres

                        Roches Douvres are under French jurisdiction

—423 5   Devon, Plymouth City, Torbay

                        Class here *Exe River, *Tamar River

                        Subdivisions are added for Devon, Plymouth City, Torbay together; for
                        Devon alone

—423 51   Torridge District

—423 52   North Devon District

—423 53   West Devon Borough

                            Class here *Dartmoor

—423 54   Mid Devon District

—423 55   Teignbridge District

—423 56   Exeter City

                            Class here Exeter

—423 57   East Devon District

—423 58   Plymouth City

                            Unitary authority

                            Class here Plymouth

—423 59   South Hams District and Torbay

—423 592   South Hams District

                                Class here *Dart River

—423 595   Torbay

                                Unitary authority

                                Class here Torbay

—423 7   Cornwall and Isles of Scilly

                        Cornwall is a unitary authority

                        Subdivisions are added for Cornwall and Isles of Scilly together, for
                        Cornwall alone

—[423 71–423 78]   Former districts of Cornwall, former Restormel Borough

                            Numbers discontinued; class in —4237

—423 79   Isles of Scilly

*For a specific part of this jurisdiction, region, or feature, see the part and follow instructions under
  —4–9

—423 8	Somerset
—423 81	Sedgemoor District
—423 83	Mendip District
	Class here *Mendip Hills
—423 85	West Somerset District
	Class here *Exmoor; *Quantock Hills
—423 87	Taunton Deane District
	Class here *Blackdown Hills
—423 89	South Somerset District
—423 9	Bristol and neighboring unitary authorities
	Class here former Avon; *Lower (Bristol) Avon River
—423 91	South Gloucestershire
	Unitary authority
	Including former Kingswood Borough, former Northavon District
—423 93	Bristol City
	Unitary authority
	Class here Bristol
—423 96	North Somerset
	Former name: Woodspring District
	Unitary authority
—423 98	Bath and North East Somerset District
	Unitary authority
	Including former Wansdyke District
	Class here Bath
—424	Midlands of England
	Class here West Midlands; *Welsh Marches (Welsh Borders); *Severn River
	For East Midlands, see —425
—424 1	Gloucestershire
—424 12	Tewkesbury Borough
—424 13	Forest of Dean District

*For a specific part of this jurisdiction, region, or feature, see the part and follow instructions under —4–9

—424 14   Gloucester City

                       Class here Gloucester

—424 16   Cheltenham Borough

                       Class here Cheltenham

—424 17   Cotswold District

                       Class here *Cotswold Hills

—424 19   Stroud District

—424 2   Herefordshire

                   Unitary authority

                   Including former Hereford City, former Leominster District

                       *For parts of former Leominster District in Malvern Hills District,
                       see —42447*

—424 4   Worcestershire

                   Class here former Hereford and Worcester; *Upper (Warwickshire)
                   Avon River

                       For Herefordshire, see —4242

—424 41   Wyre Forest District

—424 42   Bromsgrove District

—424 43   Redditch Borough

                       Class here Redditch

—424 47   Malvern Hills District

—424 48   Worcester City

                       Class here Worcester

—424 49   Wychavon District

—424 5   Shropshire, and Telford and Wrekin

                   Subdivisions are added for Shropshire, and Telford and Wrekin
                   together, for Shropshire alone

—424 51   Oswestry Borough

—424 53   North Shropshire District

—424 54   Shrewsbury and Atcham Borough

—424 56   Telford and Wrekin

                   Unitary authority

—424 57   South Shropshire District

*For a specific part of this jurisdiction, region, or feature, see the part and follow instructions under
   —4–9

—424 59	Bridgnorth District
—424 6	Staffordshire and Stoke-on-Trent City

Subdivisions are added for Staffordshire and Stoke-on-Trent City together, for Staffordshire alone

—424 61	Staffordshire Moorlands District
—424 62	Newcastle-under-Lyme Borough
—424 63	Stoke-on-Trent City

Unitary authority

Class here Stoke-on-Trent

—424 64	Stafford Borough
—424 65	East Staffordshire Borough
—424 66	South Staffordshire District
—424 67	Cannock Chase District
—424 68	Lichfield District
—424 69	Tamworth Borough

Class here Tamworth

—424 8	Warwickshire
—424 81	North Warwickshire Borough
—424 83	Nuneaton and Bedworth Borough
—424 85	Rugby Borough
—424 87	Warwick District
—424 89	Stratford-on-Avon District
—424 9	Birmingham and neighboring metropolitan boroughs

Class here Black Country

—424 91	Wolverhampton Metropolitan Borough

Class here Wolverhampton

—424 92	Walsall Metropolitan Borough

Including Walsall

—424 93	Dudley Metropolitan Borough
—424 94	Sandwell Metropolitan Borough
—424 96	Birmingham City

Class here Birmingham

—424 97	Solihull Metropolitan Borough

—424 98	Coventry City

Class here Coventry

—425	East Midlands of England

Class here *Chiltern Hills; *Trent River

SUMMARY

—425 1	**Derbyshire and Derby City**
—425 2	**Nottinghamshire and Nottingham City**
—425 3	**Lincolnshire**
—425 4	**Leicestershire, Leicester City, Rutland County**
—425 5	**Northamptonshire**
—425 6	**Bedfordshire and Luton Borough**
—425 7	**Oxfordshire**
—425 8	**Hertfordshire**
—425 9	**Buckinghamshire and Milton Keynes**

—425 1	Derbyshire and Derby City

Class here *Derwent River of Derbyshire

Subdivisions are added for Derbyshire and Derby City together, for Derbyshire alone

—425 11	High Peak Borough

Class here *Peak District

—425 12	Chesterfield Borough
—425 13	Derbyshire Dales District

Class here *Dove River

—425 14	North East Derbyshire District
—425 15	Bolsover District
—425 16	Amber Valley Borough
—425 17	Derby City

Unitary authority

Class here Derby

—425 18	Erewash Borough
—425 19	South Derbyshire District
—425 2	Nottinghamshire and Nottingham City

Subdivisions are added for Nottinghamshire and Nottingham City together, for Nottinghamshire alone

—425 21	Bassetlaw District
—425 23	Mansfield District

*For a specific part of this jurisdiction, region, or feature, see the part and follow instructions under —4–9

—425 24	Newark and Sherwood District
	Class here *Sherwood Forest
—425 25	Ashfield District
—425 26	Broxtowe Borough
—425 27	Nottingham City
	Unitary authority
	Class here Nottingham
—425 28	Gedling Borough
—425 29	Rushcliffe Borough
—425 3	Lincolnshire
	Class here *Lincoln Heath; *the Wash; *Witham River
—425 31	West Lindsey District
	Class here former *Parts of Lindsey
—425 32	East Lindsey District
	Class here *Lincoln Wolds
—425 34	Lincoln City
	Class here Lincoln
—425 35	North Kesteven District
	Class here former *Parts of Kesteven
—425 37	Boston Borough
—425 38	South Kesteven District
—425 39	South Holland District
	Class here former *Parts of Holland; *Welland River
—425 4	Leicestershire, Leicester City, Rutland County
	Subdivisions are added for Leicestershire, Leicester City, Rutland County together; for Leicestershire alone
—425 41	Blaby District
—425 42	Leicester City
	Unitary authority
	Class here Leicester
—425 43	Oadby and Wigston Borough
—425 44	Harborough District

*For a specific part of this jurisdiction, region, or feature, see the part and follow instructions under —4–9

—425 45	Rutland County
	Unitary authority
—425 46	Melton Borough
—425 47	Charnwood Borough
—425 48	North West Leicestershire District
—425 49	Hinckley and Bosworth Borough
—425 5	Northamptonshire
	Class here *Nene River
—425 51	Corby Borough
—425 52	Kettering Borough
—425 54	East Northamptonshire District
—425 56	Daventry District
	Class here *Northampton Uplands
—425 57	Northampton Borough
	Class here Northampton
—425 58	Wellingborough Borough
—425 59	South Northamptonshire District
—425 6	Bedfordshire and Luton Borough
	Subdivisions are added for Bedfordshire and Luton Borough together, for Bedfordshire alone
—425 61	Bedford Borough
—425 63	Mid Bedfordshire District
—425 65	South Bedfordshire District
—425 67	Luton Borough
	Unitary authority
	Class here Luton
—425 7	Oxfordshire
—425 71	West Oxfordshire District
—425 73	Cherwell District
—425 74	Oxford City
	Class here Oxford
—425 76	Vale of White Horse District

*For a specific part of this jurisdiction, region, or feature, see the part and follow instructions under
—4–9

—425 79	South Oxfordshire District
—425 8	Hertfordshire
—425 81	North Hertfordshire District
—425 82	Stevenage Borough
	Class here Stevenage
—425 83	East Hertfordshire District
—425 84	Dacorum Borough
—425 85	St. Albans City and District
—425 86	Welwyn Hatfield District
—425 87	Broxbourne Borough
—425 88	Three Rivers District
—425 89	Watford Borough and Hertsmere Borough
—425 892	Watford Borough
	Class here Watford
—425 895	Hertsmere Borough
—425 9	Buckinghamshire and Milton Keynes

Subdivisions are added for Buckinghamshire and Milton Keynes together, for Buckinghamshire alone

—425 91	Milton Keynes
	Unitary authority
	Class here Milton Keynes
—425 93	Aylesbury Vale District
—425 95	Wycombe District
—425 97	Chiltern District
—425 98	South Bucks District
—426	Eastern England

Class here East Anglia; *The Fens; *Great Ouse River

>	—426 1–426 5 East Anglia

Class comprehensive works in —426

—426 1	Norfolk

Class here *Yare River

*For a specific part of this jurisdiction, region, or feature, see the part and follow instructions under —4–9

—426 12	North Norfolk District
—426 13	King's Lynn and West Norfolk Borough
—426 14	Breckland District
—426 15	Norwich City
	Class here Norwich
—426 17	Broadland District
	Class here *Norfolk Broads
—426 18	Great Yarmouth Borough
—426 19	South Norfolk District
	Class here *Waveney River
—426 4	Suffolk
—426 41	Waveney District
—426 43	Forest Heath District
—426 44	Saint Edmundsbury Borough
—426 45	Mid Suffolk District
—426 46	Suffolk Coastal District
—426 48	Babergh District
—426 49	Ipswich Borough
	Class here Ipswich
—426 5	Cambridgeshire and Peterborough City
	Subdivisions are added for Cambridgeshire and Peterborough City together, for Cambridgeshire alone
—426 51	Peterborough City
	Unitary authority
—426 53	Fenland District
	Class here Isle of Ely
	See also —42656 for Ely
—426 54	Huntingdonshire District
—426 56	East Cambridgeshire District
	Including Ely
	See also —42653 for Isle of Ely
—426 57	South Cambridgeshire District

*For a specific part of this jurisdiction, region, or feature, see the part and follow instructions under —4–9

—426 59	Cambridge City
	Class here Cambridge
—426 7	Essex, Thurrock, Southend-on-Sea Borough

Subdivisions are added for Essex, Thurrock, Southend-on-Sea Borough together; for Essex alone

—426 71	Uttlesford and Braintree Districts
—426 712	Uttlesford District
—426 715	Braintree District
—426 72	Colchester Borough and Tendring District
—426 723	Colchester Borough
—426 725	Tendring District
—426 73	Harlow District
	Class here Harlow
—426 74	Epping Forest District
—426 75	Chelmsford Borough and Maldon District
—426 752	Chelmsford Borough
—426 756	Maldon District
—426 76	Brentwood Borough
—426 77	Basildon District and Rochford District
—426 772	Basildon District
	Including Basildon
—426 775	Rochford District
—426 78	Thurrock
	Unitary authority
	Including Thurrock
—426 79	Castle Point Borough and Southend-on-Sea Borough
—426 792	Castle Point Borough
—426 795	Southend-on-Sea Borough
	Unitary authority
	Class here Southend-on-Sea
—427	Northwestern England and Isle of Man

Class here comprehensive works on northern England

Subdivisions are added for northwestern England and Isle of Man together, for northwestern England alone

For northeastern England, see —428

—427 1　　　　　Cheshire, Halton Borough, Warrington Borough

> Subdivisions are added for Cheshire, Halton Borough, Warrington Borough together; for Cheshire alone

—427 12　　　　Crewe and Nantwich Borough

—427 13　　　　Congleton Borough

—427 14　　　　Chester City

—427 15　　　　Vale Royal Borough

—427 16　　　　Macclesfield Borough

—427 17　　　　Ellesmere Port and Neston Borough

—427 18　　　　Halton Borough

> Unitary authority

—427 19　　　　Warrington Borough

> Unitary authority

—427 3　　　　　Manchester and neighboring metropolitan boroughs

—427 31　　　　Trafford Metropolitan Borough

—427 32　　　　Salford City

—427 33　　　　Manchester City

> Class here Manchester

—427 34　　　　Stockport Metropolitan Borough

—427 35　　　　Tameside Metropolitan Borough

—427 36　　　　Wigan Metropolitan Borough

—427 37　　　　Bolton Metropolitan Borough

—427 38　　　　Bury Metropolitan Borough

—427 39　　　　Rochdale Metropolitan Borough and Oldham Metropolitan Borough

—427 392　　　　Rochdale Metropolitan Borough

—427 393　　　　Oldham Metropolitan Borough

—427 5　　　　　Liverpool and neighboring metropolitan boroughs

> Class here former Merseyside; *Mersey River

—427 51　　　　Wirral Metropolitan Borough

—427 53　　　　Liverpool City

> Class here Liverpool

—427 54　　　　Knowsley Metropolitan Borough

---

*For a specific part of this jurisdiction, region, or feature, see the part and follow instructions under —4–9

—427 57	St. Helens Metropolitan Borough
—427 59	Sefton Metropolitan Borough
—427 6	**Lancashire, Blackburn with Darwen Borough, Blackpool Borough**
	Subdivisions are added for Lancashire, Blackburn with Darwen Borough, Blackpool Borough together; for Lancashire alone
—427 61	West Lancashire District and Chorley Borough
—427 612	West Lancashire District
—427 615	Chorley Borough
—427 62	Blackburn with Darwen Borough and Hyndburn Borough
—427 623	Blackburn with Darwen Borough
	Unitary authority
—427 625	Hyndburn Borough
—427 63	Rossendale Borough
—427 64	Burnley Borough and Pendle Borough
—427 642	Burnley Borough
—427 645	Pendle Borough
—427 65	Blackpool Borough
	Unitary authority
	Class here Blackpool
—427 66	Fylde Borough and Preston Borough
—427 662	Fylde Borough
	Class here *The Fylde
—427 665	Preston Borough
—427 67	South Ribble Borough
—427 68	Wyre Borough and Ribble Valley Borough
—427 682	Wyre Borough
—427 685	Ribble Valley Borough
	Class here *Forest of Bowland; *Ribble River
—427 69	Lancaster City
—427 8	**Cumbria**
	Class here Lake District; Cumbrian Mountains
—427 81	Barrow-in-Furness Borough

*For a specific part of this jurisdiction, region, or feature, see the part and follow instructions under —4–9

—427 83	South Lakeland District
—427 84	Copeland Borough
—427 86	Eden District
	Class here *Eden River
—427 87	Allerdale District
	See also —16337 for Solway Firth
—427 89	Carlisle City
—427 9	Isle of Man
—428	Northeastern England
	Class here the *Pennines
—428 1	Leeds and neighboring metropolitan boroughs
	Class here former West Yorkshire; former *Yorkshire
—428 12	Calderdale Metropolitan Borough
—428 13	Kirklees Metropolitan Borough
—428 15	Wakefield City
	Class here *Aire River
—428 17	Bradford City
—428 19	Leeds City
—428 2	Sheffield and neighboring metropolitan boroughs
	Class here former South Yorkshire
—428 21	Sheffield City
—428 23	Rotherham Metropolitan Borough
—428 25	Barnsley Metropolitan Borough
—428 27	Doncaster Metropolitan Borough
—428 3	Kingston upon Hull and neighboring unitary authorities
	Class here former Humberside; *Yorkshire Wolds; *Humber River
—428 32	North Lincolnshire
	Unitary authority
	Including former Glanford Borough, former Scunthorpe Borough

*For a specific part of this jurisdiction, region, or feature, see the part and follow instructions under
   —4–9

—428 34	North East Lincolnshire
	Unitary authority
	Including former Cleethorpes Borough, former Great Grimsby Borough
—428 37	Kingston upon Hull City
	Unitary authority
	Class here Hull
—428 39	East Riding of Yorkshire
	Unitary authority
	Including former Beverley Borough, former *Boothferry Borough, former East Yorkshire Borough, former Holderness Borough

—428 4   **North Yorkshire and York City**

          Class here *Yorkshire Dales; *Derwent River of Yorkshire, *Ouse River

          Subdivisions are added for North Yorkshire and York City together, for North Yorkshire alone

—428 41	Craven District
—428 42	Harrogate Borough
—428 43	York City
	Unitary authority
	Class here York
—428 45	Selby District
—428 46	Ryedale District
	Class here *North Yorkshire Moors
—428 47	Scarborough Borough
—428 48	Richmondshire District
	Class here *Swale River, *Ure River
—428 49	Hambleton District
	Class here *Cleveland Hills

—428 5   **Middlesbrough and neighboring unitary authorities**

          Class here former Cleveland; *Tees River

—428 51	Stockton-on-Tees Borough
	Unitary authority

*For a specific part of this jurisdiction, region, or feature, see the part and follow instructions under —4–9

—428 53	Middlesbrough
	Unitary authority
—428 54	Redcar and Cleveland Borough
	Former name: Langbaurgh-on-Tees Borough
	Unitary authority
—428 57	Hartlepool Borough
	Unitary authority
—428 6	Durham and Darlington Borough
	Class here *Wear River
	Subdivisions are added for Durham and Darlington Borough together, for Durham alone
—428 61	Teesdale District
—428 62	Sedgefield Borough
—428 63	Darlington Borough
	Unitary authority
—428 64	Wear Valley District
—428 65	Durham City
—428 67	Easington District
—428 68	Derwentside District
—428 69	Chester-le-Street District
—428 7	Newcastle upon Tyne and neighboring metropolitan boroughs
	Class here former Tyne and Wear; *Tyne River
—428 71	Sunderland Metropolitan Borough
—428 73	Gateshead Metropolitan Borough
—428 75	South Tyneside Metropolitan Borough
—428 76	Newcastle upon Tyne City
	Class here Newcastle upon Tyne
—428 79	North Tyneside Metropolitan Borough
—428 8	Northumberland
	Class here *Cheviot Hills
—428 81	Tynedale District
—428 83	Castle Morpeth Borough

*For a specific part of this jurisdiction, region, or feature, see the part and follow instructions under —4–9

—428 84	Blyth Valley Borough
—428 86	Wansbeck District
—428 87	Alnwick District
	Class here *Coquet River
—428 89	Berwick-upon-Tweed Borough
—429	Wales

Class here *Cambrian Mountains

(Option: Class here Wales to 410; prefer —3629)

—429 1	North Wales

For northwestern Wales, see —4292; for northeastern Wales, see —4293

—429 2	Northwestern Wales

Class here former Gwynedd County

—429 21	Isle of Anglesey County

Former name: Ynys Môn Borough

—429 25	Gwynedd

Including former Arfon Borough, former Dwyfor District, former Meirionnydd District

Class here *Snowdonia

—429 27	Conwy County Borough

Including former Aberconwy Borough

—429 3	Northeastern Wales

Class here former Clwyd County

—429 33	Flintshire County

Including former Alyn and Deeside District, former Delyn Borough

—429 37	Denbighshire County

Including former Rhuddlan Borough

Class here former *Glyndŵr District

—429 39	Wrexham County Borough
—429 4	South Wales

For Powys County, see —4295; for southwestern Wales, see —4296; for central southern Wales, see —4297; for City and County of Swansea, Neath Port Talbot County Borough, Cardiff County, Vale of Glamorgan, see —4298; for southeastern Wales, see —4299

---

*For a specific part of this jurisdiction, region, or feature, see the part and follow instructions under —4–9

—429 5   Powys County

             Class here *mid Wales; *Wye River

—429 51   Northern Powys County

             Area north of Wye River

             Including former *Radnor District; Severn River in Wales

             Class here former Montgomery District

—429 56   Southern Powys County

             Area south of Wye River

             Class here former Brecknock Borough

—429 6   Southwestern Wales

             Class here former Dyfed County

—429 61   Ceredigion County

—429 62   Pembrokeshire County

             Including former Preseli District

—429 65   Carmarthenshire County

             Including former Dinefwr Borough, former Llanelli Borough

—429 7   Central southern Wales

             Class here former county of *Mid Glamorgan

               For City and County of Swansea, Neath Port Talbot County Borough, Cardiff County, Vale of Glamorgan, see —4298

—429 71   Bridgend County Borough

               Class here former *Ogwr Borough

—429 75   Merthyr Tydfil County Borough

—429 76   Caerphilly County Borough

               Including former Islwyn Borough, former Rhymney Valley District

—429 78   Rhondda Cynon Taff County Borough

               Including former *Taff-Ely Borough

—429 8   City and County of Swansea, Neath Port Talbot County Borough, Cardiff County, Vale of Glamorgan

—429 82   City and County of Swansea

               Including former *Lliw Valley Borough; Swansea; Gower Peninsula

               Class here former county of *West Glamorgan

---

*For a specific part of this jurisdiction, region, or feature, see the part and follow instructions under —4–9

—429 85	Neath Port Talbot County Borough
	Including former Afan Borough
—429 87	Cardiff County
	Class here former county of *South Glamorgan; Cardiff
—429 89	Vale of Glamorgan
—429 9	Southeastern Wales
	Class here former *Gwent, former *Monmouthshire
—429 91	Newport County Borough
—429 95	Blaenau Gwent County Borough
—429 97	Torfaen County Borough
—429 98	Monmouthshire County

—43 **Germany and neighboring central European countries**

Class here *Holy Roman Empire; *central Europe, *Germanic regions

Class central eastern Europe in —437

For Switzerland, see —494

(Option: Class here Germanic regions to 481, Germany to 481; prefer —363)

SUMMARY

—431	Northeastern Germany
—432	Saxony and Thuringia
—433	Bavaria (Bayern)
—434	Southwestern Germany
—435	Northwestern Germany
—436	Austria and Liechtenstein
—437	Czech Republic and Slovakia
—438	Poland
—439	Hungary

> **—431–435 Germany**

Class comprehensive works in —43

—431 Northeastern Germany

Class here former German Democratic Republic (East Germany); *Elbe River

For Saxony and Thuringia, see —432

*For a specific part of this jurisdiction, region, or feature, see the part and follow instructions under —4–9

—431 5   Brandenburg and Berlin

> Subdivisions are added for Brandenburg and Berlin together, for Brandenburg alone

---

\>   —431 51–431 54   Brandenburg

> Class comprehensive works in —4315

—431 51   Southern Brandenburg

> Including Dahme-Spreewald county (Dahme-Spreewald Landkreis), Elbe-Elster county (Elbe-Elster Landkreis), Oberspreewald-Lausitz county (Oberspreewald-Lausitz Landkreis), Spree-Neisse county (Spree-Neisse Landkreis); Cottbus

> Class here *Lausitz-Spreewald planning region (Lausitz-Spreewald Raumordnungsregion); former *Cottbus district (Cottbus Bezirk); *Lusatia, Lower Lusatia

—431 53   Eastern Brandenburg

> Including *Oderland-Spree planning region (Oderland-Spree Raumordnungsregion), *Uckermark-Barnim planning region (Uckermark-Barnim Raumordnungsregion); Barnim (Barnim Landkreis), Märkisch-Oderland (Märkisch-Oderland Landkreis), Oder-Spree (Oder-Spree Landkreis), Uckermark county (Uckermark Landkreis)

> Class here former *Frankfurt an der Oder district (Frankfurt an der Oder Bezirk)

—431 532   Frankfurt an der Oder

—431 54   Western Brandenburg

> Including *Havelland-Fläming planning region (Havelland-Fläming Raumordnungsregion), *Prignitz-Oberhavel planning region (Prignitz-Oberhavel Raumordnungsregion); Havelland county (Havelland Landkreis), Oberhavel county (Oberhavel Landkreis), Ostprignitz-Ruppin county (Ostprignitz-Ruppin Landkreis), Potsdam-Mittelmark county (Potsdam-Mittelmark Landkreis), Prignitz county (Prignitz Landkreis), Teltow-Fläming county (Teltow-Fläming Landkreis); Brandenburg an der Havel

> Class here former *Potsdam district (Potsdam Bezirk)

—431 546   Potsdam

—431 55   Berlin

—431 552   Eastern Berlin

> Class here former East Berlin

---

*For a specific part of this jurisdiction, region, or feature, see the part and follow instructions under —4–9

—431 554   Western Berlin

                                 Class here former West Berlin

—431 7   Mecklenburg-Vorpommern

                                 Class here former Mecklenburg

—431 72   Eastern Mecklenburg

                                 Including Demmin county (Demmin Landkreis),
                                 Mecklenburg-Strelitz county (Mecklenburg-Strelitz Landkreis),
                                 Müritz county (Müritz Landkreis); Neubrandenburg

                                 Class here former *Neubrandenburg district (Neubrandenburg
                                 Bezirk)

—431 74   Central Mecklenburg

                                 Including Bad Doberan county (Bad Doberan Landkreis), Güstrow
                                 county (Güstrow Landkreis)

                                 Class here former *Rostock district (Rostock Bezirk)

—431 745   Rostock

—431 76   Western Mecklenburg

                                 Including Ludwigslust county (Ludwigslust Landkreis),
                                 Nordwestmecklenburg county (Nordwestmecklenburg Landkreis),
                                 Parchim county (Parchim Landkreis); Schwerin, Wismar

                                 Class here former *Schwerin district (Schwerin Bezirk)

—431 78   German Pomerania (Vorpommern)

                                 Including southern part of German Pomerania; northern part of
                                 German Pomerania; Nordvorpommern county (Nordvorpommern
                                 Landkreis), Ostvorpommern county (Ostvorpommern Landkreis),
                                 Rügen county (Rügen Landkreis), Uecker-Randow county
                                 (Uecker-Randow Landkreis); Greifswald, Stralsund

—431 8   Saxony-Anhalt (Sachsen-Anhalt)

                                 Class here former Prussian Saxony

—431 82   Northern Saxony-Anhalt

                                 Including *Harz Mountains

                                 Class here former *Magdeburg district (Magdeburg
                                 Regierungsbezirk)

—431 822   Magdeburg

—431 84   Southern Saxony-Anhalt

                                 Class here former *Halle district (Halle Regierungsbezirk); *Saale
                                 River

—431 848   Halle

*For a specific part of this jurisdiction, region, or feature, see the part and follow instructions under
    —4–9

—431 86	Eastern Saxony-Anhalt
	Class here former Dessau district (Dessau Regierungsbezirk), Anhalt
—432	Saxony and Thuringia
—432 1	Saxony (Sachsen)
—432 12	Leipzig district (Leipzig Direktionsbezirk)
	Class here former Leipzig district (Leipzig Regierungsbezirk)
—432 122	Leipzig
—432 14	Dresden district (Dresden Direktionsbezirk)
	Class here former Dresden district (Dresden Regierungsbezirk)
—432 142	Dresden
—432 16	Chemnitz district (Chemnitz Direktionsbezirk)
	Class here former Chemnitz district (Chemnitz Regierungsbezirk); *Erzgebirge in Germany
—432 162	Chemnitz
—432 2	Thuringia (Thüringen)
—432 22	Eastern Thuringia
	Including Altenburger Land county (Altenburger Land Landkreis), Greiz county (Greiz Landkreis), Saale-Holzlandkreis county (Saale-Holzlandkreis Landkreis), Saale-Orla-Kreis county (Saale-Orla-Kreis Landkreis), Saalfeld-Rudolstadt county (Saalfeld-Rudolstadt Landkreis); Gera, Jena
	Class here former *Gera district (Gera Bezirk)
—432 24	Northern Thuringia
	Including Eichsfeld county (Eichsfeld Landkreis), Gotha county (Gotha Landkreis), Kyffhäuserkreis county (Kyffhäuserkreis Landkreis), Nordhausen county (Nordhausen Landkreis), Sömmerda county (Sömmerda Landkreis), Unstrut-Hainich-Kreis county (Unstrut-Hainich-Kreis Landkreis), Weimarer Land county (Weimarer Land Landkreis)
	Class here former *Erfurt district (Erfurt Bezirk)
—432 241	Weimar
—432 248	Erfurt

*For a specific part of this jurisdiction, region, or feature, see the part and follow instructions under —4–9

—432 26	Southern Thuringia

     Including Hildburghausen county (Hildburghausen Landkreis), Ilm-Kreis county (Ilm-Kreis Landkreis), Schmalkalden-Meiningen county (Schmalkalden-Meiningen Landkreis), Sonneberg county (Sonneberg Landkreis), Wartburgkreis county (Wartburgkreis Landkreis); Eisenach, Suhl; Thuringian Forest

     Class here former *Suhl district (Suhl Bezirk)

—433	Bavaria (Bayern)

     Class here Franconian Jura; *Danube River in Germany

     (Option: Class here Bavaria to 481, Vindelicia; prefer —3633)

—433 1	Upper Franconia (Oberfranken)
—433 11	Coburg
—433 15	Bayreuth
—433 18	Bamberg
—433 2	Middle Franconia (Mittelfranken)
—433 22	Erlangen
—433 24	Nuremberg (Nürnberg)
—433 3	Lower Franconia (Unterfranken)

     Including *Rhön Mountains

—433 31	Aschaffenburg
—433 36	Schweinfurt
—433 39	Würzburg
—433 4	Upper Palatinate (Oberpfalz)
—433 47	Regensburg
—433 5	Lower Bavaria (Niederbayern)

     Class here *Bavarian Forest, *Bohemian Forest in Germany

     Class comprehensive works on Bohemian Forest in —43714

—433 55	Passau
—433 58	Landshut
—433 6	Upper Bavaria (Oberbayern)

     Class here *Bavarian Alps

—433 62	Ingolstadt
—433 64	Munich (München)

*For a specific part of this jurisdiction, region, or feature, see the part and follow instructions under —4–9

—433 7   Swabia district (Schwaben Regierungsbezirk)

—433 75   Augsburg

—434   Southwestern Germany

        Class here *Main River, *Rhine River

—434 1   Hesse (Hessen)

—434 12   Kassel district (Kassel Regierungsbezirk)

—434 124   Kassel

—434 14   Giessen district (Giessen Regierungsbezirk)

        Including *Lahn River

—434 16   Darmstadt district (Darmstadt Regierungsbezirk)

        Including *Taunus Mountains

—434 163   Offenbach am Main

—434 164   Frankfurt am Main

—434 165   Wiesbaden

—434 167   Darmstadt

—434 2   Saarland

        Class here *Saar River

—434 21   Saarbrücken district (Saarbrücken Regionalverband)

        Class here former Saarbrücken district (Saarbrücken Stadtverband)

—434 3   Rhineland-Palatinate (Rheinland-Pfalz)

        Class here Rhine Province (Rhenish Prussia); *Moselle River

        For Saarland, see —4342; for North Rhine-Westphalia, see —4355

—434 31   Western Rhineland-Palatinate

        Class here former Trier district (Trier Regierungsbezirk)

—434 313   Trier

—434 32   Northern Rhineland-Palatinate

        Class here former Koblenz district (Koblenz Regierungsbezirk)

—434 323   Koblenz

—434 35   Southern Rhineland-Palatinate

        Class here former Rheinhessen-Pfalz district (Rheinhessen-Pfalz Regierungsbezirk); Palatinate; Pfälzerwald Mountains

        For Upper Palatinate, see —4334

---

*For a specific part of this jurisdiction, region, or feature, see the part and follow instructions under —4–9

—434 351	Mainz
—434 352	Worms
—434 353	Ludwigshafen am Rhein and Rhein-Pfalz-Kreis county (Rhein-Pfalz-Kreis Landkreis)
—434 353 2	Ludwigshafen am Rhein
—434 6	Baden-Württemberg

Class here comprehensive works on Swabia; *Black Forest

For Swabia district of Bavaria, see —4337; for Stuttgart and Tübingen districts, see —4347

—434 62	Freiburg district (Freiburg Regierungsbezirk)

Including *Lake Constance (Bodensee)

—434 626	Südlicher Oberrhein Region

Including Breisgau-Hochschwarzwald county (Breisgau-Hochschwarzwald Landkreis), Emmendingen county (Emmendingen Landkreis), Ortenaukreis county (Ortenaukreis Landkreis)

—434 626 2	Freiburg im Breisgau
—434 64	Karlsruhe district (Karlsruhe Regierungsbezirk)

Class here former *Baden

—434 643	Mittlerer Oberrhein Region

Including Karlsruhe county (Karlsruhe Landkreis), Rastatt county (Rastatt Landkreis); Baden-Baden

—434 643 6	Karlsruhe
—434 645	Unterer Neckar area

Former heading: Unterer Neckar Region

Including Neckar-Odenwald-Kreis county (Neckar-Odenwald-Kreis Landkreis), Rhein-Neckar-Kreis county (Rhein-Neckar-Kreis Landkreis)

Class here *Rhein-Neckar Region (Rhein-Neckar Metropolregion); *Neckar River

—434 645 2	Mannheim
—434 645 4	Heidelberg
—434 7	Stuttgart district and Tübingen district

Class here former *Württemberg

---

*For a specific part of this jurisdiction, region, or feature, see the part and follow instructions under —4–9

—434 71	Stuttgart district (Stuttgart Regierungsbezirk)
	Class here Stuttgart Region
—434 715	Stuttgart
—434 73	Tübingen district (Tübingen Regierungsbezirk)
	Including former *Hohenzollern
	Class here *Swabian Jura
—435	Northwestern Germany
—435 1	Schleswig-Holstein and Hamburg
—435 12	Schleswig-Holstein
	Including North Friesland; *North Frisian Islands
—435 123	Kiel
—435 125	Lübeck
—435 15	Hamburg
—435 2	Bremen
	Class here Bremen city
—435 21	Bremerhaven
—435 5	North Rhine-Westphalia (Nordrhein-Westfalen)
	Class here *Ruhr River
	For Münster, Arnsberg, Detmold districts, see —4356
—435 51	Cologne district (Köln Regierungsbezirk)
—435 511	Aachen
—435 514	Cologne (Köln)
—435 518	Bonn
—435 53	Düsseldorf district (Düsseldorf Regierungsbezirk)
—435 532	Wuppertal
—435 534	Düsseldorf
—435 535	Mönchengladbach and Krefeld
—435 535 3	Mönchengladbach
—435 535 7	Krefeld
—435 536	Duisburg
—435 537	Mülheim an der Ruhr and Oberhausen

*For a specific part of this jurisdiction, region, or feature, see the part and follow instructions under —4–9

—435 537 3	Mülheim an der Ruhr
—435 537 7	Oberhausen
—435 538	Essen
—435 6	**Münster district, Arnsberg district, Detmold district**
	Class here Westphalia; *Lippe River
—435 61	Münster district (Münster Regierungsbezirk)
	Class here *Münsterland
—435 614	Münster
—435 618	Gelsenkirchen
—435 63	Arnsberg district (Arnsberg Regierungsbezirk)
—435 632	Bochum
—435 633	Dortmund
—435 635	Hagen
—435 65	Detmold district (Detmold Regierungsbezirk)
	Class here *Teutoburg Forest
—435 655	Bielefeld
—435 9	**Lower Saxony (Niedersachsen)**
	Class here *Weser River
—435 91	Northwestern Lower Saxony
	Class here former Weser-Ems district (Weser-Ems Regierungsbezirk)
—435 911	Osnabrück
—435 914	Oldenburg
—435 917	East Friesland region
	Including Aurich county (Aurich Landkreis), Friesland county (Friesland Landkreis), Leer county (Leer Landkreis), Wittmund county (Wittmund Landkreis); Emden, Wilhelmshaven; *East Frisian Islands
—435 93	Northeastern Lower Saxony
	Class here former Lüneburg district (Lüneburg Regierungsbezirk)
—435 95	Southwestern Lower Saxony
	Class here former Hannover district (Hannover Regierungsbezirk)

*For a specific part of this jurisdiction, region, or feature, see the part and follow instructions under —4–9

—435 954	Hannover Region
	Class here Hannover
—435 97	Southern Lower Saxony
	Class here former *Braunschweig state; former Braunschweig district (Braunschweig Regierungsbezirk)
—435 976	Braunschweig
—436	Austria and Liechtenstein

Class here *Austrian Empire, *Dual Monarchy of Austria-Hungary

Subdivisions are added for Austria and Liechtenstein together, for Austria alone

(Option: Class here Austria to 476, Noricum; prefer —3636)

—436 1	Eastern Austria
—436 12	Lower Austria (Niederösterreich)
	Class here *Danube River in Austria
—436 13	Vienna (Wien)
—436 15	Burgenland
—436 2	Upper Austria (Oberösterreich)
—436 24	Linz
—436 3	Salzburg province (Salzburg Land)
—436 32	Salzburg
—436 4	Western Austria, and Liechtenstein

Subdivisions are added for western Austria, and Liechtenstein together; for western Austria alone

Class here *Alpine region of Austria, *Eastern Alps

For Salzburg province, see —4363

(Option: Class here western Austria to 476, Raetia in Austria; prefer —3634)

—436 42	Tyrol (Tirol)
	Class here *Inn River
—436 424	Innsbruck
—436 45	Vorarlberg

*For a specific part of this jurisdiction, region, or feature, see the part and follow instructions under —4–9

—436 48	Liechtenstein
	Independent principality
	(Option: Class here Liechtenstein to 476; prefer —36348)
—436 5	Styria (Steiermark)
—436 55	Graz
—436 6	Carinthia (Kärnten)
—437	Czech Republic and Slovakia
	Class here Czechoslovakia, central eastern Europe
	Class central Europe in —43; class eastern Europe in —47
	For Poland, see —438; for Hungary, see —439
—437 1	Czech Republic
	Including Sudetenland
	Class here Bohemia
	For Moravia, see —4372
—437 11	Středočeský Region (Středočeský Kraj)
—437 12	Prague (Praha)
—437 13	Jihočeský Region (Jihočeský Kraj)
	Former name: Budějovický Region (Budějovický Kraj)
—437 14	Plzeňský Region (Plzeňský Kraj)
	Class here former *Západočeský Region (Západočeský Kraj), *Bohemian Forest (Český Les)
—437 15	Karlovarský Region (Karlovarský Kraj)
	Including *Erzgebirge
—437 16	Ústecký Region (Ústecký Kraj)
	Class here former *Severočeský Region (Severočeský Kraj)
—437 17	Liberecký Region (Liberecký Kraj)
—437 18	Královéhradecký Region (Královéhradecký Kraj)
	Class here former *Východočeský Region (Východočeský Kraj)
—437 19	Pardubický Region (Pardubický Kraj)
—437 2	Moravia
—437 22	Vysočina Region (Vysočina Kraj)
	Former name: Jihlavský Region (Jihlavský Kraj)

*For a specific part of this jurisdiction, region, or feature, see the part and follow instructions under —4–9

—437 24   Jihomoravský Region (Jihomoravský Kraj)

                Former name: Brněnský Region (Brněnský Kraj)

—437 25   Zlínský Region (Zlínský Kraj)

—437 27   Olomoucký Region (Olomoucký Kraj)

—437 28   Moravskoslezský Region (Moravskoslezský Kraj)

                Former name: Ostravský Region (Ostravský Kraj)

                Class here Czech Silesia, former *Severomoravský Region (Severomoravský Kraj)

—437 3   Slovakia

                Class here *Carpathian Mountains in Slovakia

—437 31   Bratislava Region (Bratislava Kraj)

                Class here Bratislava

—437 32   Trnavský Region (Trnavský Kraj)

—437 33   Nitriansky Region (Nitriansky Kraj)

                Class here former *Západoslovenský Region (Západoslovenský Kraj)

—437 34   Banskobystrický Region (Banskobystrický Kraj)

                Class here former *Banskobystrický Region (Banskobystrický Kraj)

—437 35   Košický Region (Košický Kraj)

                Class here former *Východoslovenský Region (Východoslovenský Kraj)

—437 36   Prešovský Region (Prešovský Kraj)

—437 37   Žilinský Region (Žilinský Kraj)

—437 38   Trenčiansky Region (Trenčiansky Kraj)

—438   Poland

—438 1   Northwestern Poland

—438 12   Lubuskie Province (Lubuskie Voivodeship)

                Including former *Gorzów Wielkopolski Province (Gorzów Wielkopolski Voivodeship), former *Zielona Góra Province (Zielona Góra Voivodeship)

*For a specific part of this jurisdiction, region, or feature, see the part and follow instructions under
—4–9

—438 16   Zachodniopomorskie Province (Zachodniopomorskie Voivodeship)

Including former Koszalin Province (Koszalin Voivodeship), former Szczecin Province (Szczecin Voivodeship)

Class here *Pomerania, *Polish Pomerania

For German Pomerania, see —4317

—438 2   North central Poland

Class here *West Prussia

—438 22   Pomorskie Province (Pomorskie Voivodeship)

Including former Gdańsk Province (Gdańsk Voivodeship), former *Słupsk Province (Słupsk Voivodeship)

Class here Pomerelia

—438 26   Kujawsko-Pomorskie Province (Kujawsko-Pomorskie Voivodeship)

Including former Bydgoszcz Province (Bydgoszcz Voivodeship), former *Toruń Province (Toruń Voivodeship), former Włocławek Province (Włocławek Voivodeship)

—438 3   Northeastern Poland

—438 32   Warmińsko-Mazurskie Province (Warmińsko-Mazurskie Voivodeship)

Including former *Elbląg Province (Elbląg Voivodeship), former Olsztyn Province (Olsztyn Voivodeship), former *Suwałki Province (Suwałki Voivodeship)

Class here comprehensive works on East Prussia

For Kaliningrad province of Russia, see —4724

—438 36   Podlaskie Province (Podlaskie Voivodeship)

Including former Białystok Province (Białystok Voivodeship), former *Łomża Province (Łomża Voivodeship)

—438 4   Central Poland

—438 41   Mazowieckie Province (Mazowieckie Voivodeship)

Including former *Ciechanów Province (Ciechanów Voivodeship), former *Ostrołęka Province (Ostrołęka Voivodeship), former *Płock Province (Płock Voivodeship), former Radom Province (Radom Voivodeship), former *Siedlce Province (Siedlce Voivodeship), former Warsaw Province (Warsaw Voivodeship)

—438 43   Lubelskie Province (Lubelskie Voivodeship)

Including former *Biała Podlaska Province (Biała Podlaska Voivodeship), former Chełm Province (Chełm Voivodeship), former Lublin Province (Lublin Voivodeship), former Zamość Province (Zamość Voivodeship)

*For a specific part of this jurisdiction, region, or feature, see the part and follow instructions under —4–9

—438 45   Świętokrzyskie Province (Świętokrzyskie Voivodeship)

Including former *Kielce Province (Kielce Voivodeship)

—438 47   Łódzkie Province (Łódzkie Voivodeship)

Including former Łódź Province (Łódź Voivodeship), former *Piotrków Trybunalski Province (Piotrków Trybunalski Voivodeship), former Sieradz Province (Sieradz Voivodeship), former *Skierniewice Province (Skierniewice Voivodeship)

—438 49   Wielkopolskie Province (Wielkopolskie Voivodeship)

Including former *Kalisz Province (Kalisz Voivodeship), former Konin Province (Konin Voivodeship), former *Leszno Province (Leszno Voivodeship), former *Piła Province (Piła Voivodeship), former Poznań Province (Poznań Voivodeship)

—438 5   Southwestern Poland

Class here Silesia

For Czech Silesia, see —4372

—438 52   Dolnośląskie Province (Dolnośląskie Voivodeship)

Including former Jelenia Góra Province (Jelenia Góra Voivodeship), former Legnica Province (Legnica Voivodeship), former Wałbrzych Province (Wałbrzych Voivodeship), former Wrocław Province (Wrocław Voivodeship)

—438 55   Opolskie Province (Opolskie Voivodeship)

Class here former Opole Province (Opole Voivodeship)

—438 58   Śląskie Province (Śląskie Voivodeship)

Including former *Bielsko Province (Bielsko Voivodeship), former *Częstochowa Province (Częstochowa Voivodeship), former *Katowice Province (Katowice Voivodeship)

—438 6   Southeastern Poland

Class here Galicia

For East Galicia, see —4779

—438 62   Małopolskie Province (Małopolskie Voivodeship)

Including former Kraków Province (Kraków Voivodeship), former Nowy Sącz Province (Nowy Sącz Voivodeship), former *Tarnów Province (Tarnów Voivodeship)

—438 66   Podkarpackie Province (Podkarpackie Voivodeship)

Including former *Krosno Province (Krosno Voivodeship), former Przemyśl Province (Przemyśl Voivodeship), former Rzeszów Province (Rzeszów Voivodeship), former *Tarnobrzeg Province (Tarnobrzeg Voivodeship)

*For a specific part of this jurisdiction, region, or feature, see the part and follow instructions under —4–9

—439   Hungary

(Option: Class here Hungary to ca. 640, Pannonia; prefer —3639)

—439 1   Pest county and Budapest

Variant name: Pest Megye

Subdivisions are added for Pest county and Budapest together, for Pest county alone

—439 12   Budapest

—439 7   Hungary west of Danube

Including Baranya county (Baranya Megye), Fejér county (Fejér Megye), Győr-Moson-Sopron county (Győr-Moson-Sopron Megye), Komárom-Esztergom county (Komárom-Esztergom Megye), Somogy county (Somogy Megye), Tolna county (Tolna Megye), Vas county (Vas Megye), Veszprém county (Veszprém Megye), Zala county (Zala Megye)

For Pest county, see —4391

—439 8   Hungary east of Danube

Including Bács-Kiskun county (Bács-Kiskun Megye), Csongrád county (Csongrád Megye), Heves county (Heves Megye), Jász-Nagykun-Szolnok county (Jász-Nagykun-Szolnok Megye), Nógrád county (Nógrád Megye)

For Pest county, see —4391; for easternmost Hungary, see —4399

—439 9   Easternmost Hungary

Including Békés county (Békés Megye), Borsod-Abaúj-Zemplén county (Borsod-Abaúj-Zemplén Megye), Hajdú-Bihar county (Hajdú-Bihar Megye), Szabolcs-Szatmár-Bereg county (Szabolcs-Szatmár-Bereg Megye)

—44   **France and Monaco**

Subdivisions are added for France and Monaco together, for France alone

For a specific overseas department of France, see the department, e.g., Martinique —72982

(Option: Class here Celtic regions to 486, France to 486, Gaul [Gallia Transalpina]; prefer —364)

SUMMARY

—441	Brittany (Bretagne) and Pays de la Loire

Class here northwestern France

Subdivisions are added for Brittany (Bretagne) and Pays de la Loire together, for Brittany (Bretagne) alone

---

>	—441 1–441 5 Brittany (Bretagne)

Class comprehensive works in —441

—441 1	Finistère department
—441 12	Brest
—441 2	Côtes-d'Armor department
—441 3	Morbihan department
—441 5	Ille-et-Vilaine department
—441 54	Rennes
—441 6	Pays de la Loire

Class here *Maine

For Sarthe department, see —4417; for Maine-et-Loire department, see —4418

—441 62	Mayenne department
—441 67	Loire-Atlantique department
—441 675	Nantes
—441 69	Vendée department
—441 7	Sarthe department
—441 8	Maine-et-Loire department

Class here *Anjou

—441 84	Angers
—442	Basse-Normandie, Haute-Normandie, Picardie, Nord-Pas-de-Calais

Class here Normandy (Normandie)

>	—442 1–442 5 Normandy (Normandie)

Class comprehensive works on Normandy (Normandie) in —442

---

*For a specific part of this jurisdiction, region, or feature, see the part and follow instructions under —4–9

—442 1	Basse-Normandie

> *For Calvados department, see —4422; for Orne department, see —4423*

—442 12	Manche department

> *For Chausey Islands, see —42348; for Roches Douvres, see —42349*

—442 2	Calvados department
—442 24	Caen
—442 3	Orne department
—442 4	Haute-Normandie

> *For Seine-Maritime department, see —4425*

—442 42	Eure department
—442 5	Seine-Maritime department
—442 52	Rouen
—442 6	Picardy (Picardie)
—442 62	Somme department
—442 625	Amiens
—442 64	Oise department
—442 66	Aisne department
—442 7	Nord-Pas-de-Calais

Class here *northern France

> *For Nord department, see —4428*

—442 72	Pas-de-Calais department

Class here Artois

—442 8	Nord department

Class here French Flanders

—442 84	Lille
—443	Champagne-Ardenne, Ile-de-France, Lorraine, Alsace

Class here *Marne River; northeastern France

—443 1	Champagne-Ardenne

Class here *Champagne

> *For Marne department, see —4432; for Aube department and Haute-Marne department, see —4433*

*For a specific part of this jurisdiction, region, or feature, see the part and follow instructions under —4–9

—443 12	Ardennes department
—443 2	Marne department
—443 22	Reims
—443 3	Aube department and Haute-Marne department
—443 31	Aube department
—443 32	Haute-Marne department
—443 6	Ile-de-France

> Class here Région parisienne; Paris metropolitan area; *Seine River
>
> Class Paris department in —44361
>
> *For Seine-et-Marne department, see* —4437

—443 61	Paris department (Paris)

> Class Paris metropolitan area in —4436

—443 62	Seine-Saint-Denis department
—443 63	Val-de-Marne department
—443 64	Hauts-de-Seine department
—443 65	Essonne department
—443 66	Yvelines department
—443 663	Versailles
—443 67	Val-d'Oise department
—443 7	Seine-et-Marne department
—443 8	Lorraine
—443 81	Meuse department

> Including *Argonne

—443 82	Meurthe-et-Moselle department
—443 823	Nancy
—443 85	Moselle department
—443 853	Metz
—443 89	Vosges department

> Including *Vosges Mountains

---

*For a specific part of this jurisdiction, region, or feature, see the part and follow instructions under —4–9

—443 9	Alsace

> *For territory of Belfort, see —44455*
>
> (Option: Class here Alsace to 486, Germania Superior; prefer —364)

—443 93	Haut-Rhin department
—443 933	Mulhouse
—443 95	Bas-Rhin department
—443 954	Strasbourg
—444	Burgundy and Franche-Comté

Class here *eastern France, *Saône River

—444 1	Burgundy (Bourgogne)

> *For Côte-d'Or department, see —4442; for Saône-et-Loire department, see —4443*

—444 12	Yonne department
—444 16	Nièvre department
—444 2	Côte-d'Or department
—444 26	Dijon
—444 3	Saône-et-Loire department
—444 5	Franche-Comté

Class here *Jura Mountains in France

> *For Doubs department, see —4446; for Jura department, see —4447*

—444 53	Haute-Saône department
—444 55	Territory of Belfort
—444 6	Doubs department

Class here *Doubs River

—444 66	Besançon
—444 7	Jura department
—445	Centre, Rhône-Alpes, Auvergne

Class here *Loire River; central France

(Option: Class here central France to 486, Lugdunensis; prefer —364)

—445 1	*Centre

Class here *Orléanais

—445 12	Eure-et-Loir department

---

*For a specific part of this jurisdiction, region, or feature, see the part and follow instructions under —4–9

—445 124	Chartres
—445 2	Loiret department
—445 27	Orléans
—445 3	Loir-et-Cher department
	Including *Sologne
—445 4	Indre-et-Loire department
	Class here Touraine
	For Indre and Cher departments, see —4455
—445 45	Tours
—445 5	Indre department and Cher department
	Class here Berry
—445 51	Indre department
—445 52	Cher department
—445 525	Bourges
—445 8	Rhône-Alpes
	Class here *Alps in France; *Rhône River
—445 81	Loire department
	Class comprehensive works on Lyonnais in —44582
—445 817	Saint-Etienne
—445 82	Rhône department
	Class here Lyonnais
	For Loire department, see —44581
—445 823	Lyon
—445 83	Ain department
—445 84	Haute-Savoie department
	Class comprehensive works on Savoy in —44585
—445 85	Savoie department
	Including Vanoise National Park
	Class here Savoy
	For Haute-Savoie department, see —44584

*For a specific part of this jurisdiction, region, or feature, see the part and follow instructions under —4–9

—445 86   Isère department

                 Class here Dauphiné

                         *For Drôme department, see —44587; for Hautes-Alpes
                         department, see —4497*

—445 865   Grenoble

—445 87   Drôme department

—445 88   Valréas

                 Exclave of Vaucluse department

—445 89   Ardèche department

—445 9   Auvergne

                 Class here *Massif Central

—445 91   Puy-de-Dôme department

—445 914   Clermont-Ferrand

—445 92   Cantal department

—445 95   Haute-Loire department

—445 97   Allier department

                 Class here *Bourbonnais

—446   Poitou-Charentes and Limousin

                 Class here Poitou, *western France

                 Subdivisions are added for Poitou-Charentes and Limousin together, for
                 Poitou-Charentes alone

—446 2   Deux-Sèvres department

—446 3   Vienne department

—446 34   Poitiers

—446 4   Charente-Maritime department

                 Including Aunis

                 Class here *Saintonge

—446 42   La Rochelle

—446 5   Charente department

                 Class here *Angoumois; *Charente River

—446 6   Limousin

                         *For Corrèze department, see —4467; for Creuse department, see
                         —4468*

*For a specific part of this jurisdiction, region, or feature, see the part and follow instructions under
   —4–9

—446 62	Haute-Vienne department
—446 624	Limoges
—446 7	Corrèze department
—446 8	Creuse department
	Class here *Marche
—447	Aquitaine and Midi-Pyrénées
	Class here *Guyenne; *Garonne River; southwestern France
	(Option: Class here southwestern France to 486, Aquitania; prefer —364)
—447 1	Aquitaine
	For Dordogne department, see —4472
—447 14	Gironde department
—447 144	Bordeaux
—447 15	Landes department
—447 16	Pyrénées-Atlantiques department
	Class here Béarn, Pays Basque
—447 18	Lot-et-Garonne department
—447 2	Dordogne department
	Class here *Périgord
—447 3	*Midi-Pyrénées
	Class here *Gascony (Gascogne); *Pyrenees Mountains in France
—447 33	Lot department
—447 35	Ariège department
	Class here *Foix
—447 36	Haute-Garonne department
—447 367	Toulouse
—447 37	Tarn department
—447 4	Aveyron department
	Class here *Rouergue
—447 5	Tarn-et-Garonne department
—447 7	Gers department
—447 8	Hautes-Pyrénées department
	Including *Pyrenees National Park

*For a specific part of this jurisdiction, region, or feature, see the part and follow instructions under —4–9

—448   Languedoc-Roussillon

> Class here *Languedoc; *southern France

> *See also —16382 for Gulf of Lions*

> (Option: Class here Languedoc-Roussillon to 486, Narbonensis; prefer —364)

—448 1   Lozère department

> Including *Cévennes National Park; *Cévennes Mountains

—448 3   Gard department

—448 37   Nîmes

—448 4   Hérault department

—448 42   Montpellier

—448 7   Aude department

—448 9   Pyrénées-Orientales department

> Class here Roussillon

—449   Provence-Alpes-Côte d'Azur, Monaco, Corsica

> Former name for Provence-Alpes-Côte d'Azur: Provence-Côte d'Azur

> Class here Provence; southeastern France

> Subdivisions are added for Provence-Alpes-Côte d'Azur, Monaco, Corsica together; for Provence-Alpes-Côte d'Azur alone

—449 1   Bouches-du-Rhône department

—449 12   Marseilles (Marseille)

—449 18   Arles

—449 2   Vaucluse department

> *For Valréas, see —44588*

—449 22   Avignon

—449 3   Var department

> Including Port Cros National Park

—449 4   Alpes-Maritimes department and Monaco

> Including *Mercantour National Park

> Class here Nice (county); *Riviera (Côte d'Azur)

> Subdivisions are added for Alpes-Maritimes department and Monaco together, for Alpes-Maritimes department alone

> Class Nice (city) in —44941

---

*For a specific part of this jurisdiction, region, or feature, see the part and follow instructions under —4–9

—449 41   Nice (city)

> Class Nice (county) in —4494

—449 49   Monaco

> Independent principality, enclave in Alpes-Maritimes

—449 5   Alpes de Haute-Provence department

—449 7   Hautes-Alpes department

> Including *Ecrins National Park

—449 9   Corsica (Corse)

> (Option: Class here Corsica to 453; prefer —3799)

—449 92   Corse-de-Sud department

> (Option: Class here Corse-de-Sud department to 453; prefer —37992)

—449 96   Haute-Corse department

> (Option: Class here Haute-Corse department to 453; prefer —37996)

—45   **Italy, San Marino, Vatican City, Malta**

> Class here Italian Peninsula; *Apennines

> Subdivisions are added for Italy, San Marino, Vatican City, Malta together; for Italy alone

> (Option: Class here Italian Peninsula and adjacent territories to 476, Roman Empire; prefer —37)

SUMMARY

—451	**Northwestern Italy**	
—452	**Lombardy (Lombardia) region**	
—453	**Northeastern Italy**	
—454	**Emilia-Romagna region and San Marino**	
—455	**Tuscany (Toscana) region**	
—456	**Central Italy and Vatican City**	
—457	**Southern Italy**	
—458	**Sicily and adjacent islands**	
—459	**Sardinia**	

—451   Northwestern Italy

> Class here Piedmont (Piemonte) region, *northern Italy, *Alps in Italy

> (Options: Class here Gallia Cisalpina [Cisalpine Gaul]; prefer —372. Class here northwestern Italy to 476; prefer —3722. Class here Piedmont region to 476; prefer —37222)

—451 1   Valle d'Aosta region

> (Option: Class here Valle d'Aosta region to 476; prefer —37221)

*For a specific part of this jurisdiction, region, or feature, see the part and follow instructions under —4–9

—451 11   Aosta

                   (Option: Class here Aosta to 476; prefer —372211)

___

>   —451 2–451 7 Piedmont (Piemonte) region

       Class comprehensive works in —451

—451 2   Turin (Torino) province

                   (Option: Class here Turin province to 476; prefer —37222)

—451 21   Turin

                   (Option: Class here Turin to 476; prefer —372221)

—451 3   Cuneo province

                   (Option: Class here Cuneo province to 476; prefer —3716)

—451 4   Alessandria province

                   (Option: Class here Alessandria province to 476; prefer —3718)

—451 5   Asti province

                   (Option: Class here Asti province to 476; prefer —3717)

—451 6   Novara province and Verbania province

                   Subdivisions are added for Novara province and Verbania province
                   together, for Novara province alone

                   (Option: Class here Novara province to 476; prefer —37224)

—451 65   Verbania (Verbano-Cusio-Ossola) province

                   Including *Lake Maggiore

                   (Option: Class here Verbania province to 476; prefer —372245)

—451 7   Vercelli province and Biella province

                   Subdivisions are added for Vercelli province and Biella province
                   together, for Vercelli province alone

                   (Option: Class here Vercelli province to 476; prefer —37223)

—451 76   Biella province

                   (Option: Class here Biella province to 476; prefer —372236)

—451 8   Liguria region

                   Class here *Italian Riviera (Ligurian Riviera)

                   See also —16382 for Ligurian Sea

                   (Option: Class here Liguria to 476; prefer —371)

___

*For a specific part of this jurisdiction, region, or feature, see the part and follow instructions under
   —4–9

—451 82	Genoa (Genova) province
	(Option: Class here Genoa province to 476; prefer —3712)
—451 821	Genoa
	(Option: Class here Genoa to 476; prefer —37121)
—451 83	La Spezia province
	(Option: Class here La Spezia province to 476; prefer —3711)
—451 84	Savona province
	(Option: Class here Savona province to 476; prefer —3713)
—451 87	Imperia province
	(Option: Class here Imperia province to 476; prefer —3714)
—452	Lombardy (Lombardia) region

Class here *Po River

(Option: Class here Lombardy region to 476, Gallia Transpadana [Transpadane Gaul]; prefer —3722)

—452 1	Milan (Milano) province and Lodi province

Subdivisions are added for Milan (Milano) province and Lodi province together, for Milan (Milano) province alone

(Option: Class here Milan province to 476; prefer —37227)

Monza-Brianza province, formerly part of Milan province, relocated to —45228

—452 11	Milan
	(Option: Class here Milan to 476; prefer —372271)
—452 19	Lodi province
	(Option: Class here Lodi province to 476; prefer —37228)
—452 2	Varese province and Monza-Brianza province

Subdivisions are added for Varese province and Monza-Brianza province together, for Varese province alone

(Option: Class here Varese province to 476; prefer —37225)

—452 28	Monza-Brianza province [*formerly* —4521]

(Option: Class here Monza-Brianza province to 476; prefer —372262)

*For a specific part of this jurisdiction, region, or feature, see the part and follow instructions under —4–9

—452 3   Como and Lecco province

           Subdivisions are added for Como province and Lecco province together, for Como province alone

           (Option: Class here Como province to 476; prefer —372264)

—452 31   Como

           (Option: Class here Como to 476; prefer —3722641)

—452 37   Lecco province

           (Option: Class here Lecco province to 476; prefer —372265)

—452 4   Bergamo province

           (Option: Class here Bergamo province to 476; prefer —372268)

—452 41   Bergamo

           (Option: Class here Bergamo to 476; prefer —3722681)

—452 5   Sondrio province

           (Option: Class here Sondrio province to 476; prefer —372266)

—452 6   Brescia province

           Including *Lake Garda

           (Option: Class here Brescia province to 476; prefer —37312)

—452 61   Brescia

           (Option: Class here Brescia to 476; prefer —373121)

—452 7   Cremona province

           (Option: Class here Cremona province to 476; prefer —37315)

—452 71   Cremona

           (Option: Class here Cremona to 476; prefer —37315)

—452 8   Mantua (Mantova) province

           (Option: Class here Mantua (Mantova) province to 476; prefer —37318)

—452 81   Mantua

           (Option: Class here Mantua to 476; prefer —373181)

—452 9   Pavia province

           (Option: Class here Pavia province to 476; prefer —37229)

*For a specific part of this jurisdiction, region, or feature, see the part and follow instructions under —4–9

—453	Northeastern Italy

Class here Veneto region; *Adige River, *Piave River

See also —16385 for Gulf of Venice

(Option: Class here northeastern Italy to 476, Venetia; prefer —373)

>	—453 1–453 7 Veneto region

Class comprehensive works in —453

—453 1	Venice (Venezia) province

(Option: Class here Venice (Venezia) province to 476; prefer —3735)

—453 11	Venice

(Option: Class here Venice to 476; prefer —3735)

—453 2	Padua (Padova) province

(Option: Class here Padua (Padova) province to 476; prefer —3734)

—453 21	Padua

(Option: Class here Padua to 476; prefer —37341)

453 3	Rovigo province

Class here Polesine

(Option: Class here Rovigo province to 476; prefer —3733)

—453 4	Verona province

(Option: Class here Verona province to 476; prefer —3732)

—453 41	Verona

(Option: Class here Verona to 476; prefer —37321)

—453 5	Vicenza province

(Option: Class here Vicenza province to 476; prefer —37362)

—453 51	Vicenza

(Option: Class here Vicenza to 476; prefer —37362)

—453 6	Treviso province

(Option: Class here Treviso province to 476; prefer —37365)

—453 61	Treviso

(Option: Class here Treviso to 476; prefer —37365)

*For a specific part of this jurisdiction, region, or feature, see the part and follow instructions under
  —4–9

—453 7   Belluno province

        (Option: Class here Belluno province to 476; prefer —37368)

—453 8   Trentino-Alto Adige region

        (Option: Class here Trentino-Alto Adige region to 476; prefer —3737)

—453 83   Bolzano province

        Class here Alto Adige, Bozen, South Tyrol, Südtirol

        (Option: Class here Bolzano province to 476; prefer —37373)

—453 85   Trento province

        Including Trento

        (Option: Class here Trento province to 476; prefer —37375)

—453 9   Friuli-Venezia Giulia region

        (Option: Class here Friuli-Venezia Giulia region to 476; prefer —3738)

—453 91   Udine province

        (Option: Class here Udine province to 476; prefer —37381)

—453 92   Gorizia province

        (Option: Class here Gorizia province to 476; prefer —37382)

—453 93   Trieste province

        (Option: Class here Trieste province to 476; prefer —3739)

—453 931   Trieste

        (Option: Class here Trieste to 476; prefer —37391)

—453 94   Pordenone province

        (Option: Class here Pordenone province to 476; prefer —37394)

—454   Emilia-Romagna region and San Marino

        Class here *Tuscan Apennines (Appennino Tosco-Emiliano)

        Subdivisions are added for Emilia-Romagna region and San Marino together, for Emilia-Romagna region alone

        (Option: Class here Emilia-Romagna region to 476, Gallia Cispadana; prefer —3726)

—454 1   Bologna province

        (Option: Class here Bologna province to 476; prefer —37261)

—454 11   Bologna

        (Option: Class here Bologna to 476; prefer —372611)

---

*For a specific part of this jurisdiction, region, or feature, see the part and follow instructions under —4–9

—454 2   Modena province

                    (Option: Class here Modena province to 476; prefer —37262)

—454 21   Modena

                        (Option: Class here Modena to 476; prefer —372621)

—454 3   Reggio Emilia (Reggio nell'Emilia) province

                    (Option: Class here Reggio Emilia (Reggio nell'Emilia) province to
                    476; prefer —37263)

—454 4   Parma province

                    (Option: Class here Parma province to 476; prefer —37264)

—454 41   Parma

                        (Option: Class here Parma to 476; prefer —37264)

—454 5   Ferrara province

                    (Option: Class here Ferrara province to 476; prefer —37265)

—454 51   Ferrara

                        (Option: Class here Ferrara to 476; prefer —372651)

—454 6   Piacenza province

                    (Option: Class here Piacenza province to 476; prefer —37266)

—454 7   Ravenna province

                    (Option: Class here Ravenna province to 476; prefer —37267)

—454 71   Ravenna

                        (Option: Class here Ravenna to 476; prefer —372671)

—454 8   Forlì-Cesena province and Rimini province

                    Class here former Forlì province

                    Subdivisions are added for Forlì-Cesena province and Rimini province
                    together, for Forlì-Cesena province alone

                    (Option: Class here Forlì-Cesena province, to 476; prefer —37268)

—454 86   Rimini province

                        (Option: Class here Rimini province to 476; prefer —372686)

—454 9   San Marino

                    Independent state

                    (Option: Class here San Marino to 476; prefer —37269)

—455   Tuscany (Toscana) region

Class here *Arno River

(Option: Class here Tuscany (Toscana) region to 476, Etruria; prefer —375)

—455 1   Florence (Firenze) province and Prato province

Subdivisions are added for Florence (Firenze) province and Prato province together, for Florence (Firenze) province alone

(Option: Class here Florence (Firenze) province to 476; prefer —3751)

—455 11   Florence

(Option: Class here Florence to 476; prefer —37511)

—455 19   Prato province

(Option: Class here Prato province to 476; prefer —37519)

—455 2   Pistoia province

(Option: Class here Pistoia province to 476; prefer —3752)

—455 3   Lucca province

(Option: Class here Lucca province to 476; prefer —3753)

—455 4   Massa-Carrara (Massa e Carrara) province

(Option: Class here Massa-Carrara (Massa e Carrara) province to 476; prefer —3754)

—455 5   Pisa province

(Option: Class here Pisa province to 476; prefer —3755)

—455 51   Pisa

(Option: Class here Pisa to 476; prefer —3755)

—455 6   Livorno province

Including Elba island

(Option: Class here Livorno province to 476; prefer —37562)

—455 7   Grosseto province

Class here *Maremma

(Option: Class here Grosseto province to 476; prefer —37564)

—455 8   Siena province

(Option: Class here Siena province to 476; prefer —37566)

—455 81   Siena

(Option: Class here Siena to 476; prefer —37566)

*For a specific part of this jurisdiction, region, or feature, see the part and follow instructions under —4–9

—455 9   Arezzo province

          (Option: Class here Arezzo province to 476; prefer —37568)

—456   Central Italy and Vatican City

          Class here former *Papal States (States of the Church)

          Subdivisions are added for central Italy and Vatican City together, for central Italy alone

—456 2   Lazio region

              For Rome province, see —4563

          (Option: Class here Lazio region to 476, Latium; prefer —376)

—456 22   Frosinone province

          (Option: Class here Frosinone province to 476; prefer —3767)

—456 23   Latina province

          Including Pontine Islands

          Class here Pontine Marshes

          (Option: Class here Latina province to 476; prefer —3765)

—456 24   Rieti province

          Class here Sabina

          (Option: Class here Rieti province to 476, Sabina to 476; prefer —37735)

—456 25   Viterbo province

          (Option: Class here Viterbo province to 476; prefer —3758. Class here Vulci; prefer —37582. Class here Volsinii Novi; prefer —37582)

—456 251   Viterbo

          (Option: Class here Viterbo to 476; prefer —3758)

—456 3   Rome (Roma) province and Vatican City

          Subdivisions are added for Rome (Roma) province and Vatican City together, for Rome (Roma) province alone

          (Option: Class here Rome province in Etruria to 476; prefer —3759. Class here Veii; prefer —37595. Class here Rome province to 476, Ostia to 476, Praeneste (Palestrina) to 476; prefer —3763)

—456 32   Rome

          (Option: Class here Rome to 476; prefer —3763)

---

*For a specific part of this jurisdiction, region, or feature, see the part and follow instructions under —4–9

—456 34   Vatican City

           Independent papal state, enclave in Rome

           (Option: Class here Vatican City to 476; prefer —3763)

—456 5   Umbria region

           (Options: Class here Umbria and Picenum; prefer —374. Class here Umbria region to 476; prefer —3742. Class here Umbria region in Etruria to 476; prefer —3757)

—456 51   Perugia province

           (Options: Class here Perugia province to 476; prefer —3743. Class here Perugia province in Etruria to 476; prefer —37573)

—456 511   Perugia

           (Option: Class here Perugia to 476; prefer —375731)

—456 52   Terni province

           (Options: Class here Terni province to 476; prefer —3744. Class here Terni province in Etruria to 476; prefer —37576)

—456 7   Marches (Marche) region

           (Option: Class here Marches region to 476, Picenum; prefer —3745)

—456 71   Ancona province

           Including Ancona

           (Option: Class here Ancona province to 476; prefer —3745)

—456 73   Macerata province

           (Option: Class here Macerata province to 476; prefer —3746)

—456 74   Fermo province [*formerly* —45675]

           (Option: Class here Fermo province to 476; prefer —3747)

—456 75   Ascoli Piceno province

           (Option: Class here Ascoli Piceno province to 476; prefer —3748)

           Fermo province, formerly part of Ascoli Piceno province, relocated to —45674

—456 77   Pesaro e Urbino province

           (Option: Class here Pesaro e Urbino province to 476; prefer —3742)

—457   Southern Italy

           For Sicily, see —458

           (Option: Class here southern Italy to 476, Magna Graecia; prefer —377)

—457 1   Abruzzo region and Molise region

> Subdivisions are added for Abruzzo region and Molise region together, for Abruzzo region alone
>
> (Option: Class here Abruzzo region to 476, Samnium; prefer —3773)

\>   —457 11–457 17   Abruzzo region

Class comprehensive works in —4571

—457 11   Aquila (L'Aquila) province

> Including L'Aquila
>
> (Option: Class here Aquila province to 476; prefer —37734)

—457 13   Chieti province

> (Option: Class here Chieti province to 476; prefer —37737)

—457 15   Teramo province

> (Option: Class here Teramo province to 476; prefer —3749)

—457 17   Pescara province

> (Option: Class here Pescara province to 476; prefer —37736)

—457 19   Molise region

> (Option: Class here Molise region to 476; prefer —37733)

—457 192   Campobasso province

> Including Campobasso
>
> (Option: Class here Campobasso province to 476; prefer —37738)

—457 194   Isernia province

> (Option: Class here Isernia province to 476; prefer —37733)

—457 2   Campania region

> *For Naples province, see —4573; for Salerno province, see —4574*
>
> (Option: Class here Campania to 476; prefer —3772)

—457 21   Avellino province

> (Option: Class here Avellino province to 476; prefer —37731)

—457 23   Benevento province

> Including Beneventum (Benevento) to 476
>
> (Option: Class here Benevento province to 476, Beneventum (Benevento) to 476; prefer —37732)

—457 25   Caserta province

> (Option: Class here Caserta province to 476; prefer —37723)

—457 3	Naples (Napoli) province

Including Capri Island, Ischia Island

(Options: Class here Naples province to 476, Puteoli (Pozzuoli) to 476; prefer —37725. Class here Cumae; prefer —377252. Class here Nola to 476; prefer —377255. Class here Herculaneum; prefer —3772564. Class here Pompeii; prefer —3772568. Class here Stabiae; prefer —377258)

—457 31	Naples

(Option: Class here Naples to 476; prefer —377251)

—457 4	Salerno province

(Options: Class here Salerno province to 476; prefer —37727. Class here Salerno province in Lucania to 476; prefer —37777. Class here Paestum; prefer —377773)

—457 41	Salerno

(Option: Class here Salerno [Salernum] to 476; prefer —377271)

—457 5	Puglia (Apulia) region

See also —16386 for Gulf of Taranto

(Option: Class here Puglia region to 476; prefer —3775)

—457 51	Bari province

(Option: Class here Bari province to 476; prefer —37758)

Southern part of Barletta-Andria-Trani province, formerly part of Bari province, relocated to —45759

—457 511	Bari

(Option: Class here Bari to 476; prefer —377581)

—457 53	Lecce province

(Option: Class here Lecce province to 476; prefer —37765)

—457 54	Brindisi province

(Options: Class here Calabria [Roman region]; prefer —3776. Class here Brindisi province to 476; prefer —37763)

—457 541	Brindisi

(Option: Class here Brindisi to 476; prefer —377631)

—457 55	Taranto province

(Option: Class here Taranto province to 476; prefer —37767)

—457 57	Foggia province

(Options: Class here Apuli [Roman region]; prefer —3775. Class here Foggia province to 476; prefer —37753)

Northern part of Barletta-Andria-Trani province, formerly part of Foggia province, relocated to —45759

—457 59   Barletta-Andria-Trani province

> Including northern part of Barletta-Andria-Trani province [*formerly* —45757*]

> Class here southern part of Barletta-Andria-Trani province [*formerly* —45751*]

> (Option: Class here Barletta-Andria-Trani province to 476; prefer —37756)

—457 7   Basilicata (Lucania) region

> *See also —16386 for Gulf of Taranto*

> (Option: Class here Basilicata region to 476, Lucania; prefer —3777)

—457 71   Potenza province

> (Option: Class here Potenza province to 476; prefer —37775)

—457 72   Matera province

> Including Metaponto

> (Option: Class here Matera province to 476, Metaponto to 476; prefer —37773)

—457 8   Calabria region

> *See also —16386 for Gulf of Taranto, Strait of Messina*

> (Option: Class here Calabria region to 476, Bruttium; prefer —3778)

—457 81   Catanzaro province

> (Option: Class here Catanzaro province to 476; prefer —37781)

—457 82   Vibo Valentia province

> (Option: Class here Vibo Valentia province to 476; prefer —37782)

—457 83   Reggio di Calabria province

> (Option: Class here Reggio di Calabria province to 476; prefer —37783)

—457 831   Reggio di Calabria

> (Option: Class here Reggio di Calabria to 476; prefer —377831)

—457 85   Cosenza province

> (Option: Class here Cosenza province to 476; prefer —37785)

—457 87   Crotone province

> (Option: Class here Crotone province to 476; prefer —37787)

—458   Sicily and adjacent islands

> Subdivisions are added for Sicily and adjacent islands together, for Sicily alone

> (Option: Class here Sicily to 476; prefer —378)

>   —458 1–458 2 Sicily region

         Class comprehensive works in —458

—458 1   Eastern Sicily

         (Option: Class here eastern Sicily to 476; prefer —3781)

—458 11   Messina province

         Including Lipari Islands

           See also —16386 for Strait of Messina

         (Option: Class here Messina province to 476; prefer —37811)

—458 111   Messina

         (Option: Class here Messina to 476; prefer —378111)

—458 12   Enna province

         (Option: Class here Enna province to 476; prefer —37812)

—458 13   Catania province

         Including Mount Etna

         (Option: Class here Catania province to 476; prefer —37813)

—458 131   Catania

         (Option: Class here Catania to 476; prefer —378131)

—458 14   Syracuse (Siracusa) province

         (Option: Class here Syracuse province to 476; prefer —37814)

—458 141   Syracuse

         (Option: Class here Syracuse to 476; prefer —378141)

—458 15   Ragusa province

         (Option: Class here Ragusa province to 476; prefer —37815)

—458 2   Western Sicily

         (Option: Class here western Sicily to 476; prefer —3782)

—458 21   Caltanissetta province

         (Option: Class here Caltanissetta province to 476; prefer —37821)

—458 22   Agrigento province

         Including Pelagian Islands

         (Option: Class here Agrigento province to 476; prefer —37822)

—458 221   Agrigento

         (Option: Class here Agrigento to 476; prefer —378221)

—494 539	Sense district (Sense Bezirk, Singine district)
—494 54	Bern canton
	Class here *Aar River
—494 541	Berner Oberland administrative region (Berner Oberland Verwaltungsregion)
	Class here *Bernese Alps (Berner Alpen)
—494 541 2	Obersimmental-Saanen district (Obersimmental-Saanen Verwaltungskreis)
—494 541 5	Frutigen-Niedersimmental district (Frutigen-Niedersimmental Verwaltungskreis)
	Including *Lake of Thun (Thuner See)
—494 541 8	Interlaken-Oberhasli district (Interlaken-Oberhasli Verwaltungskreis)
—494 542	Berner-Mitteland administrative region (Berner-Mitteland Verwaltungsregion)
	Class here Berner-Mitteland district (Berner-Mitteland Verwaltungskreis)
—494 542 4	Bern
—494 545	Seeland administrative region (Seeland Verwaltungsregion)
—494 545 3	Seeland district (Seeland Verwaltungskreis)
—494 545 7	Biel district (Biel Verwaltungskreis, Bienne district)
—494 547	Berner Jura administrative region (Berner Jura Verwaltungsregion)
	Class here Berner Jura district (Berner Jura Verwaltungskreis)
—494 549	Emmental-Oberaargau administrative region (Emmental-Oberaargau Verwaltungsregion)
—494 549 3	Oberaargau district (Oberaargau Verwaltungskreis)
—494 549 7	Emmental district (Emmental Verwaltungskreis)
—494 55	Lucerne canton (Luzern canton)
—494 551	Entlebuch district (Entlebuch Amt)
—494 553	Willisau district (Willisau Amt)
—494 555	Sursee district (Sursee Amt)
—494 557	Lucerne district (Luzern Amt)
	Class here *Lake Lucerne (Vierwaldstätter See)
—494 557 4	Lucerne (Luzern)

*For a specific part of this jurisdiction, region, or feature, see the part and follow instructions under —4–9

—494 559	Hochdorf district (Hochdorf Amt)
—494 56	Aargau canton
—494 562	Western Aargau
—494 562 2	Zofingen district (Zofingen Bezirk)
—494 562 3	Kulm district (Kulm Bezirk)
—494 562 5	Lenzburg district (Lenzburg Bezirk)
—494 562 6	Brugg district (Brugg Bezirk)
—494 562 8	Aarau district (Aarau Bezirk)
—494 562 84	Aarau
—494 564	Northern Aargau
	Class here *Hochrhein
—494 564 3	Rheinfelden district (Rheinfelden Bezirk)
—494 564 5	Laufenburg district (Laufenburg Bezirk)
—494 564 7	Zurzach district (Zurzach Bezirk)
—494 566	Eastern Aargau
	Class here *Reuss River
—494 566 3	Baden district (Baden Bezirk)
—494 566 5	Bremgarten district (Bremgarten Bezirk)
—494 566 7	Muri district (Muri Bezirk)
—494 57	Zürich canton
—494 572	Western Zürich
	Class here *Lake of Zurich
—494 572 1	Affoltern district (Affoltern Bezirk)
—494 572 2	Dietikon district (Dietikon Bezirk)
—494 572 3	Dielsdorf district (Dielsdorf Bezirk)
—494 572 4	Bülach district (Bülach Bezirk)
—494 572 6	Zürich district (Zürich Bezirk)
	Class here Zurich
—494 572 8	Horgen district (Horgen Bezirk)
—494 572 9	Meilen district (Meilen Bezirk)
—494 574	Eastern Zürich

*For a specific part of this jurisdiction, region, or feature, see the part and follow instructions under —4–9

—494 574 1	Uster district (Uster Bezirk)
—494 574 3	Hinwil district (Hinwil Bezirk)
—494 574 5	Pfäffikon district (Pfäffikon Bezirk)
—494 574 7	Winterthur district (Winterthur Bezirk)
—494 574 9	Andelfingen district (Andelfingen Bezirk)

—494 58   Schaffhausen canton

—494 586   Schaffhausen

—494 59   Thurgau canton

         Class here *Thur River

—494 591	Frauenfeld district (Frauenfeld Bezirk)
—494 591 8	Frauenfeld
—494 593	Münchwilen district (Münchwilen Bezirk)
—494 595	Weinfelden district (Weinfelden Bezirk)
—494 597	Kreuzlingen district (Kreuzlingen Bezirk)

         Class here *Lake Constance (Bodensee) in Switzerland

—494 599   Arbon district (Arbon Bezirk)

—494 7   Alpine region cantons

         Class here *Alps

         (Option: Class here Alpine region cantons to 486, Raetia; prefer —36947)

SUMMARY

—494 71	**Appenzell Ausser-Rhoden canton and Appenzell Inner-Rhoden canton**
—494 72	**Saint Gall canton**
—494 73	**Graubünden canton (Grisons canton)**
—494 74	**Glarus canton**
—494 75	**Schwyz canton and Zug canton**
—494 76	**Nidwalden canton and Obwalden canton**
—494 77	**Uri canton**
—494 78	**Ticino canton (Tessin canton)**
—494 79	**Valais canton (Wallis canton)**

—494 71   Appenzell Ausser-Rhoden canton and Appenzell Inner-Rhoden canton

         Class here former Appenzell canton; *Alpstein

—494 712   Appenzell Ausser-Rhoden canton

—494 712 6   Herisau

—494 714   Appenzell Inner-Rhoden canton

*For a specific part of this jurisdiction, region, or feature, see the part and follow instructions under —4–9

—494 714 4	Appenzell
—494 72	Saint Gall canton
—494 721	Rheintal constituency (Rheintal Wahlkreis)
—494 722	Rorschach constituency (Rorschach Wahlkreis)
—494 723	Saint Gall constituency (Sankt Gallen Wahlkreis)
—494 723 4	Saint Gall
—494 725	Wil constituency (Wil Wahlkreis)
—494 726	Toggenburg constituency (Toggenburg Wahlkreis)
—494 727	See-Gaster constituency (See-Gaster Wahlkreis)
	Including *Walensee
—494 728	Werdenberg constituency (Werdenberg Wahlkreis)
—494 729	Sarganserland constituency (Sarganserland Wahlkreis)
—494 73	Graubünden canton (Grisons canton)
—494 732	Eastern Graubünden
	Class here *Rhaetian Alps
—494 732 1	Landquart district (Landquart Bezirk)
—494 732 2	Plessur district (Plessur Bezirk)
—494 732 24	Chur
—494 732 4	Albula district (Albula Bezirk)
—494 732 5	Prättigau-Davos district (Prättigau-Davos Bezirk)
	Including *Rätikon Mountains
—494 732 7	Inn district (Inn Bezirk)
	Including Swiss National Park
	Class here *Inn River in Switzerland
—494 732 8	Maloja district (Maloja Bezirk, Maloggia Distretto)
—494 732 9	Bernina district (Bernina Bezirk)
—494 735	Western Graubünden
—494 735 2	Moësa district (Moësa Bezirk)
—494 735 4	Hinterrhein district (Hinterrhein Bezirk)
—494 735 6	Imboden district (Imboden Bezirk)
—494 735 8	Surselva district (Surselva Bezirk)

*For a specific part of this jurisdiction, region, or feature, see the part and follow instructions under —4–9

—494 74	Glarus canton
	Class here *Glarner Alps
—494 744	Glarus
—494 75	Schwyz canton and Zug canton
—494 752	Schwyz canton
—494 752 1	March district (March Bezirk)
—494 752 3	Höfe district (Höfe Bezirk)
—494 752 4	Einsiedeln district (Einsiedeln Bezirk)
—494 752 6	Schwyz district (Schwyz Bezirk)
—494 752 64	Schwyz
—494 752 8	Gersau district (Gersau Bezirk)
—494 752 9	Küssnacht district (Küssnacht Bezirk)
—494 756	Zug canton
	Class here *Lake Zug (Zuger See)
—494 756 4	Zug
—494 76	Nidwalden canton and Obwalden canton
—494 762	Nidwalden canton
—494 762 4	Stans
—494 764	Obwalden canton
—494 764 4	Saren
—494 77	Uri canton
—494 774	Altdorf
—494 78	Ticino canton (Tessin canton)
	Class here *Lepontine Alps
—494 781	Leventina district (Leventina Distretto)
—494 782	Blenio district (Blenio Distretto)
—494 783	Riviera district (Riviera Distretto)
—494 784	Bellinzona district (Bellinzona Distretto)
—494 784 4	Bellinzona
—494 785	Lugano district (Lugano Distretto)
	Class here *Lake Lugano

*For a specific part of this jurisdiction, region, or feature, see the part and follow instructions under
—4–9

—494 786	Mendrisio district (Mendrisio Distretto)
—494 788	Locarno district (Locarno Distretto)
	Class here *Lake Maggiore in Switzerland
—494 789	Vallemaggia district (Vallemaggia Distretto)
—494 79	Valais canton (Wallis canton)
	Class here *Rhône River in Switzerland, *Pennine Alps
—494 794	Upper Valais
—494 794 1	Goms district (Goms Bezirk)
—494 794 2	Östlich Raron district (Östlich Raron Bezirk)
—494 794 3	Brig district (Brig Bezirk)
—494 794 5	Westlich Raron district (Westlich Raron Bezirk)
—494 794 6	Visp district (Visp Bezirk)
—494 794 8	Leuk district (Leuk Bezirk)
—494 796	Upper Valais
—494 796 1	Sierre district
—494 796 3	Hérens district
—494 796 4	Sion district
—494 796 44	Sion
—494 796 5	Conthey district
—494 796 6	Entremont district
—494 796 7	Martigny district
—494 796 8	Saint-Maurice district
—494 796 9	Monthey district
—495	Greece
	See also —16388 for Aegean Sea
	(Option: Class here Greece to 323; prefer —38)
—495 1	Attica region, Central Greece region, Aetolia and Acarnania department

---

*For a specific part of this jurisdiction, region, or feature, see the part and follow instructions under
—4–9

—495 12   Attica region (Attikē periphereia)

           Class here Athens

             For Peloponnesus portion of Attica region, Kythēra Island, see —4952

             (Option: Class here Attica to 323, Athens to 323, Marathon; prefer —385)

—495 15   Central Greece region (Sterea Hellada periphereia)

             Including Boeotia department (Voiōtia nome), Euboea department (Euvoia nome), Eurytania department (Eurytania nome), Phocis department (Phōkis nome), Phthiōtis department (Phthiōtis nome); Euboea Island, Skyros Island

             (Options: Class here Eurytania department to 323, Phocis department to 323, Phthiōtis department to 323, Doris, Locris, Malis, Phocis, Amphissa, Delphi; prefer —383. Class here Eurytania department to 323, Boeotia to 323, Euboea Island to 323, Chalcis, Thebes; prefer —384. Class here Skyros Island to 323; prefer —3911)

—495 18   Aetolia and Acarnania department (Aitōlia kai Akarnania nome)

             (Option: Class here Aetolia and Acarnania department to 323, Aetolia, Acarnania; prefer —383)

—495 2   Peloponnesus and Isthmus of Corinth

             Including Peloponnesus portion of Attica region, Kythēra Island

             Subdivisions are added for Peloponnesus and Isthmus of Corinth together, for Peloponnesus alone

             See also —16386 for Gulf of Corinth; also —49522 for Peloponnesus region (Peloponnēsos periphereia)

             (Option: Class here Peloponnesus to 323; prefer —386)

—495 22   Peloponnesus region (Peloponnēsos periphereia)

             Including Arcadia department (Arkadia nome), Argolis department (Argolis nome), Corinth department ((Korinthia nome), Laconia department (Lakōnia nome), Messēnia department (Messēnia nome); Isthmus of Corinth

             See also —4952 for Peloponnesus

             (Options: Class here Megaris to 323; prefer —384. Class here Corinth to 323; prefer —387. Class here Arcadia to 323, Argolis to 323, Mycenae, Tiryns; prefer —388. Class here Laconia to 323, Messenia to 323, Sparta to 323; prefer —389)

—495 27   Western Greece region (Dytikē Hellada periphereia)

             Including Achaea department (Achaia nome), Elis department (Ēleia nomes)

             For Aetolia and Acarnania department, see —49518

             (Options: Class here Achaea to 323; prefer —387. Class here Elis to 323, Olympia, Phigalia; prefer —388)

—495 3   Epirus region (Ēpeiros periphereia)

> Including Arta department (Arta nome), Iōannina department (Iōannina nome), Preveza department (Preveza nome), Thesprōtia department (Thesprōtia nome)

> Class here comprehensive works on Epirus; *Pindus Mountains

>> *For Albanian Epirus, see —4965*

> (Option: Class here Epirus to 323; prefer —382)

—495 4   Thessaly region (Thessalia periphereia)

> Including Karditsa department (Karditsa nome), Larisa department (Larisa nome), Magnēsia department (Magnēsia nome), Trikala department (Trikala nome); Northern Sporades

>> *For Skyros Island, see —49515*

> (Options: Class here Thessaly to 323; prefer —382. Class here Northern Sporades to 323; prefer —3911)

—495 5   Ionian Islands region (Ionioi Nēsoi periphereia)

> Including Cefalonia department (Kephallēnia nome), Corfu department (Kerkyra nome), Leukas department (Leukas nome), Zante department (Zakynthos nome); Ithaca Island

> Class here Ionian Islands

> (Options: Class here Ionian Islands to 323, northern Ionian Islands to 323; prefer —382. Class here Ithaca Island to 323; prefer —383. Class here southern Ionian Islands to 323; prefer —386)

—495 6   Former Macedonia region (Makedonia periphereia)

> Class here comprehensive works on Macedonia region

>> *For country of Macedonia, see —4976; for Macedonia in Bulgaria, see —4998*

> (Option: Class here comprehensive works on Macedonia to 323; prefer —381)

—495 62   Western Macedonia region (Dytikē Makedonia periphereia)

> Including Flórina department (Phlorina nome), Grevena department (Grevena nome), Kastoria department (Kastoria nome), Kozanē department (Kozanē nome)

> (Option: Class here Western Macedonia region to 323; prefer —381)

---

*For a specific part of this jurisdiction, region, or feature, see the part and follow instructions under —4–9

—495 65   Central Macedonia region (Kentrikē Makedonia periphereia)

> Including Chalkidikē department (Chalkidikē nome), Hematheia department (Ēmathia nome), Kilkis department (Kilkis nome), Pella department (Pella nome), Pieria department (Pieria nome), Serrai department (Serrai nome), Thessalonikē department (Thessalonikē nome); Mount Athos

> (Option: Class here Central Macedonia region to 323; prefer —381)

—495 7   Eastern Macedonia and Thrace region (Anatolikē Makedonia kai Thrakē periphereia)

> Including Drama department (Drama nome), Evros department (Evros nome), Kavala department (Kavala nome), Rodopē department (Rhodope) nome), Xanthē department (Xanthē nome); Samothrace Island, Thasos Island

> Class here comprehensive works on Thrace

> *For Eastern Thrace, see —4961; for Bulgarian Thrace, see —4995*

> (Options: Class here Eastern Macedonia and Thrace region to 323; prefer —381. Class here Samothrace Island to 323, Thasos Island to 323; prefer —3911. Class here Thrace to 323; prefer —39861)

—495 8   Former Aegean Islands region (Aigaio Nēsoi periphereia)

> Class here *Aegean Islands, *Sporades

> *See also —16388 for Aegean Sea*

> (Option: Class here Aegean Islands to 323, Sporades to 323; prefer —391)

—495 82   Northern Aegean region (Voreio Aigaio periphereia)

> Including Chios department (Chios nome), Lesvos department (Lesbos nome), Samos department (Samos nome)

> (Options: Class here Lemnos Island to 323, Northern Aegean Islands to 323; prefer —3911. Class here Lesvos department to 323, Lesbos Island to 323; prefer —3912. Class here Chios department to 323, Chios Island to 323; prefer —3913. Class here Samos department to 323, Samos Island to 323; prefer —3914)

—495 85   Cyclades department (Kyklades nome)

> Class here Southern Aegean region (Notio Aigaio periphereia)

> *For Dodecanese department, see —49587*

> (Option: Class here Cyclades to 323; prefer —3915)

---

*For a specific part of this jurisdiction, region, or feature, see the part and follow instructions under —4–9

—495 87   Dodecanese department (Dōdekanēsos nome)

Class here Southern Sporades

(Options: Class here Dodecanese to 323, Rhodes to 323, Southern Sporades to 323; prefer —3916. Class here Karpathos Island to 323; prefer —3917)

—495 9   Crete region (Krētē periphereia)

Including Chania department (Canea nome), Hērakleion department (Hērakleion nome), Lasithi department (Lasithi nome), Rethymnē department (Rethymnē nome)

(Option: Class here Crete to 323, Knossos; prefer —3918)

—496   *Balkan Peninsula

Class here *Danube River

See also —56 for Ottoman Empire

(Option: Class here southeastern Europe to ca. 640; prefer —398)

—496 1   Turkey in Europe (Eastern Thrace)

See also —16389 for Dardanelles, Sea of Marmara

(Option: Class here Turkey in Europe (Eastern Thrace) to 323; prefer —39861)

—496 12   European portion of Çanakkale Province (Çanakkale İli)

Class here Gallipoli peninsula (Gelibolu)

Class comprehensive works on Çanakkale Province (Çanakkale İli) in —5622

—496 14   Edirne Province (Edirne İli)

Including Edirne (Adrianople)

—496 15   Kırklareli Province (Kırklareli İli)

—496 16   Tekirdağ Province (Tekirdağ İli)

—496 18   İstanbul Province (İstanbul İli)

Class here Istanbul (Constantinople)

For Asian portion of İstanbul Province, see —5632

See also —16389 for Bosporus

(Option: Class here İstanbul Province to 640, Constantinople to 640; prefer —398618)

—496 5   Albania

(Option: Class here Albania to ca. 640; prefer —39865)

*For a specific part of this jurisdiction, region, or feature, see the part and follow instructions under —4–9

—497   Serbia, Croatia, Slovenia, Bosnia and Hercegovina, Montenegro, Macedonia

> Class here Yugoslavia (1918–1991), comprehensive works on former Yugoslavia
>
> Class Yugoslavia (1991–2003) in —4971
>
> (Option: Class here former Yugoslavia to ca. 640, Illyria, Illyricum; prefer —3987)

—497 1   Serbia

> Including Belgrade, Kosovo i Metohija, Voivodina, Yugoslav Banat
>
> Class here Yugoslavia (1991–2003), Serbia and Montenegro (2003–2006)
>
> *For Montenegro, see —49745*
>
> (Option: Class here Serbia to ca. 640; prefer —39871)

—497 2   Croatia

> Including Dalmatia, *Istria, Slavonia
>
> (Options: Class here Istria in Croatia to 476, comprehensive works on Istria; prefer —3739. Class here Croatia to ca. 640; prefer —39872)

—497 3   Slovenia

> (Options: Class here Istria in Slovenia to 476; prefer —3739. Class here Slovenia to ca. 640; prefer —39873)

—497 4   Bosnia and Hercegovina, Montenegro

—497 42   Bosnia and Hercegovina

> Including Sarajevo
>
> (Option: Class here Bosnia and Hercegovina to ca. 640; prefer —398742)

—497 45   Montenegro

> (Option: Class here Montenegro to ca. 640; prefer —398745)

—497 6   Macedonia

> Class here Vardar River
>
> Class comprehensive works on Macedonia region in —4956
>
> (Option: Class here Macedonia to ca. 640; prefer —39876)

—498   Romania

> (Option: Class here Romania to ca. 640, Dacia; prefer —398)

---

*For a specific part of this jurisdiction, region, or feature, see the part and follow instructions under —4–9

—498 1   Northeast Romania

Including Bacău district (Bacău judeţ), Botoşani district (Botoşani judeţ), Brăila district (Brăila judeţ), Galaţi district (Galaţi judeţ), Iaşi district (Iaşi judeţ), Neamţ district (Neamţ judeţ), Suceava district (Suceava judeţ), Vaslui district (Vaslui judeţ), Vrancea district (Vrancea judeţ)

Class here *Moldavia

—498 2   Walachia (Southeast Romania)

Including Argeş district (Argeş judeţ), Bucureşti district (Bucureşti judeţ), Buzău district (Buzău judeţ), Călăraşi district (Călăraşi judeţ), Dîmboviţa district (Dîmboviţa judeţ), Giurgiu district (Giurgiu judeţ), Ialomiţa district (Ialomiţa judeţ), Olt district (Olt judeţ), Prahova district (Prahova judeţ), Teleorman district (Teleorman judeţ), Vîlcea district (Vîlcea judeţ)

Including Ploieşti

For Black Sea area, see —4983

—498 3   Black Sea area

Including Constanţa district (Constanţa judeţ), Tulcea district (Tulcea judeţ)

Class here *Dobruja

For South Dobruja, see —4994

See also —16389 for Black Sea

(Option: Class here Black Sea area of Romania to 640, Scythia; prefer —3951)

—498 4   Central and west Romania

Including Alba district (Alba judeţ), Arad district (Arad judeţ), Bihor district (Bihor judeţ), Bistriţa-Năsăud district (Bistriţa-Năsăud judeţ), Braşov district (Braşov judeţ), Caraş-Severin district (Caraş-Severin judeţ), Cluj district (Cluj judeţ), Covasna district (Covasna judeţ), Dolj district (Dolj judeţ), Gorj district (Gorj judeţ), Harghita district (Harghita judeţ), Hunedoara district (Hunedoara judeţ), Maramureş district (Maramureş judeţ), Mehedinţi district (Mehedinţi judeţ), Mureş district (Mureş judeţ), Sălaj district (Sălaj judeţ), Satu Mare district (Satu Mare judeţ), Sibiu district (Sibiu judeţ), Timiş district (Timiş judeţ)

Including Oltenia, Transylvania

Class here *Banat, *Bukovina

For North Bukovina, see —4779; for Yugoslav Banat, see —4971

*For a specific part of this jurisdiction, region, or feature, see the part and follow instructions under —4–9

—499	Bulgaria

        Class here *Balkan Mountains

        (Option: Class here Bulgaria to ca. 640, Moesia; prefer —398)

—499 1	Montana region (Montana oblast)
—499 2	Lovech region (Loveshka oblast)
—499 3	Ruse region (Rusenska oblast)
—499 4	Varna region (Varnenska oblast)

        Including South Dobruja

—499 5	Burgas region (Burgaska oblast)

        Including Bulgarian Thrace

—499 6	Khaskovo region (Khaskovska oblast)
—499 7	Plovdiv region (Plovdivska oblast)

        Class here *Rhodope Mountains

—499 8	Sofia region (Sofiĭska oblast)

        Including Bulgarian Macedonia

—499 9	Sofia city

        Class here comprehensive works on historic region of Sofia

        For parts of historic region of Sofia in Sofia region (Sofiĭska oblast), see —4998

—5	**Asia**

        Class here Eurasia, Far East, Orient

        For Europe, see —4

SUMMARY

—51	**China and adjacent areas**
—52	**Japan**
—53	**Arabian Peninsula and adjacent areas**
—54	**India and neighboring south Asian countries**
—55	**Iran**
—56	**Middle East (Near East)**
—57	**Siberia (Asiatic Russia)**
—58	**Central Asia**
—59	**Southeast Asia**

*For a specific part of this jurisdiction, region, or feature, see the part and follow instructions under —4–9

—51   **China and adjacent areas**

Class here People's Republic of China

Subdivisions are added for China and adjacent areas together, for China alone

(Option: Class here China to 420; prefer —31)

—511   Northeastern China

Class here Northern Region; *Yellow River (Huang He)

For Inner Mongolia Autonomous Region, see —5177; for Manchuria, see —518

See also —16456 for Yellow Sea

—511 3   Shanghai Municipality and Jiangsu Province

—511 32   Shanghai Municipality (Shanghai Shi)

—511 36   Jiangsu Province (Jiangsu Sheng)

Including Nanjing

—511 4   Shandong Province (Shandong Sheng)

—511 5   Hebei Province, Tianjin Municipality, Beijing Municipality

—511 52   Hebei Province (Hebei Sheng)

—511 54   Tianjin Municipality (Tianjin Shi)

—511 56   Beijing Municipality (Beijing Shi)

—511 7   Shanxi Province (Shanxi Sheng)

—511 8   Henan Province (Henan Sheng)

—512   Southeastern China and adjacent areas

Class here Eastern and Central-Southern Regions; *Yangtze River

Subdivisions are added for southeastern China and adjacent areas together, for southeastern China alone

For Shanghai Municipality, see —51132; for Jiangsu Province, see —51136; for Shandong Province, see —5114; for Henan Province, see —5118

—512 1   Hubei Province and Hunan Province

—512 12   Hubei Province (Hubei Sheng)

—512 15   Hunan Province (Hunan Sheng)

—512 2   Jiangxi Province and Anhui Province

—512 22   Jiangxi Province (Jiangxi Sheng)

—512 25   Anhui Province (Anhui Sheng)

---

*For a specific part of this jurisdiction, region, or feature, see the part and follow instructions under —4–9

—512 4	East China Sea area

           See also —16457 for East China Sea

—512 42	Zhejiang Province (Zhejiang Sheng)
—512 45	Fujian Province (Fujian Sheng)

           See also —16457 for Formosa Strait

—512 49	Taiwan (Formosa) and adjacent islands

           Republic of China (Nationalist China)

           Subdivisions are added for Taiwan (Formosa) and adjacent islands together, for Taiwan (Formosa) alone

           See also —16457 for Formosa Strait

           (Option: Class here Taiwan (Formosa) to 420; prefer —31249)

—512 5	Hong Kong
—512 6	Macau
—512 7	Guangdong Province (Guangdong Sheng)
—512 75	Guangzhou (Canton)
—512 8	Guangxi Zhuangzu Autonomous Region (Guangxi Zhuangzu Zizhiqu)

           See also —16472 for Gulf of Tonkin

–512 9	Hainan Province (Hainan Sheng)
—513	Southwestern China (South-Western Region)

           For Tibet, see —515

—513 4	Guizhou Province (Guizhou Sheng)
—513 5	Yunnan Province (Yunnan Sheng)
—513 8	Sichuan Province (Sichuan Sheng)

           Including Chongqing

—514	Northwestern China (North-Western Region)

           For Xinjiang Uygur Autonomous Region, see —516; for Ningsia Huizu Autonomous Region, see —5175

—514 3	Shaanxi Province (Shaanxi Sheng)
—514 5	Gansu Province (Gansu Sheng)
—514 7	Qinghai Province (Qinghai Sheng)
—515	Tibet Autonomous Region (Xizang Zizhiqu)

—516   Xinjiang Uygur Autonomous Region (Xinjiang Uygur Zizhiqu)

       Including *Tien Shan

—517   Mongolia

—517 3   Outer Mongolia (Mongolian People's Republic)

       Independent state

       Including *Gobi Desert; *Altai Mountains

—517 5   Ningxia Huizu Autonomous Region (Ningxia Huizu Zizhiqu)

—517 7   Inner Mongolia Autonomous Region (Nei Monggol Zizhiqu)

—518   Manchuria

       Class here North-Eastern Region

—518 2   Liaoning Province (Liaoning Sheng)

—518 4   Heilongjiang Province (Heilongjiang Sheng)

—518 8   Jilin Province (Jilin Sheng)

—519   Korea

       See also —16456 for Yellow Sea

—519 3   North Korea (People's Democratic Republic of Korea)

—519 5   South Korea (Republic of Korea)

—52   **Japan**

—521   Honshū (Honsyū)

—521 1   Tōhoku region (Tōhoku chihō)

       See also —16454 for Tsugaru Strait

—521 12   Aomori prefecture (Aomori-ken)

       Including *Towada Lake

—521 13   Akita prefecture (Akita-ken)

—521 14   Iwate prefecture (Iwate-ken)

—521 15   Miyagi prefecture (Miyagi-ken)

—521 16   Yamagata prefecture (Yamagata-ken)

—521 17   Fukusima prefecture (Fukusima-ken)

—521 3   Kantō region (Kantō chihō)

       Including *Tone River

—521 31   Ibaraki prefecture (Ibaraki-ken)

*For a specific part of this jurisdiction, region, or feature, see the part and follow instructions under —4–9

—521 32	Tochigi prefecture (Tochigi-ken)
—521 33	Gumma prefecture (Gumma-ken)
—521 34	Saitama prefecture (Saitama-ken)
—521 35	Tōkyō prefecture (Tōkyō-to)

Class here Tokyo

For Bonin (Ogasawara) Islands, see —528

—521 36	Kanagawa prefecture (Kanagawa-ken)
—521 364	Yokohama
—521 37	Chiba prefecture (Chiba-ken)
—521 5	**Hokuriku region (Hokuriku chihō)**
—521 52	Niigata prefecture (Niigata-ken)

Class here *Shinano River

—521 53	Toyama prefecture (Toyama-ken)
—521 54	Ishikawa prefecture (Ishikawa-ken)
—521 55	Fukui prefecture (Fukui-ken)
—521 6	**Chūbu region (Chūbu chihō)**

Including *Akaishi Mountains

For Hokuriku region, see —5215

—521 62	Gifu prefecture (Gifu-ken)
—521 63	Nagano prefecture (Nagano-ken)
—521 64	Yamanashi prefecture (Yamanashi-ken)
—521 65	Shizuoka prefecture (Shizuoka-ken)

For Mount Fuji, see —52166

—521 66	Mount Fuji (Fuji-san, Fujiyama)
—521 67	Aichi prefecture (Aichi-ken)
—521 674	Nagoya
—521 8	**Kinki region (Kinki chihō)**
—521 81	Mie prefecture (Mie-ken)
—521 82	Wakayama prefecture (Wakayama-ken)
—521 83	Ōsaka prefecture (Ōsaka-fu)

Class here *Yodo River

*For a specific part of this jurisdiction, region, or feature, see the part and follow instructions under —4–9

—521 834	Ōsaka
—521 84	Nara prefecture (Nara-ken)
—521 85	Shiga prefecture (Shiga-ken)
—521 86	Kyōto prefecture (Kyōto-fu)
—521 864	Kyōto
—521 87	Hyōgo prefecture (Hyōgo-ken)
—521 874	Kōbe
—521 9	Chūgoku region (Chūgoku chihō)

See also —*16455 for Inland Sea (Seto-naikai)*

—521 93	Tottori prefecture (Tottori-ken)
—521 94	Okayama prefecture (Okayama-ken)
—521 95	Hiroshima prefecture (Hiroshima-ken)
—521 954	Hiroshima
—521 96	Shimane prefecture (Shimane-ken)
—521 97	Yamaguchi prefecture (Yamaguchi-ken)
—522	Kyusyu region (Kyūshū chihō)

———————

>	—522 2–522 8 Kyusyu (Kyūshū) island

Class comprehensive works in —522

—522 2	Fukuoka prefecture (Fukuoka-ken)
—522 3	Saga prefecture (Saga-ken)
—522 4	Nagasaki prefecture (Nagasaki-ken)
—522 44	Nagasaki
—522 5	Kumamoto prefecture (Kumamoto-ken)
—522 6	Kagoshima prefecture (Kagoshima-ken)
—522 7	Miyazaki prefecture (Miyazaki-ken)
—522 8	Ōita prefecture (Ōita-ken)
—522 9	Okinawa prefecture (Okinawa-ken)

Class here Ryukyu Islands

—522 94	Okinawa island
—523	Shikoku
—523 2	Ehime prefecture (Ehime-ken)
—523 3	Kōchi prefecture (Kōchi-ken)

—523 4	Tokushima prefecture (Tokushima-ken)
—523 5	Kagawa prefecture (Kagawa-ken)
—524	Hokkaidō

> Including Etorofu, Kunashiri (islands claimed by both Japan and Russia)
>
> *See also —16453 for La Perouse Strait; also —16454 for Tsugaru Strait*

—528	Bonin (Ogasawara) Islands
—53	**Arabian Peninsula and adjacent areas**

> Including Arabia Deserta, 622–637 [*formerly* —3947]
>
> Class here Persian Gulf region
>
> Subdivisions are added for Arabian Peninsula and adjacent areas together, for Arabian Peninsula alone
>
> *For Iran, see —55; for Iraq, see —567*
>
> *See also —16533 for Red Sea; also —16535 for Persian Gulf*
>
> (Options: Class here Arabia Petraea; prefer —3948. Class here Arabia Deserta, Arabia Felix, Arabian Peninsula to 622, Persian Gulf region to 622; prefer —3949)

—531	Sinai Peninsula

> Including Janūb Sīnā' Province, Shamāl Sīnā' Province; Gaza Strip
>
> Class Suez Canal in —6215
>
> (Option: Class here Sinai Peninsula to 622; prefer —3948)

—533	Yemen

> Class here Republic of Yemen
>
> (Option: Class here Yemen to 622; prefer —3949)

—533 2	Northern Yemen

> Class here Yemen Arab Republic

—533 5	Southern Yemen

> Class here Federation of South Arabia, People's Democratic Republic of Yemen

—535	Oman and United Arab Emirates
—535 3	Oman

> *See also —16536 for Gulf of Oman*
>
> (Option: Class here Oman to 622; prefer —3949)

—535 7	United Arab Emirates

> Including Abu Dhabi, 'Ajmān, Dubai, Fujairah, Ras al Khaimah, Shārjah, Umm al-Qaiwain
>
> (Option: Class here United Arab Emirates to 622; prefer —3949)

—536	Persian Gulf States

> *For Oman and United Arab Emirates, see —535*

—536 3	Qatar

> (Option: Class here Qatar to 622; prefer —3949)

—536 5	Bahrain

> (Option: Class here Bahrain to 622; prefer —3949)

—536 7	Kuwait

> (Option: Class here Kuwait to 622; prefer —3949)

—538	Saudi Arabia

> Including Hejaz, Nejd; Mecca; *Rub'al-Khali, Syrian Desert in Saudi Arabia
>
> (Option: Class here Saudi Arabia to 622; prefer —3949)

—54   **India and neighboring south Asian countries**

> Class here south Asia
>
> Subdivisions are added India and neighboring south Asian countries together, for India alone
>
> *For southeast Asia, see —59*
>
> (Option: Class here India to 647, South Asia to 647; prefer —34)

SUMMARY

—541	**Northeastern India**
—542	**Uttar Pradesh**
—543	**Madhya Pradesh**
—544	**Rajasthan**
—545	**Northwestern India**
—546	**Jammu and Kashmir**
—547	**Western India**
—548	**Southern India**
—549	**Other jurisdictions**

>	—541–548 India

> Class comprehensive works in —54

—541	Northeastern India

> Including *Ganges River

—541 2	Bihar and Jharkhand
—541 23	Bihar

---

*For a specific part of this jurisdiction, region, or feature, see the part and follow instructions under —4–9

—541 27	Jharkhand
—541 3	Orissa and Chhattīsgarh
—541 33	Orissa
—541 37	Chhattīsgarh
—541 4	West Bengal

Class here former province of Bengal

For former East Bengal, see —5492

—541 47	Calcutta
—541 5	Tripura
—541 6	Far northeast of India

Class here *Brahmaputra River in India

For Manipur, see —5417

—541 62	Assam
—541 63	Arunāchal Pradesh
—541 64	Meghalaya
—541 65	Nāgāland
—541 66	Mizoram
—541 67	Sikkim
—541 7	Manipur
—542	Uttar Pradesh
—543	Madhya Pradesh
—544	Rajasthan

Class here *Thar (Great Indian) Desert

—545	Northwestern India

Class here former province of Punjab

For Jammu and Kashmir, see —546; for Punjab Province of Pakistan, see —54914

—545 1	Uttarakhand

Former name: Uttaranchal

—545 2	Himachal Pradesh
—545 5	Punjab and Haryana

Class here former Punjab state

---

*For a specific part of this jurisdiction, region, or feature, see the part and follow instructions under
 —4–9

—545 52		Punjab
		Including Chandīgarh
—545 58		Haryana
—545 6	Delhi	
		Class here Delhi, New Delhi
—546	Jammu and Kashmir	
		Class here comprehensive works on Kashmir
		Including *Karakoram Range
		For area of Kashmir controlled by Pakistan, see —54913
—547	Western India	
—547 5		Gujarat
—547 6		Dādra and Nagar Haveli
—547 7		Daman and Diu
		Class comprehensive works on Portuguese India in —5478
—547 8		Goa
		Class here Portuguese India
		For Daman and Diu, see —5477
—547 9		Maharashtra
—547 92		Bombay (Mumbai)
—548	Southern India	
		Class here *Deccan
—548 1		Lakshadweep
—548 2		Tamil Nadu
		Including Madras
—548 3		Kerala
—548 4		Andhra Pradesh
		Including Hyderabad
		Class here former state of Hyderabad
		For Maharashtra, see —54792; for Karnataka, see —5487
—548 6		Puducherry
		Former name: Pondicherry
—548 7		Karnataka

*For a specific part of this jurisdiction, region, or feature, see the part and follow instructions under
—4–9

—548 8   Andaman and Nicobar Islands

—549   Other jurisdictions

                   Class here Pakistan (West and East, 1947–1971)

—549 1   Pakistan

                       Class here *Indus River

                       (Option: Class here Pakistan to 647; prefer —3491)

—549 11   Federally Administered Tribal Areas

—549 12   Khyber-Pakhtunkhwa

                           Former name: North-West Frontier Province

—549 122   Districts and agencies north of Peshawar

                               Including Chitrāl, Dīr, Kalam, Swat

—549 123   Peshawar District

                               Class here Peshawar

—549 124   Districts south of Peshawar

                               Including Dera Ismāīl Khān District

—549 13   Northern Areas and Azad Kashmir

                           Class here area of Kashmir controlled by Pakistan

                           Class comprehensive works on Kashmir in —546

—549 132   Northern Areas

—549 138   Azad Kashmir

—549 14   Punjab Province and Islāmābād Capital Territory

                           Including Multān, Sargodha Districts

                           Subdivisions are added for Punjab Province and Islāmābād Capital Territory together, for Punjab Province alone

                           For Bahāwalpur District, see —54916

—549 142   Rāwalpindi District

—549 143   Lahore District

                               Class here Lahore

—549 149   Islāmābād Capital Territory

                               Class here Islāmābād

*For a specific part of this jurisdiction, region, or feature, see the part and follow instructions under —4–9

—549 15	Baluchistan Province
	Class here comprehensive works on Baluchistan
	For Iranian Baluchistan, see —5583
—549 152	Quetta District
—549 153	Kalāt District
—549 16	Bahāwalpur District
—549 17	Khairpūr District
—549 18	Sindh Province
	For Khairpūr District, see —54917
—549 182	Hyderabad District
	Class here Hyderabad
—549 183	Karachi District
	Class here Karachi
—549 2	Bangladesh
	Class here comprehensive works on *Brahmaputra River
	(Option: Class here Bangladesh to 647; prefer —3492)
—549 22	Dhaka Division
	Class here Dhaka
—549 23	Chittagong Division
	Class here Chittagong
—549 24	Rājshāhi Division
—549 25	Khulna Division
—549 26	Barisāl Division
—549 27	Sylhet Division
—549 29	Chittagong Hill Tracts Region
—549 3	Sri Lanka
	Including Colombo
—549 5	Maldives
—549 6	Nepal
	Class here *Himalaya Mountains
—549 8	Bhutan

*For a specific part of this jurisdiction, region, or feature, see the part and follow instructions under —4–9

—55	**Iran**
	(Option: Class here Iranian Plateau to 637; prefer —35)
—551	Ardabīl province, Gīlān province, Zanjān province, Qazvīn province
—551 2	Ardabīl province
—551 4	Gīlān province
—551 6	Zanjān province
—551 8	Qazvīn province
—552	Golestān province, Māzandarān province, Semnān province, Tehran province, Qum province, Markazī province
—552 2	Golestān province
—552 3	Māzandarān province
	(Option: Class here Māzandarān province to 637, Hyrcania; prefer —396)
—552 4	Semnān province
—552 5	Tehran province
	Class here Tehran
—552 6	Qum province
—552 7	Markazī province
—553	East Azerbaijan (Āzarbāyjān-i Khāvarī) province
	Class here Azerbaijan region
	For country of Azerbaijan, see —4754; for West Azerbaijan province of Iran, see —554
—554	West Azerbaijan (Āzarbāyjān-i Bākhtarī) province
—555	Hamadān province, Kordestān province, Kermānshāhān province, Īlām province
	(Option: Class here Hamadān province to 637, Kordestān province to 637, Kermānshāhān province to 637, Īlām province to 637, Media; prefer —3575)
—555 2	Hamadān province
	(Option: Class here Hamadān province to 637, Ecbatana; prefer —35752)
—555 4	Kordestān province
	Class comprehensive works on Kurdistan in —5667
—555 6	Kermānshāhān province
—555 8	Īlām province
—556	Lorestān province, Khūzestān province, Kohkīlūyeh va Boyer Ahmadī province

—556 2   Lorestān province

—556 4   Khūzestān province

> (Option: Class here Khūzestān province to 637, Elam [Susiana], Susa; prefer —35764)

—556 8   Kohkīlūyeh va Boyer Ahmadī province

> Former name: Boyer Ahmadī va Kohkīlūyeh province

—557   Fārs province, Būshehr province, Hormozgān province

—557 2   Fārs province

> (Option: Class here Fārs province to 637, Persia, Pasargadae, Persepolis; prefer —35772)

—557 4   Būshehr province

—557 5   Hormozgān province

—558   Kermān province and Sīstān va Balūchestān province

—558 2   Kermān province

—558 3   Sīstān va Balūchestān province

> Class comprehensive works on Baluchistan in —54915

—559   North Khorāsān province, Razavi Khorāsān province, South Khorāsān province, Yazd province, Eṣfahān province, Chahār Mahāll va Bakhtīarī province

—559 2   North Khorāsān province (Khorāsān-e Jonūbī province), Razavi Khorāsān province (Khorāsān-e Razavī province), South Khorāsān province (Khorāsān-e Shomālī province)

> Former name: Khorāsān province

—559 4   Yazd province

—559 5   Eṣfahān province

—559 7   Chahār Mahāll va Bakhtīarī province

—56   *Middle East (Near East)

> Class here *Ottoman Empire

> (Option: Class here Middle East to 640; prefer —394)

---

*For a specific part of this jurisdiction, region, or feature, see the part and follow instructions under —4–9

SUMMARY

—561   Turkey

Class here Asia Minor

For divisions of Turkey, see —562–566

(Options: Class here Turkey to 640, Asia Minor to 640, western Asia Minor to 640; prefer —392. Class here eastern Asia Minor to 640, Diocese of Pontus; prefer —393)

>   —562–566 Divisions of Turkey

Class comprehensive works in —561

For Turkey in Europe, see —4961

—562   Western Turkey

—562 2   Çanakkale Province (Çanakkale İli)

Including Bozca (Tenedos) Island, Gökçeada (İmroz, Imbros) Island

For European portion of Çanakkale Province, see —49612

See also —16389 for Dardanelles

(Options: Class here Bozca (Tenedos) Island to 323, Gökçeada (İmroz, Imbros) Island to 323; prefer —3911. Class here Çanakkale Province to 640, Hellespontus Province, Troas, Troy; prefer —3921)

—562 3   Balıkesir Province (Balıkesir İli)

(Option: Class here Balıkesir Province to 640, Cyzicus, Mysia; prefer —3921)

—562 4   Manisa Province (Manisa İli)

(Option: Class here Manisa Province to 640, Lydia, Sardis; prefer —3922)

—562 5   İzmir Province (İzmir İli)

Including Bergama (Pergamum)

(Option: Class here İzmir Province to 640, Asia Province, Ionia, Ephesus, Pergamum, Smyrna; prefer —3923)

—562 6   Aydın Province (Aydın İli)

(Option: Class here Aydın Province to 640, Magnesia ad Maeandrum, Miletus; prefer —3923)

—562 7 Burdur Province (Burdur İli), Denizli Province (Denizli İli), Muğla Province (Muğla İli)

(Option: Class here Burdur Province to 640, Denizli Province to 640, Muğla Province to 640, Caria Province, Halicarnassus; prefer —3924)

—562 8 Afyon Province (Afyon İli), Kütahya Province (Kütahya İli), Uşak Province (Uşak İli)

(Option: Class here Afyon Province to 640, Kütahya Province to 640, Uşak Province to 640, Phrygia Province, Phrygia Pacatiana Province; prefer —3926)

—563 North central Turkey

See also —16389 for Bosporus, Sea of Marmara

(Option: Class here Bithynia Province to 640; prefer —39313)

—563 1 Bursa Province (Bursa İli)

(Option: Class here Bursa Province to 640; prefer —39313)

—563 2 Asian portion of İstanbul Province (İstanbul İli)

(Option: Class here Asian portion of İstanbul Province to 640; prefer —39313)

—563 3 Kocaeli Province (Kocaeli İli) and Yalova Province (Yalova İli)

Including İzmit (Nicomedia)

(Option: Class here Kocaeli Province to 640, Yalova Province to 640; prefer —39313)

—563 4 Bilecik Province (Bilecik İli), Bolu Province (Bolu İli), Düzce Province (Düzce İli), Sakarya Province (Sakarya İli)

(Option: Class here Bilecik Province to 640, Bolu Province to 640, Düzce Province to 640, Sakarya Province to 640, Honorias Province; prefer —39315)

—563 5 Eskişehir Province (Eskişehir İli)

(Option: Class here Eskişehir Province to 640, Phrygia Salutaris Province; prefer —3926)

—563 6 Ankara Province (Ankara İli)

(Option: Class here Ankara Province to 640, Galatia, Galatia Prima Province, Galatia Salutaris Province; prefer —3932)

—563 7 Bartın Province (Bartın İli), Çankırı Province (Çankırı İli), Karbük Province (Karbük İli), Kastamonu Province (Kastamonu İli), Zonguldak Province (Zonguldak İli)

(Option: Class here Bartın Province to 640, Çankırı Province to 640, Karbük Province to 640, Kastamonu Province to 640, Zonguldak Province to 640, Paphlagonia Province; prefer —39317)

—563 8   Amasya Province (Amasya İli), Çorum Province (Çorum İli), Kırıkkale Province (Kırıkkale İli), Samsun Province (Samsun İli), Sinop Province (Sinop İli), Yozgat Province (Yozgat İli)

> (Options: Class here Kırıkkale Province to 640; prefer —3932. Class here Amasya Province to 640, Samsun Province to 640, Sinop Province to 640, Yozgat Province to 640, Helenopontus Province; prefer —39332)

—563 83   Çorum Province (Çorum İli)

> (Option: Class here Çorum Province to 640; prefer —39332)

—564   South central Turkey

> Including *Taurus Mountains (Toros Dağları)

—564 1   Aksaray Province (Aksaray İli), Kayseri Province (Kayseri İli), Kırşehir Province (Kırşehir İli), Nevşehir Province (Nevşehir İli), Niğde Province (Niğde İli)

> (Option: Class here Aksaray Province to 640, Kırşehir Province to 640, Niğde Province to 640, Cappadocia to 640, Cappadocia Prima Province, Cappadocia Secunda Province; prefer —3934)

—564 12   Kayseri Province (Kayseri İli)

> (Option: Class here Kayseri province to 640; prefer —3934)

—564 14   Nevşehir Province (Nevşehir İli)

> (Option: Class here Nevşehir province to 640; prefer —3934)

—564 2   Konya Province (Konya İli)

> (Option: Class here Konya Province to 640, Lycaonia Province, Pisidia Province; prefer —3927)

—564 3   Isparta Province (Isparta İli)

> (Option: Class here Isparta Province to 640; prefer —3927)

—564 4   Antalya Province (Antalya İli)

> (Options: Class here western part of Antalya Province to 640, Lycia; prefer —3928. Class here eastern part of Antalya Province to 640, Pamphylia; prefer —3929)

—564 5   Karaman Province (Karaman İli)

> (Option: Class here Karaman Province to 640; prefer —3927)

—564 6   Mersin Province (Mersin İli)

> Former name: İçel Province (İçel İli)
>
> Including Tarsus
>
> (Option: Class here Mersin Province to 640, Cilicia Prima Province, Isauria Province; prefer —3935)

---

*For a specific part of this jurisdiction, region, or feature, see the part and follow instructions under —4–9

—564 7　　　　　　Adana Province (Adana İli) and Osmaniye Province (Osmaniye İli)

　　　　　　　　　(Option: Class here Adana Province to 640, Osmaniye Province to 640, Cilicia Secunda Province; prefer —3935)

—564 8　　　　　　Hatay Province (Hatay İli)

　　　　　　　　　Including Antioch (Antakya)

　　　　　　　　　(Option: Class here Hatay Province, Antioch to 640; prefer —39431)

—564 9　　　　　　Gaziantep Province (Gaziantep İli) and Kilis Province (Kilis İli)

　　　　　　　　　(Option: Class here Gaziantep Province to 640, Kilis Province to 640, Cyrrhestica; prefer —3936)

—565　　　　　　　East central Turkey

　　　　　　　　　(Options: Class here Pontus; prefer —3933. Class here Pontus Polemoniacus Province; prefer —39337)

—565 1　　　　　　Şanlıurfa Province (Şanlıurfa İli)

　　　　　　　　　Variant name: Urfa Province (Urfa İli)

　　　　　　　　　(Option: Class here Şanlıurfa Province to 640, Osroene; prefer —3942)

—565 2　　　　　　Adıyaman Province (Adıyaman İli)

　　　　　　　　　(Option: Class here Adıyaman Province to 640, Commagene; prefer —3936)

—565 3　　　　　　Kahramanmaraş Province (Kahramanmaraş İli)

　　　　　　　　　Former name: Maraş Province (Maraş İli)

　　　　　　　　　(Option: Class here Kahramanmaraş Province to 640, northern part of Euphratensis Province, comprehensive works on Euphratensis Province; prefer —3936)

—565 4　　　　　　Malatya Province (Malatya İli)

　　　　　　　　　(Option: Class here Malatya Province to 640; prefer —3936)

—565 5　　　　　　Sivas Province (Sivas İli)

　　　　　　　　　(Option: Class here Sivas Province to 640; prefer —3955)

—565 6　　　　　　Ordu Province (Ordu İli) and Tokat Province (Tokat İli)

　　　　　　　　　(Option: Class here Ordu Province to 640, Tokat Province to 640; prefer —39337)

—565 7　　　　　　Bayburt Province (Bayburt İli), Giresun Province (Giresun İli), Gümüşhane Province (Gümüşhane İli)

　　　　　　　　　(Option: Class here Bayburt Province to 640, Giresun Province to 640, Gümüşhane Province to 640; prefer —39337)

—565 8　　　　　　Trabzon Province (Trabzon İli)

　　　　　　　　　Former name: Trebizond

　　　　　　　　　(Option: Class here Trabzon Province to 640; prefer —39337)

—566　　　　　　　Eastern Turkey

—566 2   Northeastern Turkey

Class here comprehensive works on Armenia region

For country of Armenia, see —4756

(Option: Class here Armenia region to 640, Armenia [ancient kingdom]; prefer —3955)

—566 22   Ardahan Province (Ardahan İli), Artvin Province (Artvin İli), Rize Province (Rize İli)

(Option: Class here Ardahan Province to 640, Artvin Province to 640, Rize Province to 640; prefer —39337)

—566 24   Erzurum Province (Erzurum İli)

(Option: Class here Erzurum Province to 640; prefer —3955)

—566 26   Ağrı Province (Ağrı İli), Iğdır Province (Iğdır İli), Kars Province (Kars İli)

(Option: Class here Ağrı Province to 640, Iğdır Province to 640, Kars Province to 640; prefer —3955)

—566 28   Hakkâri Province (Hakkâri İli) and Van Province (Van İli)

(Option: Class here Hakkâri Province to 640, Van Province to 640; prefer —3955)

—566 7   Southeast central Turkey

Class here comprehensive works on Kurdistan

For Iranian Kurdistan, see —5554; for Iraqi Kurdistan, see —5672

(Option: Class here southeast central Turkey to 640; prefer —3942)

—566 72   Bitlis Province (Bitlis İli) and Muş Province (Muş İli)

(Option: Class here Bitlis Province to 640, Muş Province to 640; prefer —3942)

—566 73   Bingöl Province (Bingöl İli)

(Option: Class here Bingöl Province to 640; prefer —3942)

—566 74   Erzincan Province (Erzincan İli)

(Option: Class here Erzincan Province to 640; prefer —3942)

—566 75   Tunceli Province (Tunceli İli)

(Option: Class here Tunceli Province to 640; prefer —3942)

—566 76   Elazığ Province (Elazığ İli)

(Option: Class here Elazığ Province to 640; prefer —3942)

—566 77   Diyarbakır Province (Diyarbakır İli)

(Option: Class here Diyarbakır Province to 640; prefer —3942)

—566 78   Batman Province (Batman İli), Mardin Province (Mardin İli), Siirt Province (Siirt İli), Şirnak Province (Şirnak İli)

                 (Option: Class here Batman Province to 640, Mardin Province to 640, Siirt Province to 640, Şirnak Province to 640; prefer —3942)

—567   Iraq

        Class here Mesopotamia

        (Options: Class here Iraq to 637, Mesopotamia to 637, Assyria, Chaldean Empire, Persian Empire, Sassanian Empire, Seleucid Empire; prefer —35. Class here Arabia Deserta; prefer —3947)

—567 2   Kurdish Autonomous Region

           Including Dahūk Province, Irbīl Province, Sulaymānīyah Province

           Class comprehensive works on Kurdistan in —5667

           (Option: Class here Kurdish Autonomous Region to 637; prefer —352)

—567 4   Upper Mesopotamia

           Including Anbār Province, Diyālá Province, Nīnawá (Nineveh) Province, Şalāḥ ad-Dīn Province, Ta'mim Province; Mosul; Syrian Desert in Iraq

           (Option: Class here Upper Mesopotamia to 637, Ashur, Nineveh; prefer —354)

—567 47   Baghdād Province

           Class here Baghdad

—567 5   Lower Mesopotamia

           Including Bābil Province, Başrah Province, Dhī Qār Province, Karbalā' Province, Maysān Province, Muthanná Province, Najaf, Qādisīyah Province, Wāsiṭ (Kūt) Province

           (Option: Class here Lower Mesopotamia to 637, Akkad, Babylon, Babylonia, Sumer, Ur; prefer —355)

—569   Syria, Lebanon, Cyprus, Israel, Jordan

        Class here *Syrian Desert

—569 1   Syria

        (Option: Class here Syria to 640; prefer —3943)

—569 12   Desert provinces of Syria

           Including Dayr al-Zawr, Ḥasakah, Ḥimş, Raqqah

           Class here Syrian Desert in Syria

           (Option: Class here desert provinces to 640, Palmyra, southern part of Euphratensis Province, southern part of Cyrrhestica; prefer —39432)

*For a specific part of this jurisdiction, region, or feature, see the part and follow instructions under —4–9

—569 13	Northwest provinces of Syria

            Including Aleppo (Ḥalab), Ḥamāh, Idlib, Latakia, Ṭarṭūs

            (Option: Class here northwest provinces to 640, Ebla, Ugarit; prefer —3943)

—569 14	Southwest provinces of Syria and city of Damascus

            Including Damascus (Dimashq) Province, Darʻā Province, Qunayṭirah Province, Suwaydāʼ Province; *Anti-Lebanon

            Subdivisions are added for southwest provinces and city of Damascus together, for southwest provinces alone

            (Option: Class here southwest provinces to 640; prefer —3943)

—569 144	City of Damascus

            (Option: Class here Damascus to 640; prefer —394344)

—569 2	Lebanon

            (Option: Class here Lebanon to 640, Phoenicia, Coelesyria, Baalbek, Byblos, Sidon, Tyre; prefer —3944)

—569 25	Beirut
—569 3	Cyprus

            (Option: Class here Cyprus to 640; prefer —3937)

—569 4	Palestine; Israel

            Palestine: area covering Israel, Gaza Strip, and West Bank of Jordan

            Including *Jordan River; *Dead Sea

            For Gaza Strip, see —531; for West Bank, see —56951–56953

            (Options: Class here Palestine to 70; prefer —33. Class here Israel to 70; prefer —334)

—569 44	Jerusalem district

            (Option: Class here Jerusalem district to 70; prefer —3344)

—569 442	Jerusalem

            (Option: Class here Jerusalem to 70; prefer —33442)

—569 45	Tsafon district

            Class here Galilee

            (Option: Class here Tsafon district to 70, Galilee to 70; prefer —3345)

—569 46	Haifa district

            (Option: Class here Haifa district to 70; prefer —3346)

---

*For a specific part of this jurisdiction, region, or feature, see the part and follow instructions under —4–9

—569 47   Merkaz district

                 (Option: Class here Merkaz district to 70; prefer —3347)

—569 48   Tel Aviv district

                 Class here Tel Aviv

                 (Option: Class here Tel Aviv district to 70, Tel Aviv to 70; prefer
                 —3348)

—569 49   Darom district

                 Class here Negev

                 (Options: Class here Darom district to 70, Judah, Judaea; prefer
                 —3349. Class here Darom district in Edom to 70, Edom; prefer
                 —3946. Class here Darom district in Arabia Petraea to 622; prefer
                 —3948)

—569 5   Jordan and West Bank

                 Subdivisions are added for Jordan and West Bank together, for Jordan
                 alone

                 (Option: Class here Jordan to 70; prefer —335)

>   —569 51–569 53 West Bank

         Class comprehensive works in —56953

—569 51   Hebron district

                 (Option: Class here Hebron Province to 70; prefer —3351)

—569 52   Jerusalem district

                 Class city of Jerusalem in —569442

                 (Option: Class here Jerusalem Province to 70; prefer —3352)

—569 53   Nablus district

                 Class here comprehensive works on West Bank, area administered
                 by Palestinian National Authority

                     *For Gaza Strip, see —531; for Hebron district, see —56951; for
                     Jerusalem district, see —56952*

                 (Option: Class here Nablus district to 70, West Bank to 70, Samaria;
                 prefer —3353)

>   —569 54–569 59 Jordan

         Class comprehensive works in —5695

—569 54   Irbid Province, 'Ajlūn Province, Jarash Province

                 (Option: Class here Irbid Province to 70, 'Ajlūn Province to 70,
                 Jarash Province to 70; prefer —3354)

—569 542 Irbid Province

> (Option: Class here Irbid Province to 70; prefer —33542)

—569 546 'Ajlūn Province

> (Option: Class here 'Ajlūn Province to 70; prefer —33546)

—569 548 Jarash Province

> (Option: Class here Jarash Province to 70; prefer —33548)

—569 55 Balqā' Province

> (Option: Class here Balqā' Province to 70; prefer —3355)

—569 56 Ma'dabā Province, Karak Province, Ṭafīlah Province

—569 562 Ma'dabā Province

> (Option: Class here Ma'dabā Province to 70; prefer —39462)

—569 563 Karak Province

> (Option: Class here Karak Province to 70, Moab; prefer —39462)

—569 567 Ṭafīlah Province

> (Option: Class here Ṭafīlah Province to 70; prefer —39464)

—569 57 'Aqabah Province and Ma'ān Province

> (Option: Class here 'Aqabah Province to 70 and Ma'ān Province to 70; prefer —39464)

—569 572 'Aqabah Province

> (Options: Class here 'Aqabah Province in Edom to 70; prefer —39464. Class here 'Aqabah Province to 622; prefer —3948)

—569 577 Ma'ān Province

> (Option: Class here Ma'ān Province to 622, Petra; prefer —3948)

—569 58 Amman Province

Class here Amman

> (Option: Class here Amman Province to 70; prefer —3358)

—569 59 Zarqā' Province and Mafraq Province

Class here *Syrian Desert in Jordan

> (Option: Class here Zarqā' Province to 70 and Mafraq Province to 70; prefer —3359)

—569 593 Zarqā' Province

> (Option: Class here Zarqā' Province to 70; prefer —33593)

*For a specific part of this jurisdiction, region, or feature, see the part and follow instructions under —4–9

—569 597   Mafraq Province

         (Option: Class here Mafraq Province to 70; prefer —33597)

—57   **Siberia (Asiatic Russia)**

—573   Western Siberia

         Including Kemerovo province (Kemerovskaĭa oblast'), Kurgan province (Kurganskaĭa oblast'), Novosibirsk province (Novosibirskaĭa oblast'), Omsk province (Omskaĭa oblast'), Tomsk province (Tomskaĭa oblast'), Tyumen province (Tĭumenskaĭa oblast'); Altay territory (Altaĭskiĭ kraĭ); Gorno-Altay (Gorno-Altaĭ) republic; Khantia-Mansia autonomous district (Khanty-Mansiĭskiĭ avtonomnyĭ okrug), Yamal-Nenets autonomous district (Yamal-Nenetskiĭ avtonomnyĭ okrug)

         For Chelyabinsk province, Sverdlovsk province, see —4743

—575   Eastern Siberia

         Including Chita province (Chitinskaĭa oblast'), Irkutsk province (Irkutskaĭa oblast'); Krasnoyarsk territory (Krasnoĭarskiĭ kraĭ); Buryatia (Burĭatiĭa) republic, Khakassia (Khakasskaĭa) republic, Sakha (Yakutia, ĬAkutiĭa) republic, Tuva republic; Agin Burĭat autonomous district (Agin Burĭatskiĭ avtonomnyĭ okrug), Evenki autonomous district (Evenskiĭ avtonomnyĭ okrug), Taĭmyr autonomous district (Taĭmyrskiĭ avtonomnyĭ okrug), Ust-Orda Burĭat autonomous district (Ust-Orda Burĭatskiĭ avtonomnyĭ okrug); *Sayan Mountains

         For Far Eastern Siberia, see —577; for Severnaya Zemlya, see —987; for New Siberian Islands, see —988

—577   Far Eastern Siberia

         Including Amur province (Amurskaĭa oblast'), Kamchatka province (Kamchatskaĭa oblast'), Magadan province (Magadanskaĭa oblast'), Sakhalin province (Sakhalinskaĭa oblast'); Khabarovsk territory (Khabarovskiĭ kraĭ), Primor'ye territory (Primorskiĭ kraĭ); Jewish autonomous region (Evreĭskaĭa avtonomnaĭa oblast, Yevrey avtonomnaĭa oblast); Chukchi autonomous district (Chukotskiĭ avtonomnyĭ okrug), Korĭak autonomous district (Korĭakskiĭ avtonomnyĭ okrug); Komandorski Islands, Kuril Islands, Wrangel Island; *Amur River

         See also —16451 for Bering Strait; also —16453 for Sea of Okhotsk; also —16454 for Tatar Strait

—58   **Central Asia**

         (Option: Class here Central Asia to ca. 640; prefer —396)

—581   Afghanistan

         Class here *Hindu Kush

         (Option: Class here Afghanistan to ca. 640, Ariana, Bactria, Parthia; prefer —396)

---

*For a specific part of this jurisdiction, region, or feature, see the part and follow instructions under —4–9

—584	Turkestan

        Class Sinkiang in —516

          For Turkmenistan, see —585; for Tajikistan, see —586; for Uzbekistan, see —587

—584 3	Kyrgyzstan

        Including *Tien Shan

—584 5	Kazakhstan
—585	Turkmenistan

        (Option: Class here Turkmenistan to ca. 640, Margiana; prefer —396)

—586	Tajikistan

        Including Gorno-Badakhshan autonomous province (oblast)

        Class here *Pamir

—587	Uzbekistan

        Including Karakalpak autonomous republic; *Aral Sea

        (Option: Class here Uzbekistan to ca. 640, Sogdiana; prefer —396)

—59	**Southeast Asia**

        Including Paracel Islands, Spratly Islands

        Class here *Indochina (southeast peninsula of Asia), *Mekong River

        Class works about "Indochina" when used to equate with French Indochina in —597

—591	Myanmar
—593	Thailand

        See also —16472 for Gulf of Thailand

—594	Laos
—595	Malaysia, Brunei, Singapore

        Subdivisions are added for Malaysia, Brunei, Singapore together; for Malaysia alone

—595 1	Peninsular Malaysia (Malaya, West Malaysia)

        Including Johor state, Kedah state, Kelantan state, Malacca (Melaka) state, Negeri Sembilan state, Pahang state, Perak state, Perlis state, Pinang (Pulau Pinang) state, Selangor state, Terengganu state; Kuala Lumpur

        Class here *Malay Peninsula

---

*For a specific part of this jurisdiction, region, or feature, see the part and follow instructions under —4–9

—595 3   Sabah

> State of Malaysia
>
> Including Labuan
>
> Class here northern Borneo, East Malaysia
>
> *For Sarawak, see —5954; for Brunei, see —5955*

—595 4   Sarawak

> State of Malaysia

—595 5   Brunei

—595 7   Singapore

> Independent republic
>
> *See also —16472 for Singapore Strait*

—596   Cambodia

—597   Vietnam

> Class here *French Indochina (Indochina)
>
> Class works about "Indochina" when used to equate with the southeast peninsula of Asia in —59
>
> Use of this number for comprehensive works on Mekong River discontinued; class in —59

—597 1   Mountain region of northern Vietnam

> Including Bắc Kạn province, Cao Bằng province, Điện Biên province, Hà Giang province, Hòa Bình province, Lai Châu province, Lạng Sơn province, Lào Cai province, Sơn La province, Thái Nguyên province, Tuyên Quang province, Yên Bái province

—597 2   Midland region of northern Vietnam

> Including Bắc Giang province, Bắc Ninh province, Phú Thọ province, Quảng Ninh province, Vĩnh Phúc province

—597 3   *Red River Delta region

> Including Hà Nam province, Hà Tây province, Hải Dương province, Hưng Yên province, Nam Định province, Ninh Bình province, Thái Bình province; Haiphong municipality, Hanoi municipality
>
> Class here *Red River, *North Vietnam (1954–1975), comprehensive works on northern Vietnam
>
> *For mountain region of northern Vietnam, see —5971; for midland region of northern Vietnam, see —5972*

---

*For a specific part of this jurisdiction, region, or feature, see the part and follow instructions under —4–9

—597 4   North coastal region of central Vietnam

Including Hà Tĩnh province, Nghệ An province, Quảng Bình province, Quảng Trị province, Thanh Hóa province, Thừa Thiên-Huế province

Class here *Trường Sơn Mountain Range (Chaine Annamitique); comprehensive works on central Vietnam, on coastal area of central Vietnam

For south coastal region of central Vietnam, see —5975; for western highlands region of central Vietnam, see —5976

—597 5   South coastal region of central Vietnam

Including Bình Định province, Bình Thuận province, Khánh Hòa province, Ninh Thuận province, Phú Yên province, Quảng Nam province, Quảng Ngãi province; Đà Nẵng municipality

See also —59 for Paracel Islands, Spratly Islands

—597 6   Western highlands region of central Vietnam

Including Đắc Lắc (Dak Lak) province, Đắc Nông (Dak Nông) province, Gia Lai province, Kon Tum province, Lâm Đồng province

—597 7   Eastern region of southern Vietnam

Including Bà Rịa-Vũng Tàu province, Bình Dương province, Bình Phước province, Đồng Nai province, Tây Ninh province; Ho Chi Minh City

Class here *South Vietnam (1954–1975), comprehensive works on southern Vietnam

For Mekong River Delta region, see —5978

—597 8   *Mekong River Delta region

Including Bến Tre province, Đồng Tháp province, Long An province, Tiền Giang province, Trà Vinh province, Vĩnh Long province

For southern Mekong River Delta region, see —5979

—597 9   Southern Mekong River Delta region

Including An Giang province, Bạc Liêu province, Cà Mau province, Hậu Giang province, Kiên Giang province, Sóc Trăng province; Cần Thơ municipality

—598   Indonesia and East Timor

Class here Malay Archipelago, Sunda Islands

Subdivisions are added for Indonesia and East Timor together, for Indonesia alone

For Philippines, see —599; for western New Guinea, see —951

See also —16473 for inner sea of Malay Archipelago; also —16474 for seas adjoining southern Sunda Islands

---

*For a specific part of this jurisdiction, region, or feature, see the part and follow instructions under —4–9

> —598 1–598 6 Indonesia

Class comprehensive works in —598

—598 1   Sumatra and neighboring islands

Subdivisions are added for Sumatra and neighboring islands together, for Sumatra alone

> —598 11–598 18 Sumatra

Class comprehensive works in —5981

—598 11   Aceh (Nanggroe Aceh Darussalam)

—598 12   North Sumatra (Sumatera Utara)

—598 13   West Sumatra (Sumatera Barat)

—598 14   Riau

—598 15   Jambi

—598 16   South Sumatra (Sumatera Selatan)

—598 17   Bengkulu

—598 18   Lampung

—598 19   Riau Islands and Bangka Belitung

—598 192   Riau Islands (Kepulauan Riau)

Including Anambas Islands, Lingga Islands, Natuna Islands

—598 196   Bangka Belitung (Kepulauan Bangka Belitung)

Including Belitung

Class here Bangka

—598 2   Java and neighboring islands

Subdivisions are added for Java and neighboring islands together, for Java alone

—598 22   Jakarta

—598 23   Banten

—598 24   West Java (Jawa Barat)

—598 26   Central Java (Jawa Tengah)

—598 27   Yogyakarta

—598 28   East Java (Jawa Timur)

Including Madura

—598 3   Kalimantan

                   Class here Borneo

                   For northern Borneo, see —5953

—598 32   West Kalimantan (Kalimantan Barat)

—598 34   Central Kalimantan (Kalimantan Tengah)

—598 36   South Kalimantan (Kalimantan Selatan)

—598 38   East Kalimantan (Kalimantan Timur)

—598 4   Celebes (Sulawesi)

—598 42   North Sulawesi (Sulawesi Utara)

—598 43   Gorontalo

—598 44   Central Sulawesi (Sulawesi Tengah)

—598 46   West Sulawesi (Sulawesi Barat)

—598 47   South Sulawesi (Sulawesi Selatan)

—598 48   South-East Sulawesi (Sulawesi Tenggara)

—598 5   Moluccas

—598 52   Maluku

                   Including Ambon Island, Wetar Island

—598 56   North Maluku (Maluku Utara)

                   Including Halmahera

—598 6   Lesser Sunda Islands (Nusa Tenggara)

—598 62   Bali

—598 65   West Nusa Tenggara (Nusa Tenggara Barat)

                   Including Lombok, Sumbawa

—598 68   East Nusa Tenggara (Nusa Tenggara Timur)

                   Including West Timor; Flores Island, Sumba Island, *Timor Island

—598 7   East Timor

—599   Philippines

                   See also —16471 for inner seas of Philippines

---

*For a specific part of this jurisdiction, region, or feature, see the part and follow instructions under —4–9

—599 1   Luzon island and adjacent islands

>   Including Abra province, Albay province, Bataan province, Batanes
>   province, Batangas province, Benguet province, Bulacan province,
>   Cagayan province, Camarines Norte province, Camarines Sur province,
>   Catanduanes province, Cavite province, Ifugao province, Ilocos Norte
>   province, Ilocos Sur province, Isabela province, Kalinga-Apayao
>   province, La Union province, Laguna province, Marinduque province,
>   Mountain province, Nueva Ecija province, Nueva Vizcaya province,
>   Pampanga province, Pangasinan province, Quezon province, Rizal
>   province, Sorsogon province, Tarlac province, Zambales province
>
>   Subdivisions are added for Luzon island and adjacent islands together,
>   for Luzon island alone
>
>   *See also —16458 for Luzon Strait*

—599 16   Manila

—599 3   Mindoro island and adjacent islands

>   Including Occidental Mindoro province, Oriental Mindoro province
>
>   Subdivisions are added for Mindoro island and adjacent islands
>   together, for Mindoro island alone

—599 4   Palawan Island and adjacent islands (Palawan province)

>   Subdivisions are added for Palawan and adjacent islands together, for
>   Palawan Island alone

—599 5   Visayan Islands

>   Including Aklan province, Antique province, Bohol province, Capiz
>   province, Cebu province, Eastern Samar province, Iloilo province,
>   Leyte province, Masbate province, Negros Occidental province, Negros
>   Oriental province, Northern Samar province, Romblon province,
>   Southern Leyte province, Western Samar province
>
>   Including Cebu Island, Leyte Island, Negros Island, Panay Island,
>   Samar Island

—599 7   Mindanao Island and adjacent islands

>   Including Agusan del Norte province, Agusan del Sur province, Basilan
>   province, Bukidnon province, Camiguin province, Davao del Norte
>   province, Davao del Sur province, Davao Oriental province, Lanao
>   del Norte province, Lanao del Sur province, Maguindanao province,
>   Misamis Occidental province, Misamis Oriental province, North
>   Cotabato province, South Cotabato province, Sultan Kudarat province,
>   Surigao del Norte province, Surigao del Sur province, Zamboanga del
>   Norte province, Zamboanga del Sur province
>
>   Including Basilan Island, Dinagat Island
>
>   Subdivisions are added for Mindanao Island and adjacent islands
>   together, for Mindanao Island alone

—599 9   Sulu Archipelago

>   Including Sulu province, Tawitawi province
>
>   *See also —16473 for Sulu Sea*

—6   Africa

SUMMARY

—61   Tunisia and Libya

Class here *Barbary States, *North Africa

(Option: Class here North Africa to ca. 640; prefer —397)

—611   Tunisia

Including Bizerte, Tunis

(Option: Class here Tunisia to 647, Byzacium, Carthage, Proconsular Africa; prefer —3973)

—612   Libya

Including Banghāzī, Tripoli; *Libyan Desert

(Options: Class here Libya to 644, Tripolis, Leptis Magna, Oea, Sabrata; prefer —3974. Class here Cyrenaica; prefer —3975. Class here Marmarica; prefer —3976)

—62   Egypt and Sudan

Class here Federation of Arab Republics state (wilāyat), *Nile River

Subdivisions are added for Egypt and Sudan together, for Egypt alone

For Syria, see —5691; for Libya, see —612

(Option: Class here Egypt to 640; prefer —32)

>   —621–623 Egypt

Class comprehensive works in —62

For Sinai, see —531

*For a specific part of this jurisdiction, region, or feature, see the part and follow instructions under —4–9

—621   Lower Egypt

              Including Alexandria province, Buḥayrah province, Damietta province
              (Dumyāṭ province), Daqahlīyah province, Gharbīyah province, Kafr
              al-Shaykh province, Marsá Maṭrūḥ province (Maṭrūḥ province), Minūfīyah
              province, Mudīrīyat al-Sharqīyah province (Sharqīyah province),
              Qalyūbīyah province

              Class here Nile River Delta

              (Option: Class here lower Egypt to 640, Alexandria to 640; prefer —32)

—621 5   Isthmus of Suez

                  Including Ismailia province, Port Said province (Būr Saʻīd province),
                  Suez province (Suways province); Suez Canal

                  See also —16533 for Gulf of Suez

—621 6   Cairo province (Qāhirah province)

                  Class here Cairo

—622   Middle Egypt

              Including Asyūṭ province, Banī Suwayf province, Fayyūm province, Jīzah
              province, Minyā province, Wādī al-Jadīd province; *Western Desert,
              *Qattara Depression

              (Option: Class here middle Egypt to 640, Giza, Memphis; prefer —32)

—623   Upper Egypt

              Including Aswān province, Baḥr al-Aḥmar province, Qinā province, Sūhāj
              province; *Eastern Desert (Arabian Desert); *Lake Nasser

              (Option: Class here upper Egypt to 640, Abydos, Karnak, Luxor, Thebes;
              prefer —32)

—624   Sudan

                  For states of Sudan, see —625–629

              _____

>   —625–629 States of Sudan

              Class comprehensive works in —624

—625   Northern states of Sudan

                  Including Kassalā state (Kassalā wilāyat), Northern state (Shamālīyah
                  wilāyat), Qaḍārif state (Qaḍārif wilāyat), Red Sea state (Baḥr al-Aḥmar
                  wilāyat), River Nile state (Nahr an Nīl wilāyat); Port Sudan

                  See also —16533 for Red Sea

                  (Option: Class here northern states of Sudan to 500, Nubia, Ethiopia, Kush;
                  prefer —3978)

*For a specific part of this jurisdiction, region, or feature, see the part and follow instructions under
  —4–9

—626   Khartoum state and east central states of Sudan

—626 2   Khartoum state (Kharṭūm wilāyat)

>   Class here Khartoum

—626 4   East central states of Sudan

>   Including Blue Nile state (Nīl al Azraq wilāyat), Gezira state (Jazīrah wilāyat), Sinnār state (Sinnār wilāyat), White Nile state (Nīl al-Abyaḍ wilāyat)
>
>   Class here *Blue Nile River
>
>   Class comprehensive works on White Nile River in —6293

—627   Darfur region

>   Including Northern Darfur state (Shamāl Dārfūr wilāyat), Southern Darfur state (Janūb Dārfūr wilāyat), Western Darfur state (Gharb Dārfūr wilāyat)

—628   Kordofan region

>   Including Northern Kordofan state (Shamāl Kurdufān wilāyat), Southern Kordofan state (Janūb Kurdufān wilāyat), Western Kordofan state (Gharb Kurdufān wilāyat)

—629   Southern states of Sudan

—629 3   Upper Nile states

>   Including Junqalī state (Junqalī wilāyat), Upper Nile state (Aʻālī al-Nīl wilāyat), Waḥdah state (Waḥdah wilāyat)
>
>   Class here *White Nile River
>
>   *See also —6264 for White Nile state*

—629 4   Southwestern states of Sudan

>   Including Lakes state (Buḥayrāt wilāyat), Northern Bahr al Ghazal state (Shamāl Baḥr al Ghazal wilāyat), Warab state (Warab wilāyat), Western Bahr al Ghazal state (Gharb Baḥr al Ghazāl wilāyat)

—629 5   Equatoria states

>   Including Baḥr al Jabal state (Baḥr al Jabal wilāyat), East Equatoria state (Sharq al-Istiwāʼīyah wilāyat), West Equatoria state (Gharb al-Istiwāʼīyah wilāyat)

—63   Ethiopia and Eritrea

>   Class here Horn of Africa
>
>   Subdivisions are added for Ethiopia and Eritrea together, for Ethiopia alone
>
>   *For Djibouti and Somalia, see —677*
>
>   *See also —3978 for ancient Ethiopia (a part of what is now modern Sudan, not modern Ethiopia)*

---

*For a specific part of this jurisdiction, region, or feature, see the part and follow instructions under —4–9

> —632–634 Ethiopia

Class comprehensive works in —63

—632 Central Ethiopia and eastern Ethiopia

Including Dirē Dawa Administrative Region (Dirē Dawa Āwraja); Hārerī Hizb federal state (Hārerī Hizb kelel), Oromiyā federal state (Oromiyā kelel), Somali federal state (Somali kelel)

—633 Western Ethiopia

Including Addis Ababa administrative region (Addis Ababa Āwraja); Benishangul-Gumuz Federal State (Benishangul-Gumuz kelel); Southern Nations, Nationalities, and Peoples Federal State (YaDabub behér béhérasbočenā hezboč kelel); Gambella Federal State (Gambēla Āstedader Ākababī)

Class Oromiyā federal state (Oromiyā kelel) in —632

—634 Northern Ethiopia

Including 'Afār federal state ('Afār kelel), 'Amāra federal state ('Amāra kelel), Tigray federal state (Tigray kelel)

—635 Eritrea

Including Asmara

—64 **Morocco, Ceuta, Melilla, Western Sahara, Canary Islands**

Class here *Atlas Mountains

Subdivisions are added for Morocco, Ceuta, Melilla, Western Sahara, Canary Islands together; for Morocco alone

(Option: Class here Morocco to 647, Mauretania Tingitana; prefer —39712)

—641 Ceuta and Melilla

Autonomous communities of Spain

(Option: Class here Ceuta to 647, Melilla to 647; prefer —39712)

> —642–646 Morocco

Class Western Sahara, claimed by Morocco, in —648; class comprehensive works in —64

—642 Tangier-Tétouan region

Including Chefchaouen province (Chaouen province), Larache province, Tétouan province; Tangier-Assilah prefecture, Fahs-Beni Makada prefecture

Class here former *Spanish Morocco

*For a specific part of this jurisdiction, region, or feature, see the part and follow instructions under —4–9

—643   Northern regions of Morocco

> *For Tangier-Tétouan region, see —642*

—643 2   Taza-Al Hoceïma-Taounate region

> Including Hoceïma province, Taounate province, Taza province; *Rif Mountains

—643 3   Oriental region

> Including Berkane province, Jerada province, Figuig province, Nador province, Taourirt province; Oujda-Angad prefecture

—643 4   Fès-Boulemane region

> Including Boulemane province, Sefrou province; Fez-Jdid Dar-Dbibegh prefecture, Fez-Medina prefecture, Zouagha-Moulay Yacoub prefecture

—643 5   Gharb-Chrarda-Béni Hsen region

> Including Kénitra province, Sidi Kacem province

—643 6   Rabat-Salé-Zemmour-Zaër region

> Including Khémisset province; Rabat prefecture, Salé prefecture, Skhirate-Témara prefecture; Rabat

—643 8   Grand Casablanca region

> Including Aïn Chok-Hay Hassani prefecture, Aïn Scbaâ-Hay Mohamed prefecture, Ben M'sik-Sidi Othmane prefecture, Casablanca-Anfa prefecture, Fida-Derb Soltane prefecture, Méchouar de Casablanca prefecture, Mohammedia prefecture, Sidi Bernoussi-Zenata prefecture; Casablanca

—643 9   Chaouia-Ouardigha region

> Including Ben Slimane province, Khouribga province, Settat province

—644   Tadla-Azilal region

> Including Azilal province, Béni Mellal province

> Class here *High Atlas Mountains

—645   Meknès-Tafilalt region

> Including Errachidia province (Rachidia province), Hajeb province, Ifrane province, Khénifra province; Ismaïlia prefecture, Meknès-El Menzeh prefecture

—646   Southwestern regions of Morocco

> *For regions in Western Sahara, claimed by Morocco, see —648*

—646 2   Doukkala-Abda region

> Including Jadīda province, Safi province

---

*For a specific part of this jurisdiction, region, or feature, see the part and follow instructions under —4–9

—646 4   Marrakech-Tensift-El Haouz region

> Including Chichaoua province, Essaouira province, Haouz province, Kelâat Es-Sraghna province (Kelaa des Srarhna province); Marrakech-Médina prefecture, Marrakech-Ménara prefecture, Sidi-Youssef-Ben-Ali prefecture

—646 6   Souss Massa-Draâ region

> Including Ouarzazate province, Taroudant province, Tiznit province, Zagora province; Agadir Idda Outanane prefecture, Chtouka-Aït Baha prefecture, Inezgane-Aït Melloul prefecture

—646 8   Guelmim-Es Semara region

> Including Assa-Zag province, Guelmim province, Tan-Tan province, Tata province

> *For Es Semara province (Smara province), see —648*

—648   Western Sahara

> Claimed by Morocco

> Including Laâyoune-Bojador-Sakia El-Hamra region, Oued Eddahab-Lagouira region; Ad Dakhla province, Bojador province (Boujdour province), Es Semara province (Smara province), Laâyoune province

—649   Canary Islands

> Including Las Palmas province of Spain, Santa Cruz de Tenerife province of Spain

—65   **Algeria**

> (Options: Class here Mauretania; prefer —3971. Class here Algeria to 647, Mauretania Caesariensis; prefer —39714)

—651   Northwestern provinces of Algeria

> Including Aïn Temouchent, Mascara, Mostaganem, Oran, Relizane, Saïda, Sidi Bel Abbès, Tiaret, Tissemsilt, Tlemcen

—653   North central provinces of Algeria

> Including Aïn Defla, Algiers (Jaza'ir), Blida (Boulaida), Bouira, Boumerdes, Cheliff (Chlef, El Asnam, Orléansville), Djelfa, Médéa, Tipaza, Tizi-Ouzou

—655   Northeastern provinces of Algeria

> Including Annaba (Bône), Batna, Bejaïa (Bougie), Biskra, Bordj Bou Arréridj, Constantine (Qacentina), Guelma, Jījil (Jijel), Khenchela, Mila, M'Sila, Oum el Bouaghi, Sétif, Skikda, Souk Ahras, Tarf, Tébessa

> (Option: Class here northeastern provinces of Algeria to 647, Numidia; prefer —3972)

—657   Sahara provinces of Algeria

> Including Adrar, Bayadh, Béchar, Ghardaia, Illizi, Laghouat, Naâma, Ouargla, Oued, Tamanrasset, Tindouf

> (Option: Class here Sahara provinces of Algeria to 647, Gaetulia; prefer —3977)

—66   **West Africa and offshore islands**

> Class here *Sahara Desert, *Sahel

> Subdivisions are added for west Africa and offshore islands together, for west Africa alone

SUMMARY

—**661**	**Mauritania**
—**662**	**Mali, Burkina Faso, Niger**
—**663**	**Senegal**
—**664**	**Sierra Leone**
—**665**	**Gambia, Guinea, Guinea-Bissau, Cape Verde**
—**666**	**Liberia and Côte d'Ivoire**
—**667**	**Ghana**
—**668**	**Togo and Benin**
—**669**	**Nigeria**

—661   Mauritania

> Including Nouakchott

—662   Mali, Burkina Faso, Niger

> Class here *Niger River

—662 3   Mali

> Including Bamako

—662 5   Burkina Faso

> Including Bobo-Dioulasso, Ouagadougou

—662 6   Niger

> Including Niamey

—663   Senegal

> Including Dakar region, Diourbel region, Fatick region, Kaolack region, Kolda region, Louga region, Saint-Louis region, Tambacounda region, Thiès region, Ziguinchor region

> Class here Senegambia

> *For Gambia, see —6651*

—664   Sierra Leone

> Including Freetown

*For a specific part of this jurisdiction, region, or feature, see the part and follow instructions under —4–9

—665   Gambia, Guinea, Guinea-Bissau, Cape Verde

       Class here *Upper Guinea area

—665 1   Gambia

       Including Banjul

       Class here *Gambia River

—665 2   Guinea

       Including Conakry, Kankan

—665 7   Guinea-Bissau

       Including Bissau

—665 8   Cape Verde

       Including Praia

       Class here Cape Verde Islands

—666   Liberia and Côte d'Ivoire

—666 2   Liberia

       Including Monrovia

—666 8   Côte d'Ivoire (Ivory Coast)

       Including Abidjan, Bouaké, Yamoussoukro

—667   Ghana

       Including Accra, Kumasi; British Togoland

       Class here *Volta River

—668   Togo and Benin

—668 1   Togo

       Including Lomé

       Class here French Togoland, comprehensive works on Togoland

       For British Togoland, see —667

—668 3   Benin

       Including Cotonou, Porto-Novo

—669   Nigeria

—669 1   Lagos State

       Class here Lagos

—669 2   Western states of Nigeria

—669 23   Ogun State

*For a specific part of this jurisdiction, region, or feature, see the part and follow instructions under —4–9

—669 25	Oyo State
	Including Ibadan
—669 26	Osun State
—669 27	Ekiti State
—669 28	Ondo State
—669 3	Bendel states
—669 32	Edo State
	Including Benin City
—669 36	Delta State
—669 4	Eastern states of Nigeria
—669 41	Bayelsa State
—669 42	Rivers State
	Including Port Harcourt
—669 43	Akwa Ibom State
—669 44	Cross River State
	Including Calabar
—669 45	Abia State
—669 46	Imo State
—669 47	Ebonyi State
—669 48	Anambra State
—669 49	Enugu State
	Including Enugu
—669 5	Plateau State, Nassarawa State, Benue State, Kwara State
—669 52	Plateau State
	Including Jos
—669 53	Nassarawa State
—669 54	Benue State
	Including Makurdi
—669 56	Kogi State
—669 57	Kwara State
	Including Ilorin
—669 6	Zamfara State, Sokoto State, Kebbi State, Niger State; Federal Capital Territory
—669 61	Zamfara State

—669 62	Sokoto State
	Including Sokoto
—669 63	Kebbi State
—669 65	Niger State
	Including Minna
—669 68	Federal Capital Territory
	Class here Abuja
—669 7	Kaduna State, Katsina State, Jigawa State, Kano State
—669 73	Kaduna State
	Including Kaduna
—669 76	Katsina State
—669 77	Jigawa State
—669 78	Kano State
	Including Kano
—669 8	Bauchi State, Gombe State, Borno State, Yobe State, Adamawa State, Taraba State
—669 82	Bauchi State
—669 84	Gombe State
—669 85	Borno State
	Including Maiduguri
—669 87	Yobe State
—669 88	Adamawa State
—669 89	Taraba State

—67   **Central Africa and offshore islands**

Class here *Black Africa, *Sub-Saharan Africa (Africa south of the Sahara)

Subdivisions are added for central Africa and offshore islands together, for central Africa alone

*For a specific part of this jurisdiction, region, or feature, see the part and follow instructions under —4–9

SUMMARY

—671   Cameroon, Sao Tome and Principe, Equatorial Guinea

Class here Islands of Gulf of Guinea, *Lower Guinea area

See also —16373 for Gulf of Guinea

—671 1   Cameroon

Including Douala, Yaoundé

—671 5   Sao Tome and Principe

Including São Tomé

—671 8   Equatorial Guinea

—671 83   Río Muni

—671 86   Bioko island (Fernando Po island) and Annobón island (Pagalu island)

Including Malabo

—672   Gabon and Republic of the Congo

—672 1   Gabon

Including Libreville

—672 4   Republic of the Congo

Including Brazzaville

See also —6751 for Democratic Republic of the Congo

—673   Angola

—673 1   Cabinda province

Exclave of Angola

—673 2   Northern provinces of Angola

Including Bengo, Cuanza Norte, Cuanza Sul, Luanda, Uíge, Zaire; Luanda (capital city)

For Cabinda province, see —6731

*For a specific part of this jurisdiction, region, or feature, see the part and follow instructions under —4–9

—673 4	Central provinces of Angola
	Including Benguela, Bié, Huambo, Lunda Norte, Lunda Sul, Malanje, Moxico
—673 5	Southern provinces of Angola
	Including Cuando Cubango (Kuando Kubango), Cunene (Kunene), Huíla, Namibe
—674	Central African Republic and Chad
—674 1	Central African Republic
	Including Bangui
—674 3	Chad
	Including Djamena
—675	Democratic Republic of the Congo, Rwanda, Burundi
—675 1	Democratic Republic of the Congo
	Former name: Zaire
	Class here *Congo (Zaire) River
	See also —6724 for Republic of the Congo
—675 11	Bas-Congo province, Bandundu province, Kinshasa
—675 112	Kinshasa
—675 114	Bas-Congo province
—675 116	Bandundu province
—675 12	Kasaï-Occidental province and Kasaï-Oriental province
—675 123	Kasaï-Occidental province
—675 126	Kasaï-Oriental province
—675 13	Équateur province
—675 15	Orientale province
—675 17	Maniema province, Nord-Kivu province, Sud-Kivu province
	Including *Lake Kivu
—675 18	Katanga province
	Including Lubumbashi; *Lake Mweru
—675 7	Rwanda and Burundi
—675 71	Rwanda
	Including Kigali

*For a specific part of this jurisdiction, region, or feature, see the part and follow instructions under —4–9

—675 72	Burundi
	Including Bujumbura
—676	Uganda and Kenya
	Class here *East Africa, *Great Rift Valley
—676 1	Uganda
	Including Kampala
—676 2	Kenya
—676 22	North-Eastern Province
—676 23	Coast Province
	Including Mombasa
—676 24	Eastern Province
—676 25	Nairobi
—676 26	Central Province
—676 27	Rift Valley Province
	Including *Lake Turkana (Rudolf)
—676 28	Western Province
—676 29	Nyanza Province
—677	Djibouti and Somalia
	Class here Somaliland
—677 1	Djibouti
	Including Djibouti (city)
—677 3	Somalia
	Including Mogadishu
—678	Tanzania
—678 1	Zanzibar Region and Pemba Region
	Including Pemba North, Pemba South, Zanzibar Central/South, Zanzibar North, Zanzibar Urban/West
—678 2	Mainland regions of Tanzania
	Former name: Tanganyika
—678 22	Tanga Region
—678 23	Dar es Salaam Region and Pwani Region
	Variant name for Pwani Region: Coast Region

*For a specific part of this jurisdiction, region, or feature, see the part and follow instructions under
  —4–9

—678 232	Dar es Salaam Region
	Class here Dar es Salaam
—678 24	Lindi Region and Mtwara Region
—678 25	South central regions of Tanzania
	Including Iringa Region, Morogoro Region, Ruvuma Region
—678 26	North central regions of Tanzania
	Including Arusha Region, Dodoma Region, Kilimanjaro Region, Singida Region; Kilimanjaro National Park; *Mount Kilimanjaro
—678 27	Regions of Tanzania adjacent to Lake Victoria
	Including Kagera Region (West Lake Region, Ziwa Magharibi Region), Mara Region, Mwanza Region; Serengeti National Park
	Class here *Lake Victoria
—678 28	Western regions of Tanzania
	Including Kigoma Region, Mbeya Region, Rukwa Region, Shinyanga Region, Tabora Region; *Lake Tanganyika
—679	Mozambique
	Including *Zambezi River
—679 1	Maputo province
	Class here Maputo; *Komati River; Pongola River (Rio Maputo) in Mozambique
—679 2	Gaza province
	Class here *Limpopo River
—679 3	Inhambane province
—679 4	Manica province and Sofala province
—679 5	Tete province
—679 6	Zambézia province
—679 7	Nampula province
—679 8	Cabo Delgado province
—679 9	Niassa province
—68	**Republic of South Africa and neighboring southern African countries**
	Class here southern Africa
	Subdivisions are added for Republic of South Africa and neighboring southern African countries together, for Republic of South Africa alone

*For a specific part of this jurisdiction, region, or feature, see the part and follow instructions under —4–9

SUMMARY

—682	**Gauteng, North-West, Limpopo, Mpumalanga, former homelands (national states) of Republic of South Africa**
—684	**KwaZulu-Natal**
—685	**Free State**
—687	**Northern Cape, Western Cape, Eastern Cape**
—688	**Namibia, Botswana, Lesotho, Swaziland**
—689	**Zimbabwe, Zambia, Malawi**

>   —682–687   Republic of South Africa

Class comprehensive works on Republic of South Africa in —68; class comprehensive works on Orange River in —6871

—682   Gauteng, North-West, Limpopo, Mpumalanga, former homelands (national states) of Republic of South Africa

Class here former Transvaal; *Highveld regions of South Africa; *Vaal River

—682 2   Gauteng

Class here Witwatersrand

—682 21   Johannesburg district

Including Soweto

Class here Johannesburg

—682 22   Krugersdorp district, Oberholzer district, Randfontein district, Roodepoort district, Westonaria district

Class here *West Rand, Far Western Rand

—682 23   Heidelberg district, Vanderbijlpark district, Vereeniging district

Class here *Vaal Triangle

—682 24   Brakpan district, Nigel district, Springs district

Class here *Ekurhuleni (East Rand)

—682 25   Alberton district, Benoni district, Boksburg district, Germiston district, Kempton Park district

—682 26   Randburg district

—682 27   Pretoria district

Class here Pretoria, *Tshwane

—682 28   Soshanguve district and Wonderboom district

—682 29   Bronkhorstspruit district and Cullinan district

*For a specific part of this jurisdiction, region, or feature, see the part and follow instructions under —4–9

—682 4   North-West

                        Class here former *Bophuthatswana

—682 41   Bafokeng district, Brits district, Moretele I district, Odi district, Rustenburg district

                        See also —68275 for Moretele II district

—682 42   Koster district, Potchefstroom district, Ventersdorp district

—682 43   Klerksdorp district

—682 44   Coligny district, Delareyville district, Ditsobotla district, Lichtenburg district

—682 45   Bloemhof district, Christiana district, Schweizer-Reneke district, Wolmaransstad district

—682 46   Ganyesa district, Kudumane district (Thlaping Tlaro district), Taung district, Vryburg district

—682 47   Molopo district

—682 48   Northern districts of North-West

                        Including Lehurutshe district, Madikwe district, Mankwe district, Marico district, Swartruggens district; Pilanesberg National Park; *Marico River

—682 5   Limpopo

                        Class here *Limpopo River in South Africa

—682 51   Bela-Bela district and Thabazimbi district

                        Former name of Bela-Bela district: Warmbad district (Warmbaths district)

—682 53   Lephlale district (Ellisras district), Mokerong district, Mokopane district (Potgietersrus district), Waterberg district

                        Including *Mogalakwena River

—682 55   Nebo district, Sekhukhuneland district, Thabamoopo district

                        Including Sekhukhuneberg Range

                        Class here former *Lebowa

—682 56   Bochum district, Polokwane district, Seshego district

—682 57   Northeastern districts of Limpopo

                        Including Dzanani district, Hlanganani district, Malamulele district, Musina district (Messina district), Mutale district, Sekgosese district, Soutpansberg district, Thohoyandou district, Vuwani district

                        Class here former Venda; Soutpansberg

---

*For a specific part of this jurisdiction, region, or feature, see the part and follow instructions under —4–9

—682 59   Southeastern districts of Limpopo

> Including Bolobedu district, Giyani district, Letaba district, Lulekani district, Mapulaneng district, Mhala district, Namakgale district, Naphuno district, Phalaborwa district, Ritavi district

> Class here former *Gazankulu; *Lowveld regions of South Africa

—682 7   Mpumalanga

> Class here *Drakensberg Mountains in Mpumalanga

—682 71   Nsikazi district, Pelgrimsrus 1 district (Pilgrim's Rest 1 district), Witrivier district (White River district)

> Including *Lebombo Mountains; *Crocodile River, *Sabie River

> Class here *Kruger National Park

> *See also —68274 for Pelgrimsrus 2 district (Pilgrim's Rest 2 district)*

—682 72   Barberton district, Eerstehoek district, Nkomazi district (Kamhlushwa district)

> Including *Komati River in South Africa

> Class here former KaNgwane

> *For Nsikazi district, see —68271*

—682 73   Nelspruit district

—682 74   Belfast district, Lydenburg district, Pelgrimsrus 2 district (Pilgrim's Rest 2 district), Waterval-Boven district

> *See also —68271 for Pelgrimsrus 1 district (Pilgrim's Rest 1 district)*

—682 75   Northwestern districts of Mpumalanga

> Including Groblersdal district, Kwamhlanga district, Mbibana district, Mdutjana district, Mkobola district, Mortele II district, Moutse district

> Class here former KwaNdebele

> *See also —68241 for Moretele I district*

—682 76   Middelburg district and Witbank district

—682 77   Balfour district, Delmas district, Hoëveldrif district (Highveld Ridge district), Kriel district

—682 78   Bethal district, Carolina district, Ermelo district

—682 79   Southern districts of Mpumalanga

> Including Amersfoort district, Piet Retief district, Standerton district, Volksrust district, Wakkerstroom district

---

*For a specific part of this jurisdiction, region, or feature, see the part and follow instructions under —4–9

—682 9   Former homelands (Former national states)

                Use only if the work covers pre-1997 periods

                For a specific homeland or part of a homeland, see the homeland or the part, e.g., Ciskei —68755

—684   KwaZulu-Natal

                Former name: Natal

                Province of Republic of South Africa

                Class here former KwaZulu; Zululand; *Tugela River

—684 1   Northwestern districts of KwaZulu-Natal

                Including Dannhauser district, Dundee district, Glencoe district, Newcastle district, Utrecht district

                Class here *Blood River

—684 2   North central districts of KwaZulu-Natal

                Including Babanango district, Ngotshe district, Nqutu district, Paulpietersburg district, Simdlangentsha district, Vryheid districts; *Pongola River

                For Pongola River (Rio Maputo) in Mozambique, see —6791

—684 3   Northeastern districts of KwaZulu-Natal

                Including Hlabisa district, Ingwavuma district, Lower Umfolozi district, Mhlabatini district, Mtonjaneni district, Nongoma district, Ubombo district; Maputaland, Tongaland; Hluhluwe Game Reserve, Mkuze Game Reserve, Ndumu Game Reserve, Umfolozi Game Reserve; Greater Saint Lucia Wetland Park

—684 4   *North Coast districts

                Including Eshowe district, Inanda district, Lower Tugela district, Mapumulu district, Mtunzini district, Ndwedwe district

—684 5   Southern coastal districts of KwaZulu-Natal

                Including Chatsworth district, Pinetown district, Port Shepstone district, Umbumbulu district, Umlazi district, Umzinto district; Oribi Gorge Nature Reserve

                Class here *South Coast (area south of Durban to Port Edward)

—684 55   Durban district

                Including Amanzimtoti, Kingsburgh

                Class here Durban; *Durban-Pinetown industrial area

—684 6   Alfred district and Mount Currie district

                Class here *Griqualand East

*For a specific part of this jurisdiction, region, or feature, see the part and follow instructions under —4–9

—684 7   Natal Midlands district

                          Including Bergville district, Camperdown district, Estcourt district, Impendle district, Ixopo district, Kliprivier district, Kranskop district, Lions River district, Mooirivier district, Msinga district, New Hanover district, Nkandla district, Polela district, Richmond district, Umvoti district, Underberg district, Weenen districts

                          Including Natal Drakensberg Park, Royal Natal National Park; Giant's Castle Game Reserve; *Mgeni River

                          Class here *Drakensberg Mountains

—684 75   Pietermaritzburg district

                          Including Albert Falls and Nature Reserve

—685   Free State

                          Former name: Orange Free State

                          Province of Republic of South Africa

—685 1   Northeastern districts of Free State

                          Including Bethlehem district, Ficksburg district, Fouriesburg district, Frankfort district, Harrismith district, Lindley district, Reitz district, Senekal district, Vrede districts, Witsieshoek district; former homelands of Orange Free State, former Qwaqwa; Golden Gate Highlands National Park

                          Class here *Northeastern Orange Free State

—685 2   Northern districts of Free State

                          Including Bothaville district, Heilbron district, Koppies district, Kroonstad district, Parys district, Viljoenskroon district, Vredefort district

                          Class here *Northern Orange Free State

—685 25   Sasolburg district

—685 3   North central districts of Free State

                          Including Brandfort district, Bultfontein district, Hennenman district, Hoopstad district, Odendaalsrus district, Theunissen district, Ventersburg district, Virginia district, Wesselsbron district, Winburg district; Willem Pretorius Game Reserve

—685 35   Welkom district

—685 4   Bloemfontein district

—685 5   East central districts of Free State

                          Including Clocolan district, Excelsior district, Ladybrand district, Marquard district, Thaba Nchu district

*For a specific part of this jurisdiction, region, or feature, see the part and follow instructions under
   —4–9

—685 6   Southeastern districts of Free State

                  Including Botshabelo district, Dewetsdorp district, Reddersburg district,
                  Rouxville district, Smithfield district, Wepener district, Zastron district

                  Class here *Caledon River

                  For Caledon River in Lesotho, see —6885

—685 7   Southwestern districts of Free State

                  Including Bethulie district, Edenburg district, Fauresmith district,
                  Jagersfontein district, Petrusburg district, Philippolis district,
                  Trompsburg district

—685 8   Boshof district, Jacobsdal district, Koffiefontein district

—687   Northern Cape, Western Cape, Eastern Cape

                  Provinces of Republic of South Africa

                  Class here former Cape of Good Hope

—687 1   Northern Cape

                  Class here *Orange River

—687 11   Northeastern districts of Northern Cape

                  Including Barkly West district, Hartswater district, Hay district,
                  Herbert district, Kimberley district, Kuruman district, Postmasburg
                  district, Warrenton district; Vaalbos National Park; *Harts River

                  Class here *Kalahari Desert in South Africa

                  Class comprehensive works on Kalahari Desert in —6883

—687 12   Gordonia district, Kenhardt district, Prieska district

                  Including Augrabies National Park, Kgalagadi Transfrontier Park
                  (Kalahari Gemsbok National Park)

—687 13   Eastern Upper Karoo districts

                  Including Britstown district, Colesberg district, De Aar district,
                  Hanover district, Hopetown district, Noupoort district, Philipstown
                  district, Richmond district; *Vanderkloof (P. K. le Roux) Dam

                  Class here *Upper Karoo

                  For western Upper Karoo districts, see —68717

—687 17   Western Upper Karoo districts

                  Including Calvinia district, Carnarvon district, Fraserburg district,
                  Sutherland district, Victoria West district, Williston district;
                  Tankwa-Karoo National Park; *Bokkeveld Range, *Nuweveld
                  Range, *Roggeveld Range

---

*For a specific part of this jurisdiction, region, or feature, see the part and follow instructions under
  —4–9

—687 19   Namaqualand district

                        Including Ais-Ais/Richtersveld Transfrontier Park (Richtersveld
                        National Park)

—687 3   Western Cape

—687 31   Clanwilliam district, Vanrhynsdorp district, Vredendal district

                        Class here *Cedarberg

—687 32   West central districts of Western Cape

                        Including Hopefield district, Malmesbury district, Moorreesburg
                        district, Piquetberg district, Vredenburg district; West Coast National
                        Park

—687 33   North central districts of Western Cape

                        Including Ceres district, Montagu district, Robertson district,
                        Tulbagh district, Worcester district

—687 34   Paarl district, Somerset West district, Stellenbosch district, Strand
                        district, Wellington district

                        Including *Boland

—687 35   Cape Peninsula districts

                        Including Bellville district, Goodwood district, Kuils River district,
                        Mitchell's Plain district, Simonstown district, Wynberg district;
                        Crossroads; Cape of Good Hope; Robben Island

                        Class here Cape Metropolitan Area

—687 355   Cape district

                        Including Kirstenbosch Botanic Gardens, Table Mountain

                        Class here Cape Town

—687 36   South central districts of Western Cape

                        Including Bredasdorp district, Caledon district, Heidelberg district,
                        Hermanus district, Swellendam district; Bontebok National Park;
                        Overberg

—687 37   Southeastern districts of Western Cape

                        Including George district, Knysna district, Mosselbaai (Mossel Bay)
                        district, Riversdale district; Knysna National Lake Area (Knysna
                        Lakes National Park), Wilderness National Park

                        Class here *Garden Route

—687 38   Little Karoo

                        Including Calitzdorp district, Ladismith district, Oudtshoorn district,
                        Uniondale district

---

*For a specific part of this jurisdiction, region, or feature, see the part and follow instructions under
  —4–9

—687 39   Great Karoo districts

                           Including Beaufort West district, Laingsburg district, Murraysburg
                           district, Prince Albert district; Karoo National Park

                           Class here *Great Karoo, the *Karoo

—687 5   Eastern Cape

                           Class here homelands (national states [South Africa]); Kaffraria

—687 51   Southwestern districts of Eastern Cape

                           Including Hankey district, Humansdorp district, Jansenville district,
                           Joubertina district, Steytlerville district, Willowmore district;
                           Tsitsikamma National Park (Tsitsikamma Forest and Coastal
                           National Park)

—687 52   Port Elizabeth district and Uitenhage district

                           Class here Nelson Mandela Bay Municipality (Port
                           Elizabeth-Uitenhage-Despatch industrial area)

—687 53   Southeastern districts of Eastern Cape

                           Including Adelaide district, Albany district, Alexandria district,
                           Bathurst district, Bedford district, Fort Beaufort district, Kirkwood
                           district, Somerset East district; Addo Elephant National Park,
                           Zuurberg National Park

—687 54   Northwestern districts of Eastern Cape

                           Including Aberdeen district, Cradock district, Graaff-Reinet district,
                           Middelburg district, Pearston district; Mountain Zebra National Park

—687 55   Central districts of Eastern Cape

                           Including Cathcart district, Hewu district, Keiskammahoek district,
                           King William's Town district, Komga district, Mdantsane district,
                           Middledrift district, Molteno district, Mpofu district, Ntabethemba
                           district, Peddie district, Queenstown district, Sterkstroom district,
                           Stutterheim district, Tarka district, Victoria East district, Zwelitsha
                           district; *Stormberg

                           Class here former Ciskei

—687 555   East London district

—687 56   North central districts of Eastern Cape

                           Including Albert district, Aliwal North district, Hofmeyr district,
                           Lady Grey district, Sterkspruit district (Herschel district), Steynsburg
                           district, Venterstad district

—687 57   Northeastern districts of Eastern Cape

                           Including Barkly East district, Elliot district, Indwe district, Maclear
                           district, Wodehouse district

*For a specific part of this jurisdiction, region, or feature, see the part and follow instructions under
   —4–9

—687 58   Former Transkei

Including Butterworth district, Cala district, Cofimvaba district, Elliotdale district, Engcobo district, Idutywa district, Kentani district, Lady Frere district, Libode district, Mqanduli district, Mthatha (Umtata) district, Ngqeleni district, Nqamakwe district, Port St. Johns district, Qumbu district, Tsolo district, Tsomo district, Willowvale district; *Great Kei River

Class here Pondoland

For Sterkspruit district, see —68756; for Bizana district, Flagstaff district, Lusikisiki district, Maluti district, Mount Ayliff district, Mount Fletcher district, Mount Frere district, Tabankulu district, Umzimkulu district, see —68759

—687 59   Eastern districts of Eastern Cape

Including Bizana district, Flagstaff district, Lusikisiki district, Maluti district, Mount Ayliff district, Mount Fletcher district, Mount Frere district, Tabankulu district, Umzimkulu district

—688   Namibia, Botswana, Lesotho, Swaziland

—688 1   Namibia

Including Windhoek

—688 3   Botswana

Including Gaborone

Class here *Kalahari Desert

—688 5   Lesotho

Including Maseru

—688 7   Swaziland

Including Mbabane

—689   Zimbabwe, Zambia, Malawi

—689 1   Zimbabwe

Including Manicaland Province, Mashonaland Central Province, Mashonaland East Province, Mashonaland West Province, Masvingo Province, Matabeleland North Province, Matabeleland South Province, Midlands Province; Bulawayo, Harare; Victoria Falls

For Victoria Falls in Zambia, see —6894

—689 4   Zambia

Including Central Province, Copperbelt Province, Eastern Province, Luapula Province, Lusaka Province, North-Western Province, Northern Province, Southern Province, Western Province; Lusaka

---

*For a specific part of this jurisdiction, region, or feature, see the part and follow instructions under —4–9

—689 7   Malawi

                         Including Blantyre, Lilongwe

                         Class here *Lake Nyasa (Lake Malawi)

—69   South Indian Ocean islands

—691   Madagascar

                         Including Antananarivo province, Antsiranana province, Fianarantsoa
                         province, Mahajanga province, Toamasina province, Toliara province;
                         Antananarivo (capital city)

—694   Comoro Islands

—694 1   Comoros (Federal and Islamic Republic of the Comoros)

                         Including Moroni

—694 5   Mayotte

—696   Seychelles

                         Including Victoria; Aldabra Island, Mahé Island

—697   Chagos Islands

—698   Réunion and Mauritius

                         Class here Mascarene Islands

—698 1   Réunion

                         Overseas department of France

                         Including Saint-Denis

—698 2   Mauritius

                         Including Port Louis; Cargados Carajos Shoals, Rodrigues Island

—699   Isolated islands

                         Including Amsterdam Island, Cocos Islands (Keeling Islands), Crozet
                         Islands, Kerguelen Islands, Prince Edward Islands, Saint Paul Island

—7   North America

                   Class here comprehensive works on North and South America

                   Class Western Hemisphere (North and South America, plus parts of Atlantic and
                   Pacific Oceans) in —1812

                   For South America, see —8

---

*For a specific part of this jurisdiction, region, or feature, see the part and follow instructions under
—4–9

SUMMARY

—71	**Canada**
—711	**British Columbia**
—712	**Prairie Provinces**
—713	**Ontario**
—714	**Quebec**
—715	**Atlantic Provinces**
—716	**Nova Scotia**
—717	**Prince Edward Island**
—718	**Newfoundland and Labrador, Saint Pierre and Miquelon**
—719	**Northern territories**
—72	**Mexico, Central America, West Indies, Bermuda**
—721	**Northern states of Mexico**
—722	**Lower California peninsula**
—723	**Central Pacific states of Mexico**
—724	**Central states of Mexico**
—725	**Valley of Mexico**
—726	**Southern Gulf states of Mexico**
—727	**Southern Pacific states of Mexico**
—728	**Central America**
—729	**West Indies (Antilles) and Bermuda**
—73	**United States**
—74	**Northeastern United States (New England and Middle Atlantic states)**
—741	**Maine**
—742	**New Hampshire**
—743	**Vermont**
—744	**Massachusetts**
—745	**Rhode Island**
—746	**Connecticut**
—747	**New York**
—748	**Pennsylvania**
—749	**New Jersey**
—75	**Southeastern United States (South Atlantic states)**
—751	**Delaware**
—752	**Maryland**
—753	**District of Columbia (Washington)**
—754	**West Virginia**
—755	**Virginia**
—756	**North Carolina**
—757	**South Carolina**
—758	**Georgia**
—759	**Florida**
—76	**South central United States**
—761	**Alabama**
—762	**Mississippi**
—763	**Louisiana**
—764	**Texas**
—766	**Oklahoma**
—767	**Arkansas**
—768	**Tennessee**
—769	**Kentucky**

—77	**North central United States**
—771	**Ohio**
—772	**Indiana**
—773	**Illinois**
—774	**Michigan**
—775	**Wisconsin**
—776	**Minnesota**
—777	**Iowa**
—778	**Missouri**
—78	**Western United States**
—781	**Kansas**
—782	**Nebraska**
—783	**South Dakota**
—784	**North Dakota**
—786	**Montana**
—787	**Wyoming**
—788	**Colorado**
—789	**New Mexico**
—79	**Great Basin and Pacific Slope of United States**
—791	**Arizona**
—792	**Utah**
—793	**Nevada**
—794	**California**
—795	**Oregon**
—796	**Idaho**
—797	**Washington**
—798	**Alaska**

—71   Canada

See Manual at T2—73 vs. T2—71

—711   British Columbia

Class here *Canadian Cordillera; *Rocky Mountains in Canada; *Rocky Mountain Trench

---

*For a specific part of this jurisdiction, region, or feature, see the part and follow instructions under —4–9

—711 1   Northern coastal region of British Columbia

       Coastal mainland and Coast Mountains from Alaska border to Powell River

       Including Central Coast Regional District, Skeena-Queen Charlotte Regional District; mainland part of Comox-Strathcona Regional District, mainland part of Mount Waddington Regional District; Kitimat-Stikine Regional District south of 54°30′ N

       Including Bella Coola, Kitimat, Ocean Falls, Prince Rupert; Cortes Island, Hardwicke Island, Maurelle Island, Read Island, East Redonda Island, West Redonda Island, Sonora Island, East Thurlow Island, West Thurlow Island; Bella Coola River

       Class here comprehensive works on Kitimat-Stikine Regional District; *Pacific Coast in Canada; *Coast Mountains

       For coasts of southwestern British Columbia, see —7113; for Kitimat-Stikine Regional District north of 54°30′ N, see —71185

       See also —16433 for Dixon Entrance, Hecate Strait, Inside Passage, Queen Charlotte Sound

—711 12   Haida Gwaii

       Former name: Queen Charlotte Islands

—711 2   Vancouver Island

       Including Alberni-Clayoquot Regional District, Nanaimo Regional District, Cowichan Valley Regional District; part of Comox-Strathcona Regional District on Vancouver Island, part of Mount Waddington Regional District on Vancouver Island

       Including Nanaimo; comprehensive works on Comox-Strathcona Regional District, comprehensive works on Mount Waddington Regional District; Pacific Rim National Park; Denman Island, Hope Island, Hornby Island, Malcolm Island, Nigei Island, Quadra Island; Koksilah River; Shawnigan Lake

       For mainland part of Comox-Strathcona Regional District, mainland part of Mount Waddington Regional District, see —7111

       See also —16433 for Strait of Georgia, Queen Charlotte Strait

—711 28   Victoria region

       Including Capital Regional District (Vancouver Island south of San Juan River, Koksilah River, and Shawnigan Lake)

       Including Central Saanich, Esquimalt, Metchosin, North Saanich, Oak Bay, Port Renfrew, Saanich, Sidney, Sooke, Victoria; Saanich Peninsula; *Gulf Islands; San Juan River; Sooke Lake

       See also —16432 for Strait of Juan de Fuca

—711 3   Southwestern region of British Columbia

       Class here *Fraser River, *Lillooet River

---

*For a specific part of this jurisdiction, region, or feature, see the part and follow instructions under —4–9

—711 31   Southern coastal region of British Columbia

Coastal mainland from Powell River to Howe Sound

Including Powell River Regional District, Squamish-Lillooet Regional District, Sunshine Coast Regional District

Including Lillooet, Pemberton, Powell River, Squamish, Whistler; *Garibaldi Provincial Park; Desolation Sound Provincial Marine Park; Anvil Island, Gambier Island, Hernando Island, Keats Island, Lasqueti Island, Texada Island; Malaspina Peninsula; Bridge River; Carpenter Lake, Lillooet Lake

—711 33   Metro Vancouver

Former name: Greater Vancouver Regional District

Including Burnaby, Coquitlam, Delta, Langley, Lions Bay, Maple Ridge, New Westminster, North Vancouver, Pitt Meadows, Port Coquitlam, Port Moody, Richmond, Surrey, West Vancouver, White Rock; Bowen Island

Class here Vancouver

—711 37   Fraser Valley Regional District

Including former Central Fraser Valley Regional District, former Dewdney-Alouette Regional District, former Fraser-Cheam Regional District

Including Abbotsford, Chilliwack, Hope, Mission; Golden Ears Provincial Park; Fraser Canyon; Coquihalla River, Nahatlatch River, *Pitt River; Harrison Lake

—711 5   Okanagan-Similkameen region

Including Central Okanagan Regional District, North Okanagan Regional District, Okanagan-Similkameen Regional District

Including Armstrong, Enderby, Kelowna, Osoyoos, Penticton, Princeton, Vernon; Manning Provincial Park; Shuswap River, Tulameen River; Okanagan Lake

Class here *Cascade Mountains in British Columbia

—711 6   Southeastern region of British Columbia

Class here *Columbia River in British Columbia

—711 62   West Kootenay region

Including Central Kootenay Regional District, Kootenay Boundary Regional District

Including Castlegar, Creston, Grand Forks, Greenwood, Nelson, Rossland, Trail; *Monashee Mountains; *Granby River, *Kettle River, *West Kettle River; Upper Arrow Lake, Lower Arrow Lake, Slocan Lake, Kootenay Lake

---

*For a specific part of this jurisdiction, region, or feature, see the part and follow instructions under —4–9

—711 65   East Kootenay Regional District

         Approximately the area drained by the upper Columbia River and upper Kootenay River

         Including Cranbrook, Invermere, Kimberley; Kootenay National Park

         Class here *Purcell Mountains; *Kootenay River

—711 68   Columbia-Shuswap Regional District

         Including Golden, Revelstoke, Salmon Arm; Glacier National Park, Mount Revelstoke National Park, Yoho National Park; Hamber Provincial Park; Illecillewaet River, Seymour River, Spillimacheen River; *Kinbasket (McNaughton) Lake, Shuswap Lake

         Class here *Selkirk Mountains

—711 7   Central interior region of British Columbia

         Class here *Cariboo Mountains

—711 72   Thompson-Nicola Regional District

         Approximately the area drained by the Thompson River and Nicola River

         Including Cache Creek, Chase, Clinton, Kamloops, Lytton, Merritt; Wells Gray Provincial Park; Bonaparte River, Clearwater River, Coldwater River, Nicola River, North Thompson River, South Thompson River, Thompson River; Adams Lake

—711 75   Cariboo Regional District

         Approximately the central Fraser Valley and the area drained by the Chilcotin River, Nazko River, and Quesnel River

         Including Anahim Lake, Barkerville, 100 Mile House, Quesnel, Wells, Williams Lake; Bowron Lake Provincial Park; Adams River, Chilcotin River, Chilko River, Horsefly River, Nazko River, Quesnel River, Taseko River, West Road River; Quesnel Lake

         Class here *Fraser Plateau

—711 8   Northern region of British Columbia

*For a specific part of this jurisdiction, region, or feature, see the part and follow instructions under
—4–9

—711 82   North central region of British Columbia

> Approximately the corridor formed by the Bulkley Valley, Nechako Valley, and Upper Fraser Valley

> Including Bulkley-Nechako Regional District, Fraser-Fort George Regional District

> Including Mackenzie, McBride, Prince George, Smithers, Valemount, Vanderhoof; Mount Robson Provincial Park, *Tweedsmuir Provincial Park; *Bulkley River, Chilako River, McGregor River, Morice River, Nation River, *Omineca River, Parsnip River; Morice Lake, Takla Lake; Nechako Reservoir

> Class here *Nechako Plateau; Nechako River

—711 85   Northwestern region of British Columbia

> Including Stikine Region, parts of Kitimat-Stikine Regional District north of 54°30′ N

> Including Hazelton, Stewart, Terrace; *Hazelton Mountains, *Omineca Mountains; Gataga River, Kechika River, Nass River, Osilinka River, Skeena River, Spatsizi River, *Stikine River, Sustut River

> Class here *Cassiar Mountains, *Skeena Mountains

—711 87   Northeastern region of British Columbia

> Including Northern Rockies (Fort Nelson-Liard) Regional Municipality, Peace River Regional District

> Including Dawson Creek, Fort Nelson, Fort St. John, Tumbler Ridge; Finlay River, Fort Nelson River, Ingenika River, Mesilinka River, Murray River, Pine River, Sukunka River; *Williston Lake

> Class here Peace River in British Columbia, *Liard River

—712   Prairie Provinces

> Class here *western Canada

—712 3   Alberta

—712 31   Northwestern region of Alberta

> Area north of 55° N, and west of 114° W

> Including Grande Prairie, Peace River; Lesser Slave Lake

> Class here *northern Alberta; *Peace River

—712 32   Northeastern region of Alberta

> Area north of 55° N, and east of 114° W

> Including Fort McMurray

> Class here *Wood Buffalo National Park; *Athabaska River

---

*For a specific part of this jurisdiction, region, or feature, see the part and follow instructions under —4–9

—712 33	Central region of Alberta
	Area between 55° N and 51° N
	Including Drumheller, Red Deer; Elk Island National Park; Lac La Biche
	Class here *Rocky Mountains in Alberta; *Bow River, *North Saskatchewan River, *Red Deer River
—712 332	Rocky Mountain parks region
	Including Banff; Banff National Park, Jasper National Park; Peter Lougheed Provincial Park; Willmore Wilderness Provincial Park; Kananaskis Country
	See also —71234 for Waterton Lakes National Park
—712 334	Edmonton
—712 338	Calgary
—712 34	Southern region of Alberta
	Area south of 51° N to international boundary
	Including Crowsnest Pass, Fort Macleod, Medicine Hat; Waterton Lakes National Park
712 345	Lethbridge
—712 4	Saskatchewan
—712 41	Northern region of Saskatchewan
	Area north of 55° N
	Class here *Lake Athabasca
—712 42	Central region of Saskatchewan
	Area between 55° N and 51° N
	Including Battlefords, Lloydminster, Prince Albert, Yorkton; *Lake Diefenbaker
	Class here *Saskatchewan River, *South Saskatchewan River
	For parts of Lloydminster in Alberta, see —71233
—712 425	Saskatoon
—712 43	Southwestern region of Saskatchewan
	Area south of 51° N, and west of 106° W
	Including Swift Current; *Cypress Hills

*For a specific part of this jurisdiction, region, or feature, see the part and follow instructions under —4–9

—712 44	Southeastern region of Saskatchewan
	Area south of 51° N, and east of 106° W
	Including Fort Qu'Appelle, Melville, Moose Jaw
—712 445	Regina
—712 7	Manitoba
—712 71	Northern region of Manitoba
	Area north of 55° N
	Including Churchill, Port Nelson, Thompson
	Class here *Churchill River, *Nelson River
—712 72	Central region of Manitoba
	Area between 55° N and 50° 30′ N
	Including Dauphin, Flin Flon, The Pas; Interlake region; *Lake Manitoba, *Lake Winnipeg, Lake Winnipegosis
	Class here *Canadian Shield in Manitoba
—712 73	Southwestern region of Manitoba
	Area south of 50° 30′ N, and west of 98° W
	Including Brandon, Minnedosa, Portage la Prairie
	Class here *Assiniboine River
—712 74	Southeastern region of Manitoba
	Area south of 50° 30′ N, and east of 98° W
	Including Selkirk; Whiteshell Provincial Park
	Class here *Red River of the North in Manitoba
—712 743	Winnipeg
—713	Ontario
	Including *Niagara Escarpment
	Class here *eastern Canada; *Great Lakes in Canada
	See Manual at T2—713 and T2—714
—713 1	Northern Ontario region and Georgian Bay region
	Including Patricia portion of Kenora District
	Class here Canadian Shield in Ontario, northern Ontario
	Subdivisions are added for either or both topics in heading
	See also —16327 for Hudson Bay, James Bay

*For a specific part of this jurisdiction, region, or feature, see the part and follow instructions under —4–9

>   —713 11–713 14 Northern Ontario region

    Class comprehensive works in —7131

—713 11   Northwestern Ontario

           Including *Lake of the Woods in Canada

              For Thunder Bay District, see —71312

—713 112   Kenora District

                 For Patricia portion of Kenora District, see —7131

—713 117   Rainy River District

—713 12   Thunder Bay District

           Class here *Lake Superior in Ontario

—713 13   Northeastern Ontario

              For clay belt, see —71314; for Parry Sound District, see —71315; for District Municipality of Muskoka, see —71316

—713 132   Algoma District

           Including *North Channel

—713 133   Sudbury District

           Class here City of Greater Sudbury (Regional Municipality of Sudbury)

—713 135   Manitoulin District

—713 14   Clay belt

—713 142   Cochrane District

           Including *Lake Abitibi

—713 144   Timiskaming District

—713 147   Nipissing District

           Including Algonquin Provincial Park; *Lake Nipissing

---

>   —713 15–713 18 Georgian Bay region

    Class comprehensive works in —7131

—713 15   Parry Sound District

           Class here *Georgian Bay

—713 16   District Municipality of Muskoka

---

*For a specific part of this jurisdiction, region, or feature, see the part and follow instructions under —4–9

—713 17	Simcoe County
—713 18	Grey County

>	—713 2–713 8 Southern Ontario

Class comprehensive works in —713

For Simcoe County, see —71317; for Grey County, see —71318

—713 2	Lake Huron region

Class here *Southwestern Ontario; *Lake Huron in Ontario

—713 21	Bruce County
—713 22	Huron County
—713 23	Perth County
—713 25	Middlesex County

For London, see —71326

—713 26	London
—713 27	Lambton County

Including *Saint Clair River in Ontario

—713 3	Lake Erie region

Class here *Lake Erie in Ontario

—713 31	Essex County

Including *Lake Saint Clair in Ontario

For Windsor, see —71332

—713 32	Windsor
—713 33	Municipality of Chatham-Kent

Former name: Kent County

—713 34	Elgin County
—713 36	Norfolk County

Class here former *Regional Municipality of Haldimand-Norfolk

—713 37	Haldimand County

*For a specific part of this jurisdiction, region, or feature, see the part and follow instructions under
  —4–9

—713 38	Regional Municipality of Niagara
	Including Niagara Falls (city); Niagara River; Welland Canal
	Class here *Niagara Peninsula
	For Niagara Falls (physiographic feature), see —71339; for Niagara River in New York, see —74798
—713 39	Niagara Falls
	Physiographic feature
	For Niagara Falls in New York, see —74799
—713 4	West central region of Ontario
—713 41	Dufferin County
—713 42	Wellington County
	For Guelph, see —71343
—713 43	Guelph
—713 44	Regional Municipality of Waterloo
	For Kitchener, Waterloo (city), see —71345
—713 45	Kitchener-Waterloo
	Including Waterloo (city)
	Class here Kitchener
—713 46	Oxford County
—713 47	Brant County
—713 5	Lake Ontario region
	Class here *Lake Ontario in Ontario
—713 52	City of Hamilton
	Former name: Regional Municipality of Hamilton-Wentworth
	Class here former Wentworth County; Hamilton
—713 53	Regional Municipality of Halton and Regional Municipality of Peel
—713 533	Regional Municipality of Halton
—713 535	Regional Municipality of Peel
—713 54	City of Toronto and Regional Municipality of York
	Class here former York County

*For a specific part of this jurisdiction, region, or feature, see the part and follow instructions under —4–9

—713 541	City of Toronto
	Including East York, Etobicoke, North York, Scarborough, York
	Class here Toronto
—713 547	Regional Municipality of York
—713 56	Regional Municipality of Durham
—713 57	Northumberland County
	Including *Rice Lake
—713 58	Hastings County and Prince Edward County
—713 585	Hastings County
—713 587	Prince Edward County
—713 59	Lennox and Addington County
—713 6	East central region of Ontario
—713 61	Haliburton County
—713 64	City of Kawartha Lakes
	Former name: Victoria County
	Class comprehensive works on Kawartha Lakes (physiographic feature) in —71367
—713 67	Peterborough County
	Class here *Kawartha Lakes
	See also —71364 for City of Kawartha Lakes
—713 7	Saint Lawrence River region
	Class here *Eastern Ontario; *Thousand Islands in Ontario; *Saint Lawrence River in Ontario; *Saint Lawrence Seaway in Ontario
—713 71	Frontenac County
	For Kingston, see —71372
—713 72	Kingston
—713 73	United Counties of Leeds and Grenville
—713 75	United Counties of Stormont, Dundas and Glengarry
—713 8	Ottawa River region
	Class here *Ottawa River
—713 81	Renfrew County
—713 82	Lanark County

*For a specific part of this jurisdiction, region, or feature, see the part and follow instructions under —4–9

—713 84	City of Ottawa
	Former name: Regional Municipality of Ottawa-Carleton
	Class here Ottawa; comprehensive works on National Capital Region
	For National Capital Region in Quebec province, see —714221
—713 85	United Counties of Prescott and Russell
—714	Quebec
	Class here *Canadian Shield; *Saint Lawrence River; *Saint Lawrence Seaway
	See also —16344 for Gulf of Saint Lawrence
	See Manual at T2—713 and T2—714
—714 1	Northern region of Quebec
—714 11	Nord-du-Québec region
	Former name: New Quebec
	Class here former Nouveau-Québec Administrative Region
	See also —7182 for Labrador
—714 111	Extreme northern region of Quebec
	Area north of 55° N
	Including Hudson Bay Region, Ungava Bay Region
	Class here Kativik Regional Administration, Nunavik Region
	See also —16327 for Hudson, Ungava Bays
—714 115	James Bay region
	Including Baie-James, Chibougamau, Lebel-sur-Quévillon, Matagami
	Class here mid-northern region of Quebec
—714 117	Caniapiscau Regional County Municipality
	Including Gagnon, Schefferville
—714 13	Abitibi-Témiscamingue regional county municipalities and City of Rouyn-Noranda
—714 132	Abitibi-Ouest Regional County Municipality
—714 134	Abitibi Regional County Municipality
—714 136	City of Rouyn-Noranda
—714 137	Témiscamingue Regional County Municipality
—714 139	Vallée-de-l'Or Regional County Municipality

*For a specific part of this jurisdiction, region, or feature, see the part and follow instructions under —4–9

—714 14	Lac-Saint-Jean regional county municipalities
	Class here *Saguenay-Lac-Saint-Jean Administrative Region
—714 142	Le Domaine-du-Roy Regional County Municipality
	Including Ashuapmushuam Wildlife Reserve (Chibougamau Wildlife Reserve)
—714 145	Maria-Chapdelaine Regional County Municipality
—714 148	Lac-Saint-Jean-Est Regional County Municipality
—714 16	City of Saguenay and Le Fjord-du-Saguenay Regional County Municipality
	Class here *Saguenay River
—714 162	City of Saguenay
	Including Chicoutimi, Jonquière
—714 165	Le Fjord-du-Saguenay Regional County Municipality
—714 17	Côte-Nord regional county municipalities
	See also —7182 for Labrador
—714 172	La Haute-Côte-Nord Regional County Municipality
—714 174	Manicouagan Regional County Municipality
—714 176	Sept-Rivières Regional County Municipality
—714 178	Minganie Regional County Municipality
	Le Golfe-du-Saint-Laurent Regional County Municipality, Basse-Côte-Nord region relocated to —714179
—714 178 2	Anticosti Island
—714 179	Le Golfe-du-Saint-Laurent Regional County Municipality [*formerly* —714178]
	Class here Basse-Côte-Nord region [*formerly* —714178]
—714 2	**Western region of Quebec**
	Class here *Ottawa River in Quebec Province
—714 21	Pontiac Regional County Municipality
—714 22	Outaouais regional county municipalities
	For Pontiac Regional County Municipality, see —71421

*For a specific part of this jurisdiction, region, or feature, see the part and follow instructions under —4–9

—714 221   City of Gatineau

    Former name: Outaouais Regional Community

    Including National Capital Region in Quebec province

    Class comprehensive works on National Capital Region in —71384

—714 223   Les Collines-de-l'Outaouais Regional County Municipality

    Class here Gatineau Park

—714 224   La Vallée-de-la-Gatineau Regional County Municipality

    Class here *La Vérendrye Wildlife Reserve; *Gatineau River

—714 227   Papineau Regional County Municipality

—714 23   Argenteuil Regional County Municipality

—714 24   Laurentides regional county municipalities

    Class here *Laurentians region (Laurentides region); *lower Laurentian Mountains

    Class comprehensive works on Laurentian Mountains in —7144

—714 241   Antoine-Labelle Regional County Municipality

    Class here *Papineau-Labelle Wildlife Reserve

—714 242   Les Laurentides Regional County Municipality

—714 244   Les Pays-d'en-Haut Regional County Municipality

—714 246   La Rivière-du-Nord Regional County Municipality

—714 248   Thérèse-De Blainville Regional County Municipality

—714 25   Deux-Montagnes Regional County Municipality and City of Mirabel

—714 252   Deux-Montagnes Regional County Municipality

—714 254   City of Mirabel

—714 26   Vaudreuil-Soulanges Regional County Municipality

—714 27   Montréal Metropolitan Community

    Class here Montréal region

    For a specific part of Montréal Metropolitan Community not provided for here, see the part, e.g., City of Montréal —71428, La Vallée-du-Richelieu Regional County Municipality —714365

—714 271   City of Laval

    Class here Jésus Island

*For a specific part of this jurisdiction, region, or feature, see the part and follow instructions under —4–9

—714 28   Urban agglomeration of Montréal

                        Including Baie-D'Urfé, Beaconsfield, Côte-Saint-Luc, Dollard-des-Ormeaux, Dorval, Hampstead, Kirkland, L'Île-Dorval, Mont-Royal, Montréal-Est, Montréal-Ouest, Pointe-Claire, Sainte-Anne-de-Bellevue, Senneville, Westmount

                        Class here City of Montréal, Montréal; Montréal Island

—714 3   Southwestern region of Quebec

                        Area south of Saint Lawrence River, and Richelieu River valley and westward

                        Class here *Montérégie region; Richelieu River

—714 31   Le Haut-Saint-Laurent Regional County Municipality

—714 32   Beauharnois-Salaberry Regional County Municipality

—714 34   Roussillon Regional County Municipality

                        Class here former *Châteauguay County, former *Laprairie County

—714 35   Les Jardins-de-Napierville Regional County Municipality

—714 36   Lajemmerais Regional County Municipality and La Vallée-du-Richelieu Regional County Municipality

—714 362   Lajemmerais Regional County Municipality

—714 365   La Vallée-du-Richelieu Regional County Municipality

                        Class here former *Chambly County

—714 37   Urban agglomeration of Longueuil

                        Former name: Champlain Regional County Municipality

                        Including Brossard, Saint-Bruno-de-Montarville, Saint-Lambert

                        Former Chambly County relocated to —714365

—714 371   Boucherville

—714 373   Longueuil

—714 38   Le Haut-Richelieu Regional County Municipality

                        Class here former Iberville County, former Saint-Jean County

—714 39   Le Bas-Richelieu Regional County Municipality

—714 4   North central region of Quebec

                        Area north of Saint Lawrence River from Montréal to Saguenay River

                        Class here *Laurentian Mountains

—714 41   Lanaudière regional county municipalities

—714 412   Les Moulins Regional County Municipality

*For a specific part of this jurisdiction, region, or feature, see the part and follow instructions under —4–9

—714 415	Montcalm Regional County Municipality
—714 416	L'Assomption Regional County Municipality
—714 418	Matawinie Regional County Municipality
	Class here *Mont-Tremblant National Park
—714 42	Joliette Regional County Municipality
—714 43	D'Autray Regional County Municipality
—714 44	Maskinongé Regional County Municipality
—714 45	Mauricie regional county municipalities
	Class here *Saint-Maurice River
—714 451	City of Trois-Rivières
	Including Cap-de-la-Madeleine
	Class here former Francheville Regional County Municipality
—714 453	City of Shawinigan
	Former name: Le Centre-de-la-Mauricie Regional County Municipality
	Including *La Mauricie National Park
—714 455	Les Chenaux Regional County Municipality
	Class here former *Champlain County
—714 457	Mékinac Regional County Municipality
—714 459	Urban agglomeration of La Tuque
	Former heading: Le Haut-Saint-Maurice Regional County Municipality
	Including La Bostonnais; Lac-Édouard
—714 46	Portneuf Regional County Municipality
	Including Portneuf Wildlife Reserve
—714 47	*Québec Metropolitan Community
	Class here *Capitale-Nationale region
—714 471	Urban agglomeration of Québec
	Including L'Ancienne-Lorette, Notre-Dame-des-Anges, Saint-Augustin-de-Desmaures
	Class here Québec
—714 474	La Jacques-Cartier Regional County Municipality
	Class here *Jacques-Cartier River

*For a specific part of this jurisdiction, region, or feature, see the part and follow instructions under —4–9

—714 476	L'Île-d'Orléans Regional County Municipality
	Class here Isle of Orléans
—714 48	La Côte-de-Beaupré Regional County Municipality
	Class here *Laurentides Wildlife Reserve (Laurentides Provincial Park)
—714 49	Charlevoix regional county municipalities
—714 492	Charlevoix Regional County Municipality
	Including Île aux Coudres
—714 494	Charlevoix-Est Regional County Municipality
—714 5	South central region of Quebec
	Area south of Saint Lawrence River, and east of Richelieu River valley
	Class here *Centre-du-Québec region
	For southern border area, see —7146
—714 52	Les Maskoutains Regional County Municipality and Acton Regional County Municipality
—714 523	Les Maskoutains Regional County Municipality
—714 525	Acton Regional County Municipality
—714 53	Rouville Regional County Municipality
—714 54	Nicolet-Yamaska Regional County Municipality
—714 55	Bécancour Regional County Municipality
—714 56	Drummond Regional County Municipality and Arthabaska Regional County Municipality
—714 563	Drummond Regional County Municipality
—714 565	Arthabaska Regional County Municipality
	Class here *Bois-Francs region
—714 57	Les Sources Regional County Municipality and L'Érable Regional County Municipality
—714 573	Les Sources Regional County Municipality
	Former names: Asbestos Regional County Municipality, L'Or-Blanc Regional County Municipality
—714 575	L'Érable Regional County Municipality
—714 58	Lotbinière Regional County Municipality

*For a specific part of this jurisdiction, region, or feature, see the part and follow instructions under
—4–9

—714 59   City of Lévis

                   Including former Les Chutes-de-la-Chaudière Regional County
                   Municipality, former Desjardins Regional County Municipality

—714 6   Southern region of Quebec

                   Southern border area east of Richelieu River valley

                   Class here *Eastern Townships (Cantons-de-l'Est), *Estrie
                   Administrative Region; *Saint-François River

—714 62   Brome-Missisquoi Regional County Municipality

—714 63   La Haute-Yamaska Regional County Municipality

—714 64   Memphrémagog Regional County Municipality

                       Class here *Lake Memphrémagog

—714 65   Le Val-Saint-François Regional County Municipality

—714 66   City of Sherbrooke

                   Former names: La Région-Sherbrookoise Regional County
                   Municipality, Sherbrooke Regional County Municipality

—714 67   Coaticook Regional County Municipality

—714 68   Le Haut-Saint-François Regional County Municipality

—714 69   Le Granit Regional County Municipality

—714 7   Eastern region of Quebec

                   Area south of Saint Lawrence River from Lévis to Gulf of Saint
                   Lawrence

                   Class here *Notre-Dame Mountains

—714 71   Les Appalaches Regional County Municipality, Beauce-Sartigan
                   Regional County Municipality, Robert-Cliche Regional County
                   Municipality, La Nouvelle-Beauce Regional County Municipality

                       Class here *Beauce region, *Chaudière-Appalaches region;
                       *Chaudière River

—714 712   Les Appalaches Regional County Municipality

                       Former name: L'Amiante Regional County Municipality

—714 714   Beauce-Sartigan Regional County Municipality

—714 716   Robert-Cliche Regional County Municipality

—714 718   La Nouvelle-Beauce Regional County Municipality

—714 72   Les Etchemins Regional County Municipality

—714 73   Bellechasse Regional County Municipality and Montmagny Regional
                   County Municipality

*For a specific part of this jurisdiction, region, or feature, see the part and follow instructions under
   —4–9

—714 733	Bellechasse Regional County Municipality
—714 735	Montmagny Regional County Municipality
	Including Île aux Grues, Grosse Île
—714 74	L'Islet Regional County Municipality
—714 75	Kamouraska Regional County Municipality
—714 76	Témiscouata Regional County Municipality, Rivière-du-Loup Regional County Municipality, Les Basques Regional County Municipality
	Class here *Bas-Saint-Laurent region
—714 762	Témiscouata Regional County Municipality
—714 764	Rivière-du-Loup Regional County Municipality
	Including Île Verte
—714 766	Les Basques Regional County Municipality
—714 77	Gaspé Peninsula regional county municipalities

Class here Gaspésie region; Gaspésie-Îles-de-la-Madeleine Administrative Region, former Bas-Saint-Laurent-Gaspésie Administrative Region; *Gaspé Peninsula

For Bas-Saint-Laurent region, see —71476; for Avignon Regional County Municipality and Bonaventure Regional County Municipality, see —71478; for Gaspé regional county municipalities and Municipality of Les Îles-de-la-Madeleine, see —71479

—714 771	Rimouski-Neigette Regional County Municipality
—714 773	La Mitis Regional County Municipality
—714 775	Matane Regional County Municipality
—714 778	La Matapédia Regional County Municipality
—714 78	Avignon Regional County Municipality and Bonaventure Regional County Municipality
—714 783	Avignon Regional County Municipality
—714 785	Bonaventure Regional County Municipality
—714 79	Gaspé regional county municipalities and Municipality of Les Îles-de-la-Madeleine
—714 791	La Haute-Gaspésie Regional County Municipality

Former name: Denis-Riverin Regional County Municipality

Class here *Gaspésie National Park

---

*For a specific part of this jurisdiction, region, or feature, see the part and follow instructions under —4–9

—714 793	La Côte-de-Gaspé Regional County Municipality
	Including Forillon National Park
—714 795	Le Rocher-Percé Regional County Municipality
	Former name: Pabok Regional County Municipality
—714 797	Municipality of Les Îles-de-la-Madeleine
	Class here Magdalen Islands

—715 Atlantic Provinces

Class here Maritime Provinces

For Nova Scotia, see —716; for Prince Edward Island, see —717; for Newfoundland and Labrador, see —718

See also —16344 for Gulf of Saint Lawrence, Northumberland Strait

—715 1 New Brunswick

For eastern counties, see —7152; for southern counties, see —7153; for central counties, see —7154; for western counties, see —7155

>	—715 11–715 12 Northern counties of New Brunswick
	Class comprehensive works in —7151
—715 11	Restigouche County
	Including *Restigouche River
—715 12	Gloucester County
	Including Bathurst

—715 2 Eastern counties of New Brunswick

—715 21	Northumberland County
	Class here *Miramichi River
—715 22	Kent County
—715 23	Westmorland County
	Including Sackville
—715 235	Moncton

—715 3 Southern counties of New Brunswick

See also —16345 for Bay of Fundy

—715 31	Albert County
—715 32	Saint John County

*For a specific part of this jurisdiction, region, or feature, see the part and follow instructions under —4–9

—715 33	Charlotte County
	Including Grand Manan Island; *Saint Croix River in New Brunswick
—715 4	Central counties of New Brunswick
—715 41	Kings County
—715 42	Queens County
—715 43	Sunbury County
—715 5	Western counties of New Brunswick
	Class here *Saint John River
—715 51	York County
—715 515	Fredericton
—715 52	Carleton County
—715 53	Victoria County
—715 54	Madawaska County
—716	Nova Scotia
—716 1	Northern counties of Nova Scotia
—716 11	Cumberland County
	Including Amherst
—716 12	Colchester County
	Including Truro
—716 13	Pictou County
	Including New Glasgow, Pictou
—716 14	Antigonish County
—716 2	Southern counties of Nova Scotia
—716 21	Guysborough County
—716 22	Halifax Regional Municipality
—716 225	Halifax-Dartmouth metropolitan area
	Class here Dartmouth, Halifax
—716 23	Lunenburg County
—716 24	Region of Queens Municipality
—716 25	Shelburne County

*For a specific part of this jurisdiction, region, or feature, see the part and follow instructions under —4–9

—716 3	Bay of Fundy counties

See also —16345 for Bay of Fundy

—716 31	Yarmouth County
—716 32	Digby County
—716 33	Annapolis County

Including Kejimkujik National Park

For Kejimkujik National Park in Queens County, see —71624

—716 34	Kings County

Including Wolfville

—716 35	Hants County

Including Windsor

—716 9	Cape Breton Island and Sable Island

Class here *Bras d'Or Lake

Subdivisions are added for Cape Breton Island and Sable Island together, for Cape Breton Island alone

---

>	—716 91–716 98 Cape Breton Island

Class comprehensive works in —7169

—716 91	Inverness County

Including Cape Breton Highlands National Park

For Cape Breton Highlands National Park in Victoria County, see —71693

—716 93	Victoria County
—716 95	Cape Breton Regional Municipality
—716 955	Louisbourg

Class here Fortress of Louisbourg National Historic Site

—716 98	Richmond County
—716 99	Sable Island
—717	Prince Edward Island
—717 1	Prince County
—717 4	Queens County

For Charlottetown, see —7175

*For a specific part of this jurisdiction, region, or feature, see the part and follow instructions under —4–9

—717 5   Charlottetown

—717 7   Kings County

—718   Newfoundland and Labrador, Saint Pierre and Miquelon

               Class here Newfoundland

               See also —16344 for Grand Banks of Newfoundland

—718 1   St. John's

—718 2   Labrador

—718 8   Saint Pierre and Miquelon

               Overseas territory of France

—719   Northern territories

               Class here Canadian Arctic

               See also —16327 for Beaufort Sea, Canadian Arctic waters, Northwest Passage

—719 1   Yukon

               Including Dawson, Whitehorse

—719 2   *Northwest Territories (1870–1999)

               See also —7193 for Northwest Territories (1999–)

—719 3   Northwest Territories (1999–)

               Including *Fort Smith Region, Inuvik Region

               Including Aklavik, Colville Lake, Déline (Fort Franklin), Fort Simpson, Fort Smith, Hay River, Holman, Inuvik, Lutselk'e, Paulatuk, Pine Point, Rae Lakes, Reliance, Sachs Harbour, Tuktoyaktuk, Tulita (Fort Norman), Wrigley, Yellowknife; Nahanni National Park, Tuktut Nogait National Park; *Thelon Game Sanctuary; Cape Baring, Cape Wollaston; Banks Island, *Borden Island, *Mackenzie King Island; Mackenzie Mountains; Slave River; Great Bear Lake, Great Slave Lake

               Class here former *Mackenzie District; Mackenzie River

               See also —7192 for Northwest Territories (1870–1999)

—719 5   Nunavut

*For a specific part of this jurisdiction, region, or feature, see the part and follow instructions under —4–9

—719 52   Baffin Region (Qikiqtaaluk Region)

          Baffin Island, Bylot Island, Mansel Island, Nottingham Island, Salisbury Island, Somerset Island, Wales Island; Ellesmere Island and all other islands east of 106° W and north of M'Clure Strait, Viscount Melville Sound, and Lancaster Sound; all islands in Hudson Bay, James Bay, Ungava Bay, and Hudson Strait; Melville Peninsula

          Including Arctic Bay (Tununirusiq), Cape Dorset (Kinngait), Grise Fiord (Ausuittuq), Hall Beach (Sanirajak), Igloolik (Iglulik), Iqaluit, Pangnirtung (Pannirtuuq), Pond Inlet (Mittimatalik), Resolute (Qausuittuq), Sanikiluaq; Auyuittuq National Park

          Class here former Franklin District; *Canadian Arctic Archipelago

          See also —16327 for Hudson Bay, James Bay, Ungava Bay

—719 55   Kitikmeot Region

          Mainland within Nunavut north of 66° N and west of 87° W; King William Island, Prince of Wales Island, *Victoria Island

          Including Bathurst Inlet (Kingaok), Cambridge Bay (Ikaluktutiak), Coppermine (Kugluktuk), Gjoa Haven (Oqsuqtooq), Pelly Bay (Aqvilgjuaq), Spence Bay (Talurqjuak), Umingmaktok; Boothia Peninsula, Simpson Peninsula; *Contwoyto Lake

—719 58   Keewatin Region (Kivallik Region)

          Mainland within Nunavut between 60° N and 66° N, and east of 106° W; land surrounding Repulse Bay; Coats Island, Southampton Island

          Including Baker Lake (Qamani'tuaq), Chesterfield Inlet (Igluligaarjuk), Coral Harbour (Salliq), Rankin Inlet (Kangiqsliniq), Repulse Bay (Naujaat); *Dubawnt Lake; *Thelon River

          Class here former Keewatin District

—72   **Mexico, Central America, West Indies, Bermuda**

          Class here Middle America

          Subdivisions are added for Mexico, Central America, West Indies, Bermuda together; for Mexico alone

SUMMARY

—721	**Northern states of Mexico**
—722	**Lower California peninsula**
—723	**Central Pacific states of Mexico**
—724	**Central states of Mexico**
—725	**Valley of Mexico**
—726	**Southern Gulf states of Mexico**
—727	**Southern Pacific states of Mexico**
—728	**Central America**
—729	**West Indies (Antilles) and Bermuda**

*For a specific part of this jurisdiction, region, or feature, see the part and follow instructions under —4–9

>   —721–727 Mexico

               Class comprehensive works in —72

—721   Northern states of Mexico

               Class here *Mexican-American Border Region

                  For Lower California peninsula, see —722

—721 2   Tamaulipas

—721 3   Nuevo León

—721 4   Coahuila

—721 5   Durango

—721 6   Chihuahua

—721 7   Sonora

               Class here *Sonoran Desert

                  See also —1641 for Gulf of California

—722   Lower California peninsula

                  See also —1641 for Gulf of California

—722 3   Baja California Norte

—722 4   Baja California Sur

—723   Central Pacific states of Mexico

               Class here *Sierra Madre Occidental

—723 2   Sinaloa

—723 4   Nayarit

—723 5   Jalisco

—723 6   Colima

—723 7   Michoacán

—724   Central states of Mexico

               Class here *Sierra Madre Oriental

                  For Valley of Mexico, see —725

—724 1   Guanajuato

—724 2   Aguascalientes

—724 3   Zacatecas

---

*For a specific part of this jurisdiction, region, or feature, see the part and follow instructions under —4–9

—724 4	San Luis Potosí
—724 5	Querétaro
—724 6	Hidalgo
—724 7	Tlaxcala
—724 8	Puebla
—724 9	Morelos
—725	*Valley of Mexico
—725 2	Mexico state
—725 3	Distrito Federal

Class here Mexico City

—726	Southern Gulf states of Mexico
—726 2	Veracruz
—726 3	Tabasco
—726 4	Campeche
—726 5	Yucatán
—726 7	Quintana Roo
—727	Southern Pacific states of Mexico
—727 3	Guerrero

Class here *Sierra Madre del Sul

—727 4	Oaxaca
—727 5	Chiapas
—728	Central America

SUMMARY

—728 1	**Guatemala**
—728 2	**Belize**
—728 3	**Honduras**
—728 4	**El Salvador**
—728 5	**Nicaragua**
—728 6	**Costa Rica**
—728 7	**Panama**

—728 1	Guatemala
—728 11	Guatemala department

Class here Guatemala City

—728 12	Petén department

*For a specific part of this jurisdiction, region, or feature, see the part and follow instructions under
—4–9

—728 13	Izabal department and Zacapa department
—728 131	Izabal department
—728 132	Zacapa department
—728 14	Southeastern departments of Guatemala
—728 141	Chiquimula department
—728 142	Jalapa department
—728 143	Jutiapa department
—728 144	Santa Rosa department
—728 15	North central departments of Guatemala
—728 151	Alta Verapaz department
—728 152	Baja Verapaz department
—728 153	El Progreso department
—728 16	South central departments of Guatemala
—728 161	Chimaltenango department
—728 162	Sacatepéquez department
—728 163	Escuintla department
—728 164	Sololá department
—728 165	Suchitepéquez department
—728 17	Huehuetenango department and Quiché department
—728 171	Huehuetenango department
—728 172	Quiché department
—728 18	Southwestern departments of Guatemala
—728 181	Totonicapán department
—728 182	Quezaltenango department
—728 183	Retalhuleu department
—728 184	San Marcos department
—728 2	Belize
—728 21	Corozal District
—728 22	Belize District
—728 23	Stann Creek District
—728 24	Toledo District
—728 25	Cayo District
—728 26	Orange Walk District

—728 3	Honduras
—728 31	Northern departments of Honduras
—728 311	Cortés
—728 312	Atlántida
—728 313	Colón
—728 314	Yoro
—728 315	Islas de la Bahía
—728 32	Gracias a Dios department
—728 33	Olancho department
—728 34	El Paraíso department
—728 35	Southern departments of Honduras
—728 351	Choluteca
—728 352	Valle
—728 36	La Paz department
—728 37	Central departments of Honduras
—728 371	Francisco Morazán
	Class here Tegucigalpa
—728 372	Comayagua
—728 38	Western departments of Honduras
—728 381	Intibucá
—728 382	Lempira
—728 383	Ocotepeque
—728 384	Copán
—728 385	Santa Bárbara
—728 4	El Salvador
—728 41	Western departments of El Salvador
—728 411	Ahuachapán
—728 412	Santa Ana
—728 413	Sonsonate
—728 42	Central departments of El Salvador
—728 421	Chalatenango
—728 422	La Libertad
—728 423	San Salvador
	Class here San Salvador

—728 424	Cuscatlán
—728 425	La Paz
—728 426	Cabañas
—728 427	San Vicente
—728 43	Eastern departments of El Salvador
—728 431	Usulután
—728 432	San Miguel
—728 433	Morazán
—728 434	La Unión
—728 5	Nicaragua
—728 51	Pacific departments of Nicaragua
—728 511	Chinandega
—728 512	León
—728 513	Managua
	Class here Managua
—728 514	Masaya
—728 515	Granada
—728 516	Carazo
—728 517	Rivas
	Class here *Lake Nicaragua
—728 52	Central departments of Nicaragua
—728 521	Nueva Segovia
—728 522	Jinotega
—728 523	Madriz
—728 524	Estelí
—728 525	Matagalpa
—728 526	Boaco
—728 527	Chontales
—728 53	Atlantic region of Nicaragua
—728 531	Río San Juan department
—728 532	Región Autónoma del Atlántico Sur

*For a specific part of this jurisdiction, region, or feature, see the part and follow instructions under
  —4–9

—728 537   Región Autónoma del Atlántico Norte

—728 6   Costa Rica

—728 61   Limón province

—728 62   Cartago province

—728 63   San José province

                    Class here San José

—728 64   Heredia province

—728 65   Alajuela province

—728 66   Guanacaste province

—728 67   Puntarenas province

—728 7   Panama

                    See also —1641 for Gulf of Panama

—728 71   Western Panama

—728 711   Chiriquí province

—728 712   Bocas del Toro province

—728 717   Ngöbe Buglé comarca

—728 72   Central Panama

                        For Panamá province and Colón province, see —72873

—728 721   Coclé province

—728 722   Veraguas province

—728 723   Los Santos province

—728 724   Herrera province

—728 73   Panamá province and Colón province

                        For Canal Area, see —72875

—728 731   Panamá province

                        Class here Panama City

—728 732   Colón province

—728 75   Canal Area

                    Class here Panama Canal

—728 77   Eastern Panama

—728 772   Kuna Yala comarca

—728 773   Kuna de Madungandí comarca

—728 774   Kuna de Wargandi comarca

—728 776   Emberá comarca

—728 778		Darién province

—729   West Indies (Antilles) and Bermuda

> Class here *Caribbean Area

> Subdivisions are added for West Indies (Antilles) and Bermuda together, for West Indies (Antilles) alone

> *See also —16365 for Caribbean Sea*

SUMMARY

—729 1	Cuba
—729 2	Jamaica and Cayman Islands
—729 3	Dominican Republic
—729 4	Haiti
—729 5	Puerto Rico
—729 6	Bahama Islands
—729 7	Leeward Islands
—729 8	Windward Islands and other southern islands
—729 9	Bermuda

>   —729 1–729 5   Greater Antilles

> Class comprehensive works in —729

—729 1   Cuba

—729 11   Pinar del Río province

—729 12   Ciudad da La Habana province (Havana), Havana province, Isla de la Juventud

—729 123   Ciudad da La Habana province (Havana)

—729 124   Havana province

—729 125   Isla de la Juventud

—729 13   Matanzas province

—729 14   Villa Clara province, Cienfuegos province, Sancti Spíritus province

—729 142   Villa Clara province

—729 143   Cienfuegos province

—729 145   Sancti Spíritus province

—729 15   Ciego de Ávila province and Camagüey province

—729 153   Ciego de Ávila province

—729 156   Camagüey province

—729 16   Eastern Cuba

---

*For a specific part of this jurisdiction, region, or feature, see the part and follow instructions under —4–9

—729 162	Las Tunas province
—729 163	Granma province
—729 164	Holguín province
—729 165	Santiago de Cuba province
—729 167	Guantánamo province

—729 2   **Jamaica and Cayman Islands**

> Subdivisions are added for Jamaica and Cayman Islands together, for Jamaica alone

—729 21   Cayman Islands

—729 3   **Dominican Republic**

> Class here comprehensive works on Hispaniola
>
> *For Haiti, see —7294*

—729 32	Southwestern provinces of Dominican Republic
—729 323	Pedernales
—729 324	Barahona
—729 325	Independencia
—729 326	Baoruco (Bahoruco)
—729 34	Western provinces of Dominican Republic
—729 342	San Juan
—729 343	Elísa Piña
—729 345	Dajabón
—729 35	Northwestern provinces of Dominican Republic
—729 352	Monte Cristi
—729 353	Santiago Rodríguez
—729 356	Santiago
—729 357	Valverde
—729 358	Puerto Plata
—729 36	North central provinces of Dominican Republic
—729 362	Espaillat
—729 363	Salcedo
—729 364	María Trinidad Sánchez
—729 365	Samaná
—729 367	Duarte
—729 368	Sánchez Ramírez

—729 369	Monseñor Nouel province and La Vega province
—729 369 3	Monseñor Nouel
—729 369 7	La Vega
—729 37	South central provinces of Dominican Republic
—729 372	Azua
—729 373	Peravia
—729 374	San Cristóbal
—729 375	Distrito Nacional
	Class here Santo Domingo
—729 377	Monte Plata
—729 38	Eastern provinces of Dominican Republic
—729 381	Hato Mayor
—729 382	San Pedro de Macorís
—729 383	La Romana
—729 384	El Seibo
—729 385	La Altagracia
—729 4	Haiti
—729 42	Nord-Ouest département
	Including Ile de la Tortue
—729 43	Nord département and Nord-Est département
—729 432	Nord département
—729 436	Nord-Est département
—729 44	Centre département and Artibonite département
—729 442	Centre département
—729 446	Artibonite département
—729 45	Ouest département and Sud-Est département
—729 452	Ouest département
	Class here Port-au-Prince
—729 456	Sud-Est département
—729 46	Sud département and Grand'Anse département
—729 462	Sud département
—729 466	Grand'Anse département
—729 5	Puerto Rico

—729 51	San Juan district
	Class here San Juan
—729 52	Bayamón district
—729 53	Arecibo district
—729 54	Aguadilla district
—729 56	Mayagüez district
—729 57	Ponce district
—729 58	Guayama district
—729 59	Humacao district
	Including Vieques Island
—729 6	Bahama Islands
—729 61	Turks and Caicos Islands

>   —729 7–729 8   Lesser Antilles (Caribbees)

Class comprehensive works in —729

—729 7   Leeward Islands

For Dominica, see —729841

—729 72   Virgin Islands

—729 722   Virgin Islands of the United States

         Including Saint Croix, Saint John, Saint Thomas; Virgin Islands National Park

–729 725   British Virgin Islands

         Including Tortola, Virgin Gorda

—729 73   Anguilla and Saint Kitts-Nevis

         Class here West Indies Associated States

For Antigua, see —72974; for Windward Islands, see —72984

—729 74   Antigua and Barbuda

—729 75   Montserrat

—729 76	Guadeloupe

Overseas department of France

Including Basse Terre island, Désirade island, Grande Terre island, Marie Galante island, Saint Barthélemy island, Saintes Islands, northern part of Saint Martin

Class here French West Indies, comprehensive works on Saint Martin

> *For southern part of Saint Martin, see —72977; for Martinique, see —72982*

—729 77	Leeward Netherlands islands

Including Saba, Saint Eustatius, southern part of Saint Martin

Class comprehensive works on former Netherlands Antilles in —72986

—729 8	Windward Islands and other southern islands

> *For Nueva Esparta, Venezuela, see —8754*

—729 81	Barbados
—729 82	Martinique

Overseas department of France

—729 83	Trinidad and Tobago
—729 84	Windward Islands
—729 841	Dominica
—729 843	Saint Lucia
—729 844	Saint Vincent and the Grenadines

> *For Carriacou, see —729845*

—729 845	Grenada and Carriacou
—729 86	Netherlands islands

Including Aruba, Bonaire, Curaçao

Class here former Netherlands Antilles

> *For Leeward Netherlands islands, see —72977*

—729 9	Bermuda
—73	**United States**

> *For specific states, see —74–79*

> *See Manual at T2—73 vs. T2—71*

—(734–739)   Specific states

        (Optional numbers; prefer —74–79)

        Add to base number —73 the numbers following —7 in notation 74–79 of this table, e.g., Pennsylvania —7348

>   **—74–79 Specific states of United States**

        Class comprehensive works in —73

        For Hawaii, see —969

        (Option: Class in —734–739)

—74   **Northeastern United States (New England and Middle Atlantic states)**

        Class here United States east of Allegheny Mountains, east of Mississippi River; *Appalachian Mountains; *Connecticut River

        For southeastern United States, see —75; for south central United States, see —76; for north central United States, see —77

SUMMARY

—741	Maine
—742	New Hampshire
—743	Vermont
—744	Massachusetts
—745	Rhode Island
—746	Connecticut
—747	New York
—748	Pennsylvania
—749	New Jersey

>   —741–746 New England

        Class comprehensive works in —74

—741   Maine

—741 1   Aroostook County

—741 2   Northwestern counties of Maine

        Including Moosehead Lake

—741 22   Somerset County

        Class here *Kennebec River

—741 25   Piscataquis County

---

*For a specific part of this jurisdiction, region, or feature, see the part and follow instructions under —4–9

—741 3	Penobscot County
	Including Bangor
	Class here *Penobscot River
—741 4	Southeastern counties of Maine
—741 42	Washington County
	Class here *Saint Croix River
—741 45	Hancock County
	Including Mount Desert Island
	Class here Acadia National Park

                            For Acadia National Park in Knox County, see —74153

—741 5	South central counties of Maine
—741 52	Waldo County
—741 53	Knox County
—741 57	Lincoln County
—741 6	Kennebec County
	Including Augusta
—741 7	West central counties of Maine
	Class here *Rangeley Lakes
—741 72	Franklin County
—741 75	Oxford County
—741 8	Southwest central counties of Maine
	Class here *Androscoggin River
—741 82	Androscoggin County
—741 85	Sagadahoc County
—741 9	Southwestern counties of Maine
—741 91	Cumberland County
	Class here Portland
—741 95	York County
—742	New Hampshire
—742 1	Coos County
—742 2	*White Mountains

*For a specific part of this jurisdiction, region, or feature, see the part and follow instructions under —4–9

—742 3	Grafton County
—742 4	Counties bordering *Lake Winnipesaukee
—742 42	Carroll County
—742 45	Belknap County
—742 5	Strafford County
—742 6	Rockingham County
	Including Portsmouth
—742 7	West central counties of New Hampshire
—742 72	Merrimack County
	Including Concord
	Class here *Merrimack River
—742 75	Sullivan County
—742 8	Hillsborough County
	Including Manchester
—742 9	Cheshire County
—743	Vermont
	Class here *Green Mountains
—743 1	Northwestern counties of Vermont
	Class here *Lake Champlain in Vermont
—743 12	Grand Isle County
—743 13	Franklin County
—743 17	Chittenden County
	Including Burlington
	Class here *Winooski River
—743 2	Northeastern counties of Vermont
—743 23	Orleans County
—743 25	Essex County
—743 3	North central counties of Vermont
—743 34	Caledonia County
—743 35	Lamoille County

*For a specific part of this jurisdiction, region, or feature, see the part and follow instructions under
  —4–9

—743 4	Washington County
	Including Montpelier
—743 5	Addison County
—743 6	East central counties of Vermont
—743 63	Orange County
—743 65	Windsor County
—743 7	Rutland County
—743 8	Bennington County
—743 9	Windham County
—744	Massachusetts
—744 1	Berkshire County
	Class here *Berkshire Hills
—744 2	Connecticut River counties
—744 22	Franklin County
—744 23	Hampshire County
—744 26	Hampden County
	Including Springfield
—744 3	Worcester County
—744 4	Middlesex County
	Including Cambridge, Lexington, Lowell; *Charles River
—744 5	Essex County
—744 6	Suffolk County
—744 61	Boston
—744 7	Norfolk County
—744 8	Southeastern counties of Massachusetts
	For counties bordering Nantucket Sound, see —7449
	See also —16345 for Cape Cod Bay
—744 82	Plymouth County
—744 85	Bristol County
—744 9	Counties bordering Nantucket Sound
	See also —16346 for Nantucket Sound

---

*For a specific part of this jurisdiction, region, or feature, see the part and follow instructions under
—4–9

—744 92   Barnstable County (Cape Cod)

                           See also —16345 for Cape Cod Bay

—744 94   Dukes County

                           Including Elizabeth Islands, Martha's Vineyard

—744 97   Nantucket County

                           Class here Nantucket Island

—745   Rhode Island

                           See also —16346 for Rhode Island Sound, Narragansett Bay

—745 1   Providence County

                           For Providence, see —7452

—745 2   Providence

—745 4   Kent County

—745 5   Bristol County

—745 6   Newport County

                           For Newport, see —7457

—745 7   Newport

—745 8   Block Island

—745 9   Washington County

                           For Block Island, see —7458

—746   Connecticut

                           See also —16346 for Long Island Sound

—746 1   Litchfield County

—746 2   Hartford County

                           For Hartford, see —7463

—746 3   Hartford

—746 4   Northeastern counties of Connecticut

—746 43   Tolland County

—746 45   Windham County

—746 5   New London County

—746 6   Middlesex County

—746 7   New Haven County

                           For New Haven, see —7468

—746 8   New Haven

—746 9   Fairfield County

         Including Stamford

>   —747–749   Middle Atlantic states

         Class comprehensive works in —74

—747   New York

—747 1   New York

         Class here Borough of Manhattan (Manhattan Island, New York County)

           For borough of Brooklyn, see —74723; for borough of Queens, see —747243; for borough of Richmond, see —74726; for borough of the Bronx, see —747275

           See also —16346 for New York Bay

—747 2   Other parts of New York metropolitan area

           For Fairfield County, Connecticut, see —7469; for New Jersey counties of metropolitan area, see —7493

—747 21   Long Island

           For specific parts of Long Island, see —74723–74725

           See also —16346 for Long Island Sound

>   —747 23–747 25   Specific parts of Long Island

         Class comprehensive works in —74721

—747 23   Borough of Brooklyn (Kings County)

—747 24   Queens County and Nassau County

—747 243   Borough of Queens (Queens County)

—747 245   Nassau County

—747 25   Suffolk County

—747 26   Staten Island (Borough of Richmond, Richmond County)

—747 27   Borough of the Bronx and Westchester County

—747 275   Borough of the Bronx (Bronx County)

—747 277   Westchester County

—747 28   Rockland County

—747 3	Other southeastern counties of New York
	Class here *Hudson River
—747 31	Orange County
—747 32	Putnam County
—747 33	Dutchess County
—747 34	Ulster County
—747 35	Sullivan County
—747 36	Delaware County
—747 37	Greene County
—747 38	*Catskill Mountains
—747 39	Columbia County
—747 4	Middle eastern counties of New York
—747 41	Rensselaer County
—747 42	Albany County
	For Albany, see —74743
—747 43	Albany
—747 44	Schenectady County
—747 45	Schoharie County
—747 46	Montgomery County
—747 47	Fulton County
—747 48	Saratoga County
—747 49	Washington County
—747 5	Northern counties of New York
	Class here *Adirondack Mountains
—747 51	Warren County
	Including *Lake George
—747 52	Hamilton County
—747 53	Essex County
—747 54	Clinton County
	Class here *Lake Champlain
—747 55	Franklin County

*For a specific part of this jurisdiction, region, or feature, see the part and follow instructions under
—4–9

—747 56	Saint Lawrence County
	Including *Saint Lawrence River in New York
—747 57	Jefferson County
—747 58	*Thousand Islands
—747 59	Lewis County
—747 6	North central counties of New York
	Class here *Mohawk River
—747 61	Herkimer County
—747 62	Oneida County
	Including *Oneida Lake
—747 64	Madison County
—747 65	Onondaga County
	For Syracuse, see —74766
—747 66	Syracuse
—747 67	Oswego County
—747 68	Cayuga County
	Including *Cayuga Lake
—747 69	Seneca County
—747 7	South central counties of New York
—747 71	Tompkins County
	Class here Ithaca
—747 72	Cortland County
—747 73	Chenango County
—747 74	Otsego County
—747 75	Broome County
—747 77	Tioga County
—747 78	Chemung County
—747 8	West central counties of New York
	Class here *Finger Lakes
—747 81	Schuyler County
—747 82	Yates County
	Class here *Keuka Lake

*For a specific part of this jurisdiction, region, or feature, see the part and follow instructions under
—4–9

—747 83	Steuben County
—747 84	Allegany County
—747 85	Livingston County
—747 86	Ontario County
—747 87	Wayne County
—747 88	Monroe County

Class here *Genesee River

For Rochester, see —74789

—747 89	Rochester
—747 9	Western counties of New York

Class here *Lake Ontario

—747 91	Orleans County
—747 92	Genesee County
—747 93	Wyoming County
—747 94	Cattaraugus County
—747 95	Chautauqua County
—747 96	Erie County

For Buffalo, see —74797

—747 97	Buffalo
—747 98	Niagara County

Including *Niagara River in New York, Niagara Falls (city)

Class Niagara Falls (physiographic feature) in —74799

—747 99	Niagara Falls in New York

Physiographic feature

—748	Pennsylvania

Class here *Susquehanna River

—748 1	Southeastern counties of Pennsylvania

Class here *Schuylkill River

—748 11	Philadelphia County (Philadelphia)
—748 12	Montgomery County
—748 13	Chester County

*For a specific part of this jurisdiction, region, or feature, see the part and follow instructions under
   —4–9

—748 14	Delaware County
—748 15	Lancaster County
—748 16	Berks County
—748 17	Schuylkill County
—748 18	Dauphin County
	Including Harrisburg
—748 19	Lebanon County
—748 2	Eastern counties of Pennsylvania
	Class here *Pocono Mountains
—748 21	Bucks County
—748 22	Northampton County
—748 23	Wayne County
	Including *Lake Wallenpaupack
—748 24	Pike County
—748 25	Monroe County
	Including *Delaware Water Gap
—748 26	Carbon County
—748 27	Lehigh County
—748 3	Northeastern counties of Pennsylvania
—748 31	Northumberland County
—748 32	Luzerne County
—748 34	Susquehanna County
—748 35	Wyoming County
—748 36	Lackawanna County
	For Scranton, see —74837
—748 37	Scranton
—748 38	Columbia County
—748 39	Montour County
—748 4	Southeast central counties of Pennsylvania
—748 41	York County
—748 42	Adams County

*For a specific part of this jurisdiction, region, or feature, see the part and follow instructions under
—4–9

—748 43	Cumberland County
—748 44	Franklin County
—748 45	Perry County
	Class here *Juniata River
—748 46	Mifflin County
—748 47	Juniata County
—748 48	Union County
—748 49	Snyder County
—748 5	Northeast central counties of Pennsylvania
	Class here *West Branch of Susquehanna River
—748 51	Lycoming County
—748 53	Centre County
—748 54	Clinton County
—748 55	Potter County
—748 56	Tioga County
748 57	Bradford County
—748 59	Sullivan County
—748 6	Northwest central counties of Pennsylvania
	Class here *Allegheny River
—748 61	Clearfield County
—748 62	Jefferson County
—748 63	McKean County
—748 65	Elk County
—748 66	Cameron County
—748 67	Warren County
—748 68	Forest County
—748 69	Clarion County
—748 7	Southwest central counties of Pennsylvania
	Class here *Allegheny Mountains
—748 71	Bedford County
—748 72	Fulton County

*For a specific part of this jurisdiction, region, or feature, see the part and follow instructions under
  —4–9

—748 73	Huntingdon County
—748 75	Blair County
—748 77	Cambria County
—748 79	Somerset County
—748 8	Southwestern counties of Pennsylvania

Class here *Monongahela River

—748 81	Westmoreland County
—748 82	Washington County
—748 83	Greene County
—748 84	Fayette County
—748 85	Allegheny County

For Pittsburgh, see —74886

—748 86	Pittsburgh
—748 88	Armstrong County
—748 89	Indiana County
—748 9	Northwestern counties of Pennsylvania
—748 91	Butler County
—748 92	Beaver County
—748 93	Lawrence County
—748 95	Mercer County
—748 96	Venango County
—748 97	Crawford County
—748 99	Erie County
—749	New Jersey

Class here *Delaware River

—749 2	Northeastern counties of New Jersey
—749 21	Bergen County

Class here *Hackensack River

—749 23	Passaic County
—749 26	Hudson County

For Jersey City, see —74927

*For a specific part of this jurisdiction, region, or feature, see the part and follow instructions under —4–9

—749 27	Jersey City
—749 3	*Counties of New Jersey in New York metropolitan area
	Class here *Passaic River
—749 31	Essex County
	For Newark, see —74932; for The Oranges, see —74933
—749 32	Newark
—749 33	The Oranges
	Including East Orange, Maplewood, Orange, South Orange, West Orange
—749 36	Union County
—749 4	East central counties of New Jersey
	See also —16346 for New York Bay
—749 41	Middlesex County
	For New Brunswick, see —74942
—749 42	New Brunswick
—749 44	Somerset County
	Class here *Raritan River
—749 46	Monmouth County
—749 48	Ocean County
—749 6	West central counties of New Jersey
—749 61	Burlington County
	Including *Mullica River
	Class here *Pine Barrens
—749 65	Mercer County
	For Trenton, see —74966
—749 66	Trenton
—749 7	Northwestern counties of New Jersey
—749 71	Hunterdon County
—749 74	Morris County
—749 76	Sussex County
—749 78	Warren County
—749 8	South central counties of New Jersey

*For a specific part of this jurisdiction, region, or feature, see the part and follow instructions under —4–9

—749 81	Gloucester County
—749 84	Atlantic County

For Atlantic City, see —74985

—749 85	Atlantic City
—749 87	Camden County
—749 9	Southern counties of New Jersey

See also —16346 for Delaware Bay

—749 91	Salem County
—749 94	Cumberland County
—749 98	Cape May County

—75 Southeastern United States (South Atlantic states)

Class here southern states, *Piedmont, *Atlantic Coastal Plain

For south central United States, see —76

SUMMARY

—751	Delaware
—752	Maryland
—753	District of Columbia (Washington)
—754	West Virginia
—755	Virginia
—756	North Carolina
—757	South Carolina
—758	Georgia
—759	Florida

—751	Delaware

See also —16346 for Delaware Bay

—751 1	New Castle County

For Wilmington, see —7512

—751 2	Wilmington
—751 4	Kent County

Including Dover

—751 7	Sussex County
—752	Maryland

Class here *Potomac River

See also —16347 for Chesapeake Bay

*For a specific part of this jurisdiction, region, or feature, see the part and follow instructions under —4–9

—752 1   Eastern Shore

                      Class here *Delmarva Peninsula

                      For southern counties of Eastern Shore, see —7522; for northern counties of Eastern Shore, see —7523

—752 2   Southern counties of Eastern Shore

—752 21   Worcester County

                      Including *Assateague Island

—752 23   Somerset County

—752 25   Wicomico County

—752 27   Dorchester County

—752 3   Northern counties of Eastern Shore

—752 31   Caroline County

                      Class here *Choptank River

—752 32   Talbot County

—752 34   Queen Annes County

                      Class here *Chester River

—752 36   Kent County

—752 38   Cecil County

\>   —752 4–752 9   Maryland west of Chesapeake Bay

                 Class comprehensive works in —752

—752 4   Southern counties of Maryland

                      Class here *Patuxent River

—752 41   Saint Marys County

—752 44   Calvert County

—752 47   Charles County

—752 5   South central counties of Maryland

—752 51   Prince George's County

—752 55   Anne Arundel County

                      For Annapolis, see —75256

—752 56   Annapolis

—752 6   Independent city of Baltimore

---

*For a specific part of this jurisdiction, region, or feature, see the part and follow instructions under —4–9

—752 7	North central counties of Maryland
	Class here *Piedmont in Maryland
—752 71	Baltimore County
—752 74	Harford County
	Including *Susquehanna River in Maryland
—752 77	Carroll County
—752 8	West central counties of Maryland
—752 81	Howard County
—752 84	Montgomery County
—752 87	Frederick County
—752 9	Western counties of Maryland
—752 91	Washington County
—752 94	Allegany County
—752 97	Garrett County
—753	District of Columbia (Washington)
—754	West Virginia
—754 1	Northern Panhandle counties
	Class here *Ohio River in West Virginia
—754 12	Hancock County
—754 13	Brooke County
—754 14	Ohio County
	Class here Wheeling
—754 16	Marshall County
—754 18	Wetzel County
—754 19	Tyler County
—754 2	Little Kanawha Valley counties
	Class here *Little Kanawha River
—754 21	Pleasants County
—754 22	Wood County
—754 24	Ritchie County
—754 26	Wirt County

*For a specific part of this jurisdiction, region, or feature, see the part and follow instructions under —4–9

—754 27	Gilmer County
—754 29	Calhoun County
—754 3	Kanawha Valley counties
	Class here *Kanawha River
—754 31	Jackson County
—754 33	Mason County
—754 35	Putnam County
—754 36	Roane County
—754 37	Kanawha County
	Including Charleston
—754 39	Boone County
—754 4	Southwestern border counties of West Virginia
	Including *Tug Fork
	Class here *Guyandotte River
—754 42	Cabell County
—754 43	Lincoln County
—754 44	Logan County
—754 45	Wyoming County
—754 47	Wayne County
	Including *Big Sandy River
—754 48	Mingo County
—754 49	McDowell County
—754 5	Monongahela Valley counties
	Class here *Monongahela River in West Virginia
—754 52	Monongalia County
—754 54	Marion County
—754 55	Taylor County
—754 56	Doddridge County
—754 57	Harrison County
—754 59	Barbour County
—754 6	Central counties of West Virginia

*For a specific part of this jurisdiction, region, or feature, see the part and follow instructions under
   —4–9

—754 61	Lewis County
—754 62	Upshur County
—754 65	Webster County
—754 66	Braxton County
—754 67	Clay County
—754 69	Nicholas County

> Class here *Gauley River

—754 7   New River Valley counties

> Class here *New River

—754 71	Fayette County
—754 73	Raleigh County
—754 74	Mercer County
—754 76	Summers County
—754 78	Monroe County

—754 8   Allegheny Crest counties

> Class here *Allegheny Mountains in West Virginia; *Cheat River

—754 82	Preston County
—754 83	Tucker County
—754 85	Randolph County
—754 87	Pocahontas County
—754 88	Greenbrier County

> Class here *Greenbrier River

—754 9   Eastern Panhandle counties

> Class here *Potomac Valley of West Virginia

—754 91	Pendleton County
—754 92	Grant County
—754 93	Hardy County
—754 94	Mineral County
—754 95	Hampshire County
—754 96	Morgan County
—754 97	Berkeley County

*For a specific part of this jurisdiction, region, or feature, see the part and follow instructions under
—4–9

—754 99	Jefferson County
—755	Virginia
	Class here *Blue Ridge
—755 1	Northampton County, Accomack County, Chesapeake Bay Region
	Class here *Tidewater Virginia
—755 15	Northampton County
—755 16	Accomack County
—755 18	*Chesapeake Bay Region
	See also —16347 for Chesapeake Bay
—755 2	Potomac-Rappahannock region
	Including Northern Neck
	Class here *Rappahannock River
—755 21	Northumberland County
—755 22	Lancaster County
—755 23	Richmond County
—755 24	Westmoreland County
—755 25	King George County
—755 26	Stafford County
—755 27	Prince William County, Fauquier County, Manassas, Manassas Park
—755 273	Prince William County, Manassas, Manassas Park
—755 273 2	Prince William County
—755 273 4	Independent city of Manassas
—755 273 6	Independent city of Manassas Park
—755 275	Fauquier County
—755 28	Loudoun County
—755 29	Washington metropolitan area of Virginia
—755 291	Fairfax County
—755 292	Independent city of Fairfax
—755 293	Independent city of Falls Church
—755 295	Arlington County
—755 296	Independent city of Alexandria

*For a specific part of this jurisdiction, region, or feature, see the part and follow instructions under —4–9

—755 572	Greensville County
—755 573	Independent city of Emporia
—755 575	Brunswick County
—755 58	Dinwiddie County, Prince George County, Petersburg, Hopewell
—755 581	Independent city of Petersburg
—755 582	Dinwiddie County
—755 585	Prince George County
—755 586	Independent city of Hopewell
—755 59	Chesterfield County and Colonial Heights
—755 594	Chesterfield County
—755 595	Independent city of Colonial Heights
—755 6	South central region of Virginia
	Class here *Piedmont in Virginia; *Roanoke River in Virginia
—755 61	Powhatan County and Cumberland County
—755 612	Powhatan County
—755 615	Cumberland County
—755 62	Buckingham County and Appomattox County
—755 623	Buckingham County
—755 625	Appomattox County
—755 63	Prince Edward County, Amelia County, Nottoway County
—755 632	Prince Edward County
—755 634	Amelia County
—755 637	Nottoway County
—755 64	Lunenburg County and Mecklenburg County
—755 643	Lunenburg County
—755 645	Mecklenburg County
—755 65	Charlotte County
—755 66	Halifax County, Pittsylvania County, Danville
—755 661	Halifax County
—755 665	Pittsylvania County
—755 666	Independent city of Danville

*For a specific part of this jurisdiction, region, or feature, see the part and follow instructions under —4–9

—755 67	Campbell County, Bedford County, Lynchburg, Bedford
—755 671	Independent city of Lynchburg
—755 672	Campbell County
—755 675	Bedford County
—755 676	Independent city of Bedford
—755 68	Franklin County
—755 69	Henry County, Patrick County, Martinsville
—755 692	Henry County
—755 693	Independent city of Martinsville
—755 695	Patrick County
—755 7	Southwestern region of Virginia
—755 71	Floyd County, Carroll County, Grayson County, Galax
—755 712	Floyd County
—755 714	Carroll County
—755 715	Independent city of Galax
—755 717	Grayson County
—755 72	Smyth County, Washington County, Bristol
—755 723	Smyth County
—755 725	Washington County
—755 726	Independent city of Bristol
—755 73	Scott County and Lee County
—755 732	Scott County
—755 735	Lee County
—755 74	Wise County, Dickenson County, Norton
—755 743	Wise County
—755 744	Independent city of Norton
—755 745	Dickenson County
—755 75	Buchanan County and Russell County
—755 752	Buchanan County
—755 755	Russell County
—755 76	Tazewell County and Bland County
—755 763	Tazewell County
—755 765	Bland County

—755 77	Wythe County and Pulaski County
—755 773	Wythe County
—755 775	Pulaski County
—755 78	Giles County, Montgomery County, Radford
—755 782	Giles County
—755 785	Montgomery County
—755 786	Independent city of Radford
—755 79	Roanoke County, Craig County, Roanoke, Salem
—755 791	Independent city of Roanoke
—755 792	Roanoke County
—755 793	Independent city of Salem
—755 795	Craig County
—755 8	**Central western region of Virginia**
—755 81	Alleghany County and Covington
—[755 811]	Clifton Forge
	Relocated to —755816
—755 812	Independent city of Covington
—755 816	Alleghany County
	Including Clifton Forge [*formerly* —755811]
—755 83	Botetourt County
—755 85	Rockbridge County, Buena Vista, Lexington
—755 851	Independent city of Buena Vista
—755 852	Rockbridge County
—755 853	Independent city of Lexington
—755 87	Bath County
—755 89	Highland County
—755 9	**Northwestern region of Virginia**
	Class here *Shenandoah National Park; *Shenandoah Valley
—755 91	Augusta County, Staunton, Waynesboro
—755 911	Independent city of Staunton
—755 912	Independent city of Waynesboro

*For a specific part of this jurisdiction, region, or feature, see the part and follow instructions under —4–9

—755 916	Augusta County
—755 92	Rockingham County and Harrisonburg
—755 921	Independent city of Harrisonburg
—755 922	Rockingham County
—755 94	Page County
—755 95	Shenandoah County
—755 97	Warren County
—755 98	Clarke County
—755 99	Frederick County and Winchester
—755 991	Independent city of Winchester
—755 992	Frederick County
—756	North Carolina
—756 1	Northeast coastal plain counties of North Carolina

Class here *Coastal Plain in North Carolina; *Outer Banks

See also —16348 for Albemarle Sound, Pamlico Sound

—756 13	Currituck County and Camden County
—756 132	Currituck County
—756 135	Camden County

Including *Dismal Swamp in North Carolina

—756 14	Pasquotank County, Perquimans County, Chowan County
—756 142	Pasquotank County
—756 144	Perquimans County
—756 147	Chowan County
—756 15	Gates County and Hertford County

Class here *Chowan River

—756 153	Gates County
—756 155	Hertford County
—756 16	Bertie County and Washington County

Class here *Roanoke River

—756 163	Bertie County
—756 165	Washington County

*For a specific part of this jurisdiction, region, or feature, see the part and follow instructions under —4–9

—756 17	Tyrrell County and Dare County
—756 172	Tyrrell County
—756 175	Dare County
	Including Roanoke Island; Cape Hatteras
—756 18	Hyde County and Beaufort County
—756 184	Hyde County
—756 186	Beaufort County
—756 19	Craven County, Pamlico County, Carteret County
	Class here *Neuse River
—756 192	Craven County
—756 194	Pamlico County
—756 197	Carteret County
—756 2	Southeast coastal plain counties of North Carolina
	Class here *Cape Fear River
—756 21	Jones County
—756 23	Onslow County
—756 25	Pender County
—756 27	New Hanover County
	Class here Wilmington
—756 29	Brunswick County
—756 3	Southwest coastal plain counties of North Carolina
—756 31	Columbus County
—756 32	Bladen County
—756 33	Robeson County and Scotland County
—756 332	Robeson County
—756 335	Scotland County
—756 34	Richmond County
—756 35	Moore County and Lee County
—756 352	Moore County
—756 355	Lee County
—756 36	Harnett County and Hoke County

*For a specific part of this jurisdiction, region, or feature, see the part and follow instructions under
—4–9

—756 362	Harnett County
—756 365	Hoke County
—756 37	Cumberland County and Sampson County
—756 373	Cumberland County
—756 375	Sampson County
—756 38	Duplin County and Lenoir County
—756 382	Duplin County
—756 385	Lenoir County
—756 39	Greene County and Wayne County
—756 393	Greene County
—756 395	Wayne County
—756 4	Northwest coastal plain counties of North Carolina
—756 41	Johnston County
—756 43	Wilson County
—756 44	Pitt County
—756 45	Martin County
—756 46	Edgecombe County
—756 47	Nash County
—756 48	Halifax County
—756 49	Northampton County
—756 5	Northeast Piedmont counties
	Class here *Piedmont in North Carolina
—756 52	Warren County
—756 53	Vance County and Granville County
—756 532	Vance County
—756 535	Granville County
—756 54	Franklin County
—756 55	Wake County
	Class here Raleigh
—756 56	Durham County and Orange County
—756 563	Durham County

*For a specific part of this jurisdiction, region, or feature, see the part and follow instructions under —4–9

—756 565	Orange County
—756 57	Person County and Caswell County
—756 573	Person County
—756 575	Caswell County
—756 58	Alamance County
—756 59	Chatham County
—756 6	Northwest Piedmont counties
—756 61	Randolph County
—756 62	Guilford County
—756 63	Rockingham County
—756 64	Stokes County
—756 65	Surry County
—756 66	Yadkin County
—756 67	Forsyth County
—756 68	Davidson County
	Class here *Yadkin River
—756 69	Davie County
—756 7	Southern Piedmont counties
—756 71	Rowan County
—756 72	Cabarrus County
—756 73	Stanly County
—756 74	Montgomery County
—756 75	Anson County and Union County
—756 753	Anson County
—756 755	Union County
—756 76	Mecklenburg County
	Class here Charlotte
—756 77	Gaston County and Cleveland County
—756 773	Gaston County
—756 775	Cleveland County
—756 78	Lincoln County and Catawba County

*For a specific part of this jurisdiction, region, or feature, see the part and follow instructions under —4–9

—756 782	Lincoln County
—756 785	Catawba County
—756 79	Iredell County and Alexander County
—756 793	Iredell County
—756 795	Alexander County
—756 8	Northern Appalachian region counties

Class here *Blue Ridge in North Carolina, *Appalachian region in North Carolina

—756 82	Wilkes County
—756 83	Alleghany County and Ashe County
—756 832	Alleghany County
—756 835	Ashe County
—756 84	Watauga County and Caldwell County
—756 843	Watauga County
—756 845	Caldwell County
—756 85	Burke County
—756 86	Avery County and Mitchell County
—756 862	Avery County
—756 865	Mitchell County
—756 87	Yancey County and Madison County
—756 873	Yancey County
—756 875	Madison County
—756 88	Buncombe County

Including Asheville

—756 89	McDowell County
—756 9	Southern Appalachian region
—756 91	Rutherford County and Polk County
—756 913	Rutherford County
—756 915	Polk County
—756 92	Henderson County
—756 93	Transylvania County
—756 94	Haywood County

*For a specific part of this jurisdiction, region, or feature, see the part and follow instructions under —4–9

—756 95	Jackson County
—756 96	Swain County
	Class here *Great Smoky Mountains in North Carolina
—756 97	Graham County
—756 98	Macon County and Clay County
—756 982	Macon County
—756 985	Clay County
—756 99	Cherokee County
—757	South Carolina
—757 2	Mountain counties of South Carolina
	Class here *Blue Ridge in South Carolina
—757 21	Oconee County
—757 23	Pickens County
—757 25	Anderson County
—757 27	Greenville County
—757 29	Spartanburg County
—757 3	Southwest Piedmont counties
	Class here *Piedmont in South Carolina
—757 31	Laurens County
—757 33	Greenwood County
—757 35	Abbeville County
—757 36	McCormick County
—757 37	Edgefield County
—757 38	Saluda County
—757 39	Newberry County
—757 4	Northeast Piedmont counties
	Class here *Broad River
—757 41	Union County
—757 42	Cherokee County
—757 43	York County

*For a specific part of this jurisdiction, region, or feature, see the part and follow instructions under —4–9

—757 45	Lancaster County
	Class here *Catawba River
—757 47	Chester County
—757 49	Fairfield County
—757 6	Northeast counties of sand hills and upper pine belt of South Carolina
	Class here *Coastal Plain in South Carolina
—757 61	Kershaw County
—757 63	Chesterfield County
—757 64	Marlboro County
—757 66	Darlington County
—757 67	Lee County
—757 69	Sumter County
—757 7	Southwest counties of sand hills and upper pine belt of South Carolina
—757 71	Richland County
	Class here Columbia
—757 72	Calhoun County
—757 73	Lexington County
—757 75	Aiken County
—757 76	Barnwell County
—757 77	Allendale County
—757 78	Bamberg County
—757 79	Orangeburg County
—757 8	Northeast counties of lower pine belt of South Carolina
	Including *Black River, *Santee River
	Class here *Pee Dee River
—757 81	Clarendon County
—757 83	Williamsburg County
—757 84	Florence County
—757 85	Dillon County
—757 86	Marion County

*For a specific part of this jurisdiction, region, or feature, see the part and follow instructions under
—4–9

—757 87	Horry County
—757 89	Georgetown County
—757 9	Southwest counties of lower pine belt of South Carolina
	Including *Edisto River; *Savannah River in South Carolina
—757 91	Charleston County
—757 915	Charleston
—757 93	Berkeley County
—757 94	Dorchester County
—757 95	Colleton County
—757 97	Hampton County
—757 98	Jasper County
—757 99	Beaufort County
	Class here *Sea Islands
—758	Georgia
	Class here *Chattahoochee River
—758 1	Northeastern counties of Georgia
	Class here *Savannah River
—758 12	Rabun County and Habersham County
—758 123	Rabun County
—758 125	Habersham County
—758 13	Stephens County and Franklin County
—758 132	Stephens County
—758 135	Franklin County
—758 14	Banks County and Jackson County
—758 143	Banks County
—758 145	Jackson County
—758 15	Madison County and Hart County
—758 152	Madison County
—758 155	Hart County
—758 16	Elbert County and Lincoln County
—758 163	Elbert County

*For a specific part of this jurisdiction, region, or feature, see the part and follow instructions under
—4–9

—758 165	Lincoln County
—758 17	Wilkes County and Oglethorpe County
—758 172	Wilkes County
—758 175	Oglethorpe County
—758 18	Clarke County
	Class here Athens
—758 19	Oconee County and Barrow County
—758 193	Oconee County
—758 195	Barrow County
—758 2	North central counties of Georgia
	Class here *Blue Ridge in Georgia
—758 21	Walton County and Rockdale County
—758 212	Walton County
—758 215	Rockdale County
—758 22	Gwinnett County and De Kalb County
—758 223	Gwinnett County
—758 225	De Kalb County
—758 23	Fulton County
—758 231	Atlanta
—758 24	Douglas County and Cobb County
—758 243	Douglas County
—758 245	Cobb County
—758 25	Cherokee County and Pickens County
—758 253	Cherokee County
—758 255	Pickens County
—758 26	Dawson County and Forsyth County
—758 263	Dawson County
—758 265	Forsyth County
—758 27	Hall County, Lumpkin County, White County
—758 272	Hall County
—758 273	Lumpkin County

*For a specific part of this jurisdiction, region, or feature, see the part and follow instructions under
  —4–9

—758 277	White County
—758 28	Towns County and Union County
—758 282	Towns County
—758 285	Union County
—758 29	Fannin County and Gilmer County
—758 293	Fannin County
—758 295	Gilmer County
—758 3	Northwestern counties of Georgia
—758 31	Murray County
—758 32	Whitfield County and Catoosa County
—758 324	Whitfield County
—758 326	Catoosa County
—758 33	Walker County
—758 34	Dade County and Chattooga County
—758 342	Dade County
	Class here *Lookout Mountain in Georgia
—758 344	Chattooga County
—758 35	Floyd County
—758 36	Gordon County and Bartow County
—758 362	Gordon County
—758 365	Bartow County
—758 37	Paulding County and Polk County
—758 373	Paulding County
—758 375	Polk County
—758 38	Haralson County
—758 39	Carroll County
—758 4	West central counties of Georgia
	Class here *Piedmont in Georgia
—758 42	Heard County, Coweta County, Fayette County
—758 422	Heard County
—758 423	Coweta County

*For a specific part of this jurisdiction, region, or feature, see the part and follow instructions under
　—4–9

—758 426	Fayette County
—758 43	Clayton County and Henry County
—758 432	Clayton County
—758 435	Henry County
—758 44	Spalding County and Lamar County
—758 443	Spalding County
—758 446	Lamar County
—758 45	Pike County and Meriwether County
—758 453	Pike County
—758 455	Meriwether County
—758 46	Troup County and Harris County
—758 463	Troup County
—758 466	Harris County
—758 47	Muscogee County and Chattahoochee County
—758 473	Muscogee County
—758 476	Chattahoochee County
—758 48	Marion County, Talbot County, Upson County
—758 482	Marion County
—758 483	Talbot County
—758 486	Upson County
—758 49	Taylor County and Schley County
—758 493	Taylor County
—758 495	Schley County
—758 5	Central counties of Georgia
—758 51	Macon County and Houston County
—758 513	Macon County
—758 515	Houston County
—758 52	Pulaski County and Bleckley County
—758 523	Pulaski County
—758 525	Bleckley County
—758 53	Dodge County and Laurens County
—758 532	Dodge County
—758 535	Laurens County

—758 54	Wilkinson County and Twiggs County
—758 543	Wilkinson County
—758 545	Twiggs County
—758 55	Bibb County and Peach County
—758 552	Bibb County
	Class here Macon
—758 556	Peach County
—758 56	Crawford County, Monroe County, Jones County
—758 562	Crawford County
—758 563	Monroe County
—758 567	Jones County
—758 57	Baldwin County and Putnam County
—758 573	Baldwin County
—758 576	Putnam County
—758 58	Jasper County and Butts County
—758 583	Jasper County
—758 585	Butts County
—758 59	Newton County and Morgan County
—758 593	Newton County
—758 595	Morgan County
—758 6	**East central counties of Georgia**
	Including *Oconee River
	Class here *Ogeechee River
—758 61	Greene County and Taliaferro County
—758 612	Greene County
—758 616	Taliaferro County
—758 62	Hancock County and Warren County
—758 623	Hancock County
—758 625	Warren County
—758 63	McDuffie County and Columbia County
—758 632	McDuffie County

*For a specific part of this jurisdiction, region, or feature, see the part and follow instructions under
 —4–9

—758 635	Columbia County
—758 64	Richmond County
	Class here Augusta
—758 65	Burke County
—758 66	Jefferson County and Glascock County
—758 663	Jefferson County
—758 666	Glascock County
—758 67	Washington County and Johnson County
—758 672	Washington County
—758 676	Johnson County
—758 68	Treutlen County and Emanuel County
—758 682	Treutlen County
—758 684	Emanuel County
—758 69	Jenkins County and Screven County
—758 693	Jenkins County
—758 695	Screven County
—758 7	Southeastern counties of Georgia
	Including *Sea Islands of Georgia
—758 72	Effingham County and Chatham County
—758 722	Effingham County
—758 724	Chatham County
	Class here Savannah
—758 73	Bryan County, Liberty County, McIntosh County
—758 732	Bryan County
—758 733	Liberty County
—758 737	McIntosh County
—758 74	Glynn County and Camden County
—758 742	Glynn County
—758 746	Camden County
—758 75	Charlton County, Brantley County, Wayne County

*For a specific part of this jurisdiction, region, or feature, see the part and follow instructions under
  —4–9

—758 752	Charlton County
	Class here *Okefenokee Swamp
—758 753	Brantley County
—758 756	Wayne County
—758 76	Long County, Evans County, Bulloch County
—758 762	Long County
—758 763	Evans County
—758 766	Bulloch County
—758 77	Candler County and Tattnall County
—758 773	Candler County
—758 775	Tattnall County
—758 78	Toombs County, Appling County, Bacon County
—758 782	Toombs County
—758 784	Appling County
—758 787	Bacon County
—758 79	Pierce County and Ware County
—758 792	Pierce County
—758 794	Ware County
—758 8	South central counties of Georgia
—758 81	Clinch County, Echols County, Lanier County
—758 812	Clinch County
—758 814	Echols County
—758 817	Lanier County
—758 82	Atkinson County, Coffee County, Jeff Davis County
—758 822	Atkinson County
—758 823	Coffee County
—758 827	Jeff Davis County
—758 83	Montgomery County and Wheeler County
—758 832	Montgomery County
—758 835	Wheeler County
—758 84	Telfair County and Wilcox County

*For a specific part of this jurisdiction, region, or feature, see the part and follow instructions under
—4–9

—758 843	Telfair County
—758 845	Wilcox County
—758 85	Ben Hill County and Irwin County
—758 852	Ben Hill County
—758 855	Irwin County
—758 86	Berrien County and Lowndes County
—758 862	Berrien County
—758 864	Lowndes County
—758 87	Brooks County and Cook County
—758 874	Brooks County
—758 876	Cook County
—758 88	Tift County and Turner County
—758 882	Tift County
—758 885	Turner County
—758 89	Crisp County and Dooly County
—758 893	Crisp County
—758 895	Dooly County
—758 9	Southwestern counties of Georgia
	Class here *Flint River
—758 91	Sumter County and Webster County
—758 913	Sumter County
—758 916	Webster County
—758 92	Stewart County, Quitman County, Clay County
—758 922	Stewart County
—758 924	Quitman County
—758 927	Clay County
—758 93	Randolph County and Terrell County
—758 932	Randolph County
—758 935	Terrell County
—758 94	Lee County and Worth County
—758 943	Lee County

*For a specific part of this jurisdiction, region, or feature, see the part and follow instructions under —4–9

—758 945	Worth County
—758 95	Dougherty County and Calhoun County
—758 953	Dougherty County
—758 956	Calhoun County
—758 96	Early County, Miller County, Baker County
—758 962	Early County
—758 964	Miller County
—758 967	Baker County
—758 97	Mitchell County and Colquitt County
—758 973	Mitchell County
—758 975	Colquitt County
—758 98	Thomas County and Grady County
—758 984	Thomas County
—758 986	Grady County
—758 99	Decatur County and Seminole County
—758 993	Decatur County
—758 996	Seminole County
—759	Florida
—759 1	Northeastern counties of Florida
	Class here *Saint Johns River
—759 11	Nassau County
	Class here *Saint Marys River
—759 12	Duval County
	Class here Jacksonville
—759 13	Baker County
—759 14	Union County
—759 15	Bradford County
—759 16	Clay County
—759 17	Putnam County
—759 18	Saint Johns County
—759 19	Flagler County

*For a specific part of this jurisdiction, region, or feature, see the part and follow instructions under —4–9

—759 2	East central counties of Florida
—759 21	Volusia County
—759 22	Lake County
—759 23	Seminole County
—759 24	Orange County
—759 25	Osceola County
—759 27	Brevard County
—759 28	Indian River County
—759 29	Saint Lucie County
—759 3	Southeastern counties of Florida
—759 31	Martin County
—759 32	Palm Beach County
—759 35	Broward County
	Including Fort Lauderdale
—759 38	Dade County
—759 381	Miami and Miami Beach
—759 39	*The Everglades and *Lake Okeechobee
	Class here *Everglades National Park
—759 4	Southwestern counties of Florida
—759 41	Monroe County
	Including Key West
	Class here *Florida Keys
—759 44	Collier County
	Including *Ten Thousand Islands
	Class here *Big Cypress Swamp
—759 46	Hendry County
—759 48	Lee County
	Class here *Caloosahatchee River
—759 49	Charlotte County
—759 5	South central counties of Florida
—759 51	Glades County

*For a specific part of this jurisdiction, region, or feature, see the part and follow instructions under —4–9

—759 53	Okeechobee County
	Class here *Kissimmee River
—759 55	Highlands County
—759 57	Hardee County
	Class here *Peace River
—759 59	De Soto County
—759 6	Southern west central counties of Florida
—759 61	Sarasota County
—759 62	Manatee County
—759 63	Pinellas County
—759 65	Hillsborough County
	Class here Tampa
—759 67	Polk County
—759 69	Pasco County
—759 7	Northern west central counties of Florida
	Class here *Withlacoochee River
—759 71	Hernando County
—759 72	Citrus County
—759 73	Sumter County
—759 75	Marion County
—759 77	Levy County
—759 78	Gilchrist County
—759 79	Alachua County
—759 8	North central counties of Florida
	Class here *Suwannee River
—759 81	Dixie County and Lafayette County
—759 812	Dixie County
—759 816	Lafayette County
—759 82	Suwannee County
—759 83	Columbia County
—759 84	Hamilton County

*For a specific part of this jurisdiction, region, or feature, see the part and follow instructions under —4–9

—759 85	Madison County
—759 86	Taylor County
—759 87	Jefferson County
—759 88	Leon County
	Including Tallahassee
—759 89	Wakulla County
—759 9	Panhandle counties
—759 91	Franklin County
—759 92	Liberty County and Gadsden County
	Including *Apalachicola River
—759 923	Liberty County
—759 925	Gadsden County
—759 93	Jackson County
—759 94	Calhoun County and Gulf County
—759 943	Calhoun County
—759 947	Gulf County
—759 95	Bay County
—759 96	Washington County and Holmes County
—759 963	Washington County
—759 965	Holmes County
—759 97	Walton County
—759 98	Okaloosa County and Santa Rosa County
—759 982	Okaloosa County
—759 985	Santa Rosa County
—759 99	Escambia County
	Including Pensacola
—76	**South central United States**
	Class here Gulf Coast states, Old Southwest

*For a specific part of this jurisdiction, region, or feature, see the part and follow instructions under
   —4–9

—761 5	*Piedmont counties
	Class here *Tallapoosa River
—761 52	Elmore County
—761 53	Tallapoosa County
	Class here *Lake Martin
—761 55	Lee County
—761 56	Chambers County
—761 57	Randolph County
—761 58	Clay County
—761 59	Coosa County
—761 6	Coosa Valley counties
	Class here *Coosa River
—761 61	Talladega County
—761 63	Calhoun County
—761 64	Cleburne County
—761 65	Cherokee County
—761 66	De Kalb County
—761 67	Etowah County
—761 69	Saint Clair County
—761 7	Central plateau and basin counties of Alabama
—761 72	Blount County
—761 73	Cullman County
—761 74	Winston County
—761 76	Walker County
—761 78	Jefferson County
—761 781	Birmingham
—761 79	Shelby County
—761 8	Central pine belt counties of Alabama
—761 81	Chilton County
—761 82	Bibb County
—761 84	Tuscaloosa County

*For a specific part of this jurisdiction, region, or feature, see the part and follow instructions under
  —4–9

—761 85	Pickens County
—761 86	Lamar County
—761 87	Fayette County
—761 89	Marion County
—761 9	Tennessee Valley counties

Class here *Tennessee River in Alabama

—761 91	Franklin County and Colbert County
—761 913	Franklin County
—761 915	Colbert County
—761 92	Lawrence County
—761 93	Morgan County
—761 94	Marshall County

Class here *Guntersville Lake

—761 95	Jackson County
—761 97	Madison County

Class here Huntsville

—761 98	Limestone County

Class here *Wheeler Lake

—761 99	Lauderdale County
—762	Mississippi
—762 1	Southeastern counties of Mississippi
—762 12	Jackson County
—762 13	Harrison County
—762 14	Hancock County
—762 15	Pearl River County
—762 16	Stone County and George County
—762 162	Stone County
—762 165	George County
—762 17	Greene County and Perry County
—762 173	Greene County
—762 175	Perry County

*For a specific part of this jurisdiction, region, or feature, see the part and follow instructions under —4–9

—762 18	Forrest County
—762 19	Lamar County
—762 2	Southwestern counties of Mississippi
—762 21	Marion County
—762 22	Walthall County
—762 23	Pike County
—762 24	Amite County
—762 25	Wilkinson County
—762 26	Adams County
	Class here Natchez
—762 27	Franklin County
—762 28	Jefferson County and Claiborne County
—762 283	Jefferson County
—762 285	Claiborne County
—762 29	Warren County
—762 4	West central counties of Mississippi
	Class here *Big Black River, *Yazoo River; Yazoo Mississippi Delta
—762 41	Issaquena County and Sharkey County
—762 412	Issaquena County
—762 414	Sharkey County
—762 42	Washington County
—762 43	Bolivar County
—762 44	Coahoma County
—762 45	Quitman County and Tallahatchie County
—762 453	Quitman County
—762 455	Tallahatchie County
—762 46	Leflore County
—762 47	Sunflower County
—762 48	Humphreys County
—762 49	Yazoo County

*For a specific part of this jurisdiction, region, or feature, see the part and follow instructions under
—4–9

—762 5	South central counties of Mississippi
	Class here *Piney Woods (region), *Pearl River
—762 51	Hinds County
	Class here Jackson
—762 52	Copiah County
—762 53	Lincoln County and Lawrence County
—762 534	Lincoln County
—762 536	Lawrence County
—762 54	Jefferson Davis County and Covington County
—762 543	Jefferson Davis County
—762 545	Covington County
—762 55	Jones County
—762 57	Wayne County and Jasper County
—762 573	Wayne County
—762 575	Jasper County
—762 58	Smith County and Simpson County
—762 582	Smith County
—762 585	Simpson County
—762 59	Rankin County
—762 6	Central and east central counties of Mississippi
—762 62	Madison County and Holmes County
—762 623	Madison County
—762 625	Holmes County
—762 63	Carroll County and Grenada County
—762 633	Carroll County
—762 635	Grenada County
—762 64	Montgomery County and Attala County
—762 642	Montgomery County
—762 644	Attala County
—762 65	Leake County and Scott County
—762 653	Leake County

*For a specific part of this jurisdiction, region, or feature, see the part and follow instructions under —4–9

—762 655	Scott County
—762 67	Newton County, Clarke County, Lauderdale County
—762 672	Newton County
—762 673	Clarke County
—762 676	Lauderdale County
	For Meridian, see —762677
—762 677	Meridian
—762 68	Kemper County and Neshoba County
—762 683	Kemper County
—762 685	Neshoba County
—762 69	Winston County, Choctaw County, Webster County
—762 692	Winston County
—762 694	Choctaw County
—762 697	Webster County
—762 8	Northwestern counties of Mississippi
—762 81	Calhoun County
—762 82	Yalobusha County
—762 83	Lafayette County
—762 84	Panola County
—762 85	Tate County
—762 86	Tunica County
—762 87	De Soto County
—762 88	Marshall County
—762 89	Benton County
—762 9	Northeastern counties of Mississippi
—762 92	Tippah County and Union County
—762 923	Tippah County
—762 925	Union County
—762 93	Pontotoc County and Lee County
—762 932	Pontotoc County
—762 935	Lee County
—762 94	Chickasaw County and Clay County
—762 942	Chickasaw County

—762 945	Clay County
—762 95	Oktibbeha County and Noxubee County
—762 953	Oktibbeha County
—762 955	Noxubee County
—762 97	Lowndes County and Monroe County
—762 973	Lowndes County
—762 975	Monroe County
—762 98	Itawamba County and Prentiss County
—762 982	Itawamba County
—762 985	Prentiss County
—762 99	Alcorn County and Tishomingo County
—762 993	Alcorn County
—762 995	Tishomingo County
—763	Louisiana
—763 1	Eastern parishes of Louisiana
—763 11	Washington Parish
—763 12	Saint Tammany Parish
—763 13	Tangipahoa Parish
—763 14	Livingston Parish
—763 15	Saint Helena Parish
—763 16	East Feliciana Parish
—763 17	West Feliciana Parish
—763 18	East Baton Rouge Parish
	Class here Baton Rouge
—763 19	Ascension Parish
—763 3	Southeastern parishes of Louisiana
	Class here Mississippi Delta
—763 31	Saint James Parish
—763 32	Saint John the Baptist Parish
	Including *Lake Maurepas
—763 33	Saint Charles Parish

*For a specific part of this jurisdiction, region, or feature, see the part and follow instructions under —4–9

—763 34	*Lake Pontchartrain
—763 35	Orleans Parish (New Orleans)
—763 36	Saint Bernard Parish
—763 37	Plaquemines Parish
—763 38	Jefferson Parish
—763 39	Lafourche Parish
—763 4	South central parishes of Louisiana
—763 41	Terrebonne Parish
—763 42	Saint Mary Parish
—763 43	Assumption Parish
—763 44	Iberville Parish
—763 45	West Baton Rouge Parish and Pointe Coupee Parish
—763 452	West Baton Rouge Parish
—763 454	Pointe Coupee Parish
—763 46	Saint Landry Parish
—763 47	Lafayette Parish
—763 48	Saint Martin Parish
—763 49	Iberia Parish
—763 5	Southwestern parishes of Louisiana
—763 51	Vermilion Parish
—763 52	Cameron Parish
	Including Calcasieu Lake, *Sabine Lake
—763 54	Calcasieu Parish
—763 55	Jefferson Davis Parish
—763 56	Acadia Parish
—763 57	Evangeline Parish
—763 58	Allen Parish
—763 59	Beauregard Parish
—763 6	West central parishes of Louisiana
	Class here *Red River in Louisiana
—763 61	Vernon Parish

*For a specific part of this jurisdiction, region, or feature, see the part and follow instructions under —4–9

—763 62	Sabine Parish
	Class here *Toledo Bend Reservoir
—763 63	De Soto Parish
—763 64	Red River Parish
—763 65	Natchitoches Parish
—763 66	Winn Parish
—763 67	Grant Parish
—763 69	Rapides Parish
—763 7	East central parishes of Louisiana
	Class here *Ouachita River
—763 71	Avoyelles Parish
—763 73	Concordia Parish
—763 74	Catahoula Parish
—763 75	La Salle Parish
—763 76	Caldwell Parish
—763 77	Franklin Parish
—763 79	Tensas Parish
—763 8	Northeastern parishes of Louisiana
—763 81	Madison Parish
—763 82	East Carroll Parish
—763 83	West Carroll Parish
—763 84	Morehouse Parish
—763 86	Richland Parish
—763 87	Ouachita Parish
—763 89	Union Parish
—763 9	Northwestern parishes of Louisiana
—763 91	Lincoln Parish
—763 92	Jackson Parish
—763 93	Bienville Parish
—763 94	Claiborne Parish
—763 96	Webster Parish

*For a specific part of this jurisdiction, region, or feature, see the part and follow instructions under —4–9

—763 97	Bossier Parish
—763 99	Caddo Parish
	Including *Caddo Lake
	Class here Shreveport
—764	Texas
	Class here *Brazos River, *Colorado River
—764 1	Coastal plains of Texas

For East Texas timber belt and blackland prairie, see —7642; for Rio Grande Plain, see —7644

—764 11	Nueces County and neighboring counties
	Class here *Nueces River
—764 113	Nueces County
	Class here Corpus Christi
—764 115	San Patricio County
—764 117	Bee County
—764 119	Refugio County
—764 12	Calhoun County and neighboring counties
	Class here *Guadalupe River, *San Antonio River
—764 121	Calhoun County
—764 122	Aransas County
—764 123	Goliad County
—764 125	Victoria County
—764 127	Jackson County
—764 13	Matagorda County and neighboring counties
—764 132	Matagorda County
—764 133	Wharton County
—764 135	Fort Bend County
—764 137	Brazoria County
—764 139	Galveston County
—764 14	Harris County and neighboring counties
	Class here *East Texas; *Sabine River, *Trinity River
—764 141	Harris County

*For a specific part of this jurisdiction, region, or feature, see the part and follow instructions under —4–9

—764 141 1	Houston
—764 143	Chambers County
—764 145	Jefferson County
—764 147	Orange County
—764 15	Montgomery County and neighboring counties
	Class here *Neches River
—764 153	Montgomery County
—764 155	Liberty County
—764 157	Hardin County
—764 159	Jasper County
—764 16	Newton County and neighboring counties
—764 162	Newton County
—764 163	Tyler County
—764 165	Polk County
—764 167	San Jacinto County
—764 169	Walker County
—764 17	Trinity County and neighboring counties
—764 172	Trinity County
—764 173	Angelina County
—764 175	San Augustine County
—764 177	Sabine County
—764 179	Shelby County
—764 18	Nacogdoches County and neighboring counties
—764 182	Nacogdoches County
—764 183	Cherokee County
—764 185	Rusk County
—764 187	Panola County
—764 189	Gregg County
—764 19	Harrison County and neighboring counties
—764 192	Harrison County
—764 193	Marion County

*For a specific part of this jurisdiction, region, or feature, see the part and follow instructions under
   —4–9

—764 195	Cass County
—764 197	Bowie County
—764 2	East Texas timber belt and blackland prairie
	For Austin-San Antonio region, see —7643
—764 21	Red River County and neighboring counties
—764 212	Red River County
—764 213	Franklin County
—764 215	Titus County
—764 217	Morris County
—764 219	Camp County
—764 22	Upshur County and neighboring counties
—764 222	Upshur County
—764 223	Wood County
—764 225	Smith County
—764 227	Henderson County
—764 229	Anderson County
—764 23	Freestone County and neighboring counties
—764 232	Freestone County
—764 233	Leon County
—764 235	Houston County
—764 237	Madison County
—764 239	Robertson County
—764 24	Burleson County and neighboring counties
—764 241	Burleson County
—764 242	Brazos County
—764 243	Grimes County
—764 245	Washington County
—764 247	Lee County
—764 249	Waller County
—764 25	Fayette County and neighboring counties
—764 251	Fayette County
—764 252	Austin County
	See also —76431 for Austin (city)
—764 253	Colorado County

—764 255	Lavaca County
—764 257	Gonzales County
—764 259	De Witt County
—764 26	Lamar County and Fannin County
	Class here *blackland prairie
—764 263	Lamar County
—764 265	Fannin County
—764 27	Hunt County and neighboring counties
—764 272	Hunt County
—764 273	Delta County
—764 274	Hopkins County
—764 275	Rains County
—764 276	Van Zandt County
—764 277	Kaufman County
—764 278	Rockwall County
—764 28	Dallas County and neighboring counties
—764 281	Dallas County and Ellis County
—764 281 1	Dallas County
	For Dallas, see —7642812
—764 281 2	Dallas
	Class here Dallas-Fort Worth metropolitan area
	For Fort Worth, see —7645315
—764 281 5	Ellis County
—764 282	Navarro County
—764 283	Hill County
—764 284	McLennan County
—764 285	Limestone County
—764 286	Falls County
—764 287	Bell County
—764 288	Milam County
—764 289	Williamson County

*For a specific part of this jurisdiction, region, or feature, see the part and follow instructions under —4–9

—764 3	Austin-San Antonio region

For Comal County, see —764887; for Hays County, see —764888

—764 31	Travis County

Class here Austin

See also —764252 for Austin County

—764 32	Bastrop County
—764 33	Caldwell County
—764 34	Guadalupe County
—764 35	Bexar County
—764 351	San Antonio
—764 4	Rio Grande Plain (Lower Rio Grande Valley)

Class here *Rio Grande

—764 42	Medina County
—764 43	Uvalde County and neighboring counties
—764 432	Uvalde County
—764 433	Kinney County
—764 435	Maverick County
—764 437	Zavala County
—764 44	Frio County and neighboring counties
—764 442	Frio County
—764 443	Atascosa County
—764 444	Karnes County
—764 445	Wilson County
—764 447	Live Oak County
—764 45	McMullen County and neighboring counties
—764 452	McMullen County
—764 453	La Salle County
—764 455	Dimmit County
—764 46	Webb County and neighboring counties
—764 462	Webb County
—764 463	Duval County

*For a specific part of this jurisdiction, region, or feature, see the part and follow instructions under —4–9

—764 465	Jim Wells County
—764 47	Kleberg County and neighboring counties
	Class here *Padre Island
—764 472	Kleberg County
—764 473	Kenedy County
—764 475	Brooks County
—764 48	Jim Hogg County and neighboring counties
—764 482	Jim Hogg County
—764 483	Zapata County
—764 485	Starr County
—764 49	Hidalgo County and neighboring counties
—764 492	Hidalgo County
—764 493	Willacy County
—764 495	Cameron County
—764 5	North central plains of Texas

For Burnet-Llano region, see —7646; for northwestern lowland counties, see —7647

—764 51	Mills County and neighboring counties
	Class here *Grand Prairie
—764 512	Mills County
—764 513	Lampasas County
—764 515	Coryell County
—764 518	Bosque County
—764 52	Somervell County and neighboring counties
—764 521	Somervell County
—764 522	Hood County
—764 524	Johnson County
—764 53	Tarrant County and neighboring counties
—764 531	Tarrant County
—764 531 5	Fort Worth

Class comprehensive works on Dallas-Fort Worth metropolitan area in —7642812

*For a specific part of this jurisdiction, region, or feature, see the part and follow instructions under —4–9

—764 532	Wise County
—764 533	Cooke County
—764 54	Montague County and neighboring counties
—764 541	Montague County
—764 542	Clay County
—764 543	Archer County
—764 544	Jack County
—764 545	Young County
—764 546	Stephens County
—764 547	Eastland County
—764 548	Brown County
—764 549	Hamilton County
—764 55	Erath County and neighboring counties
—764 551	Erath County
—764 552	Palo Pinto County
—764 553	Parker County
—764 554	Comanche County
—764 555	Denton County
—764 556	Collin County
—764 557	Grayson County
—764 6	Burnet-Llano region
—764 62	Llano County
—764 63	Burnet County
—764 64	Blanco County
—764 65	Gillespie County
—764 66	Mason County
—764 67	McCulloch County
—764 68	San Saba County
—764 7	Northwestern lowland counties of Texas
—764 71	Concho County
—764 72	Tom Green County and neighboring counties
—764 721	Tom Green County
—764 723	Coke County

—764 724	Runnels County
—764 725	Coleman County
—764 726	Callahan County
—764 727	Taylor County
—764 728	Nolan County
—764 729	Mitchell County
—764 73	Scurry County and neighboring counties
—764 731	Scurry County
—764 732	Fisher County
—764 733	Jones County
—764 734	Shackelford County
—764 735	Throckmorton County
—764 736	Haskell County
—764 737	Stonewall County
—764 738	Kent County
—764 74	Dickens County and neighboring counties
—764 741	Dickens County
—764 742	King County
—764 743	Knox County
—764 744	Baylor County
—764 745	Wichita County
—764 746	Wilbarger County
—764 747	Hardeman County
—764 748	Foard County
—764 75	Cottle County and neighboring counties
—764 751	Cottle County
—764 752	Motley County
—764 753	Hall County
—764 754	Childress County
—764 8	Great Plains

Class here *Llano Estacado

*For a specific part of this jurisdiction, region, or feature, see the part and follow instructions under —4–9

>	—764 81–764 83 Panhandle counties
	Class comprehensive works in —7648
—764 81	Northern Panhandle counties
—764 812	Dallam County
—764 813	Sherman County
—764 814	Hansford County
—764 815	Ochiltree County
—764 816	Lipscomb County
—764 817	Hemphill County
—764 818	Roberts County
—764 82	Middle Panhandle counties
—764 821	Hutchinson County
—764 822	Moore County
—764 823	Hartley County
—764 824	Oldham County
—764 825	Potter County
—764 826	Carson County
—764 827	Gray County
—764 828	Wheeler County
—764 83	Southern Panhandle counties
—764 831	Collingsworth County
—764 832	Donley County
—764 833	Armstrong County
—764 834	Randall County
—764 835	Deaf Smith County
—764 836	Parmer County
—764 837	Castro County
—764 838	Swisher County
—764 839	Briscoe County
—764 84	Floyd County and neighboring counties
—764 841	Floyd County
—764 842	Hale County

—764 843	Lamb County
—764 844	Bailey County
—764 845	Cochran County
—764 846	Hockley County
—764 847	Lubbock County
—764 848	Crosby County
—764 849	Yoakum County
—764 85	Lynn County and neighboring counties
—764 851	Lynn County
—764 852	Garza County
—764 853	Borden County
—764 854	Dawson County
—764 855	Gaines County
—764 856	Andrews County
—764 857	Martin County
—764 858	Howard County
—764 859	Terry County
—764 86	Midland County and neighboring counties
—764 861	Midland County
—764 862	Ector County
—764 863	Upton County
—764 87	*Edwards Plateau counties
—764 871	Sterling County
—764 872	Glasscock County
—764 873	Reagan County
—764 874	Irion County
—764 875	Crockett County
—764 876	Schleicher County
—764 877	Menard County
—764 878	Kimble County
—764 879	Sutton County

*For a specific part of this jurisdiction, region, or feature, see the part and follow instructions under —4–9

—764 88	Val Verde County and neighboring counties
—764 881	Val Verde County
—764 882	Edwards County
—764 883	Real County
—764 884	Kerr County
—764 885	Bandera County
—764 886	Kendall County
—764 887	Comal County
—764 888	Hays County

—764 9	Western mountain and basin region of Texas

Class here *Pecos River

—764 91	Pecos Basin counties
—764 912	Loving County
—764 913	Winkler County
—764 914	Ward County
—764 915	Crane County
—764 92	Stockton Plateau counties
—764 922	Terrell County
—764 923	Pecos County
—764 924	Reeves County
—764 93	Big Bend Region counties
—764 932	Brewster County

Including Big Bend National Park

—764 933	Presidio County
—764 934	Jeff Davis County
—764 94	Culberson County

Including Guadalupe Mountains National Park

For Guadalupe Mountains National Park in Hudspeth County, see —76495

—764 95	Hudspeth County
—764 96	El Paso County

Class here El Paso; *upper Rio Grande of Texas

---

*For a specific part of this jurisdiction, region, or feature, see the part and follow instructions under —4–9

—766	Oklahoma
	Class here *Canadian River
—766 1	Northwestern counties of Oklahoma
	Class here former *Oklahoma Territory; *North Canadian River
—766 13	Panhandle counties
	For Beaver County, see —76614
—766 132	Cimarron County
—766 135	Texas County
—766 14	Beaver County
—766 15	Harper County and Ellis County
—766 153	Harper County
—766 155	Ellis County
—766 16	Roger Mills County
—766 17	Custer County
—766 18	Dewey County
766 19	Woodward County
—766 2	North central counties of Oklahoma
—766 21	Woods County
—766 22	Alfalfa County
—766 23	Grant County
—766 24	Kay County
—766 25	Osage County
—766 26	Pawnee County
—766 27	Noble County
—766 28	Garfield County
—766 29	Major County
—766 3	Central counties of Oklahoma
—766 31	Blaine County
—766 32	Kingfisher County
—766 33	Logan County
—766 34	Payne County

*For a specific part of this jurisdiction, region, or feature, see the part and follow instructions under
—4–9

—766 35	Lincoln County
—766 36	Pottawatomie County
—766 37	Cleveland County
—766 38	Oklahoma County
	Class here Oklahoma City
—766 39	Canadian County
—766 4	Southwestern counties of Oklahoma
—766 41	Caddo County
—766 42	Washita County
—766 43	Beckham County
—766 44	Greer County and Harmon County
—766 443	Greer County
—766 445	Harmon County
—766 45	Jackson County
—766 46	Tillman County
—766 47	Kiowa County
—766 48	Comanche County
—766 49	Cotton County
—766 5	South central counties of Oklahoma
	Class here former *Indian Territory; *Arbuckle Mountains; *Washita River
—766 52	Jefferson County
—766 53	Stephens County
—766 54	Grady County
—766 55	McClain County
—766 56	Garvin County
—766 57	Murray County
	Including Platt National Park
—766 58	Carter County
—766 59	Love County
—766 6	Southeastern counties of Oklahoma
	Class here *Ouachita Mountains; *Red River

*For a specific part of this jurisdiction, region, or feature, see the part and follow instructions under
  —4–9

—766 61	Marshall County
	Class here *Lake Texoma
—766 62	Bryan County
—766 63	Choctaw County
—766 64	McCurtain County
—766 65	Pushmataha County
—766 66	Atoka County
—766 67	Coal County
—766 68	Johnston County
—766 69	Pontotoc County
—766 7	Southeast central counties of Oklahoma
—766 71	Seminole County
—766 72	Hughes County
—766 73	Okfuskee County
—766 74	McIntosh County
—766 75	Pittsburg County
—766 76	Latimer County
—766 77	Haskell County
—766 79	Le Flore County
—766 8	Northeast central counties of Oklahoma
	Class here *Ozark Plateau in Oklahoma; *Boston Mountains in Oklahoma; *Arkansas River in Oklahoma
—766 81	Sequoyah County
—766 82	Muskogee County
—766 83	Okmulgee County
—766 84	Creek County
—766 86	Tulsa County
	Class here Tulsa
—766 87	Wagoner County
	Class here *Fort Gibson Reservoir
—766 88	Cherokee County
—766 89	Adair County

*For a specific part of this jurisdiction, region, or feature, see the part and follow instructions under —4–9

—766 9	Northeastern counties of Oklahoma
—766 91	Delaware County
—766 93	Mayes County
—766 94	Rogers County
—766 96	Washington County
—766 97	Nowata County
—766 98	Craig County
—766 99	Ottawa County
—767	Arkansas
—767 1	Northwestern counties of Arkansas
	Class here *Ozark Mountains, *Ozark Plateau
—767 13	Benton County
—767 14	Washington County
—767 15	Madison County
—767 16	Newton County
—767 17	Carroll County
—767 18	Boone County
—767 19	Marion County and Searcy County
—767 193	Marion County
	Class here *Bull Shoals Lake
—767 195	Searcy County
—767 2	North central counties of Arkansas
	Class here *White River
—767 21	Baxter County
—767 22	Fulton County
—767 23	Sharp County
—767 24	Randolph County
—767 25	Lawrence County
—767 26	Independence County
—767 27	Izard County
—767 28	Stone County and Cleburne County

*For a specific part of this jurisdiction, region, or feature, see the part and follow instructions under
  —4–9

—767 283	Stone County
—767 285	Cleburne County
—767 29	Van Buren County
—767 3	Northwest central counties of Arkansas
	Class here *Arkansas River
—767 31	Conway County
—767 32	Pope County
—767 33	Johnson County
—767 34	Franklin County
—767 35	Crawford County
—767 36	Sebastian County
—767 37	Logan County
—767 38	Yell County
—767 39	Perry County
—767 4	Southwest central counties of Arkansas
	Class here *Ouachita Mountains in Arkansas
—767 41	Garland County
	Including Hot Springs National Park
—767 42	Hot Spring County
—767 43	Montgomery County
—767 44	Scott County
—767 45	Polk County
—767 47	Sevier County
—767 48	Howard County and Pike County
—767 483	Howard County
—767 485	Pike County
—767 49	Clark County
—767 5	Southwestern counties of Arkansas
—767 52	Nevada County
—767 54	Hempstead County
—767 55	Little River County

*For a specific part of this jurisdiction, region, or feature, see the part and follow instructions under
  —4–9

—767 56	Miller County
—767 57	Lafayette County
—767 59	Columbia County
—767 6	South central counties of Arkansas
—767 61	Union County
—767 63	Bradley County
—767 64	Calhoun County
—767 66	Ouachita County
—767 67	Dallas County
—767 69	Cleveland County
—767 7	Central counties of Arkansas
—767 71	Grant County
—767 72	Saline County
—767 73	Pulaski County
	Class here Little Rock
—767 74	Faulkner County
—767 76	White County
—767 77	Prairie County
—767 78	Lonoke County
—767 79	Jefferson County
—767 8	Southeastern counties of Arkansas
	Class here *Mississippi River in Arkansas
—767 82	Lincoln County and Drew County
—767 823	Lincoln County
—767 825	Drew County
—767 83	Ashley County
—767 84	Chicot County
—767 85	Desha County
—767 86	Arkansas County
—767 87	Monroe County
—767 88	Phillips County

*For a specific part of this jurisdiction, region, or feature, see the part and follow instructions under —4–9

—767 89	Lee County
—767 9	Northeastern counties of Arkansas
—767 91	Saint Francis County
—767 92	Woodruff County
—767 93	Cross County
—767 94	Crittenden County
—767 95	Mississippi County
—767 96	Poinsett County
—767 97	Jackson County
—767 98	Craighead County
—767 99	Greene County and Clay County
—767 993	Greene County
—767 995	Clay County
—768	Tennessee

Class here *Tennessee River

—768 1	Mississippi Valley counties
—768 12	Lake County

Including *Reelfoot Lake

—768 13	Obion County
—768 15	Dyer County
—768 16	Lauderdale County
—768 17	Tipton County
—768 19	Shelby County

Class here Memphis

—768 2	West Tennessee Plain counties
—768 21	Fayette County
—768 22	Haywood County and Crockett County
—768 223	Haywood County
—768 225	Crockett County
—768 23	Gibson County
—768 24	Weakley County

*For a specific part of this jurisdiction, region, or feature, see the part and follow instructions under —4–9

—768 25	Carroll County
—768 26	Henderson County and Chester County
—768 263	Henderson County
—768 265	Chester County
—768 27	Madison County
—768 28	Hardeman County
—768 29	McNairy County
—768 3	Western Tennessee River Valley counties
—768 31	Hardin County
—768 32	Decatur County
—768 33	Benton County
—768 34	Henry County
—768 35	Stewart County
—768 36	Houston County
—768 37	Humphreys County
—768 38	Perry County
—768 39	Wayne County
—768 4	West Highland Rim counties

Class here comprehensive works on Highland Rim counties

For east Highland Rim counties, see —7686

—768 42	Lawrence County
—768 43	Lewis County and Hickman County
—768 432	Lewis County
—768 434	Hickman County

Class here *Duck River

—768 44	Dickson County
—768 45	Montgomery County
—768 46	Cheatham County and Robertson County
—768 462	Cheatham County
—768 464	Robertson County
—768 47	Sumner County

*For a specific part of this jurisdiction, region, or feature, see the part and follow instructions under —4–9

—768 48	Trousdale County and Macon County
—768 482	Trousdale County
—768 484	Macon County
—768 49	Clay County
	Class here *Dale Hollow Lake
—768 5	Central Basin counties
	Class here *Cumberland River
—768 51	Jackson County
—768 52	Smith County
—768 53	De Kalb County and Cannon County
—768 532	De Kalb County
	Class here *Center Hill Lake
—768 535	Cannon County
—768 54	Wilson County
—768 55	Davidson County
	Class here Nashville
—768 56	Williamson County
—768 57	Rutherford County
—768 58	Bedford County and Marshall County
—768 583	Bedford County
—768 585	Marshall County
—768 59	Maury County
—768 6	East Highland Rim counties
—768 61	Giles County
—768 62	Lincoln County and Moore County
—768 624	Lincoln County
—768 627	Moore County
—768 63	Franklin County
—768 64	Coffee County
—768 65	Warren County and Van Buren County
—768 653	Warren County

*For a specific part of this jurisdiction, region, or feature, see the part and follow instructions under —4–9

—768 657	Van Buren County
—768 66	White County
—768 67	Putnam County
—768 68	Overton County and Pickett County
—768 684	Overton County
—768 687	Pickett County
—768 69	Fentress County
—768 7	*Cumberland Plateau counties
—768 71	Scott County
—768 72	Campbell County
—768 73	Anderson County
	Class here *Clinch River
—768 74	Morgan County
—768 75	Cumberland County
—768 76	Bledsoe County
—768 77	Sequatchie County
	Class here *Sequatchie River
—768 78	Grundy County
—768 79	Marion County
—768 8	Southeastern counties of Tennessee
—768 82	Hamilton County
	Including *Lookout Mountain
	Class here Chattanooga; *Chickamauga Lake
—768 83	Rhea County and Meigs County
—768 834	Rhea County
—768 836	Meigs County
—768 84	Roane County
—768 85	Knox County
	Including *Fort Loudoun Lake
	Class here Knoxville
—768 86	Loudon County and McMinn County

*For a specific part of this jurisdiction, region, or feature, see the part and follow instructions under —4–9

—768 863	Loudon County
—768 865	McMinn County
—768 87	Bradley County and Polk County
—768 873	Bradley County
—768 875	Polk County
—768 88	Monroe County and Blount County
—768 883	Monroe County
—768 885	Blount County
—768 89	*Great Smoky Mountains area
	Class here *Great Smoky Mountains National Park
—768 893	Sevier County
—768 895	Cocke County
	Class here *French Broad River
—768 9	Northeastern counties of Tennessee
—768 91	Greene County
—768 92	Hamblen County and Jefferson County
—768 923	Hamblen County
—768 924	Jefferson County
—768 93	Grainger County and Union County
—768 932	Grainger County
—768 935	Union County
	Class here *Norris Lake
—768 94	Claiborne County and Hancock County
—768 944	Claiborne County
	Class here *Cumberland Mountains in Tennessee
—768 946	Hancock County
—768 95	Hawkins County
—768 96	Sullivan County
—768 97	Washington County
—768 98	Unicoi County and Carter County
—768 982	Unicoi County

*For a specific part of this jurisdiction, region, or feature, see the part and follow instructions under
—4–9

—768 984	Carter County
—768 99	Johnson County
—769	Kentucky
—769 1	Southern mountain region counties of Kentucky
	Including *Cumberland Plateau in Kentucky
	Class here *Cumberland Mountains
—769 12	Bell County and Knox County
—769 123	Bell County
—769 125	Knox County
—769 13	Whitley County and McCreary County
—769 132	Whitley County
—769 135	McCreary County
—769 14	Laurel County and Clay County
—769 143	Laurel County
—769 145	Clay County
—769 15	Leslie County and Harlan County
—769 152	Leslie County
—769 154	Harlan County
—769 16	Letcher County and Knott County
—769 163	Letcher County
—769 165	Knott County
—769 17	Perry County and Owsley County
—769 173	Perry County
—769 176	Owsley County
—769 18	Jackson County and Lee County
—769 183	Jackson County
—769 185	Lee County
—769 19	Breathitt County
—769 2	Northern mountain region counties of Kentucky
	Class here *Big Sandy River and *Tug Fork in Kentucky
—769 21	Wolfe County and Magoffin County

*For a specific part of this jurisdiction, region, or feature, see the part and follow instructions under
 —4–9

—769 213	Wolfe County
—769 215	Magoffin County
—769 22	Floyd County
—769 23	Pike County
—769 24	Martin County and Johnson County
—769 243	Martin County
—769 245	Johnson County
—769 25	Morgan County and Elliott County
—769 253	Morgan County
—769 255	Elliott County
—769 26	Lawrence County
—769 27	Boyd County
—769 28	Carter County
—769 29	Greenup County and Lewis County
—769 293	Greenup County
—769 295	Lewis County
—769 3	Northern Bluegrass counties
	Class here *Bluegrass region, *Kentucky River
—769 32	Mason County and Bracken County
—769 323	Mason County
—769 325	Bracken County
—769 33	Pendleton County
—769 34	Campbell County
—769 35	Kenton County
—769 36	Boone County and Gallatin County
—769 363	Boone County
—769 365	Gallatin County
—769 37	Carroll County and Trimble County
—769 373	Carroll County
—769 375	Trimble County
—769 38	Oldham County and Henry County

*For a specific part of this jurisdiction, region, or feature, see the part and follow instructions under —4–9

—769 383	Oldham County
—769 385	Henry County
—769 39	Owen County and Grant County
—769 393	Owen County
—769 395	Grant County
—769 4	Southern Bluegrass counties
—769 41	Harrison County, Robertson County, Nicholas County
—769 413	Harrison County
—769 415	Robertson County
—769 417	Nicholas County
—769 42	Bourbon County and Scott County
—769 423	Bourbon County
—769 425	Scott County
—769 43	Franklin County and Shelby County
—769 432	Franklin County
	Including Frankfort
—769 435	Shelby County
—769 44	Jefferson County
	Class here Louisville
—769 45	Bullitt County and Spencer County
—769 453	Bullitt County
—769 455	Spencer County
—769 46	Anderson County and Woodford County
—769 463	Anderson County
—769 465	Woodford County
—769 47	Fayette County
	Class here Lexington
—769 48	Jessamine County and Mercer County
—769 483	Jessamine County
—769 485	Mercer County
—769 49	Washington County and Nelson County
—769 493	Washington County
—769 495	Nelson County
—769 5	The Knobs counties

—769 51	Marion County
—769 52	Boyle County and Garrard County
—769 523	Boyle County
—769 525	Garrard County
—769 53	Madison County
—769 54	Clark County
—769 55	Montgomery County and Bath County
—769 553	Montgomery County
—769 555	Bath County
—769 56	Fleming County
—769 57	Rowan County
—769 58	Menifee County and Powell County
—769 583	Menifee County
—769 585	Powell County
—769 59	Estill County
—769 6	Eastern Pennyroyal counties
	Class here *Highland Rim in Kentucky, *Pennyroyal Plateau
—769 62	Rockcastle County and Lincoln County
—769 623	Rockcastle County
—769 625	Lincoln County
—769 63	Pulaski County
	Class here *Lake Cumberland
—769 64	Wayne County
—769 65	Clinton County and Russell County
—769 653	Clinton County
—769 655	Russell County
—769 66	Casey County
—769 67	Taylor County and Adair County
—769 673	Taylor County
—769 675	Adair County
—769 68	Cumberland County and Monroe County

*For a specific part of this jurisdiction, region, or feature, see the part and follow instructions under
—4–9

—769 683	Cumberland County
—769 685	Monroe County
—769 69	Metcalfe County and Green County
—769 693	Metcalfe County
—769 695	Green County
—769 7	Western Pennyroyal counties
—769 71	Larue County and Hart County
—769 713	Larue County
—769 715	Hart County
—769 72	Barren County
—769 73	Allen County and Simpson County
—769 732	Allen County
—769 735	Simpson County
—769 74	Warren County
—769 75	Edmonson County, Butler County, Mammoth Cave National Park
—769 752	Edmonson County
—769 754	*Mammoth Cave National Park
—769 755	Butler County
—769 76	Logan County
—769 77	Todd County
—769 78	Christian County
—769 79	Trigg County
	Class here *Land Between the Lakes; *Lake Barkley
—769 8	Western basin counties of Kentucky
	Class here *Green River
—769 81	Lyon County and Caldwell County
—769 813	Lyon County
—769 815	Caldwell County
—769 82	Hopkins County and McLean County
—769 823	Hopkins County
—769 826	McLean County

*For a specific part of this jurisdiction, region, or feature, see the part and follow instructions under —4–9

—769 83	Muhlenberg County and Ohio County
—769 832	Muhlenberg County
—769 835	Ohio County
—769 84	Grayson County and Hardin County
—769 842	Grayson County
—769 845	Hardin County
—769 85	Meade County and Breckinridge County
—769 852	Meade County
—769 854	Breckinridge County
—769 86	Hancock County and Daviess County
—769 862	Hancock County
—769 864	Daviess County
	Class here Owensboro
—769 87	Henderson County
—769 88	Webster County and Union County
—769 883	Webster County
—769 885	Union County
—769 89	Crittenden County and Livingston County
—769 893	Crittenden County
—769 895	Livingston County
	Class here *Kentucky Lake
—769 9	Counties west of Tennessee River
—769 91	Marshall County
—769 92	Calloway County
—769 93	Graves County
—769 95	McCracken County
—769 96	Ballard County
—769 97	Carlisle County
—769 98	Hickman County
—769 99	Fulton County

*For a specific part of this jurisdiction, region, or feature, see the part and follow instructions under —4–9

—77   **North central United States**

Class here Lake states; *Middle West; *Mississippi River, *Ohio River; *Great Lakes

SUMMARY

—771	**Ohio**
—772	**Indiana**
—773	**Illinois**
—774	**Michigan**
—775	**Wisconsin**
—776	**Minnesota**
—777	**Iowa**
—778	**Missouri**

>   —771–776 Lake states

Class comprehensive works in —77

For New York, see —747; for Pennsylvania, see —748

—771   Ohio

—771 1   Northwestern counties of Ohio

Class here *Maumee River

—771 11   Williams County and Fulton County

—771 113   Williams County

—771 115   Fulton County

—771 12   Lucas County

For Toledo, see —77113

—771 13   Toledo

—771 14   Defiance County

—771 15   Henry County

—771 16   Wood County

—771 17   Paulding County

—771 18   Putnam County

—771 19   Hancock County

—771 2   North central counties of Ohio

Class here *Lake Erie

—771 21   Ottawa County and Sandusky County

*For a specific part of this jurisdiction, region, or feature, see the part and follow instructions under —4–9

—771 212	Ottawa County
—771 214	Sandusky County
	Class here *Sandusky Bay
—771 22	Erie County
—771 23	Lorain County
—771 24	Seneca County
—771 25	Huron County
—771 26	Wyandot County
—771 27	Crawford County
—771 28	Richland County
—771 29	Ashland County
—771 3	Northeastern counties of Ohio
—771 31	Cuyahoga County
	Class here *Cuyahoga River
	For Cleveland, see —77132
—771 32	Cleveland
—771 33	Lake County and Geauga County
—771 334	Lake County
—771 336	Geauga County
—771 34	Ashtabula County
—771 35	Medina County
—771 36	Summit County
	Class here Akron
—771 37	Portage County
—771 38	Trumbull County
—771 39	Mahoning County
	Class here Youngstown; *Mahoning River
—771 4	West central counties of Ohio
—771 41	Van Wert County and Mercer County
—771 413	Van Wert County

*For a specific part of this jurisdiction, region, or feature, see the part and follow instructions under —4–9

—771 415	Mercer County
	Class here *Grand Lake (Lake Saint Marys)
—771 42	Allen County
—771 43	Auglaize County
—771 44	Hardin County
—771 45	Shelby County
—771 46	Logan County and Champaign County
—771 463	Logan County
—771 465	Champaign County
—771 47	Darke County
—771 48	Miami County
—771 49	Clark County
—771 5	Central counties of Ohio
	Class here *Scioto River
—771 51	Marion County and Morrow County
—771 514	Marion County
—771 516	Morrow County
—771 52	Knox County
—771 53	Union County and Delaware County
—771 532	Union County
—771 535	Delaware County
—771 54	Licking County
—771 55	Madison County
—771 56	Franklin County
	For Columbus, see —77157
—771 57	Columbus
—771 58	Fairfield County
—771 59	Perry County
—771 6	East central counties of Ohio
—771 61	Wayne County
—771 62	Stark County

*For a specific part of this jurisdiction, region, or feature, see the part and follow instructions under —4–9

—771 63	Columbiana County
—771 64	Holmes County
—771 65	Coshocton County
—771 66	Tuscarawas County
—771 67	Carroll County
—771 68	Harrison County
—771 69	Jefferson County
—771 7	Southwestern counties of Ohio

  Class here *Miami River

—771 71	Preble County
—771 72	Montgomery County

  For Dayton, see —77173

—771 73	Dayton
—771 74	Greene County
—771 75	Butler County
—771 76	Warren County and Clinton County
—771 763	Warren County
—771 765	Clinton County
—771 77	Hamilton County

  For Cincinnati, see —77178

—771 78	Cincinnati
—771 79	Clermont County and Brown County
—771 794	Clermont County
—771 796	Brown County
—771 8	South central counties of Ohio
—771 81	Fayette County and Pickaway County
—771 813	Fayette County
—771 815	Pickaway County
—771 82	Ross County
—771 83	Hocking County and Vinton County
—771 835	Hocking County

*For a specific part of this jurisdiction, region, or feature, see the part and follow instructions under
  —4–9

—771 837	Vinton County
—771 84	Highland County and Pike County
—771 845	Highland County
—771 847	Pike County
—771 85	Jackson County
—771 86	Adams County
—771 87	Scioto County
—771 88	Lawrence County
—771 89	Gallia County
—771 9	Southeastern counties of Ohio
—771 91	Muskingum County
	Class here *Muskingum River
—771 92	Guernsey County
—771 93	Belmont County
—771 94	Morgan County
—771 95	Noble County
—771 96	Monroe County
—771 97	Athens County
	Class here *Hocking River
—771 98	Washington County
—771 99	Meigs County
—772	Indiana
—772 1	Southeastern counties of Indiana
—772 11	Dearborn County
—772 12	Ohio County and Switzerland County
—772 123	Ohio County
—772 125	Switzerland County
—772 13	Jefferson County
—772 14	Ripley County
—772 15	Franklin County
—772 16	Decatur County

*For a specific part of this jurisdiction, region, or feature, see the part and follow instructions under
—4–9

—772 17	Jennings County
—772 18	Scott County and Clark County
—772 183	Scott County
—772 185	Clark County
—772 19	Floyd County
—772 2	South central counties of Indiana
—772 21	Harrison County
—772 22	Washington County
—772 23	Jackson County
—772 24	Bartholomew County
—772 25	Brown County and Monroe County
—772 253	Brown County
—772 255	Monroe County
—772 26	Lawrence County
—772 27	Orange County
—772 28	Crawford County
—772 29	Perry County
—772 3	Southwestern counties of Indiana
	Class here *White River
—772 31	Spencer County
—772 32	Warrick County
—772 33	Vanderburgh County
—772 34	Posey County
—772 35	Gibson County
—772 36	Pike County
—772 37	Dubois County
—772 38	Martin County and Daviess County
—772 382	Martin County
—772 385	Daviess County
—772 39	Knox County

*For a specific part of this jurisdiction, region, or feature, see the part and follow instructions under
—4–9

—772 4	West central counties of Indiana
	Class here *Wabash River
—772 41	Sullivan County
—772 42	Greene County
—772 43	Owen County
—772 44	Clay County
—772 45	Vigo County
—772 46	Vermillion County and Parke County
—772 462	Vermillion County
—772 465	Parke County
—772 47	Fountain County
—772 48	Montgomery County
—772 49	Putnam County
—772 5	Central counties of Indiana
—772 51	Morgan County and Johnson County
—772 513	Morgan County
—772 515	Johnson County
—772 52	Marion County
	Class here Indianapolis
—772 53	Hendricks County
—772 54	Boone County
—772 55	Clinton County and Tipton County
—772 553	Clinton County
—772 555	Tipton County
—772 56	Hamilton County
—772 57	Madison County
—772 58	Hancock County
—772 59	Shelby County
—772 6	East central counties of Indiana
—772 61	Rush County
—772 62	Fayette County and Union County

*For a specific part of this jurisdiction, region, or feature, see the part and follow instructions under —4–9

—772 623	Fayette County
—772 625	Union County
—772 63	Wayne County
—772 64	Henry County
—772 65	Delaware County
	Including Muncie
—772 66	Randolph County
—772 67	Jay County
—772 68	Blackford County
—772 69	Grant County
—772 7	Northeastern counties of Indiana
—772 71	Huntington County
—772 72	Wells County
—772 73	Adams County
—772 74	Allen County
	Class here Fort Wayne
—772 75	Whitley County
—772 76	Noble County
—772 77	De Kalb County
—772 78	Steuben County
—772 79	Lagrange County
—772 8	North central counties of Indiana
—772 81	Elkhart County
—772 82	Kosciusko County
—772 83	Wabash County
—772 84	Miami County
—772 85	Howard County
—772 86	Cass County
—772 87	Fulton County
—772 88	Marshall County
—772 89	Saint Joseph County
	Class here South Bend
—772 9	Northwestern counties of Indiana
—772 91	La Porte County

—772 92	Starke County and Pulaski County
—772 923	Starke County
—772 925	Pulaski County
—772 93	White County
—772 94	Carroll County
—772 95	Tippecanoe County
—772 96	Warren County
—772 97	Benton County, Newton County, Jasper County
—772 972	Benton County
—772 974	Newton County
—772 977	Jasper County
—772 98	Porter County
—772 99	Lake County
	Including Gary
—773	Illinois
—773 1	Cook County
—773 11	Chicago
—773 2	Northeastern counties of Illinois
	Class here *Des Plaines River
	For Cook County, see —7731
—773 21	Lake County
—773 22	McHenry County
—773 23	Kane County
—773 24	DuPage County
—773 25	Will County
—773 26	Kendall County and Grundy County
—773 263	Kendall County
—773 265	Grundy County
—773 27	La Salle County
—773 28	De Kalb County
—773 29	Boone County

*For a specific part of this jurisdiction, region, or feature, see the part and follow instructions under —4–9

—773 3	Northwestern counties of Illinois
	Class here *Rock River
—773 31	Winnebago County
—773 32	Ogle County
—773 33	Stephenson County
—773 34	Jo Daviess County and Carroll County
—773 343	Jo Daviess County
—773 345	Carroll County
—773 35	Whiteside County
—773 36	Lee County
—773 37	Bureau County and Putnam County
—773 372	Bureau County
—773 375	Putnam County
—773 38	Henry County
—773 39	Rock Island County and Mercer County
—773 393	Rock Island County
	Class comprehensive works on Davenport-Rock Island-Moline tri-city area in —77769
—773 395	Mercer County
—773 4	West central counties of Illinois
—773 41	Henderson County and Warren County
—773 413	Henderson County
—773 415	Warren County
—773 42	McDonough County
—773 43	Hancock County
—773 44	Adams County
—773 45	Pike County and Scott County
—773 453	Pike County
—773 455	Scott County
—773 46	Morgan County and Cass County
—773 463	Morgan County
—773 465	Cass County

*For a specific part of this jurisdiction, region, or feature, see the part and follow instructions under —4–9

—773 47	Brown County and Schuyler County
—773 473	Brown County
—773 475	Schuyler County
—773 48	Fulton County
—773 49	Knox County
—773 5	**Central counties of Illinois**
	Class here *Illinois River
—773 51	Stark County and Marshall County
—773 513	Stark County
—773 515	Marshall County
—773 52	Peoria County
—773 53	Woodford County
—773 54	Tazewell County
—773 55	Mason County and Menard County
	Class here *Sangamon River
—773 553	Mason County
—773 555	Menard County
—773 56	Sangamon County
	Including Springfield
—773 57	Logan County
—773 58	Macon County and De Witt County
—773 582	Macon County
—773 585	De Witt County
—773 59	McLean County
—773 6	**East central counties of Illinois**
—773 61	Livingston County
—773 62	Ford County
—773 63	Kankakee County
—773 64	Iroquois County
—773 65	Vermilion County
—773 66	Champaign County

*For a specific part of this jurisdiction, region, or feature, see the part and follow instructions under
—4–9

—773 67	Piatt County and Moultrie County
—773 673	Piatt County
—773 675	Moultrie County
—773 68	Douglas County
—773 69	Edgar County
—773 7	Southeastern and south central counties of Illinois

>	—773 71–773 78 Southeastern counties of Illinois
	Class comprehensive works in —7737
—773 71	Clark County
—773 72	Coles County
—773 73	Cumberland County
—773 74	Jasper County
—773 75	Crawford County
—773 76	Lawrence County
—773 77	Richland County
—773 78	Wabash County
—773 79	South central counties of Illinois
—773 791	Edwards County
—773 792	Wayne County
—773 793	Jefferson County
—773 794	Marion County
—773 795	Clay County
—773 796	Effingham County
—773 797	Fayette County
—773 798	Shelby County
—773 8	Southwestern counties of Illinois
—773 81	Christian County
—773 82	Montgomery County
—773 83	Macoupin County
—773 84	Greene County
—773 85	Calhoun County and Jersey County
—773 853	Calhoun County

—773 855	Jersey County
—773 86	Madison County
—773 87	Bond County and Clinton County
—773 873	Bond County
—773 875	Clinton County
—773 88	Washington County
—773 89	Saint Clair County
—773 9	Southern counties of Illinois
—773 91	Monroe County
—773 92	Randolph County
—773 93	Perry County
—773 94	Franklin County
—773 95	Hamilton County
—773 96	White County
—773 97	Gallatin County
—773 98	Hardin County
—773 99	Southernmost counties of Illinois
—773 991	Pope County
—773 992	Saline County
—773 993	Williamson County
—773 994	Jackson County
—773 995	Union County
—773 996	Johnson County
—773 997	Massac County
—773 998	Pulaski County
—773 999	Alexander County
—774	Michigan

Class here *Lake Huron, *Lake Michigan

> —774 1–774 8 Lower Peninsula

Class comprehensive works in —774

*For a specific part of this jurisdiction, region, or feature, see the part and follow instructions under —4–9

—774 1	Southwestern counties of Lower Peninsula
—774 11	Berrien County
—774 12	Cass County
—774 13	Van Buren County
—774 14	Allegan County
—774 15	Ottawa County
	Class here *Grand River
—774 16	Barry County
—774 17	Kalamazoo County
—774 19	Saint Joseph County
—774 2	South central counties of Lower Peninsula
—774 21	Branch County
—774 22	Calhoun County
—774 23	Eaton County
—774 24	Clinton County
—774 25	Shiawassee County
—774 26	Ingham County
	For Lansing and East Lansing, see —77427
—774 27	Lansing and East Lansing
—774 28	Jackson County
—774 29	Hillsdale County
—774 3	Southeastern counties of Lower Peninsula
—774 31	Lenawee County
—774 32	Monroe County
—774 33	Wayne County
	Including Dearborn; *Detroit River
	For Detroit, see —77434
—774 34	Detroit
—774 35	Washtenaw County
	Including Ann Arbor
—774 36	Livingston County

*For a specific part of this jurisdiction, region, or feature, see the part and follow instructions under
  —4–9

—774 37	Genesee County
	Including Flint
—774 38	Oakland County
—774 39	Macomb County
	Including *Lake Saint Clair
—774 4	Southeast central counties of Lower Peninsula
—774 41	Saint Clair County
	Including *Saint Clair River
—774 42	Lapeer County
—774 43	Sanilac County
—774 44	Huron County
—774 45	Tuscola County
—774 46	Saginaw County
—774 47	Bay County
	Class here *Saginaw River; *Saginaw Bay
—774 48	Midland County
—774 49	Gratiot County
—774 5	Southwest central counties of Lower Peninsula
—774 51	Isabella County
—774 52	Mecosta County
—774 53	Montcalm County
—774 54	Ionia County
—774 55	Kent County
	For Grand Rapids, see —77456
—774 56	Grand Rapids
—774 57	Muskegon County
—774 58	Newaygo County
—774 59	Oceana County
—774 6	Northwest central counties of Lower Peninsula
—774 61	Mason County
—774 62	Manistee County

*For a specific part of this jurisdiction, region, or feature, see the part and follow instructions under —4–9

—774 63	Benzie County and Leelanau County
—774 632	Benzie County
—774 635	Leelanau County
—774 64	Grand Traverse County
	Class here *Grand Traverse Bay
—774 65	Kalkaska County
—774 66	Missaukee County
—774 67	Wexford County
—774 68	Lake County
—774 69	Osceola County
—774 7	Northeast central counties of Lower Peninsula
	Class here *Au Sable River
—774 71	Clare County
—774 72	Gladwin County
—774 73	Arenac County
—774 74	Iosco County
—774 75	Ogemaw County
—774 76	Roscommon County
—774 77	Crawford County
—774 78	Oscoda County
—774 79	Alcona County
—774 8	Northern counties of Lower Peninsula
—774 81	Alpena County
—774 82	Presque Isle County
—774 83	Montmorency County
—774 84	Otsego County
—774 85	Antrim County
—774 86	Charlevoix County
—774 87	Cheboygan County
—774 88	Emmet County

*For a specific part of this jurisdiction, region, or feature, see the part and follow instructions under
—4–9

—774 9	Upper Peninsula
	Class here *Lake Superior
—774 91	Chippewa County
	Including *Saint Marys River; *Whitefish Bay
—774 92	Mackinac County and Luce County
—774 923	Mackinac County
	Including *Straits of Mackinac
—774 925	Luce County
—774 93	Alger County and Schoolcraft County
—774 932	Alger County
—774 935	Schoolcraft County
—774 94	Delta County
—774 95	Menominee County and Dickinson County
—774 953	Menominee County
—774 955	Dickinson County
—774 96	Marquette County
—774 97	Baraga County and Iron County
—774 973	Baraga County
—774 975	Iron County
—774 98	Gogebic County and Ontonagon County
—774 983	Gogebic County
—774 985	Ontonagon County
—774 99	Houghton County and Keweenaw County
	Class here Keweenaw Peninsula
—774 993	Houghton County
—774 995	Keweenaw County
	For Isle Royale, see —774997
—774 997	Isle Royale (Isle Royale National Park)
—775	Wisconsin
	Class here *Wisconsin River

---

*For a specific part of this jurisdiction, region, or feature, see the part and follow instructions under —4–9

—775 1	Northwestern counties of Wisconsin
	Class here *Saint Croix River
—775 11	Douglas County
	Including Superior
	Class comprehensive works on Duluth and Superior in —776771
—775 13	Bayfield County
—775 14	Burnett County
—775 15	Washburn County
—775 16	Sawyer County
—775 17	Polk County
—775 18	Barron County
—775 19	Rusk County
—775 2	North central counties of Wisconsin
—775 21	Ashland County
—775 22	Iron County
—775 23	Vilas County
—775 24	Price County
—775 25	Oneida County
—775 26	Taylor County
—775 27	Lincoln County
—775 28	Clark County
—775 29	Marathon County
—775 3	Northeastern counties of Wisconsin
—775 31	Forest County
—775 32	Florence County
—775 33	Marinette County
—775 35	Langlade County and Menominee County
—775 354	Langlade County
—775 356	Menominee County
—775 36	Shawano County
—775 37	Oconto County

*For a specific part of this jurisdiction, region, or feature, see the part and follow instructions under
—4–9

—775 38	Waupaca County
—775 39	Outagamie County
—775 4	West central counties of Wisconsin
	Class here *Chippewa River
—775 41	Saint Croix County
—775 42	Pierce County
—775 43	Dunn County
—775 44	Chippewa County
—775 45	Eau Claire County
—775 47	Pepin County
—775 48	Buffalo County
—775 49	Trempealeau County
—775 5	Central counties of Wisconsin
—775 51	Jackson County
—775 52	Wood County
—775 53	Portage County
—775 54	Monroe County
—775 55	Juneau County
—775 56	Adams County
—775 57	Waushara County
—775 58	Marquette County
—775 59	Green Lake County
—775 6	East central counties of Wisconsin
	Class here *Fox River
—775 61	Brown County
	Including Green Bay (city)
	See also —77563 for Green Bay (physiographic feature)
—775 62	Kewaunee County
—775 63	Door County
	Class here *Green Bay (physiographic feature)
	See also —77561 for Green Bay (city)

*For a specific part of this jurisdiction, region, or feature, see the part and follow instructions under —4–9

—775 64	Winnebago County
	Class here *Lake Winnebago
—775 66	Calumet County
—775 67	Manitowoc County
—775 68	Fond du Lac County
—775 69	Sheboygan County
—775 7	Southwestern counties of Wisconsin
—775 71	La Crosse County
—775 73	Vernon County
—775 74	Crawford County
—775 75	Richland County
—775 76	Sauk County
—775 77	Grant County
—775 78	Iowa County
—775 79	Lafayette County
—775 8	South central counties of Wisconsin
—775 81	Columbia County
—775 82	Dodge County
—775 83	Dane County
	Class here Madison
—775 85	Jefferson County
—775 86	Green County
—775 87	Rock County
—775 89	Walworth County
—775 9	Southeastern counties of Wisconsin
—775 91	Washington County
—775 92	Ozaukee County
—775 93	Waukesha County
—775 94	Milwaukee County
	For Milwaukee, see —77595
—775 95	Milwaukee

*For a specific part of this jurisdiction, region, or feature, see the part and follow instructions under —4–9

—775 96	Racine County
—775 98	Kenosha County
—776	Minnesota
—776 1	Southeastern counties of Minnesota
—776 11	Houston County
—776 12	Winona County
—776 13	Wabasha County
—776 14	Goodhue County
—776 15	Dodge County and Olmsted County
—776 153	Dodge County
—776 155	Olmsted County
—776 16	Fillmore County
—776 17	Mower County
—776 18	Freeborn County
—776 19	Steele County and Waseca County
—776 193	Steele County
—776 195	Waseca County
—776 2	Southwestern counties of Minnesota
—776 21	Blue Earth County
—776 22	Faribault County
—776 23	Martin County and Jackson County
—776 232	Martin County
—776 235	Jackson County
—776 24	Nobles County
—776 25	Rock County
—776 26	Pipestone County
—776 27	Murray County
—776 28	Cottonwood County
—776 29	Watonwan County
—776 3	Southwest central counties of Minnesota
	Class here *Minnesota River

*For a specific part of this jurisdiction, region, or feature, see the part and follow instructions under —4–9

—776 31	Brown County
—776 32	Nicollet County
—776 33	Sibley County
—776 34	Renville County
—776 35	Redwood County
—776 36	Lyon County and Lincoln County
—776 363	Lyon County
—776 365	Lincoln County
—776 37	Yellow Medicine County
—776 38	Lac qui Parle County
—776 39	Chippewa County
—776 4	West central counties of Minnesota
—776 41	Swift County
—776 42	Stevens County
—776 43	Big Stone County and Traverse County
—776 432	Big Stone County
—776 435	Traverse County
—776 44	Grant County
—776 45	Douglas County
—776 46	Pope County
—776 47	Stearns County
—776 48	Kandiyohi County
—776 49	Meeker County
—776 5	Southeast central counties of Minnesota
—776 51	Wright County
—776 52	McLeod County
—776 53	Carver County
—776 54	Scott County
—776 55	Le Sueur County and Rice County
—776 553	Le Sueur County
—776 555	Rice County
—776 56	Dakota County
—776 57	Hennepin County

—776 579	Minneapolis
	Class here Twin Cities
	For Saint Paul, see —776581
—776 58	Ramsey County
—776 581	Saint Paul
	Class comprehensive works on Twin Cities in —776579
—776 59	Washington County
—776 6	East central counties of Minnesota
—776 61	Chisago County
—776 62	Pine County
—776 63	Kanabec County
—776 64	Isanti County
—776 65	Anoka County
—776 66	Sherburne County
—776 67	Benton County
—776 68	Mille Lacs County
—776 69	Morrison County
—776 7	Northeastern counties of Minnesota
—776 71	Crow Wing County
—776 72	Aitkin County
—776 73	Carlton County
—776 75	Cook County
—776 76	Lake County
—776 77	Saint Louis County
	Including Voyageurs National Park; *Mesabi Range
	For Voyageurs National Park in Koochiching County, see —77679
—776 771	Duluth
	Class here comprehensive works on Duluth and Superior, Wisconsin
	For Superior, see —77511
—776 78	Itasca County

*For a specific part of this jurisdiction, region, or feature, see the part and follow instructions under —4–9

—776 79	Koochiching County
	Including *Rainy River; *Rainy Lake
—776 8	North central counties of Minnesota
—776 81	Lake of the Woods County
	Class here *Lake of the Woods
—776 82	Beltrami County
—776 83	Clearwater County
—776 84	Becker County
—776 85	Hubbard County
—776 86	Cass County
—776 87	Wadena County
—776 88	Todd County
—776 89	Otter Tail County
—776 9	Northwestern counties of Minnesota
	Class here *Red River of the North in Minnesota
—776 91	Wilkin County
—776 92	Clay County
—776 93	Norman County
—776 94	Mahnomen County
—776 95	Polk County
—776 96	Red Lake County and Pennington County
—776 963	Red Lake County
—776 965	Pennington County
—776 97	Marshall County
—776 98	Roseau County
—776 99	Kittson County
—777	Iowa
	Class here *Des Moines River
—777 1	Northwestern counties of Iowa
	Including *Big Sioux River in Iowa
—777 11	Lyon County and Osceola County

*For a specific part of this jurisdiction, region, or feature, see the part and follow instructions under —4–9

—777 114	Lyon County
—777 116	Osceola County
—777 12	Dickinson County and Emmet County
—777 123	Dickinson County
—777 125	Emmet County
—777 13	Sioux County
—777 14	O'Brien County
—777 15	Clay County and Palo Alto County
—777 153	Clay County
—777 155	Palo Alto County
—777 16	Plymouth County
—777 17	Cherokee County
—777 18	Buena Vista County
—777 19	Pocahontas County
—777 2	North central counties of Iowa
—777 21	Kossuth County
—777 22	Winnebago County
—777 23	Worth County and Mitchell County
—777 232	Worth County
—777 234	Mitchell County
—777 24	Hancock County
—777 25	Cerro Gordo County
—777 26	Floyd County
—777 27	Humboldt County and Wright County
—777 272	Humboldt County
—777 274	Wright County
—777 28	Franklin County
—777 29	Butler County
—777 3	Northeastern counties of Iowa
—777 31	Howard County and Chickasaw County
—777 312	Howard County
—777 315	Chickasaw County
—777 32	Winneshiek County

—777 33	Allamakee County
—777 34	Bremer County
—777 35	Fayette County
—777 36	Clayton County
—777 37	Black Hawk County
—777 38	Buchanan County and Delaware County
—777 382	Buchanan County
—777 385	Delaware County
—777 39	Dubuque County
—777 4	West central counties of Iowa
—777 41	Woodbury County
	Including Sioux City
—777 42	Ida County and Sac County
—777 422	Ida County
—777 424	Sac County
—777 43	Calhoun County
—777 44	Monona County
—777 45	Crawford County
—777 46	Carroll County and Greene County
—777 465	Carroll County
—777 466	Greene County
—777 47	Harrison County
—777 48	Shelby County and Audubon County
—777 484	Shelby County
—777 486	Audubon County
—777 49	Guthrie County
—777 5	Central counties of Iowa
—777 51	Webster County
—777 52	Hamilton County
—777 53	Hardin County and Grundy County
—777 535	Hardin County
—777 537	Grundy County
—777 54	Boone County and Story County

—777 544	Boone County
—777 546	Story County
—777 55	Marshall County
—777 56	Tama County
—777 57	Dallas County
—777 58	Polk County
	Class here Des Moines
—777 59	Jasper County and Poweshiek County
—777 594	Jasper County
—777 596	Poweshiek County
—777 6	East central counties of Iowa
	Class here *Iowa River
—777 61	Benton County
—777 62	Linn County
—777 63	Jones County
—777 64	Jackson County
—777 65	Iowa County and Johnson County
—777 653	Iowa County
—777 655	Johnson County
—777 66	Cedar County
—777 67	Clinton County
—777 68	Muscatine County
—777 69	Scott County
	Class here Davenport-Rock Island-Moline tri-city area
	For Rock Island County, Illinois, see —773393
—777 7	Southwestern counties of Iowa
—777 71	Pottawattamie County
—777 72	Cass County
—777 73	Adair County
—777 74	Mills County
—777 75	Montgomery County

*For a specific part of this jurisdiction, region, or feature, see the part and follow instructions under —4–9

—777 76	Adams County
—777 77	Fremont County
—777 78	Page County
—777 79	Taylor County
—777 8	South central counties of Iowa
—777 81	Madison County
—777 82	Warren County
—777 83	Marion County
—777 84	Mahaska County
—777 85	Union County and Clarke County
—777 853	Union County
—777 856	Clarke County
—777 86	Lucas County and Monroe County
—777 863	Lucas County
—777 865	Monroe County
—777 87	Ringgold County and Decatur County
—777 873	Ringgold County
—777 875	Decatur County
—777 88	Wayne County
—777 89	Appanoose County
—777 9	Southeastern counties of Iowa
—777 91	Keokuk County
—777 92	Washington County and Louisa County
—777 923	Washington County
—777 926	Louisa County
—777 93	Wapello County
—777 94	Jefferson County
—777 95	Henry County
—777 96	Des Moines County
—777 97	Davis County
—777 98	Van Buren County
—777 99	Lee County

—778	Missouri
	Class here *Missouri River in Missouri
—778 1	Northwestern counties of Missouri
—778 11	Atchison County and Holt County
—778 113	Atchison County
—778 115	Holt County
—778 12	Nodaway County and Andrew County
—778 124	Nodaway County
—778 126	Andrew County
—778 13	Buchanan County and Platte County
—778 132	Buchanan County
—778 135	Platte County
—778 14	Worth County and Gentry County
—778 143	Worth County
—778 145	Gentry County
—778 15	De Kalb County and Clinton County
—778 153	De Kalb County
—778 155	Clinton County
—778 16	Clay County
—778 17	Harrison County
—778 18	Daviess County and Caldwell County
—778 183	Daviess County
—778 185	Caldwell County
—778 19	Ray County
—778 2	North central counties of Missouri
	Class here *Chariton River, *Grand River
—778 21	Mercer County and Grundy County
—778 213	Mercer County
—778 215	Grundy County
—778 22	Livingston County and Carroll County
—778 223	Livingston County

*For a specific part of this jurisdiction, region, or feature, see the part and follow instructions under
  —4–9

—778 225	Carroll County
—778 23	Putnam County and Sullivan County
—778 232	Putnam County
—778 235	Sullivan County
—778 24	Linn County
—778 25	Chariton County
—778 26	Schuyler County and Adair County
—778 262	Schuyler County
—778 264	Adair County
—778 27	Macon County
—778 28	Randolph County and Howard County
—778 283	Randolph County
—778 285	Howard County
—778 29	Boone County
—778 3	Northeastern counties of Missouri
—778 31	Scotland County and Knox County
—778 312	Scotland County
—778 315	Knox County
—778 32	Shelby County and Monroe County
—778 323	Shelby County
—778 325	Monroe County
—778 33	Audrain County and Callaway County
—778 332	Audrain County
—778 335	Callaway County
—778 34	Clark County and Lewis County
—778 343	Clark County
—778 345	Lewis County
—778 35	Marion County and Ralls County
—778 353	Marion County
—778 355	Ralls County
—778 36	Pike County
—778 37	Lincoln County
—778 38	Montgomery County and Warren County

—778 382	Montgomery County
—778 386	Warren County
—778 39	Saint Charles County
—778 4	**West central counties of Missouri**
—778 41	Jackson County
—778 411	Kansas City

Class here Greater Kansas City

For Wyandotte County, Kansas, see —78139

—778 42	Cass County
—778 43	Bates County
—778 44	Vernon County
—778 45	Lafayette County and Johnson County
—778 453	Lafayette County
—778 455	Johnson County
—778 46	Henry County and Saint Clair County
—778 462	Henry County
—778 466	Saint Clair County
—778 47	Saline County
—778 48	Pettis County
—778 49	Benton County and Hickory County
—778 493	Benton County

Class here *Lake of the Ozarks

—778 496	Hickory County
—778 5	**Central counties of Missouri**
—778 51	Cooper County
—778 52	Moniteau County
—778 53	Morgan County
—778 54	Camden County
—778 55	Cole County

Including Jefferson City

—778 56	Miller County

*For a specific part of this jurisdiction, region, or feature, see the part and follow instructions under —4–9

—778 57	Pulaski County
—778 58	Osage County
—778 59	Maries County and Phelps County
—778 592	Maries County
—778 594	Phelps County
—778 6	East central counties of Missouri
—778 61	Gasconade County
—778 62	Crawford County
—778 63	Franklin County
—778 64	Washington County
—778 65	Saint Louis County
—778 66	Independent city of Saint Louis
—778 67	Jefferson County
—778 68	Saint Francois County
—778 69	Sainte Genevieve County and Perry County
—778 692	Sainte Genevieve County
—778 694	Perry County
—778 7	Southwestern counties of Missouri
—778 71	Barton County
—778 72	Jasper County
—778 73	Newton County and McDonald County
—778 732	Newton County
—778 736	McDonald County
—778 74	Cedar County and Dade County
—778 743	Cedar County
—778 745	Dade County
—778 75	Lawrence County
—778 76	Barry County
—778 77	Polk County
—778 78	Greene County
—778 79	Christian County, Stone County, Taney County
—778 792	Christian County
—778 794	Stone County

—778 797	Taney County
—778 8	**South central counties of Missouri**
	Class here *Ozark Plateau in Missouri
—778 81	Dallas County and Laclede County
—778 813	Dallas County
—778 815	Laclede County
—778 82	Webster County and Wright County
—778 823	Webster County
—778 825	Wright County
—778 83	Douglas County and Ozark County
—778 832	Douglas County
—778 835	Ozark County
—778 84	Texas County
—778 85	Howell County
—778 86	Dent County
—778 87	Shannon County and Oregon County
—778 873	Shannon County
—778 875	Oregon County
—778 88	Iron County and Reynolds County
—778 883	Iron County
—778 885	Reynolds County
—778 89	Carter County and Ripley County
—778 892	Carter County
—778 894	Ripley County
—778 9	**Southeastern counties of Missouri**
—778 91	Madison County
—778 92	Wayne County
—778 93	Butler County
—778 94	Bollinger County
—778 95	Stoddard County
—778 96	Cape Girardeau County

*For a specific part of this jurisdiction, region, or feature, see the part and follow instructions under —4–9

—778 97	Scott County
—778 98	Mississippi County and New Madrid County
—778 983	Mississippi County
—778 985	New Madrid County
—778 99	Dunklin County and Pemiscot County
—778 993	Dunklin County
—778 996	Pemiscot County

—78   **Western United States**

Class here the West; *Great Plains; *Rocky Mountains; *Missouri River

For Great Basin and Pacific Slope, see —79

SUMMARY

—781	**Kansas**
—782	**Nebraska**
—783	**South Dakota**
—784	**North Dakota**
—786	**Montana**
—787	**Wyoming**
—788	**Colorado**
—789	**New Mexico**

—781	Kansas

Class here *Arkansas River in Kansas

—781 1	Northwestern counties of Kansas
—781 11	Cheyenne County and Sherman County
—781 112	Cheyenne County
—781 115	Sherman County
—781 12	Wallace County and Rawlins County
—781 123	Wallace County
—781 125	Rawlins County
—781 13	Thomas County and Logan County
—781 132	Thomas County
—781 135	Logan County
—781 14	Decatur County and Sheridan County
—781 143	Decatur County
—781 145	Sheridan County

*For a specific part of this jurisdiction, region, or feature, see the part and follow instructions under —4–9

—781 15	Gove County and Norton County
—781 152	Gove County
—781 155	Norton County
—781 16	Graham County and Trego County
—781 163	Graham County
—781 165	Trego County
—781 17	Phillips County
—781 18	Rooks County
—781 19	Ellis County
—781 2	North central counties of Kansas
	Class here *Republican River, *Solomon River
—781 21	Smith County and Osborne County
—781 213	Smith County
—781 215	Osborne County
—781 22	Jewell County
—781 23	Mitchell County
—781 24	Republic County
—781 25	Cloud County
—781 26	Ottawa County
—781 27	Washington County and Clay County
—781 273	Washington County
—781 275	Clay County
—781 28	Riley County
—781 29	Geary County
—781 3	Northeastern counties of Kansas
	Class here *Kansas (Kaw) River
—781 31	Marshall County
—781 32	Pottawatomie County
—781 33	Nemaha County and Jackson County
—781 332	Nemaha County
—781 335	Jackson County

*For a specific part of this jurisdiction, region, or feature, see the part and follow instructions under —4–9

—781 34	Brown County
—781 35	Doniphan County
—781 36	Atchison County
—781 37	Jefferson County
—781 38	Leavenworth County
—781 39	Wyandotte County
	Class here Kansas City
	Class comprehensive works on Greater Kansas City in —778411
—781 4	West central counties of Kansas
—781 41	Greeley County and Hamilton County
—781 413	Greeley County
—781 415	Hamilton County
—781 42	Wichita County and Kearny County
—781 423	Wichita County
—781 425	Kearny County
—781 43	Scott County
—781 44	Finney County
—781 45	Lane County
—781 46	Ness County
—781 47	Hodgeman County
—781 48	Rush County
—781 49	Pawnee County
—781 5	Central counties of Kansas
—781 51	Russell County
—781 52	Barton County
—781 53	Lincoln County and Ellsworth County
—781 532	Lincoln County
—781 535	Ellsworth County
—781 54	Rice County and Saline County
—781 543	Rice County
—781 545	Saline County
—781 55	McPherson County
—781 56	Dickinson County

—781 57	Marion County
—781 58	Morris County
—781 59	Chase County
—781 6	East central counties of Kansas
—781 61	Wabaunsee County
—781 62	Lyon County
—781 63	Shawnee County
	Class here Topeka
—781 64	Osage County and Coffey County
—781 643	Osage County
—781 645	Coffey County
—781 65	Douglas County
—781 66	Franklin County
—781 67	Anderson County and Johnson County
—781 672	Anderson County
—781 675	Johnson County
—781 68	Miami County
—781 69	Linn County
—781 7	Southwestern counties of Kansas
—781 71	Stanton County and Morton County
—781 712	Stanton County
—781 715	Morton County
—781 72	Grant County and Stevens County
—781 723	Grant County
—781 725	Stevens County
—781 73	Haskell County and Seward County
—781 732	Haskell County
—781 735	Seward County
—781 74	Gray County
—781 75	Meade County
—781 76	Ford County
—781 77	Clark County
—781 78	Edwards County and Kiowa County

—781 782	Edwards County
—781 785	Kiowa County
—781 79	Comanche County
—781 8	South central counties of Kansas
—781 81	Stafford County and Pratt County
—781 813	Stafford County
—781 815	Pratt County
—781 82	Barber County
—781 83	Reno County
—781 84	Kingman County and Harper County
—781 843	Kingman County
—781 845	Harper County
—781 85	Harvey County
—781 86	Sedgwick County
	Class here Wichita
—781 87	Sumner County
—781 88	Butler County
—781 89	Cowley County
—781 9	Southeastern counties of Kansas
—781 91	Greenwood County, Elk County, Chautauqua County
—781 913	Greenwood County
—781 915	Elk County
—781 918	Chautauqua County
—781 92	Woodson County and Wilson County
—781 923	Woodson County
—781 925	Wilson County
—781 93	Montgomery County
—781 94	Allen County
—781 95	Neosho County
—781 96	Labette County
—781 97	Bourbon County
—781 98	Crawford County
—781 99	Cherokee County

—782	Nebraska
	Class here *Platte River
—782 2	Missouri River lowland counties
—782 22	Dixon County, Dakota County, Thurston County
—782 223	Dixon County
—782 224	Dakota County
—782 227	Thurston County
—782 23	Cuming County and Dodge County
—782 232	Cuming County
—782 235	Dodge County
—782 24	Burt County and Washington County
—782 243	Burt County
—782 245	Washington County
—782 25	Douglas County and Sarpy County
—782 254	Douglas County
	Class here Omaha
—782 256	Sarpy County
—782 27	Cass County and neighboring counties
—782 272	Cass County
—782 273	Otoe County
—782 276	Johnson County
—782 278	Nemaha County
—782 28	Richardson County, Pawnee County, Gage County
—782 282	Richardson County
—782 284	Pawnee County
—782 286	Gage County
—782 29	Lancaster County and Saunders County
—782 293	Lancaster County
	Class here Lincoln
—782 296	Saunders County
—782 3	South central counties of Nebraska

*For a specific part of this jurisdiction, region, or feature, see the part and follow instructions under —4–9

—782 32	Butler County, Seward County, Saline County
—782 322	Butler County
—782 324	Seward County
—782 327	Saline County
—782 33	Jefferson County and Thayer County
—782 332	Jefferson County
—782 335	Thayer County
—782 34	Fillmore County and York County
—782 342	Fillmore County
—782 345	York County
—782 35	Polk County, Hamilton County, Clay County
—782 352	Polk County
—782 354	Hamilton County
—782 357	Clay County
—782 37	Nuckolls County, Webster County, Franklin County
	Class here *Republican River in Nebraska
—782 372	Nuckolls County
—782 374	Webster County
—782 377	Franklin County
—782 38	Harlan County, Furnas County, Gosper County
—782 382	Harlan County
—782 384	Furnas County
—782 387	Gosper County
—782 39	Phelps County, Kearney County, Adams County
—782 392	Phelps County
—782 394	Kearney County
—782 397	Adams County
—782 4	Central counties of Nebraska
—782 41	Hall County
—782 42	Merrick County and Nance County
—782 423	Merrick County

*For a specific part of this jurisdiction, region, or feature, see the part and follow instructions under —4–9

—782 425	Nance County
—782 43	Howard County
—782 44	Sherman County
—782 45	Buffalo County
—782 46	Dawson County
—782 47	Custer County
—782 48	Valley County
—782 49	Greeley County
—782 5	Northeast central counties of Nebraska
—782 51	Boone County
—782 52	Platte County
—782 53	Colfax County and Stanton County
—782 532	Colfax County
—782 535	Stanton County
—782 54	Madison County
—782 55	Antelope County
—782 56	Pierce County
—782 57	Wayne County
—782 58	Cedar County
—782 59	Knox County
—782 7	North central counties of Nebraska
	Class here *Niobrara River
—782 72	Boyd County and Keya Paha County
—782 723	Boyd County
—782 725	Keya Paha County
—782 73	Cherry County and Brown County
—782 732	Cherry County
—782 736	Brown County
—782 74	Rock County and Holt County
—782 743	Rock County
—782 745	Holt County

*For a specific part of this jurisdiction, region, or feature, see the part and follow instructions under —4–9

—782 76	Wheeler County, Garfield County, Loup County
—782 762	Wheeler County
—782 764	Garfield County
—782 767	Loup County
—782 77	Blaine County, Thomas County, Hooker County
—782 772	Blaine County
—782 774	Thomas County
—782 777	Hooker County
—782 78	Grant County and Arthur County
—782 783	Grant County
—782 785	Arthur County
—782 79	McPherson County and Logan County
—782 793	McPherson County
—782 795	Logan County
—782 8	Southwestern counties of Nebraska
—782 82	Lincoln County
—782 83	Hayes County and Frontier County
—782 832	Hayes County
—782 835	Frontier County
—782 84	Red Willow County and Hitchcock County
—782 843	Red Willow County
—782 845	Hitchcock County
—782 86	Dundy County
—782 87	Chase County
—782 88	Perkins County
—782 89	Keith County
—782 9	Panhandle counties
—782 91	Deuel County and Garden County
—782 913	Deuel County
—782 915	Garden County
—782 92	Sheridan County
—782 93	Dawes County
—782 94	Box Butte County

—782 95	Morrill County
—782 96	Cheyenne County
—782 97	Kimball County and Banner County
—782 973	Kimball County
—782 975	Banner County
—782 98	Scotts Bluff County
—782 99	Sioux County
—783	South Dakota
—783 1	Northeastern counties of South Dakota
—783 12	Roberts County
—783 13	Marshall County
—783 14	Day County and Brown County
—783 142	Day County
—783 144	Brown County
—783 15	Edmunds County
—783 16	McPherson County
—783 17	Campbell County
—783 18	Walworth County
—783 19	Potter County
—783 2	East central counties of South Dakota
—783 21	Faulk County and Spink County
—783 213	Faulk County
—783 217	Spink County
—783 22	Clark County
—783 23	Codington County
—783 24	Grant County
—783 25	Deuel County
—783 26	Hamlin County
—783 27	Brookings County, Kingsbury County, Beadle County
—783 272	Brookings County
—783 273	Kingsbury County
—783 274	Beadle County
—783 28	Hand County, Hyde County, Sully County

—783 282	Hand County
—783 283	Hyde County
—783 284	Sully County
—783 29	Hughes County
	Including Pierre
—783 3	Southeastern counties of South Dakota
	Class here *Missouri River in South Dakota, *James River
—783 31	Buffalo County
—783 32	Jerauld County
—783 33	Sanborn County
—783 34	Miner County
—783 35	Lake County
—783 36	Moody County
—783 37	Minnehaha County and neighboring counties
—783 371	Minnchaha County
	Including Sioux Falls
—783 372	McCook County
—783 373	Hanson County
—783 374	Davison County
—783 375	Aurora County
—783 38	Brule County and neighboring counties
	Class here *Lake Francis Case
—783 381	Brule County
—783 382	Charles Mix County
—783 383	Douglas County
—783 384	Hutchinson County
—783 385	Turner County
—783 39	Lincoln County and neighboring counties
	Class here *Big Sioux River
—783 391	Lincoln County
—783 392	Union County

*For a specific part of this jurisdiction, region, or feature, see the part and follow instructions under —4–9

—783 393	Clay County
—783 394	Yankton County
—783 395	Bon Homme County
—783 4	Northwestern counties of South Dakota
—783 42	Harding County
—783 43	Butte County
—783 44	Meade County
—783 45	Perkins County
—783 5	Central counties of South Dakota
	Class here *Lake Oahe
—783 52	Corson County
—783 53	Ziebach County
—783 54	Dewey County
—783 55	Stanley County
—783 56	Haakon County
—783 57	Jackson County and Jones County
—783 572	Jackson County
—783 577	Jones County
—783 58	Lyman County
—783 59	Gregory County
—783 6	South central counties of South Dakota
—783 61	Tripp County
—783 62	Todd County
—783 63	Mellette County
—783 64	Washabaugh County
—783 65	Bennett County
—783 66	Shannon County
—783 9	Southwestern counties of South Dakota
	Class here *Black Hills
—783 91	Lawrence County

*For a specific part of this jurisdiction, region, or feature, see the part and follow instructions under —4–9

—783 93   Pennington County

                 Including Badlands National Park

                   For Badlands National Park in Jackson County, see —783572; for Badlands National Park in Shannon County, see —78366

—783 95   Custer County

                 Including Wind Cave National Park

—783 97   Fall River County

—784   North Dakota

—784 1   Red River Valley counties

                 Class here *Red River of the North

—784 12   Richland County

—784 13   Cass County

                 Including Fargo

—784 14   Traill County

—784 16   Grand Forks County

—784 18   Walsh County

—784 19   Pembina County

—784 3   Sheyenne River Valley and adjacent counties

                 Class here *Sheyenne River

—784 31   Sargent County and Ransom County

—784 314   Sargent County

—784 315   Ransom County

—784 32   Barnes County

—784 33   Steele County

—784 34   Griggs County

—784 35   Nelson County

—784 36   Ramsey County

—784 37   Cavalier County

—784 38   Towner County

—784 39   Benson County

—784 5   James River Valley and adjacent counties

                 Class here *James River in North Dakota

*For a specific part of this jurisdiction, region, or feature, see the part and follow instructions under —4–9

—784 51	Eddy County and Foster County
—784 512	Eddy County
—784 516	Foster County
—784 52	Stutsman County
—784 53	La Moure County
—784 54	Dickey County
—784 55	McIntosh County
—784 56	Logan County
—784 57	Kidder County
—784 58	Wells County
—784 59	Pierce County and Rolette County
—784 591	Pierce County
—784 592	Rolette County
—784 6	Souris River Valley counties
	Class here *Souris River
—784 61	Bottineau County
—784 62	McHenry County
—784 63	Ward County
—784 64	Renville County
—784 7	Counties of North Dakota north and east of Missouri River
	Class here *Missouri River in North Dakota
—784 71	Divide County
—784 72	Burke County
—784 73	Williams County
—784 74	Mountrail County
—784 75	McLean County
	Class here *Lake Sakakawea (Garrison Reservoir)
—784 76	Sheridan County
—784 77	Burleigh County
	Including Bismarck
—784 78	Emmons County

*For a specific part of this jurisdiction, region, or feature, see the part and follow instructions under —4–9

—784 8	Counties of North Dakota south and west of Missouri River

For Badlands counties, see —7849

—784 81	McKenzie County
—784 82	Dunn County
—784 83	Mercer County
—784 84	Oliver County and Stark County
—784 843	Oliver County
—784 844	Stark County
—784 85	Morton County
—784 86	Hettinger County
—784 87	Grant County
—784 88	Sioux County
—784 89	Adams County
—784 9	Badlands counties
—784 92	Bowman County
—784 93	Slope County
—784 94	Billings County
—784 95	Golden Valley County

>	—786–789 Rocky Mountains states

Class comprehensive works in —78

For Idaho, see —796

—786	Montana

Class here *Missouri River in Montana

—786 1	North central counties of Montana

Class here *Great Plains in Montana; *Milk River

—786 12	Toole County
—786 13	Liberty County
—786 14	Hill County
—786 15	Blaine County
—786 16	Phillips County

*For a specific part of this jurisdiction, region, or feature, see the part and follow instructions under —4–9

—786 17	Valley County
	Class here *Fort Peck Lake
—786 2	Northeastern and central plains counties of Montana
—786 21	Daniels County and Sheridan County
—786 213	Daniels County
—786 218	Sheridan County
—786 22	Roosevelt County
—786 23	Richland County
—786 24	Dawson County
—786 25	Prairie County
—786 26	McCone County
—786 27	Garfield County
—786 28	Petroleum County
—786 29	Fergus County and Chouteau County
—786 292	Fergus County
—786 293	Chouteau County
—786 3	Southeastern counties of Montana
	Class here *Yellowstone River
—786 31	Golden Valley County, Musselshell County, Treasure County
—786 311	Golden Valley County
—786 312	Musselshell County
—786 313	Treasure County
—786 32	Rosebud County
—786 33	Custer County
—786 34	Wibaux County
—786 35	Fallon County
—786 36	Carter County
—786 37	Powder River County
—786 38	Big Horn County
—786 39	Yellowstone County

*For a specific part of this jurisdiction, region, or feature, see the part and follow instructions under —4–9

—786 5	Northwest central counties of Montana
	Class here *Rocky Mountains in Montana
—786 52	Glacier County
	Including *Glacier National Park, *Waterton-Glacier International Peace Park
—786 53	Pondera County
—786 55	Teton County
—786 6	Southwestern and central mountain counties of Montana
—786 61	Cascade County, Meagher County, Lewis and Clark County
—786 611	Cascade County
—786 612	Meagher County
—786 615	Lewis and Clark County
	Including Helena
—786 62	Judith Basin County
—786 63	Wheatland County
—786 64	Sweet Grass County
—786 65	Stillwater County and Carbon County
—786 651	Stillwater County
—786 652	Carbon County
—786 66	Park County and neighboring counties
—786 661	Park County
	Including Yellowstone National Park in Montana
	For Yellowstone National Park in Gallatin County, see —786662
—786 662	Gallatin County
—786 663	Madison County
—786 664	Broadwater County
—786 67	Jefferson County
—786 68	Silver Bow County
	Including Butte
—786 69	Beaverhead County

*For a specific part of this jurisdiction, region, or feature, see the part and follow instructions under —4–9

—786 8	Northwestern counties of Montana
	Class here *Bitterroot Range
—786 81	Lincoln County
—786 82	Flathead County
—786 83	Lake County and Sanders County
—786 832	Lake County
	Class here *Flathead Lake
—786 833	Sanders County
—786 84	Mineral County
—786 85	Missoula County
—786 86	Powell County
—786 87	Deer Lodge County
—786 88	Granite County
—786 89	Ravalli County
—787	Wyoming
—787 1	Eastern counties of Wyoming
	Class here *Great Plains in Wyoming
—787 12	Campbell County
—787 13	Crook County
—787 14	Weston County
—787 15	Niobrara County
—787 16	Converse County
	Class here *North Platte River
—787 17	Platte County
—787 18	Goshen County
—787 19	Laramie County
	Including Cheyenne
—787 2	*Rocky Mountains in Wyoming
—787 3	*Big Horn Mountains counties
—787 32	Sheridan County
—787 33	Big Horn County

*For a specific part of this jurisdiction, region, or feature, see the part and follow instructions under —4–9

—787 34	Washakie County
—787 35	Johnson County
—787 4	*Absaroka Range counties
—787 42	Park County
—787 43	Hot Springs County
	Including *Owl Creek Mountains
—787 5	Yellowstone National Park and Teton County
—787 52	*Yellowstone National Park
—787 55	Teton County
	Including Grand Teton National Park; *Teton Range
	Class here *Snake River in Wyoming
—787 6	*Wind River Range counties
—787 63	Fremont County
—787 65	Sublette County
—787 8	Southwestern counties of Wyoming
—787 82	Lincoln County
—787 84	Uinta County
—787 85	Sweetwater County
	Including *Green River in Wyoming
—787 86	Carbon County
	Class here *Medicine Bow Range
—787 9	*Laramie Mountains counties
—787 93	Natrona County
—787 95	Albany County
—788	Colorado
	Class here *Rocky Mountains in Colorado
—788 1	Northern Colorado Plateau counties
	Class here *Colorado Plateau
—788 12	Moffat County
	Class here Dinosaur National Monument
	For Dinosaur National Monument in Uintah County, Utah, see —79221

*For a specific part of this jurisdiction, region, or feature, see the part and follow instructions under —4–9

—788 14	Routt County
—788 15	Rio Blanco County
—788 16	Garfield County
—788 17	Mesa County
	Class here *Colorado River in Colorado
—788 18	Delta County
—788 19	Montrose County
	Including Black Canyon of the Gunnison National Park
—788 2	Southern Colorado Plateau counties
—788 22	Ouray County
—788 23	San Miguel County
—788 25	San Juan County
—788 26	Dolores County
—788 27	Montezuma County
	Including Mesa Verde National Park
—788 29	La Plata County
—788 3	Southern Rocky Mountains counties
	Class here *San Juan Mountains; *San Luis Valley; *Rio Grande in Colorado
—788 32	Archuleta County
—788 33	Conejos County
—788 35	Costilla County
—788 36	Alamosa County
—788 37	Rio Grande County
—788 38	Mineral County
—788 39	Hinsdale County
—788 4	West central Rocky Mountains counties
—788 41	Gunnison County
—788 43	Pitkin County
—788 44	Eagle County
—788 45	Summit County
—788 46	Lake County

*For a specific part of this jurisdiction, region, or feature, see the part and follow instructions under
—4–9

—788 47	Chaffee County
—788 49	Saguache County
	Including Great Sand Dunes National Park and Preserve; *Sangre de Cristo Mountains
	For Great Sand Dunes National Park and Preserve in Alamosa County, see —78836
—788 5	East central Rocky Mountains counties
—788 51	Huerfano County
—788 52	Custer County
—788 53	Fremont County
—788 55	Pueblo County
—788 56	El Paso County
	Class here Colorado Springs
—788 58	Teller County
—788 59	Park County
—788 6	Northern Rocky Mountains counties
	Class here *Front Range
—788 61	Clear Creek County
—788 62	Gilpin County
—788 63	Boulder County
—788 64	Broomfield County
—788 65	Grand County
—788 66	Jackson County
	Class here *Park Range
—788 68	Larimer County
—788 69	*Rocky Mountain National Park
—788 7	Northern Great Plains counties
	Class here *Great Plains in Colorado; *South Platte River
—788 72	Weld County
—788 74	Morgan County
—788 75	Logan County
—788 76	Sedgwick County

*For a specific part of this jurisdiction, region, or feature, see the part and follow instructions under —4–9

—788 77	Phillips County
—788 78	Yuma County
—788 79	Washington County
—788 8	Central Great Plains counties
—788 81	Adams County
—788 82	Arapahoe County
—788 83	Denver County (Denver)
—788 84	Jefferson County
—788 86	Douglas County
—788 87	Elbert County
—788 89	Lincoln County
—788 9	Southern Great Plains counties
	Class here *Arkansas River in Colorado
—788 91	Kit Carson County
—788 92	Cheyenne County
—788 93	Kiowa County
—788 94	Crowley County
—788 95	Otero County
—788 96	Las Animas County
—788 97	Bent County
—788 98	Prowers County
—788 99	Baca County
—789	New Mexico
—789 2	Northeastern counties of New Mexico
	Class here *Great Plains in New Mexico
—789 22	Colfax County
—789 23	Union County
—789 24	Harding County
—789 25	Guadalupe County
—789 26	Quay County
—789 27	Curry County

*For a specific part of this jurisdiction, region, or feature, see the part and follow instructions under —4–9

—789 3	Roosevelt County and Lea County
	Class here *Llano Estacado in New Mexico
—789 32	Roosevelt County
—789 33	Lea County
—789 4	Pecos Valley counties
	Class here *Pecos River in New Mexico
—789 42	Eddy County
	Including Carlsbad Caverns National Park
—789 43	Chaves County
—789 44	De Baca County
—789 5	*Rocky Mountains counties
—789 52	Rio Arriba County
—789 53	Taos County
—789 54	Mora County
—789 55	San Miguel County
—789 56	Santa Fe County
	Class here Santa Fe
—789 57	Sandoval County
—789 58	Los Alamos County
—789 6	Basin and Range region counties
	Class here *Rio Grande in New Mexico
—789 61	Bernalillo County
	Class here Albuquerque
—789 62	Socorro County
	Including *Elephant Butte Reservoir
—789 63	Torrance County
—789 64	Lincoln County
—789 65	Otero County
	Including White Sands National Monument; *Sacramento Mountains
	For White Sands National Monument in Doña Ana County, see —78966
—789 66	Doña Ana County

*For a specific part of this jurisdiction, region, or feature, see the part and follow instructions under —4–9

—789 67	Sierra County
	Class here *San Andres Mountains
—789 68	Luna County
—789 69	Grant County and Hidalgo County
—789 692	Grant County
—789 693	Hidalgo County
	Class here *Peloncillo Mountains
—789 8	Northwestern counties of New Mexico
—789 82	San Juan County
—789 83	McKinley County
—789 9	West central counties of New Mexico
—789 91	Cibola County
—789 92	Valencia County
—789 93	Catron County

—79   **Great Basin and Pacific Slope of United States**

Class here *new Southwest, Pacific Coast states

SUMMARY

—791	**Arizona**
—792	**Utah**
—793	**Nevada**
—794	**California**
—795	**Oregon**
—796	**Idaho**
—797	**Washington**
—798	**Alaska**

—791	Arizona
—791 3	Colorado Plateau region
	Class here *Colorado River
—791 32	*Grand Canyon National Park
—791 33	Coconino County
	Class here *Painted Desert; *Little Colorado River
—791 35	Navajo County

*For a specific part of this jurisdiction, region, or feature, see the part and follow instructions under
—4–9

—791 37	Apache County
	Including Petrified Forest National Park
	For Petrified Forest National Park in Navajo County, see —79135
—791 5	Mountain region of Arizona
—791 51	Greenlee County
—791 53	Cochise County
—791 54	Graham County
—791 55	Gila County
—791 57	Yavapai County
—791 59	Mohave County
—791 7	Plains region of Arizona
	Class here *Sonoran Desert in United States, *Gila River
—791 71	Yuma County
—791 72	La Paz County
—791 73	Maricopa County
	Class here Phoenix
—791 75	Pinal County
—791 77	Pima County
—791 776	Tucson
—791 79	Santa Cruz County
—792	Utah
—792 1	Wyoming Basin region
—792 12	Cache County
—792 13	Rich County
—792 14	Summit County
	Including *Uinta Mountains
—792 15	Daggett County
—792 2	Rocky Mountains region
	Class here *Wasatch Range
—792 21	Uintah County
—792 22	Duchesne County

*For a specific part of this jurisdiction, region, or feature, see the part and follow instructions under —4–9

—792 23	Wasatch County
—792 24	Utah County
—792 25	Salt Lake County
—792 258	Salt Lake City
—792 26	Morgan County
—792 27	Davis County
—792 28	Weber County
—792 4	Great Basin region
—792 42	Box Elder County

> Class here *Great Salt Lake

—792 43	Tooele County

> Class here *Great Salt Lake Desert

—792 44	Juab County
—792 45	Millard County
—792 46	Beaver County
—792 47	Iron County
—792 48	Washington County

> Class here Zion National Park

>> *For Zion National Park in Iron County, see —79247; for Zion National Park in Kane County, see —79251*

—792 5	Colorado Plateau region

> Class here *Colorado River in Utah, *Green River

—792 51	Kane County

> Including Grand Staircase-Escalante National Monument

>> *For Grand Staircase-Escalante National Monument in Garfield County, see —79252*

—792 52	Garfield County

> Including Bryce Canyon National Park

>> *For Bryce Canyon National Park in Kane County, see —79251*

—792 53	Piute County
—792 54	Wayne County

> Including *Capitol Reef National Park

---

*For a specific part of this jurisdiction, region, or feature, see the part and follow instructions under —4–9

—792 55	Sevier County
—792 56	Sanpete County and Carbon County
—792 563	Sanpete County
—792 566	Carbon County
—792 57	Emery County
—792 58	Grand County
	Including Arches National Park
—792 59	San Juan County
	Including Canyonlands National Park; *Glen Canyon National Recreation Area; *San Juan River; *Lake Powell
	Class here *Four Corners Region
	For Canyonlands National Park in Wayne County, see —79254
—793	Nevada
—793 1	Eastern region of Nevada
—793 12	*Lake Mead National Recreation Area
—793 13	Clark County
—793 135	Las Vegas
—793 14	Lincoln County
—793 15	White Pine County
	Including Great Basin National Park
—793 16	Elko County
	Class here *Humboldt River
—793 3	Central region of Nevada
—793 32	Eureka County
—793 33	Lander County
—793 34	Nye County
—793 35	Esmeralda County
—793 5	Western region of Nevada
—793 51	Mineral County
—793 52	Churchill County
—793 53	Pershing County

*For a specific part of this jurisdiction, region, or feature, see the part and follow instructions under —4–9

—793 54	Humboldt County
	Including *Black Rock Desert
—793 55	Washoe County
	Including Reno
—793 56	Storey County
	Including Virginia City
—793 57	Carson City
	Including *Lake Tahoe in Nevada
—793 58	Lyon County
—793 59	Douglas County
—794	California
—794 1	Northwestern counties of California
	Class here *Coast Ranges in California
—794 11	Del Norte County
—794 12	Humboldt County
	Including Redwood National Park
	For Redwood National Park in Del Norte County, see —79411
—794 14	Trinity County
—794 15	Mendocino County
—794 17	Lake County
—794 18	Sonoma County
—794 19	Napa County
—794 2	Northeastern counties of California
	Class here *Cascade Range in California
—794 21	Siskiyou County
	Including Lava Beds National Monument
	Class here *Klamath Mountains in California
	For Lava Beds National Monument in Modoc County, see —79423
—794 23	Modoc County
—794 24	Shasta County
	Including *Lassen Volcanic National Park

*For a specific part of this jurisdiction, region, or feature, see the part and follow instructions under —4–9

—794 26	Lassen County
—794 27	Tehama County
—794 29	Plumas County
—794 3	North central counties of California
—794 31	Glenn County
—794 32	Butte County
—794 33	Colusa County
—794 34	Sutter County
—794 35	Yuba County
—794 36	Sierra County
—794 37	Nevada County
—794 38	Placer County
	Including *Lake Tahoe
—794 4	East central counties of California
	Class here *Sierra Nevada
—794 41	El Dorado County
—794 42	Amador County
—794 43	Alpine County
—794 44	Calaveras County
—794 45	Tuolumne County
—794 46	Mariposa County
—794 47	*Yosemite National Park
—794 48	Mono County
—794 5	Central counties of California
	Class here *Central Valley (Great Valley); *Sacramento River
—794 51	Yolo County
—794 52	Solano County
—794 53	Sacramento County
	For Sacramento, see —79454
—794 54	Sacramento
—794 55	San Joaquin County

*For a specific part of this jurisdiction, region, or feature, see the part and follow instructions under —4–9

—794 57	Stanislaus County
—794 58	Merced County
—794 6	**West central counties of California**

Class here *San Francisco Bay Area

See also —16432 for San Francisco Bay

—794 61	San Francisco County (San Francisco)
—794 62	Marin County
—794 63	Contra Costa County
—794 65	Alameda County

For Oakland, see —79466; for Berkeley, see —79467

—794 66	Oakland
—794 67	Berkeley
—794 69	San Mateo County
—794 7	**Southern Coast Range counties**
—794 71	Santa Cruz County
—794 73	Santa Clara County

For San Jose, see —79474

—794 74	San Jose
—794 75	San Benito County
—794 76	Monterey County

Class here *Salinas River

See also —16432 for Monterey Bay

—794 78	San Luis Obispo County

Class here *Santa Lucia Range

—794 8	**South central counties of California**

Class here *San Joaquin River

—794 81	Madera County
—794 82	Fresno County

Including Kings Canyon National Park

For Fresno, see —79483; for Kings Canyon National Park in Tulare County, see —79486

—794 83	Fresno

*For a specific part of this jurisdiction, region, or feature, see the part and follow instructions under —4–9

—794 85	Kings County
—794 86	Tulare County
	Including Sequoia National Park; *Mount Whitney
—794 87	Inyo County
	Class here *Death Valley National Park
—794 88	Kern County
—794 9	Southern California
—794 91	Santa Barbara County
	Including Channel Islands National Park; *Santa Barbara Islands
	For Anacapa Island, see —79492
—794 92	Ventura County
—794 93	Los Angeles County
	Including Pasadena; *San Gabriel Mountains
	For Los Angeles, see —79494
—794 94	Los Angeles
—794 95	San Bernardino County
	Including *San Bernardino Mountains
	Class here *Mojave Desert
—794 96	Orange County
	Including *Santa Ana Mountains
—794 97	Riverside County
	Including Joshua Tree National Park
	For Joshua Tree National Park in San Bernardino County, see —79495
—794 98	San Diego County
—794 985	San Diego
—794 99	Imperial County
	Including *Salton Sea
	Class here *Imperial Valley; *Colorado Desert

*For a specific part of this jurisdiction, region, or feature, see the part and follow instructions under —4–9

—795   Oregon

> Class here Pacific Northwest; *Cascade Range

> *For British Columbia, see —711; for Idaho, see —796; for Washington, see —797*

—795 1   *Western Oregon

> Class here *Coast Ranges

—795 2   Southwestern counties of Oregon

> Class here *Klamath Mountains

—795 21   Curry County

> Class here *Rogue River

—795 23   Coos County

—795 25   Josephine County

—795 27   Jackson County

—795 29   Douglas County

> Class here Umpqua River

—795 3   West central counties of Oregon

> Class here *Willamette River

—795 31   Lane County

—795 33   Lincoln County

—795 34   Benton County

—795 35   Linn County

—795 37   Marion County

> Including Salem

—795 38   Polk County

—795 39   Yamhill County

—795 4   Northwestern counties of Oregon

> Class here *Columbia River in Oregon

—795 41   Clackamas County

—795 43   Washington County

—795 44   Tillamook County

—795 46   Clatsop County

—795 47   Columbia County

*For a specific part of this jurisdiction, region, or feature, see the part and follow instructions under —4–9

—795 49	Multnomah County
	Class here Portland
—795 5	*Eastern Oregon
—795 6	North central counties of Oregon
—795 61	Hood River County
	Including *Mount Hood
—795 62	Wasco County
	Class here *Deschutes River
—795 64	Sherman County
—795 65	Gilliam County
—795 67	Morrow County
—795 69	Umatilla County
—795 7	Northeastern counties of Oregon
	Class here *Blue Mountains; *Snake River in Oregon
—795 71	Union County
—795 73	Wallowa County
	Including *Wallowa Mountains
—795 75	Baker County
—795 78	Grant County
—795 8	Central counties of Oregon
—795 81	Wheeler County
—795 83	Crook County
—795 85	Jefferson County
—795 87	Deschutes County
—795 9	Southeastern counties of Oregon
—795 91	Klamath County
—795 915	Crater Lake National Park
—795 93	Lake County
—795 95	Harney County
—795 97	Malheur County
—796	Idaho

*For a specific part of this jurisdiction, region, or feature, see the part and follow instructions under —4–9

—796 1	*Southern Idaho
	Class here *Snake River
—796 2	Southwestern counties of Idaho
—796 21	Owyhee County
—796 23	Canyon County
—796 24	Payette County
—796 25	Washington County
—796 26	Adams County
—796 27	Gem County
—796 28	Ada County
	Including Boise
—796 29	Elmore County
	Including *Sawtooth Range
	Class comprehensive works on Sawtooth Mountains in —79672
—796 3	South central counties of Idaho
—796 31	Camas County
—796 32	Blaine County
—796 33	Minidoka County
—796 34	Lincoln County
—796 35	Jerome County
—796 36	Gooding County
—796 37	Twin Falls County
—796 39	Cassia County
—796 4	Southeastern counties of Idaho
—796 41	Oneida County
—796 42	Franklin County
—796 44	Bear Lake County
	Including *Wasatch Range in Idaho
—796 45	Caribou County
—796 47	Bannock County
—796 49	Power County

*For a specific part of this jurisdiction, region, or feature, see the part and follow instructions under —4–9

—796 5	Northeastern counties of southern Idaho
—796 51	Bingham County
—796 53	Bonneville County
—796 54	Teton County
—796 55	Madison County
—796 56	Fremont County
—796 57	Clark County
—796 58	Jefferson County
—796 59	Butte County

Including Craters of the Moon National Monument

For Craters of the Moon National Monument in Blaine County, see —79632

—796 6	*Central Idaho

Class here *Bitterroot Range in Idaho

—796 7	South central counties of Idaho

Class here *Salmon River Mountains

—796 72	Custer County

Including *Sawtooth Mountains

See also —79629 for Sawtooth Range

—796 74	Boise County
—796 76	Valley County
—796 78	Lemhi County
—796 8	North central counties of Idaho
—796 82	Idaho County

Class here *Salmon River

—796 84	Lewis County
—796 85	Nez Perce County

Including *Clearwater River

—796 86	Latah County
—796 88	Clearwater County
—796 9	Northern Idaho

*For a specific part of this jurisdiction, region, or feature, see the part and follow instructions under —4–9

—796 91	Shoshone County
	Including *Coeur d'Alene Mountains
—796 93	Benewah County
—796 94	Kootenai County
—796 96	Bonner County
—796 98	Boundary County
—797	Washington
	Class here *Columbia River
—797 1	*Eastern Washington
—797 2	Northeastern counties of Washington
—797 21	Pend Oreille County
—797 23	Stevens County
	Including *Franklin D. Roosevelt Lake
—797 25	Ferry County
—797 28	Okanogan County
—797 3	East central counties of Washington
—797 31	Douglas County
—797 32	Grant County
—797 33	Franklin County
—797 34	Adams County
—797 35	Lincoln County
—797 37	Spokane County
	Class here Spokane
—797 39	Whitman County
	Class here *Palouse River
—797 4	Southeastern counties of Washington
	Class here *Snake River in Washington
—797 42	Asotin County
—797 44	Garfield County
—797 46	Columbia County
	Including *Blue Mountains in Washington

*For a specific part of this jurisdiction, region, or feature, see the part and follow instructions under
—4–9

—797 48	Walla Walla County
—797 5	Central counties of Washington
	Class here *Cascade Range in Washington
—797 51	Benton County
—797 53	Klickitat County
—797 55	Yakima County
	Class here *Yakima River
—797 57	Kittitas County
—797 59	Chelan County
—797 6	*Western Washington
—797 7	Puget Sound counties

See also —16432 for Puget Sound

—797 71	Snohomish County
—797 72	Skagit County
—797 73	Whatcom County

Including North Cascades National Park

For North Cascades National Park in Chelan County, see —79759; for North Cascades National Park in Skagit County, see —79772

—797 74	San Juan County
—797 75	Island County
—797 76	Kitsap County
—797 77	King County
—797 772	Seattle
—797 78	Pierce County
—797 782	Mount Rainier National Park

For Mount Rainier National Park in Lewis County, see —79782

—797 788	Tacoma
—797 79	Thurston County

Including Olympia

—797 8	Southwest central counties of Washington

*For a specific part of this jurisdiction, region, or feature, see the part and follow instructions under —4–9

—797 82	Lewis County

Class here *Cowlitz River

—797 84	Skamania County
—797 86	Clark County
—797 88	Cowlitz County
—797 9	Coastal counties of Washington

Class here *Coast Ranges in Washington

—797 91	Wahkiakum County
—797 92	Pacific County
—797 94	*Olympic Peninsula

Class here *Olympic Mountains

—797 95	Grays Harbor County
—797 97	Mason County
—797 98	Jefferson County

Class here Olympic National Park

For Olympic National Park in Mason County, see —79797; for Olympic National Park in Clallam County, see —79799

—797 99	Clallam County

See also —16432 for Strait of Juan de Fuca

—798	Alaska
—798 2	Panhandle region

Including Haines Borough, Juneau Borough, Ketchikan Gateway Borough, Sitka Borough, Yakutat Borough; Glacier Bay National Park and Preserve, Misty Fjords National Monument

—798 3	South central region of Alaska

Pacific Coast area from Icy Bay to Cape Douglas, inland to crest of Alaska and Aleutian Ranges

Including Kenai Peninsula Borough, Matanuska-Susitna Borough; *Denali National Park and Preserve, Kenai Fjords National Park, *Wrangell-Saint Elias National Park and Preserve; Kenai Peninsula; *Alaska Range

See also —16434 for Gulf of Alaska, Cook Inlet; also —7986 for Denali Borough

—798 35	Greater Anchorage Area Borough

*For a specific part of this jurisdiction, region, or feature, see the part and follow instructions under —4–9

—798 4   Southwestern region of Alaska

                      Area from Cape Douglas to Stuart Island

                      Including Aleutians East Borough, Bristol Bay Borough, Kodiak Island Borough, Lake and Peninsula Borough; Katmai National Park and Preserve; Aleutian Islands, Kodiak Island; *Kuskokwim River

                           See also —16434 for Bristol Bay

—798 6   Central region of Alaska

                      Area from the crest of Alaska Range to North Slope Borough

                      Including Denali Borough, Fairbanks North Star Borough, Northwest Arctic Borough; Gates of the Arctic National Park and Preserve, Kobuk Valley National Park, Lake Clark National Park and Preserve; Seward Peninsula

                      Class here *Yukon River

                      Class comprehensive works on Denali National Park and Preserve in —7983

                         For Gates of the Arctic National Park and Preserve in North Slope Borough, see —7987

                         See also —16434 for Norton Sound

—798 7   North Slope Borough

                      Including Brooks Range

—8   South America

            Class here Latin America, Spanish America, the *Andes

               For Middle America, see —72

SUMMARY

—81	**Brazil**
—82	**Argentina**
—83	**Chile**
—84	**Bolivia**
—85	**Peru**
—86	**Colombia and Ecuador**
—87	**Venezuela**
—88	**Guiana**
—89	**Paraguay and Uruguay**

—81   Brazil

—811   Northern region of Brazil

                    Class here *Amazon River

—811 1   Rondônia state

---

*For a specific part of this jurisdiction, region, or feature, see the part and follow instructions under —4–9

—811 2	Acre state
—811 3	Amazonas state
—811 4	Roraima state
—811 5	Pará state
—811 6	Amapá state
—811 7	Tocantins state
—812	Maranhão state and Piauí state
—812 1	Maranhão state
—812 2	Piauí state
—813	Northeastern region of Brazil

> *For Maranhão state and Piauí state, see —812; for Sergipe state and Bahia state, see —814*

—813 1	Ceará state
—813 2	Rio Grande do Norte state
—813 3	Paraíba state
—813 4	Pernambuco state

> Including Fernando de Noronha archipelago

—813 5	Alagoas state
—814	Sergipe state and Bahia state
—814 1	Sergipe state
—814 2	Bahia state

> Class here *São Francisco River

—815	Southeastern region of Brazil

> *For São Paulo state, see —8161*

—815 1	Minas Gerais state
—815 2	Espírito Santo state
—815 3	Rio de Janeiro state

> Class here Rio de Janeiro

—816	São Paulo state and southern region of Brazil

> Class here *Paraná River in Brazil

> Subdivisions are added for São Paulo state and southern region of Brazil together, for southern region of Brazil alone

---

*For a specific part of this jurisdiction, region, or feature, see the part and follow instructions under —4–9

—816 1   São Paulo state

                    Class here São Paulo

\>   —816 2–816 5 Southern region of Brazil

                    Class comprehensive works in —816

—816 2   Paraná state

—816 4   Santa Catarina state

—816 5   Rio Grande do Sul state

—817   West central region of Brazil

—817 1   Mato Grosso do Sul state

—817 2   Mato Grosso state

—817 3   Goiás state

—817 4   Federal District of Brazil

                    Including Brasília

—82   **Argentina**

—821   South central region of Argentina

—821 1   Capital Federal

                    Including Buenos Aires

—821 2   Buenos Aires province

                    See also —16368 for Bahía Blanca Estuary, Río de la Plata

—821 3   La Pampa province

—822   Mesopotamian provinces

                    Class here *Paraná River, *Uruguay River

—822 1   Entre Ríos

—822 2   Corrientes

—822 3   Misiones

—822 4   Santa Fe

—823   Northeastern provinces of Argentina

—823 4   Chaco

—823 5   Formosa

—824   Northwestern provinces of Argentina

*For a specific part of this jurisdiction, region, or feature, see the part and follow instructions under —4–9

—824 1	Jujuy
—824 2	Salta
—824 3	Tucumán
—824 5	Catamarca
—824 6	La Rioja
—825	North central provinces of Argentina
—825 2	Santiago del Estero
—825 4	Córdoba
—826	Central Highland provinces
—826 2	San Luis
—826 3	San Juan
—826 4	Mendoza
—827	Patagonian region

Class here comprehensive works on Patagonia

For Patagonian region in Chile, see —83644

—827 2	Neuquén province
—827 3	Río Negro province

See also —16368 for Gulf of San Matías

—827 4	Chubut province

See also —16368 for Gulf of San Jorge

—827 5	Santa Cruz province

See also —16368 for Bahía Grande, Gulf of San Jorge

—827 6	Tierra del Fuego province

Class here comprehensive works on Tierra del Fuego archipelago, Isla Grande de Tierra del Fuego

Class south Atlantic Ocean islands claimed by Argentina in —9711

For Tierra del Fuego province of Chile, see —83646

—83	**Chile**
—831	Tarapacá region, Antofagasta region, Atacama region
—831 2	Tarapacá region
—831 23	Arica province
—831 27	Iquique province
—831 3	Antofagasta region
—831 32	Tocopilla province

—831 35	El Loa province
—831 38	Antofagasta province
—831 4	Atacama region
—831 42	Chañaral province
—831 45	Copiapó province
—831 48	Huasco province
—832	Coquimbo region and Valparaíso region
—832 3	Coquimbo region
—832 32	Elqui province
—832 35	Limarí province
—832 38	Choapa province
—832 4	Valparaíso region

> *For Quillota province, Valparaíso province, San Antonio province, see —8325; for Easter Island, see —9618*

—832 42	Los Andes province
—832 45	San Felipe province
—832 48	Petorca province
—832 5	Quillota province, Valparaíso province, San Antonio province

Class comprehensive works on Valparaíso region in —8324

—832 52	Quillota province
—832 55	Valparaíso province
—832 58	San Antonio province
—833	Central regions
—833 1	Metropolitana region
—833 15	Santiago
—833 2	Cachapoal province

Class here Libertador General Bernardo O'Higgins region

> *For Colchagua province, see —8333*

—833 3	Colchagua province
—833 4	Curicó province
—833 5	Talca province

Class here Maule region

> *For Curicó province, see —8334; for Linares province, see —8337*

—833 7	Linares province

—833 8	Ñuble province
—833 9	Concepción province
—834	Bíobío region and Araucanía region
—834 1	Bíobío (Bío-Bío) region

> For *Ñuble province, see* —8338; *for Concepción province, see* —8339; *for Arauco province, see* —8342; *for Bío-Bío province, see* —8343

—834 2	Arauco province
—834 3	Bío-Bío province
—834 5	Malleco province
—834 6	Cautín province

> Class here Araucanía region

> For *Malleco province, see* —8345

—835	Los Lagos region
—835 2	Valdivia province
—835 3	Osorno province
—835 4	Llanquihue province
—835 6	Chiloé province
—836	Aisén del General Carlos Ibáñez del Campo region and Magallanes y Antártica Chilena region
—836 2	Aisén del General Carlos Ibáñez del Campo region
—836 22	Aisén province
—836 25	General Carrera province
—836 28	Capitán Prat province
—836 4	Magallanes y Antártica Chilena region
—836 42	Ultima Esperanza province
—836 44	Magallanes province

> *See also* —1674 *for Strait of Magellan*

—836 46	Tierra del Fuego province

> Class comprehensive works on Tierra del Fuego archipelago in —8276

—836 48	Antártica Chilena province
—84	**Bolivia**
—841	Mountain region departments of Bolivia

—841 2	La Paz

         Class here La Paz; *Lake Titicaca

—841 3	Oruro
—841 4	Potosí
—842	Valley region departments of Bolivia
—842 3	Cochabamba
—842 4	Chuquisaca

         Including Sucre

—842 5	Tarija
—843	Santa Cruz department

         Class here plains region

—844	Amazon region departments
—844 2	El Beni (Beni)
—844 3	Pando
—85	**Peru**
—851	Northern departments of Peru
—851 2	Tumbes department

         Class here Grau region

           For Piura department, see —8513

—851 3	Piura department
—851 4	Lambayeque department

         Class here Nor Oriental del Marañón region

           For Cajamarca department, see —8515; for Amazonas department, see —8546

—851 5	Cajamarca department
—851 6	La Libertad department (La Libertad region)
—852	Central departments of Peru
—852 1	Ancash department (Chavín Region)
—852 2	Huánuco department

         Class here Andrés Avelino Cáceres region

           For Pasco department, see —8523; for Junín department, see —8524

*For a specific part of this jurisdiction, region, or feature, see the part and follow instructions under —4–9

—852 3	Pasco department
—852 4	Junín department
—852 5	Lima department
	Class here Lima
—852 6	Callao constitutional province
—852 7	Ica department
	Class here Los Libertadores Wari region

> *For Huancavelica department, see —8528; for Ayacucho department, see —8529*

—852 8	Huancavelica department
—852 9	Ayacucho department
—853	Southern departments of Peru
—853 2	Arequipa department (Arequipa region)
—853 4	Moquegua department
	Class here Mariátegui region

> *For Tacna department, see —8535; for Puno department, see —8536*

—853 5	Tacna department
—853 6	Puno department
	Including Lake Titicaca in Peru
—853 7	Cuzco department
	Class here Inca region

> *For Apurímac department, see —8538; for Madre de Dios department, see —8542*

—853 8	Apurímac department
—854	Eastern departments of Peru
—854 2	Madre de Dios department
—854 3	Ucayali department (Ucayali region)
—854 4	Loreto department (Amazonas region)
	Class here *Amazon River in Peru

> *See also —8546 for Amazonas department*

—854 5	San Martín department (San Martín region)

*For a specific part of this jurisdiction, region, or feature, see the part and follow instructions under —4–9

—854 6   Amazonas department

           See also —8544 for Amazonas region

—86   **Colombia and Ecuador**

—861   Colombia

           Class here *Magdalena River

—861 1   Caribbean Region

—861 11   San Andrés y Providencia

           Islands in Caribbean Sea

—861 12   Córdoba

           Including *San Jorge River

—861 13   Sucre

—861 14   Bolívar

—861 15   Atlántico

861 16   Magdalena

           Including *Sierra Nevada de Santa Marta National Park

—861 17   La Guajira

—861 18   Cesar

\>   —861 2–861 4   Andean Region

       Class comprehensive works in —8612

—861 2   Northern departments of Andean Region

           Class here Andean Region

           For southwestern departments of Andean Region, see —8613; for southeastern departments of Andean Region, see —8614

—861 24   Norte de Santander

           Including *Tama National Park

—861 25   Santander

—861 26   Antioquia

           Including *Paramillo National Park

—861 3   Southwestern departments of Andean Region

—861 32   Risaralda

—861 34   Quindío

*For a specific part of this jurisdiction, region, or feature, see the part and follow instructions under —4–9

—861 35	Caldas
—861 36	Tolima
—861 39	Huila
	Including *Nevado del Huila National Park
—861 4	Southeastern departments of Andean Region
—861 44	Boyacá
	Including *El Cocuy National Park; *Cocuy Range
—861 46	Cundinamarca
	Including *Sumapaz National Park
—861 48	Capital District of Santa Fe de Bogotá
	Class here Bogotá
—861 5	*Pacific Coast Region
	Class here *Cordillera Occidental
—861 51	Chocó
	Including *Atrato River
—861 52	Valle del Cauca
	Including Farallones de Cali National Park
—861 53	Cauca
	Including *Puracé National Park; *Coconucos Range
—861 58	Nariño
	Including Sanquianga National Park
—861 6	Amazon Region
	For Amazonas, see —8617
—861 63	Putumayo
—861 64	Caquetá
—861 65	Vaupés
—861 66	Guaviare
—861 67	Guainía
—861 7	Amazonas
—861 9	Orinoquia Region
—861 92	Vichada
	Including El Tuparro National Park

*For a specific part of this jurisdiction, region, or feature, see the part and follow instructions under —4–9

—861 94	Meta
	Including *Los Picahos National Park, Serrania de La Macarena National Park
—861 96	Casanare
—861 98	Arauca
—866	Ecuador
—866 1	Sierra Region
	For southern provinces of Sierra Region, see —8662
—866 11	Carchi
—866 12	Imbabura
—866 13	Pichincha
	Including Quito
—866 14	Cotopaxi
—866 15	Tungurahua
—866 16	Bolívar
—866 17	Chimborazo
—866 2	Southern provinces of Sierra Region
—866 23	Cañar
—866 24	Azuay
—866 25	Loja
—866 3	Costa Region
—866 31	El Oro
—866 32	Guayas
	See also —1641 for Gulf of Guayaquil
—866 33	Los Ríos
—866 34	Manabí
—866 35	Esmeraldas
—866 4	Oriente Region
—866 41	Sucumbíos province and Napo province
—866 412	Sucumbíos
—866 416	Napo
—866 42	Pastaza

*For a specific part of this jurisdiction, region, or feature, see the part and follow instructions under —4–9

—866 43	Morona-Santiago
—866 44	Zamora-Chinchipe
—866 5	Galapagos Islands (Colón)

—87   **Venezuela**

Class here *Orinoco River

—871	Southwestern states of Venezuela
—871 2	Táchira
—871 3	Mérida
—871 4	Trujillo
—872	Northwestern states of Venezuela
—872 3	Zulia

Class here *Lake Maracaibo

—872 4	Falcón

See also —16365 for Gulf of Venezuela

—872 5	Lara
—872 6	Yaracuy
—873	North central states of Venezuela

Including Federal Dependencies

For Distrito Federal, see —877

—873 2	Carabobo
—873 4	Aragua
—873 5	Miranda
—874	Central states of Venezuela
—874 2	Apure
—874 3	Barinas
—874 5	Portuguesa
—874 6	Cojedes
—874 7	Guárico
—875	Northeastern states of Venezuela
—875 2	Anzoátegui

*For a specific part of this jurisdiction, region, or feature, see the part and follow instructions under —4–9

—875 3	Sucre

See also —16366 for Gulf of Paria

—875 4	Nueva Esparta
—875 6	Monagas
—876	Southeastern states of Venezuela
—876 2	Delta Amacuro
—876 3	Bolívar
—876 4	Amazonas
—877	Distrito Federal

Including Caracas

—88	**Guiana**
—881	Guyana
—881 1	Barima-Waini Region
—881 2	Pomeroon-Supenaam Region
—881 3	Essequibo Islands-West Demerara Region
—881 4	Upper Demerara-Berbice Region
—881 5	Demerara-Mahaica Region

Including Georgetown

—881 6	Mahaica-Berbice Region
—881 7	East Berbice-Corentyne Region
—881 8	Upper Takutu-Upper Essequibo region and Potaro-Siparuni region
—881 84	Upper Takutu-Upper Essequibo Region
—881 87	Potaro-Siparuni Region
—881 9	Cuyuni-Mazaruni Region
—882	French Guiana (Guyane)

Overseas department of France

Including Cayenne and Saint-Laurent du Maroni arrondissements

Class here Inini

—883	Suriname
—883 1	Nickerie district
—883 2	Coronie district
—883 3	Saramacca district
—883 4	Para district

—883 5	Paramaribo district and Wanica district
—883 52	Paramaribo district
	Class here Paramaribo
—883 57	Wanica district
—883 7	Commewijne district
—883 8	Marowijne district
—883 9	Brokopondo district and Sipaliwini district
—883 92	Brokopondo district
—883 95	Sipaliwini district
—89	**Paraguay and Uruguay**
—892	Paraguay
	Class here *Paraguay River
—892 1	Oriental region
—892 12	Asunción Capital District and southern departments of Oriental region

Subdivisions are added for Asunción Capital District and southern departments of Oriental region together, for southern departments of Oriental region alone

—892 121	Asunción Capital District

>	—892 122–892 128 Southern departments of Oriental region

Class comprehensive works in —89212

—892 122	Central
—892 123	Paraguarí
—892 124	Ñeembucú
—892 125	Misiones
—892 126	Itapúa
—892 127	Caazapá
—892 128	Guairá
—892 13	Northern departments of Oriental region
—892 132	Alto Paraná
—892 133	Canindeyú
—892 134	Caaguazú

*For a specific part of this jurisdiction, region, or feature, see the part and follow instructions under —4–9

—892 135	Cordillera
—892 136	San Pedro
—892 137	Amambay
—892 138	Concepción
—892 2	Occidental region

Class here *Chaco Boreal

—892 23	Presidente Hayes
—892 24	Boquerón
—892 27	Alto Paraguay
—895	Uruguay

Class here *Uruguay River in Uruguay

—895 1	Coastal departments of Uruguay

See also —16368 for Río de la Plata

—895 11	Colonia
—895 12	San José
—895 13	Montevideo

Class here Montevideo

—895 14	Canelones
—895 15	Maldonado
—895 16	Rocha
—895 2	Central departments of Uruguay
—895 21	Lavalleja
—895 22	Treinta y Tres
—895 23	Cerro Largo
—895 24	Durazno
—895 25	Florida
—895 26	Flores
—895 27	Soriano
—895 28	Río Negro
—895 3	Northern departments of Uruguay
—895 31	Paysandú

*For a specific part of this jurisdiction, region, or feature, see the part and follow instructions under —4–9

—895 32	Tacuarembó
—895 34	Rivera
—895 35	Salto
—895 36	Artigas

—9   Australasia, *Pacific Ocean islands, Atlantic Ocean islands, Arctic islands, Antarctica, extraterrestrial worlds

Subdivisions are added for Australasia, Pacific Ocean islands, Atlantic Ocean islands, Arctic islands, Antarctica, extraterrestrial worlds together; for Australasia alone; Pacific Ocean islands alone

SUMMARY

—93	New Zealand
—94	Australia
—95	New Guinea and neighboring countries of Melanesia
—96	Polynesia and other Pacific Ocean islands
—97	Atlantic Ocean islands
—98	Arctic islands and Antarctica
—99	Extraterrestrial worlds

>   —93–96 Australasia and Pacific Ocean islands

Class comprehensive works in —9

—93   New Zealand

See Manual at T2—93

SUMMARY

—931	North Island
—932	Auckland Region
—933	Waikato Region
—934	Bay of Plenty Region, Gisborne Region, Hawke's Bay Region, Taranaki Region
—935	Manawatu-Wanganui Region
—936	Wellington Region
—937	South Island
—938	Canterbury Region
—939	Otago Region, Southland Region, outlying islands

—931	*North Island
—931 2	Former *Auckland Province

>   —931 3–931 8 Northland Region

Class comprehensive works in —9313

---

*For a specific part of this jurisdiction, region, or feature, see the part and follow instructions under —4–9

—931 3   Far North District

                  Class here Northland Region

                      For Whangarei District, see —9316; for Kaipara District, see —9318

—931 6   Whangarei District

—931 8   Kaipara District

—932   Auckland Region

—932 1   Rodney District

                  Including Kawau Island

—932 2   North Shore City

                  Class here Takapuna

—932 3   Waitakere City

—932 4   Auckland City

                  Including Great Barrier Island, Little Barrier Island, Waiheke Island

                  Class here Auckland

—932 5   Manukau City

—932 6   Papakura District

—932 7   Franklin District in Auckland Region

—933   Waikato Region

—933 1   Franklin District

                      For Franklin District in Auckland Region, see —9327

—933 2   Thames Coromandel District and Hauraki District

—933 23   Thames Coromandel District

                  Class here Coromandel Peninsula

—933 27   Hauraki District

—933 3   Waikato District

—933 4   Hamilton City

                  Class here Hamilton

—933 5   Matamata Piako District and Waipa District

—933 53   Matamata Piako District

—933 57   Waipa District

—933 6   South Waikato District, and Rotorua District in Waikato Region

—933 63   South Waikato District

—933 67   Rotorua District in Waikato Region

—933 7   Otorohanga District

—933 8   Waitomo District

> *For Waitomo District in Manawatu-Wanganui Region, see —93517*

—933 9   Taupo District

> Including Lake Taupo

> *For Taupo District in Bay of Plenty Region, see —93424; for Taupo District in Hawke's Bay Region, see —93463; for Taupo District in Manawatu-Wanganui Region, see —93513*

—934   Bay of Plenty Region, Gisborne Region, Hawke's Bay Region, Taranaki Region

—934 2   Bay of Plenty Region

—934 21   Tauranga District

—934 22   Western Bay of Plenty District

—934 23   Rotorua District

> *For Rotorua District in Waikato Region, see —93367*

—934 24   Taupo District in Bay of Plenty Region

—934 25   Whakatane District

> Including Urewera National Park

> *For Urewera National Park in Wairoa District, see —93462*

—934 26   Kawerau District

> Class here Kawerau

—934 28   Opotiki District

—934 4   Gisborne Region (Gisborne District)

—934 6   Hawke's Bay Region

—934 62   Wairoa District

—934 63   Taupo District in Hawke's Bay Region

—934 64   Rangitikei District in Hawke's Bay Region

—934 65   Hastings District

—934 67   Napier City

—934 69   Central Hawke's Bay District

—934 8   Taranaki Region

—934 82   New Plymouth District

> Including Egmont National Park

> *For Egmont National Park in Stratford District, see —93485; for Egmont National Park in South Taranaki District, see —93488*

—934 85	Stratford District

> *For Stratford District in Manawatu-Wanganui Region, see —9353*

—934 88	South Taranaki District
—935	Manawatu-Wanganui Region

> *For Taupo District, see —9339*

—935 1	Taupo District in Manawatu-Wanganui Region and Waitomo District in Manawatu-Wanganui Region
—935 13	Taupo District in Manawatu-Wanganui Region
—935 17	Waitomo District in Manawatu-Wanganui Region
—935 2	Ruapehu District

Including Tongariro National Park, Whanganui National Park

> *For Tongariro National Park in Taupo District, see —9339; for Whanganui National Park in Wanganui District, see —9354*

—935 3	Stratford District in Manawatu-Wanganui Region
—935 4	Wanganui District
—935 5	Rangitikei District

> *For Rangitikei District in Hawke's Bay Region, see —93464*

—935 6	Manawatu District
—935 7	Tararua District

> *For Tararua District in Wellington Region, see —9369*

—935 8	Palmerston North City

Class here Palmerston North

—935 9	Horowhenua District
—936	Wellington Region
—936 1	Kapiti Coast District
—936 2	Porirua City
—936 3	Wellington City

Class here Wellington

—936 4	Lower Hutt City
—936 5	Upper Hutt City

>	—936 6–936 9 Wairarapa

Class comprehensive works in —9366

—936 6   South Wairarapa District

         Class here Wairarapa

            For Carterton District, see —9367; for Masterton District, see —9368; for Tararua District in Wellington Region, see —9369

—936 7   Carterton District

—936 8   Masterton District

—936 9   Tararua District in Wellington Region

—937   South Island

            For Canterbury Region, see —938; for Otago and Southland Regions, see —939

\>   —937 1–937 4   West Coast Region

         Class comprehensive works in —9371

—937 1   Westland District

         Including *Mount Aspiring National Park, Westland National Park

         Class here West Coast Region, *Southern Alps

            For Grey District, see —9372; for Buller District, see —9373; for Tasman District in West Coast Region, see —9374

—937 2   Grey District

—937 3   Buller District

         Including Paparoa National Park

            For Paparoa National Park in Grey District, see —9372

—937 4   Tasman District in West Coast Region

         Including Nelson Lakes National Park

\>   —937 5–937 9   Nelson-Marlborough Region

         Class comprehensive works in —9375

—937 5   Marlborough District

         Class here Nelson-Marlborough Region

            For Nelson City, see —9376; for Tasman District, see —9377; for Kaikoura District, see —9378; for Hurunui District in Nelson-Marlborough Region, see —9379

—937 6   Nelson City

---

*For a specific part of this jurisdiction, region, or feature, see the part and follow instructions under —4–9

—937 7   Tasman District

>   Including Abel Tasman National Park

>   *For Tasman District in West Coast Region, see —9374*

—937 8   Kaikoura District

—937 9   Hurunui District in Nelson-Marlborough Region

—938   Canterbury Region

—938 1   Hurunui District

>   Including Arthur's Pass National Park

>   *For Arthur's Pass National Park in Grey District, see —9372; for Arthur's Pass National Park in Selwyn District, see —9385; for Hurunui District in Nelson-Marlborough Region, see —9379*

—938 2   Waimakariri District

—938 3   Christchurch City

>   Class here Christchurch

—938 4   Banks Peninsula District

>   Class here Banks Peninsula

—938 5   Selwyn District

—938 6   Ashburton District

—938 7   Timaru District

—938 8   MacKenzie District

>   Including Mount Cook National Park; Lake Pukaki

>   *For Mount Cook National Park in Westland District, see —9371*

—938 9   Waimate District, and Waitaki District in Canterbury Region

—938 93   Waimate District

—938 97   Waitaki District in Canterbury Region

>   Including Lake Ohau

—939   Otago Region, Southland Region, outlying islands

>   —939 1–939 5 Otago Region

>   Class comprehensive works in —9391

—939 1   Waitaki District

>   Class here Otago Region

>   *For Waitaki District in Canterbury Region, see —93897; for Dunedin City, see —9392; for Clutha District, see —9393; for Central Otago District, see —9394; for Queenstown-Lakes District, see —9395*

—939 2	Dunedin City
—939 3	Clutha District
—939 4	Central Otago District
—939 5	Queenstown-Lakes District

        Including Lake Hawea, Lake Wakatipu, Lake Wanaka

>   —939 6–939 8   Southland Region

        Class comprehensive works in —9396

—939 6   Southland District

        Including Fiordland National Park; Stewart Island; Lake Manapouri, Lake Te Anau

        Class here Southland Region

          For Gore District, see —9397; for Invercargill District, see —9398

—939 7	Gore District
—939 8	Invercargill District
—939 9	Outlying islands

        Including Chatham Islands, Kermadec Islands, Subantarctic Islands (Antipodes Islands, Auckland Islands, Bounty Islands, Campbell Island, Snares Islands, Traps Islands)

—94   **Australia**

        Class here *Great Dividing Range

SUMMARY

—941	**Western Australia**
—942	**Central Australia**
—943	**Queensland**
—944	**New South Wales**
—945	**Victoria**
—946	**Tasmania**
—947	**Australian Capital Territory**
—948	**Outlying islands**

—941	Western Australia
—941 1	Perth metropolitan district

        Including Fremantle

---

*For a specific part of this jurisdiction, region, or feature, see the part and follow instructions under —4–9

—941 2   Southwestern district

           Including Albany, Bunbury, Collie, Geraldton, Katanning, Manjimup, Narrogin, Northam; Kalbarri National Park, Nelson and Hay National Park, Nornalup National Park, Stirling Range National Park; Darling Range, Stirling Range; Blackwood River, Swan River

           For Perth metropolitan district, see —9411

—941 3   Northwestern district

           Including Port Hedland; Barrow Island National Park, Bernier and Dorre Islands National Park, Cape Range National Park; Gascoyne River

—941 4   Kimberley district

           Including Broome, Wyndham; Ord River

—941 5   North central district

           Class here Gibson Desert, Great Sandy Desert, *Great Victoria Desert

—941 6   South central district

           Including Coolgardie, Kalgoorlie

—941 7   Southern district

           Including Esperance, Norseman; Cape Le Grand National Park, Esperance National Park

—942   Central Australia

—942 3   South Australia

—942 31   Adelaide metropolitan district

—942 32   Central district

           Including Angaston, Clare, Gawler, Murray Bridge, Port Pirie, Salisbury, Victor Harbour; Chaunceys Line Reserve National Park; Mount Lofty Ranges

           For Adelaide metropolitan district, see —94231

—942 33   Eastern district

           Including Barmera, Berri, Loxton, Renmark

—942 34   Southern district

           Including Mount Gambier; Canunda National Park

—942 35   West central district

           Including Flinders Chase National Park; Yorke Peninsula; Kangaroo Island

—942 36   North central district

           Including Quorn

*For a specific part of this jurisdiction, region, or feature, see the part and follow instructions under —4–9

—942 37	Northern district
	Class here *Flinders Ranges; *Coopers Creek
—942 38	Western district
	Including Port Augusta, Port Lincoln, Whyalla; Lincoln National Park; Eyre Peninsula; Lake Eyre, Lake Gairdner
—942 9	Northern Territory
	Class here northern Australia
	For Western Australia, see —941; for Queensland, see —943
—942 91	Southern district
	Including Alice Springs; Ormiston Gorge National Park, Palm Valley National Park, Uluru (Ayers Rock)-Mount Olga National Park; Davenport Range; Ayers Rock
—942 95	Northern district
	Including Darwin, Katherine, Tennant Creek; Cobourg Peninsula National Park, Katherine Gorge National Park; Arnhem Land; Groote Eylandt; Daly River, Roper River
—943	Queensland
	Class here *Great Barrier Reef
—943 1	Brisbane metropolitan district
—943 2	Southeastern district
	Including Bundaberg, Gympie, Ipswich, Kingaroy, Maryborough, Southport, Surfers Paradise; Bunya Mountains National Park, Cooloola National Park, Lamington National Park, Mount Barney National Park; Fraser Island
	Class here *Brisbane River
	For Brisbane metropolitan district, see —9431
—943 3	Downs district
	Including Dalby, Millmerran, Oakey, Stanthorpe, Toowoomba; Granite Belt National Park; Darling Downs
—943 4	Southwestern district
	Including Charleville, Mitchell
—943 5	Central district
	Including Barcaldine, Blackall, Clermont, Gladstone, Longreach, Monto, Rockhampton, Yeppoon; Carnarvon National Park, Dipperu National Park, Isla Gorge National Park, Robinson Gorge National Park, Salvator Rosa National Park; Fitzroy River

*For a specific part of this jurisdiction, region, or feature, see the part and follow instructions under —4–9

—943 6   Northeastern district

                Including Atherton, Bowen, Cairns, Charters Towers, Ingham, Innisfail,
                Mackay, Mareeba, Townsville; Bellenden Ker National Park, Conway
                Range National Park, Eungella National Park, Hinchinbrook Island
                National Park, Mount Elliott National Park, Mount Spec National Park,
                Whitsunday Island National Park, Windsor Tableland National Park;
                Whitsunday Islands; Burdekin River

—943 7   Northwestern district

                Including Mount Isa; Simpson Desert National Park

                See also —16475 for Gulf of Carpentaria

—943 8   Peninsula and Torres Strait Islands

                Including Cape York Peninsula

—944   New South Wales

                Class here *Australian Alps; *Murray River

                For Lord Howe Island, see —9481

—944 1   Sydney metropolitan district

                Including Parramatta, Penrith; Ku-ring-gai Chase National Park

—944 2   Lower north coast district

                Including Cessnock, Forster, Gloucester, Gosford, Maitland,
                Muswellbrook, Newcastle, Port Macquarie, Singleton, Taree; Brisbane
                Water National Park; Hawkesbury River, Hunter River

—944 3   Upper north coast district

                Including Ballina, Casino, Coffs Harbour, Grafton, Kempsey, Kyogle,
                Lismore, Murwillumbah; Gibraltar Range National Park; Richmond
                River

                Class here *Macleay River

—944 4   North central district

                Including Armidale, Coonabarabran, Glen Innes, Inverell, Tamworth,
                Tenterfield; Mount Kaputar National Park, New England National Park

                Class here *Gwydir River

—944 5   Central district

                Including Bathurst, Cowra, Dubbo, Forbes, Gilgandra, Katoomba,
                Lithgow, Mudgee, Orange, Wellington; Blue Mountains National Park;
                *Blue Mountains

—944 6   Upper south coast district

                Including Camden, Campbelltown, Port Kembla, Wollongong; Morton
                National Park, Royal National Park; Nepean River

*For a specific part of this jurisdiction, region, or feature, see the part and follow instructions under
  —4–9

—944 7	Southeastern district

> Including Batemans Bay, Bega, Bombala, Eden, Goulburn, Moruya, Narooma, Nowra, Queanbeyan, Yass; Kosciusko National Park, Shoalhaven National Park; Shoalhaven River

> Class here *Snowy Mountains

> Class Australian Capital Territory in —947

—944 8	Southern district

> Including Albury, Cootamundra, Corowa, Griffith, Junee, Leeton, Wagga Wagga; Cocoparra National Park; Wakool River

> Class here Murrumbidgee River

—944 9	Western district

> Including Bourke, Broken Hill, Cobar, Nyngan, Walgett, Warren; Menindee Lake

> Class here *Lachlan River

—945	Victoria
—945 1	Melbourne metropolitan district
—945 2	Central district

> Including Geelong, Healesville, Mornington, Queenscliff, Sorrento, Sunbury, Torquay, Werribee; Kinglake National Park; French Island, Phillip Island

> Class here Yarra River

> *For Melbourne metropolitan district, see —9451*

—945 3	North central district

> Including Castlemaine, Creswick, Daylesford, Heathcote, Maldon, Maryborough, Woodend

—945 4	Northern district

> Including Bendigo, Echuca, Inglewood, Kyabram, Nathalia, Rushworth, Shepparton

> Class here *Goulburn River

—945 5	Northeastern district

> Including Beechworth, Benalla, Corryong, Euroa, Rutherglen, Wangaratta, Wodonga; Mount Buffalo National Park

> Class here *Ovens River

*For a specific part of this jurisdiction, region, or feature, see the part and follow instructions under —4–9

—945 6   Gippsland district

> Including Bairnsdale, Lakes Entrance, Moe, Morwell, Traralgon, Warragul; Mallacoota Inlet National Park, Wilsons Promontory National Park

—945 7   Western district

> Including Ararat, Ballarat, Colac, Hamilton, Port Fairy, Portland, Warrnambool

—945 8   Wimmera district

> Including Horsham, Stawell

—945 9   Mallee district

> Including Merbein, Mildura, Swan Hill; Hattah Lakes National Park, Wyperfeld National Park; *Wimmera River

—946   Tasmania

—946 1   Hobart metropolitan district

—946 2   Southern district

> Including Kingston, New Norfolk, Port Cygnet; Hartz Mountains National Park, Lake Pedder National Park, Mount Field National Park; Bruny Island

> *For Hobart metropolitan district, see —9461*

—946 3   Central district

> Including Deloraine, Oatlands; Cradle Mountain-Lake Saint Clair National Park; Cradle Mountain; Great Lake; Lake Saint Clair

—946 4   Eastern district

> Including Port Arthur, Scottsdale; Ben Lomond National Park, Freycinet National Park, Maria Island National Park; Tasman Peninsula

—946 5   Northwestern district

> Including Beaconsfield, Burnie, Devonport, Launceston, Smithton, Stanley, Wynyard

> Class here *Tamar River

—946 6   Western district

> Including Queenstown; Frenchmans Cap National Park

—946 7   Bass Strait Islands

> Including Furneaux Islands

—947   Australian Capital Territory

—947 1   Canberra

---

*For a specific part of this jurisdiction, region, or feature, see the part and follow instructions under —4–9

—948	Outlying islands

       Including Christmas Island, Coral Sea Islands

       For Cocos Islands, see —699

—948 1	Lord Howe Island
—948 2	Norfolk Island
—95	**New Guinea and neighboring countries of Melanesia**

       Class here Oceania

       Subdivisions are added for New Guinea and neighboring countries of Melanesia together, for New Guinea alone

       For Polynesia, Micronesia, see —96

———————————

>	—951–957 New Guinea

       Class comprehensive works in —95

—951	Western New Guinea (Irian Barat)

       Variant names: Irian Jaya, West Papua

       Part of Indonesia

       Class here former Papua province

—951 2	West Irian Jaya (Irian Jaya Barat)

       Province of Indonesia

       Class here Bird's Head Peninsula

—951 6	Papua

       Province of Indonesia

—953	Papua New Guinea

       Class here former German New Guinea, former territory of New Guinea; New Guinea region of Papua New Guinea

       For Papuan region, see —954; for Highlands region, see —956; for Momase region, see —957; for Bismarck Archipelago, see —958; for North Solomons Province, see —9592

—954	Papuan region of Papua New Guinea
—954 1	Milne Bay Province

       Including D'Entrecasteaux Islands, Murua (Woodlark) Island, Trobriand Islands

—954 2	Northern (Oro) Province
—954 5	National Capital District

       Class here Port Moresby

—954 6   Central Province

                    Including Bereina

—954 7   Gulf Province

                    Class here *Purari River

—954 9   Western (Fly River) Province

—956   Highlands region of Papua New Guinea

                    Class here *Bismarck Range

—956 1   Southern Highlands Province

—956 3   Enga Province

—956 5   Western Highlands Province

                    Class here Jimi River

—956 7   Simbu (Chimbu) Province

—956 9   Eastern Highlands Province

                    Including Goroka

—957   Momase (Northern coastal) region of Papua New Guinea

—957 1   Morobe Province

                    Including Lae; Siassi Islands; Markham River

—957 3   Madang Province

—957 5   East Sepik Province

                    Class here *Sepik River, *Yuat River

—957 7   West Sepik (Sandaun) Province

—958   Bismarck Archipelago

                    Part of Papua New Guinea

—958 1   Manus Province

                    Including Admiralty Islands

—958 3   New Ireland Province

                    Including Kavieng

—958 5   East New Britain Province

                    Including Rabau

                    Class here comprehensive works on New Britain

                    For West New Britain Province, see —9587

—958 7   West New Britain Province

---

*For a specific part of this jurisdiction, region, or feature, see the part and follow instructions under
    —4–9

—959	Other parts of Melanesia
—959 2	North Solomons Province

Part of Papua New Guinea

Including Bougainville, Buka islands

—959 3	Solomon Islands

Independent nation

—959 31	Western Province
—959 33	Guadalcanal Province
—959 35	Central Province
—959 36	Isabel Province
—959 37	Malaita Province
—959 38	Makira and Ulawa Province
—959 39	Temotu Province
—959 5	Vanuatu
—959 7	New Caledonia

Including Loyalty Islands

—96 Polynesia and other Pacific Ocean islands

Subdivisions are added for Polynesia and other Pacific Ocean islands together, for Polynesia alone

—961	Southwest central Pacific Ocean islands, isolated islands of southeast Pacific Ocean

Subdivisions are added for southwest central Pacific Ocean islands, isolated islands of southeast Pacific Ocean together; for southwest central Pacific Ocean islands alone

—961 1	Fiji
—961 2	Tonga (Friendly Islands)
—961 3	American Samoa

Class here comprehensive works on Samoan Islands

For Samoa, see —9614

—961 4	Samoa

Class comprehensive works on Samoan Islands in —9613

—961 5	Tokelau (Union) Islands
—961 6	Wallis and Futuna Islands
—961 8	Isolated islands of southeast Pacific Ocean

Including Easter Island, Oeno Island, Pitcairn Island

—962	South central Pacific Ocean islands

Class here French Polynesia

For Marquesas Islands, see —9631; for Tuamotu Islands, see —9632

—962 1	Society Islands
—962 11	Tahiti
—962 2	Gambier Islands and Tubuai (Austral) Islands
—962 3	Cook Islands

For Manihiki Atoll, see —9624

—962 4	Manihiki Atoll

Part of Cook Islands

—962 6	Niue
—963	Southeast central Pacific Ocean islands

For isolated islands of southeast Pacific Ocean, see —9618

—963 1	Marquesas Islands

Part of French Polynesia

—963 2	Tuamotu Islands (Low Archipelago)

Part of French Polynesia

For Gambier Islands, see —9622

—964	Line Islands (Equatorial Islands)

Including Kiritimati (Christmas)

For Palmyra, see —9699

—965	*West central Pacific Ocean islands (Micronesia)

Including Wake Island

—966	Federated States of Micronesia and Republic of Palau

Including Truk Islands

Class here Caroline Islands

—967	Mariana Islands

Including Guam, Saipan, Tinian

Class here Commonwealth of the Northern Mariana Islands

—968	Islands of eastern Micronesia

*For a specific part of this jurisdiction, region, or feature, see the part and follow instructions under
—4–9

—968 1	Kiribati
	Including Gilbert Islands
	For Line Islands, see —964
—968 2	Tuvalu
	Class here Ellice Islands
—968 3	Marshall Islands
	Including Bikini Atoll, Enewetak Atoll, Kwajalein Atoll
—968 5	Nauru (Pleasant Island)
—969	Hawaii and neighboring north central Pacific Ocean islands

Subdivisions are added for Hawaii and neighboring north central Pacific Ocean islands together, for Hawaii alone

---

>	—969 1–969 4 Hawaii

State of the United States of America

Class comprehensive works in —969

—969 1	Hawaii County (Hawaii Island)
—969 2	Maui County
—969 21	Maui Island
—969 22	Kahoolawe Island
—969 23	Lanai Island
—969 24	Molokai Island
	Including Kalawao County
—969 3	Honolulu County (Oahu Island)
—969 31	Honolulu
—969 4	Kauai County
—969 41	Kauai Island
—969 42	Niihau Island
—969 9	Outlying islands
	Including Howland Island, Johnston Island, Midway Islands, Palmyra Atoll
—97	***Atlantic Ocean islands**

*For a specific part of this jurisdiction, region, or feature, see the part and follow instructions under —4–9

—971   Falkland Islands, South Georgia and South Sandwich Islands, Bouvet Island

—971 1   Falkland Islands (Islas Malvinas)

—971 2   South Georgia and South Sandwich Islands

           Class here South Georgia Island, South Sandwich Islands

—971 3   Bouvet Island

—973   Saint Helena and dependencies

           Including Ascension Island; Tristan da Cunha Islands

           Subdivisions are added for Saint Helena and dependencies together, for Saint Helena alone

—98   **Arctic islands and Antarctica**

           Subdivisions are added for Arctic islands and Antarctica together, for Arctic islands alone

---

>   —981–988 *Arctic islands

           Class comprehensive works in —98

—981   Svalbard

           Including Spitsbergen Island

—982   Greenland

—983   Jan Mayen Island

—985   Franz Josef Land

           Part of Arkhangel´sk province of Russia

—986   Novaya Zemlya

           Part of Arkhangel´sk province of Russia

—987   Severnaya Zemlya

           Part of Krasnoyarsk territory of Russia

—988   New Siberian Islands

           Part of Yakutia republic of Russia

—989   Antarctica

           Including British Antarctic Territory; Dronning Maud (Queen Maud) Land, Ellsworth Land, Enderby Land; South Orkney Islands, South Shetland Islands; South Pole

*For a specific part of this jurisdiction, region, or feature, see the part and follow instructions under —4–9

—99	**Extraterrestrial worlds**

Worlds other than Earth

Class space in —19

See Manual at T2—99 vs. T2—19

>	—991–994 Solar system

Class comprehensive works in —99

—991	Earth's moon
—992	Planets of solar system and their satellites
—992 1	Mercury
—992 2	Venus
—992 3	Mars
—992 4	Asteroids (Planetoids)
—992 5	Jupiter
—992 6	Saturn
—992 7	Uranus
—992 8	Neptune
—992 9	Trans-Neptunian objects

Former heading: Pluto and transplutonian planets

Including Pluto

—993	Meteoroids and comets
—994	Sun

Table 3. Subdivisions for the Arts, for Individual Literatures, for Specific Literary Forms

Notation from Table 3 is never used alone, but may be used as required by add notes under subdivisions of individual literatures or with base numbers for individual literatures identified by * under 810–890. It is never used for individual literatures that lack instructions to add from Table 3; the number for works of or about such literatures ends with the language notation, e.g., Newari poetry 895.49

Notation from Table 3 may also be used where instructed in 700.4, 791.4, 808–809

Table 3 is divided into three subtables:

Table 3A for description, critical appraisal, biography, single or collected works of an individual author

Table 3B for description, critical appraisal, biography, collected works of two or more authors; also for rhetoric in specific literary forms

Table 3C for additional elements used in number building within Table 3B and as instructed in 700.4, 791.4, 808–809

Turn to Table 3A or 3B for full instructions on building numbers for individual literatures, to 808–809 for other uses of Table 3B and 3C for literature, to 700.4 for uses of Table 3C for the arts, to 791.4 for uses of Table 3C for motion pictures, radio, television

See Manual at Table 3

Table 3A. Subdivisions for Works by or about Individual Authors

Procedures for building numbers for individual authors:

1.   Look in the schedule 810–890 to find the base number for the language. The base number may be identified in an add note, e.g., at 821–828 ("add to base number 82") or another note, e.g., at 896 ("896.392 Swahili"); otherwise, it is the number given for the literature, e.g., Dutch-language literature 839.31. If there is a specific literary form, go to step 2; if not, go to the instructions under —8 in Table 3A

2.   In Table 3A find the correct subdivision for the literary form, e.g., poetry —1. Add this to the base number, e.g., Swahili poetry 896.3921, Dutch poetry 839.311. If the literary form appears as a subdivision of —8 Miscellaneous writings, go to the instructions under —8 in Table 3A; otherwise, go to step 3

3.   Turn back to the appropriate number in the schedule 810–890 to see whether there is an applicable period table. If there is one, go to step 4; if not, complete the class number by inserting a decimal point between the third and fourth digits, e.g., Khmer (Cambodian) poetry by a 20th-century author 895.9321
     (Option: Where optional period tables are available for countries that share the same language, either [1] use initial letters to distinguish the separate countries, or [2] use the special number designated for literature of those countries that are not preferred. Then use the optional period tables, e.g., drama in English by a 20th-century New Zealand author NZ822.2 or 828.993322. Full instructions for optional period tables appear under 811–818, 819, 821–828, 828.99, 841–848, 848.99, 861–868, 868.99, 869, 869.899. If the option is used, go to step 4)
     (Option: Where optional period tables are not available for countries that share the same language, use initial letters to distinguish the separate countries. Then use the standard period table for the language if one is available. If a period table is available, go to step 4)

4.   Select the appropriate period number. Add this number to the number already derived; always insert a point after the third digit. The class number is complete (*except* for William Shakespeare), since standard subdivisions are never added for individual authors, e.g., Spenser's *Faerie Queene* 821.3 (821 English poetry + 3 Elizabethan period)

   See Manual at Table 3A; also at Table 3B vs. Table 3A; also at 800: Literary criticism

> ## —1–8   Specific forms

Unless other instructions are given, observe the following table of preference for works combining two or more literary forms, e.g., drama written in verse —2 (*not* —1):

Drama	—2
Poetry	—1
Class epigrams in verse in —8	
Fiction	—3
Essays	—4
Speeches	—5
Letters	—6
Miscellaneous writings	—8

A single work of humor or satire, or a collection of humor or satire by an individual author in one form is classed with the form, e.g., satirical fiction —3. Humor or satire without identifiable form is classed according to the instructions at —8, plus notation 07 from the table under —81–89 if there is an applicable period table. A collection of humor or satire by an individual author in more than one form is classed according to the instructions at —8, plus notation 09 from the add table under —81–89 if there is an applicable period table

Class comprehensive works (description, critical appraisal, biography, or collected works that cover two or more forms of literature by an individual author) with the form with which the author is chiefly identified, e.g., a biography that discusses the poetry and fiction of a mid-19th-century American writer known primarily as a novelist 813.3

If the author is not chiefly identified with any one form, class comprehensive works as instructed at —8, plus notation 09 from the table under —81–89 if there is an applicable period table, e.g., the collected poetry and fiction of a mid-19th-century American writer not chiefly identified with any one form 818.309

See Manual at Table 3A

(Option: Class description, critical appraisal, biography, single and collected works of all individual authors regardless of form in —8)

—1   Poetry

Class epigrams in verse in —8

See Manual at T3A—2, T3B—2 vs. T3A—1, T3B—102

—11–19   Poetry of specific periods

Add to base number —1 notation from the period table for the specific literature in 810–890, e.g., earliest period —11; do not add standard subdivisions. If there is no applicable period table, add nothing to —1, e.g., Mongolian poetry by an author of the earliest period 894.231 (*not* 894.2311)
    (Option: Where two or more countries share the same language, follow one of the options given after step 3 at beginning of Table 3A, e.g., poetry in English by an Australian author of the earliest period A821.1 or 828.993411)

—2   Drama

Class here closet drama, drama written in poetry

See Manual at T3A—2, T3B—2 vs. T3A—1, T3B—102

—21–29   Specific periods

Add to base number —2 notation from the period table for the specific
literature in 810–890, e.g., earliest period —21; do not add standard
subdivisions. If there is no applicable period table, add nothing to —2, e.g.,
Mongolian drama by an author of the earliest period 894.232 (*not* 894.2321)
(Option: Where two or more countries share the same language, follow
one of the options given after step 3 at beginning of Table 3A, e.g., drama
in English by a New Zealand author of the earliest period NZ822.1 or
828.993321)

—3   Fiction

Class here novels, novelettes, short stories

Class graphic novels in 741.5

—31–39   Specific periods

Add to base number —3 notation from the period table for the specific
literature in 810–890, e.g., earliest period —31; do not add standard
subdivisions. If there is no applicable period table, add nothing to —3, e.g.,
Mongolian fiction by an author of the earliest period 894.233 (*not* 894.2331)
(Option: Where two or more countries share the same language, follow one
of the options given after step 3 at beginning of Table 3A, e.g., fiction in
French by a Canadian author of the colonial period C843.3 or 848.99233)

—4   Essays

Texts, collections, discussions of works with literary value

See Manual at 800: Choice between literature and nonliterary subject

—41–49   Specific periods

Add to base number —4 notation from the period table for the specific
literature in 810–890, e.g., earliest period —41; do not add standard
subdivisions. If there is no applicable period table, add nothing to —4,
e.g., Macedonian essays by an author of the earliest period 891.8194 (*not*
891.81941)
(Option: Where two or more countries share the same language, follow one
of the options given after step 3 at beginning of Table 3A, e.g., essays in
Spanish by a 19th-century Mexican author M864.2 or 868.992142)

—5   Speeches

Texts, collections, discussions of works with literary value

See Manual at 800: Choice between literature and nonliterary subject

—51–59   **Specific periods**

> Add to base number —5 notation from the period table for the specific literature in 810–890, e.g., earliest period —51; do not add standard subdivisions. If there is no applicable period table, add nothing to —5, e.g., Mongolian speeches by an author of the earliest period 894.235 (*not* 894.2351)
>> (Option: Where two or more countries share the same language, follow one of the options given after step 3 at beginning of Table 3A, e.g., speeches in Spanish by a 19th-century Chilean author Ch865.2 or 868.993352)

—6   Letters

> Texts, collections, discussions of works with literary value

> Class collections of the letters of an individual author as biography with the form with which the author is chiefly identified, e.g., letters of a mid-19th-century American known primarily as a novelist 813.3

> *See Manual at 800: Choice between literature and nonliterary subject*

—61–69   **Specific periods**

> Add to base number —6 notation from the period table for the specific literature in 810–890, e.g., earliest period —61; do not add standard subdivisions. If there is no applicable period table, add nothing to —6, e.g., Tibetan letters by an author of the earliest period 895.46 (*not* 895.461)
>> (Option: Where two or more countries share the same language, follow one of the options given after step 3 at beginning of Table 3A, e.g., letters in Portuguese by a 20th-century Brazilian author B869.64 or 869.899264)

—8   Miscellaneous writings

> Procedures for building numbers:

> 1.   To the base number add notation 8, e.g., miscellaneous writings in English 828. Go to step 2

> 2.   Turn back to the appropriate number in the schedule 810–890 to see whether there is an applicable period table. If there is one, go to step 3; if not, complete the class number by inserting a decimal point between the third and fourth digits, e.g., miscellaneous writings in Khmer (Cambodian) by a 20th-century writer 895.9328
>> (Option: Where optional period tables are available for countries that share the same language, either [1] use initial letters to distinguish the separate countries, or [2] use the special number designated for literature of those countries that are not preferred. Then use the optional period tables, e.g., miscellaneous writings in English by a 20th-century New Zealand author NZ828.2 or 828.993382. Full instructions for optional period tables appear under 811–818, 819, 821–828, 828.99, 841–848, 848.99, 861–868, 868.99, 869, 869.899. If the option is used, go to step 3)
>> (Option: Where optional period tables are not available for countries that share the same language, use initial letters to distinguish the separate countries. Then use the standard period table for the language if one is available. If a period table is available, go to step 3)

> 3.   Select the appropriate period number, e.g., the Victorian period in the English literature of Great Britain 8. Then follow the instructions under —81–89

> (Option: Class here description, critical appraisal, biography, single and collected works of all individual authors regardless of form; prefer —1–8)

—81–89   **Specific periods**

Add to base number —8 notation from the period table for the specific literature in 810–890, e.g., earliest period —81; then add further as follows, but in no case add standard subdivisions:

02   Anecdotes, epigrams, graffiti, jokes, jests, quotations, riddles, tongue twisters

Class anonymous riddles from the oral tradition in 398.6; class anonymous jokes and jests from the oral tradition in 398.7; class anonymous tongue twisters from the oral tradition in 398.8

See Manual at T1—0207 vs. T3B—7, T3A—8 + 02, T3B—802, T3B—8 + 02, T3A—8 + 07, T3B—807, T3B—8 + 07; also at T3A—8 + 02, T3B—802, T3B—8 + 02 vs. 398.6, 793.735

03   Diaries, journals, notebooks, reminiscences

See Manual at T3A—8 + 03 and T3B—803, T3B—8 + 03

07   Works without identifiable literary form

Class here experimental and nonformalized works, works that mimic nonliterary forms and genres for literary purposes, not conveying useful information (e.g., humorous or fantasy works in the form of dictionaries, self-help books, travel guides)

Class experimental works with an identifiable literary form with the form, e.g., experimental novels —3; class works without identifiable literary form that are linked with a specific literary work with the work, e.g., a history of an imaginary game associated with a specific novel with the novel in —3; class works that convey useful information on a nonliterary topic with the topic even if linked with a specific literary work, e.g., literary cookbooks with real recipes inspired by or derived from literary sources 641.5

See Manual at T1—0207 vs. T3B—7, T3A—8 + 02, T3B—802, T3B—8 + 02, T3A—8 + 07, T3B—807, T3B—8 + 07

08   Prose literature

Collections or discussions of works in more than one prose form

Class here collections and criticism of selected prose works of an individual author that do not include the author's main literary form, e.g., a collection of the prose works of an English Victorian poet 828.808, a collection of the stories and plays of an English essayist of the romantic period 828.708

Class prose without identifiable literary form in 07. Class a specific form of prose literature with the form, e.g., essays —4; class comprehensive collections or criticisms of an author's work with the the author's main literary number, either with the predominant literary form or in 09 for individual authors not limited to or chiefly identifiable with one specific form, e.g., a comprehensive collection of the works of an English Victorian writer known primarily as a novelist 823.8

09   Individual authors not limited to or chiefly identifiable with one specific form

Class here description, critical appraisal, biography, collected works

(continued)

—81–89   **Specific periods (continued)**

If there is no applicable period table, add nothing to —8, e.g., Mongolian prose literature by an author of the later 20th century 894.238 (*not* 894.23808)

(Option: Where two or more countries share the same language, follow one of the options given after step 2 under —8, e.g., prose literature in English by an Indian author of the later 20th century In828.308 or 828.99358308)

Table 3B. Subdivisions for Works by or about More than One Author

Table 3B is followed and supplemented by Table 3C, which provides additional elements for building numbers within Table 3B

Procedures for building numbers for works by or about more than one author, limited to literatures of specific languages:

1. Look in the schedule 810–890 to find the base number for the language. The base number may be identified in an add note, e.g., at 821–828 ("add to base number 82") or another note, e.g., at 896 ("896.392 Swahili"); otherwise, it is the number given for the literature, e.g., Dutch-language literature 839.31. If there is a specific literary form, go to step 2; if not, go to step 8

2. In Table 3B find the subdivision for the literary form, e.g., poetry —1. Add this to the base number, e.g., English poetry 821, Dutch poetry 839.311. If the literary form appears as a subdivision of —8 Miscellaneous writings, go to the instructions under —8 in Table 3B. If the work deals with poetry, drama, fiction, or speech of specific media, scope, kinds for which there is special notation in Table 3B (e.g., —1042 sonnets), go to step 3. For other works that deal with or fall within a limited time span, go to step 4. A limited time span is (1) fewer than three literary periods or (2) a single century. For other works not limited by time period, go to step 7

3. Use the notation in Table 3B for the kind of poetry, drama, fiction, or speech, e.g., sonnets in English literature 821.042. Insert a point after the third digit. Check whether the specific form is (1) the sole kind in a heading identified by * or (2) is named in a subdivisions-are-added note as a kind for which subdivisions may be added or (3) appears in a class-here note under a heading identified by *. If none of these conditions holds, the number is complete, e.g., collections of English-language clerihews 821.07

If one of the three conditions does hold, follow the instructions in the table under —102–107 in Table 3B. Following these instructions will involve using Table 3C for literature of specific periods, literature displaying specific features or emphasizing specific subjects, and literature for and by groups of people, e.g., collections of English sonnets 821.04208, collections of English sonnets about love 821.042083543

(continued)

Table 3B. Subdivisions for Works by or about More than One Author (continued)

4.   Turn back to the appropriate number in the schedule 810–890 to see whether there is an applicable period table. If there is one, go to step 5; if not, complete the class number by inserting a point between the third and fourth digits, e.g., Khmer (Cambodian) poetry by 20th-century authors 895.9321

   (Option: Where optional period tables are available for countries that share the same language, either [1] use initial letters to distinguish the separate countries, or [2] use the special number designated for literature of those countries that are not preferred. Then use the optional period tables, e.g., 20th-century drama in English by New Zealand authors NZ822.2 or 828.993322. Full instructions for optional period tables appear under 811–818, 819, 821–828, 828.99, 841–848, 848.99, 861–868, 868.99, 869, 869.899. If the option is used, go to step 5)

   (Option: Where optional period tables are not available for countries that share the same language, use initial letters to distinguish the separate countries. Then use the standard period table for the language if one is available. If a period table is available, go to step 5)

5.   Select the appropriate period number. Add this number to the number already derived, e.g., English poetry of the Elizabethan period 821.3; always insert a decimal point after the third digit. Go to step 6

6.   Under the number for the literary form in Table 3B, go to the subdivisions for specific periods, e.g., under —2 for drama go to —21–29. Follow the instructions given there, which will lead to adding the numbers following —10 in notation 1001–1009 of this table. For literature displaying specific features, literature emphasizing subjects, and literature for and by groups of people, the instructions at —1001–1009 will lead to use of Table 3C, e.g., critical appraisal of idealism in English Elizabethan drama 822.30913

7.   If the work is not limited by time period, go to the first subdivisions under the particular form in Table 3B, e.g., under —2 for drama go to —2001–2009. Follow the instructions given there to add the numbers following —100 in notation 1001–1009 of this table. For literature displaying specific features, literature emphasizing subjects, and literature for and by groups of people, the instructions at —1001–1009 will lead to use of Table 3C, e.g., collections of English poetry about war 821.00803581, collections of English poetry by rural authors 821.008091734

(continued)

Table 3B. Subdivisions for Works by or about More than One Author (continued)

8. If the work is not limited to a specific literary form, consult —01–09 in Table 3B. Follow the instructions at the number selected, making use of Table 3C when specified, e.g., collections of English literature in many forms about holidays 820.80334. Use period notation 08001–08009 and —09001–09009 only if there is an applicable period table

> (Option: Where optional period tables are available for countries that share the same language, either [1] use initial letters to distinguish the separate countries, or [2] use the special number designated for literature of those countries that are not preferred. Then use the optional period tables, e.g., 20th-century drama in English by New Zealand authors NZ822.2 or 828.993322. Full instructions for optional period tables appear under 811–818, 819, 821–828, 828.99, 841–848, 848.99, 861–868, 868.99, 869, 869.899)

> (Option: Where optional period tables are not available for countries that share the same language, use initial letters to distinguish the separate countries. Then use the standard period table for the language if one is available)

The procedures described above require the use of schedule 810–890, Table 3B, and Table 3C in varying order. Sometimes also other tables are used. Example:

82	English (810–890)
1	poetry (Table 3B)
914	of later 20th century (810–890)
080	collections (Table 3B)
32	about travel (Table 3C)
4253	Lincolnshire (Table 2)

Thus, collections of later-20th-century English-language poetry about travel in Lincolnshire 821.914080324253

Note that literary form —8 Miscellaneous writings is arranged first by period and then by specific miscellaneous forms

Instructions in the use of notation from Table 3B for rhetoric in specific literary forms, collections of literary texts from more than two literatures, and history, description, critical appraisal of more than two literatures are found in 808–809

See Manual at Table 3B; also at Table 3B vs. Table 3A; also at 800

SUMMARY

—01–09	[Standard subdivisions; collections of literary texts in more than one form; history, description, critical appraisal of works in more than one form]
—1	Poetry
—2	Drama
—3	Fiction
—4	Essays
—5	Speeches
—6	Letters
—7	Humor and satire
—8	Miscellaneous writings

—01–07   **Standard subdivisions**

> Standard subdivisions are used for general works consisting equally of literary texts and history, description, critical appraisal, e.g., a serial consisting equally of literary texts and history, description, critical appraisal of a variety of literature in English 820.5. Works limited to specific topics found in Table 3C are classed in —08, plus notation from Table 3C

> Class collections of literary texts in —08; class history, description, critical appraisal in —09

—08   **Collections of literary texts in more than one form**

> Do not use for groups of people; class in —0808–0809

> Class history, description, critical appraisal of a specific literature in —09

> *See Manual at T3B—08 and T3B—09*

—080 001–080 008   Standard subdivisions

—080 009   History and geographic treatment

—080 009 01–080 009 05   Historical periods

> Do not use for literature of a specific language; class in —08001–08009

—080 01–080 09   Specific periods

> Add to base number —080 notation from the period table for the specific literature, e.g., earliest period —08001. If there is no applicable period table, this provision for indicating period cannot be used, e.g., collection of 20th-century literary works in Amharic 892.8708

> Works consisting equally of literary texts and history, description, critical appraisal of a specific literature are classed here if limited to specific periods, e.g., texts and criticism of 19th-century English-language literary works 820.8008

—080 1–080 9   **Literature displaying specific features, or emphasizing subjects, or for and by groups of people**

> Add to base number —080 notation 1–9 from Table 3C, e.g., collections of literary texts about holidays —080334

> Works consisting equally of literary texts and history, description, critical appraisal of a specific literature are classed here if limited to specific topics found in Table 3C, e.g., texts and criticism of English-language literary works about war 820.803581

—09   **History, description, critical appraisal of works in more than one form**

> Notation —09 from Table 1 as modified below

> Do not use for geographic treatment; class in —090009

> Class here collected biography of authors, individual and collected biography of critics

> *See Manual at T3B—08 and T3B—09*

—090 001–090 008   Standard subdivisions

—090 009   Geographic treatment

> Do not use for history without subdivision, biography; class in
> —09. Do not use for historical periods; class in —09001–09009

—090 009 3–090 009 9   Specific continents, countries, localities

> Do not use for literature for and by residents of specific
> continents countries, localities; class in —0993–0999

—090 01–090 09   Literature from specific periods

> Add to base number —0900 notation from the period table for
> the specific literature, e.g., earliest period —09001. If there is no
> applicable period table, this provision for indicating period cannot be
> used, e.g., history of early Cornish literature 891.6709
> (Option: Use notation from an optional period table, e.g., history
> of literature in Spanish by Chilean authors of early 20th century
> Ch860.90042 or 868.9933090042; prefer —0993–0999, e.g.,
> history of literature in Spanish by Chilean authors 860.9983,
> history of literature in Spanish by Chilean authors of early 20th
> century 860.998309041. Full instructions appear under 811–818,
> 819, 821–828, 828.99, 841–848, 848.99, 861–868, 868.99, 869,
> and 869.899)

> *See Manual at T3B—091–099 vs. T3B—09001–09009*

—[090 1–090 9]   Historical periods

> Do not use; class in —09001–09009

—091–099   Literature displaying specific features or emphasizing subjects, and for
                          and by groups of people

> Add to base number —09 notation 1–9 from Table 3C, e.g., history and
> description of literature on Faust —09351, history of literature in Spanish
> by Chilean authors 860.9983, history of literature in Spanish by Chilean
> authors of early 20th century 860.998309041

> *See Manual at T3B—091–099 vs. T3B—09001–09009*

> (Option: Class literature from specific periods in —09001–09009, using
> notation from an optional period table)

> ## —1–8 Specific forms

Unless other instructions are given, observe the following table of preference for works combining two or more literary forms, e.g., poetic drama —2 (*not* —1):

Drama	—2
Poetry	—1
Class epigrams in verse in —8	
Fiction	—3
Essays	—4
Speeches	—5
Letters	—6
Miscellaneous writings	—8
Humor and satire	—7

Class comprehensive works on prose literature in —808. Class comprehensive works on two or more forms with the base number for the individual literature, plus notation 01–09 from Table 3B if applicable, adding 0 when required to make a three-figure number, e.g., comprehensive works on English poetry and fiction 820

—1   Poetry

Including greeting card verse

Class here folk poetry, prose poems

Class anonymous nursery rhymes and related rhymes and rhyming games from the oral tradition in 398.8

See Manual at T3B—1

—100 1–100 7   Standard subdivisions

Standard subdivisions are used for general works consisting equally of literary texts and history, description, critical appraisal, e.g., a serial consisting equally of literary texts and history, description, critical appraisal of poetry in English 821.005. Works limited to specific topics found in Table 3C are classed in —100801–100809

Class collections of literary texts in —1008; class history, description, critical appraisal in —1009

—100 8   Collections of literary texts

Do not use for groups of people; class in —100808–100809

General works consisting equally of literary texts and history, description, critical appraisal are classed in —1001–1007, in the number for the specific form, or the specific form plus literary period. Works limited to specific topics found in Table 3C are classed in —100801–100809

—100 800 1–100 800 7   Standard subdivisions

—[100 800 8]   Groups of people

Do not use; class in —100808–100809

—[100 800 9]   History, geographic treatment, biography

> Do not use for collections by and for persons resident in specific areas; class in —100809. Do not use for history, description, critical appraisal; class in —1009

—100 801–100 809   Collections of literary texts displaying specific features or emphasizing specific subjects, for and by specific groups of people

> Add to base number —10080 notation 1–9 from Table 3C, e.g., collections of poetry dealing with travel —1008032

> Works consisting equally of literary texts and history, description, critical appraisal are classed here if limited to specific topics found in Table 3C

—100 9   History, description, critical appraisal

> Notation —09 from Table 1 as modified below

> Do not use for geographic treatment; class in —10099

> Class here collected biography of authors, individual and collected biography of critics

> Follow the instructions under —1008 for works consisting equally of literary texts and history, description, critical appraisal

—100 901–100 907   Standard subdivisions

—[100 908]   Groups of people

> Do not use; class in —10098–10099

—[100 909]   History, geographic treatment, biography

> Do not use for history, biography; class in —1009. Do not use for geographic treatment; class in —10099

—100 91–100 99   History, description, critical appraisal of poetry displaying specific features or emphasizing specific subjects, for and by specific groups of people

> Add to base number —1009 notation 1–9 from Table 3C, e.g., critical appraisal of poetry by children —10099282

>   —102–107   Specific kinds of poetry

Limited to the kinds provided for below

Except for modifications shown under specific entries, add to each subdivision identified by * as follows:

01–07	Standard subdivisions
	Standard subdivisions are used for general works consisting equally of literary texts and history, description, critical appraisal, e.g., a serial consisting equally of literary texts and history, description, critical appraisal of narrative poetry in English —10305. Works limited to specific topics found in Table 3C are classed in 08, plus notation from Table 3C
	Class collections of literary texts in 08; class history, description, critical appraisal in 09
08	Collections of literary texts
08001–08008	Standard subdivisions
08009	History and geographic treatment
0800901–0800905	Historical periods
	Do not use for literature of a specific language; class in 0801–0809
0801–0809	Specific periods
	Add to 080 notation from the period table for the specific literature, e.g., Elizabethan period of English literature 0803, collections of English sonnets of the Elizabethan period 821.0420803. If there is no applicable period table, this provision for indicating period cannot be used, e.g., collection of 20th-century Slovak narrative poetry 891.8710308
	Works consisting equally of literary texts and history, description, critical appraisal of a specific literature are classed here if limited to specific periods, e.g., texts and criticism of English sonnets of the Elizabethan period 821.0420803
081–089	Literature displaying specific features, or emphasizing subjects, or for and by groups of people
	Add to 08 notation 1–9 from Table 3C, e.g., collections dealing with love 083543, collections of English sonnets dealing with love 821.042083543
	Works consisting equally of literary texts and history, description, critical appraisal of the form in a specific kind are classed here if limited to specific topics found in Table 3C, e.g., texts and criticism of narrative poems about war —103083581
09	History, description, critical appraisal
	Class here collected biography
09001–09008	Standard subdivisions
09009	History and geographic treatment
0900901–0900905	Historical periods
	Do not use for literature of a specific language; class in 0901–0909

(continued)

651

>   —102–107   Specific kinds of poetry (continued)

0901–0909	Specific periods Add to 090 notation from the period table for the specific literature, e.g., Elizabethan period of English literature 0903, collections of English sonnets of the Elizabethan period 821.0420903. If there is no applicable period table, this provision for indicating period cannot be used, e.g., history and criticism of 20th-century Pashto (Afghan) lyric poetry 891.59310409 Follow the instructions under 0801–0809 for works consisting equally of literary texts and history, description, critical appraisal
091–099	Literature displaying specific features, or emphasizing subjects, or for and by groups of people Add to 09 notation 1–9 from Table 3C, e.g., critical appraisal of works about seasons 0933, critical appraisal of French lyric poetry about seasons 841.040933 Follow the instructions under 081–089 for works consisting equally of literary texts and history, description, critical appraisal

Class epigrams in verse in —8; class comprehensive works in —1

See Manual at T3B—102–107, T3B—205, T3B—308 vs. T3C—1, T3C—3

—102   *Dramatic poetry

Including dramatic monologues

See also —2 for poetic plays

See Manual at T3A—2, T3B—2 vs. T3A—1, T3B—102

—103   *Narrative poetry

Including fabliaux

For ballads, see —1044

—103 2   *Epic poetry

—103 3   *Medieval metrical romances

See also —3 for prose versions of medieval romances

—104   *Lyric and balladic poetry

Including concrete poetry

Class here poetry of minnesingers and troubadours

Subdivisions are added for lyric and balladic poetry together, for lyric poetry alone

Class dramatic lyric poems in —102

*Add as instructed under —102–107

—104 1	*Haiku
—104 2	*Sonnets
—104 3	*Odes
—104 4	*Ballads
—105	*Didactic poetry
—107	*Humorous and satirical poetry

> Including clerihews
>
> Class here light verse
>
> Subdivisions are added for either or both topics in heading
>
> Class humor and satire in two or more literary forms, including both verse and prose, in —7

—107 5	*Limericks
—11–19	**Poetry of specific periods**

> Add to base number —1 notation from the period table for the specific literature in 810–890, e.g., earliest period —11; then add the numbers following —10 in notation 1001–1009 of this table, e.g., collections from the earliest period dealing with travel —1108032
>
> If there is no applicable period table, add nothing to —1, e.g., collections of Mongolian poetry by authors of the earliest period 894.231 (*not* 894.231108)
>
> Class specific kinds of poetry from specific periods in —102–107
>
> (Option: Where two or more countries share the same language, follow one of the options given after step 4 at beginning of Table 3B, e.g., collections of poetry in English by Australian authors of the earliest period A821.108 or 828.99341108)

—2   Drama

> Class here closet drama, drama written in poetry, folk drama
>
> *See Manual at T3B—2; also at T3A—2, T3B—2 vs. T3A—1, T3B—102*

—200 1–200 9	Standard subdivisions; collections; history, description, critical appraisal

> Add to base number —200 the numbers following —100 in notation 1001–1009 of this table, e.g., collections of drama dealing with travel —2008032

>	—202–205 Drama of specific media, scope, kinds

> Add to each subdivision identified by * as instructed under —102–107, e.g., collections of comedies dealing with travel —205230832
>
> Class comprehensive works in —2

---

*Add as instructed under —102–107

>	—202–203 Drama for mass media
	Class comprehensive works in —2
—202	Drama for radio and television
—202 2	*Drama for radio
—202 5	*Drama for television
—203	*Drama for motion pictures
—204	Drama of restricted scope
	Class drama of restricted scope for mass media in —202–203
—204 1	*One-act plays
	Including interludes, sketches
—204 5	*Monologues
—205	Specific kinds of drama
	Limited to the kinds provided for below
	Including masques
	Class specific kinds of drama for mass media in —202–203; class specific kinds of drama of restricted scope in —204
	See Manual at T3B—102–107, T3B—205, T3B—308 vs. T3C—1, T3C—3
—205 1	*Serious drama
	Class here Nō plays
—205 12	*Tragedy
	Class tragicomedy in —20523
—205 14	*Historical drama
—205 16	*Religious and morality plays
	Not limited to medieval plays
	Class here miracle, mystery, passion plays
	Subdivisions are added for either or both topics in heading
—205 2	*Comedy and melodrama
—205 23	*Comedy
	Including tragicomedy
	Class humor and satire in two or more literary forms, including both verse and prose, in —7

*Add as instructed under —102–107

—205 232	*Farce
—205 27	*Melodrama

         Including modern detective and mystery (suspense) drama

—205 7	*Variety drama

—21–29   **Drama of specific periods**

Add to base number —2 notation from the period table for the specific literature in 810–890, e.g., earliest period —21; then add the numbers following —10 in notation 1001–1009 of this table, e.g., critical appraisal of drama of earliest period —2109

If there is no applicable period table, add nothing to —2, e.g., collections of Mongolian drama by authors of the earliest period 894.232 (*not* 894.232108)

Class drama of specific media, scope, kinds from specific periods in —202–205

(Option: Where two or more countries share the same language, follow one of the options given after step 4 at beginning of Table 3B, e.g., collections of drama in English by New Zealand authors of the earliest period NZ822.108 or 828.99332108)

—3   **Fiction**

Class here novelettes and novels

Class graphic novels in 741.5

See Manual at T3B—3

—300 1–300 9   Standard subdivisions; collections; history, description, critical appraisal

Add to base number —300 the numbers following —100 in notation 1001–1009 of this table, e.g., collections of fiction dealing with travel —3008032

>   —301–308 Fiction of specific scope and kinds

Add to each subdivision identified by * as instructed under —102–107, e.g., collections of short stories dealing with travel —3010832

Class comprehensive works in —3

—301   *Short stories

Class short stories of specific kinds in —308

*Add as instructed under —102–107

—308   Specific kinds of fiction

> Limited to the kinds provided for below
>
> Unless other instructions are given, observe the following table of preference, e.g., historical adventure fiction —3081 (*not* —3087):

Autobiographical and biographical fiction	—3082
Historical and period fiction	—3081
Adventure fiction	—3087
Love and romance	—3085
Psychological, realistic, sociological fiction	—3083

> *See Manual at T3B—102–107, T3B—205, T3B—308 vs. T3C—1, T3C—3*

—308 1   *Historical and period fiction

> Subdivisions are added for either or both topics in heading
>
> Class alternative histories in —308768

—308 2   *Autobiographical and biographical fiction

> Subdivisions are added for either or both topics in heading

—308 3   *Psychological, realistic, sociological fiction

> Subdivisions are added for any or all topics in heading

—308 5   *Love and romance

> Modern romantic fiction
>
> Subdivisions are added for either or both topics in heading
>
> Class medieval prose romances in —3

—308 7   *Adventure fiction

> Unless other instructions are given, observe the following table of preference, e.g., Gothic horror fiction —308729 (*not* —308738):

Alternative histories	—308768
Science fiction	—308762
Gothic fiction	—308729
Western fiction	—30874
Detective, mystery, suspense, spy fiction (*except* —308729)	—30872
Ghost fiction	—308733
Horror fiction	—308738
Fantasy fiction	—308766
Picaresque fiction	—30877

—308 72   *Detective, mystery, suspense, spy, Gothic fiction

> Subdivisions are added for a combination of two or more topics in heading, for detective fiction alone, for mystery fiction alone, for suspense fiction alone, for spy fiction alone

*Add as instructed under —102–107

—308 729	*Gothic fiction
	Class modern romantic fiction in which the supernatural has little or no role in —3085
—308 73	*Ghost and horror fiction
—308 733	*Ghost fiction
—308 738	*Horror fiction
—308 74	*Western fiction
—308 76	*Science and fantasy fiction, alternative histories
—308 762	*Science fiction
—308 766	*Fantasy fiction
—308 768	*Alternative histories
	Class historical and period fiction in —3081
—308 77	*Picaresque fiction

—31–39   Fiction of specific periods

Add to base number —3 notation from the period table for the specific literature in 810–890, c.g., earliest period —31; then add the numbers following —10 in notation 1001–1009 of this table, e.g., critical appraisal of fiction of earliest period —3109

If there is no applicable period table, add nothing to —3, e.g., collections of Mongolian fiction by authors of the earliest period 894.233 (*not* 894.233108)

Class specific scope and kinds from specific periods in —301–308

(Option: Where two or more countries share the same language, follow one of the options given after step 4 at beginning of Table 3B, e.g., collections of fiction in French by Canadian authors of the earliest period C843.108 or 848.9923108)

—4   Essays

Collections or discussions of works with literary value

See Manual at 800: Choice between literature and nonliterary subject

—400 1–400 9   Standard subdivisions; collections; history, description, critical appraisal

Add to base number —400 the numbers following —100 in notation 1001–1009 of this table, e.g., collections of essays dealing with travel —4008032

---

*Add as instructed under —102–107

—41–49   **Essays of specific periods**

> Add to base number —4 notation from the period table for the specific literature in 810–890, e.g., earliest period —41; then add the numbers following —10 in notation 1001–1009 of this table, e.g., critical appraisal of essays of the earliest period —4109
>
> If there is no applicable period table, add nothing to —4, e.g., collections of Mongolian essays by authors of the earliest period 894.234 (*not* 894.234108)
>
> (Option: Where two or more countries share the same language, follow one of the options given after step 4 at beginning of Table 3B, e.g., collections of essays in Spanish by Mexican authors of the 19th century M864.208 or 868.99214208)

—5   Speeches

> Collections or discussions of works with literary value
>
> *See Manual at 800: Choice between literature and nonliterary subject*

—500 1–500 9   Standard subdivisions; collections; history, description, critical appraisal

> Add to base number —500 the numbers following —100 in notation 1001–1009 of this table, e.g., collections of speeches dealing with travel —5008032

\>   **—501–506 Specific kinds of speeches**

> Limited to the kinds provided for below
>
> Add to each subdivision identified by * as instructed under —102–107, e.g., collections of recitations dealing with travel —5040832
>
> Class comprehensive works in —5

—501   *Public speeches (Oratory)

> Including after-dinner, platform, television speeches; speeches and toasts for special occasions
>
> *For debates, see —503*

—503   *Debates

> Class here public discussion of opposing views

—504   *Recitations

—505   *Texts for choral speaking

—506   *Conversations

*Add as instructed under —102–107

—51–59   Speeches of specific periods

> Add to base number —5 notation from the period table for the specific literature in 810–890, e.g., earliest period —51; then add the numbers following —10 in notation 1001–1009 of this table, e.g., critical appraisal of speeches of the earliest period —5109
>
> If there is no applicable period table, add nothing to —5, e.g., collections of Mongolian speeches by authors of the earliest period 894.235 (*not* 894.235108)
>
> Class specific kinds from specific periods in —501–506
>
> (Option: Where two or more countries share the same language, follow one of the options given after step 4 at beginning of Table 3B, e.g., collections of speeches in Spanish by Chilean authors of the 19th century Ch865.208 or 868.99335208)

—6   Letters

> Collections or discussions of works with literary value
>
> *See Manual at 800: Choice between literature and nonliterary subject*

—600 1–600 9   Standard subdivisions; collections; history, description, critical appraisal

> Add to base number —600 the numbers following —100 in notation 1001–1009 of this table, e.g., collections of letters dealing with travel —6008032

—61–69   Letters of specific periods

> Add to base number —6 notation from the period table for the specific literature in 810–890, e.g., earliest period —61; then add the numbers following —10 in notation 1001–1009 of this table, e.g., critical appraisal of letters of the earliest period —6109
>
> If there is no applicable period table, add nothing to —6, e.g., collections of Tibetan letters by authors of the earliest period 895.46 (*not* 895.46108)
>
> (Option: Where two or more countries share the same language, follow one of the options given after step 4 at beginning of Table 3B, e.g., collections of letters in Portuguese by Brazilian authors of the 20th century B869.6408 or 869.89926408)

—7   Humor and satire

> Limited to collections and criticism of works in two or more literary forms including both verse and prose
>
> Class here parody
>
> Subdivisions are added for either or both topics in heading
>
> *See also —808 for humor and satire in two or more prose forms*
>
> *See Manual at T1—0207 vs. T3B—7, T3A—8 + 02, T3B—802, T3B—8 + 02, T3A—8 + 07, T3B—807, T3B—8 + 07*
>
> (Option: Give precedence to humor and satire over all other literary forms)

—700 1–700 9   Standard subdivisions; collections; history, description, critical appraisal

> Add to base number —700 the numbers following —100 in notation 1001–1009 of this table, e.g., collections of humor and satire dealing with travel —7008032

—71–79   Humor and satire of specific periods

> Add to base number —7 notation from the period table for the specific literature in 810–890, e.g., earliest period —71; then add the numbers following —10 in notation 1001–1009 of this table, e.g., critical appraisal of humor and satire of the earliest period —7109

> If there is no applicable period table, add nothing to —7, e.g., collections of Turkmen humor and satire by authors of the earliest period 894.3647 (*not* 894.3647108)

> (Option: Where two or more countries share the same language, follow one of the options given after step 4 at beginning of Table 3B, e.g., collections of humor and satire in English by Australian authors of the earliest period A827.108 or 828.99347108)

—8   Miscellaneous writings

Procedures for building numbers:

1.   To the base number for the literature add notation 8, e.g., miscellaneous writings in English 828. If the work covers a limited time span (fewer than three literary periods, unless a single century spans three periods, then a single century), go to step 2; if not, go to step 4

2.   Turn back to the appropriate number in the schedule 810–890 to see whether there is an applicable period table. If there is one, go to step 3; if not, go to step 4
(Option: Where optional period tables are available for countries that share the same language, either [1] use initial letters to distinguish the separate countries, or [2] use the special number designated for literature of those countries that are not preferred. Then use the optional period tables, e.g., miscellaneous writings in English by 20th-century New Zealand authors NZ828.2 or 828.993382. Full instructions for optional period tables appear under 811–818, 819, 821–828, 828.99, 841–848, 848.99, 861–868, 868.99, 869, 869.899. If the option is used, go to step 3)
(Option: Where optional period tables are not available for countries that share the same language, use initial letters to distinguish the separate countries. Then use the standard period table for the language if one is available. If a period table is available, go to step 3)

3.   Select the appropriate period number, e.g., the Victorian period in English literature 8. Then follow the instructions under —81–89

4.   If the work does not cover a limited time period, or if there is no applicable period table, consider whether the work is limited to one of the forms of miscellaneous writing listed in —802–808. If it is limited to one of those forms, go to step 5; if not, complete the class number by inserting a decimal point between the third and fourth digits, e.g., miscellaneous writings in Russian from many time periods 891.78, miscellaneous writings in Khmer (Cambodian) by 20th-century authors 895.9328

5.   Class the work in the appropriate number from the span —802–808, then complete the number by inserting a point between the third and fourth digits, e.g., prose literature in Russian from many time periods 891.7808, prose literature in Khmer (Cambodian) by 20th-century authors 895.932808

See Manual at Table 3B: Number building

—800 1–800 9   Standard subdivisions; collections; history, description, critical appraisal

> Add to base number —800 the numbers following —100 in notation 1001–1009 of this table, e.g., critical appraisal of miscellaneous writings from more than one period —8009

\>   —802–808 Specific kinds of miscellaneous writings

Limited to kinds provided for below

Class in each number without further subdivision history, description, critical appraisal, biography, collections of works of authors from more than one period

Class comprehensive works in —8

—802   Anecdotes, epigrams, graffiti, jokes, jests, quotations, riddles, tongue twisters

>   Standard subdivisions are added for any or all topics in heading

>   Class humor and satire in two or more literary forms, including both verse and prose, in —7; class anonymous riddles from the oral tradition in 398.6; class anonymous jokes and jests from the oral tradition in 398.7; class anonymous tongue twisters from the oral tradition in 398.8

>> *See Manual at T1—0207 vs. T3B—7, T3A—8 + 02, T3B—802, T3B—8 + 02, T3A—8 + 07, T3B—807, T3B—8 + 07; also at T3A—8 + 02, T3B—802, T3B—8 + 02 vs. 398.6, 793.735*

—803   Diaries, journals, notebooks, reminiscences

>   Standard subdivisions are added for any or all topics in heading

>   Class interdisciplinary collections of diaries in 900. Class diaries, journals, notebooks, reminiscences of nonliterary authors with the appropriate subject, e.g., diary of an astronomer 520.92

>> *See Manual at T3A—8 + 03 and T3B—803, T3B—8 + 03*

—807   Works without identifiable literary form

>   Class here experimental and nonformalized works, works that mimic nonliterary forms and genres for literary purposes, not conveying useful information (e.g., humorous or fantasy works in the form of dictionaries, self-help books, travel guides)

>   Class experimental works with an identifiable literary form with the form, e.g., experimental novels —3; class works that convey useful information on a nonliterary topic with the topic, e.g., literary cookbooks with real recipes inspired by or derived from literary sources 641.5

>> *See Manual at T1—0207 vs. T3B—7, T3A—8 + 02, T3B—802, T3B—8 + 02, T3A—8 + 07, T3B—807, T3B—8 + 07*

—808   Prose literature

>   Collections and discussions of works in more than one literary form

>   Class prose without identifiable literary form in —807. Class a specific form of prose literature with the form, e.g., essays —4

—81–89   **Miscellaneous writings of specific periods**

Add to base number —8 notation from the period table for the specific literature in 810–890, e.g., earliest period —81; then add further as follows:

001–009   Standard subdivisions; collections; history, description, critical appraisal

Add to 00 the numbers following —100 in notation 1001–1009 from Table 3B, e.g., collections 008

02   Anecdotes, epigrams, graffiti, jokes, jests, quotations, riddles, tongue twisters

Add to 02 the numbers following —10 in notation 1001–1009 from Table 3B, e.g., collections 0208

Subdivisions are added for any or all topics in heading

Class humor and satire in two or more literary forms, including both verse and prose, in —7; class anecdotes, epigrams, graffiti, jokes, jests, quotations, riddles, tongue twisters from specific periods in —802 if there is no applicable period table; class anonymous riddles from the oral tradition in 398.6; class anonymous jokes and jests from the oral tradition in 398.7; class anonymous tongue twisters from the oral tradition in 398.8

See Manual at T1—0207 vs. T3B—7, T3A—8 + 02, T3B—802, T3B—8 + 02, T3A—8 + 07, T3B—807, T3B—8 + 07; also at T3A—8 + 02, T3B—802, T3B—8 + 02 vs. 398.6, 793.735

03   Diaries, journals, notebooks, reminiscences

Add to 03 the numbers following —10 in notation 1001–1009 from Table 3B, e.g., collections 0308

Subdivisions are added for any or all topics in heading

Class diaries, journals, notebooks, reminiscences from specific periods in —803 if there is no applicable period table

See Manual at T3A—8 + 03 and T3B—803, T3B—8 + 03

07   Works without identifiable literary form

Class here experimental and nonformalized works, works that mimic nonliterary forms and genres for literary purposes, not conveying useful information (e.g., humorous or fantasy works in the form of dictionaries, self-help books, travel guides)

Add to 07 the numbers following —10 in notation 1001–1009 from Table 3B, e.g., collections of stream of consciousness writings 0708025

Class works without identifiable literary form from specific periods in —807 if there is no applicable period table. Class experimental works with an identifiable literary form with the form, e.g., experimental novels —3; class works that convey useful information on a nonliterary topic with the topic, e.g., literary cookbooks with real recipes inspired by or derived from literary sources 641.5

See Manual at T1—0207 vs. T3B—7, T3A—8 + 02, T3B—802, T3B—8 + 02, T3A—8 + 07, T3B—807, T3B—8 + 07

(continued)

—81–89   **Miscellaneous writings of specific periods (continued)**

08   Prose literature

Collections and discussions of works in more than one·literary form

Add to 08 the numbers following —10 in notation 1001–1009 from Table 3B, e.g., collections 0808

Class prose without identifiable literary form in 07. Class a specific form of prose literature with the form, e.g., essays —4

Class prose literature from specific periods in —808, e.g., collections of 20th-century Albanian prose literature 891.991808

(Option: Use the notation from an optional period table with either option given after step 2 under —8 in Table 3B, e.g., prose literature in English by Australian authors of early 20th century A828.20808 or 828.9934820808)

Table 3C. Notation to Be Added Where Instructed in Table 3B, 700.4, 791.4, 808–809

See Manual at Table 3B: Preference order

SUMMARY

—001–009	**Standard subdivisions**
—01–09	**Specific periods**
—1	**Arts and literature displaying specific qualities of style, mood, viewpoint**
—2	**Literature displaying specific elements**
—3	**Arts and literature dealing with specific themes and subjects**
—4	**Literature emphasizing subjects**
—8	**Literature for and by ethnic and national groups**
—9	**Literature for and by groups of people with specific attributes, residents of specific areas**

—001–007   Standard subdivisions

—[008]   Groups of people

> Do not use; class in —8–9

—009   History and geographic treatment

> Do not use for biography; class in base number. Do not use for literature for and by persons resident in specific areas; class in —9

—009 01–009 05   Historical periods

> Do not use for literature of a specific language; class in —01–09

—01–09   Specific periods

> Add to base number —0 notation from the period table for the specific literature, e.g., earliest period —01

—1   Arts and literature displaying specific qualities of style, mood, viewpoint

> Do not use if redundant, e.g., horror (—164) in horror fiction (—308738 in Table 3B)

> Class literature displaying specific elements and specific qualities in —2; class arts and literature dealing with specific themes and subjects and displaying specific qualities in —3

> *See Manual at T3B—102–107, T3B—205, T3B—308 vs. T3C—1, T3C—3*

—11   **Nontraditional viewpoints**

Including impressionism

Class here avant-garde, experimental approaches in the arts

> *For a specific type of avant-garde or experimental approach not provided for here, see the type, e.g., experimental literary works without identifiable literary form —807 in Table 3B*

—112   Modernism

—113   Postmodernism

—114   Futurism

—115   Expressionism

—116   Dadaism and surrealism

—116 2   Dadaism

—116 3   Surrealism

—12   **Realism and naturalism**

Including determinism

—13   **Idealism**

—14   **Classicism and romanticism**

Class pastoral arts and literature in —358209734

—142   Classicism

—145   Romanticism

Including primitivism

—15   **Symbolism, allegory, fantasy, myth**

Standard subdivisions are added for any or all topics in heading

Including the grotesque, science fiction in the arts

Class symbolism, allegory, fantasy, myth associated with a specific style or viewpoint with the style or viewpoint, e.g., surrealism —1163

> *For science fiction as a type of fiction, see —308762 in Table 3B*

> *See Manual at T3C—37 vs. T3C—15*

—16   **Tragedy and horror**

—162   Tragedy

> *For tragedy as a kind of drama, see —20512 in Table 3B*

—164   Horror

> *For horror fiction, see —308738 in Table 3B*

—17   **Comedy**

> Comic style or viewpoint
>
> Class collections and criticism of humor and satire in two or more literary forms in —7 in Table 3B; class jokes in —802 in Table 3B
>
> *For comedy as a kind of drama, see —20523 in Table 3B*

—18   **Irony**

—2   **Literature displaying specific elements**

> Class literature dealing with specific themes and subjects and displaying specific elements in —3

—22   **Description**

> Including setting

—23   **Narrative**

—24   **Plot**

—25   **Stream of consciousness**

—26   **Dialogue**

—27   **Characters**

> Including the "double" (Doppelgänger) in literature

—3   **Arts and literature dealing with specific themes and subjects**

> Personifications of a specific theme or subject are classed with the theme or subject, e.g., personifications of death —3548
>
> Do not use if redundant, e.g., historical themes (—358) in historical fiction (—3081 in Table 3B)
>
> *See Manual at T3B—102–107, T3B—205, T3B—308 vs. T3C—1, T3C—3*

—32   **Travel and geography**

> Standard subdivisions are added for either or both topics in heading
>
> Class here hotels
>
> Add to base number —32 notation 1–9 from Table 2, e.g., ocean travel —32162, ancient geography —323, travel in California —32794
>
> Class specific persons associated with travel and geography in —351; class historical and political themes in —358; class supernatural, mythological, legendary places in —372. Class religious aspects of travel and geography with the topic, e.g., travel on pilgrimages —3820351, geography in the Bible —3822091
>
> Civilization of places, comprehensive works on places relocated to —358; landscapes relocated to —36

—33   **Times**

Including seasons; parts of day, e.g., dawn

Class specific persons associated with times in —351; class times (historical periods) in —3582–3589

See also —384 for time (philosophic concept)

—334   Holidays

Including religious holidays, e.g., Christmas

—34   **Language**

Class here comprehensive works on language and literature

Class specific persons associated with language in —351

For literature, see —357. For the language of a specific subject, see the subject, e.g., language of science —36

—35   **Humanity**

Class here autobiography, biography, human existence, works dealing with contemporary viewpoints

Unless other instructions are given, observe the following table of preference, e.g., women —3522 (*not* —3552):

Specific persons	—351
Specific groups of people	—352
Historical, political, military themes	—358
Life cycle	—354
Social themes	—355
Artistic, recreational, literary themes	—357
Technical themes	—356
Human characteristics and activities	—353

—351   Specific persons

Individual real, fictional, legendary, mythological persons

Including Count Dracula, Don Juan, Faust, Joan of Arc, Job, Julius Caesar, King Arthur, Odysseus, Pierrot

See also —382 for specific gods and goddesses

—352   Specific groups of people

Including heroes

See also —375 for paranatural beings of human and semihuman form; also —8–9 for literature for and by groups of people

—352 1–352 7   Groups of people by miscellaneous attributes

Add to base number —352 the numbers following —08 in notation 081–087 from Table 1, e.g., women —3522

—[352 8]   Occupational and religious groups

> A specific occupational group relocated to the group in —3, e.g., lawyers —3554; a specific religious group relocated to the group in —382, e.g., Buddhists —382943

—352 9   Ethnic and national groups

—352 905–352 909   Ethnic and national groups with ethnic origins from more than one continent, of European descent

> Add to base number —3529 notation 05–09 from Table 5, e.g., people of mixed African, Asian, and European ancestry —352905

—352 91–352 99   Specific ethnic and national groups

> Add to base number —3529 notation 1–9 from Table 5, e.g., Chinese —3529951

\>   —353–358   Specific human, social, technical, artistic, recreational, literary, historical, political, military themes

Class comprehensive works in —35

Specific human, social, technical, artistic, recreational, literary, historical, political, military themes related to a specific group of people, other than people associated with a specific occupational or religious group, relocated to the group of people in —352, e.g., people with disabilities —3527

—353   Human characteristics and activities

Including alienation, chivalry, dreams, fear, friendship, happiness, heroism, justice, melancholy, personal beauty and ugliness, pride, snobbishness, success, vices, virtues

Class here ethical and psychological themes

Class love in —3543; class legal justice in —3554; class mental illness, comprehensive works on human body in —3561

—353 8   Sex

Class here erotica, sexuality

Class sexual orientation in —353

—354   Life cycle

Including birth, adolescence, aging

Class a specific social group associated with life cycle with the social group in —352, e.g., adolescents —35235

—354 3   Love and marriage

Standard subdivisions are added for either or both topics in heading

—354 8   Death

—355   Social themes

Class here everyday life

> *For political themes, see —3581. For a specific aspect of everyday life, see the aspect, e.g., home and family management —3564, recreation —3579*

Military science relocated to —3581; comprehensive works on adventure relocated to —3582

—355 2   Sociology and anthropology

Standard subdivisions are added for either or both topics in heading

Including exile, violence

Class sex in —3538; class social problems and services in —3556; class war and peace in —3581. Class themes associated with a specific social group with the social group in —352, e.g., feminism —3522, homophobia —352664; class themes associated with life cycle with the theme in —354, e.g., birth, adolescence, aging —354, love and marriage —3543, death —3548

—355 3   Economics

Including commerce, environment, industry, labor; accounting, management, public relations

—355 4   Law

—355 6   Social problems and services

Standard subdivisions are added for either or both topics in heading

Including crime, poverty

> *For social welfare problems of and services for people with physical illness, mental illness, substance abuse, mental retardation, physical disabilities, see —3561*

—355 7   Education

—355 8   Communications and transportation

> *For communications and transportation engineering, see —356*

> *See also —3553 for commerce*

—355 9   Customs, etiquette, folklore

> *For holidays, see —334. For customs of specific subjects, see the subject, e.g., customs of life cycle —354, customs of peace and war, —3581; for specific themes in folklore, see the theme, e.g., real animals —362, legendary animals —374*

Customs of costume, dwellings, food relocated to —3564

—356   Technical themes

> Including communications, computer, military, transportation engineering
>
> Class accounting, management, public relations in —3553; class comprehensive works on communications and transportation in —3558; class scientific themes, comprehensive works on scientific and technical themes in —36; class comprehensive works on computer science in —39
>
> *For agriculture, see —36*

—356 1   Medicine, health, human body

> Standard subdivisions are added for any or all topics in heading
>
> Including human anatomy, physiology, diseases; mental illness; social welfare problems of and services for people with physical illness, mental illness, substance abuse, mental retardation, physical disabilities; human form and shape, nudity
>
> Class birth, development, aging in —354; class death in —3548
>
> *For personal beauty and ugliness, see —353*

—356 4   Home and family management

> Including customs of costume, dwellings, food [*all formerly* —3559]; beauty shops, restaurants
>
> Class hotels in —32; class personal beauty and ugliness in —353

—357   Artistic, recreational, literary themes

> Including architecture, painting
>
> Class comprehensive works on language and literature in —34; class gardens in —364
>
> Books relocated to —39

—357 8   Music

—357 9   Recreational and performing arts

> Including dancing, sports

—358   Historical, political, military themes

> Standard subdivisions are added for historical, political, military themes together; for historical themes alone
>
> Class here civilization of places, comprehensive works on places [*both formerly* —32], historical events
>
> Class history with respect to ethnic and national groups in —3529; class historical fiction in literature in —3081 in Table 3B. Class historical themes in religion with religious themes in —382, e.g., history of Biblical events —3822095
>
> *For geography of places, see —32*

—358 1   Political and military themes

         Standard subdivisions are added for either or both topics in heading

         Including nationalism, peace, war

         Class here military science [*formerly* —355]

> *For military engineering, see —356; for political and military themes limited to general historical periods, see —358207–358208; for political and military themes limited to areas, regions, places in general, see —358209; for political and military themes limited to specific historical periods, see —35821–35828; for political and military themes limited to ancient world, to specific continents, countries, localities, to extraterrestrial worlds, see —3583–3589*

—358 2   World historical themes

         Civilization and events not limited by continent, country, locality

         Including comprehensive works on adventure [*formerly* —355]

         Class here military themes, political themes not limited by continent, country, locality

         Class adventure fiction in literature in —3087 in Table 3B; class historical, military, political themes limited by continent, country, locality in —3583–3589; class comprehensive works on political themes, on military themes in —3581

> *For specific kinds of adventure, see the kind, e.g., detective adventures —3556, Westerns —35878*

—[358 200 1–358 200 9]   Standard subdivisions

         Do not use; class in —35801–35809

>   —358 207–358 208   General historical periods

         Class here general historical themes covering three or more continents (or three or more countries if not on the same continent)

         Class specific historical periods in —35821–35828; class comprehensive works in —3582

> *For ancient history, see —3583*

—358 207   Ca. 500–1450/1500

         Including comprehensive works on Crusades

         Class history of a place during the period of the Crusades with the history of the place, e.g., history of Europe during the period of Crusades —3584018

> *For comprehensive works on a specific Crusade, see the history of the country or region in which most of the fighting took place, e.g., First Crusade —35856014, Fourth Crusade —35849503*

—358 208   Modern history, 1450/1500–

—358 209	Areas, regions, places in general
	Not limited by continent, country, locality
—358 209 01–358 209 09	Standard subdivisions
—358 209 1–358 209 9	Specific areas, regions, places in general

Add to base number —358209 the numbers following —1 in notation 11–19 from Table 2, e.g., urban civilization —358209732, pastoral themes —358209734

—358 21–358 28	Specific historical periods

Add to base number —3582 the numbers following 909 in 909.1–909.8, e.g., 19th century —358281

Class general historical periods in —358207–358208

—358 3–358 9	Historical themes of ancient world; of specific continents, countries, localities; of extraterrestrial worlds

Class here military themes, political themes limited geographically

Add to base number —358 the numbers following 9 in 930–990, e.g., World War II —3584053, history and civilization of U.S. West —35878

Class western fiction as a type of fiction in —30874 in Table 3B

—36   Natural and physical phenomena; mathematics

Standard subdivisions are added for natural and physical phenomena, mathematics together; for natural and physical phenomena together; for natural phenomena alone

Including fire, weather

Class here landscapes [*formerly* —32], agriculture, nature, scientific themes, comprehensive works on scientific and technical themes

Class science fiction in literature in —308762 in Table 3B; class science fiction in the arts in —15; class times (e.g., seasons, times of day) in —33; class specific persons associated with natural and physical phenomena, with mathematics in —351. Class animals or plants for a specific purpose with the purpose, e.g., medicinal plants —3561, meat —3564

> *For human anatomy, physiology, diseases, see* —3561

—362	Animals

Class here pets

Add to base number —362 the numbers following 59 in 592–599, e.g., cats —3629752

Class supernatural, mythological, legendary animals in —374

> *See Manual at 800, T3C—362 vs. 398.245, 590, 636*

—364   Plants

> Class here gardens
>
> Add to base number —364 the numbers following 58 in 582–588, e.g., trees —364216, roses —3643734
>
> Class supernatural, mythological, legendary plants in —37

—37   **The supernatural, mythological, legendary**

> Standard subdivisions are added for any or all topics in heading
>
> Including spiritualism
>
> Class here monsters
>
> Class specific legendary and mythological persons in —351; class specific groups of legendary and mythological people in —352; class religious mythology in —382013
>
>> *See Manual at T3C—37 vs. T3C—15*

—372   Places

> Including Atlantis, dystopias, utopias
>
> Class religious treatment of places associated with life after death in —382023
>
>> *See also —382035 for religious treatment of sacred places*

—374   Animals

> Including dragons, werewolves

—375   Paranatural beings of human and semihuman form

> Including centaurs, fairies, ghosts, vampires
>
> Class gods, goddesses, other objects of worship and veneration in —382
>
>> *For ghost fiction as a kind of fiction, see —308733 in Table 3B; for specific paranatural beings of human and semihuman form, see —351; for werewolves, see —374*

—377   Magic and witchcraft

> Standard subdivisions are added for either or both topics in heading
>
> Class wicca in —3829994

—38   **Philosophic and abstract themes**

—382   Religious themes

> Add to base number —382 the numbers following 2 in 201–299, e.g., Buddhism —382943; however, for religious holidays, see —334; for specific natural persons connected with religion, see —351
>
>> *See also —42 for religious works not basically belletristic but discussed as literature*

—384   Philosophic themes

> Including existentialism, humanism, nihilism, time, transcendentalism
>
> Class specific persons associated with philosophic themes in —351
>
> > *For ethical themes, see —353*
> >
> > *See also —33 for times (e.g., seasons, times of day)*

—39   **Computer science, information, general works**

> Including books [*formerly* —357], journalism, library and information sciences, museology
>
> Class specific persons associated with computer science, information, or general works in —351; class supernatural, mythological, legendary phenomena in —37. Class computer applications in a specific subject with the subject, e.g., computer applications in economics —3553
>
> > *For computer engineering, see —356*

—4   **Literature emphasizing subjects**

> Works not basically belletristic discussed as literature, where the real interest is in the literary quality of the text rather than the subject of the text
>
> Add to base number —4 notation 001–999, e.g., religious works as literature —42, biography as literature —492
>
> Class literary examination of a text in order to reach conclusions about its meaning, structure, authorship, date, where the real interest is in the subject of the text with the text, e.g., literary criticism of Bible 220.66

>   **—8–9 Literature for and by groups of people**

> Do not use if redundant, e.g., collections of English-language poetry for and by the English 821.008 (*not* 821.0080821)
>
> Unless other instructions are given, observe the following table of preference, e.g., literature for or by Roman Catholic girls —92827088282 (*not* —921282083 or —9287):

People by age group	—9282–9285
People by gender or sex	—9286–9287
People by relationships, people by miscellaneous social attributes, people with disabilities and illnesses, gifted people	—9205–9207
Occupational and religious groups	—921
Ethnic and national groups	—8
Residents of specific continents, countries, localities	—93–99
Residents of specific regions	—91

> Class literature displaying specific features for and by groups of people in —1–3; class comprehensive works in the appropriate number in Table 3B

—8   Literature for and by ethnic and national groups

Class literature for and by ethnic and national groups in continents, countries, localities where the groups predominate in —93–99

See Manual at T3C—93–99, T3C—9174 vs. T3C—8

—805–809   Ethnic and national groups with ethnic origins from more than one continent, of European descent

Add to base number —8 notation 05–09 from Table 5, e.g., literature by people of mixed African, native American, and Asian descent —805

—81–89   Specific ethnic and national groups

Add to base number —8 notation 1–9 from Table 5, e.g., literature by Africans and people of African descent —896, literature by Africans and people of African descent in Brazil —896081

—9   Literature for and by groups of people with specific attributes, residents of specific areas

—91   Literature for and by residents of specific regions

Not limited by continent, country, locality

Add to base number —91 the numbers following —1 in notation 11–19 from Table 2, e.g., literature by rural authors —91734

See Manual at T3C—93–99, T3C—9174 vs. T3C—8

—92   Literature for and by groups of people with specific attributes

—920 5–920 7   People by relationships, people by miscellaneous social attributes, people with disabilities and illnesses, gifted people

Miscellaneous social attributes not provided for elsewhere

Add to base number —920 the numbers following —08 in notation 085–087 from Table 1, e.g., literature by mothers —92052, literature by convicts —9206927

—921   Occupational and religious groups

Add to base number —921 notation 001–999, e.g., literature by Catholics —921282, literature by painters —92175

—928   People by age group, gender, or sex

> **—928 2–928 5 Age groups**

Class comprehensive works in —928

—928 2   Children

—928 26   Boys

—928 27   Girls

—928 3   Young people twelve to twenty

—928 36	Males twelve to twenty
—928 37	Females twelve to twenty
—928 5	People in late adulthood

>	—928 6–928 7 People by gender or sex

Class comprehensive works in —928

For transgender and intersex people, see —92067

—928 6	Men
—928 7	Women

—93–99 Literature for and by residents of specific continents, countries, localities

Class here literature for and by ethnic and national groups in continents, countries, localities where the groups predominate

Add to base number —9 notation 3–9 from Table 2, e.g., literature (other than in Japanese language) by residents of Japan —952, a collection of Japanese-language literature by residents of Hokkaidō 895.60809524, a collection of English literature by residents of Australia 820.80994

See Manual at T3C—93–99; also at T3C—93–99, T3C—9174 vs. T3C—8

(Option: Do not use for literatures of specific countries if the literatures are separately identified in accordance with options given under 811–818, 819, 821–828, 828.99, 841–848, 848.99, 861–868, 868.99, 869, 869.899)

Table 4. Subdivisions of Individual Languages and Language Families

The following notation is never used alone, but may be used as required by add notes under subdivisions of specific languages or language families, or with the base numbers for individual languages identified by * under 420–490, e.g., Norwegian (base number 439.82) grammar (—5 in this table): 439.825. Where instructed to do so elsewhere, add 0 to the base number for the language before adding notation from this table, e.g., dictionary of Spanish Sign Language 419.46003. A decimal point is inserted following the third digit of any number thus constructed that is longer than three digits

Notation from Table 1 is added to the notation in Table 4 when appropriate, e.g., —509 history of grammar, 439.82509 history of Norwegian grammar

See Manual at 410

SUMMARY

—01–09	**Standard subdivisions and special topics of subdivisions of individual languages and language families**
—1	**Writing systems, phonology, phonetics of the standard form of the language**
—2	**Etymology of the standard form of the language**
—3	**Dictionaries of the standard form of the language**
—5	**Grammar of the standard form of the language**
—7	**Historical and geographic variations, modern nongeographic variations**
—8	**Standard usage of the language (Prescriptive linguistics)**

—01   **Philosophy and theory**

Notation —01 from Table 1 as modified below

Do not use for schools and theories of linguistics; class in —018

—014   Communication; semantics, pragmatics, languages for special purposes

Notation —014 from Table 1 as modified below

Class here lexicology

For dictionaries, see —3; for lexicography, see —3028; for discursive works on terminology intended to teach vocabulary, see —81; for spelling and pronunciation in applied linguistics, see —813

See Manual at T4—3 vs. T4—81

—014 1   Discourse analysis

Including pragmatics in discourse analysis

Class discourse analysis of languages for special purposes in —0147

Use of this number for content analysis, semiotics discontinued; class in —014

—[014 2]   Etymology

Do not use; class in —2

—014 3	Semantics

        For history of word meanings, see —2

        See Manual at 401.43 vs. 306.44, 401.45, 401.9, 412, 415

—014 302 85	Computer applications
—014 302 856 35	Natural language processing

        Class here word sense disambiguation

—014 5	Pragmatics

        For pragmatics in discourse analysis, see —0141; for pragmatics in psycholinguistics, see —019

—014 52	Speech acts

        Class here illocutionary acts

—014 54	Presupposition

        Class here implication, entailment

—014 56	Reference

        Class here anaphora, deixis

—014 7	Languages for special purposes

        Class here sublanguages, discourse analysis of languages for special purposes

        Class teaching of languages for special purposes as second languages in —80071; class translation of languages for special purposes in —803. Class dictionaries of languages for special purposes with the purpose, plus notation 03 from Table 1, e.g., medical dictionaries 610.3

—[014 8]	Abbreviations, acronyms, symbols

        Do not use for abbreviations, acronyms, symbols as part of writing systems; class in —11. Do not use for dictionaries of abbreviations, acronyms, symbols; class in —315

—018	Schools, theories, methodologies

        Including functionalism, structural linguistics

        For works on schools, theories, methodologies that stress syntax, or syntax and phonology, see —5018

—018 8	Corpus linguistics

        Including language data samples collected as corpora to support corpus-based analysis, corpus linguistics applied to texts in a specific subject

        Class corpus linguistics applied to a specific topic in linguistics with the topic, e.g., corpus-based discourse analysis —0141, corpus-based analysis of noun phrases —55; class corpus linguistics applied to a specific work or the works of a specific author with the work or author, e.g., versions of the Bible 220.4, Shakespeare's works 822.33

—019 Psychological principles

> Including language acquisition, speech errors
>
> Class here psycholinguistics
>
> Class psychological principles of a specific topic with the topic, e.g., psycholinguistics of reading a specific language —84019
>
> > *See Manual at 407.1, T1—071 vs. 401.93, T4—019, 410.71, 418.0071, T4—80071*

—02 **Miscellany**

—028 5 Computer applications

> Class computer applications in corpus linguistics in —0188

—028 563 5 Natural language processing

> Class here computational linguistics

—03 **Encyclopedias and concordances**

> Do not use for dictionaries of standard form of language; class in —3. Do not use for dictionaries of historical and geographic variations of modern nongeographic variations in the language; class in —7

—04 **Special topics of subdivisions of individual languages and language families**

—042 Bilingualism

> Class here multilingualism
>
> Add to base number —042 notation 2–9 from Table 6 for the language that is not dominant in the area in which the linguistic interaction occurs, e.g., works dealing with the dominant language and English —04221, works dealing with French as the dominant language and English 440.4221
>
> > *See also 306.446 for sociology of bilingualism and multilingualism*

—05–06 **Standard subdivisions**

—07 **Education, research, related topics**

—071 Education

> > *See Manual at 407.1, T1—071 vs. 401.93, T4—019, 410.71, 418.0071, T4—80071*

—072 Research

—072 1 Research methods

> Class corpus-based research methods in —0188

—08 **Groups of people**

—09 **History, geographic treatment, biography**

> Do not use for works that stress distinctive characteristics of historical and geographic variations from the standard form of the language; class in —7

—————

> ## —1–5 Description and analysis of the standard form of the language

Class writing systems, phonology, etymology, dictionaries, grammar of historical and geographic variations, of modern nongeographic variations of the language in —7; class standard usage, prescriptive and applied linguistics in —8; class comprehensive works in the base number for the language (adding 0 when required to make a three-figure number), e.g., comprehensive works on phonology, etymology, dictionaries, grammar of standard French 440

See Manual at T4—1–5, T4—8 vs. T4—7

—1 Writing systems, phonology, phonetics of the standard form of the language

Class writing systems, phonology, phonetics of historical and geographic variations, of modern nongeographic variations of languages in —7

—11 Writing systems

Including alphabets, ideographs, syllabaries; braille; abbreviations, acronyms, symbols; capitalization, punctuation, transliteration

Class here paleography and epigraphy limited to study of ancient and medieval handwriting and inscriptions

Class dictionaries of abbreviations, acronyms, symbols in —315; class paleography covering all aspects of early writings in the base number for the language (adding 0 when required to make a three-digit number), e.g., Latin paleography 470; class paleography of historical and geographic variations, of modern nongeographic variations of the language in —7, e.g., paleography of postclassical Latin 477; class books meant to teach the alphabet in —813; class prescriptive works on punctuation in —823; class manual alphabets in —891

For spelling, see —152

—15 Phonology, phonetics, spelling

Standard subdivisions are added for phonology, phonetics, spelling together; for phonology and phonetics together; for phonology alone

Class here consonants, vowels; morphophonology, morphophonemics, phonemics

Class comprehensive works on phonology, morphology, syntax; on phonology and morphology; on phonology and syntax in —5

For suprasegmental features, see —16

See also —3 for dictionaries

—152	**Spelling (Orthography) and pronunciation**

Standard subdivisions are added for either or both topics in heading

Class here description and analysis of the nature, history, and function of spelling and pronunciation

Class specialized spelling and pronouncing dictionaries in —31; class training in standard spelling and pronunciation in —813; class fingerspelling in —891; class speech training for public speaking, debating, conversation in 808.5; class comprehensive works on writing systems in —11

—158	Phonetics
—16	**Suprasegmental features**

Phonology and phonetics of vocal effects extending over more than one sound segment

Including juncture (pauses), pitch, stress

Class here intonation

—2   Etymology of the standard form of the language

Class etymology of historical and geographic variations, of modern nongeographic variations of languages in —7

—203	Dictionaries, encyclopedias, concordances

Including dictionaries of eponyms [*formerly* —31]

Class dictionaries of foreign words and phrases in —2403; class bilingual dictionaries of etymology in —32–39

—24	**Elements from foreign languages**
—240 3	Dictionaries, encyclopedias, concordances

Class here dictionaries of foreign words and phrases

Class dictionaries of foreign words and phrases from a specific language with the language in —241–249, plus notation 03 from Table 1, e.g., dictionaries of foreign words and phrases from French —244103, dictionaries of foreign words and phrases from French in English 422.44103

—241–249	Elements from specific foreign languages

Add to base number —24 notation 1–9 from Table 6, e.g., French words in the language —2441, French words in English 422.441, dictionary of French words in English 422.44103

—3   Dictionaries of the standard form of the language

Including dictionaries with pictures of sign-language signs

Class dictionaries of historical and geographic variations, of modern nongeographic variations of languages in —7

See Manual at T4—3 vs. T4—81

—302 8   Auxiliary techniques and procedures; apparatus, equipment,
                      materials

                      Class here basic techniques and procedures; lexicography

—31   Specialized dictionaries

                      Including dictionaries of clichés, homonyms, paronyms; pronouncing
                      dictionaries, reverse dictionaries (dictionaries with words clustered by themes
                      or that allow searching by definitions or that arrange words in reverse order
                      of spelling), rhyming dictionaries; speller-dividers (ready-reference lists of
                      words)

                      Class etymological dictionaries in —203; class dictionaries of foreign
                      words and phrases in —2403; class reverse dictionaries (dictionaries of
                      antonyms) in —312; class bilingual specialized dictionaries in —32–39; class
                      crossword-puzzle dictionaries in 793.73203. Class subject dictionaries with the
                      subject, plus notation 03 from Table 1, e.g., dictionary of medicine 610.3

                      *See also —813 for spellers (spelling books with exercises to teach how to
                      spell)*

                      Dictionaries of eponyms relocated to —203

—312   Dictionaries of synonyms and antonyms

                      Standard subdivisions are added for either or both topics in heading

                      Class here reverse dictionaries (dictionaries of antonyms)

                      Class reverse dictionaries (dictionaries with words clustered by themes or
                      that allow searching by definitions or that arrange words in reverse order of
                      spelling) in —31

—313   Dictionaries of idioms

—315   Dictionaries of abbreviations, acronyms, symbols

                      Standard subdivisions are added for any or all topics in heading

—317   Picture dictionaries

                      Limited to dictionaries with pictures of what words represent

                      See also —3 for dictionaries with pictures of sign-language signs

—32–39   Bilingual dictionaries

                      Add to base number —3 notation 2–9 from Table 6, e.g., dictionaries of the
                      language and English —321, dictionary of French and English 443.21

                      A bilingual dictionary with entry words in only one language is classed
                      with that language, e.g., an English-French dictionary 423.41. A bilingual
                      dictionary with entry words in both languages aimed at speakers of only
                      one of the languages is classed with the other language, e.g., a bilingual
                      dictionary with entry words in French and English but with introduction and
                      explanatory apparatus only in French is classed with English in 423.41. A
                      bilingual dictionary with entry words in both languages aimed at speakers of
                      both languages is classed with the language coming later in 420–490, e.g.,
                      French-German, German-French dictionaries 443.31

—5 Grammar of the standard form of the language

Class here grammatical categories, sentences, syntax, topic and comment, word order; comprehensive works on phonology, morphology, syntax; on phonology and morphology; on phonology and syntax

Class grammar of historical and geographic variations, of modern nongeographic variations of languages in —7

Unless other instructions are given, class a subject with aspects in two or more subdivisions of —5 in the number coming last, e.g., number expressed by verbs —56 (*not* —55)

For phonology, see —15; for prescriptive grammar, see —82

—501	Philosophy and theory

Notation —01 from Table 1 as modified below

Do not use for schools and theories of grammar; class in —5018

—501 8	Schools, theories, methodologies

Including case, categorial, relational grammar

—501 82	Generative grammar
—501 84	Dependency grammar
—502 85	Computer applications
—502 856 35	Natural language processing

Class here part-of-speech tagging, parsing

>	**—55–57 Word classes**

Class here parts of speech

Class comprehensive works in —5

—55	**Nouns, pronouns, adjectives, articles**

Including case, number, person

Class here noun phrases

—554	Nouns
—555	Pronouns
—56	**Verbs**

Including modality, mood, voice; comprehensive works on words derived from verbs, on infinitives, on participles

Class here verb phrases

Class works that treat a specific function (other than the verb function) of words derived from verbs with the function, e.g., gerunds as nouns —554

—562	Tense

—563   Aspect

—57   **Miscellaneous word classes**

Including conjunctions, interjections, particles, prepositions, prepositional phrases

Class clitics in —592

—576   Adverbs

Including adverbials

—59   **Morphology**

Class morphophonology, morphophonemics in —15

For morphology of specific word classes, see —55–57

—592   Word formation

Including affixes (infixes, prefixes, suffixes), clitics; formation of compound words

Class here derivational morphology

Class etymology in —2

—595   Inflection

For inflectional schemata designed for use as aids in learning a language, see —82

—7   **Historical and geographic variations, modern nongeographic variations**

Class here early forms; dialects, patois, provincialisms; pidgins, creoles, mixed languages; argot, cant, jargon, slang

Subdivisions of —7 are given under some individual languages in 420–490

Use notation 7 only for works that stress differences among the forms of a language

Works on writing systems, etymology, dictionaries, phonology, phonetics, grammar, applied linguistics are classed here when applied to historical and geographic variations, to modern nongeographic variations, e.g., paleography and epigraphy of an early form of the language, the distinctive grammatical characteristics of a particular dialect

See Manual at T4—7; also at T4—1–5, T4—8 vs. T4—7

—8   Standard usage of the language (Prescriptive linguistics)

General, formal, informal usage

Class here applied linguistics, works for people learning a second language, works for native speakers who are learning the acceptable patterns of their own language

Class purely descriptive linguistics in —1–5; class dictionaries in —3; class prescriptive and applied linguistics applied to historical and geographic variations, to modern nongeographic variations of the language in —7

For rhetoric, see 808.04

See Manual at T4—1–5, T4—8 vs. T4—7; also at 410

—800 1–800 9   Standard subdivisions

See Manual at 407.1, T1—071 vs. 401.93, T4—019, 410.71, 418.0071, T4—80071

—800 71   Education

Class here second language teaching

See Manual at 407.1, T1—071 vs. 401.93, T4—019, 410.71, 418.0071, T4—80071

—802   Translating to and from other languages

Class here interpreting

Use the base number for the language being translated into, for works on translating into a specific language. Use the base number coming later in 420–490 for works on translating in both directions between two languages. Use the base number for the language being translated from, for works on translating from one language into many languages

Add to base number —802 notation 2–9 from Table 6 for the language being translated from, e.g., translating from Chinese into a specific language —802951, translating from Chinese into English 428.02951, translating from Chinese into English and English into Chinese 495.180221, translating from Chinese into many languages 495.1802

Except for collections of texts intended for teaching the art of translating, translations themselves are classed with the works translated

Translating materials on specific subjects relocated to —803; translating literature (belles-lettres) and rhetoric relocated to —804

—802 028 5   Computer applications

—802 028 563 5   Natural language processing

Class here machine translation

—803   Translating materials on specific subjects [*formerly* —802]

Class here interpreting materials on specific subjects

Use the base number for the language being translated into, for works on translating into a specific language. Use the base number coming later in 420–490 for works on translating in both directions between two languages. Use the base number for the language being translated from, for works on translating from one language into many languages

Add to base number —803 three-digit numbers 001–999 (but stop before any zero that follows a non-zero number), e.g., translating natural history materials —8035 (*not* —803508), translating medical materials —80361; then, for translating from a specific language, add 0* and to the result add notation 2–9 from Table 6, e.g., translating medical materials from German —80361031, translating medical materials from German into English 428.0361031; however, for translating literature (belles-lettres) and rhetoric, see —804
Notation for language may be added for any topic, even if the subject of the work does not approximate the whole

Class translating a specific work or the works of a specific author with the work, translations of the work, or author, e.g., translating the Bible 220, translating the Bible into English 220.52, translating the works of Aristotle 185

Except for collections of texts intended for teaching the art of translating, translations themselves are classed with the works translated, e.g., German translations of the Bible 220.531, translations of Julius Caesar's De Bello Gallico 936.402

—804   Translating literature (belles-lettres) and rhetoric [*formerly* —802]

Standard subdivisions are added for translating literature (belles-lettres) and rhetoric together, for translating literature (belles-lettres) alone

Class here interpreting literature and rhetoric, translating works about literature, rhetoric

Use the base number for the language being translated into, for works on translating into a specific language. Use the base number coming later in 420–490 for works on translating in both directions between two languages. Use the base number for the language being translated from, for works on translating from one language into many languages

Class translating a specific work or the works of a specific author with the work or author, e.g., translating the Aeneid 873.01, translating the works of Shakespeare 822.33

Except for collections of texts intended for teaching the art of translating, translations themselves are classed with the works translated, e.g., translation of the Divina Commedia by Dante Alighieri 851.1

—804 001–804 009   Standard subdivisions

---

*Add 00 for standard subdivisions; see instructions at beginning of Table 1

—804 02–804 09   Translating literature from a specific language

> Add to base number —8040 notation 2–9 from Table 6, e.g., translating French literature —804041, translating French literature into English 428.04041

—804 1–804 8   Translating specific forms of literature

> Add to base number —804 one-digit notation 1–8 from Table 3B, e.g., translating poetry —8041, translating tragedy —8042 (*not* —80420512); then, for translating from a specific language, add 0* and to the result add notation 2–9 from Table 6, e.g., translating Spanish poetry —8041061, translating Spanish poetry into English 428.041061
>> Notation for language may be added for any topic, even if the subject of the work does not approximate the whole

> Class translating a specific work or the works of a specific author with the work, translations of the work, or author, e.g., translating the Bible 220, translating the Bible into English 220.52, translating the works of Aristotle 185

—81   Words

> Class here discursive works on terminology intended to teach vocabulary

> Class formal presentation of vocabulary for those whose native language is different in —824; class audio-lingual presentation of vocabulary for those whose native language is different in —834; class comprehensive works on terminology in —014

> *See also —3 for dictionaries*

> *See Manual at T4—3 vs. T4—81*

—813   Spelling (Orthography) and pronunciation

> Standard subdivisions are added for either or both topics in heading

> Including books meant to teach the alphabet

> Class here pronunciation of consonants, vowels; spellers (spelling books with exercises to teach how to spell)

> *See also —152 for nonprescriptive treatment of spelling and pronunciation; also —31 for speller-dividers (ready-reference lists of words); also 783.043 for pronunciation for singing*

—82   Structural approach to expression

> Formal (traditional) presentation of grammar, vocabulary, reading selections

> Class here prescriptive grammar, verb tables and inflectional schemata designed for use as aids in learning a language

> *For words, see —81; for reading, see —84*

—823   Punctuation

---

*Add 00 for standard subdivisions; see instructions at beginning of Table 1

—824   Structural approach to expression for people whose native language is
                    different

> Add to —824 notation 2–9 from Table 6, e.g., the language for
> Spanish-speaking people —82461, English for Spanish-speaking people
> 428.2461

—83   **Audio-lingual approach to expression**

> Class here the "hear-speak" school of learning a language
>
> *For pronunciation, see —813*

—834   Audio-lingual approach to expression for people whose native
                    language is different

> Class here bilingual phrase books
>
> Add to —834 notation 2–9 from Table 6, e.g., the language for
> Spanish-speaking people —83461, English for Spanish-speaking people
> 428.3461

—84   **Reading**

> *For readers, see —86*

—842   Remedial reading

> Correcting faulty habits and increasing the proficiency of poor readers

—843   Developmental reading

> Including reading power and efficiency of good readers

—843 2   Rapid reading (Speed reading)

—86   **Readers**

> Graded selections with emphasis on structure and vocabulary as needed
>
> Including readers compiled for training college students in reading
> comprehension
>
> Class here texts intended primarily for practice in reading a language
>
> (Option: Class primary readers in 372.4122)

—862   Readers for new literates

> Regardless of subject

—864   Readers for people whose native language is different from the
                    language of the reader

—864 024   Readers for people in specific occupations

> Class here readers intended to instill a knowledge of the special
> vocabulary of a specific subject
>
> Add to base number —864024 notation 001–999, e.g.,
> engineering readers for people whose native language is different
> —86402462, English-language engineering readers for people
> whose native language is not English 428.6402462

—864 2–864 9   Readers for speakers of specific native languages

> Add to base number —864 notation 2–9 from Table 6, e.g., readers (in language other than Spanish) for Spanish-speaking people —86461, English-language readers for Spanish-speaking people 428.6461; then add further as follows:
>
> > 024   Readers for people in specific occupations
> >
> > > Class here readers intended to instill a knowledge of the special vocabulary of a specific subject
> > >
> > > Add to base number 024 notation 001–999, e.g., engineering readers (in language other than Spanish) for Spanish-speaking people —8646102462, English-language engineering readers for Spanish-speaking people 428.646102462

—89   **Use of a spoken language or a manually coded form of a spoken language for communication with and by deaf people**

—891   Manually coded language

> Class here use of signs and fingerspelling to represent specific standard spoken languages
>
> Class signs and fingerspelling used as part of sign languages in 419
>
> *See also —8955 for cued speech*

—891 4–891 9   Specific systems of manual coding

> Add to base number —891 notation 4–9 from Table 2, e.g., British systems of signing and fingerspelling —89141

—895   Lipreading, cued speech, oral interpretation (lipspeaking)

—895 4   Lipreading (Speechreading)

—895 5   Cued speech

Table 5. Ethnic and National Groups

The following numbers are never used alone, but may be used as required (either directly when so noted or through the interposition of notation 089 from Table 1) with any number from the schedules, e.g., civil and political rights (323.11) of Navajo Indians (—9726 in this table): 323.119726; ceramic arts (738) of Jews (—924 in this table): 738.089924. They may also be used when so noted with numbers from other tables, e.g., notation 174 from Table 2

In this table racial groups are mentioned in connection with a few broad ethnic groupings, e.g., a note to class Blacks of African origin at —96 Africans and people of African descent. Concepts of race vary. A work that emphasizes race should be classed with the ethnic group that most closely matches the concept of race described in the work

Except where instructed otherwise, and unless it is redundant, add 0 to the number from this table and to the result add notation 1 or —3–9 from Table 2 for area in which a group is or was located, e.g., Germans in Brazil —31081, but Germans in Germany —31; Jews in Germany or Jews from Germany —924043. If notation from Table 2 is not added, use 00 for standard subdivisions; see below for complete instructions on using standard subdivisions

Notation from Table 2 may be added if the number in Table 5 is limited to speakers of only one language even if the group discussed does not approximate the whole of the group specified by the Table 5 number, e.g., Bavarians in Brazil —31081 (because German is the primary language spoken by Bavarians), but Amhara in United States —928 (*not* —928073 because Amharic is not the only language spoken by the peoples included in —928)

Notation from Table 2 may be added for either present or past specific location of the group discussed if only one specific location is relevant, e.g., sociology of Jews from many different countries now in United States 305.8924073, contributions to music around the world of Jews who previously lived in Poland 780.899240438

If both present and past specific locations of the group discussed are relevant, then notation from Table 2 is added only for present location of the group, e.g., Jews from Germany in the United States —924073 (*not* —924043). An exception occurs when the present location of the group is defined by the class number to which ethnic or national group notation is added, e.g., Jews in United States history 973.04924. The area notation added to Table 5 numbers is then available to show the past location of the group, e.g., Jews from Germany in United States history 973.04924043, Jews from Germany in United States higher education 378.73089924043

Standard subdivisions may be added to Table 5 notation when that notation is added directly to the base number, e.g., periodicals about sociology of Irish Americans 305.8916207305. However, standard subdivisions are not added to Table 5 notation when that notation is used through interposition of notation 089 from Table 1, e.g., an exhibition of ceramic arts of Russian Jews 738.089924047 (*not* 738.089924047074)

(continued)

691

Table 5. Ethnic and National Groups (continued)

When Table 5 notation is not followed by 0 plus notation from Table 2, use 00 for standard subdivisions, e.g., periodicals about sociology of Japanese 305.8956005, collected biography of Irish Americans in New York City 974.71004916200922. When Table 5 notation is followed by 0 plus notation from Table 2, however, use 0 for standard subdivisions, e.g., periodicals about sociology of Japanese Americans 305.895607305. (For the purpose of this rule, notation 96073 African Americans is treated as Table 5 notation, e.g., periodicals on sociology of African Americans 305.896073005, periodicals on sociology of African Americans in Ohio 305.896073077105)

Except where instructed otherwise, give preference to ethnic group over nationality, e.g., United States citizens of Serbian descent —9182073 (*not* —13). In this table "ethnic group" most often means a group with linguistic ties, but it can also mean a group with other cultural ties

Except where instructed otherwise, when choosing between two ethnic groups, give preference to the group for which the notation is different from that for the nationality of the people, e.g., a work treating equally Hispanic and native American heritage of bilingual Spanish-Guaraní mestizos of Paraguay —9838220892 (*not* —68892)

Except where instructed otherwise, when choosing between two national groups, give preference to the former or ancestral national group, e.g., people from the former Soviet Union who became United States citizens —917073 (*not* —13)

See Manual at Table 5

SUMMARY

—05–09	[People of mixed ancestry with ethnic origins from more than one continent; Europeans and people of European descent]
—1	North Americans
—2	British, English, Anglo-Saxons
—3	Germanic peoples
—4	Modern Latin peoples
—5	Italians, Romanians, related groups
—6	Peoples who speak, or whose ancestors spoke, Spanish, Portuguese, Galician
—7	Other Italic peoples
—8	Greeks and related groups
—9	Other ethnic and national groups

—05   **People of mixed ancestry with ethnic origins from more than one continent**

Limited to works that emphasize such mixed ancestry

Class works about people of mixed ancestry that do not emphasize mixture with the ethnic groups stressed in the works or with the groups with which the people are most closely identified, e.g., works about Métis that emphasize their North American native roots —97 (*not* —0597009); class works that stress the kind of mixed ethnic heritage (e.g., language, customs, food, but not genetics) that results when people of one continent move to another continent and raise their children in the new location with the ethnic group of origin, plus notation from Table 2 as instructed at beginning of Table 5 to show the new location, e.g., people who have Chinese parents and were raised in the United Kingdom —951041

For people of mixed North and South American native ancestry, see —97

—050 9   Europeans and people of European descent with ethnic origins from more than one continent

> Limited to works that emphasize European ancestry and mixed ancestry with ethnic origins from more than one continent

> Add to base number —0509 notation 1–9 from Table 5, e.g., people with European and Asian ancestry —0509095, people with European and Asian ancestry in Hawaii —05090950969, people with European and Chinese ancestry —05090951

> Works that emphasize mixed ancestry but give equal emphasis to European and non-European origins, or give more emphasis to non-European origins, are classed in —051–059, e.g., works about mixed Asian and European ancestry that give equal emphasis to both groups —0595009, works about mixed Chinese and European ancestry that emphasize Chinese ancestry —05951009

—051–059   Specific ethnic and national groups

> Add to base number —05 notation 1–9 from Table 5 for the group only, e.g., American native peoples of mixed ancestry with ethnic origins from more than one continent —0597; then, for each group having its own number, add 0 and to the result add as follows:
>
> 001–009   Standard subdivisions
>
> 09   Europeans and people of European descent
>   Here are classed people whose mixed ancestry includes Europeans, Indo-European peoples, or white people generally, e.g., people of mixed American native and European ancestry —0597009, people of mixed American native and European ancestry in Canada —0597009071
>   *For a specific ethnic or regional group, see 1–9*
>
> 1–9   Specific ethnic and national groups
>   Add notation 1–9 from Table 5, e.g., people of mixed American native and French ancestry —0597041, people of mixed American native and French ancestry in Canada —0597041071, people of mixed Aleut and Russian ancestry —05971909171

> Give priority in notation to the ethnic group emphasized. If emphasis is equal, give priority to the one coming last in Table 5

—09   **Europeans and people of European descent**

> Class here people who speak or whose ancestors spoke languages traditionally spoken in Europe; comprehensive works on Indo-European peoples; comprehensive works on whites

> Class works that emphasize mixed ancestry with origins from more than one continent in —05, e.g., works emphasizing mixed Hindi-English ancestry —059143021

> *For a specific ethnic or regional group, see the group, e.g., Germans —31, Bengali —9144, Arabs —927, people of Middle Eastern origins —94*

> ## —1–9 Specific ethnic and national groups

By origin or situation

Class people of mixed ancestry with ethnic origins from more than one continent in —05; class comprehensive works on Europeans, on Indo-European peoples in —09; class comprehensive works in 001–999 without adding notation from Table 5

See Manual at Table 5

(Option: To give local emphasis and a shorter number to a specific group, place it first by use of a letter or other symbol, e.g., Arabs —A [preceding —1]. Another option is given at —1)

—1   North Americans

For Spanish Americans, see —68; for North American regional and national groups of largely African descent, see —9697, e.g., West Indians —969729, Haitians —9697294; for North American native peoples, see —97. For North Americans of other origins, see the ethnic group of origin, e.g., North Americans of Celtic (Irish, Scots, Manx, Welsh, Cornish) origin —91607

(Option: To give local emphasis and a shorter number to a specific group, e.g., Sinhalese, class it in this number; in that case class North Americans in —2. Another option is given at —1–9)

—11   Canadians

Class here people of Canada as a national group

For Canadians not of British or French origin, see the ethnic group of origin, e.g., Canadians of German origin —31071, Inuit —9712071

—112   Canadians of British origin

See Manual at T5—112, T5—114 vs. T5—2, T5—41

—114   Canadians of French origin

See Manual at T5—112, T5—114 vs. T5—2, T5—41

—13   People of United States ("Americans")

Class here United States citizens of British origin, people of United States as a national group

For United States citizens of other origins, see the ethnic group of origin, e.g., German Americans —31073, African Americans —96073

See Manual at T5—13 vs. T5—2073, T5—21073

—2   British, English, Anglo-Saxons

Subdivisions are added for British, English, Anglo-Saxons together; for British as an ethnic group; for English as an ethnic group

For North Americans of British origin, see —1; for Anglo-Indians (Indian citizens of British origin), see —91411; for people of Celtic (Irish, Scots, Manx, Welsh, Cornish) origin, see —916

See Manual at Table 5; also at T5—112, T5—114 vs. T5—2, T5—41; also at T5—13 vs. T5—2073, T5—21073; also at T5—201–209 vs. T5—2101–2109

—21   People of British Isles

Class here United Kingdom citizens of British origin, people of United Kingdom as a national group

Class New Zealanders of British origin in —23; class Australians of British origin in —24; class South Africans of British origin in —28

For United Kingdom citizens of other origins, see the ethnic group of origin, e.g., United Kingdom citizens of Indian origin —91411041

See Manual at T5—13 vs. T5—2073, T5—21073; also at T5—201–209 vs. T5—2101–2109

—23   New Zealanders

Class here New Zealanders of British origin, New Zealanders as a national group

For New Zealanders of other origins, see the ethnic group of origin, e.g., New Zealanders of Irish origin —9162093, Maori —99442

—24   Australians

Class here Australians of British origin, Australians as a national group

For Australians of other origins, see the ethnic group of origin, e.g., Australians of Italian origin —51094, Aboriginal Australians —9915

—28   South Africans of British origin

Class South Africans as a national group in —968

See also —2106891 for Zimbabweans of British origin

—3   Germanic peoples

For English, Anglo-Saxons, see —2

—31   Germans

—35   Swiss

Class here Swiss Germans, comprehensive works on people of Switzerland as a national group

For Swiss citizens of other ethnic groups, see the ethnic group, e.g., French-speaking Swiss —410494, Romansh-speaking Swiss —59960494, Italian-speaking Swiss —510494

—36   Austrians

—39	**Other Germanic peoples**

Including Goths, Vandals

—392	Friesians
—393	Netherlandish peoples
—393 1	Dutch
—393 2	Flemings (Flemish)

Class here comprehensive works on Belgians as a national group

For Walloons, see —42

—393 6	Afrikaners

Class South Africans as a national group in —968

—395	Scandinavians

Class here comprehensive works on peoples of the Nordic countries

For Icelanders and Faroese, see —396; for Swedes, see —397; for Danes and Norwegians, see —398; for Finns, see —94541; for Sámi, see —9457

—396	Icelanders and Faroese
—396 1	Icelanders
—396 9	Faroese
—397	Swedes
—398	Danes and Norwegians
—398 1	Danes
—398 2	Norwegians

—4	**Modern Latin peoples**

For Italians, Romanians, related groups, see —5; for peoples who speak, or whose ancestors spoke, Spanish, Portuguese, Galician, see —6

—41	**French**

Class Canadians of French origin in —114

For Corsicans, see —59984; for Basques, see —9992

See Manual at T5—112, T5—114 vs. T5—2, T5—41

—42	**Walloons**
—49	**Catalans**
—5	**Italians, Romanians, related groups**
—51	**Italians**

—[56]   **Sardinians**

>   Relocated to —59982

—57   **Dalmatians**

—[58]   **Corsicans**

>   Relocated to —59984

—59   **Romanians; peoples who speak, or whose ancestors spoke, Rhaetian languages; Sardinians, Corsicans**

—591   Romanians

—599   Peoples who speak, or whose ancestors spoke, Rhaetian languages; Sardinians, Corsicans

—599 2   Friulians

—599 4   Ladins

—599 6   Romansch

—599 8   Sardinians and Corsicans

—599 82   Sardinians [*formerly* —56]

—599 84   Corsicans [*formerly* —58]

—6   **Peoples who speak, or whose ancestors spoke, Spanish, Portuguese, Galician**

—61   **People of Spain**

>   *For Catalans, see —49; for Basques, see —9992*

—68   **Spanish Americans**

>   Class here comprehensive works on Latin Americans

>   *For Latin American peoples not provided for here, see the people, e.g., Brazilians —698*

>   *See also —9141 for people of Guyana and Suriname as national groups; also —96972 for Central American and Caribbean national groups of majority African origin, e.g., —9697282 for Belizeans, —9697294 for Haitians*

—687–688   Regional and national groups

>   Citizens of independent and partly independent jurisdictions having a Spanish-speaking majority or Spanish as an official language; former citizens and descendants of citizens of these jurisdictions

>   Add to base number —68 notation 7–8 from Table 2, e.g., Central Americans —68728, Puerto-Ricans —687295, Chileans —6883; then add further as instructed at beginning of Table 5, e.g., Chileans in United States and U.S. citizens of Chilean origin —6883073; however, for comprehensive works on Spanish Americans in jurisdictions where they are a minority, see —6804–6809, e.g., Spanish Americans in United States —68073

—69 **Peoples who speak, or whose ancestors spoke, Portuguese and Galician**

Subdivisions are added for peoples who speak, or whose ancestors spoke, Portuguese and Galician together; for peoples who speak, or whose ancestors spoke Portuguese alone

—691 People of Portugal

—698 Brazilians

Class here Brazilians of Portuguese origin, Brazilians as a national group

For Brazilian citizens of other origins, see the ethnic group of origin, e.g., Brazilians of Italian origin —51081, Brazilians of African origin —96081

—699 People who speak, or whose ancestors spoke, Galician

—7 **Other Italic peoples**

For Etruscans, see —9994

—71 **Ancient Romans**

—79 **Osco-Umbrians**

—8 **Greeks and related groups**

Subdivisions are added for Greeks and related groups together, for Greeks as an ethnic group alone

See also —91819 for Slavic Macedonians

—81 **Ancient Greeks**

Class here comprehensive works on ancient Greeks and Romans

For ancient Romans, see —71

—89 **Modern Greeks and related groups**

—893 Greek nationals

—895 Cypriots

Class here comprehensive works on people of Cyprus

For Turkish Cypriots, see —943505693

—9 **Other ethnic and national groups**

SUMMARY

—91	Other Indo-European peoples
—92	Semites
—93	Non-Semitic Afro-Asiatic peoples
—94	Peoples of north and west Asian origin or situation; Dravidians; peoples who speak, or whose ancestors spoke, miscellaneous languages of south Asia
—95	East and southeast Asian peoples; Munda
—96	Africans and people of African descent
—97	North American native peoples
—98	South American native peoples
—99	Papuans; Aboriginal Australians and Tasmanians; Malayo-Polynesian and related peoples; miscellaneous peoples

—91   Other Indo-European peoples

SUMMARY

—914	South Asians
—915	Peoples who speak, or whose ancestors spoke, Iranian languages
—916	Celts
—917	East Slavs
—918	Slavs
—919	Balts and other Indo-European peoples

—914   South Asians

Class here Indo-Aryans (peoples who speak, or whose ancestors spoke, Indo-Aryan languages)

For Dravidians and peoples who speak, or whose ancestors spoke, miscellaneous languages of south Asia, see —948; for south Asians who speak, or whose ancestors spoke, languages closely related to languages of east and southeast Asia, see —95; for Andamanese, see —959

See also notation 08621 in Table 1 for Brahmans as an elite social group; also notation 0882945 in Table 1 for Brahmans as a religious group

—914 1   National groups

Citizens of independent and partly independent jurisdictions of south Asia and of largely south Asian origin; former citizens and descendants of citizens of these jurisdictions

Including Guyanese, Mauritians, Surinamers

Class nationals of a specific ethnolinguistic group with the group, e.g., Tamil —94811

For Nepalese national group, see —91495

See also —96972983 for Trinidadian national group; also —9959 for Fijian national group

Maldivians as a national group relocated to —91489

—914 11	Indians
	Including Anglo-Indians (Indian citizens of British origin), post-1975 Sikkimese
	Class comprehensive works on Sikkimese in —91417
—914 12	Pakistanis and people of Bangladesh
—914 122	Pakistanis
—914 126	People of Bangladesh
—914 13	Sri Lankans (Ceylonese)
	For Sinhalese as an ethnic group, see —9148; for Tamil as an ethnic group, see —94811
—914 17	Sikkimese
	For post-1975 Sikkimese, see —91411
—914 18	Bhutanese
	Class Bhotia as an ethnic group in —9541
—914 2	Punjabis and Sindhi
—914 21	Punjabis
—914 25	Sindhi [*formerly* —948]
—914 3	Peoples who speak, or whose ancestors spoke, Western Hindi languages
	Class here comprehensive works on Hindi-speaking peoples
	For peoples who speak, or whose ancestors spoke, languages of east central zone of Indo-Aryan languages (Eastern Hindi languages), see —91492
—914 4	Bengali
	For Bengali of Bangladesh, see —914126
—914 5	Assamese, Bihari, Oriya
—914 51	Assamese
—914 54	Bihari
—914 56	Oriya
—914 6	Maratha and Konkani
—914 61	Maratha [*formerly* —948]
—914 69	Konkani [*formerly* —9149]
—914 7	Gujarati and Bhil; people who speak, or whose ancestors spoke, Rajasthani
—914 71	Gujarati

—914 79   People who speak, or whose ancestors spoke, Rajasthani

                  Including Gujar

—914 8   Sinhalese, Vedda, Maldivians

                  Subdivisions are added for Sinhalese, Vedda, Maldivians together; for Sinhalese alone

—914 89   Maldivians

                  Peoples who speak, or whose ancestors spoke, Divehi (Maldivian)

                  Class here Maldivians as a national group [*formerly* —9141]

—914 9   Other Indo-Aryan peoples

                  Including peoples who speak, or whose ancestors spoke, Nuristani languages

                  Konkani relocated to —91469

—914 92   Peoples who speak, or whose ancestors spoke, east central zone languages (Eastern Hindi languages)

                  Including speakers of Awadhi, Bagheli, Chattisgarhi

                  Speakers of Fijian Hindustani (Fiji Hindi) are of many south Asian ethnic groups; use —91409611 for Fijian citizens from south Asia

—914 95   Nepali

                  Class here Nepali as an ethnic group, comprehensive works on people of Nepal as a national group

                      For citizens of Nepal belonging to other ethnic groups, see the ethnic group, e.g., Bihari —91454, Chepang and Newar —9549

—914 96   Pahari

                  Class here peoples who speak, or whose ancestors spoke, northern zone languages, Pahari languages

                      For people who speak, or whose ancestors spoke, Nepali, see —91495

—914 97   Romany people

—914 99   Dardic peoples

                  Including Kashmiris, Kohistanis

                  Class Romany people in —91497

—915   Peoples who speak, or whose ancestors spoke, Iranian languages

                  Including Kushans, Scythians

—915 5   Persians

                  Class here Persians as an ethnic group, comprehensive works on people of Iran as a national group

                      For citizens of Iran belonging to other ethnic groups, see the ethnic group, e.g., Azerbaijani —94361055

—915 7	Tajik
	Including Galcha
—915 9	Other Iranian peoples
	Including Ossets, Pamiri
—915 93	Afghans (Pashtun)

Class here Afghans as an ethnic group, comprehensive works on people of Afghanistan as a national group

For citizens of Afghanistan belonging to other ethnic groups, see the ethnic group, e.g., Tajik —91570581

—915 97	Kurds
—915 98	Baluchi
—916	Celts
	Including Gauls
—916 2	Irish
—916 3	Scots
—916 4	Manx
—916 6	Welsh (Cymry)
—916 7	Cornish
—916 8	Bretons
—917	East Slavs

Class here people of Commonwealth of Independent States, of former Soviet Union as national groups

Class comprehensive works on Slavs in —918

For a specific ethnic group of Commonwealth of Independent States or former Soviet Union, see the group, e.g., Uzbek —94325

—917 1	Russians
—917 14	Cossacks
—917 9	Ukrainians, Ruthenians, Belarusians
—917 91	Ukrainians and Ruthenians

Subdivisions are added for Ukrainians and Ruthenians together, for Ukrainians alone

See also notation 0882815 in Table 1 for Ruthenians as a religious group

—917 99	Belarusians
—918	Slavs

For east Slavs, see —917

—918 1   Bulgarians and Macedonians

       Class here comprehensive works on South Slavs

> *For Serbs and Montenegrins, see —9182; for Croats and Bosnians, see —9183; for Slovenes, see —9184*

—918 11   Bulgarians

—918 19   Macedonians

—918 2   Serbs and Montenegrins

       Class here people of Serbia as a national group; people of former Serbia and Montenegro as a national group; people of former Yugoslavia as a national group; comprehensive works on Serbs, Montenegrins, Croats, Bosnians

       Subdivisions are added for Serbs and Montenegrins together, for Serbs alone

       Class comprehensive works on South Slavs in —9181

> *For Croats, see —9183. For citizens of Serbia of other ethnic groups, citizens of former Yugoslavia of other ethnic groups, see the ethnic group, e.g., Serbian citizens of Hungarian ancestry —9451104971*

       Bosnians relocated to —91839

—[918 22]   Serbs and Montenegrins

       Number discontinued; class in —9182

—[918 23]   Croats

       Relocated to —9183

—918 29   Montenegrins

—918 3   Croats [*formerly* —91823] and Bosnians

       Class here people of Croatia as a national group

       Subdivisions are added for Croats and Bosnians together, for Croats alone

> *For citizens of Croatia of other ethnic groups, see the ethnic group, e.g., Hungarians —9451104972*

—918 39   Bosnians [*formerly* —9182]

       Class here people who speak, or whose ancestors spoke, Bosnian; Bosniaks; Bosnian Muslims; people of Bosnia and Hercegovina as a national group

> *For citizens of Bosnia and Hercegovina of other ethnic groups, see the ethnic group, e.g., Croats —9183049742*

> *See also notation 088297 from Table 1 for Muslims as a religious group*

—918 4   Slovenes

—918 5   West Slavs

> Including Kashubs

> Class here Poles

>> *For Cossacks, see —91714; for Czechs and Moravians, see —9186; for Slovaks, see —9187; for Wends, see —9188*

—918 6   Czechs and Moravians

> Class here Czechoslovaks

> Subdivisions are added for either or both topics in heading

>> *For Slovaks, see —9187*

>> *See also notation 0882846 in Table 1 for Moravians as a religious group*

—918 7   Slovaks

—918 8   Wends (Lusatians, Sorbs)

—919   Balts and other Indo-European peoples

> Subdivisions are added for Balts and other Indo-European peoples together, for Balts alone

—919 2   Lithuanians

—919 3   Latvians (Letts)

—919 9   Albanians, Armenians, Hittites

—919 91   Albanians

—919 92   Armenians

—92   **Semites**

> Including peoples who spoke Syriac, other eastern Aramaic languages

> Class here comprehensive works on Afro-Asiatic peoples

>> *For non-Semitic Afro-Asiatic peoples, see —93*

—921   Akkadians, Amorites, Assyrians, Babylonians

—922   Aramaeans

> Including peoples who spoke western Aramaic languages

> Class peoples who spoke Syriac, other eastern Aramaic languages in —92

—924   Hebrews, Israelis, Jews

> Class here Beta Israel

> Subdivisions are added for any or all topics in heading

>> *See also notation 088296 in Table 1 for Jews as a religious group*

—926   Canaanites and Phoenicians

>> *For Amorites, see —921*

—927	Arabs and Maltese

           Subdivisions are added for Arabs and Maltese together, for Arabs alone

—927 2	Bedouins

           See also —933 for Berbers and Tuareg

—927 4	Palestinian Arabs
—927 5–927 6	Regional and national groups of Arabs

           Citizens of independent or partly independent jurisdictions having an Arab or Arabic-speaking majority or Arabic as the official language; former citizens and descendants of citizens of these jurisdictions

           Add to base number —927 notation 5–6 from Table 2, e.g., Iraqis —927567, North Africans —92761, Sudanese —927624; then add further as instructed at beginning of Table 5, e.g., Sudanese in Ethiopia and Ethiopian citizens of Sudanese ancestry —927624063; however, for comprehensive works on Arabs as a minority group in a country of Asia or Africa where Arabic is not the official language, see —92705–92706, e.g., Arabs in Iran —927055; for Mauritanians as a national group, see —9661

           Class Palestinian Arabs as an ethnic group in —9274

—927 61	Arabs of North Africa

           Number built according to instructions under —9275–9276

           Class here comprehensive works on North Africans

           For a specific North African group not provided for here, see the group, e.g., Algerians —92765, Berbers —933

—927 9	Maltese
—928	Peoples who speak, or whose ancestors spoke, Ethiopian languages

           Including Amhara, Gurage, Harari, Tigre, Tigrinya

           Class here comprehensive works on people of Ethiopia as a national group

           For Beta Israel, see —924; for Cushitic and Omotic peoples of Ethiopia, see —935; for Nilo-Saharan peoples of Ethiopia, see —965

—928 9	Eritreans

           Class here comprehensive works on people of Eritrea as a national group

           Class Eritreans who speak, or whose ancestors spoke, a specific Ethiopian language in —928

           For Cushitic peoples of Eritrea, see —935; for Nilo-Saharan peoples of Eritrea, see —965

—929	Mahri and Socotrans

           Class here South Arabic peoples

—93	**Non-Semitic Afro-Asiatic peoples**

Class here peoples who speak, or whose ancestors spoke, non-Semitic Afro-Asiatic languages

Class comprehensive works on North Africans in —92761

—931	Ancient Egyptians
—932	Copts

> *See also notation 08828172 in Table 1 for Copts as members of the Coptic Church*

—933	Berbers and Tuareg
—935	Cushitic and Omotic peoples

Including Afar, Beja

Subdivisions are added Cushitic and Omotic peoples together, for Cushitic peoples alone

Class Beta Israel in —924; class Ethiopians as a national group in —928; class Eritreans as a national group in —9289; class Djiboutians as a national group in —96771

—935 4	Somali

> Class here Somali as a national group [*formerly* —96773]

—935 5	Oromo
—935 9	Omotic peoples

Class here peoples who speak or whose ancestors spoke Omotic languages

—937	Hausa

Class the people of Niger as a national group in —96626

—94	**Peoples of north and west Asian origin or situation; Dravidians; peoples who speak, or whose ancestors spoke, miscellaneous languages of south Asia**

Class here comprehensive works on peoples of Middle Eastern origin

> *For Cypriots, see —895; for Indo-European peoples of these regions, see —91; for Semites, see —92*

—941	Tungusic peoples

Including Evenki, Nanai

—942	Peoples who speak, or whose ancestors spoke, Mongolian languages

Including Buriat (Buryat), Daur, Tu; people who speak, or whose ancestors spoke, Kalmyk-Oirat

Class here Mongols

—942 3   People who speak, or whose ancestors spoke, Mongolian proper

> Class here people who speak, or whose ancestors spoke, Halh Mongolian (Khalkha Mongolian); people of Mongolia as a national group

—943   Turkic peoples

> Add to base number —943 the numbers following —943 in notation 9431–9438 from Table 6, e.g., Turks —9435, Uzbek —94325; then add further as instructed at beginning of Table 5 , e.g., Turks in Germany —9435043; however, for Chuvashes, see —9456

> Class Cossacks in —91714

> *See Manual at T5—9435*

—944   Samoyed

—945   Finno-Ugrians

—945 1   Ugrians

> Including Ostyaks, Vogul

—945 11   Hungarians

—945 3   Permiaks, Votyak, Komi (Zyrian)

—945 4   Finnic peoples

> Including Karelians, Kven, Livonians, Veps; people who speak, or whose ancestors spoke, Tornedalen Finnish

> *For Permiaks, Votyak, Komi, see —9453; for Cheremis, Chuvashes, Mordvin, see —9456; for Sámi, see —9457*

—945 41   Finns

> Class Kven and people who speak, or whose ancestors spoke, Tornedalen Finnish in —9454

—945 45   Estonians

—[945 5]   Sámi

> Relocated to —9457

—945 6   Mari, Chuvashes, Mordvin

—945 7   Sámi [*formerly* —9455]

> Add to base number —9457 the numbers following —9457 in notation 94572–94578 from Table 6, e.g., people who speak or whose ancestors spoke Lule Sámi —945743; then add further as instructed at beginning of Table 5, e.g., Lule Sámi in Sweden —9457430485

—946   Paleo-Asiatic (Paleosiberian) peoples

> Including Ainu (Utari); peoples who speak or whose ancestors spoke Chukotko-Kamchatkan (Luorawetlin), Yukaghir languages; Nivkh (Gilyak), Ket (Yenisei Ostyak)

—948	**Dravidians and and peoples who speak, or whose ancestors spoke, miscellaneous languages of south Asia**

Class here peoples who speak, or whose ancestors spoke, Dravidian languages

Subdivisions are added for Dravidians and peoples who speak, or whose ancestors spoke, miscellaneous languages of south Asia together, for Dravidians alone

Use of this number for Scytho-Dravidians discontinued because without meaning in context

Sindhi relocated to —91425; Maratha relocated to —91461

—948 1	**South Dravidians**

Including Toda

Class here peoples who speak, or whose ancestors spoke, south Dravidian languages

—948 11	Tamil
—948 12	Malayalis
—948 14	Kanarese
—948 2	**Central Dravidians**

Class here peoples who speak, or whose ancestors spoke, central Dravidian languages

—948 23	Gond
—948 24	Kandh (Kondh, Kui)
—948 27	Telugu
—948 3	**North Dravidians**

Including Oraon (Kurux, Kurukh)

Class here Brahui; peoples who speak, or whose ancestors spoke, north Dravidian languages

—948 9	**Peoples who speak, or whose ancestors spoke, miscellaneous languages of south Asia**

Only those peoples provided for below

Including people who speak, or whose ancestors spoke, Nihali

Class south Asians who speak, or whose ancestors spoke, languages closely related to east and southeast Asian languages in —95; class Andamanese in —959; class Indo-Aryans, comprehensive works on south Asians in —914

—948 92	Burusho

Class here people who speak, or whose ancestors spoke, Burushaski

—95   **East and southeast Asian peoples; Munda**

Including Karen

Class here east Asians; south Asian peoples who speak, or whose ancestors spoke, languages closely related to languages of east and southeast Asia; comprehensive works on Asian peoples

For a specific Asian people not provided for here, see the people, e.g., Persians —9155, Malays —9928

—951   Chinese

Class here Han Chinese; people who speak or whose ancestors spoke Mandarin Chinese (Putonghua), Beijing dialect; comprehensive works on people of China as a national group

For Chinese citizens of other ethnic groups, see the ethnic group, e.g., Mongol —942051

—951 7   Hakka

Class here people who speak or whose ancestors spoke Hakka dialects

—954   Tibeto-Burman peoples

Including Naxi

Class here peoples who speak, or whose ancestors spoke, Tibeto-Burman languages

Class Karen in —95

For Burmese, see —958

—954 1   Tibetans

Class here Bhotia as an ethnic group

See also —91418 for Bhutanese as a national group

—954 9   Eastern Himalayan peoples

Including Chepang, Newar

Class here peoples who speak, or whose ancestors spoke, eastern Himalayan languages

See also —91495 for Nepali

—956   Japanese

Including Ryukyuans

For Ainu, see —946

—957   Koreans

—958   Burmese

—959   Miscellaneous southeast Asian peoples; Munda

> Only those peoples provided for below

> Including Andamanese [*formerly* —9911]; peoples who speak, or whose ancestors spoke, Kadai languages, Kam-Sui languages

> Class here peoples who speak, or whose ancestors spoke, Daic languages

—959 1   Tai peoples

> Class here peoples who speak, or whose ancestors spoke, Tai languages

—959 11   Thai (Siamese)

—959 19   Other Tai peoples

> Including Shan

> *For Viet-Muong peoples, see —9592*

—959 191   Lao

—959 2   Viet-Muong peoples

> Class here peoples who speak, or whose ancestors spoke, Viet-Muong languages

> Class comprehensive works on Montagnards of Vietnam in —9593

—959 22   Vietnamese

—959 3   Austroasiatic peoples

> Including Semang [*formerly* —9911]; comprehensive works on Montagnards of Vietnam

> Class here peoples who speak, or whose ancestors spoke, Austroasiatic languages, Mon-Khmer languages

> *For Viet-Muong peoples, see —9592; for Munda, see —9595. For Montagnards of a specific ethnic group, see the ethnic group, e.g., Rhade —9922*

—959 32   Khmer

> Class here Khmer as an ethnic group, comprehensive works on people of Cambodia as a national group

> *For citizens of Cambodia belonging to another ethnic group, see the ethnic group, e.g., Jarai —9922*

—[959 4]   Hmong and Yao peoples

> Relocated to —9597

—959 5   Munda

—959 7   Hmong and Yao peoples [*formerly* —9594]

> Class here peoples who speak, or whose ancestors spoke, Hmong-Mien (Miao-Yao) languages

—959 72   Hmong (Miao)

—959 78   Yao

—96   **Africans and people of African descent**

Class here Blacks of African origin

For peoples who speak or whose ancestors spoke Ethiopian languages, see —928; for non-Semitic Afro-Asiatic peoples, see —93; for Malagasy, see —993

—960 67   Africans of Central Africa and offshore islands

Number built according to instructions at beginning of Table 5

Class here comprehensive works on African pygmies

For specific groups of African pygmies, see the specific ethnic group, e.g., Baka —96361

—960 73   African Americans (United States Blacks)

Unless it is redundant, add 0* to —96073 and to the result add notation 1–9 from Table 2 for area, e.g., African Americans in England —96073042, African Americans in New York —960730747, but African Americans in United States —96073

See Manual at T5—96073

—961   Khoikhoi and San

—963   Peoples who speak, or whose ancestors spoke, Niger-Congo languages

Including peoples who speak, or whose ancestors spoke, Ijoid languages, Kordofanian languages; Dogon

Add to base number —963 the numbers following —963 in notation 9632–9639 from Table 6, e.g., Zulu —963986; then add further as instructed at beginning of Table 5 , e.g., Zulu in Malawi —96398606897

—963 91   Peoples who speak, or whose ancestors spoke, central Bantu languages

Number built according to instructions under —963

Peoples who speak, or whose ancestors spoke, Fipa-Mambwe languages relocated to —96394

—963 915   Peoples who speak, or whose ancestors spoke, languages of Bemba group

Number built according to instructions under —963

People who speak, or whose ancestors spoke, Bwile relocated to —96393

—963 93   Peoples who speak, or whose ancestors spoke, central western Bantu languages

Number built according to instructions under —963

Including people who speak, or whose ancestors spoke, Bwile [*formerly* —963915]

---

*Add 00 for standard subdivisions; see instructions at beginning of Table 5

—963 94   Peoples who speak, or whose ancestors spoke, northern Bantu languages

Number built according to instructions under —963

Including peoples who speak, or whose ancestors spoke, Fipa-Mambwe languages [*formerly* —96391]

—965   Peoples who speak, or whose ancestors spoke, Nilo-Saharan languages

Including Nilotic peoples, Nubians, Luo, Songhai

Class here peoples who speak or whose ancestors spoke Chari-Nile (Macrosudanic) languages

—966–968   Regional and national groups in Africa

Citizens of independent and partly independent jurisdictions; former citizens and descendants of citizens of these jurisdictions

Add to base number —96 the numbers following —6 in notation 66–68 from Table 2, e.g., West Africans —966, Nigerians —9669; then add further as instructed at beginning of Table 5 , e.g., Nigerians in the United Kingdom and British citizens of Nigerian origin —9669041; however, Somali as a national group relocated from —96773 to —9354

Class nationals of a specific ethnolinguistic group with the group, e.g., South Africans of British origin —28, Nigerian Hausa —9370669, Nigerian Igbo —963320669

See also —9276 for national groups of African Arabs, e.g., modern Egyptians —92762, Sudanese —927624; also —928 for Ethiopians as a national group; also —9289 for Eritreans as a national group; also —931 for ancient Egyptians as a national group

—969   Other regional and national groups of largely African descent

Citizens of independent and partly independent jurisdictions outside Africa; former citizens and descendants of citizens of these jurisdictions

Add to base number —969 notation 4–9 from Table 2, e.g., West Indians —969729, Haitians —9697294, Virgin Islanders —96972972; then add further as instructed at beginning of Table 5, e.g., Haitians in the United States —9697294073

Class Cubans in —687291; class Dominicans (Dominican Republic) in —687293; class Puerto Ricans in —687295; class minority groups of African descent in —9604–9609, plus notation from Table 2 as instructed at beginning of Table 5 to show where the groups are located, e.g., people of African descent in Canada —96071. Class nationals of a specific ethnolinguistic group with the group, e.g., Bahamians of English origin —2107296

—969 729   Caribbean peoples of largely African descent

Number built according to instructions under —969

Class here comprehensive works on Caribbean peoples

For Caribbean peoples of other ethnic groups, see the ethnic group, e.g., Spanish Americans —68729

—97	**North American native peoples**

Class here peoples who speak, or whose ancestors spoke, North American native languages; comprehensive works on Woodland Indians, on North and South American native peoples

Class national groups of modern Central America where Spanish is an official language in —68728 even if the majority of their population is of North American native origin, e.g., Guatemalans as a national group —687281. Class a specific group of Woodland Indians with the group according to the language that the Indians speak or their ancestors spoke, e.g., Iroquois —9755

For South American native peoples, see —98

—970 78	Indians of Western United States

Number built according to instructions at beginning of Table 5

Class here Plains Indians

For a specific group of Plains Indians, see the group according to the language that the Indians speak or their ancestors spoke, e.g., Cheyenne —97353

—971	Peoples who speak, or whose ancestors spoke, Inuit, Yupik, Aleut languages

Class here peoples who speak, or whose ancestors spoke, Eskimo languages

—971 2	Peoples who speak, or whose ancestors spoke, Inuit (Inuktitut) languages

Including Greenlandic Inuit, Inupiat

Class comprehensive works on peoples who speak, or whose ancestors spoke, Inuit and Yupik languages in —971

—971 24	Eastern Canadian Inuit
—971 4	Peoples who speak, or whose ancestors spoke, Yupik languages

Including peoples who speak, or whose ancestors spoke, Siberian Yupik languages; Yuit

—971 9	Aleut
—972	Peoples who speak, or whose ancestors spoke, Na-Dene languages

Including Chipewyan, Gwich'in, Hupa, Koyukon, Tinne

Class here peoples who speak, or whose ancestors spoke, Athapaskan languages

—972 5	Peoples who speak, or whose ancestors spoke, Apachean languages

Including Jicarilla Apache, Kiowa Apache

Class here Apache

For Navajo, see —9726

See also —97492 for Kiowa

—972 56	Chiricahua Apache and Mescalero Apache
	Subdivisions are added for either or both topics in heading
—972 6	Navajo (Diné)
—972 7	Tlingit
—972 8	Haida
—973	Peoples who speak, or whose ancestors spoke, Algic, Muskogean languages

Including Lumbee, Yurok

Class here peoples who speak, or whose ancestors spoke, Algonquian languages

Subdivisions are added for peoples who speak, or whose ancestors spoke, Algic languages and peoples who speak, or whose ancestors spoke, Muskogean languages together; for peoples who speak, or whose ancestors spoke, Algic languages alone

---

>	—973 1–973 5 Peoples who speak, or whose ancestors spoke, Algonquian languages

Class comprehensive works in —973

—973 1	Peoples who speak, or whose ancestors spoke, Central Algonquian languages

For peoples who speak, or whose ancestors spoke, Cree-Montaignais-Naskapi languages, see —9732; for peoples who speak, or whose ancestors spoke, Ojibwa languages, see —9733

—973 12	Kickapoo
—973 13	Menomini
—973 14	Mesquakie
	Class here Fox
—973 149	Sauk (Sac)
—973 15	Miami
	Including Illinois
—973 16	Potawatomi
—973 17	Shawnee
—973 2	Peoples who speak, or whose ancestors spoke, Cree-Montagnais-Naskapi languages
	Class here Innu
—973 23	Cree

—973 3	Peoples who speak, or whose ancestors spoke, Ojibwa languages
	Including Algonquin
—973 33	Ojibwa
	Class here Chippewa
—973 36	Ottawa
—973 4	Peoples who speak, or whose ancestors spoke, eastern Algonquian languages
	Including Abnaki, Malecite, Passamaquoddy
—973 43	Micmac
—973 44	Mohegan, Montauk, Narragansett, Pequot, Stockbridge
	Subdivisions are added for a combination of two or more topics in heading, for Mohegan alone, for Montauk alone, for Narragansett alone, for Pequot alone
—973 449	Stockbridge
—973 45	Delaware (Lenni Lenape)
	Including Munsee
—973 47	Powhatan
—973 48	Wampanoag
	Including Massachuset
—973 5	Peoples who speak, or whose ancestors spoke, Plains Algonquian languages
—973 52	Blackfoot
	Class here Kainah, Piegan, Siksika
—973 53	Cheyenne
—973 54	Peoples who speak, or whose ancestors spoke, Arapaho languages
	Including Gros Ventre (Atsina)
	Class here Arapaho
—973 8	Peoples who speak, or whose ancestors spoke, Muskogean languages
	Including Koasati, Mikasuki
—973 85	Muskogee (Creek) and Seminole
	Subdivisions are added for Muskogee and Seminole together, for Muskogee alone
—973 859	Seminole
—973 86	Chickasaw

—973 87   Choctaw

—974   **Peoples who speak, or whose ancestors spoke, Penutian, Mayan, Mixe-Zoque, Uto-Aztecan, Kiowa Tanoan languages**

Class here Pueblo Indians

Class a specific group of Pueblo Indians with the group according to the language that the Indians speak or their ancestors spoke, e.g., Zuni —97994

—974 1   **Peoples who speak, or whose ancestors spoke, Penutian languages**

Including Chinook, Maidu

Class Zuni in —97994; class peoples who speak, or whose ancestors spoke, Araucanian languages in —9872; class peoples who speak, or whose ancestors spoke, Uru-Chipaya languages in —989

—974 12   Peoples who speak, or whose ancestors spoke, Plateau Penutian, Tsimshian languages

Including Niska, Umatilla

—974 122   Klamath and Modoc

Subdivisions are added for either or both topics in heading

—974 124   Nez Percé

—974 127   Yakama

—974 128   Tsimshian

—974 13   Peoples who speak, or whose ancestors spoke, Yok-Utian languages

Including Costanoan, Yokuts

—974 133   Miwok

—974 2   **Peoples who speak, or whose ancestors spoke, Mayan languages**

Including Huastec, Kekchí, Mam, Tzutujil

Class here Mayas; peoples who speak, or whose ancestors spoke, Quichean-Mamean, Quichean languages

—974 22   Cakchikel

—974 23   Quiché

—974 27   Peoples who speak, or whose ancestors spoke, Yucatecan languages

Including Itzá, Lacandón, Mopán

Class here Yucatecan Maya

—974 28   Peoples who speak, or whose ancestors spoke, Cholan-Tzeltalan languages

Including Tzeltal

—974 287   Tzotzil

—974 3　　　Peoples who speak, or whose ancestors spoke, Mixe-Zoque languages

—974 5　　　Peoples who speak, or whose ancestors spoke, Uto-Aztecan languages

　　　　　　Including Cahuilla, Luiseño

—974 52　　Peoples who speak, or whose ancestors spoke, Aztecan languages

　　　　　　Class here Nahuas (Aztecs)

—974 54　　Peoples who speak, or whose ancestors spoke, Sonoran languages

　　　　　　For peoples who speak, or whose ancestors spoke, Tepiman languages, see —97455

—974 542　　Yaqui

—974 544　　Huichol

—974 546　　Peoples who speak, or whose ancestors spoke, Tarahumaran languages

　　　　　　Class here Tarahumara

—974 55　　Peoples who speak, or whose ancestors spoke, Tepiman languages

—974 552　　Tohono O'Odham and Akimel O'Odham

　　　　　　Subdivisions are added for Tohono O'Odham and Akimel O'Odham together, for Tohono O'Odham alone

—974 552 9　　Akimel O'Odham (Pima)

—974 57　　Peoples who speak, or whose ancestors spoke, Numic languages

　　　　　　Including Mono

—974 572　　Comanche

—974 574　　Shoshoni

—974 576　　Ute and Southern Paiute

　　　　　　Including Chemehuevi

　　　　　　Subdivisions are added for Ute and Southern Paiute together, for Ute alone

—974 576 9　　Southern Paiute

　　　　　　Class here comprehensive works on Paiute

　　　　　　For Northern Paiute, see —974577

—974 577　　Northern Paiute

　　　　　　Class here Bannock

　　　　　　Class comprehensive works on Paiute in —9745769

—974 58　　Hopi

—974 9	Peoples who speak, or whose ancestors spoke, Kiowa Tanoan languages (Tanoan languages)
—974 92	Kiowa

See also —9725 for Kiowa Apache

—974 94	Tewa
—974 96	Northern Tiwa

Class here Taos, comprehensive works on Northern and Southern Tiwa

For Southern Tiwa, see —97497

—974 97	Southern Tiwa

Class here Isleta

Class comprehensive works on Northern and Southern Tiwa in —97496

—975	Peoples who speak, or whose ancestors spoke, Siouan, Iroquoian, Hokan, Chumash, Yuki languages

Class peoples who speak, or whose ancestors spoke, Keresan languages in —979; class peoples who speak, or whose ancestors spoke, Caddoan languages in —9793

See also —979 for Yuchi

—975 2	Peoples who speak, or whose ancestors spoke, Siouan languages

Including Catawba, Iowa, Oto

—975 22	Mandan
—975 24	Peoples who speak, or whose ancestors spoke, Dakota languages

Including Assiniboine

—975 243	Dakota
—975 244	Lakota (Teton)

Class here Oglala

—975 25	Peoples who speak, or whose ancestors spoke, Dhegiha languages

Including Kansa, Quapaw

—975 253	Omaha and Ponca

Subdivisions are added for Omaha and Ponca together, for Omaha alone

—975 253 9	Ponca
—975 254	Osage

—975 26	Winnebago
	Class here Ho-Chunk
—975 27	Peoples who speak, or whose ancestors spoke, Missouri Valley Siouan languages
—975 272	Crow
—975 274	Hidatsa
—975 5	Peoples who speak, or whose ancestors spoke, Iroquoian languages
	Including Tuscarora
	Class here Iroquois
—975 54	Peoples who speak, or whose ancestors spoke, Five Nations languages
	Including Cayuga, Onondaga
—975 542	Mohawk
—975 543	Oneida
—975 546	Seneca
—975 55	Wyandot
	Class here Huron
—975 57	Cherokee
—975 7	Peoples who speak, or whose ancestors spoke, Hokan languages
	Including Seri
—975 72	Peoples who speak, or whose ancestors spoke, Yuman languages
	Including Diegueño, Maricopa, Quechan (Yuma)
—975 722	Mohave
—975 724	Havasupai, Walapai, Yavapai
	Subdivisions are added for any or all topics in heading
—975 74	Peoples who speak, or whose ancestors spoke, Pomo languages
—975 76	Washo
—975 8	Peoples who speak, or whose ancestors spoke, Chumash languages
—976	Peoples who speak, or whose ancestors spoke, Oto-Manguean languages
	Including Mazatec, Otomí
—976 3	Peoples who speak, or whose ancestors spoke, Mixtecan languages
	Class here Mixtec

—976 8   Peoples who speak, or whose ancestors spoke, Zapotecan languages

         Class here Zapotec

—978   Peoples who speak, or whose ancestors spoke, Chibchan languages of Central America, Misumalpan languages

         Subdivisions are added for peoples who speak, or whose ancestors spoke, Chibchan languages of Central America and peoples who speak, or whose ancestors spoke, Misumalpan languages together; for peoples who speak, or whose ancestors spoke, Chibchan languages of Central America alone

         Class comprehensive works on peoples who speak, or whose ancestors spoke, Chibchan languages in —982

—978 3   San Blas Kuna (San Blas Cuna)

—978 8   Peoples who speak, or whose ancestors spoke, Misumalpan languages

—978 82   Mískito

—979   Peoples who speak, or whose ancestors spoke, other North American languages

         Including peoples who speak, or whose ancestors spoke, Chimakuan, Coahuiltecan, Gulf, Huavean, Keres, Subtiaba-Tlapanec, Totonacan languages; peoples who speak, or whose ancestors spoke, Choco languages of Central America

         Including Cuitlateco, Lenca, Xinca, Yuchi

         Class comprehensive works on peoples who speak, or whose ancestors spoke, Choco languages in —989

         See also —975 for peoples who speak, or whose ancestors spoke, Yuki languages

—979 2   Peoples who speak, or whose ancestors spoke, Arawakan languages of Central America and West Indies

         Including Garífuna (Black Carib)

         Class comprehensive works on peoples who speak, or whose ancestors spoke, Arawakan languages in —9839

         See also —9842 for peoples who speak, or whose ancestors spoke, Carib languages

—979 22   Taino

—979 3   Peoples who speak, or whose ancestors spoke, Caddoan languages

         Including Caddo, Wichita

—979 32   Arikara

—979 33   Pawnee

—979 4   Peoples who speak, or whose ancestors spoke, Salishan languages

—979 43	Peoples who speak, or whose ancestors spoke, Interior Salish languages
	Including Coeur d'Alene (Skitswish), Shuswap, Spokane
—979 435	Kalispel and Pend d'Oreille (Salish)
	Subdivisions are added for either or both topics in heading
—979 5	Peoples who speak, or whose ancestors spoke, Wakashan languages
—979 53	Kwakiutl
—979 54	Makah
—979 55	Nootka
—979 6	Peoples who speak, or whose ancestors spoke, Tarascan languages
	Class here Purépecha (Tarasco)
—979 9	Kutenai and Zuni
—979 92	Kutenai
—979 94	Zuni

—98   **South American native peoples**

Class here peoples who speak, or whose ancestors spoke, South American native languages

Class national groups of modern South America where Spanish is an official language in —688 even if the majority of their population is of South American native origin, e.g., Peruvians as a national group —6885

—982   Peoples who speak, or whose ancestors spoke, Chibchan, Barbacoan languages; Paez

Class Warao in —989; class peoples who speak, or whose ancestors spoke, Yanomam languages in —9892

For peoples who speak, or whose ancestors spoke, Chibchan languages of Central America, see —978

—983   Peoples who speak, or whose ancestors spoke, Quechuan, Aymaran, Tucanoan, Jivaroan, Tupí, Arawakan languages

—983 2   Peoples who speak, or whose ancestors spoke, Quechuan and Aymaran languages

—983 23   Peoples who speak, or whose ancestors spoke, Quechuan (Kechuan) languages

Class here Incas, Quechua (Kechua)

Class peoples who speak, or whose ancestors spoke, Aymaran languages in —98324

—983 24   Peoples who speak, or whose ancestors spoke, Aymaran languages

Class here Aymara

—983 5   Peoples who speak, or whose ancestors spoke, Tucanoan languages

            Including Tucano

—983 7   Peoples who speak, or whose ancestors spoke, Jivaroan languages

            Class Yaruro in —989

—983 72   Shuar

—983 8   Peoples who speak, or whose ancestors spoke, Tupí languages

            Class here peoples who speak, or whose ancestors spoke, Tupí-Guaraní
            languages

—983 82   Peoples who speak, or whose ancestors spoke, languages in subgroups I
            and II of the Tupí-Guaraní family

                Including eastern and western Bolivian Guaraní; Mbyá Guaraní

—983 822   Paraguayan Guaraní

—[983 829]   Tupí (Nhengatu)

                   Relocated to —983832

—983 83   Peoples who speak, or whose ancestors spoke, languages in subgroup III
            of the Tupí-Guaraní family

            Including Tupinambá

—983 832   Tupí (Nhengatu) [*formerly* —983829]

—983 9   Peoples who speak, or whose ancestors spoke, Arawakan languages

            Including Goajiro

            Class here comprehensive works on peoples who speak, or whose
            ancestors spoke, Arawakan languages of South America and peoples
            who speak, or whose ancestors spoke, Arawakan languages of Central
            America and West Indies

            Class peoples who speak, or whose ancestors spoke, Guahiban
            languages in —989

                *For peoples who speak, or whose ancestors spoke, Arawakan
                languages of Central America and West Indies, see —9792*

—984   Peoples who speak, or whose ancestors spoke, Carib, Macro-Gê,
            Nambiquaran, Panoan languages

            Class peoples who speak, or whose ancestors spoke, Mataco-Guaicuru
            languages in —987; class peoples who speak, or whose ancestors spoke,
            Tacanan, Witotoan languages in —989

—984 2   Peoples who speak, or whose ancestors spoke, Carib languages

                See also —9792 for Island Carib, Black Carib

—984 22   Carib (Galibi)

—987   Peoples who speak, or whose ancestors spoke, Araucanian, Alacalufan, Chon, Lule-Vilela, Mataco-Guaicuru languages

        Including Ona

—987 2   Peoples who speak, or whose ancestors spoke, Araucanian languages

        Class here Mapudungu (Mapuche)

—989   Peoples who speak, or whose ancestors spoke, other South American languages

        Including peoples who speak, or whose ancestors spoke, Arauan, Arutani-Sape, Cahuapanan, Chapacura-Wanham, Choco, Guahiban, Harakmbet, Katukinan, Maku, Mascoian, Mosetenan, Mura, Peba-Yaguan, Salivan, Tacanan, Uru-Chipaya, Witotoan, Zamucoan, Zaparoan languages

        Including Warao, Yaruro

           For peoples who speak, or whose ancestors spoke, Choco languages of Central America, see —979

—989 2   Peoples who speak, or whose ancestors spoke, Yanomam languages

        Class here Yanomamo

—99   **Papuans; Aboriginal Australians and Tasmanians; Malayo-Polynesian and related peoples; miscellaneous peoples**

—991   Papuans; Aboriginal Australians and Tasmanians

—[991 1]   Andamanese, Semang, Aeta

        Andamanese relocated to —959; Semang relocated to —9593; Aeta relocated to —9921

—991 2   Papuans

        Class here peoples who speak, or whose ancestors spoke, Papuan languages; Papua New Guineans as a national group

        Class peoples of New Guinea who speak, or whose ancestors spoke, eastern Malayo-Polynesian languages in —995

—991 5   Aboriginal Australians and Tasmanians

        Subdivisions are added for Aboriginal Australians and Tasmanians together, for Aboriginal Australians alone

           For peoples of Australia who speak, or whose ancestors spoke, Papuan languages, see —9912

—991 59   Aboriginal Tasmanians

—992   Malayo-Polynesian and related peoples

                  Class here peoples who speak, or whose ancestors spoke,
                  Malayo-Polynesian languages; comprehensive works on peoples who
                  speak, or whose ancestors spoke, Austronesian languages

                  For Malagasy, see —993; for peoples who speak, or whose ancestors
                  spoke, eastern Malayo-Polynesian languages, see —995

—992 1   Filipinos

                  Including Aeta [*formerly* —9911]

                  Class here people of the Philippines as a national group

                  For Philippine citizens of non-Filipino ethnic groups, see the ethnic
                  group, e.g., Philippine citizens of Chinese origin —9510599

—992 2   Peoples who speak, or whose ancestors spoke, Malayo-Polynesian
                  languages of Indonesia, Malaysia, Singapore, Brunei, East Timor;
                  peoples who speak, or whose ancestors spoke, Chamic languages

                  Former heading: Peoples who speak, or whose ancestors spoke,
                  Indonesian and Chamic languages

                  Including peoples who speak, or whose ancestors spoke, central
                  Malayo-Polynesian languages; Jarai, Rhade (Rade)

                  Class here people of Indonesia as a national group; peoples who speak,
                  or whose ancestors spoke, local Malay languages

                  Class comprehensive works on Montagnards of Vietnam in —9593

                  For Formosan native peoples, see —9925; for peoples who speak, or
                  whose ancestors spoke, Malay (Bahasa Malaysia, standard Malay)
                  or other Malayo-Polynesian languages of Peninsular Malaysia, and
                  Malaysians as a national group, see —9928

                  See also —9912 for peoples who speak, or whose ancestors spoke,
                  non-Austronesian languages of New Guinea; also —995 for peoples
                  who speak, or whose ancestors spoke, eastern Malayo-Polynesian
                  languages

—992 22   People who speak, or whose ancestors spoke, Javanese

—992 23   Peoples who speak, or whose ancestors spoke, other Malayo-Polynesian
                  languages of Java and Bali

                  Class people who speak, or whose ancestors spoke, Indonesian
                  (Bahasa Indonesia) in —9922

—992 232   Sundanese (People who speak, or whose ancestors spoke, Sunda)

—992 234   Madurese (People who speak, or whose ancestors spoke, Madura)

—992 238   Balinese (People who speak, or whose ancestors spoke, Bali)

—992 24   Peoples who speak, or whose ancestors spoke, Malayo-Polynesian
                  languages of Sumatra

—992 242   Aceh (Achinese)

—992 244	Minangkabau
—992 246	Peoples who speak, or whose ancestors spoke, Batak languages
—992 246 2	Toba Batak
—992 246 6	Dairi Batak (Pakpak)
—992 248	Lampung
—992 25	Peoples who speak, or whose ancestors spoke, Malayo-Polynesian languages of Kalimantan, Sarawak, Sabah, Brunei
—992 256	Banjar (Banjarese)
—992 26	Peoples who speak, or whose ancestors spoke, Malayo-Polynesian languages of Celebes (Sulawesi)
—992 262	Bugis (Buginese)
—992 264	Makasar

—992 5　　　　Formosan native peoples

　　　　　　　Including Ami, Atayal, Bunun, Paiwan, Thao, Yami

　　　　　　　Class here peoples who speak, or whose ancestors spoke, Taiwan (Formosan) languages

　　　　　　　　See also —951 for peoples who speak, or whose ancestors spoke, Taiwanese dialect of Chinese

—992 8　　　　Malays

　　　　　　　Including Jakun, Kanaq, Seletar, Temuan, other peoples who speak, or whose ancestors spoke, Malayo-Polynesian languages of Peninsular Malaysia other than Malay (Bahasa Malaysia, Standard Malay)

　　　　　　　Class here people who speak, or whose ancestors spoke, Malay (Bahasa Malaysia, standard Malay); people of Malaysia as a national group

　　　　　　　　For citizens of Malaysia belonging to other ethnic groups, see the ethnic group, e.g., Chinese —9510595

　　　　　　　　See also —9593 for peoples who speak, or whose ancestors spoke, Semang, Senoic, other Aslian languages

—993　　　　Malagasy

—994　　　　Peoples who speak, or whose ancestors spoke, Polynesian languages

　　　　　　　Class here national groups of Polynesia; former citizens and descendants of citizens of these jurisdictions

　　　　　　　Add to base number —994 the numbers following —994 in notation 9942–9948 from Table 6, e.g., Tahitians —99444; then add further as instructed at beginning of Table 5 , e.g., Tahitians in New Zealand —99444093

　　　　　　　Comprehensive works on Pacific Islanders relocated to —995

—995   Peoples who speak, or whose ancestors spoke, eastern Malayo-Polynesian languages

> Class here comprehensive works on Pacific Islanders [*formerly* —994]; national groups of Melanesia

>> *For Papua New Guineans as a national group and peoples who speak, or whose ancestors spoke, Papuan languages, see —9912; for national groups of Polynesia and peoples who speak, or whose ancestors spoke, Polynesian languages, see —994*

—995 2   Peoples who speak, or whose ancestors spoke, Micronesian languages

> Including Chamorro, Palauans

> Class here national groups of Micronesia

—995 9   Fijians

> Class here peoples who speak, or whose ancestors spoke, eastern Fijian languages; people who speak, or whose ancestors spoke, standard Fijian; Fijians as a national group

>> *For Fijian citizens of south Asian origin, see —91409611*

—999   Miscellaneous peoples

> Limited to peoples provided for below

—999 2   Basques

—999 3   Elamites

—999 4   Etruscans

—999 5   Sumerians

—999 6   Georgians, Ingush, Chechen, Circassians, related peoples

> Class here peoples who speak, or whose ancestors spoke, Caucasian (Caucasic) languages

> Add to base number —9996 the numbers following —9996 in notation 99962–99969 from Table 6, e.g., Georgians —99969; then add further as instructed at beginning of Table 5 , e.g., Georgians in Canada —99969071

Table 6. Languages

The following notation is never used alone, but may be used with those numbers from the schedules and other tables to which the classifier is instructed to add notation from Table 6, e.g., translations of the Bible (220.5) into Dutch (—3931 in this table): 220.53931; regions (notation 175 from Table 2) where Spanish language (—61 in this table) predominates: Table 2 notation 17561. When adding to a number from the schedules, always insert a decimal point between the third and fourth digits of the complete number

Unless there is specific provision for the old or middle form of a modern language, class these forms with the modern language, e.g., Old High German —31, but Old English —29

Unless there is specific provision for a dialect of a language, class the dialect with the language, e.g., American English dialects —21, but Swiss-German dialect —35

Unless there is a specific provision for a pidgin, creole, or mixed language, class it with the source language from which more of its vocabulary comes than from its other source language(s), e.g., Crioulo language —69, but Papiamento —68. If in doubt, prefer the language coming last in Table 6, e.g., Michif —97323 (*not* —41)

The numbers in this table do not necessarily correspond exactly to the numbers used for individual languages in 420–490 and in 810–890. For example, although the base number for English in 420–490 is 42, the number for English in Table 6 is —21, not —2

(Option A: To give local emphasis and a shorter number to a specific language, place it first by use of a letter or other symbol, e.g., Arabic language —A [preceding —1]. Option B is described at —1)

See Manual at Table 6

SUMMARY

—1	**Indo-European languages**
—2	**English and Old English (Anglo-Saxon)**
—3	**Germanic languages**
—4	**Romance languages**
—5	**Italian, Dalmatian, Romanian, Rhaetian, Sardinian, Corsican**
—6	**Spanish, Portuguese, Galician**
—7	**Italic languages**
—8	**Hellenic languages**
—9	**Other languages**

—1   **Indo-European languages**

Including Nostratic hypothesis

> *For specific Indo-European languages other than east Indo-European languages and Celtic languages, see —2–8; for east Indo-European languages and Celtic languages, see —91*

(Option B: To give local emphasis and a shorter number to a specific language, e.g., Ukrainian, class it in this number, and class Indo-European languages in —91. Option A is described in the introduction to Table 6)

>   **—2–8 Specific Indo-European languages other than east Indo-European languages and Celtic languages**

Class comprehensive works in —1

—2   **English and Old English (Anglo-Saxon)**

—21   **English**

Including dialects

Class Old English in —29

—217   English-based pidgins and creoles

Including Bislama, Krio, Sea Islands Creole (Gullah), Tok Pisin

—219   Middle English, 1100–1500

—29   **Old English (Anglo-Saxon)**

> *See also —219 for Middle English*

—3   **Germanic languages**

> *For English and Old English, see —2*

—31   **German**

Class here comprehensive works on dialects of German

> *For specific dialects of German, see —32–38*

> *See also —394 for Low German*

>   **—32–38 German dialects**

Class comprehensive works in —31

> *For Low German, see —394*

—32   **Franconian dialect**

—33   **Swabian dialect**

—34   **Alsatian dialect**

—35	**Swiss-German dialect**
—38	**Pennsylvania Dutch (Pennsylvania German)**
—39	**Other Germanic languages**
—391	Yiddish

>	**—392–394 Low Germanic languages**
	Class here West Germanic languages
	Class comprehensive works in —39
—392	Frisian
—393	Netherlandish languages
—393 1	Dutch
	Including Old Low Franconian
	Class here Flemish
—393 6	Afrikaans
—394	Low German (Plattdeutsch)
	Including Old Saxon
—395	North Germanic languages (Nordic languages)

Including proto-Nordic language

Class here comprehensive works on east Scandinavian languages, comprehensive works on west Scandinavian languages, comprehensive works on modern west Scandinavian languages; comprehensive works on languages in the Nordic countries

For specific North Germanic languages, see —396–398; for Finnish, see —94541; for Sámi languages, see —9457

>	**—396–398 Specific North Germanic languages**
	Class comprehensive works in —395
—396	Old Norse (Old Icelandic), Icelandic, Faroese
	Class comprehensive works on west Scandinavian languages in —395
—396 1	Old Norse (Old Icelandic)
—396 9	Icelandic and Faroese
—396 91	Icelandic
—396 99	Faroese
—397	Swedish
—398	Danish and Norwegian

—398 1   Danish

                Class Dano-Norwegian in —3982

—398 2   Norwegian

                Class here Bokmål, Dano-Norwegian, Riksmål; New Norse, Landsmål

—399   East Germanic languages

                Including Burgundian, Gothic, Vandalic

—4   Romance languages

                Class comprehensive works on Italic languages in —7

                For Italian, Dalmatian, Romanian, Rhaetian, Sardinian, Corsican, see —5; for Spanish, Portuguese, Galician, see —6

—41   French

                Class Franco-Provençal in —49; class Occitan in —491

—417   French-based pidgins and creoles

—49   Occitan, Catalan, Franco-Provençal

—491   Occitan

                Including Auvergnat, Gascon, Languedocien, Limousin dialects; Provençal (dialect of Occitan)

                Class here Langue d'oc; Provençal (Occitan)

                See also —49 for Franco-Provençal

—499   Catalan

—5   Italian, Dalmatian, Romanian, Rhaetian, Sardinian, Corsican

                Class comprehensive works on Romance languages in —4; class comprehensive works on Italic languages in —7

—51   Italian

—[56]   Sardinian

                Relocated to —59982

—57   Dalmatian

                Class here Vegliote dialect

—59   Romanian, Rhaetian, Sardinian, Corsican

—591   Romanian

—599   Rhaetian languages; Sardinian, Corsican

—599 2   Friulian language

—599 4	Ladin language
	See also —67 for Judeo-Spanish (Ladino)
—599 6	Romansch language
—599 8	Sardinian and Corsican
—599 82	Sardinian [*formerly* —56]
—599 84	Corsican

—6   Spanish, Portuguese, Galician

Class comprehensive works on Romance languages in —4

—61   Spanish

Including Spanish-based pidgins and creoles

For Judeo-Spanish (Ladino), see —67; for Papiamento, see —68

—67   Judeo-Spanish (Ladino)

See also —5994 for Ladin

—68   Papiamento

—69   Portuguese and Galician

Standard subdivisions are added for Portuguese and Galician together, for Portuguese alone

Including Portuguese-based pidgins and creoles, e.g., Crioulo

For Papiamento, see —68

—699	Galician
	Class here Gallegan

—7   Italic languages

For Romance languages, see —4

—71   Latin

Class comprehensive works on Latin and Greek in —8

—79   Other Italic languages

—794	Latinian languages other than Latin
	Including Faliscan, Lanuvian, Praenestian, Venetic
—797	Sabellian languages
	Including Aequian, Marrucinian, Marsian, Paelignian, Sabine, Vestinian, Volscian
—799	Osco-Umbrian languages
	Including Oscan, Umbrian

—8   **Hellenic languages**

> Class here comprehensive works on classical (Greek and Latin) languages
>
> *For Latin, see —71*

—81   **Classical Greek**

—87   **Preclassical and postclassical Greek**

> Including Mycenaean Greek, Linear B; Biblical Greek, Koine (Hellenistic Greek); Byzantine Greek
>
> *See also —926 for Linear A*

—89   **Modern Greek**

> Including Demotic, Katharevusa

—9   **Other languages**

SUMMARY

—91	**East Indo-European and Celtic languages**
—92	**Afro-Asiatic languages**
—93	**Non-Semitic Afro-Asiatic languages**
—94	**Altaic, Uralic, Hyperborean, Dravidian languages, miscellaneous languages of south Asia**
—95	**Languages of east and southeast Asia**
—96	**African languages**
—97	**North American native languages**
—98	**South American native languages**
—99	**Non-Austronesian languages of Oceania, Austronesian languages, miscellaneous languages**

—91   **East Indo-European and Celtic languages**

> Class comprehensive works on Indo-European languages in —1

SUMMARY

—911	**Indo-Iranian languages**
—912	**Sanskrit**
—913	**Middle Indo-Aryan languages**
—914	**Modern Indo-Aryan languages**
—915	**Iranian languages**
—916	**Celtic languages**
—917	**East Slavic languages**
—918	**Slavic (Slavonic) languages**
—919	**Baltic and other Indo-European languages**

—911   Indo-Iranian languages

> Class here comprehensive works on languages of south Asia
>
> *For Indo-Aryan languages, see —912–914; for Iranian languages, see —915; for Dravidian languages and miscellaneous languages of south Asia, see —948; for languages of south Asia closely related to languages of east and southeast Asia, see —95; for Andamanese languages, see —959*

>	—912–914 Indo-Aryan languages
	Class comprehensive works in —911
—912	Sanskrit
—912 9	Vedic (Old Indo-Aryan)
—913	Middle Indo-Aryan languages
	Former heading: Middle Indic languages
	Class here comprehensive works on Prakrit languages
	For modern Prakrit languages, see —914
—913 7	Pali
—914	Modern Indo-Aryan languages
	Former heading: Modern Indic languages
	Class here modern Prakrit languages
	Class comprehensive works on Prakrit languages in —913
—914 1	Sindhi and Lahnda
—914 11	Sindhi
—914 19	Lahnda
	Class here Western Panjabi
	Class Eastern Panjabi in —9142
—914 2	Panjabi
	Class here Eastern Panjabi
	Class Western Panjabi in —91419
—914 3	Western Hindi languages
	Class here comprehensive works on Hindi languages
	For languages of east central zone of Indo-Aryan languages (Eastern Hindi languages), see —91492
—914 31	Standard Hindi
—914 39	Urdu
—914 4	Bengali
	Class here comprehensive works on Bengali and Assamese
	For Assamese, see —91451
—914 5	Assamese, Bihari, Oriya
—914 51	Assamese

—914 54	Bihari
	Including Bhojpuri, Magahi, Maithili
—914 56	Oriya
—914 6	Marathi and Konkani
—914 61	Marathi
—914 69	Konkani
—914 7	Gujarati, Bhili, Rajasthani
—914 71	Gujarati
—914 79	Rajasthani
	Including Jaipuri, Marwari
—914 8	Sinhalese-Maldivian languages
	Class here Sinhalese (Sinhala)
—914 89	Divehi (Maldivian)
—914 9	Other Indo-Aryan languages
	Including Nuristani (Kafiri)

See also —948 for Dravidian languages; also —954 for Tibeto-Burman languages; also —9595 for Munda languages

—914 92	Languages of east central zone of Indo-Aryan languages (Eastern Hindi languages)

         Including Awadhi, Bagheli, Chattisgarhi, Fijian Hindustani (Fiji Hindi)

         Class comprehensive works on Hindi languages in —9143

—914 95	Nepali
—914 96	Pahari languages
	Including Garhwali
	Class here languages of northern zone of Indo-Aryan languages

         For Nepali, see —91495

—914 97	Romani
—914 99	Dardic (Pisacha) languages
	Including Kashmiri, Khowar, Kohistani, Shina
—915	Iranian languages
—915 1	Old Persian
	Class here ancient west Iranian languages

         See also —9152 for Avestan language

—915 2	Avestan
	Class here ancient east Iranian languages
—915 3	Middle Iranian languages
	Including Khotanese (Saka), Pahlavi (Middle Persian), Sogdian
—915 5	Modern Persian (Farsi)
	Class Dari in —9156; class Tajik in —9157
—915 6	Dari
—915 7	Tajik
—915 9	Other modern Iranian languages
	Including Pamir languages; Osetin (Ossetic)
—915 93	Pashto (Afghan)
—915 97	Kurdish languages
	Including central and southern Kurdish
	Class here Kurdish (Kurmanji, northern Kurdish)
—915 98	Baluchi
—916	Celtic languages
	Including Gaulish
—916 2	Irish Gaelic
—916 3	Scottish Gaelic
—916 4	Manx
—916 6	Welsh (Cymric)
—916 7	Cornish
—916 8	Breton
—917	East Slavic languages
	Class comprehensive works on Slavic (Slavonic) languages in —918
—917 1	Russian
—917 9	Ukrainian and Belarusian
—917 91	Ukrainian
—917 99	Belarusian
—918	Slavic (Slavonic) languages
	Including Common Slavic
	Class here comprehensive works on Balto-Slavic languages
	For East Slavic languages, see —917; for Baltic languages, see —919

—918 1	South Slavic languages

> *For Serbian, see —9182; for Croatian and Bosnian, see —9183; for Slovenian, see —9184*

—918 11	Bulgarian
—918 17	Old Bulgarian (Church Slavic)
—918 19	Macedonian
—918 2	Serbian

Class here Serbo-Croatian (languages of Serbs, Croats, and Bosnians treated together as a single language)

Croatian relocated to —9183; Bosnian relocated to —91839

—918 3	Croatian [*formerly* —9182] and Bosnian

Standard subdivisions are added for Croatian and Bosnian together, for Croatian alone

—918 39	Bosnian [*formerly* —9182]
—918 4	Slovenian
—918 5	West Slavic languages

Including Kashubian

> *For Czech, see —9186; for Slovak, see —9187; for Wendish, see —9188; for Polabian, see —9189*

—918 51	Polish
—918 6	Czech

Including Moravian dialects

—918 7	Slovak
—918 8	Wendish (Lusatian, Sorbian)
—918 9	Polabian
—919	Baltic and other Indo-European languages

Standard subdivisions are added for Baltic and other Indo-European languages together, for Baltic languages alone

---

>	—919 1–919 3 Baltic languages

Class comprehensive works in —919

—919 1	Old Prussian
—919 2	Lithuanian
—919 3	Latvian (Lettish)
—919 9	Other Indo-European languages
—919 91	Albanian

—919 92		Armenian
—919 93		Illyrian and Thraco-Phrygian languages

          Including Ligurian, Messapian, Phrygian, Thracian

—919 94   Tocharian

—919 98   Anatolian languages

          Including Luwian, Lycian, Lydian, Palaic

          Class here Hittite

          Class a non-Indo-European language spoken in ancient Anatolia with the language, e.g., Hurrian —999

—92   **Afro-Asiatic languages**

         Class here Semitic languages

          For non-Semitic Afro-Asiatic languages, see —93

—921   East Semitic languages

         Including Assyrian, Babylonian

         Class here Akkadian (Assyro-Babylonian)

          For Eblaite, see —926

          See also —9995 for Sumerian

\>   —922–929   West Semitic languages

         Class comprehensive works in —92

—922   Aramaic languages

          For Eastern Aramaic languages, see —923

—922 9   Western Aramaic languages

          Including Biblical Aramaic (Chaldee) and Samaritan

—923   Eastern Aramaic languages

         Class here Syriac

—924   Hebrew

—926   Canaanite languages

         Including Ammonite, Eblaite, Moabite, Phoenician; Linear A and its language

         Class here comprehensive works on Canaanitic languages

          For Hebrew, see —924

          See also —87 for Linear B

          See Manual at T6—926

—926 7	Ugaritic
—927	Arabic and Maltese

Standard subdivisions are added for Arabic and Maltese together, for Arabic alone

Including Judeo-Arabic

Class here classical Arabic

See also —929 for South Arabian languages

—927 9	Maltese
—928	Ethiopian languages

Including Gurage, Harari

Class here comprehensive works on South Semitic languages

For South Arabian languages, see —929

—928 1	Ge'ez
—928 2	Tigré
—928 3	Tigrinya (Tigrigna)
—928 7	Amharic
—929	South Arabian languages

Including Mahri, Sokotri

Class comprehensive works on South Semitic languages in —928

See also —927 for Arabic

—93	**Non-Semitic Afro-Asiatic languages**
—931	Egyptian

Including Demotic Egyptian

For Coptic, see —932

—932	Coptic
—933	Berber languages

Including Rif, Siwa

—933 3	Tamazight
—933 4	Kabyle
—933 8	Tamashek
—935	Cushitic and Omotic languages

Standard subdivisions are added for Cushitic and Omotic languages together, for Cushitic languages alone

Including Afar, Beja

—935 4	Somali
—935 5	Oromo
—935 9	Omotic languages
—937	Chadic languages
	Including Angas
—937 2	Hausa

—94   **Altaic, Uralic, Hyperborean, Dravidian languages, miscellaneous languages of south Asia**

SUMMARY

—941	Tungusic languages
—942	Mongolian languages
—943	Turkic languages
—944	Samoyedic languages
—945	Finno-Ugric languages
—946	Hyperborean (Paleosiberian) languages
—948	Dravidian languages and miscellaneous languages of south Asia

---

>   —941–943   Altaic languages

       Class comprehensive works in —94

         For Ainu, see —946; for Japanese, see —956; for Korean, see —957

—941	Tungusic languages
	Including Even (Lamut), Evenki (Tungus), Manchu, Nanai (Goldi)
—942	Mongolian languages
	Including Buriat (Buryat), Daur, Kalmyk-Oirat, Tu
—942 3	Mongolian proper
	Class here Halh Mongolian (Khalkha Mongolian)
—943	Turkic languages
—943 1	Old Turkic and Chuvash
—943 15	Chuvash
—943 2	Eastern Turkic languages

         For northeast Turkic languages, see —9433; for southern Turkic languages, see —9436

—943 23	Uighur
—943 25	Uzbek

—943 3   Northern Turkic languages

           Including Tuva-Altai languages; Dolgan

           Class here northeast Turkic languages

           Class Old Turkic in —9431

             For eastern Turkic languages, see —9432

—943 32   Yakut

             Use of this number for Dolgan discontinued; class in —9433

—943 4   Central Turkic languages

           Including Kara-Kalpak, Nogai

—943 45   Kazakh

—943 47   Kyrgyz

—943 5   Turkish (Osmanli)

           Class here Ottoman Turkish

—943 6   Southern Turkic languages

           Including Gagauz, Khalaj, Salar

           Class here southwest Turkic languages

             For Turkish, see —9435; for western Turkic languages, see —9438

—943 61   Azerbaijani

—943 64   Turkmen

             Including Chagatai

—943 8   Western Turkic languages

           Including Bashkir, Karachay-Balkar, Karaim

           Class here northwest Turkic languages

             For northern Turkic languages, see —9433; for Kara-Kalpak, Nogai, see —9434; for Kazakh, see —94345; for Kyrgyz, see —94347

—943 87   Tatar

           Class here comprehensive works on Tatar languages

             For Crimean Tatar, see —94388

—943 88   Crimean Tatar

—944   Samoyedic languages

           Including Nganasan, Ostyak Samoyed, Yenisei Samoyed (Enets), Yurak Samoyed (Nenets)

             See also —9451 for Khanty (Ostyak); also —946 for Ket (Yenisei Ostyak)

—945   Finno-Ugric languages

Class here comprehensive works on Uralic languages, on Uralic and Yukaghir languages

For Samoyedic languages, see —944; for Yukaghir languages, see —946

—945 1   Ugric languages

Including Khanty (Ostyak), Vogul

See also —944 for Ostyak Samoyed; also —946 for Ket (Yenisei Ostyak)

—945 11   Hungarian (Magyar)

—945 3   Permic languages

Including Votyak (Udmurt), Zyrian (Komi)

—945 4   Finnic languages

Including Karelian, Kven Finnish, Livonian, Tornedalen Finnish, Veps

For Permian languages, see —9453; for Middle Volga languages, see —9456; for Sámi languages, see —9457

—945 41   Finnish (Suomi)

Class Kven Finnish, Tornedalen Finnish in —9454

—945 45   Estonian

—[945 5]   Sámi (Saami) languages

Relocated to —9457

—945 6   Middle Volga languages

Including Mari, Mordvin

—945 7   Sámi (Saami) languages [*formerly* —9455]

—945 72   Southern group of western Sámi languages

Including Ume Sámi

Class here comprehensive works on western Sámi languages

For northern group of western Sámi languages, see —94574

—945 722   South Sámi

—945 74   Northern group of western Sámi languages

Including Pite Sámi

—945 743   Lule Sámi

—945 745   North Sámi

—945 76   Eastern Sámi languages

Including Akkala Sámi, Inari Sámi, Kildin Sámi, Skolt Sámi, Ter Sámi

—946	Hyperborean (Paleosiberian) languages

Including Chukotko-Kamchatkan (Luorawetlin), Yukaghir languages; Ainu, Nivkh (Gilyak), Ket (Yenisei Ostyak)

Class comprehensive works on the Uralic and Yukaghir languages in —945

See also —944 for Ostyak Samoyed, Yenisei Samoyed; also —9451 for Ostyak; also —9714 for Yupik languages; also —9719 for Aleut language

—948	Dravidian languages and miscellaneous languages of south Asia

Standard subdivisions are added for Dravidian languages and miscellaneous languages of south Asia together, for Dravidian languages alone

—948 1	South Dravidian languages

Including Kota, Toda

Class here Dravida group

—948 11	Tamil
—948 12	Malayalam
—948 14	Kannada (Kanarese)
—948 2	Central Dravidian languages
—948 23	Gondi
—948 24	Kui (Khond, Kandh)
—948 27	Telugu
—948 3	North Dravidian languages

Including Kurux (Kurukh, Oraon), Sauria Paharia (Malto)

Class here Brahui

—948 9	Miscellaneous languages of south Asia

Only those languages provided for below

Including Nihali

Class languages of south Asia closely related to languages of east and southeast Asia in —95; class Andamanese languages in —959; class Indo-Iranian languages of south Asia and comprehensive works on languages of south Asia in —911

—948 92	Burushaski
—948 99	Language of Indus script

—95   **Languages of east and southeast Asia**

Including Karen

Here are classed languages of south Asia closely related to languages of east and southeast Asia

Class here Sino-Tibetan languages

For Austronesian languages of east and southeast Asia, see —992

—951   Chinese

—951 1   Mandarin (Putonghua)

Class here Beijing dialect

—951 7   Chinese dialects

Including Gan, Hakka, Min, Wu, Xiang, Yue (Cantonese) dialects

For Beijing, Mandarin dialects, see —9511

—954   Tibeto-Burman languages

Including Baric, Bodish, Loloish languages

Class Karen in —95

For Burmese, see —958

—954 1   Tibetan

—954 9   Eastern Himalayan languages

Including Chepang, Limbu, Magari, Sunwar; Newari

Class here Kiranti languages, Mahakiranti languages

See also —91495 for Nepali

—956   Japanese

—957   Korean

—958   Burmese

—959   Miscellaneous languages of southeast Asia; Munda languages

Only those languages provided for below

Including Andamanese languages, Kadai languages, Kam-Sui languages

Class here Daic languages

Class Austroasiatic languages in —9593

For Austronesian languages, see —992

—959 1   Tai languages

—959 11   Thai (Siamese)

—959 19		Other Tai languages

Including Shan

For Viet-Muong languages, see —9592

—959 191		Lao
—959 2	Viet-Muong languages	
—959 22		Vietnamese
—959 3	Austroasiatic languages	

Including Semang, Senoic languages; Khasi, Mon, Sedang, Srê

Class here Mon-Khmer languages

For Viet-Muong languages, see —9592; for Munda languages, see —9595

—959 32		Khmer (Cambodian)
—959 5	Munda languages	

Including Gadaba, Ho, Mundari, Santali

—959 7	Hmong-Mien (Miao-Yao) languages	
—959 72		Hmong (Miao)
—959 78		Yao
—96	**African languages**	

Class an African creole having a non-African primary source language with the source language, e.g., Krio —217

For Afrikaans, see —3936; for Ethiopian languages, see —928; for non-Semitic Afro-Asiatic languages, see —93; for Malagasy, see —993

SUMMARY

—961	**Khoisan languages**
—963	**Niger-Congo languages**
—965	**Nilo-Saharan languages**

—961	Khoisan languages

Including Khoikhoi, San

—963	Niger-Congo languages

Including Ijoid, Kordofanian languages; Dogon

SUMMARY

—963 2	**West Atlantic languages**
—963 3	**Igboid, Defoid, Edoid, Idomoid, Nupoid, Akpes, Oko, Ukaan languages; Kwa languages; Kru languages**
—963 4	**Mande languages**
—963 5	**Gur (Voltaic) languages**
—963 6	**Benue-Congo and Adamawa-Ubangi languages**
—963 9	**Bantu languages**

—963 2	West Atlantic languages
—963 21	Senegambian languages
	Former heading: Senegal group
	Including Serer (Serer-Sine)
	For Fula, see —96322
—963 214	Wolof
—963 22	Fula (Fulani)
—963 3	Igboid, Defoid, Edoid, Idomoid, Nupoid, Akpes, Oko, Ukaan languages; Kwa languages; Kru languages
	Class comprehensive works on Benue-Congo languages in —9636
—963 32	Ibo (Igbo)
—963 33	Yoruboid languages
	Class here Yoruba
—963 37	Kwa languages
	Including Adangme
	For Tano (Volta-Comoe) languages, see —96338
—963 374	Ewe
	Use of this number for Ewe group discontinued; class in —96337
—963 378	Gã
—963 38	Tano (Volta-Comoe) languages
	Including Anyi, Baoulé, Nzima
—963 385	Akan
	Class here Fante, Twi
	Use of this number for central Tano subgroup discontinued; class in —96338
—963 4	Mande languages
—963 45	Manding-Mokole languages
	Class here Mandekan languages
—963 452	Bambara
—963 48	Mende-Bandi languages
	Including Bandi (Gbandi)
	Class here Mende
—963 5	Gur (Voltaic) languages
	Including Dagomba, Moré, Senufo
	Class Dogon in —963

—963 6	Benue-Congo and Adamawa-Ubangi languages

Standard subdivisions are added for Benue-Congo and Adamawa-Ubangi languages together, for Benue-Congo languages alone

Including Bamileke

Class here Bantoid languages

Class Mbam languages (from zone A) in —96396

> *For Igboid, Defoid, Edoid, Idomoid, Nupoid, Akpes, Oko, Ukaan languages, see —9633; for Bantu languages, see —9639*

—963 61	Adamawa-Ubangi languages

Including Gbaya, Zande

—963 616	Sango
—963 64	Cross River languages

Including Ibibio

—963 642	Efik
—963 9	Bantu languages

Bantu proper (Narrow Bantu)

> *See also —9636 for Bantoid languages other than Bantu proper*

> *See Manual at T6—9639*

—963 91	Central Bantu languages

Including Bena-Kinga, Gogo, Pogoro, Shambala, Zigula-Zaramo groups (from zone G); Bisa-Lamba, Lenje-Tonga, Nyakyusa, Nyika-Safwa groups (from zone M); Manda, Senga-Sena, Tumbuka groups (from zone N)

Class here central eastern Bantu languages

> *For Swahili group, see —96392; for central western Bantu languages, see —96393*

Fipa-Mambwe languages relocated to —96394

—963 915	Bemba group

Class here Bemba

Bwile relocated to —96393

—963 918	Nyanja group

Class here Nyanja, Chichewa (Chewa)

—963 92	Swahili group

Class here Swahili

—963 93	Central western Bantu languages	—963 9
	Including Bwile [*formerly* —963915]; Hu zone H); Holu, Mbala, Salampasu-Ndemb Kaonde, Luba, Nkoya, Songye groups (fro	—963 9
	Class Chokwe-Luchazi, Diriku, Kwangwa,	—963 9
—963 931	Kongo group	
	Class here Kongo (Koongo)	—963 9
—963 932	Mbundu group	
	Limited to zone H	
	Class here Mbundu (Kimbundu)	
—963 94	Northern Bantu languages	
	Including Fipa-Mambwe languages [*formerly* Bira-Huku, Enya, Lega-Kalanga, Nyanga grou Nyilamba-Langi, Sukuma-Nyamwezi, Tongwe Konzo, Shi-Havu groups (from zone J)	—963
	Class here northeastern Bantu languages	—963
	For north northeastern Bantu languages, see northwestern Bantu languages, see —96396	—963
—963 946	Rwanda-Rundi group	
—963 946 1	Rwanda (Kinyarwanda)	—96
—963 946 5	Rundi	
—963 95	North northeastern Bantu languages	—9
	Including Chaga, Kuria, Nyika groups (from zone Masaba-Luyia groups (from zone J)	—9
	Class Konzo, Shi-Havu groups in —96394	—9
—963 953	Kikuyu-Kamba group	
	For Kikuyu, see —963954	—
—963 954	Kikuyu	
—963 956	Nyoro-Ganda group	—
	Including Chiga, Nyankore	
	For Ganda (Luganda), see —963957	
—963 957	Ganda (Luganda)	
—963 96	Northwestern Bantu languages	—
	Including Bafia, Basaa, Bube-Benga, Kako, Lundu-Bal Makaa-Njem, Mbam (Sanaga, West, Yambasa), Yaunde groups (from zone A); Kele, Mbere, Myene, Njebi, Sira, Tsogo, Yanzi groups (zone B); Bushong, Kele, Mbosi, N Ngando, Ngombe, Ngundi, Tetela groups (from zone C)	

2	Duala group
	Class here Duala
8	Bangi-Ntomba group
8 6	Lingala languages
	Class here Lingala
7	Southern Bantu languages

Including Makua, Matumbi, Yao groups (zone P); Chopi group (from zone S)

Class here southeastern Bantu languages

For Nguni group, see —96398; for southwestern Bantu languages, Lozi, see —96399

975	Shona group
	Class here Shona
976	Venda (Tshivenda)
977	Sotho Tswana group
	Class here Sotho languages
	Class Lozi in —96399
977 1	Northern Sotho

Class comprehensive works on Northern and Southern Sotho in —963977

3 977 2	Southern Sotho
3 977 5	Tswana
3 978	Tswa-Ronga group
	Class here Tsonga
3 98	Nguni group
	Including Ndebele (Zimbabwe)
63 985	Xhosa
	Class Fanakalo in —963986
63 986	Zulu
	Including Fanakalo
963 987	Swazi (siSwati)
963 989	Ndebele (South Africa)

—963 99	Southwestern Bantu languages

> Including Chokwe-Luchazi, Diriku, Kwangwa, Subia groups (from zone K); Herero, Ndonga, South Mbundu, Yeye groups (zone R); Lozi

> Class Holu, Mbala, Salampasu-Ndembo groups in —96393

—965	Nilo-Saharan languages

> Including Nilotic, Nubian languages; Luo, Songhai

> Class here Chari-Nile (Macrosudanic) languages

—97	**North American native languages**

> Class here comprehensive works on North and South American native languages

> *For South American native languages, see —98*

—971	Inuit, Yupik, Aleut languages

> Class here Eskimo languages

—971 2	Inuit (Inuktitut) languages

> Including Inupiatun, Kalâtdlisut (Greenlandic)

> Class comprehensive works on Inuit and Yupik languages in —971

—971 24	Eastern Canadian Inuktitut
—971 4	Yupik languages

> Including Siberian Yupik languages; Yuit

—971 9	Aleut
—972	Na-Dene languages

> Including Chipewyan, Hupa, Koyukon

> Class here Athapaskan languages

—972 5	Apachean languages

> Including Jicarilla Apache, Kiowa Apache

> *For Navajo, see —9726*

> *See also —97492 for Kiowa*

—972 56	Mescalero-Chiricahua Apache

> Class here Chiricahua, Mescalero

—972 6	Navajo (Diné)
—972 7	Tlingit
—972 8	Haida

—973	Algic and Muskogean languages

Standard subdivisions are added for Algic and Muskogean languages together, for Algic languages alone

Including Lumbee, Yurok

Class here Algonquian languages

>	—973 1–973 5 Algonquian languages

Class comprehensive works in —973

—973 1	Central Algonquian languages

For Cree-Montagnais-Naskapi languages, see —9732; for Ojibwa languages, see —9733

—973 12	Kickapoo
—973 13	Menomini
—973 14	Mesquakie

Class here Fox

—973 149	Sauk (Sac)
—973 15	Miami

Including Illinois

—973 16	Potawatomi
—973 17	Shawnee
—973 2	Cree-Montagnais-Naskapi languages
—973 23	Cree

Including Michif

—973 3	Ojibwa languages
—973 33	Ojibwa

Class here Chippewa

—973 36	Ottawa
—973 4	Eastern Algonquian languages

Including Abnaki, Malecite-Passamaquoddy

—973 43	Micmac
—973 44	Mohegan-Montauk-Narragansett

Class here Mohegan, Montauk, Narragansett, Pequot

—973 449	Stockbridge

—973 45	Unami and Munsee
	Standard subdivisions are added for Unami and Munsee together, for Unami alone
	Variant names for Unami: Delaware, Lenni Lenape
	Variant name for Munsee: Delaware
—973 47	Powhatan
—973 48	Wampanoag
	Including Massachuset
—973 5	Plains Algonquian languages
—973 52	Blackfoot
	Class here Siksika
—973 53	Cheyenne
—973 54	Arapaho languages
	Including Gros Ventre (Atsina)
	Class here Arapaho
—973 8	Muskogean languages
	Including Koasati, Mikasuki
—973 85	Muskogee (Creek) and Seminole
	Standard subdivisions are added for Muskogee and Seminole together, for Muskogee alone
—973 859	Seminole
—973 86	Chickasaw
—973 87	Choctaw
—974	Penutian, Mayan, Mixe-Zoque, Uto-Aztecan, Kiowa Tanoan languages
—974 1	Penutian languages
	Including Chinook, Maidu
	Class Zuni in —97994; class Araucanian languages in —9872; class Uru-Chipaya languages in —989
—974 12	Plateau Penutian and Tsimshian languages
	Including Umatilla
—974 122	Klamath-Modoc
	Class here Klamath, Modoc
—974 124	Nez Percé
—974 127	Yakama
—974 128	Tsimshian

—974 13	Yok-Utian languages
	Including Costanoan, Yokuts
—974 133	Miwok
—974 2	Mayan languages
	Including Kekchí, Mam, Tzutujil
	Class here Quichean-Mamean, Quichean languages
—974 22	Cakchikel
—974 23	Quiché
—974 27	Yucatecan languages
	Including Itzá, Lacandón, Mopán
	Class here Maya, Yucatec Maya
—974 28	Cholan-Tzeltalan languages
	Including Tzeltal
—974 287	Tzotzil
—974 3	Mixe-Zoque languages
—974 5	Uto-Aztecan languages
	Including Cahuilla, Luiseño
—974 52	Aztecan languages
	Class here Nahuatl (Aztec)
—974 54	Sonoran languages
	For Tepiman languages, see —97455
—974 542	Yaqui
—974 544	Huichol
—974 546	Tarahumaran languages
	Class here Tarahumara
—974 55	Tepiman languages
—974 552	Tohono O'odham and Akimel O'odham
	Standard subdivisions are added for Tohono O'odham and Akimel O'odham together, for Tohono O'odham alone
—974 552 9	Akimel O'odham (Pima)
—974 57	Numic languages
	Including Mono
—974 572	Comanche
—974 574	Shoshoni

—974 576	Ute and Southern Paiute
	Standard subdivisions are added for Ute and Southern Paiute together, for Ute alone
	Including Chemehuevi
—974 576 9	Southern Paiute
	Class here comprehensive works on Paiute
	For Northern Paiute, see —974577
—974 577	Northern Paiute
	Class here Bannock
	Class comprehensive works on Paiute in —9745769
—974 58	Hopi
—974 9	Kiowa Tanoan languages (Tanoan languages)
—974 92	Kiowa
	See also —9725 for Kiowa Apache
—974 94	Tewa
—974 96	Northern Tiwa
	Class here Taos, comprehensive works on Northern and Southern Tiwa
	For Southern Tiwa, see —97497
—974 97	Southern Tiwa
	Class here Isleta
	Class comprehensive works on Northern and Southern Tiwa in —97496
—975	Siouan, Iroquoian, Hokan, Chumash, Yuki languages
	Class Keresan languages in —979; class Caddoan languages in —9793
	See also —979 for Yuchi
—975 2	Siouan languages
	Including Catawba, Iowa, Oto
—975 22	Mandan
—975 24	Dakota languages
	Including Assiniboine
—975 243	Dakota
—975 244	Lakota (Teton)
—975 25	Dhegiha languages

—975 253	Omaha and Ponca
	Standard subdivisions are added for Omaha and Ponca together, for Omaha alone
—975 253 9	Ponca
—975 254	Osage
—975 26	Winnebago
—975 27	Missouri Valley Siouan languages
—975 272	Crow
—975 274	Hidatsa

—975 5   Iroquoian languages

Including Tuscarora

—975 54	Five Nations languages
	Including Cayuga, Onondaga
—975 542	Mohawk
—975 543	Oneida
—975 546	Seneca
—975 55	Wyandot
	Class here Huron
—975 57	Cherokee

—975 7   Hokan languages

—975 72	Yuman languages
	Including Maricopa, Quechan (Yuma)
—975 722	Mohave
—975 724	Havasupai-Walapai-Yavapai
	Class here Havasupai, Walapai, Yavapai
—975 74	Pomo languages
—975 76	Washo

—975 8   Chumash languages

—976   Oto-Manguean languages

Including Otomí

—976 3   Mixtecan languages

Class here Mixtec

—976 8   Zapotecan languages

Class here Zapotec

—978   Chibchan languages of Central America, Misumalpan languages

> Standard subdivisions are added for Chibchan languages of Central America and Misumalpan languages together, for Chibchan languages of Central America alone
>
> Class comprehensive works on Chibchan languages in —982

—978 3   San Blas Kuna (San Blas Cuna)

—978 8   Misumalpan languages

—978 82   Mískito

—979   Other North American languages

> Including Chimakuan, Coahuiltecan, Gulf, Huavean, Keres, Subtiaba-Tlapanec, Totonacan languages; Choco languages of Central America; Cuitlateco, Lenca, Xinca, Yuchi
>
> Class comprehensive works on Choco languages in —989
>
> *See also —975 for Yuki languages*

—979 2   Arawakan languages of Central America and West Indies

> Including Garífuna (Black Carib)
>
> Class comprehensive works on Arawakan languages in —9839
>
> *See also —9842 for Carib languages*

—979 22   Taino

—979 3   Caddoan languages

> Including Caddo, Wichita

—979 32   Arikara

—979 33   Pawnee

—979 4   Salishan languages

—979 43   Interior Salish languages

> Including Coeur d'Alene (Skitswish), Shuswap, Spokane

—979 435   Kalispel-Pend d'Oreille (Salish)

> Class here Kalispel, Pend d'Oreille

—979 5   Wakashan languages

—979 53   Kwakiutl

—979 54   Makah

—979 55   Nootka

—979 6   Tarascan languages

> Class here Purépecha (Tarasco)

—979 9   Kutenai and Zuni

—979 92   Kutenai

—979 94   Zuni

—98   **South American native languages**

—982   Chibchan and Barbacoan languages; Paez

Class Warao in —989; class Yanomam languages in —9892

For Chibchan languages of Central America, see —978

—983   Quechuan, Aymaran, Tucanoan, Jivaroan, Tupí, Arawakan languages

—983 2   Quechuan and Aymaran languages

—983 23   Quechuan (Kechuan) languages

Class here Quechua (Kechua)

Class Aymaran languages in —98324

—983 24   Aymaran languages

Class here Aymara

—983 5   Tucanoan languages

Including Tucano

—983 7   Jivaroan languages

Class Yaruro in —989

—983 72   Shuar

—983 8   Tupí languages

Class here Tupí-Guaraní languages

—983 82   Languages in subgroups I and II of the Tupí-Guaraní family

Including eastern and western Bolivian Guaraní; Mbyá Guaraní

—983 822   Paraguayan Guaraní

—[983 829]   Tupí (Nhengatu)

Relocated to —983832

—983 83   Languages in subgroup III of the Tupí-Guaraní family

Including Tupinambá

—983 832   Tupí (Nhengatu) [*formerly* —983829]

—983 9   Arawakan languages

Class here comprehensive works on Arawakan languages of South America and of Central America and West Indies

Class Guahiban languages in —989

For Arawakan languages of Central America and West Indies, see —9792

—999 64　　　　　　　Nakho-Daghestan (Northeast Caucasian) languages

　　　　　　　　　　　　Including Avaro-Andi-Dido group; Avaric, Dargwa, Lak, Lezghian, Tabasaran

　　　　　　　　　　　　Class here Daghestan languages

—999 641　　　　　　Nakh languages

　　　　　　　　　　　　　Including Chechen, Ingush

　　　　　　　　　　　　　Class here north central Caucasian languages

—999 68　　　　　　　Kartvelian (South Caucasian) languages

　　　　　　　　　　　　Including Laz, Svan

　　　　　　　　　　　　For Georgian, see —99969

—999 69　　　　　　　Georgian

—999 8　　　　　　　Sign languages

　　　　　　　　　　　　Including sign languages used primarily for purposes other than communication of deaf people

　　　　　　　　　　　　Class comprehensive works on sign languages in 419

—999 84–999 89　　　Sign languages used primarily for communication among deaf people or between hearing and deaf people

　　　　　　　　　　　　Class here indigenous sign languages of deaf communities

　　　　　　　　　　　　Add to base number —9998 notation 4–9 from Table 2, e.g., British Sign Language —999841, Spanish Sign Language —999846, Catalonian Sign Language —9998467, American Sign Language —99987

—999 9　　　　　　　Artificial languages

　　　　　　　　　　　　Including Afrihili, Klingon

—999 92　　　　　　　Esperanto

—999 93　　　　　　　Interlingua

Relocations and Discontinuations

In Edition 23, relocation and discontinuation notes usually follow other types of notes at the former location (the location from which a topic or group of topics has been shifted) in the schedules and tables.

The following two lists show all the relocations and discontinuations since Edition 22.

The column headed Edition 22 indicates in numerical order each number in that edition from which a topic or group of topics has been shifted; the column headed Edition 23 indicates each corresponding number in the present edition to which those topics or groups of topics have been shifted. If two or more topics have been shifted from one number to two or more numbers, each separate shift is shown.

Numbers in the Edition 22 column enclosed in square brackets are no longer in use; those not enclosed in brackets have lost part of their meaning through relocation or discontinuation, but still retain some of their original meaning.

In the following lists, the same abbreviations employed in the Relative Index are used for Tables 1–6, e.g., T1 means Table 1 Standard Subdivisions.

Relocations

In a relocation, one or more topics are shifted to a number differing form the old in respects other than length. If the relocation is partial, the original number remains valid; but if it is total, the original number is no longer used. Relocations are described and explained in the Introduction.

Relocations that have appeared previously in an interim update prior to publication of Edition 23 are indicated by * next to the Edition 22 number. Relocations that eliminate dual provision for the same topic or topics are indicated by † next to the Edition 22 number.

For example, in Table 2 one of the topics that was in —364 in Edition 22 has been relocated to —3692 in Edition 23; all of the topics in —3925 have been relocated to —39313. All the topics in —992 have been relocated to —9952 to eliminate dual provision. Scattered within 305–306 means that the topic has been relocated to so many numbers throughout that span that it is not feasible to name them all. A number or number range following a colon is an element of an add table. For example, 839.7:6 refers to notation 6 in the add table at 839.7.

For details of the specific relocated topics the classifier should consult the appropriate entries in the tables and schedules.

Edition 22	Edition 23	Edition 22	Edition 23
T1—0722*	T1—0723	T3C—357*	T3C—39
T1—079*	T1—0681	T4—31*	T4—203
T1—079*	T1—074	T4—802*	T4—803
[T1—0863]	T1—0862	T4—802*	T4—804
[T1—08633]	T1—08694	[T5—56]*	T5—59982
T1—08655	T1—08656	[T5—58]*	T5—59984
T1—0866	T1—0867	T5—9141*	T5—91489
T1—0922–0923	T1—0925–0928	T5—9149*	T5—91469
T2—363	T2—368	T5—9182*	T5—91839
T2—363	T2—36921	[T5—91823]*	T5—9183
T2—363	T2—36947	[T5—9455]	T5—9457
T2—364	T2—3692	T5—948*	T5—91425
T2—364	T2—3693	T5—948*	T5—91461
T2—364	T2—36943	[T5—9594]*	T5—9597
T2—374*	T2—37576	T5—96391	T5—96394
T2—376*	T2—37583	T5—963915	T5—96393
T2—376*	T2—37595	[T5—96773]*	T5—9354
T2—3921	T2—3923	[T5—983829]*	T5—983832
[T2—3925]	T2—39313	[T5—9911]*	T5—959
[T2—3947]	T2—354	[T5—9911]*	T5—9921
[T2—3947]	T2—355	T5—994*	T5—995
[T2—3947]	T2—3949	[T6—56]*	T6—59982
[T2—3947]	T2—53	T6—9182*	T6—9183
T2—398	T2—3639	[T6—9455]	T6—9457
T2—4521*	T2—45228	T6—96391	T6—96394
T2—45675*	T2—45674	T6—963915	T6—96393
T2—45751*	T2—45759	[T6—983829]*	T6—983832
T2—45757*	T2—45759	T6—992*†	T6—9952
T2—4591*	T2—4596	T6—994*	T6—995
T2—4591*	T2—4598	[001.432]*	001.433
T2—4592*	T2—45937	[001.432]*	907.2
T2—46912*	T2—46911	004.1	006.22
T2—46931*	T2—46932	004.165*	004.1675
T2—46935*	T2—46934	004.678*	025.042
T2—46942*	T2—46941	005.72	005.717
T2—46942*	T2—46944	005.74*†	006.312
T2—46952*	T2—46951	005.741	005.72
T2—476	T2—3988	005.757*	005.756
T2—487*	T2—4881	006.33*	005.74015113
T2—48973*	T2—48971	006.42	006.242
T2—48973*	T2—48972	017	025.31
T2—48975*	T2—48971	[017.5–.8]	017.1–.4
T2—714178	T2—714179	[018]	017
[T2—755811]*	T2—755816	[019]	017
T3C—32*	T3C—358	025.4028*	025.41
T3C—32*	T3C—36	025.48*	025.47
[T3C—3528]*	Scattered within T3C—3	[025.482]*	025.47
T3C—353–358*	T3C—352	[025.484]*	025.47
T3C—355*	T3C—3581	025.49*	025.47
T3C—355*	T3C—3582	025.7*	025.84
T3C—3559*	T3C—3564	027.65*	027.5

*Previously published
†Eliminates dual provision

Edition 22	Edition 23	Edition 22	Edition 23
037.82*	037.83	320.54092	320.54091:092
[149.96]	149.97	320.54092*	320.54093–.54099:092
[155.334]	155.343	[320.5490947]	320.540947
155.418	155.4192	[320.549096]	320.54096
155.4228	155.42292	324.24–.29:02	324.24–.29:03–08
155.4238	155.42392	324.24102*	324.24104–.24109
155.4248	155.424192	324.24302*	324.24303–.24308
155.518	155.5192	324.243602*	324.243603–.243608
155.6	152	324.243608*	324.243603
155.6	153	324.249402*	324.249403–.249408
155.6	155.2	324.2494082*	324.249404
155.6	155.3	324.2494082*	324.249407
155.6	155.7	324.2494083*	324.249403
155.6	155.9	324.27102*	324.27104–.27109
155.6	158	324.2732*	324.2733–.2738
[155.60866]	155.34	324.29402*	324.29404–.29409
[155.6089]	155.82	[331.11423]	331.1144
155.6093–.6099	155.89	[331.1143]	331.08
[155.63]	155.33	[331.1143]	331.133
155.6718	155.67192	[331.69]	331.63
174	175	[331.6905–331.699]	Scattered within 331.133
197	199.4754	[341.2424]	341.242224
197	199.4756	343.0812	343.0811
197	199.4758	346.01664*	346.042
197	199.476	347.08	345.0144
197	199.477	362.5081	362.592
197	199.478	[362.50835]	362.77569
197	199.4793	[362.5086941]	362.594
197	199.4796	[362.608]	362.69
197	199.4798	362.7085	362.7874
238.19	238.15	[362.7086]	362.77
238.19	238.16	[362.70866]	362.786
238.19	238.18	[362.7089]	362.778
[297.09023]	297.09022	[362.820835]	362.787
[297.09024]	297.09022	[362.8208653]†	362.8294
297.124	297.125	[362.8208654]†	362.8293
302.2308	Scattered within 305–306	362.8294	363.8293
[305.389623]	305.3823	[362.8308]†	362.839
[305.3896942]	305.38442	[362.830835]	362.7083
305.42	304.2082	[362.8392]	362.787432
[305.48962]	305.482	[362.8392]	362.839532
[305.48963]	305.482	362.84	362.5089
[305.48969]	305.484	362.84	362.778
[305.556]	305.96513	362.84	362.82089
305.568	305.569	[362.850835]	362.77562
306.44*	401.45	363.33*†	363.1798
320.508	320.56	[363.3497]*	363.1798
320.5401–.5407	320.54091:01–07	[363.3497]*	363.32
320.5401–.5407*	320.54093–.54099:01–07	363.46*	362.19888
320.5408	320.54091:08	363.58*	362.583
320.5408*	320.54093–.54099:08	366*	369

*Previously published
†Eliminates dual provision

Edition 22	Edition 23	Edition 22	Edition 23
371.01	371.05	469.791	469.794699
[371.823]	371.8211	469.794	469.9
[371.823]	371.822	[469.7996657]	469.796657
[372.82]	372.37	[469.7996658]	469.796658
372.83	372.89	[491.43001–.43009]	491.4301–.4309
373.224	373.215	[491.81001–.81009]	491.8101–.8109
[373.242]	373.241	491.82*	491.83
379.26	370.8	[491.85001–.85009]	491.8501–.8509
[380.01–.09]*	380.1–.9	[495.171–.178]	495.179511–495.179518
[382.913]	382.91093	[495.4001–.4009]	495.401–.409
385.5	388.44	[495.91001–.91009]	495.9101–.9109
385.5	388.46	[512.9001–.9009]*	512.901–.909
[387.001–.009]*	387.01–.09	[522.3]	522.2
388.44	388.42	[522.4]	522.2
388.46	388.42	[522.4]	527.0284
391.1–.3	391.46	523.48*	523.49
391.1–.3	391.47	602.18	389.6
391.1–.3	391.48	[608.72]*†	609.2
391.41	391.44	611.0181	611.01826
391.413	391.423	611.0181	611.018276
394.15	394.1252	611.0181	611.01876
394.15	394.1253	611.0181	612.1–.9
394.15	394.1254	611.0182	612.1–.9
395.123	395.124	[611.0183]	612.7517
398.2	398.7	[611.0184]	612.751045
398.27	398.28	[611.0185]	612.11
[398.5]*	002	[611.0185]	612.42045
[398.5]*	Scattered within 001–999	[611.0186]	612.74045
398.6	808.882	611.0187	612.1–.9
398.8	808.882	[611.0188]	612.81045
410.285*	006.35	[611.0189]	612.1–.9
413.1*	412.03	611.1–.9	612.1–.9
418.02*	418.03	[612.7921]	612.793
418.02*	418.04	613.24*	613.28
[427.1–.8]	427.9421–427.9428	613.25*	613.28
[437.1–.6]	437.9431–437.9436	621.384191	621.384192
[439.6001–.6009]	439.601–.609	623.828†	623.8943
[439.69001–.69009]	439.6901–.6909	[624.17101–.17109]	624.1701–.1709
[439.776–.778]	439.779486–.779488	625.103†	625.44
[439.8171–.8175]	439.81794891–.81794895	625.146†	625.44
[439.8272–.8274]	439.8279482–.8279484	625.28†	625.44
[447.1–.8]	447.9441–447.9448	625.6	625.4
447.971	447.9714	625.6	629.2293
[457.1–.8]	457.9451–457.9458	[627.92]†	623.893
457.9*	459.982	[627.922]†	623.8942
457.95	459.984	[627.924]†	623.8944
[457.994972]	457.94972	628.96*	614.43
[467.1–.8]	467.9461–467.9468	[629.455:001–009]	629.455:01–09
[469.71–.76]	469.794691–469.794696	641.514*	641.59
[469.71–.76]	Scattered within 469.9	[641.532]	641.52
[469.78]	469.794698	641.77*	641.73

*Previously published
†Eliminates dual provision

Edition 22	Edition 23	Edition 22	Edition 23
643.53†	645.4	[771.33]	771.32
646.433	646.436	771.45	771.46
[646.43306]	646.43606	[771.47]	771.40286
658.3121*	658.3122	[771.49]	771.44
[667.8]	667.75	[775]	771.44
668.65†	632.95	[778.2]	771.48
685.36	Scattered within 688.7	[778.2]	779
[685.361]	688.7691	778.3	778.9
[685.362]	688.7621	778.4	778.9
[685.362]	688.7622	[778.53]	777
[685.363]	688.7692	[778.59]	777
[685.364]	688.7693	778.6	778.9
[685.367]	688.7	778.7	778.9
685.43	Scattered within 688.7	780.74*	780.78
687.113	687.116	780.79*	780.78
687.19	687.4	[781.284]	781.286
687.4	688.7	781.643	781.644
[697.0001–.0009]	697.001–.009	781.657	781.68175
[697.935–.938]	697.95–.98	[782.265]	782.25
704.942*	Scattered within 001–999	782.421642079	782.421642078
704.9423*	704.9421	791.45*	791.43
704.9424*	704.9421	796.15*	796.16
704.9425*	704.9421	796.325068*	796.325069
704.9426*	704.9421	796.325071*	796.325077
704.9426*	704.94979929	796.47*	796.442
[709.0501–.0508]	709.05001–.05008	[796.77]*	796.72
720.28	720.47	[796.78]*	910
720.28†	721.04	[796.79]*	910
[721.01–.03]†	720.1–.03	[808.810081–.810088]	808.81992
[721.042]†	720.48	[808.810089]	808.8198
[721.04401–.04409]	721.0401–.0409	808.810091	808.81991
[721.0467]†	720.47	808.810093–.810099	808.81993–.81999
[721.0469]†	720.49	[808.820081–.820088]	808.82992
[721.05–.09]†	720.5–.9	[808.820089]	808.8298
726.69*	726.796	808.820091	808.82991
728.92	725.37	808.820093–.820099	808.82993–.82999
728.924	727.558	[808.830081–.830088]	808.83992
[730.01–.09]	730.1–.9	[808.830089]	808.8398
[741.509]*	741.569	808.830091	808.83991
[741.509]*	741.59	808.830093–.830099	808.83993–.83999
741.59*	741.569	[808.840081–.840088]	808.84992
757	Scattered within 001–999	[808.840089]	808.8498
757.3–.6	757.2	808.840091	808.84991
757.6	758.979929	808.840093–.840099	808.84993–.84999
760	740	[808.850081–.850088]	808.85992
[760.01–.03]	740.1–.3	[808.850089]	808.8598
[760.044]	740.4	808.850091	808.85991
[760.05–.09]	740.5–.9	808.850093–.850099	808.85993–.85999
[760.0901–.0905]	740.901–.905	[808.860081–.860088]	808.86992
[760.092]	740.92	[808.860089]	808.8698
[771.33]	771.31	808.860091	808.86991

*Previously published
†Eliminates dual provision

Edition 22	Edition 23	Edition 22	Edition 23
808.860093–.860099	808.86993–.86999	945.2083*	945.2082
[808.870081–.870088]	808.87992	945.303*	945.301
[808.870089]	808.8798	945.305*	945.304
808.870091	808.87991	945.306*	945.307
808.870093–.870099	808.87993–.87999	945.3082*	945.307
839.7:6	839.7:5	945.3083*	945.3082
839.7:72	839.7:67	945.503*	945.501
891.82*	891.83	945.503*	945.504
891.82*	891.839	945.505*	945.504
[894.55]	894.57	945.507*	945.506
[930.11]	930.124	945.5082*	945.507
936.3	936.8	945.703*	945.701
936.3	936.921	945.703*	945.702
936.3	936.947	945.704*	945.703
936.4	936.92	945.704*	945.705
936.4	936.93	945.705*	945.704
936.4	936.94	945.705*	945.706
937.909*	945.901	945.706*	945.707
937.9909*	944.9901	945.7082*	945.707
[939.47]	935.4	945.7083*	945.7082
[939.47]	935.5	945.802*	945.801
[939.47]	953.02	945.803*	945.801
939.703	939.704	945.803*	945.802
939.703	939.705	945.804*	945.803
939.8	936.39	945.805*	945.804
[940.53086914]	940.53145	945.805*	945.806
[940–990:086914]	940–990:1	945.807*	945.806
941.501*	936.1502	945.8082*	945.807
941.801	936.1802	945.8083*	945.8082
941.901	936.1902	945.901*	945.902
943.031*	944.028	945.902*	945.903
943.031*	945.06	945.903*	945.902
944.027*	945.06	[945.904]*	945.903
944.028*	945.06	945.905*	945.903
[944.99021]*	944.9901	945.905*	945.906
[944.99022]*	944.9901	945.907*	945.906
[944.99025–.99029]*	944.9903	945.907*	945.9082
[944.99034]*	944.9904	945.9083*	945.9082
[944.99035]*	944.9904	947.081*	949.60387
945.03*	945.01	947.6	939.88
945.05*	945.04	958.1046*	958.1045
945.083*	945.082	959.703*	959.701
945.103*	945.101	959.703*	959.702
945.105*	945.104	959.703*	959.7041
945.106*	945.105	959.8012	959.8011
945.107*	945.106	959.8022	959.8021
945.1083*	945.1082	[959.8036]	959.8035
945.203*	945.201	[959.8036]	959.8037
945.204*	945.205	[959.8038]	959.8037
945.205*	945.206	[959.8039]	959.8037
945.207*	945.206	[959.8039]	959.8041

*Previously published

Edition 22	Edition 23
963.071	963.0721
967.73053	967.73052
968.83031	968.83032
[971.0187]*	971.5017
971.0188*	971.5017
971.601*	971.5017
972.8205	972.8204
[973.7086914]	973.714
989.2072	989.2073

* Previously published

Discontinuations

A discontinuation is the result of shifting one or more topics to a number shorter than the previous one but otherwise not differing from it. If all topics in a given number are thus shifted, the number is no longer valid. Discontinuations are described and explained in the Introduction.

In addition, several numbers have been dropped because their content in Edition 22 was meaningless within the context of Edition 23.

For example in Table 2, [—469425] has been discontinued and all of its contents moved up to the broader number —46942, while only some of the topics in —48977 have been moved up to —48. In Table 5, [—948] has been discontinued because it is without meaning.

A number or number range following a colon is an element of an add table. For example, 342–347:011 refers to notation 011 in the add table at 342–347.

For details of the specific discontinued topics the classifier should consult the appropriate entries in the tables and schedules.

Edition 22	Edition 23	Edition 22	Edition 23
[T2—42371–42378]	T2—4237	401.41	401.4
[T2—469425]*	T2—46942	[427.09]	427
T2—48977*	T2—48	[437.09]	437
T2—597*	T2—59	[447.09]	447
T4—0141	T4—014	[457.09]	457
[T5—91822]*	T5—9182	[467.09]	467
T5—948*	Without meaning	[469.709]	469.7
T6—94332*	T6—9433	[491.7709]	491.77
T6—963374*	T6—96337	[535.013]	535
T6—963385*	T6—96338	607.21*	607.2
[004.696]	004.69	607.23*	607.2
[006.336–.338]	006.33	607.24*	607.2
[025.393]*	025.39	607.25*	607.2
[025.396]*	025.39	607.26*	607.2
[027.652]*	027.65	607.27*	607.2
154.632*	154.63	607.28*	607.2
[154.634]*	154.63	607.29*	607.2
[155.32]	155.3	608*	600
[155.334]	155.33	616.3445*	616.344
155.34	155.3	624.171	624.17
201.42	201.4	636.294*	636.29
297.09021	Without meaning	[641.534]	641.53
[305.489]	305.48	[641.536]	641.53
[305.556]	305.55	[641.538]	641.53
305.56	305	[641.539]	641.53
[305.565]	305.56	[646.452]	646.45
[306.762]	306.76	[646.453]	646.45
[320.549]	320.54	[646.454]	646.45
[320.54901–.54909]	320.54	[646.457]	646.45
[324.243605]*	324.2436	[686.2255]	686.225
[324.2436082]*	324.243608	687.112	687
331.1142	331.114	[687.144–.147]	687.14
[331.114224]	331.11422	[704.9422]*	704.942
[341.22013]	341.2201	[709.04073]*	709.0407
341.2–.7:011	341.2–.7:01	[709.04077]*	709.0407
342–347:011	342–347:01	[709.04078]*	709.0407
[343.084]	343.08	[709.04079]*	709.0407
[362.2991]*	362.299	721	720
[362.299101–.299109]	362.299	[721.046]	Without meaning
[362.29911–.29918]	362.299	748.2	748
[363.3497]*	363.34	[757.22]	757.2
[371.11]	371.1	[757.23]	757
[371.823]	371.82	[760.04]	Without meaning
[372.216]	372.21	[771.33]	771.3
[372.455]	Without meaning	[775]	770
372.472	372.47	786.74	786.7
[372.832]	372.83	796.3250202*	796.32502
[378.054–.055]	378.05	808.545	808.54
378.124	378.12	[808.81008]	808.81
[378.158]	378.1	[808.82008]	808.82
388.428	388.42	[808.83008]	808.83

*Previously published

Edition 22	Edition 23
[808.84008]	808.84
[808.85008]	808.85
[808.86008]	808.86
[808.87008]	808.87
[944.99013–.99014]*	944.9901
[944.99022]*	944.9902
[944.99023–.99024]*	944.9902
[944.99025]*	944.9902
[944.99031–.99033]*	944.9903
[944.99034]*	944.9903
[945.63401–.63409]*	945.634

*Previously published

Comparative Table

The following list, arranged alphabetically by topic, shows changes in notation from Edition 22 to Edition 23 for a substantial number of topics in the revision for cinematography and videography. The tables are not substitutes for complete indexes to the revised schedules.

Topic	Edition 22	Edition 23
Aerial cinematography	778.534	777.6
Aerial videography	778.596	777.6
Amateur cinematography	778.5349	777
Amateur videography	778.59	777
Animated cartoons	778.52347	777.7
cinematography	778.5347	777.7
videography	778.592	777.7
Animation	778.52347	777.7
cinematography	778.5347	777.7
videography	778.592	777.7
Camcorders	778.5993	777.34
Cameras	778.5	777.34
amateur cinematography	778.53491	777.34
cinematography	778.5	777.34
professional cinematography	778.5	777.34
videography	778.5993	777.34
Cassettes	778.5992	777.38
Cinematographers	778.53092	777.092
Cinematography	778.53	777
Close-up cinematography	778.534	777.6
Close-up videography	778.596	777.6
Color cinematography	778.5342	777.6
Color videography	778.596	777.6
Darkroom practice (cinematography)	778.532	777.55
Discs (Recording devices)	778.5992	777.38
DVDs	778.5992	777.38
Editing	778.5235	777.55
cinematography	778.535	777.55
videography	778.593	777.55
EFP (videography)	778.594	777.5
Electronic field production (videography)	778.594	777.5
Films		
cinematography	778.53	777.38
videography	778.5992	777.38
Graphics	778.5235	777.55
cinematography	778.535	777.55
videography	778.593	777.55
High-speed cinematography	778.534	777.6
High-speed videography	778.596	777.6
Infrared cinematography	778.534	777.6
Infrared videography	778.596	777.6
Laboratory practice (cinematography)	778.532	777.55

Topic	Edition 22	Edition 23
Lighting	778.52343	777.52
cinematography	778.5343	777.52
videography	778.592	777.52
Macrography		
cinematography	778.534	777.6
videography	778.596	777.6
Micrography		
cinematography	778.534	777.6
videography	778.596	777.6
Panoramic cinematography	778.534	777.6
Panoramic videography	778.596	777.6
Post-production	778.5235	777.55
cinematography	778.535	777.55
videography	778.593	777.55
Preservation	778.528	777.58
cinematography	778.58	777.58
videography	778.597	777.58
Projection (cinematography)	778.55	777.57
Recorders	778.5993	777.36
Recording formats	778.599	777.38
Restoration	778.528	777.58
cinematography	778.58	777.58
videography	778.597	777.58
Sound	778.52344	777.53
cinematography	778.5344	777.53
videography	778.592	777.53
Space cinematography	778.534	777.6
Space videography	778.596	777.6
Special effects	778.52345	777.9
cinematography	778.5345	777.9
videography	778.593	777.9
Specific subjects	778.528	777.8
cinematography	778.598	777.8
videography	778.593	777.8
Stereoscopic cinematography	778.5341	777.65
Stereoscopic videography	778.596	777.65
Storage	778.528	777.58
cinematography	778.58	777.58
videography	778.597	777.58
Studio production (videography)	778.594	777.5
Television recorders	778.5993	777.36
Time-lapse cinematography	778.5346	777.6
Time-lapse videography	778.596	777.6
Titling	778.5235	777.55
cinematography	778.535	777.55
videography	778.593	777.55
Underwater cinematography	778.534	777.6
Underwater videography	778.596	777.6
Video cameras	778.5993	777.34
Video cassettes	778.5992	777.38
Video discs	778.5992	777.38
Video production	778.59	777

Comparative Table

Topic	Edition 22	Edition 23
Video recorders	778.5993	777.36
Video recordings	778.5992	777.38
Video records	778.5992	777.38
Video tapes	778.5992	777.38
Videocassettes	778.5992	777.38
Videodiscs	778.5992	777.38
Videography	778.59	777
Videorecordings	778.5992	777.38
Videorecords	778.5992	777.38
Videotapes	778.5992	777.38

Equivalence Tables

The following equivalence tables lead in Table A from Edition 22 numbers to Edition 23 numbers and in Table B from Edition 23 numbers to Edition 22 numbers for cinematography and videography.

In most cases, the topics in an Edition 22 number are assigned to the corresponding Edition 23 number. If the topics are assigned to different numbers, the topics are listed separately in the Notes column. For example, in Table A, both recorders and recording formats were classed in 778.599 in Edition 22, but in Edition 23 they are classed in 777.36 and 777.38, respectively.

Table A

Edition 22	Edition 23	Notes
778.52	777	
778.5232	777.55	
778.5234	777.5	Specific elements of cinematography and videography
778.5234	777.6	Specific types of cinematography and videography
778.52341	777.65	
778.52342	777.6	
778.52343	777.52	
778.52344	777.53	
778.52345	777.56	
778.52346	777.6	
778.52347	777.7	
778.52349	777	
778.523491	777.34	
778.5235	777.55	
778.5238	777.9	
778.525	777.57	
778.526	777.6	
778.528	777.58	
778.53	777	
778.53092	777.092	
778.532	777.55	
778.524	777.5	Specific elements of cinematography
778.524	777.6	Specific types of cinematography
778.5341	777.65	
778.5342	777.6	
778.5343	777.52	
778.5344	777.53	
778.5345	777.9	
778.5346	777.6	
778.5347	777.7	
778.5349	777	
778.53491	777.34	
778.535	777.55	
778.538	777.8	
778.55	777.57	
778.56	777.6	
778.58	777.58	
778.59	777	
778.592	777.5	Specific elements of video production

778.592	777.52	Lighting
778.592	777.53	Sound
778.593	777.55	
778.593	777.9	Special effects
778.594	777.5	
778.596	777.6	
778.597	777.58	
778.598	777.8	
778.599	777.36	Recorders
778.599	777.38	Recording formats
778.5992	777.38	
778.5993	777.34	Camcorders, video cameras
778.5993	777.36	Recorders

Table B

Edition 23	Edition 22	Notes
777	778.5	Cinematography and videography together
777	778.53	Cinematography
777	778.5349	Amateur cinematography
777	778.59	Videography
777.092	778.5092	Cinematography and videography together
777.092	778.53092	Cinematography
777.092	778.59092	Videography
777.3	778.5	Cinematography and videography together
777.3	778.53	Cinematography
777.3	778.599	Videography
777.34	778.5	Cinematography and videography together
777.34	778.53	Cinematography
777.34	778.53491	Amateur cinematography
777.34	778.5993	Videography
777.36	778.5993	
777.38	778.53	Cinematography and videography together
777.38	778.53	Cinematography
777.38	778.599	Videography
777.38	778.5992	Video recordings, e.g., cassettes, DVDs, tapes
777.5	778.5234	Cinematography and videography together
777.5	778.534	Cinematography
777.5	778.592	Elements—videography
777.5	778.594	Modes—videography
777.5	778.594	Electronic field and studio production
777.52	778.52343	Cinematography and videography together
777.52	778.5343	Cinematography
777.52	778.592	Videography
777.53	778.52344	Cinematography and videography together
777.53	778.5344	Cinematography
777.53	778.592	Videography
777.55	778.5235	Cinematography and videography together
777.55	778.535	Cinematography
777.55	778.593	Videography
777.57	778.55	
777.58	778.528	Cinematography and videography together
777.58	778.58	Cinematography
777.58	778.597	Videography
777.6	778.5234	Cinematography and videography together

777.6	778.534	Cinematography
777.6	778.596	Videography
777.65	778.52341	Cinematography and videography together
777.65	778.5341	Cinematography
777.65	778.596	Videography
777.7	778.52347	Cinematography and videography together
777.7	778.5347	Cinematography
777.7	778.592	Videography
777.8	778.5238	Cinematography and videography together
777.8	778.538	Cinematography
777.8	778.598	Videography
777.9	778.52345	Cinematography and videography together
777.9	778.5345	Cinematography
777.9	778.593	Videography

Reused Numbers

A reused number is a number with a total change in meaning from one edition to another. The list of reused numbers shows all Edition 22 numbers immediately reused in Edition 23.

457.91
457.94
469.791
469.798
523.481
523.482
796.3250202
796.325068

The 23rd edition of the Dewey Decimal Classification was produced using the fourth generation of the Editorial Support System (ESS), developed by OCLC Online Computer Library Center, Inc. ESS includes a print module developed by Pansoft GmbH, Karlsruhe, Germany, under an agreement with OCLC. Composition was done in Times Roman and Arial under the supervision of Michael Panzer. The book was printed and bound by Edwards Brothers, Inc., Ann Arbor, Michigan.